CENTURY OF CONFLICT

CANADIAN HISTORY SERIES

Edited by Thomas B. Costain

VOLUME TWO

CENTURY OF CONFLICT

CENTURY OF CONFLICT

The Struggle Between the French and British in Colonial America

JOSEPH LISTER RUTLEDGE

Toronto, Canada

DOUBLEDAY CANADA LIMITED

Library of Congress Catalog Card Number 56-9541

PRINTED IN THE UNITED STATES OF AMERICA

To

My Wife,

whose encouragement and forbearance lightened a long task;

My Brother Gordon Rutledge,

whose unflagging interest and innumerable helpful suggestions were a constant stimulation;

My Friend and Associate Jim Harris,

whose editorial skill helped iron out some of the rougher passages;

this book is dedicated in grateful acknowledgment.

CONTENTS

INTRODUCTION

FOR all that there have been a multitude of histories covering the century of conflict on this continent, the happenings themselves, and sometimes the actors in them, have remained cloudy and impersonal. The names fall with a sense of distant familiarity but not with any impact of reality.

That is the excuse, if excuse is needed, for the series of volumes in the making, of which this is the second. It is an attempt to make characters and events move out of the stiff formalities of history, to find flesh and blood and a sense of immediacy in the crowding events.

No history is likely to be written that must not pay tribute to the magnificent story presented by Francis Parkman, no writer but will owe a debt there to his great pioneering in the story of this continent told with such graphic mastery.

There are other historians of this era to whom grateful acknowledgment is due, some who wrote while the events they recorded were still relatively recent, and some from a more detached knowledge, or focused on some segment of the record.

But still there seems a place for a history that endeavors to relate past events to more recent happenings and attitudes. It is not easy today to understand that men could believe in the divine right of kings. Yet that thinking was half of the background of this story. It was what gave the French regime in Canada its drive and power, and it was what brought about its fall. For here was the beginning of an irrepressible conflict between autocracy and liberty at death grips in our own lands not so many centuries ago.

In those years New France, under its almost-divine King, wrote its fabulous story of initiative and devotion and almost unbelievable achievement that made her master of all but a fragment of a continent. But that conflict accomplished other results. It made freedom real and dear and meaningful to the English, who only began to fight when their backs were to the wall. It was this common love of freedom that, in face of many differences, has come to be represented by almost the only undefended border between two sovereign countries in our world today. And this fact is profoundly real, and it comes from the common roots of which this record tells, the common aspirations even in conflicting interests.

It was the Frenchmen of Canada who opened up the vast reaches of the Mississippi and founded the great cities of the Gulf of Mexico. It was the Frenchmen of Canada who first reached out into the Dakotas and Montana and Minnesota. It was the American colonists who first took Louisburg. And regiments of Royal American Infantry fought under Wolfe to make Quebec an English possession.

It is the glowing human story of France and England on this continent, of their different ways, their different concepts, and their common courage and common faith in a great continent that this book attempts to present.

JOSEPH LISTER RUTLEDGE
March 4, 1956

CENTURY OF CONFLICT

CHAPTER I

THE DEDICATED MAN

Frontenac and his vision of an empire. A conflict of ideologies, the prelude to an early cold war. The founding of Fort Frontenac. The intendant's office re-established. The challenge of the coureurs. *Their various characters. The brandy controversy leads to the Brandy Parliament.*

AUTUMN came early at Quebec that year of 1672. The tilled acres running down to the ancient highway, the great St. Lawrence, had already turned from green to gold. A hint of frost was in the air, too, and the warehouses beyond the fields were closed against it. There was an unaccustomed stir in the narrow streets this day, and more people there than gathered even on feast days or when the young blades from Upper Town came of an evening to strut about the cafés and inns where a bottle of wine was to be had for six French sous, and forty sous was the price of a pound plug from the stores that dealt in tobacco. Even the road that climbed up the cliff among the twenty-odd houses that clung there with precarious dignity had its group of people who seemed to be in no hurry to be about any business.

At the top of this street and to the right was the Bishop's Palace, rather empty now, for the bishop was in Paris and would be for some time to come. Next to it was the seminary, the finest and largest dwelling in the country. To the left, on the brow of the cliff, was the Château of St. Louis, grown a little shabby with the years, opposite it the Hospice of the Récollets. This was Upper Town. It was not the crowded and huddled place that was the town near the water. There were only fifty lots here and the only street that seemed of importance, so Father le Tac tells us, "is where the legal gentlemen live." The hospital was on the slope looking down toward the St. Charles River and there, too, the house where the intendant lived and where the Sovereign Council held its meetings.

It was not a pretentious town, though the way it climbed the cliff gave it a certain dramatic distinction. This day, outlined against the gray rocks and the forest's first crimson and purple, it seemed prepared for some great occasion. It was an occasion of sorts. A vessel dropping anchor in the wide basin before the city was always that; a sight to tempt even the diligent; a reminder of other days, of a France more settled and familiar than this vast wilderness with its brooding sense of the unknown. Today it was something more than that. A new governor was arriving, a certain Louis de Buade, Comte de Frontenac, about whom there had been a good deal of talk.

He was coming without his lady. While that was a disappointment, it was something for gossip to feed upon. Perhaps the interest of the day was more in the gossip than the governor. It was whispered about that there had been an affair between him and a certain Madame de Montespan. It was a threadbare story, even in the New World, and none too well authenticated. But the coming of Frontenac had given it a new twist. It wasn't that Madame had caught the roving eye of Louis XIV. That, perhaps, was to be expected. But gossip was quick to see that a former gallant who remained at court was no asset to an ambitious favorite. It was said that the lady had been most helpful in securing Frontenac's appointment to this distant post. There were smiles of understanding.

But there were those who had a different story. It was said in France that Madame Frontenac was ready enough to see her husband depart alone. It would have added something had there been a romantic reason. But there was none. Though she was of a lively wit and adventurous temper, no breath of scandal had come near her. The rumors did say that the lady was glad enough to have her husband far away where his arrogance and his vanities could not trouble her. The obvious fact was that the governor had come alone, lending a measure of support to these views.

So they gossiped endlessly, as was understandable. Such talk brought a flavor of other days to people hungry with remembrance.

It stirred more interest than a change of governors. Governors had come and gone, and only one of them had left more than a fleeting memory. The castle on the cliff still spoke of him—the great Champlain. He had built it, and there he had died that sad Christmas of thirty-seven years ago. No name since then had been great enough to dim that memory even for a moment. This was another change—a Frontenac for a Courcelle. What was that to New France, which had already known eight governors and was to know many more? Perhaps only the stern figure standing on the deck of the vessel that had brought him from France was likely to think of this occasion as different from many another arrival. But no occasion in which he was involved was ever insignificant to Frontenac—nor, in truth, was it.

He was not a young man, nor inexperienced. Louis de Buade, Count of Frontenac, was fifty-two years old. All of these years had been spent in the immediate shadow of the most splendid court in Europe or in the discipline of the camp. He was a godson of a king. His name of Louis had been given him by Louis XIII, son of that one-time Huguenot, white-plumed Henry of Navarre and Béarn. Both had been his father's friends. As a child Louis Buade had played with princes. As a youth of fifteen he was a junior officer in the army of the Prince of Orange in Holland. From that time his life was one of arms, in years when the proud prowess of a Condé and a Turenne was bringing new glories to the lilies of France. The arm that hung a little stiffly at the new governor's side was a relic of wounds received at the siege of Orbitello. At twenty-six years of age he was a *maréchal de camp.* Today he would have been called brigadier. It is worth remembering that when the Venetians petitioned the great Turenne to choose one to lead them against the Turks, Turenne picked Frontenac, a choice that was accepted with enthusiasm. It is evidence that his name and reputation were familiar beyond his native France. It is something, too, that he came out of that desperate and unavailing struggle without reproach and with a reputation grown greater in adversity.

There were times in Frontenac's life when his ambitions bordered on the vain and tawdry. But the New World set its mark on him. From his first glimpse of the great rock of Quebec brooding over an ancient river he was a dedicated man. History would quickly deny that even in the New World his vanity and arrogance and persistent truculence were the less, but the sense of destiny was there.

He felt himself a man in his rightful place. He had a part to play, and it was not an uncertain part.

Perhaps this was in his mind as he sat down to report to Colbert, Louis XIV's first minister. There was in his words the unaccustomed enthusiasm of one who wished to stir an answering enthusiasm in another. "I never saw anything more superb," he wrote, "than the position of this town. It could not be better situated as the capital of a great empire." There it was in the open, one man's soaring dream. Through the many vicissitudes and the innumerable mistakes to follow, it was to be a guide. It was never to leave him.

Looking back, and admitting the years and their lessons that have intervened, it still seems strange that there were so few to share this vision. A new world—yet those who thought of it at all thought of it in terms of some uncertain but personal advantage. To Louis XIV, to Colbert, his first minister, and to the fifteenth Louis who followed, New France remained a colony and trading post. Often enough they thought of it as scarcely worth the difficulties and annoyances it occasioned. If thinking went farther it was an extension in kind, a will to conserve what was already possessed rather than any broader vision. To the devoted Bishop Laval, and St. Vallier, who succeeded him, and indeed to all those gallant and earnest men of God who preceded or followed them, Canada was primarily a great mission field. There were souls to be saved, prestige to be earned for Mother Church. What more was to be asked? To men like Talon, the great intendant, it was a new field of enterprise to be explored and developed with the idea of making the existing system of government and colonial administration more workable. To Governor la Barre and many others of his ilk it was a golden opportunity to be exploited for personal gain. In the main they thought of gain as something that might be expended elsewhere than in Canada.

To the adventurous—the La Salles, the Durantayes, to Tonty and Cadillac and Du Lhut and the whole gallant company, and especially to that fabulous family of Le Moynes—it was still adventure, the excitement of new scenes, the pursuit of glory or power, the intoxication of freedom, such freedom as an old world did not know. Only in rare instances was it more than that.

Where they stopped to create, it was the creation of isolated points in a vast wilderness. These isolated points were trading posts rather than cities. There was little thought of cohesion between one and another, or of a life that was to grow in meaning and in spiritual content. The actors in the great drama thought and worked as individuals and they died with whatever vision was in them still unexpressed. Almost alone among them Frontenac, for all his shortcomings and his very human weaknesses, had something more. Beyond the present disaster or proud achievement he saw an empire.

Much of the detail of the next two decades and of the persons who played their dramatic part in the happenings of those days has appeared in a preceding volume. If it is rehearsed briefly here, it is because Frontenac, who was the dominant figure, was to continue to cast his shadow over the events to come and, to a considerable measure, set the pattern for that hundred years of irrepressible conflict whose story is still to be told. It was Frontenac who gave body to a dream of a French empire in the Americas. It was he who encouraged and supported those daring spirits who were not to be satisfied with material benefits, with the good will of King or Church, or the security of a settled abode. Frontenac was one with all those rare spirits who saw the horizon not as an end but as an entrance, a challenge to come and find.

History leaves no record whether the twenty mounted soldiers that Frontenac had convinced the King were necessary to his new dignity were present on the occasion of his arrival to take over his new authority in the early September of 1672. Louis had provided the nine thousand livres necessary for their equipment and maintenance. It was something in the neighborhood of one fourth as many dollars and, admittedly, it was provided reluctantly. The twenty-man guard was there, but to have discovered twenty horses with proper military mien would have been next to a miracle. Also, had such a cortege led the way up the Rue de la Montagne, from landing stage to Upper Town, surely someone would have made it a matter of record, and there is no such word.

Even riding alone, Frontenac would have been impressive enough. All the existing representations show him as a man standing tall, erect, and scrupulously dressed in the fashion of the day. A proud and handsome face with fierce eyes looking out from beetling brows and a great hawk nose and determined chin, force and dignity and pride and arrogance meeting in one man.

All such presentations in portrait or in stone must stem from such stray references as imagination can feed upon and the possible belief that such a man could have no other appearance. There is no contemporary portrait extant. The portrait of such a figure lying in death was believed to be that of the governor. It had indeed the facial characteristics that have become familiar to us in our thinking of the man. The same high brow, the same hawk nose, the same strong jaw and chin. But the painstaking investigation of that fine historian, Mr. Ernest Myrand, established beyond question that this was not Frontenac, however much it may have been drawn upon by those who sought to present him.

But there is no question that the portraits of Louis de Buade, Comte de Frontenac, have caught the spirit of the man, and the figure who rode that September day up the steep stretches of the Rue de la Montagne was one to be remembered.

There to meet him, too, were other memorable figures. The retiring governor, Courcelle, and Talon, the great intendant, ready for departure though reluctant to go. Probably few if any of Quebec's six hundred souls, or for that matter the equal number from the populous seigniory of Beaupré some miles down-river, would have missed the occasion. There could have been almost fifteen hundred persons present. So many at least were within reach—half the population of New France. Among them were men whose names were to be bright points of light in history's pages. There, too, the soutaned figures, the black and the gray of Jesuit and Récollet, the one a little conscious of the King's special favor and the other hopefully looking for some promise of support. And everywhere in street and doorway the smiling faces of people starved for just such a hint of magnificence as appeared in that soldierly figure riding up the steep slope to his new home.

At the top of what the English now call Mountain Hill the road passed between the Bishop's Palace and the Château of St. Louis. If Frontenac was for a moment nonplused by a palace, so little like its name, the thought could have lasted but a moment. After all, there was the memory of his own small place of Isle Savary on the Indre River near the thriving city of Blois. It, too, had been a disappointing place, but he remembered how the gardens and the fountains and the pools that he had planned, and some of which he had created, had turned it, if not into the little Versailles of his dreams, at least into a place in which he could take an honest pride. Already, probably, his mind was toying with the idea of a rebuilt château more in accordance with the King's dignity—and his own. That plan would be a weapon in the conflict that was to end in his recall, as his earlier plans had brought him almost to penury. But, even had he known this,

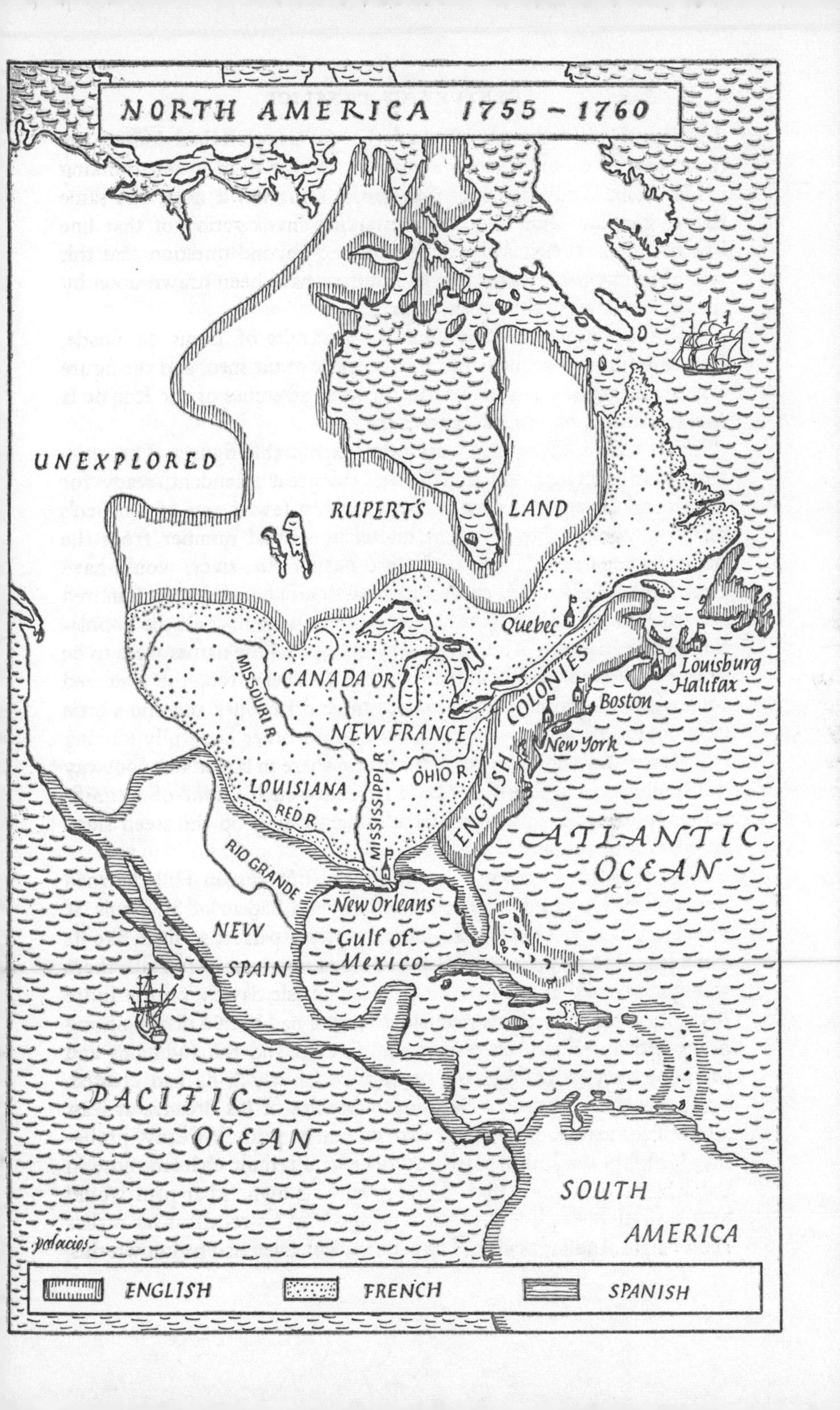
NORTH AMERICA 1755 – 1760
UNEXPLORED
RUPERT'S
LAND
Quebec
Louisburg
Halifax
Boston
New York
CANADA OR
NEW FRANCE
MISSOURI R.
MISSISSIPPI R.
OHIO R.
LOUISIANA
RED R.
RIO GRANDE
ENGLISH COLONIES
ATLANTIC
OCEAN
New Orleans
Gulf of
Mexico
NEW
SPAIN
PACIFIC
OCEAN
SOUTH
AMERICA
palacios
ENGLISH
FRENCH
SPANISH

it is doubtful that Frontenac would have changed. He was not given to bowing to opposition.

He began his governorship, as any other newly appointed executive might have done, by familiarizing himself with the situation. For the moment his native vanity was topped by his native shrewdness. He caught instant fire as Courcelle, his predecessor, whose somewhat limited gifts were crowned with some vision, told of his plan for a fort where Lake Ontario joined the St. Lawrence. Frontenac's soldier's eye was quick to see that such a fort, lying across one of the natural highways by which the Iroquois must approach, was not only a natural protection for the colony but was also a safeguard for the lake Indians who must use this highway to bring their furs to Montreal. From that moment the plan ceased to be Courcelle's and became his own.

Talon, though his duties as intendant had ended, seemed in no hurry to depart. As intendant he had been in all but absolute power over the administration of domestic affairs, just as the governor was supreme in matters relating to peace and war and the association with other nations. The quiet, soft-spoken, devoted man who had worked so assiduously to improve the fortunes of the colony was reluctant to leave his work and only too happy to explain it to the new governor.

Talon's plan was based, as were all his actions, on careful thinking. The colony could survive on the fur trade alone. It had to learn to be self-supporting. That was radical thinking for those who had been nurtured in a belief that the King would understand and provide, but it dovetailed nicely with Frontenac's growing vision of an expanding empire. Talon explained the need for more agriculture supported by better methods. He had planned and developed a modest shipbuilding plant to provide vessels for fishing or trading. He had even thought of trading with the Indies, exchanging fish and lumber for molasses and sugar. He explained the need of flour mills to meet the home demand. That was obvious enough, but it took more vision to see a brewery as perhaps the most potent force against the brandy trade that the Church was battling so fiercely. The brewery idea was a new argument to meet the one so generally used, that if the French didn't supply the Indians' demand for brandy, they would be equally debauched by English rum. There was, of course, the more effective corollary that English rum unchallenged by French brandy would remove the Indian traders from the beneficent shadow of Mother

Church and relinquish them to Protestant Calvinism. The balance leaned undoubtedly toward the lesser evil. In such thinking Frontenac and Talon were at one.

One circumstance of his governorship that did not please Frontenac was that in much of the traveling his position made necessary there was a considerable lack of dignity. It was unbecoming, he felt, that one with twenty guardsmen at his beck and call, and a natural taste for pomp, should be forced to travel crouched in a bark canoe, unable to move for fear of upsetting the fragile craft. More than once in his letters he had made this point. But rail as he might, the alternative was going afoot, a practice both inconvenient and generally dangerous.

Perhaps it was some such reflection that led him to consider how best he might present himself as the representative of the King. So thinking, it occurred to him to revive the Three Estates—clergy, nobles, and commoners—dormant in France now for a matter of sixty years. It is hard to believe that there was more than this in his decision to create a States-General in Canada. He and his father before him had been staunch King's men, and there was little in Frontenac's character, as we know it, that would suggest a wish or even a willingness to delegate any of the powers he exercised for the King. It is more probable that he thought with pleasure of himself as the central figure in a pageant of government.

It was late October when Frontenac convened his Three Estates, so it was some months before the news reached France. This was probably fortuitous, as Frontenac had not yet learned what happy leeway the slowness of communication with Paris provided for doing what he wanted without first securing permission.

When Colbert, the King's Minister of Colonies, received the governor's glowing account of the affair, he answered promptly. But there was a chilly note in his words. "It is well for you," he wrote, "to observe that you are always to follow, in the government of Canada, the forms in use here . . . you should very rarely, or, speaking more correctly, never give corporate form to the people of Canada."

Here in essence was the heart of the challenge that was building up on a continent. The rule in Canada, as in France itself, was that the King was supreme and intended so to remain. Indeed, Louis had voiced this clearly enough. "It seems to me," he had said, "as if any glory won by another was robbed from myself." There was a plain enough statement that there was no liberty as of right, but only such as might be derived from the gracious condescension of authority. And there was little enough of that, for hadn't Louis also said: "It is God's will that whoever is born a subject should not reason, but obey!"

It isn't to be imagined that Charles II or James of England valued power less than Louis or that either was more generous with his prerogatives. But Protestantism was measureably less amenable to authority than Catholicism. Then, the theory of the divine right of kings, which no one in France would have dreamed of questioning, had in England received a setback on that snowy January day in front of Whitehall when Charles I laid his head on the block. It lost still more when Cromwell showed himself ready to represent a recalcitrant Parliament at the will of the nation. These years had given to the English people, always perhaps less tractable than their neighbor, a new incentive. It was a heady draught, this suggestion of freedom to be achieved by individual yet co-operative action.

Admittedly, those who came to the New World under the English flag were those who had least to lose in the Old—the landless, the younger sons, the unfortunate, the religious zealots who would not bow the knee to any form of worship but only to God Himself. They had no thought of building a replica of the old life in the new land. Their thoughts were of a new world and a new freedom, and of opportunity hewn out of danger, threat, and hardship. So in the British colonies of the West Indies and New England and the French colonies of Canada were the two ideologies of the age—the sanctity of kingship brought at last to face the surprising doctrine of the sanctity of the individual, the belief in man's right to own himself, which was slowly emerging and becoming vocal and carrying with it intent to create a government wherein the will of all should replace the will of one. It was impossible for the proponents of one viewpoint to concede anything without first forsaking their own. Freedom and autocracy could find no common ground where they might meet. Here, then, the seeds of the irrepressible conflict that was to be.

It would be idle to assume that Frontenac was more democratically minded than his fellows. In convening the Three Estates, there had been no thought of encroaching on the royal prerogatives. After all, he was the King's representative. The governor might deal cavalierly with the King's authority, but it was not in character for him to do anything to qualify his own. He may have been somewhat more advanced in his thinking than the King, but there is nothing in his character or acts that hints at any reluctance to accept the fullest measure of autocracy. He could at times flout the King's decisions. The occasions are many, but always they represent an evasion, not a challenge, and never for any other reason than that he thought his own way the better of the two in achieving what he assumed the King desired.

It was on June 3, 1673, that Frontenac set out from Quebec to survey the domain that he governed and to do something about that fort at Cataraqui–he had already almost forgotten that the idea had come from Courcelle.

The first 185 miles to Montreal were the least troublesome of the many to be covered in that grand program to familiarize himself with the lands under his government, build a strategic post, and lay the foundation of an enduring respect among the Indian peoples.

It was almost five o'clock when the first of his canoes drew to shore and saw the little settlement of Montreal facing them. Beyond the common that fringed the river, and not so much above its level, the first scattering of houses began. They were on St. Paul Street, as it now is and as it was then. They ran back in little scattered groups of buildings for perhaps three blocks until the ground began to rise and the tilled fields reached to the fringe of the forest where the steeper sides of Mount Royal began. To the west the little town straggled out to where St. Peter Street is today and eastward from that to the square that once faced the old Place Viger station.

The governor of Montreal at the moment was a man of considerable ability and very doubtful integrity. He was François Marie Perrot and he had the advantage of being married to the niece of Talon. Though the intendant himself was scrupulous in all his actions, Perrot had no hesitancy in taking advantages where he found them, and certainly a new governor was not a windfall to be overlooked. The two were to have sharp differences later that would not add to the prestige of either, but for the moment all was amity. Perrot spared no effort to make the governor's stay pleasant and to speed the plans for the journey to Cataraqui and the building of a fort there.

In this expedition, with its evidence of the new governor's sure instinct in dealing with the Indians–so different from his often arrogant and uncompromising attitude toward his fellows—the Indians recognized qualities that were often obscure to others. Their immediate acceptance of him as the Great Onontio who warranted their continuing respect was the high point of Frontenac's early administration. Without it the record would be a dingy one. By the twenty-eighth of July the proposed fort had been completed and provisioned and in no spirit of humility named Fort Frontenac. The governor may well have had a sense of elation. The fort was built, the Indians satisfied, not one man or one canoe lost, and all for a total outlay of ten thousand francs.

It was small wonder that the governor should write a long and colorful letter to Colbert that did not overlook his own considerable part in the affair. He hoped, no doubt, that the letter would be referred to the King and gain his approbation. It was as well, perhaps, that Colbert's reply did not reach Canada until more than a year later. By that time Frontenac was well launched on a campaign of altercation at the château that demanded his attention; but even with his acknowledged ability to shed reproof, Colbert's letter, dated May 17, 1674, might well have disturbed a less sensitive man than Frontenac. There was in it no word of congratulation for a great achievement. It went instead into the slow growth of population in the colony, blamed then as later on the fact that Frontenac encouraged the more virile to adventure afield. "You will readily understand by what I have just told you," Colbert wrote, "that His Majesty's intention is not that you undertake great voyages by ascending the river St. Lawrence, nor that the inhabitants spread themselves for the future farther than they have already done. On the contrary, he desires that you labor incessantly and during the whole time you are in that country, to consolidate, concentrate, and form them into towns and villages that they may be in a better position to defend themselves successfully."

Many a man with some empire dream of his own has forgotten it all under the impact of such an extraordinary wet blanket. Apparently it disturbed Frontenac little. He did suggest that if the Minister disapproved of the fort he would go next year and tear it down. This was a palpable bluff. He knew well that Colbert, having disapproved of an expenditure of ten thousand francs to build a fort, would not countenance the expenditure of so much or any part of it to tear it down. The bluff was good and the subject was dropped.

For three years, contrary to all precedents, Frontenac had been the undisputed master of New France. Louis was somewhat more than well disposed to him. The King's letters, even under sharp provocation, show a friendly patience that was not too customary. He was as anxious as Frontenac himself that all the dignities of the supreme authority, under the King, should be assured him. More than that the King never conceded, nor did he intend to do so. At almost this exact moment a royal decree was making this very clear indeed. The decree applied to France, but the intention was no different elsewhere. "The courts are ordered," so this document read, "to register the letters of the King without any modification or restriction or condition that might cause delay or impediment in their execution." The decree pointed out that once this duty had been faithfully and submissively observed, Parliament should be permitted to ask such questions or make such observations as it might see fit. Lest this should appear to open too wide a door, the decree pointed out that once the King had made reply there could be no further discussion but only prompt obedience.

In such a mood the King was hardly likely to be patient with Frontenac's quarrelsomeness and growing pretensions. He began to think and speak of "his high and mighty lordship, the governor." There was no doubt Louis was growing impatient, and in that feeling he decided to return to the system of checks and balances that had always obtained in France and that, prior to Frontenac, had done so in Canada as well. Laval's long absence in Europe, seeking the Pope's support as well as the King's, had left Frontenac an unqualified authority. Now the bishop was returning, and with him Jacques Duchesneau to fill the post of intendant, vacant since Talon had retired.

It was never difficult to quarrel with Bishop Laval. He was stern and uncompromising. His devotion could not be questioned, nor is it possible to question a certain Messianic complex. He had been in conflict with three governors already and he returned fully armed and ready to challenge the fourth. And no one ever offered battle to Frontenac without finding a ready response.

The suggestion that Duchesneau was sent by Colbert to spy on the governor might find support in the intendant's letters but not in the replies Colbert was accustomed to send. In an autocracy it seemed advisable to have officials with somewhat overlapping authorities. It kept them from developing extravagant ideas of responsibility that autocracy could not tolerate. Probably there was no more than this.

No more was needed, governor and intendant were temperamentally geared to conflict. Autocratic and headstrong, Frontenac was a difficult man for anyone to handle, as Louis and his minister had discovered. Perhaps those two were not unhappy to realize that Duchesneau's characteristics of caution, craftiness, and dogged persistence might be useful in recalling the governor to the realization that he was the regent of authority rather than authority itself.

Intendant Duchesneau enjoyed the favor of Bishop Laval, though it could be that this favor stemmed more from the bishop's shrewd idea that the intendant might prove useful than from any warmer feeling. Still, even this tacit approval did nothing to win the favor of the governor. Temperamentally, and quite apart from this reason, Frontenac was unsuited to double harness. His domestic life had suggested this, and there was no possible likelihood that he would enjoy sharing harness with the intendant. Co-operation with the bishop was no more probable, even if the governor had not managed to get himself energetically embroiled with the Jesuits before Laval's return. Perhaps this was not too difficult a task. It wasn't that the governor was an irreligious man. No one has ever claimed that he was not a good Catholic and as devout as it was in his nature to be. But if it was difficult for the Jesuits, who had played so impressive a part in the early history of the colony, to appreciate that change was in the air and that now worldly interests were competing in the development of the New World, it was equally difficult for Frontenac not to resent their intrusion in matters that he considered practical politics.

Frontenac believed that the best way to encourage the Indians to become loyal subjects of the King was to teach them the French language. This view was shared by Louis and his minister Colbert. It did not appeal to the Jesuits at all. Primarily they were dealers in souls rather than bodies, and they did not feel that a more intimate contact with such civilization as then obtained was likely to be of spiritual benefit. That, at least, was the way the bishop explained the attitude of the Church. The governor explained it differently and more frankly, if somewhat less accurately. He wrote Colbert: "The Jesuits will not civilize the Indians because they wish to keep them in perpetual wardship. They think more of beaver skins than of souls, and their missions are pure mockeries."

Wisely the bishop forbore to retort in kind. He chose to attack policies rather than individuals. It is possible that the bishop's grapevine may have advised him of the King's mounting impatience with his representative. But Bishop Laval was much too astute to press such advantage too openly. Also, he had in mind a point of attack that seemed to be more promising.

One cannot doubt the good bishop's complete sincerity in his attitude toward the brandy traffic or that his attitude represented the thinking of virtually all the clergy. But he was human enough, no doubt, to feel that, if in uprooting an evil you discommoded a rival, that was an advantage to be accepted gracefully. But there was another phase of the brandy trade that did not escape the shrewd and determined cleric. It had to do with the *coureurs de bois*, and there the bishop knew that he was definitely in line with the thinking of His Majesty.

The *coureurs* had few friends. The Church held stubbornly to the opinion that all male citizens had better remain at home to become good husbands and fathers to the glory of God and of Mother Church. The King, intent on holding what he had instead of seeking more by adventuring afield, was of the same opinion. The colony didn't increase and was poorly safeguarded while these *coureurs* were abroad in the forest. Also, and perhaps this was a more persuasive argument, these adventurers tended to infringe on the profits of royalty and the only promising business open to the stay-at-home traders, the trade in furs. It was argued, too, that these runners of the wood debauched the Indians and endangered their own souls. This was the view of the clergy, and while the proof was not as clear and dispassionate as would be required in a present-day court of law —and partook perhaps too much the impress of devoted men sensing an evil so great that they would not be overly scrupulous to avoid an overemphasis—the argument was not without foundation.

It remained for Father Etienne de Carheil, a Norman of noble birth and a devout if somewhat myopic zealot, to lay these scattered charges on the line. He had been thirty-six years in Canada—twenty of them as missionary to the Hurons at Michilimackinac—when he wrote his all-inclusive denunciation. The years had not qualified his judgment or softened the bitterness or his scorn. True, in that August of 1702 Frontenac was dead and Governor Callières ruled in his stead. But little else had changed. Father Carheil had only a mounting anger to call upon and little more evidence, if such it was, than would have been available to him more than a dozen years earlier. In sixty or seventy pages of cramped script he enumerated the evils of the brandy traffic and the corruption it entailed. Long into the summer night his angry pen raced on, telling how this traffic debauched those it touched, especially the soldiers of the King. "All the pretended service which it is sought to make people believe that they render to the King," he wrote, "is reduced to four chief occupations. . . .

"The first consists in keeping a public tavern for the sale of brandy, wherein they trade it continually to the savages. . . . The second occupation of the soldiers consists in being sent from one post to another by the commandants in order to carry their wares and their brandy thither. . . . Their third occupation consists in making their fort a place that I am ashamed to call by its proper name, where the women have found out that their bodies might serve in lieu of merchandise and would be still better received than beaver-skins. . . ."

Despite his shame the good father did manage to steel himself to pages of precise and detailed tabulation of prodigies of viciousness. The obvious earnestness of the writer is somewhat offset by the sense of an advocate more interested in the argument than the factuality of the evidence.

"The fourth occupation of the soldiers is gambling." Father Carheil explains that it continued not only all day but all night, "even to the forgetting of the feast-days." Hour after hour the caustic and bitter summation goes on. "If occupations of this kind can be called the King's service, I admit that they have always actually rendered him one of these four services."

Bishop Laval, a sternly just and devout man, was writing in somewhat the same terms more than a dozen years in advance of good Father Carheil's tremendous blast. He wrote with ill-concealed passion of the disastrous effects of the brandy trading with the Indians. He told how they maimed and murdered one another and committed all manner of abominations while under the influence of liquor.

Colbert, to whom he wrote, was devout, too, in his own way, but it was a practical sort of devotion. It included the recognition that to challenge the brandy trade was to challenge the fur trade, and his practical view was that, minus the fur trade, Canada would hardly be worth the persistent annoyance it occasioned. He wrote the intendant asking how many crimes such as the bishop had suggested had come to his notice. Under other circumstances the request for facts rather than impassioned generalities would have roused Duchesneau's enthusiasm. He loved figures, and figures that could be neatly turned to the disadvantage of the governor would have been particularly attractive. But Duchesneau had his practical side. He knew the facts could hardly be as impressive as the bishop imagined, but to say so would be to sacrifice the good opinion of the cleric; to say otherwise would be to lose that of Colbert. Too adroit to be caught on either horn of this dilemma, Duchesneau decided to overlook the request. After all, the minister had provided his own clinching argument. "We would run the risk," Colbert had written, "if we yielded to his opinion, not only of losing this commerce but of forcing the savages to do business with the English and Dutch, who are heretics; and it would thus become impossible for us to keep them favorably disposed toward the one pure and true religion." If there was a hint of opportunism as well as unction in this thought, its soundness was beyond question.

Pressured on one side by the bishop and his clergy and on the other by his own practical common sense, Colbert decided to shrug off the problem. Centuries before that useful phrase "passing the buck" had been coined Colbert did just that. The question would be referred to important persons in the colony; persons other than the clergy, whose views were well known, would meet with the governor and the Superior Council to decide the point.

This gathering, which was to become known as the "Brandy Parliament," was the first and only mildly representative gathering in the history of New France. It would hardly be wise to assume that it represented any real divergence from the accepted absolutism. Colbert had a shrewd knowledge of how such a gathering would react. He was merely offering an opportunity for others to assume the responsibility and obloquy that otherwise would have fallen on his own shoulders.

On October 26, 1678, the most important seigneurs and merchants of the colony met to give their views. There were twenty of them. They met in the audience chamber of the Château of St. Louis, where the Council met frequently to face autocracy as they listened to the words of the King and his ministers. This day they were called to decide what authority should do. There were unaccustomed faces there. They were gathered about the long table that ran down the center of the hall to the dais at one end where, under the crossed white and gold banners of France, sat Frontenac.

But these newcomers were men who were not easily abashed. They carried their lives lightly and held opinions firmly. They recognized the importance of the occasion. The Seigneur Alexandre Bertier, who had led an expedition against the Iroquois, might be respectful of the bishop's opinions, but he felt no obligation to support them. Indeed, he promptly and bitterly protested the bishop's action in making a "reserved case" of selling liquor to the Indians. The Seigneur of Sorel joined in the protest. It was a serious point. The "reserved case" excluded from the sacraments of the Church all those who used brandy in their dealings with the Indians. Perhaps the two were not free of personal interest, at least in the tried argument that the prohibition was turning the fur trade to the English and Dutch in return for English or Dutch rum. They told of a party of Indians who had come to trade at Cataraqui with forty barrels of rum in their possession. It was a fair implication that the furs remaining for trade were the culls of the original cargo.

Louis Joliet was among the disputants. He had once leaned toward Holy Orders and had gone as far as an early clerkship before deciding to join with Father Marquette in his great explorations. Joliet was familiar with the Indians and their habits and was as determined as Bishop Laval could have wished. He urged that the fever to get brandy drove the natives to kill each other and to run into debt. He added the strange and unsupported conclusion that, recognizing their weakness, the Indians preferred to trade where liquor was not sold.

On his record Joliet was entitled to be heard with respect. But equally so was the still young, still severe and noble-looking Sieur de la Salle. He told the gathering of the instance of three hundred Indians on their way to Montreal who, hearing that no brandy was to be had there, promptly by-passed the place and took their furs to Albany, where rum was plentiful.

There was less drinking among the natives, he averred, than in a little Breton town. These familiar arguments continued for hours, but when a division was called there was no indication that anyone's opinion had been changed. Of the twenty notables whose views had been requested, fifteen voted to make no change in the practices governing the traffic.

The bishop did not take this setback lying down. That was not in his character. He went to protest personally to the minister. But for once Colbert was the good democrat. The people had spoken. He issued orders that the trade should be continued. He did offer one small sop to the bishop. Permits to go to the Indian villages should be reduced to the smallest possible number. Bishop Laval, astute and tenacious as ever, saw in this a new phase of the campaign. If Frenchmen could be restrained from going to the woods and the Indians compelled to come to well-established trading posts, both the *coureurs de bois* and the brandy traffic would be more surely under his control, and that other dream of having these hardy individualists as husbands and fathers rather than having them yearning for the freedom of the forests would be assured.

CHAPTER II

CURRENCY AND *COUREURS*

Beaver skins dominate the trade of Canada and determine the character of its life. The coureurs *and their unending conflict with authority. Various types of* coureurs*—the striking examples of Daniel du Lhut and Nicholas Perrot. The recall of Frontenac.*

THE bishop, with the King and his ministers, had small interest in an expanding domain. Their interest was in a secure and restricted community that would assure a steady flow of beaver skins through easily supervised channels. Had it been possible for them to achieve this end, the story of France in the New World would have been vastly different. Had it been possible, the whole pattern of the next century and its unending conflict might have changed too. Perhaps but for the beaver this might have been the fact. The development of the years ahead would have come in time, but not until some other incentive had taken the place of beaver skins and had helped to inspire and underwrite the adventurous urge of man.

Quite rightly is the beaver an unofficial national emblem of Canada. This intelligent and industrious animal that combined with these fine qualities an equally fine coat was the spark plug of an era. Beaver skins were almost currency in the New World. They were as negotiable, perhaps even more so, as money. The minutes of the Hudson's Bay Company of 1681 show that bundles of skins were being traded in London at 14s,6d per pound.

It was a business that fluctuated like the figures on a stockbroker's board as the news was good or bad. In the case of the Hudson's Bay Company, of course, good news boded ill for the French and vice versa. In 1688, despite hazards and uncertainty, the company declared a dividend of 50 per cent. The following year, with the Indians devastating New France and terrorizing the lesser tribes, business declined on the bay. The return of Frontenac to Quebec as governor only augmented the feeling of uncertainty. So dividends dropped to 25 per cent. But in 1690 the threat of an English attack on Quebec, which seemed to weigh the balance in favor of the English, saw cargoes of furs once more finding their way north to the bay instead of to Montreal or Quebec. In that year the company's dividend soared to 75 per cent. There seemed to be no limit to the demand for furs, and the negotiations and maneuverings to secure them were the force that set armies in motion and made conflict inevitable.

It began with the incentive of an apparently limitless source of wealth open to anyone who had the courage to defy authority and the natural threats of an unfriendly land. Not only was the promise of profit great—a few beads or a comb or a mirror might bring a return of three or four hundred times their cost—but there was adventure, and danger to be faced. It was a challenge beyond resisting to many whose only assets were courage and a certain wild recklessness.

The King might order that first offenders against his rule that no one go to the woods without license should be whipped and branded, while a second offense might condemn a man to the galley for life. The penalties were severe enough, yet they were of as little effect as if the King hadn't spoken. Perhaps the way these orders were given, blowing hot one minute and cold the next, had something to do with their lack of effect. This vacillating policy was not due to any change of opinion on the King's part but to the fact that so many defied the edicts and that too great severity might turn adventurous youth into forest outlaws or, worse still, renegades to their own particular civilization and faith. In a measure this had happened to Brulé, as has been recounted, and to Pierre Radisson, and it had not accrued to the benefit of France. These things considered, it is not surprising that men should find the temptations of the forest too great to be offset by the hard and humble duties of possessing and populating the land that Louis and his ministers had decreed for them.

If we can take the word of so special a pleader as Intendant Duchesneau, these *coureurs* represented eight hundred men out of the then total population of ten thousand. This, considering the phenomenal birth rate, meant that four out of every ten adult male citizens had taken to the woods. The figure, no doubt, includes some considerable exaggeration, but, even without, it would still be impressive.

Some years later, when Governor Denonville occupied the governorship, that well-meaning aristocrat made his own point. "You are aware, monsieur," he wrote the minister, "that the *coureurs de bois* are a great evil, but you are not aware how great that evil is. It deprives the country of its effective men; makes them indocile, debauched and incapable of discipline and turns them into pretended nobles, wearing the sword and decked out with lace, both they and their relations, who all affect to be gentlemen and ladies. As for cultivating the soil, they will not hear of it." Later he added to this an embittered footnote, commenting on their indifference to marriage; how their children, presumably because of their fathers' absence in the woods, became as unruly as Indians. But this unruliness did not apply only to children, for Denonville explains that on their return from the woods the wanderers swaggered like lords, spent all their gain in dress and drunken revelry, and despised the peasants, "whose daughters they will not deign to marry, though they are peasants themselves."

This graphic underlining of the effort of authority to keep the hewers of wood and drawers of water from encroaching on the preserves of those who toiled not was undoubtedly one of the factors in encouraging the *coureurs de bois*. The forest was a great leveler. What is perhaps not as clearly seen is that it was to be a factor in the century of conflict that was already dawning. For the checkrein on freedom that autocracy represented, while it made for the strength of a centralized authority, failed before the less capable and often clumsy direction of leaders whose shortcomings were offset by a following fired by the knowledge that the gains of victory were also their own.

Unlike England, where the difference between the nobility and commoner could be overcome by achievement or the accumulation of wealth, in France privilege was a frozen thing. It applied only to the nobility and the untitled offshoots of nobility, the group known as *gentilshommes*. As is proper, the name suggests no particular station or occupation, for usually the members of this group had none. They would not work and they could not engage in trade for fear of losing that tenuous thread that linked them to nobility. Their only possible occupation was that of arms, for courage was their one asset, and glory alone could bring added prestige. It would have seemed that the New World was made for them, but the *gentilshommes* felt no urge toward it. It liked the court, its color, its observances, its easy and decorative morals. It had no stomach for the starkness of pioneer life, nor for warfare that outraged every military tradition to which its members had been raised. To die was one thing, but to die from a shot fired from behind a tree, and quite possibly to lose one's scalp in addition, seemed to be going beyond the logical hazards of soldiering.

The very existence of this twilight class, however small a part it may have played in the drama of events, did have an influence. It was that in a new world with its less settled social boundaries the existence of this in-between class did suggest the possibility of slipping from one world into another. That was one factor that at last led the young and ambitious to try their fortune in the woods rather than accept their lot and settle down into the inescapable routine of habitant life. It was a losing fight, this effort to keep all privileges on one side of a line and all physical effort on the other. When Denonville, or the various intendants, or Bishop Laval, or the King's ministers, or even the King himself, sought to turn adventurers into plowmen, to still the craving for betterment, or to satisfy youth with a township where it had visioned a continent, each was contending for something beyond the authority of bishops or kings, as the years ahead were to prove.

The *coureurs de bois*, as a matter of fact, might be roughly divided into three groups. They resembled each other only in the courage and the spirit of adventure that animated all three. There were the men who had strayed from the settled life the King had decreed for them, in the hope of earning a competence and in the somewhat more cloudy hope that by so doing they might gradually insinuate themselves into the ranks of privilege. There were the reckless, the unstable, the indolent, and the frankly lawless, who were lured not by any promise of the future but by the present emancipation from the limited restraint of their own conscience and the somewhat more cogent all-seeing eye of the Jesuits. And there were the men who for want of a better name and a better understanding were grouped with the *coureurs* and shared the obloquy that was attached to the name.

They were traders as well as discoverers. How else could they have financed undertakings and discoveries that did not enjoy the favor of a king who wanted no part of an enlarging empire in America?

Doubtless they profited from this trading, and others with them. There is no record, however, of vast fortunes left by any of these adventurers. They were consistently at the call of the King and his governors. They worked prodigiously and took enormous risks and, for credit, they were always under the threat of the lash and the galley. Yet nothing diverted them from their purpose to go and see. They lived their rigorous, uncomfortable, and hazardous lives and, strangely enough, often managed to survive to what, even in our day, would be considered a ripe old age.

There was Daniel Greysolon du Lhut. He was described by Intendant Duchesneau as "chief among the *coureurs*," though the official's intent was to present him as chief among sinners rather than to commend. He belonged, as did Frontenac, to the middle nobility —not to one of the great houses of France, nor yet to one of the least. He was an officer of the Royal Guard, the elite even among the household troops of Louis. Even the privates in the ranks, it was said, were required to show quarterings. Apparently soldiering didn't appeal to him. It wasn't for lack of action, for the armies of Louis never suffered from stagnation. Young Du Lhut was present at the bloody battle of Seneffe when the great Condé challenged the stubborn gallantry of William of Orange and won a dubious victory at terrible cost. It was said that there were more than thirty thousand casualties. But though Du Lhut shared in the final charge of the day, he escaped the fate that befell so many. Perhaps he assumed that after so disastrous an affair there would be no further challenge to the might of France. Within a year he was in Canada, a half-pay officer still bearing his rank. He quickly made it clear that he had come to stay. He built himself a good house in Montreal—"in the best part of town," so the records say, as if he proposed to settle there for life. For some years he did stay, probably while he was learning the ways of the Indians and getting a smattering of their language and their habits. Outwardly he was the proper pattern of a conservative businessman bent on the practical matter of getting ahead.

Then, suddenly as he had come, he sold his good house and disappeared into the wilderness. To his fellow citizens, even the most broad-minded of them, it seemed a tacit announcement that in defiance of the King's orders he was prepared to follow the course that promised the most. That certainly was the viewpoint presented in the voluminous correspondence of the intendant, who didn't overlook the fact that Du Lhut was a friend of Frontenac, and what disadvantaged the one might reasonably be hoped to do the same by the other.

Du Lhut was one of the relatively few who held Frontenac's unqualified friendship. For very practical reasons, argued Intendant Duchesneau, and he argued it time and again. There were personal considerations, of course, in the friendship of the two. The trade benefits that accrued from Du Lhut's activities undoubtedly were shared and, almost as surely, Frontenac participated. In our day this would be entirely reprehensible. But in that day, if not an officially accepted practice, it was regarded with a lenient eye, provided the sharing did not bite too deeply into the revenues the King considered exclusively his own. To official eyes the practice had the advantage that it permitted salaries to be kept to an irreducible minimum. Certainly Frontenac's early salary of eight thousand livres was that. Even allowing for the different era, the two thousand dollars which this represented was unbelievably small. Frontenac had always been something of a spendthrift at heart, and Canada didn't change that. But there is no evidence that either Du Lhut or his friends benefited too largely or that they did not render more than adequate service in return. It is impossible to believe also that had the friendship been based only on co-operation for personal advantage the lifetime of effort would not have provided more than the modest competence that accrued to each.

There was another ground for understanding. In the more dramatic moments in Du Lhut's career the only person one can imagine who could have faced the situation with the same sure confidence and the same decisiveness was Frontenac. Possibly Nicholas Perrot, his fellow *coureur*, might have done so, but certainly Frontenac, and hardly another.

There is the Frontenac touch in the way Du Lhut slipped away from the fine home he had built for himself in Montreal, drawn by the pull of a parish he had dreamed of but never seen. It was the Sioux country at the head of the Great Lakes. There in a forbidden land that the Sioux had made a place of perpetual battle he, with his seven companions, faced the warrior tribes and earned their grudging respect. He had come to trade, to his own and the governor's substantial advantage, as those who had not dared the hazard were quick to say. Perhaps it was a natural skepticism. But in the perspective of history, while the suggestion may remain, it becomes insignificant in the light of the achievements of the next thirty years. For Du Lhut not only gave a name to a great city but he made the endless reaches of the Sioux country his own, gave it an uneasy peace, and made it serve the purposes of the King.

One might remember the incident that Father Louis Hennepin, with characteristic mendaciousness, turned to his own glory. Father Hennepin claimed credit for every achievement that seemed to be of outstanding significance. He had gone from the mouth of the Illinois River, so he said, to the mouth of the Mississippi and returned, a journey of over thirty-two hundred miles in a matter of thirty days, though later his Indian captors derided him because with three companions he couldn't make more than eighteen miles a day by canoe. He claimed to have been the first discoverer of the Sioux country, though when he finally reached there it was to find the plaque placed by Du Lhut the year before. He had, so to speak, rescued himself from an intolerable and dangerous situation, though he had borne the indignities and perpetual danger for three months until Du Lhut arrived on the scene. Then the good father was quick to extricate himself. Small wonder that the ever-generous Francis Parkman was to say: "This Reverend Father was the most impudent of liars."

The simple facts of this last instance were that Du Lhut, traveling the waters of the upper Mississippi, heard stories of three white men held captive by the tribes on the river below. Thinking it might be Englishmen poaching on French preserves, he determined to investigate. After paddling 160 miles with three companions he overtook a war party of a thousand warriors and discovered that it was they who were holding the captives and that these were not Englishmen but Frenchmen, and one of them Father Hennepin. "It would not do," as Du Lhut explained later to Hennepin, "to suffer an injury of such a nature without showing resentment." There was the Frontenac touch in the way Du Lhut marched to the very center of the war party, demanding to meet its chief and sternly berating him and his followers for taking the good father's robes and keeping him employed at menial tasks. Only then, it appears, did the thought of escape enter Hennepin's mind.

There was the instance while Du Lhut commanded at Fort Michilimackinac. Two Frenchmen had been killed in the woods and their fur cargoes taken by the Indians. Du Lhut set out to investigate.

Suspicion pointed to a reckless young brave strangely named Folle Avoine, who had gained a large influence over the tribes thereabout, and to Chief Achiganaga of one of the more westerly tribes and his two sons. Folle Avoine was strutting about the Sault surrounded by a coterie of followers and daring the twelve men guarding the post to do anything about it. As they perhaps wisely did nothing, Du Lhut went himself to investigate.

The general opinion among the French was that this was a place for diplomacy. Considering the prominence of the culprits and the more than probable assumption that to arrest them would set all the neighboring tribes on the warpath, it seemed wisest to forget the whole matter. After all, *coureurs* had to take their chances. There was hardly any disagreement except for Du Lhut. When he heard that Avoine was swaggering about the Sault daring anyone to arrest him and promising that at the first attempt the fort would be razed and its twelve defenders roasted, he went himself and put Avoine under arrest. The capture of the others took more time—they were hiding out with the western tribes—but finally they also were brought in.

The trial began, the trial of Indians accused of murder, but it was carried on with dignity and fairness. When it concluded, there was no further doubt. The chief was acquitted, but Folle Avoine and the chief's two sons were found guilty. The four hundred Indians who stood about watching the proceedings shouted their agreement when their elders said, "You accuse one another. Your fate is now in the hands of the Frenchmen."

This was felt to be a gesture that called for reciprocation. The culprits had been tried and found guilty. This had been admitted; the magnanimous thing now would be to forget the whole matter. When it appeared that this course was improbable, the friendliness began to disappear. The four hundred Indians gathered in angry crowds. They outnumbered the Frenchmen ten to one; the odds would be double that when the tribes hurrying through the woods reached the scene. The threat of violence grew with each passing minute.

Du Lhut explained carefully that these were not prisoners of war. Such he would be ready to spare, but not murderers. Two tribes were involved; one man from each must pay the penalty. One concession alone he would permit. The Jesuits might baptize the condemned if they so desired. But that was all.

An hour later, standing well in front of his total force of forty-two Frenchmen with four hundred maddened Indians threatening to break loose in open massacre, grim-faced Du Lhut watched as the sentence was carried out.

There was no reprisal. The Indians knew this man. He was stern and resolute in all his ways, but he was also just. He never defrauded them, never derided, and he always kept his word. With their quick eye for any hint of weakness, they knew there was no weakness here. Men had been robbed and killed, and the offenders had paid the price. Soon the stolen articles would be returned, and the chapter would be closed. For all their threats, there was no one ready to challenge the man who, they knew, would have dealt as justly and as sternly with his own.

There are other dramatic incidents in the life of this man who was branded "chief of the *coureurs*"—the blackest sin of the day. Some of them appear in this record, but it might be remembered also that at Du Lhut's death, Vaudreuil, then governor of Montreal and a man who had been anything but his friend, was to voice a grudging tribute. "He was," said Vaudreuil, "a very honest man."

Possibly had Nicholas Perrot come more prominently to the intendant's attention he, rather than Du Lhut, might have been named chief of the *coureurs*. There was little to choose between them. The lives of both emphatically deny the charges that were so readily, and often so reasonably, attached to the name of *coureur*. Both were honest and devout men. Among the treasures of the Wisconsin Historical Society is a silver monstrance. Clearly engraved on its base is the legend, "This Ostensorium was given by Monsieur Nicholas Perrot to the Mission of St. Francis Xavier at the Bay des Puants 1686." This might suggest that not all the *coureurs* were the renegades they were made to appear; that some were men of soberness and devotion—Nicholas Perrot most undoubtedly was.

That he had not always been so regarded is probably due to the fact that all too frequently he has been confused with that less admirable sharer of his name, the crafty, aggressive, unscrupulous François Marie Perrot, who for a time was governor of Montreal, prisoner of Frontenac, and owner of the trading post of Isle Perrot. There was no relationship between the two, nor any qualities in common. It would have been unthinkable that Nicholas Perrot could have traded his garments piece by piece so that an Indian garbed in his coat and hat and sword and wearing his shoes and stockings could caper about the streets of Montreal as the governor, while the real governor, Perrot, looked on with cynical interest and boasted to his boon companions that he had made thirty pistoles by the bargain.

There was a dignity about Nicholas Perrot that no one could question. He recognized it in his Indian associates as he demanded it for himself. This attitude, this recognition that he shared with Du Lhut and La Salle and Frontenac, was possibly the bond that drew them together in a friendship that overstepped authorities. It explained the hold that each maintained over the Indians. Each understood that, though forms of dignity might differ, it was as important to men of red skins as to those whose skins were white.

Nicholas Perrot was no longer in his early youth when he began to be a figure in this dangerous and violent world. He seems to have come to Canada quite unheralded and to have disappeared into the woods along with so many of the young and daring for whom the life of the city or farm offered little and the forest offered much. There was profit to be made and risks to be faced, the risk of the tomahawk and the no less authoritative risk of the displeasure of the King. Many lost their lives. Many, as the Jesuits pointed out so conscientiously, become reprobates beyond help, either spiritual or physical. They merged with the children of the forest and became lost to civilization.

Not so Nicholas Perrot. In any accounting he must be reckoned among the constructive pioneers. He was undoubtedly one of the ablest and most daring of the *coureurs*. At an age when most modern youth are being laboriously educated he had slipped into a life that, according to most of the wisdom of his day, demeaned the good and debauched the less able. To Nicholas Perrot, at least, it did neither. When he reappears he is a man ready and able to be of large service in the opening of a continent. He knew the Algonquin language like his mother tongue. He was fluent in a dozen different dialects. When he returned to civilization he had with him at least the beginnings of the manuscript *Mémoire sur les Moeurs, Coutumes et Religion des Sauvages de l'Amérique Septentrionale*, his treatise on the manners, customs, and religion of the North American Indian.

In his early youth he had been attracted to the Jesuits and had taken some early training, but the Church had not quite laid its impress on him. It had helped to make him vocal, but this vocation remained that of explorer rather than priest.

Perrot was twenty-six when he was named interpreter to the expedition sent out by Talon in 1670 under the leadership of Daumont de St. Lusson to investigate the report that copper was to be found on the shores of Lake Superior. The expedition wintered on Lake Huron's Manitoulin Island, and Perrot, having sent word to the tribes of the north that St. Lusson wished to see them at Sault Ste. Marie in the early spring, made a personal visit to the western tribes, particularly the Miami about Green Bay. All went well, and on May 1, as his memoirs tell, Perrot and his motley collection of chiefs of a dozen different tribes reached the Sault. The lake tribes, too, were gathering and St. Lusson was on hand with his party of fifteen Frenchmen.

On the morning of June 14, 1671, St. Lusson led his followers to the top of an adjoining hill. The scene had been calculated to impress. The few soldiers were under arms. The priests in their vestments stood against a background of a great cross of wood. Beside the cross was a cedar post with a metal plate bearing the arms of France. St. Lusson stepped forward, sword in one hand, a clod of earth in the other. His voice rose above the babble of tongues as he declared his purpose—"To take possession of this place Sainte Marie du Sout, as also Lakes Huron and Superior and the streams contiguous and adjacent thereto—both those which have been discovered; and those which may be discovered hereafter in all their length and breadth, bounded on the one side by the seas of the North and of the West, and on the other by the South Sea."

It was a considerable order. After some more in the same vein, guns were fired and there were shouts of "*Vive le Roi,*" while the yelps of the startled Indians added to the din.

The ceremonies over, St. Lusson and his fifteen followers, now augmented by Perrot, proceeded on their voyage to Lake Superior. The tribes, before they scattered, thoughtfully stripped the arms of France from the cedar posts. It was not because of the large claims the arms represented—which, happily, they had not understood—but probably they considered the metal plate a charm that might be all right for Frenchmen but that, for themselves, they would be as well without.

The expedition to Superior failed to find any indication of the promised copper. There was some trading. For the rest, about all these elaborate efforts succeeded in proving was a fact that had been proven time and again, that Nicholas Perrot did have the respect, the confidence, and the friendship of the Indians and that this alone held many of the tribes to their uncertain allegiance to France.

But chiefly Nicholas Perrot and Du Lhut, and especially Du Lhut, were known as the friends of Frontenac. In the official view this association did no one much credit. On the friendship of Du Lhut for Frontenac were based the charges that the governor recklessly broke the King's law by favoring the *coureurs.* But any one of a dozen men might have served the private interests of the governor as handsomely had that been the only basis of their friendship, but few others had a heart as single in its devotion to an adopted land as had Du Lhut and Frontenac.

But this was not how the friendship appeared to Intendant Duchesneau. To him it was a marriage of convenience, and in all his correspondence he presents the governor as intent upon enriching himself, even in defiance of the King's regulations. Duchesneau had a one-track mind. What he wanted to believe, he believed; what ran contrary to his thinking, he disregarded. In presenting Frontenac as an open champion of the *coureurs,* he brushed aside the known fact that the governor had petitioned the King for a galley that he might enslave for life those found guilty of illegal trading. For his part, Frontenac was never known to run from a quarrel, however trivial. Indeed, once engaged, he could never thereafter feel it a matter of small consequence. So the battle continued, the intendant growing increasingly shrill in his denunciations. The governor was protecting a host of *coureurs* who were in league with him—he was in constant communication with Du Lhut, their acknowledged leader—he had made himself master of the trade of Montreal, exacting a certain number of packs of beaver skins in return for the protection of the governor's guard. The charges suggest practices not unknown in more modern days but definitely unproven here.

The King knew this as well as anyone, but his patience was wearing too thin for him to be completely judicial. Conventional history has pictured him as a monarch devoting his life to more or less questionable pleasures. That could have been only one facet of his character, for he read and personally replied to a volume of correspondence that would stagger a present-day executive. He was intimately conversant with the scheming and rivalry and mutual recriminations that figured in the bulk of the correspondence coming from the New World.

"I see," Louis wrote the governor, "that you often turn the orders that I give you against the very object for which they are given; beware not to do so on this occasion. I shall hold you answerable for bringing the disorders of the *coureurs de bois* to an end throughout Canada." To this he added a telling warning: "Take care not to persuade yourself that what I write to you comes from the ill-office of the intendant. It results from what I fully know from everything which reaches me from Canada, proving too well what you are doing there. The bishop, the ecclesiastics, the Jesuit fathers, the Supreme Council and, in a word, everybody complains of you. . . ."

There was a momentary lull in the disputations after this, but it couldn't last long with two such inveterate battlers in the arena. During the lull Colbert retired from the troublesome and thankless task of administering the colonies and was succeeded by his son, the Marquis de Seignelay.

Frontenac was not a gifted diplomat, but it did occur to him that it might be wise to write a letter of congratulation, lest the intendant get the advantage of the first word. The congratulations did not take many words and the governor was soon launched on a familiar grievance. "I have no doubt whatever," he wrote, "that M. Duchesneau will, as usual, overwhelm you with fabrications and falsehoods to cover his own ill conduct. I send proof to justify myself, so strong and convincing that I do not see that they can leave much doubt."

Then occurs one of those strange incidents that make the character of the great governor so difficult to assess. It appears in the concluding paragraph of his letter, when it possibly occurred to him that loading the new minister with innumerable proofs of the intendant's shortcomings might not be the most ingratiating approach. So he added: "Since I fear that their great number might fatigue you, I have thought it better to send them to my wife . . . in order that she may extract and lay before you the principal portions."

This was the wife he had married in defiance of her father's will that Wednesday in October 1648; whom he had lived with four years —years marked with ever-increasing bickering—and in the thirty years that followed had scarcely seen. There is some evidence to prove that Madame Frontenac was well satisfied to have the sea between her husband and herself; that possibly to that end she had been a party to his appointment as governor; and that certainly she had no wish to have him back. Yet in this moment of trial he put the evidence of his stormy career in her hands with the certainty that she would not fail to make a better case for him than he could hope to make for himself. It was not an ill-founded confidence. Often in the past he had called for her support, as he would do in the future, and never at any time was he to find it lacking.

But the shadows were drawing close about him. No amount of pleading could disguise the fact that here was a man who was a better governor of others than he was of himself. There were more days of bickering to follow, but now they were numbered. Still the accusations continued. It was the repeated charge that governor and intendant constantly hurled at one another—that the emissaries of one or the other were carrying furs to the English settlements—that touched the King most nearly. He could overlook much—for instance, the intendant's claim that the governor's friends had spread a report of a pestilence at Montreal while his *coureurs* picked up beaver skins at depression prices. There was no shade of truth in the pestilence story, the intendant had explained virtuously—nothing more serious than that eighteen or twenty Indians had recently drunk themselves to death at Lachine. This was all familiar. So, for that matter, was the charge of trading with the English, but it was more disturbing. It involved the King's revenues. It was giving comfort to the one force he knew he had most to fear.

Each ship that left for France bore some such load of complaint, and each returning vessel brought the King's reply couched in words that grew increasingly more stern. But even sternness has a limit, and Louis had reached it. If there is any reason for surprise, it is that his patience had lasted so long. In his decision he showed no favoritism. His order of dismissal included both the disputants.

Frontenac was one of those curious anomalies whose weaknesses are also their strength. The forthright qualities that made it impossible for him to be tactful made it easy for him to lose friends among his own people, at least among the people of apparent consequence. Yet these were the characteristics that gave him his amazing hold over the Indians and the respect of the less important French citizens. There was never any question as to where he stood. He was not afraid of having opinions and of voicing them even when, quite obviously, they would not be palatable to authority. He was not devious. He did not dissemble. It is true that he was deeply conscious of his own dignity and more than ready to defend it. But he defended it against those who could strike back. There was nothing in his character to lead him to tyrannize over lesser men. When he dealt with the Indians he did so out of an instinctive understanding. They responded to many of the impulses that moved him—a sense of drama, a love of oratory and display, a dignity that wasn't a frozen sort that could not be relaxed at need, a talent for prompt decision, an ability to talk simply and, when it was a matter of moving, to move swiftly. Most of all, the Indians were quick to recognize that his word, once given, was good. He never went back on it. Out of this came a dominance over the Indian mind that no other achieved quite as fully, and only a rare few achieved at all. But for all that, had his history ended here, it would have been a history of disappointment, the record of a man of considerable talents and conspicuous weaknesses; a man with a marked ability to control those he truly understood and no ability at all to control himself.

Frontenac had been ten years in Canada when the King's mandate recalled him. He had no prospects before him. The King's favor, which once in a small way he had enjoyed, would hardly sustain one whom Majesty had come to look upon as a problem and describe with spitefulness as "his high and mighty lordship." He had grown too old for arms. If he had a place at all, it would seem to be the one he was leaving.

The day of his departure was not a day of sorrow. It was like the day of his arrival, a gala day of general rejoicing. Today they were celebrating the departure of one who seemed to have few friends. The Jesuits and all who held with them were openly exultant. This was the man who had often challenged them. They saw him depart shorn of the King's favor. If the demotion of their useful tool, the intendant, was not equally to their liking, it was possible to argue that he had served his turn. A small price to pay for a substantial reward. Perhaps the gray-gowned Récollets among the holiday crowd may have wondered what life would be like when the black gowns had no one to challenge them. But these were very minor notes in the general rejoicing.

Down the steep Rue de la Montagne, which ten years ago had echoed to the march of his twenty guardsmen, the governor walked alone. His head was held high, as always, his face stern, his back stiff with military erectness. He did not raise his eyes to the heights that once he had seen as the perfect setting for the capital of a new empire. There was no backward glance to the castle on the hill that he had planned to make another Versailles. He was a solitary figure, but not lonely as a lesser man might have been. The men who might have stood with him, the men whose vision ranged beyond the immediate and the immediately profitable—La Salle, Du Lhut, Nicholas Perrot, De la Mothe Cadillac, and Henri Tonty—were far away. Of the great, only the Le Moynes, who had never liked him, were there for his farewell.

Perhaps there was bitterness in him and uncertainty. The fact, which he must have dimly recognized, that he had brought much of his trouble on himself was a doubtful consolation. All he could see was a crowd of people and hardly a friendly face. He could not know of the sudden catch at the heart as little people vaguely sensed that with his going security had left their world. These had no part in the triumph of clergy or traders. They watched the rejoicing with troubled eyes, wondering what would happen with the strong hand withdrawn. In all the disillusionment and disappointment this fact might stand out. For some of those who watched their governor's departure would live just long enough to know how right they had been.

CHAPTER III

CONDITIONED FOR CONFLICT

France passes its peak and enters on its century-long decline. A new world power begins to emerge. A growing tension between New France and New England. The crafty dealings of La Barre and the ineffectiveness of Denonville end in an act of treachery that cuts deeply into the prestige of France.

It was a changed France to which Frontenac was returning, a France that had reached the apex of its power. It stood uncertain on that pinnacle, still confident of its great destiny but increasingly unsure how to achieve it.

Even Louis the Magnificent was not completely happy. He knew himself to be the undisputed monarch of his world. France was dominant, and he dominated France. He could say with perfect truth, "*L'état c'est moi,*" and there was no one with the will or the force to question it successfully. Yet the enemies that every absolutism engenders were increasing in numbers, both at home and abroad, and such friends as he once had were slipping away. Glory would last his time. It would continue with the semblance of the same magnificence for three quarters of a century to come. But there it would end, snuffed out at last by the impatient guillotine in the Place de la Révolution.

No one would have guessed, least of all Louis, that England, the traditional foe, was moving just as surely to an age that would be as glorious as his own. There was little to show it. For years Louis might almost have been said to hold England in the palm of his hand. Charles II of England owed much to France. It had given him asylum when his own country had driven him out. When at last he returned to his throne he was still glad to accept the uncertain bounty of Louis. For all his faults, Charles II remembered his friends. If in doing so he made his kingdom subservient to that of his benefactor, it was that the friend was more adroit, not that Charles was less loyal. And when Charles gave place to his brother James, it seemed that little had changed. James II was as responsive to Louis as his brother had been before him. Yet there was a difference, as the coming years would disclose.

Louis had changed too. By his marriage to Madame de Maintenon he had lost a trifle of his majesty and had sacrificed something of his power. Like most despots, he had his blind side and, properly approached, he was tractable enough. The new favorite, unlike so many other beauties of the court, had her heart well under control. She realized wisely that the unfamiliar was the most likely to catch and hold the fickle attentions of the King, and what more unfamiliar to Versailles than propriety and a deep interest in the Church? The Jesuits were happy to encourage, and not slow to cultivate, one who might be a powerful ally—a wife who was not a queen, yet had ample skill to bend a king to her will. They still smarted under the Edict of Nantes, which Henry of Navarre, the beloved Henry IV of France, had signed in April of 1598. It assured the Protestants, whose religious views he once had shared, perfect liberty of conscience, the administration of impartial justice, and certain other concessions that had made them almost a state within a state. One of the first and most disastrous results of the *entente cordiale* between De Maintenon and the Jesuits was the revocation of the great edict. Louis was not a man of unsullied virtue, but religion did lie near his heart. He was determined to have as subjects only those of his own faith. It was not then so much the revocation itself as the reign of bitter intolerance and cruelty that followed that brought such far-reaching consequences. It was to divide the nation, rob it of a million of its most useful craftsmen and citizens, and sow the seed of ultimate decline.

In England there was no great evidence of change. James had succeeded Charles. He had most of the vices of his brother but nothing of the former's warmth and glamor. In their place he had an added stubbornness. He had, too, a zealot strain and, strangely enough, a soaring ambition that was lacking in Charles II. Probably ambition is not quite the word. His aim was to dominate England as Louis dominated France; it was a starling masquerading as an eagle with no realization whatever that the eagle's qualities were missing. James had determination that was more an unyielding pettiness, and he had courage that bore somewhat the same character, a pettiness combined with stupidity. In still Puritan England he publicly espoused the Roman Catholic Church. England disapproved. The Test Act, which made it obligatory for civil and military officials to accept the rites of the Church of England, necessitated his relinquishment of the office of Lord High Admiral of England. The loss he could bear. The implied reproof left him unmoved, or nearly so. It did result in the minor challenge that he insisted on hearing Mass in public. Had James been a truly spiritual man, this might have evidenced an admirable devotion, but all his acts and all his character denied such an interpretation and showed it for what it was—a challenge to public opinion. It did not go unnoticed. While Charles still lived, an Exclusion Bill was proposed. Its aim was to deny the throne to anyone professing the Catholic faith. Undoubtedly it was aimed to exclude James, but the personal popularity of Charles enabled his friends to prevent its passage. By a very narrow squeak James still headed the succession. He was unmoved by this challenge. It taught him nothing. When he did ascend the throne it was with absolutism in his heart. He still wanted to be an eagle.

It was not hard for Louis to play upon these strings. His own zeal had been encouraged, at least in outer semblance, by the urging of Madame de Maintenon, and he was quick to stir up his English cousin. James needed little urging. Opposition had only served to increase his zeal. He evidenced it in a renewed persecution of the Covenanters, a move that quickly turned half of England against him. It remains a question just how much Louis' influence was instrumental in encouraging James II in the headlong career of devastating mistakes and stupidities that were to be his undoing. These mistakes brought Louis also face to face with the most implacable enemy he had on the continent, now backed by English sympathy and English might.

It is probable that Frontenac, living out shabby years buoyed up by the hope that his hands might once again turn to shaping the empire of his dreams—a hope that each day dimmed a little—was too absorbed in his own problems to realize the significance of these happenings. Not many Frenchmen would have realized how closely these events touched their lives, and Frontenac was not by nature a thoughtful man. Yet the significance was there. At the instance of representatives of the English people William of Orange, son-in-law of James II, landed at Torbay on November 5, 1688, and with a considerable army that was steadily augmented began his march on London.

James knew that he had few friends on whom he might count. He couldn't even number his daughters among them. He must have read the writing on the wall as he tossed the Great Seal of England into the Thames and fled to the support of his friend in France. He was to live there on the scant bounty of Louis for a matter of thirteen years. Louis XIV was at least a realist. He was not one to lend his support to the unfortunate or the mistaken. Doubtless he regarded James as worth a small outlay, if only for his nuisance value. Circumstances proved how right he was.

Louis was not wholly blind to the implications of his changing world. He was too shrewd not to realize that being faced with William of Orange as King of England was a different matter from having there a complaisant Charles or James. William of Orange was conversant with the French King's devious ways and he was dedicated to the set purpose of defeating them. Moreover, he had the intent and the capacity to range the nations against him. This Louis recognized without also recognizing that such a combination could challenge successfully his own omnipotence. But certainly he recognized a growing complexity in the affairs of his kingdom and its colonies.

Over in New France, which was to be the source of wealth and power that Spain had discovered in the Indies, matters were not progressing quite as Louis could have hoped. An English Company of Adventurers was encroaching on the north while Dutchmen and Englishmen had secured an uncertain footing on the continent's eastern seaboard. It was basic in French colonial policy that such infiltration should be stopped before it was well begun. The great bay was to be kept as a French preserve, while the invaders of the eastern seaboard were to be contained in that rather inhospitable section between the coast and the Alleghenies. It was thought of as inhospitable because furs were scarce in the region and the Indians none too friendly. There was always the possibility that hostile tribes, perhaps with some small persuasion, might decide to drive the interlopers into the sea.

The plan to contain the English and Dutch was a happy one. All agreed on that except the Dutch and the English. The latter, particularly, were forever slipping from their containment and setting themselves up at points where they impinged on France's growing, if unwanted, empire. On Hudson's Bay gentlemen traders actually established forts and trading posts. Time and again these were destroyed, but always they were replaced. In Newfoundland, at Louisburg, at Port Royal, there was a continuing echo of English encroachments. These aggressions had occurred in the days of peace when Louis was sure of the friendship of his English cousins. With William of Orange on the throne, the thought of the invaders on the threshold of New France troubled every waking hour. Nor were these footsteps like the stealthy, deadly footsteps of Indians, who were here today and gone tomorrow. They were more dogged and persistent. Once they came, they might be expected to return. Louis sensed that here was an inescapable threat that could not be disregarded complacently, as he brushed off so many things. These encroaching feet must be turned away or the magnificent dream of a New France could hold no reality.

But there were points of strength. France and New France each bowed to one absolute authority. Louis XIV *was* the state. What he thought, what he wished, what he did were matters beyond criticism or correction. Behind him, supporting him and being supported by him, was a church that was as autocratic as he. It was staffed by devoted zealots, the like of which the world has hardly seen. They were clamorous for sacrifice and devotedly ready for any challenge that resulted in bringing others into their particular fold. No one can discount their immeasurable service. It is part of the warp and woof of Canadian history. These were the credit items of authority.

The English were twenty times as numerous in North America as were the French. That was a fact that couldn't be overlooked. They were also men of different aspirations. Where the French dreamed of glory, the English and their close neighbors, the Dutch, thought in terms of substance. Where the scions of the old French nobility were coming to the New World for adventure and were sowing this spirit in others, they were also establishing the tradition of absolutism in this new land. They were ready to adventure anywhere and to take any risk except that of boredom or of hard, consistent, undramatic work. The less volatile Englishman, on the other hand, was busily settling himself on the land and establishing his right to it. He was building settlements and digging in for whatever might befall. Where the French were ready to accept the word of Louis as final, admitting of no argument or qualification, the English were there mainly because they were disagreers with authority, seeking a place and a life that offered them the right to disagree and to make their own opinions law.

True, in their backgrounds, in their ambitions, in their training, in their religion, the English colonists were as diverse as were their settlements of Maine and Georgia. They didn't even agree with one another. The state-rights policy that was still centuries away from being a battle cry had begun to germinate.

These were the beginnings of the thirteen colonies that were to become the United States and that for a century to come were to be in more or less open conflict with Canada. So the history of this period is the history of both. For the greater part of that period it was to be a conflict of ideologies, individual freedom ranged against authority. Where Louis was stating what was, to him, indisputable fact that "It is God's will that whoever is born a subject should not reason but obey," the English colonists were formulating a political policy of rugged individualism. They were reluctant before any authority, even that instituted for the protection of their own various units. They were reasoning sturdily on behalf of themselves and their own rights, and were ready to question any rule that seemed to qualify the freedom they desired. In a sense it was some such ideological conflict as today exists between communism and democracy, with absolute authority ranged against a system where the demand for freedom was as absolute. With such conflicting views a settled peace was hardly possible.

Something of this Louis, who was not without a native shrewdness, must have understood, if possibly only vaguely. He must have sensed the inevitability of the challenge and knew that it must be met. The English and their views must be checked decisively or their way of thought would inevitably be accepted. This, majesty could not brook.

Unfortunately for him, the emissaries that Louis sent to do his bidding were hopelessly unequal to the task. Joseph le Febvre de la

Barre, the new governor, who arrived as Frontenac was leaving, was no man to step into shoes once occupied so competently. La Barre had done well enough when confronted by the English in the West Indies. But his achievements had been legalistic rather than military. That was understandable, for he had been trained as a lawyer and was by temperament a negotiator. His greatest achievement, possibly, had been the formation of a joint stock company in Cayenne, which had served him as well as it had served the colony. But as a military man he was without distinction. He was sixty years of age when he was appointed governor of New France. It was not that his years were against him. Frontenac was a year or two older, and no one ever questioned his fitness. But whatever fire there had been in La Barre had smoldered out, leaving only a timid and crafty opportunism.

It must be admitted that he was not fortunate in the time of his arrival. To begin with, on the night of August 4 fire had swept through the little capital of Quebec, and the kettles and pails that were the only defense were hopelessly inadequate to stay the advancing flames that raced through the sun-drenched logs of home and warehouse. When the fire had finally burned itself out the Lower Town was a smoking ruin. Fifty-four homes and warehouses had been destroyed, and with the latter more goods than remained in all the rest of Canada.

Less than a month later Le Febvre de la Barre arrived with his wife and family and timidly settled himself in the château on the hill, where he remained, so his intendant tells us, in constant dread of the Indian scalping knives.

For him there was more inconvenience than danger in a town crowded beyond belief. The new intendant who had arrived with him had both danger and inconvenience. With difficulty he had found lodging on the fringes of the forest and, with more reason, he shared the governor's fears. The threat of Indian war was more than imaginary. It had been brewing before Frontenac left. It was a difficult situation even for a well-tried hand. The Iroquois had finally conquered most of the tribes adjoining and, flushed with victory, they looked for the spoils. But spoils were meager among the defeated. However, there were the tempting beaver-rich territories that were occupied by France and by the tribes who admitted French authority. The Iroquois kept an uncertain allegiance with the English and Dutch. It was a matter of trade more than of friendship, and furs were needed to make the trading possible. There may have been more than a shadow of truth in the argument that the English were encouraging their allies to look for pelts in French territory. Certainly the Senecas, who numbered as many warriors as the other members of their confederacy combined, were itching for further conquests. That was the situation as the new governor took over his post. Small wonder he was nervous.

Safe in his château at Quebec, however, he was writing the King in stirring words. "The Iroquois have twenty-six hundred warriors," he wrote belligerently. "I will attack them with twelve hundred men. They know me before seeing me," he added in modest self-appraisal. "They have been told by the English how roughly I handled them in the West Indies." Thinking this over, it seems to have occurred to him that perhaps he had been a bit rash, and he added a qualification: "If the Iroquois believe that your Majesty would have the goodness to give me some help, they will make peace, and let our allies alone, which would save the trouble and expense of an arduous war."

La Barre was always a man for second thoughts in matters of peace as well as war. He had hardly arrived when he was writing the minister that he would not follow the example of his predecessors in office in making money out of the government by trade. He coupled with this admirable sentiment a petition for larger pay. This was given him, if somewhat reluctantly, in recognition of virtues that were not present, even in the most distant sense.

Having achieved so much, he had his customary change of heart and began looking for opportunities of profit. He was not diffident in his approach and in a surprisingly short time he was in close collaboration with such shrewd and resourceful spirits as Jacques le Ber, probably the leading merchant of Montreal and married to the sister of Charles le Moyne, a valuable fact that La Barre would hardly have overlooked. There was Aubert de la Chesnaye, too, one of the wealthiest men in the colony and, in La Barre's view, usefully unburdened by scruples. He was also lucky. When Quebec's Lower Town was all but wiped out by fire, the home of La Chesnaye was the only one left unscathed.

La Barre chose with care such men, and others who had been unfriendly to the former governor and who now felt that their turn had come. La Barre, who had asserted his high principles quite profitably, now proceeded to put them on the market again. With the assistance of the anti-Frontenac clique he built a tight little trading corporation whose highly practical attitude was that not only would they encroach on the King's trading preserves but that they would deal in the furs so secured in the most profitable market, which happened to be that of the English and Dutch.

Though these operations were carried on with rather amazing openness, the emissaries of the English and Dutch even being received at the château, no one seemed to question them. No one, that is, but the intendant. Jacques de Meules had come out on the ship with La Barre to take the intendantship left vacant by Duchesneau's recall. During that long voyage the two had not risen to heights of mutual liking or respect. It did not seem to be a necessary attribute of an intendant that he should think well of a governor. It wasn't expected, and a certain amount of interofficial sniping was rather encouraged. It was thought to be a helpful attitude for keeping each under somewhat critical observation.

Even so, Meules' repeated protests over the governor's actions might have received more attention had they not been such a mixed lot and if he himself had been a man of larger caliber. But Jacques de Meules was a stubborn, incapable, and conceited man, and these are not endearing weaknesses. Even the fact that he added to these qualities a certain native shrewdness could not change that picture. Moreover, his best intention seems to have been not so much to bring credit to himself as to discredit the governor, and this was a task that La Barre was quite capable of assuming for himself.

It is a little difficult to understand what it was that entitled a man of such small capacity as Meules, of whom so little is known to history, to be given a position of such dignity and power. The intendant, not Meules alone but all the intendants, controlled the finances of the colony. The governor was assumed to know little or nothing of business, and he was not expected to interfere in it. Mainly he was supposed to be satisfied with the duties of being the King's representative and, provided he did not encroach on the kingly prerogatives, the royal power would sustain him in his acts and dignities. But even as kings are controlled in some measure by those who hold the purse strings, so the intendants exercised their restraints. They administered the business of the colony and, while they could not openly restrain the governor, they could and often did put hazards and difficulties in the way of government. They controlled the King's revenues and the assessing and gathering of taxes. They had a material influence over the judiciary and the policing power. They were a useful check on any possible usurpation of kingly attributes. A certain combativeness between governor and intendant was expected and tacitly approved. It showed that checks were operating efficiently and that no authority was outgrowing its personal breeches. But there was a nice distinction between this subdued overseeing and the open antagonism that frequently existed between the two. These differences fill the correspondence of the day with colorful charges and innuendoes that add more to the interest than to the well-being of the colony.

With such responsibilities and authority, an intendant of force and integrity could make himself of almost equal importance with the governor, as was very evident in the case of Intendant Talon. But Meules wasn't a Talon, even by the widest stretching of the imagination. He wasn't even a Duchesneau. Perhaps he held office because of what Louis would probably have considered his sound views. Hadn't he openly voiced the opinion that "the people should not be allowed to speak their mind"? It was a rather neat phrasing of autocracy's viewpoint. He seems to have been in the good graces of the clergy, too, which undoubtedly was of help. During his intendancy there was absolutely no conflict between the two. Even the conflict with the governor, while incessant, never achieved the drama and warmth and never came to the open breach that it had with Frontenac and Duchesneau.

Meules had, at least, a tidy mind. So many of his dispatches had to do with minutiae that the King and his minister might have been spared. He protested the governor's habit of holding meetings of the Sovereign Council in his own antechamber, amid the noise of servants coming and going and the clatter of the guard in the adjoining room. When this small if reasonable objection fell on deaf ears, he elaborated the details, pointing out the incongruity of the governor holding his official council "in his own chimney corner, where his wife, his children and his servants were always in the way."

However well taken this point, it did not seem to justify high official action and it got none. Even the more impressive charge that the governor not only carried on trade in his own behalf—something that he had forsworn with dignity—but that he carried it on with the English was perhaps too familiar a charge to cause undue excitement. It might, or it might not, be true.

The governor was preparing for war with the Iroquois, and this seemed of more moment. He had been energetic at it, as energetic as his character permitted. He had built certain vessels, at the King's expense and purportedly for war. Meules, however, was more than skeptical, and so reported. The vessels were to be used for trade, he said. He added that two such vessels at Fort Frontenac had been used wholly for that purpose, while the flotilla of canoes that were supposed to be carrying munitions thither were loaded with trade goods for the business of the governor and his friends. Nobody paid much attention to M. Meules. This was a pity, for with all his lacks he did have a certain native shrewdness that enabled him to assess the governor better than the King had done.

Even La Barre's proposed disciplining of the Senecas—the great gesture which he had called on all the leaders of the country to support and which seems to have been taken at face value by these leaders—did not impress the intendant Meules. Without enthusiasm he saw the governor depart on his great adventure, and sat himself down to record his views for the minister. He wrote pungently. "With all his preparations for war, and all the expense in which Monsieur the Général is involving His Majesty . . . in my belief he will content himself with going in a canoe as far as Fort Frontenac and then send for the Senecas to treat of peace with them, and deceive the people, the intendant and, if I may say so, His Majesty himself."

In an illuminating postscript he reported the actual start of the expedition with the governor tête-à-tête with a man named La Chesnaye. "Everybody says that the war is a sham, that these two will arrange things between them and, in a word, do whatever will help their trade."

It must be admitted that in every single detail of his charges Meules called his shots with commendable accuracy. True, the treaty was signed at La Famine because the Senecas would go no farther, but in all other points the intendant's forecasting was unassailably correct. There was peace in the governor's time. But the men who had come at his call, some of them from a thousand miles distant, recognized that this was no peace of dominance. It was a peace of weakness, and the prestige of France sank very low indeed.

Whether someone finally paid some attention to Meules' reports, or whether the King finally saw the mistake for himself, the result was the same. A kindly letter that stressed La Barre's age and the fatigue inseparable from high office was more generous treatment than he might have expected, but the result was the same. He was recalled.

In La Barre's place Louis sent a high-principled, pious colonel of dragoons, the Marquis de Denonville. Obviously he meant well. He tried hard. He was just and honest, but he must have known himself unequal to the need to restore the failing courage and prestige of New France that La Barre had trafficked away. St. Vallier, who was to replace the aging Bishop Laval, came to Canada on the same ship that brought Denonville and his family. He was deeply impressed by the governor's devoutness, as well he might be. "He spent nearly all his time in prayer and the reading of good books," St. Vallier records. It is not the conventional picture of the dragoon of that day. Nor, unfortunately, were prayer and good books a complete compensation for the decisiveness of character that Denonville needed and did not have. He tried hard, but for all his courage and devotion he brought the colony lower than a far lesser man had left it.

The task before him was great and his resources pitifully slim. The Iroquois, remembering how they had outwitted La Barre, were openly derisive. There was need for another Frontenac, and Denonville most certainly was not that. To meet the imminent threat of war he needed more men than the colony could provide. It is true that he came with five hundred new troops, but a hundred and fifty of them had died of fever and scurvy on the voyage out, and those who survived were poor wraiths who would not be fit for service for many weeks. The question remained, would the Indians with their new sense of mastery wait that long?

Obviously Denonville didn't think so, and he was far from certain of his ability to meet this threat. He wrote to the ministry: "If we have war, nothing can save the country but a miracle of God." Nonetheless, he set about his preparations with a steady heart, and if his judgment had been equal to his courage, all might still have been well.

Along with courage he had a certain native shrewdness. He was quick to see that the pressing problem of the colony was not alone the antagonism of the Iroquois but that plus the machinations of that astute Irishman Thomas Dongan, who was governor of New York. Governor Dongan was by nature a schemer. He was also a man of intelligence. It was evident to him that if the French policy of colonization which Frontenac had encouraged were to prevail the French would soon be masters of the continent, leaving the English only their uncertain hold on the eastern seaboard while the French established their forts along the Mississippi and the lakes and used these as starting points to reach out both east and west. Dongan's policy was to contain the French along the St. Lawrence, as the French policy was to contain the English behind the Alleghenies. The weight of numbers was undoubtedly with Dongan. But the English colonies were broken into small groups and, while their interests were one, their intentions of combining to support them were almost negligible. It was very much Dongan's fight, but even his own citizens were more intent on their individual interests than on any wide matter of policy. The French, on the other hand, had behind them an absolute authority whose instructions were that the Iroquois should be humbled and Dongan's schemes should be circumvented.

But Dongan was not a man who submitted readily to circumvention. His resources as governor of New York were scarcely greater than Denonville's, but in astuteness he was unquestionably the master. He had a way with his Indian allies. Denonville reported that Dongan had gathered all the five Iroquois nations at Orange—the present Albany—to stir their antagonism against the French. It was not difficult to do. La Barre, for all his bluster, had been both timid and stupid. When his threats were followed not by action but by a multitude of words, the Indians became convinced that the heart to take a chance wasn't there, and they judged that it was the same with France. So a shrewd suggestion here and there was all that had been necessary to put the fat in the fire. Denonville's clumsy if courageous efforts to correct this thinking were offset by one uncharacteristic act of treachery that made the breach final and complete.

Naturally Denonville felt that the strategy for restoring the prestige of France involved teaching the Iroquois a lesson. It was the same unfortunate phrase that La Barre had used. That highly vocal young captain of marines, La Hontan, who had heard the first statement and was present as La Barre attempted to carry it out, was not impressed by the repetition. "There is one thing quite clear," he said, "and that is that you can never wipe out the Iroquois; therefore, why disturb them, since they are giving us no reason to do so?"

It was a cogent question, but Denonville had his mind made up and was not to be diverted. He had the unfortunate ability to confuse stubbornness with decisiveness. The first step was to send the Jesuit priest, Jean de Lamberville, who had great influence with the Onondagas, to urge that they come to Fort Frontenac to treat with the new governor. De Lamberville was a man of extreme courage and devotion. It appears also that he was of inordinate innocence, for he took his orders at their face value, confident that what he suggested was just a friendly meeting. Denonville, good and devout man though he was, thought only in terms of deception. It was a deception that began primarily with the King, who, thinking of Indians taken captive in battle, reflected that they might be usefully employed at the oars of his galleys in France, which operated mainly against the Mediterranean pirates. The hazards were high and oarsmen difficult to secure. Denonville, though he knew that captives taken in battle were few, still gave the suggestion serious thought. Niceties of behavior did not always dominate the dealings between French and Indians, and the governor should be blamed for stupidity as much as for treachery in deciding to capture prisoners by guile. The only phase of the matter that seemed to disturb him was that it would place De Lamberville in the difficult predicament of appearing doubly to deceive his friends. "The poor father," Denonville wrote to the ministry, "knows nothing of our design. I am sorry to see him exposed to danger; but, should I recall him, his withdrawal would certainly betray our plans to the Iroquois." Counting the cost that he mistakenly assumed might have to be paid solely by the devoted priest, he decided to do nothing.

Intendant Champigny, setting out from Montreal on the first stage of the campaign against the Iroquois, was a day or two ahead of the governor and the main body. It occurred to him that this was as good a time as any to collect the captives the King had mentioned. He remembered the two villages of Quinte and Ganneious. They were the home of some of the Christian Iroquois, whose main occupation was to provide sustenance for the troops at Fort Frontenac. As a preliminary step he invited them all to a feast at the fort. Some accepted gladly; to the more suspicious he went himself to give the invitation some force. To others he sent a determined fellow named Perre whom he knew would be unlikely to take no for an answer. In all they captured, for that was the import of the invitation, thirty men and ninety women and children who had come as guests.

Among the captives were five picked up as the invitation party was returning. That was where the mischance that is shared by mice and men intervened. Among the five were the son and brother of Otréouati, the Big Mouth, a very important citizen among the Onondagas and of whom we have already heard. As soon as this contretemps was discovered the two were released and returned to Big Mouth with gifts and many kind words.

Despite this mischance Champigny was well satisfied with the venture. He was buoyed up with the thought that such prompt action on the King's suggestion would mark him out as a diligent and successful official. These various forays had netted a total of some fifty-one warriors and three times their number of women and children. For the time at least he was more interested in the stalwart prisoners who would look well in the King's galley than he was with the more practical consideration of what effect his actions might have on the patched-up peace with the Iroquois. There was always some doubt as to whether Otréouati would accept the gesture of the return of his son and brother as a full requital for those others who had been captured and had not been returned. He was an astute gentleman, this elder statesman of the Onondagas, one who could meet guile with guile; who could accept gifts and favors proudly, paying for them with promises from his generous mouth and with tongue in cheek. Some years ago Father Lamberville had warned La Barre: "He calls himself your best friend, but he is a venal creature." But La Barre had not heeded the warning, and Denonville, having learned nothing from others' mistakes, was doomed to repeat them. With all the tragic evidence before him Denonville, a more just, more able, more conscientious man, was following the same path as La Barre. He was following it with the blackness of treachery on his hands, with Big Mouth alerted and ready to sweep his people into a war fever with his impassioned oratory.

If the consciences of Denonville and Champigny troubled them at all, they put this aside, remembering with satisfaction that they were doing the King's will. They did have fifty-one captive warriors, thirty-five of whom would eventually toil at the oars of the King's galleys. The observant La Hontan tells of seeing these captives. They were tied to posts by their necks and feet so that they could neither sleep nor drive off the plague of mosquitoes. Had either relief been possible, the diversions of their Christianized fellows, who enlivened the scene by burning the fingers of the captives in the bowls of their pipes, would have discounted it.

Denonville was naturally a brave and kindly man. He had no part in these activities. But like most men of his day, he bowed to what he believed to be a necessary part of co-operation with savage allies. Perhaps it was rather that there was room for satisfaction only over the hundred and fifty women and children—or what remained of that number after excitement, distress, and disease had taken their heavy toll—rather summarily welcomed into Mother Church. The amazing devotion of the great pioneers of the Church in New France could hardly be explained but for their confident belief that baptism was an ample reward for all hardship and suffering. Certainly the devout Denonville believed this without qualification. He could see the Indian family's loss of husband and father and the forceful separation from their fellows amply offset by the fact that these women and children would be baptized and distributed among the missions of the colony.

CHAPTER IV

YOU MUST CRUSH THE WASPS

The great army and the amazing good fortune that made its concentration possible. The indecisiveness that robbed it of much of its value. Fruitless negotiations ending in the awful night at Lachine. The razing of Fort Frontenac. Denonville's recall. The nadir of New France.

NEVER before had the continent seen anything like the army that Denonville was to lead against the Senecas. It was a cross section of a continent, and the names of its leaders are a roster of the great of New France. For once, and quite unjustly, considering the unnecessary treachery with which the campaign began, everything was working with the governor.

Modern war has made us familiar with the vast problems involved in planning for concerted action. "D-Day" is one vast miracle of movements of men and munitions. With every resource of modern science, military equipment, transport, and intelligence to co-ordinate an attack, it is a matter for almost superhuman ability. Denonville's ability was average at best. Problems of strategy and logistics were almost unknown to him. The forces he was to command were scattered about the four corners of a continent, hardly closer than a thousand miles at any point and frequently more distant. Thousands of miles of forest and not a foot of finished road anywhere except the uncertain and often treacherous roads of lake and river in a hostile country. There were no communications but the toilsome and unbelievably dangerous method of delivery by hand. There was no way of co-ordinating the movements of these scattered units that could not be planned six months in advance, and who was to say who would be the friends and followers at so distant a date? Yet those scattered units that were to make up Denonville's army at Irondequoit Bay on that tenth of July of 1687 met just as planned. The meeting place was close to what is now Windsor Beach, not far from the outskirts of the city of Rochester–Rochester, which then was not even a name, not even a clearing in the limitless forest that was known as the Seneca country.

This is an achievement that must stand among the few credits that cling to Denonville's name. Perhaps it was his more in ordering than in accomplishment, but he deserves the credit that he had the courage to try. He also deserves the judgment that with great subordinate leadership he accomplished so little. He had virtually no part in the selection of these leaders. They were designated by the country they controlled at the time, but in them he was supremely fortunate.

The order that went to Henri Tonty to keep that assignment at Irondequoit Bay reached him at Fort St. Louis, whence he had followed La Salle years before and had stayed to make it his own country. He was a quiet man, though he could be stern enough at times. He had the respect of almost all and the enmity of none, not even among the Indians. He was son of Lorenzo Tonty, the Italian financier who came to Paris and there devised a scheme for benefiting the French exchequer, remembered in the tontine insurance policies of our own day. Tonty had been an adventurer even in early youth when he left his father's countinghouse to join the French navy and to take part in the Sicilian campaign. A saber cut earned in a sortee at Libisso cost him his hand and his navy career. It seemed, too, in an age that depended for security on a good right arm, that it had destined him to a return to the countinghouse. It might have been so but for a chance meeting with the young zealot La Salle, then on one of his visits to Paris. But with that meeting the pattern of Tonty's life was set. Where La Salle went, what he wished to do were Tonty's guide. It was a partnership of mutual respect between men of sharply divergent character, the one autocratic and eager for credit, the other unassuming and unassertive. Tonty was satisfied to have a part in events, let the credit go where it would.

There would be many adventures shared by La Salle and Tonty, but mainly they seemed to center in the Illinois land about Fort St.

Louis and Crèvecoeur. It was to Fort St. Louis that Tonty returned after his friend had died. There he set up what was almost a trading kingdom. No one knew the Indians better than he, or held more of their respect. He ruled with a mixture of gentleness and strength and understanding. None of it stemmed from fear, as they well knew. It was told from mouth to mouth that on those rare occasions when there was unruliness that words could not quiet there would be a quick blow with that weaponless right hand and the unruly one would trouble no more. So it was that Tonty became known to them as the "Iron Hand," not in anger, but in deep admiration and respect for such great prowess. What chief who with his hand alone could crush a skull would not have used such a great gift to his own advantage? But the Iron Hand they knew dealt with them justly, understood them fully, and had no fear. So Henri Tonty ruled his kingdom about St. Louis and Crèvecoeur.

It was here that Denonville's message reached him. He was to gather as many *coureurs* and Indians as he could and early in July was to rendezvous at Niagara and there await further instructions.

Almost the same order went to another of the same adventurous generation. It was Olivier Morel de la Durantaye, who had come to Canada as a captain in the famous regiment of Carignan-Salière and had remained for twenty exciting and profitable years. He owned the two seigniories of Bellechasse and Durantaye, from which his name derives, but he had spent little time on them. Adventurous spirits are hardly to be confined to any set group of acres. When Denonville wrote, Durantaye was commanding at that distant northern outpost of Michilimackinac.

The order was simple, but to obey it was not. The lake Indians had no enthusiasm for attacking their fellows, least of all the redoubtable Iroquois. More than that, they were holding the French in very low regard. They remembered La Barre and how they had gone to support his great expedition and how La Barre had made peace without striking a blow. They were leaning more toward joining the Iroquois than to trading blows with them, for such trading had been far from happy in days gone by, and with the French grown timid, as they supposed, a further venture held even less promise. It was only the presence of Durantaye that kept them in check, and that control was growing dangerously slight.

Fate and Colonel Dongan, New York's shrewd and crafty governor, played into Durantaye's hands, but certainly not as the doughty governor could have wished. Dongan, jealous of the rich fur trade of the northern lakes, had turned English footsteps toward that northern threshold. True, the names of the intruders he sent did not ring with any familiar English cadence. The chief emissaries of this double-barreled expedition into what had heretofore been exclusively French territory were called Rooseboom and McGregory. But despite that fact they carried Dongan's commission and were supplied with a substantial cargo of trade goods.

They were to have approached Michilimackinac in company, but something altered their plans. This was an ill-omened change for the visitors. Had they been together, their combined strength might have given a different turn to the story. As it was, Rooseboom and his canoes, carrying twenty-nine white traders and five Indians and a generous supply of trade goods, approached the fort just when La Durantaye had about given up hope of being able to support Denonville's plan and was turning his thoughts to the more practical matter of extricating himself and his followers from a situation that gave every evidence of becoming highly hazardous.

The report of Rooseboom's approach was a manifest gift from heaven. La Durantaye accepted it as such and acted promptly. Getting his small force in their canoes, he bore down upon the astonished English with every evidence of hostile intent. Rooseboom would have been quite equal to this immediate emergency. But the Indians from the Michilimackinac post, who had manned their canoes for the possible pursuit of the fleeing French, presented so impressive a force that Rooseboom, who did not know of the uncertain relations between French and Indians and saw only a cloud of enemies where he had expected delighted customers, made all haste to surrender. La Durantaye, shepherding the whole puzzled party to Michilimackinac, quickly settled matters by distributing the trade goods among the post Indians. It was a useful gesture at the moment, and the more pleasant in that it cost the donor nothing.

This sudden turn of events, this scrap of evidence that the French might still be top dog, impressed the Indians. This was more like old times when Onontio had power and didn't hesitate to use it. Before the effect could wear off, La Durantaye renewed his advances, and when a rather tenuous agreement was finally reached and before the war fervor had time to cool, he moved off down the lake in the direction of Detroit. At that rendezvous they found Du Lhut waiting with his detachment from the Sioux country, and shortly after Henri

Tonty from the mid-Mississippi area also arrived. Knowing their followers, there was no delaying. Heading into Lake Erie, the combined forces made for Niagara.

As they skirted the southern shore of the lake, fortune favored them again. It was in the person of that cool-headed English-Irishman McGregory, who certainly had no reason to expect that he would meet any enemy with whom he would not share a reasonable chance. Flight was impossible, defense even less promising. There remained the simple alternative of throwing in the hand. This McGregory did with thc bcst grace he could muster. He had with him the same number of traders as his partner Rooseboom, the same amount of trade goods, with the addition of a number of Indians captured some time before, whose restoration was to have been a happy opening for the trading. Instead, the whole party, Indians and trade goods included, was hurried off to Montreal. The incident was to provide a subject of protest by the New York governor for a good while to come, as it was to be another straw on the camel's back that would eventually lead to conflict.

La Hontan tells us that the force that Denonville himself had been able to muster around Montreal and Quebec, in militia and regulars and Indian allies, nominally Christian, numbered some fifteen hundred. Crossing the lake and skirting the southern shore with his considerable armada of canoes and bateaux, he had to face a series of storms, and keeping his fleet together was no small undertaking. It took him six days from Fort Frontenac. But the sight that greeted him as he neared Irondequoit Bay might have stirred a less sensitive heart. There were the canoes of Durantaye, Du Lhut, Perrot, Pierre de Troyes, Tonty and the rest of the adventurers and with them the savage mercenaries bright with little else than war paint.

The combined force under Denonville totaled almost three thousand where former expeditions had seemed large at two or three hundred. It was a curious assortment of fighting men. There were veterans of the French wars, regulars, in their shining steel breastplates and plumes, and with them the nobility of Canada heading the Canadian militia. Theirs was an aristocracy sweated out in danger and hardship by men who held their lives lightly yet demanded heavy payment. There were large detachments of Christian Indians, in whom Christianity was a very thin veneer laid on a savagery that still ran in the blood. And with them the savage warriors who had no veneer of any sort, but only their brown and sweat-scarred bodies streaked with red and green and white, their heads crowned with horns while backs waved as the tails of beasts kept time to their savage dancing.

This restless army had to stay two days at the fringes of the lake. Here were the hundreds of canoes and bateaux that had brought them together and remained their very vulnerable line of retreat. A fort had to be built to protect the boats, for had these been lost there was no force in all the wilds of Canada that could come to their aid.

It was the morning of July 12, 1687, that the great expedition moved off. Each man carried his own provisions. It wasn't an unbearable load—ten biscuits per man—but it was load enough. The day was a blaze of heat, such heat as Canada sometimes knows. Even the hardened *coureurs* gasped and grew faint as they fought their way through the breathless forest and into a region of waist-deep grass where the regulars in their breastplates slowly cooked in the heat. Denonville, good soldier and bit of a martinet that he was, forgot the proprieties and marched in his shirt sleeves.

It was not a very heroic enterprise, as it turned out, nor yet too capably managed. A sudden surprise attack on the vanguard resulted in throwing the main force into momentary panic that might have been its undoing. But Denonville's courage rallied them, and the Senecas soon felt the force of an attack that stemmed from shame and a desire for revenge. The Senecas had not expected such an assault and had no strategy to meet it. They slipped away into the forest, carrying as many of their dead and wounded as they could with them.

Denonville reported later that five or six of his men had been killed and perhaps twenty wounded. It was a cheap victory. He estimated the enemy losses at forty-five killed outright and added in corroboration, "Twenty-five of whom we saw butchered." This refers more probably to the aftermath of battle, when the Indians among the victors cut the dead and wounded into quarters, like butcher's meat, and put them in their kettles. It was a splendid victory.

Next morning, moving with new caution and with ranks closed, the army inched forward. No one was there to dispute the advance. The Senecas were realists. With forces so disproportionate, they would wait for another day. They had prepared for such a course, should it be necessary. When they got word of Denonville's coming they set a torch to what Abbé Belmont was to describe, in rather ambitious terms, as "the Babylon of the Senecas." The good father discovered many bits of evidence that satisfied him that "Babylon" was a gentle term. It had been a substantial town of bark huts, now in ruins. There were receptacles filled with last season's grain, and droves of hogs roamed the ruins and the forest. For ten days the work of destruction went on. Not a hog escaped, not an ear of corn in the main town of Gannagaro or in the three neighboring villages. But there was little excitement and more work in cutting down grain than cutting down enemies. Gorged on fresh pork and green corn in the blazing weather, the men began to become sick. The Indian allies were eager to be gone. "It is a miserable business," Denonville wrote, "to command savages who, as soon as they have knocked the enemy on the head, ask for nothing but to go home and carry with them the scalps which they have taken off like a skullcap."

Twelve days from the start of that momentous march from Irondequoit Bay the army was there again with nothing much to show for their trouble. The greatest gathering of troops the continent had yet seen, the greatest opportunity for decisive action it had yet known had all but slipped away. So much effort, so much planning, such fabulous, such incredible luck in their amazing concentration. Yet nothing had been accomplished, except some annoyance for Governor Dongan of New York, and nothing had been settled. Some hogs and corn destroyed, some few Indians killed and tortured, and what else? Little if anything that history can assess as gain.

It is told that just prior to Denonville's departure on this great adventure a Christian Indian had warned him, "If you upset a wasps' nest you must crush the wasps or they will sting you."

Almost two centuries later, Emerson, speaking to the youth who was to become the great Justice Holmes, put the same thought in more graphic words. Commenting on the young Holmes's highly critical essay on Plato, Emerson shook his great head. "When you shoot at a king," he said, "you must kill him." When you challenge power it cannot be with a hesitant voice. Perhaps that is the final judgment on Denonville. Good and devoted and devout and courageous man that he was, he could shoot at a king, but he lacked the final hardness to shoot to kill.

The lack of hardness that led Denonville to turn back, with his great plan of disciplining the Iroquois hardly begun, was to be a turning point in the history of New France. It was to usher out the days in which Indian and Frenchman struggle for dominion and usher in the ever-expanding conflict between French and English.

Perhaps Denonville did not see this very clearly. Perhaps no one did. There were tragic last chapters of that great conflict between France and her Indian enemies still to be written in bitterness and suffering, but the new challenge was shaping. Denonville was scarcely back from his great and purposeless expedition when the shrewd and truculent governor of New York was pointing out that if he had not destroyed the wasps he most undoubtedly had stirred up the hornets. Governor Dongan was openly charging his fellow governor with invading English territory, with killing the subjects of King James of England and despoiling his emissaries. He said it with a good deal of force and with a threat that was very thinly veiled. "I assure you, Sir," he wrote, "if my Master gives leave, I will as soon be at Quebec as you shall be at Albany."

Denonville's rather plaintive retort was that Governor Dongan had armed the Iroquois against him and that he was not encroaching on British territory, as missionary priests working among the Indians and the exploits of French *coureurs de bois* had established territorial claims for France at least as sound as anything Dongan could offer. This brought another blast from the fiery and very vocal Irishman. "The King of China," he wrote, "never goes anywhere without two Jesuits with him. I wonder you make not a like pretence to that kingdom." And he added, "You will affirm that a few loose fellowes rambling amongst Indians to keep themselves from starving gives the French a right to that countrey."

No doubt the voluble governor of New York had the advantage of the exchange of wit, but in strict truth the evidence seemed to lean toward the French view. However, again Denonville had no will to fight to a conclusion. What he wanted more than anything else was peace so that his people could get back to trading and tilling the fields without fear. Dongan was not slow to take advantage. His own hand had been immeasurably strengthened by the fact that James II had finally decided to accept the Iroquois as his subjects. Tenuous as this claim might be, Dongan made the most of it and increased his demands.

Weakening as the other grew more importunate, Denonville agreed to send back Rooseboom and McGregory, hoping this would satisfy the truculent Irishman. So desperate was he for peace that he was ready for almost any concession to secure it. Dongan raised his demands—not only the return of the two traders but the captured merchandise as well. As Durantaye, in that generous gesture, had distributed Rooseboom's trade goods among his uncertain allies and a somewhat similar fate had befallen the goods captured with McGregory, return obviously was impossible. So when Dongan countered with another demand, the immediate demolition of Fort Niagara, Denonville was already weakening. Such an agreement would solve two problems, how to placate the irritable governor, and how to defend and supply a distant outpost when it seemed hardly possible to maintain his position at home. So it was agreed.

Denonville had a moment of exaltation as he learned that Dongan had been recalled and that Sir Edmund Andros had been sent in his stead. It was a short-lived satisfaction. Sir Edmund took up the argument where Dongan had left off. It wasn't as forcefully presented. The new governor was more of a believer in the soft answer, but he didn't believe in making it so soft as to concede anything. The explosive exchanges gave way to guile. That was the only change.

The new English governor had no corner on guile, as the further record shows. Denonville, desperate for some way out of the dangers and difficulties surrounding him, was ripe for concessions. These served only part of his problem. There still remained the ever-present threat of Indian attack unless some peaceful approach could be made to them also. No doubt he had done a good deal of thinking on how to justify the perfidy of the year before at Fort Frontenac. Perhaps it was in the course of such thinking that he remembered that not all the Indians captured in Champigny's raids had been sent to the galleys in France. The women and children and a percentage of the men had been distributed among the Christian Indian villages. The thought of sending them back to their homes bearing gifts and messages of peace came to Denonville as a bit of inspired diplomacy. The shrewd old negotiator, Big Mouth—he of the persuasive words—thought of it somewhat differently. He recognized it as the counsel of desperation. He recognized, too, that French necessity might easily be turned to the advantage of the Iroquois confederacy. His plan—and a very sound plan—was to keep both France and England dangling and so secure favors from each.

It seemed to Big Mouth that of late the balance had swung rather heavily toward the English, and it was no part of his policy to have it swing too far. A dominant New England would be as hazardous as a dominant New France. He was therefore quick to seize the olive branch held out by Denonville. He traveled to Montreal accompanied by a band of twelve hundred braves. That, he was shrewd enough to know, lent force to his arguments. He made no apologies to the governor for this show of force. He spoke like a player with an all but unbeatable hand. The Iroquois knew the weakness of the French and could easily exterminate them, he assured the harassed governor. Had they not already formed a plan? Burn the houses and barns of French Canada, kill the cattle, fire the ripening grain, and, when the people were starving, attack the forts. The logic was unassailable; the ability to accomplish it was not entirely a boast.

Big Mouth grandly assured the governor that he had persuaded his people against such a course. They were subjects neither of the English nor the French; they were prepared to be friends of both. It was a masterly effort, more than it needed to be, perhaps, for Denonville was rapidly losing command of such little resolution as remained, and the preliminaries of peace were promptly begun.

There is no need to do more than review the subsequent phases of these negotiations. They have been dealt with vividly and dramatically in the preceding volume: how the renowned chief Kondiaronk–the Rat–the friend of France, heard of the all but completed peace; of his quick realization that there had been no word in the negotiation about the protection of the Huron tribe or their allies. It was peace for the French alone. For the lake Indians it spelled extermination. Freed from the threat of French interference, the Iroquois would make short work of their traditional enemies. All this the Rat was quick to see, though he gave no sign. His crafty mind was at work. The plan that came to him was a masterpiece of duplicity.

It was common knowledge that the emissaries of Big Mouth would soon be returning to continue the negotiations. The Rat heard but apparently paid no attention. He and his band moved off on their own business, which took them, not home to Michilimackinac, but across the lake to La Famine, there to await the negotiators. Four or five days they waited. Finally the canoes of the negotiators appeared. The Rat and his followers let them come to land, then met them with a blaze of musket fire. When one of the chiefs fell dead and several others were wounded, the Rat and his band rushed them and, with the exception of one warrior who managed to escape, captured the rest. Then the full flavor of his craftiness appeared. As they tied the prisoners they jeered at them for being taken so easily. What were they expecting? Didn't they know that Denonville would have warned of the coming of such a war party? Had they expected to delude the Rat as easily as they might the French?

There were hot bursts of denial. This was not a war party. Denonville knew it. Hadn't he himself arranged for their return? So emphatic were the denials that the Rat finally allowed himself to appear convinced that it was really a peace party. Anger flamed in his face and words spilled from his lips, denouncing a governor who could trick him into turning his hand against his brothers. It was a convincing act. If the governor had really planned such treachery instead of eagerly awaiting the return of the Indians' emissaries and the conclusion of peace between them, it could hardly have been given an uglier appearance. It was a black deed, the Rat contended, that would not be forgotten until Onontio had paid for it in blood. With continuing protests of regret he let the party go, urging them to return to their homes. He even pressed on them guns and powder and ball as an evidence that there was no intent to do them harm.

When they had passed out of view, the Rat and his band turned their steps again toward Fort Frontenac. He went on alone to the fort. As he left finally to rejoin his band, he was heard to mutter, "I have killed the peace. We shall see how the governor will get out of this business." Perhaps these are the most significant words in this era of Canadian history. It was true. Never was a peace more completely dead. Never did words come closer to being a death knell.

Champigny's treachery at Fort Frontenac, which the governor had either ordered or condoned, was still remembered. It had been the background of the thinking of the peace negotiators. They knew that he had permitted some of their brothers, captured by treachery, to be sent away. They didn't know that Denonville had sent them to France for the King's galleys and had not been above claiming some credit for his actions. Yet, strangely, with this known blot on his record, the final accounting rests on actions in which he certainly had no part, either in intent or accomplishment, and on treachery that was far from his imagining.

When the warrior who had managed to escape reached Fort Frontenac, he told what had happened. It was the happy chance that might have offset the Rat's crafty planning and still have saved the peace. The governor seized the chance. He sent this lone warrior back on the trail of his fellows. Only, where they bore a tale of treachery, he bore an explanation and a very generous measure of regret. Perhaps the explanations would have borne fruit. Peace might have been secured and Denonville's record might have been vastly different if, behind the explanation of one treachery, there hadn't lurked the evidence of another that could not be explained away.

For months a stubborn hush hung over forest and river and forts, and nothing happened. Denonville wrote to the ministry, with qualified optimism, that there was still a good hope of peace. But weeks dragged by and the hope grew dim. Once more his mind turned to another great expedition. If they did not want peace, then they could have war. This time he would destroy the wasps.

It was to be a two-pronged attack, one force striking across the lake against the Onondagas and Cayugas, the other to attack the Mohawks and Oneidas by way of Lake Champlain, the highway that for a hundred years to come was to be a road of war. This second attack would be over territory that was undeniably English, but Denonville was beyond being troubled by such considerations. Or perhaps it was rather that he was not too expert at entertaining more than one idea at a time, and his plan was now growing into a dominant idea. He had asked the King for an additional eight hundred regulars. Louis responded with a disappointing three hundred. But the governor was thinking now in terms of three to four thousand reinforcements. He asked for them boldly, explaining the need and elaborating on the great results that would follow. The reply came as an unbelievable shock. If the colony should be attacked again, the governor was adjured to make the best fight he could with the forces now at his disposal until the King was in a better position to help. That seemed to put an end to any hope, unless some personal approach might change the way of thinking. With this in mind the governor had a real inspiration. He sent the ever-faithful Callières to France. Callières, as governor of Montreal, was well aware of the necessities of the case and was a man in whom Denonville could put entire trust. He was to see Louis and make the argument as persuasively as he could. Having made the best decision possible, the governor set himself to await the result.

It was unhappy waiting. A sort of lethargy had settled over the colony, where nothing seemed to move or change, not even the sense of dread that was a daily companion. The hope of gain that once had seemed a justification for such hazards as must be assumed was no longer there to be a sustaining force.

Once those who were fortunate enough to be among the twenty-five who received the King's permit to trade on the lakes were happy indeed. They could turn a handsome profit by selling their licenses—perhaps for as much as six hundred crowns. The purchaser could then load the two large canoes the license permitted with a freight of trade goods. The whole transaction might show a profit of 700 per cent for the voyage. The two canoes of trade goods normally returned as four canoeloads of skins. With forty bundles of skins to a canoe and with each bundle worth some fifty crowns, the total would be eight thousand crowns. The energetic and studious La Hontan, in one of his gossipy letters, explained the profit system. There was first the six hundred crowns for the license and perhaps a thousand crowns for trade goods. For the risk involved in providing these the merchants took 40 per cent of the remaining sixty-four hundred crowns. What was left was distributed among the four or five *coureurs de bois* who had done the work at a daily risking of their lives.

Or perhaps it was the Indians themselves who came to trade, drawn by the mingled urge of avarice and the provocative appeal of French brandy. Then there was the endless haggling—four francs for a silver fox, one for a common marten, or four times as much for a quality skin. A black bearskin, properly argued, might bring seven francs. Beaver skin was another matter; sold to a merchant for Canadian francs, it brought so much, but the merchant could then sell to the Farmer-General of Public Revenue for French francs and realize 25 per cent on the transaction.

But now the warehouses were bare of furs. Instead they bulged with trade goods for the fur brigades that didn't come. There were muskets and powder and shot, hatchets and knives and kettles, fishhooks and Brazilian tobacco and thread for nets. No Indians had shown their faces in avaricious friendship for months on end. There was none of the excitement that had once accompanied the return of the *coureurs de bois*, who, weary of the long months of absence and solitude, had made the town ring with their roistering. The shops and warehouses were dark and heavy with foreboding; as despairing as the people, whom even the presence of the royal governor could not stir; as troubled as the governor himself, who did not yet know that a successor was already on the way to replace him.

The town of Montreal was early to bed that night of August 4, 1689. There was nothing to keep it awake. The night was dark with a wild wind blowing over Lake St. Louis. The clouds themselves were laced with lightning. Hail beat on the roofs and the thunder rattled the windows and crashed into the surrounding forests. At Lachine, six miles up the river from the settlement of Montreal, the storm seemed harsher. The people huddled in their beds, grateful for the rude shelter about them. They did not know, until the war whoops sounded, that at last the silence had been broken and what they had feared for many months was at their door. Fifteen hundred warriors were there. They surrounded every home. In the cold hours of early morning the bitterest and most purposeless page of Canadian history was being written in the blood of men and women and children.

There were two hundred killed immediately, according to the French historian Pierre de Charlevoix, and a hundred and twenty carried off. These were the hapless ones. For several weeks friends and relatives in Montreal and Lachine could see the nightly torture fires burning beyond the river while their fathers and wives and children lived their final brief hour of agony. But when the Indians finally left they took with them the rest of their captives so that the torture fires might burn throughout the Iroquois confederacy.

There were individuals who were not touched by the blight of fear and indecision that seemed to be everywhere; men who, given leadership, would have attempted anything with no thought of the odds against them. But leadership was no longer in Denonville. He was there in Montreal, close to the scene of danger. He was there when he could have been safely settled in his impregnable château at Quebec. No one has ever questioned his personal courage. That is something. Quite obviously he didn't lack daring, only the will to dare.

Montreal was in no immediate danger. The year before, Governor Callières had improved the long months of winter by having the inhabitants cut staves fifteen feet long. The townspeople grumbled mightily over the task, but Callières kept them at it, and when the frost was out of the ground in the spring he set them to digging trenches so that the stakes could be securely planted. There was little love for this sort of work and, until necessity arose, it was considered useless and demeaning. After all, they were traders, not diggers. The governor persisted, using his influence and his good humor to get the work done. He had had constructed, too, a series of outpost forts about six miles beyond the city in the direction of Lachine. They were small stockaded posts, lightly armed. A small garrison was always kept in each. It was a shot from one of these forts that had first alerted an encampment of two hundred regulars three miles nearer the city, who were under the command of a tough and resolute soldier, Daniel d'Auger, Sieur de Subercase. He is to have his place in the story of Canada, and it might have begun right here had he not been in Montreal waiting on Denonville.

Hearing of the disaster, Subercase set about rousing every fighting man he could find. It took time to gather the hundred inhabitants, to see them properly armed, and to ensure that Montreal itself was alert. So it was full morning before Subercase rejoined his detachment. Once he was there, the delay ended. As the three hundred passed forts, they were joined by some of the defenders. There was force enough.

Fury grew as they reached Lachine and saw the burned homes, the bloodied bodies about the doorsteps, the torture stakes still supporting the weight of the dead. Everywhere desolation and horror. This was not a stage big enough to become impersonal. The victims were people known to every member of the force. Some of them lying in their blood were relatives. Someone pointed out that the Iroquois were only half a mile away, hidden in the forest, probably still sleeping off a drunken debauch.

Sword in hand, Subercase entered the strip of forest, calling to his men to follow. Then his words were drowned in another and more authoritative voice. It was that of the Chevalier de Vaudreuil, a man of known courage who was acting as governor of Montreal in Callières' absence. He had orders, orders from the governor of New France himself, that no attack was to be made, no risks run. The forces were to remain on the defensive, nothing more.

Hot words came to Subercase's lips. This was the moment: it would not come again. Here were the men, ready and eager. There were the Indians, drunk and defenseless. But Vaudreuil did not waver. These were orders. There was no appeal short of mutiny. So the one man who seemed the man in the right place had to turn back with his forces to Fort Roland. There almost five hundred men, eager and able-bodied, waited while the prestige of France slowly died; while in the one hundred and fifty homes of Montreal —"some of them rather fine ones," as Father le Tac has recorded—stark terror reigned; while for twenty miles around the smoke of flaming homes and fields was rising; while across the river at Châteauguay the torture fires burned all night. Bewildered and benumbed, the governor waited—for what, no one can know. All that history can tell is that the ultimate hardness was lacking. The chance was there, but not the daring to put it to the touch to win or lose it all.

For more than two months the Iroquois kept the frightened populace well in hand, relieving their own monotony by torturing a few captives who, more adventurous than their fellows, stirred beyond the palisades. They waited until October came. Then the war canoes were on their way again, ninety prisoners with them, it was said. They had been prisoners for sixty days, almost within touch of their friends, who nightly must look across the river to see the torture fires burning brightly, marking the nadir of New France in its New World.

Word had come that in England James II, friend and ally of France, was fleeing to his friend for sanctuary. In his place was William of Orange, Louis' implacable foe. Soon war would be springing up between the two. Even in his demoralization the governor was shrewd enough to know that, whatever agreements might say, war would embroil the New World. Denonville had no spirit left for such thoughts. He remembered the blustering of Dongan and the quieter but no less sinister hints of Sir Edmund Andros. With threat all about him, he was planning feverishly how to weld the country into some unit that he could hold. Fort Niagara was gone. Even the eager mood in which he had planned the post was forgotten. Now he was thinking not of Niagara, but of Fort Frontenac. What chance was there of holding it against the Iroquois backed by the furtive or active support of England?

All Denonville could see was his world narrowing around him; all he could think of was to narrow it still further. That was the part of wisdom and security, or so he convinced himself. He would destroy Fort Frontenac, a post he couldn't support. The only question in his mind was how to send the order for destruction, with woods and river swarming with Iroquois. No one could be found who thought such a venture feasible. Then, just as he had decided that Fort Frontenac would have to be left to its own resources, there stepped forward a young man who seemed eager for just such a challenge, as if to show that the spirit of France had not quite died. It was the Sieur de Saint Pierre d'Arpentigny, who in most of the accounts of his hazardous venture has remained conspicuously anonymous. Courage, where courage had so generally evaporated, is worthy of comment. We do not know what was his end, but it wasn't here. Despite the almost inescapable hazards, he did reach Fort Frontenac unscathed. There he delivered his message to the commandant, Valrenne, and slipped back into the silence.

Valrenne himself was a man of tested courage. It was to show itself conspicuously in later times, but for the moment it was at an ebb. All he wanted was to get away with the consciousness of having obeyed orders and with a whole skin. Now he had the orders. He was prompt, if not completely thorough, in fulfilling them. He had a match set to everything that would burn. The few cannon were tumbled from the bastion into the lake, the walls mined, and a slow fuse set burning toward the powder magazine. In his eagerness he even fired three boats that might have served him on his return journey, and without more ado set out for Montreal believing that the destruction was complete. The party was some leagues on its way before the distant explosion seemed to write "finis" to the story of this adventurous outpost of Fort Frontenac.

Denonville's recall was not due to the orgy of massacre at Lachine. The letter of recall was on its way before the red terror seized the island of Montreal. It was not due to the surrender of Niagara or of Fort Frontenac. Neither happening was known in France, and, had it been, it would hardly have been disapproved, for old Count Frontenac remained almost alone in his defense of a far-flung empire. Denonville was recalled because a policy had changed and there was no place in a new program of aggressiveness for a waverer.

Denonville was a good and courageous soldier. When he sold his commission as colonel of the Queen's Dragoons and became governor of New France much was expected of him. He was sturdy where La Barre, whom he replaced, was aged. He had a reputation for integrity, the very last thing his predecessor could claim. He was a soldier who had distinguished himself in subordinate command. Had this been his fate, he would have graced it with fine service. But he was in full and independent command, and he lacked every quality this required—decisiveness, firmness, and the ability to meet good or ill fortune with a constant heart. He could plan; he could not execute. He was fastidious, critical, and conventional where his need was to be adaptable. He was rigid in his conception of honor—an honor empty of substance. The promise of the King's approbation meant more than the dictates of hospitality, more than his plighted word. He was scrupulously honest where dishonesty—even in a governor—was a well-beaten path. He took pride in this, while he closed his eyes to the fact that his timid but more practical wife, who hated every moment in New France, still improved these moments by keeping a room in the château for trading purposes—as a modern woman keeps a sewing room—and she missed no opportunity for profit. He must have known that one of the last acts of the *gouvernante* was a lottery to dispose of, at a profit, such goods as she could not take with her.

During Denonville's regime relations between himself and the intendant and the bishop had been warmly friendly, an almost unheard-of situation. Had he been a stronger man it might have told against him, for Louis did not approve of too much unanimity. This had no part in his recall. The saddest truth about Denonville was that there was no specific reason. Seldom had it been the King's duty to recall a man who had meant so well, had tried so sincerely, and had failed so dismally. Perhaps the failure had been a long time building and was only partially his fault.

He was not retired in disgrace. Louis gave him a curious evidence of his continued friendship: from the governorship of half a continent to the rather empty glory of the governorship of the royal children. Perhaps it would be overly cynical to suggest that a man of dignity and apparent worth had found a niche where obligations were adjusted to limitations.

So it was that Valrenne, hurrying from Fort Frontenac to assure Denonville that he had saved his defending force and had faithfully fulfilled the governor's last order, had his great surprise. He met, not the puzzled and amiable governor, but the stormy face of the one he had least expected—the one who would be least appreciative of his achievement. Then, and not until then, did he learn that Frontenac had returned.

CHAPTER V

A FIGURE OF HIGH STRATEGY

Callières in France to present Denonville's views has to accept an alternate plan, an outright attack on New York and New England. The need for strong hands to implement it. Louis remembers Frontenac. The governor returns to a country deeply depressed. The massacre at La Chesnaye makes it clear he must first face the dire threat of an Indian coalition that would isolate New France. A lone Indian becomes a sad figure of high strategy.

CALLIÈRES, though governor of Montreal, had no part in the grim happenings that had come so close to the city. He had not been touched by the spirit of defeat that had closed over New France as the torture fires died out at Lachine. He had sailed for France in the fall of 1688. Then even Denonville was still nursing plans of aggressive action–provided, of course, that the King would lend his support. It was to urge that support that he had sent his emissary to France; and Callières, who had a devotion to his superiors uncommon enough in his day, was determined to succeed. When he secured an audience he did indeed do his best. His task was not easy. It was to introduce a more hopeful note than that contained in the doleful and pleading letters that reached the King's cabinet.

His task was the more difficult in that he was not convinced of the soundness of the plan. He was to urge substantial reinforcements of from three to four thousand regulars for an offensive that once and for all would end the threat of Iroquois aggression and might take some action against the English should opportunity present itself.

Callières was not a stupid man and he sensed Louis' mounting impatience. He had given the appeal an honest and loyal try, and he wasn't prepared for the frigidity with which it was received. He had been out of touch with European politics. If he had heard that James II had left England rather hurriedly, and for his own good, the fact had made little impression. He was accustomed to the thought of people leaning on the aid of Louis, and one more, even a king, did not seem to be taxing the beneficence too much. Louis, of course, knew better, but the opportunity to use the rejected monarch, the still powerful prestige of the Stuart name, and the good will of the Catholics to make trouble for England was a chance hardly to be missed. Perhaps James could recover his throne and return to the old complaisant co-operation. The gamble was worth a try if only to keep William of Orange employed. But it would cost money and men. The shrewd Callières, once he had the drift of the thinking, knew that talk of four thousand reinforcements was futile.

He turned to an elaboration of the secondary idea in Denonville's program. It was the suggestion to mount a real offensive against the English on the American continent. Louis' interest was caught. This was a plan that dovetailed neatly with his own thinking. It made an immediate appeal to his ambition, his cautious niggardliness, and to the very real devoutness that was evidenced not so much in his life as in his support of the Catholic Church. Callières pressed his advantage shrewdly. The plan would entail little cost and no added forces, two or three war vessels at most to support a land attack on New York. The vessels would be the King's share of the undertaking. The land forces would be provided out of troops already in Canada and her own militia.

The plan was bold enough. It was to take New York with an army of perhaps sixteen hundred men, some thousand of them regulars, and an unstated number of Indians. The road would be the familiar ancient highway, up the Richelieu by canoe and bateaux to Le Merde Iroquois, which has become Lake Champlain, on to Lake St. Sacrement or, as it is now known, Lake George. Then the troublesome twelve-mile portage to the Hudson River and so to Albany. Albany once taken—a simple task, as Callières explained it—all river craft would be seized, and regulars and militia would be on their way down-river to New York.

Again Callières brushed lightly over possible obstacles, putting New York as a place of two hundred homes and perhaps four hundred fighting men. The troops having arrived, the ships cruising at the mouth of the harbor would be notified and combine in the attack. As the plan was discussed, enthusiasm grew. It was finally judged that by October New York and the surrounding country would be safely in the King's hands. The Iroquois, deprived of English support, would be at the mercy of the French and would present no further problem. New England would be bottled up—with France to the north and France in control of all New York to the south and further advantaged by having now a port that wasn't immobilized for half the year. So situated, the planners conceded, the New Englanders would come to time at the King's convenience.

It was a fabulous plan that grew as it was discussed and nowhere took count of actualities. It quickly became the King's plan and bore the marks of one whose wish was tantamount to accomplishment. As it grew it went beyond to what might come later—all lands and possessions of the defeated English were to be seized and granted under feudal tenure to French officers and privates, who would also share with the King in whatever could be secured from English officers and other persons of substance who might be thrown into prison until they had disgorged these expected benefits.

The only persons to escape this harsh judgment would be any Catholic citizens who took an oath of allegiance to Louis. All others, except such mechanics as might be useful and might be kept as prisoners, were to be removed from the colony and distributed throughout New England and Pennsylvania, and so isolated that they could not hope to reunite in any effort to recover their property. Settlements bordering on New York were to be destroyed and the more distant to pay some form of tribute. Nowhere in the plan was there any provision for possible failure. There was nothing to explain why thousands of English and Dutch would tamely submit their persons, possessions, and futures to a force of sixteen hundred men and two war vessels.

Apparently no one had gone that far in his thinking. But it did occur to Louis suddenly that the man who would normally be charged with this extravagant adventure would be Denonville, who, according to his own correspondence, was bending every thought and energy to the not too hopeful effort to hold what he had.

Obviously he was not the man. Even the loyal Callières' silence admitted it. Then it was that there came again to Louis a name that had hardly crossed his mind in seven years. The name was Frontenac, and no one was likely to say that the task was impossible for him.

These seven years are all but a blank in the history of the man who was destined to become one of the greats of Canada. There are occasional glimpses as he steps from his home, which had been his father's before him, on the Quai des Célestins in the parish of St. Paul, a tall, stalwart, aging figure grown a little shabby and more than a little pathetic in his efforts to maintain a place in the aura surrounding the Sun King. Already he was unfamiliar, even his name almost forgotten, and had his life ended here there might have been little enough to remember: a man of early promise, of courage and energy and overweening vanity and a quarrelsomeness that in the end was to make him an almost impossible servant—too troublesome for Louis' uncertain patience.

It will always remain a question as to just how Frontenac was selected for this second venture as governor of New France. He had been troublesome to the King and more than a little rebellious. That, Louis would remember. He had earned the sharp antagonism of the Jesuits, whose power was as unquestioned in France as it was in the New World.

If there was a shadow of truth in the old canard that Frontenac had been a favorite of Madame de Montespan—so that Frontenac's appointment had the double advantage of providing a governor of sound military reputation and removing a rival of the King—such a reason could apply no longer. Nor could the suggestion of Saint Simon, that Frontenac had "found it hard to bear the imperious temper of his wife; and he was given the government of Canada to deliver him from her, and afford him some means of livelihood."

Even granting such an unusual premise, it is hardly credible that it could happen twice. It seems somewhat more likely that the countess, who was a cousin of Madame de Maintenon, may have been using her influence in favor of her husband, as she had done more than once. Perhaps such intervention might have been enough to minimize any Jesuit opposition.

Obviously this is guesswork. It is more probable that Frontenac and Callières, drawn together by a common interest, may have met at court. Callières may even have called on the older man for support in his discussion with the King. This at least is possible and may have served to remind the King of a governor whose limitations were never matters of hesitancy or fear of consequences. Better than anyone else, Louis knew that if this new plan was to have any hope of success he needed such a man. Perhaps the meeting was this fortuitous. Or it may have been that Louis, making up his mind on the record of the men he had about him, sent for the old governor. The point is of little consequence. The important fact is that Louis was satisfied with his decision. "I am sending you back to Canada," he said as the aging courtier bowed before him, "where I am sure you will serve me as well as you did before; I ask no more."

Frontenac was fifty-two years old when he first landed at Quebec. He was seventy when he received his second appointment. At an age when a man may rightfully begin to lay down his burdens, here was one straightening his still broad shoulders under a heavier load. He had been in the wilderness of disuse and disappointment and declining powers. Out of favor, out of thought, out of action. Yet when Louis told him that he was to go back to Canada, restore the country, control the Iroquois, defeat the English, he accepted his task with confidence. Vanity is an expulsive quality; it leaves no place for self-depreciation. That was something that never in all his lifetime had troubled Frontenac. He didn't always succeed. His was too shrewd a mind to be confused on that point. But if he failed, he accepted the fact with equanimity, confident that success would come next time.

Having listened to the pretentious plan that Louis had built on the foundation suggested by Callières, he may not have shared in the King's assured confidence. He knew something of these stubborn English. But at least he was sure of this: while the pattern of his own plan might not parallel exactly the one he had heard, the result would be as good. Of that there was no room for doubt.

The only stipulation that we know he made was that the captives treacherously taken by Denonville and Champigny should be returned. It was not a new demand. Denonville had begged for it in plaintive appeals to the King, without result. When Frontenac asked, it was obvious that he had a sound reason. His mind was already reaching out, feeling for the strategy that would again make the name of Onontio respected and feared throughout all the broad reaches of the New World.

The voyage was not propitious. Incessant storms delayed the vessels, and it was the twelfth of September before they reached Chedabucto Bay, their immediate destination in the New World. There they changed to the little river vessel, the *François Xavier*, while La Caffinière, admiral of the two-ship navy, sailed away to prey on English shipping until the moment came to combine in that fabulous attack on New York.

But Canada was not quite the Canada for which the plans had been prepared. Stopping at Gaspé for water, the *François Xavier* came by news as well—the dreadful news of the massacre at Lachine. Hearing it for the first time, Frontenac understood better the brooding sense of people waiting—waiting for what might come tomorrow or tonight. The bold plan of ousting the English from their footing at New York must give way to holding on grimly, hoping for survival.

Dusk was falling as the *François Xavier* touched the quay at Quebec. It was October 12, 1689. The scene was familiar, yet Frontenac was not thinking of it as the setting for the capital of the New World. Perhaps the thought that was closest to him was that he had come home—to his own country, which needed him desperately.

There was rejoicing now. It was not the rejoicing of seven years ago, when all were happy to see him away. Torches were burning in the streets about the quay, and the windows of the homes that climbed up the cliff were bright with lights. From the castle on the hill came bursts of cannon and musket fire. Bishop St. Vallier, who must have shared in some measure the prejudices of his predecessor, was there to add his welcome. Massed behind him were the clergy, adding their soberer voices to the general acclaim. The members of the Sovereign Council, who in those years gone by had joined their voices with the Jesuits in demanding his recall, were now as buoyantly eager in their welcome as the humblest habitant. Then the *Te Deum* and, as it died away, a Jesuit priest stepped forward, outdoing himself in a eulogy to the man who had returned.

Frontenac was not a stupid man. Vain he was, beyond any measure, and it was easy to be vain listening to the words of welcome and remembering those other days. But seven years of hope deferred had taught him something. This was not love for him. The applause came not from men who loved but from men who feared. They did not hate the old governor the less. They had not forgotten and forgiven. They had no delusions that here was a changed man. It was just that there was no alternative. Stirring in the hearts of many was the sudden hope that this man might save New France. There was no other hope.

The stern old governor looking down from his château at the wintry river could see little change, though change was there. He was not an imaginative man, yet it could not have escaped him that the thoughts and hopes of those about him were as gray as the rain-drenched clouds that shrouded the rock. Since he had reached Canada, only one hopeful, stirring word had come to him. The incident it recorded was over and done with before he arrived. There was little question that this one decisive action in a world of drift was not born in hope but in the fear that cast its shadow over everything. The way the story kept passing from mouth to mouth showed how desperate was the need for some word of confidence that the mind could catch and hold, some word that said that courage and decision were not quite lost.

Denonville and his timid wife, safe behind the stockades of Montreal, were still tormented by the thought of the Iroquois descending on them again by way of the Ottawa and repeating at Montreal the dreadful story of Lachine. It was not an unwarranted fear, and Denonville did not lack courage or some determination. He sent out a reconnoitering party. The leaders were not his friends. For all that, he had chosen well—Greysolon du Lhut and Nicholas de Mantet, and with them twenty-eight *coureurs de bois* suddenly grown to be men to remember in these sobering hours. They had gone up the Ottawa to where it broadens into the Lake of the Two Mountains, near enough to Montreal to be a present-day pleasure ground. They were none too soon.

As they crossed the lake, two canoes came in sight. They carried twenty-two Iroquois. How many supporters were in the woods about or in the farther reaches of the river? Their warlike actions suggested that these Iroquois were not alone. The dictates of prudence suggested the wisdom of warning the governor and waiting for better odds. But prudence was a word that was little familiar to Mantet or Du Lhut or, for that matter, to the twenty-eight who followed them. The tribe of *coureurs* admittedly were imperfect men. It is not a matter of record that any of them achieved their great or graceless reputations by considering safety. Probably it never occurred to anyone there that the course of wisdom was to retire. Craftiness they understood well. It was a weapon of their trade. At best they did not calculate on living long; but they knew that, without craft, their stay would be short indeed. With a common thought the canoes were maneuvered so that to reach them the advancing Indians would have to paddle along a bright path spread by the declining sun, its blinding rays in their faces. So disposed, the Frenchmen calmly waited.

Careless of craft and drunk with past successes, the Iroquois advanced in their war canoes, the painted warriors screaming their defiance. There was a sudden blast of fire, then silence. The *coureurs* had been right. Craft had served them better than prudence. Craft meant that only one Frenchman had been wounded, but it meant, too, an enemy with empty weapons. Deliberately the French moved forward, the sun at their backs, their muskets steady. Of the twenty-two Iroquois, eighteen sprawled in their canoes dead or wounded. Only one swam ashore and escaped; the survivors went to Indian allies. They would trouble the colony no more.

When the story was recounted, courage seemed to flame again. If only there were more Mantets or Du Lhuts. But now there was Frontenac. Already he was moving with all his old-time promptness. Forgetful of the years, gathering boats, demanding men, demanding speed, pressing forward, careless of the chilling rain that drenched the countryside.

Then came the black thirteenth of November. Twenty miles down-river from Montreal the little settlement of La Chesnaye was still agog with the gossip of the governor's passing on his way up the river. Something was moving at last. Something *was* moving. It wasn't the snow that had begun to fall, blanketing the ground and deadening the whisper of approaching feet. Then it was too late, if it had ever been anything else. The houses were ablaze and could offer no security, nor could the forest. Nor could a governor in Montreal. It was three days before he even knew—before anyone told him of the twenty butchered corpses in the snow, all that remained of La Chesnaye. Not so fortunate the scores that the Iroquois took with them, the evidence of another and more desperate Lachine.

Bishop St. Vallier was not a fearful man, but he could understand fear in others, and he saw it bleak and unconcealed. "The terror is indescribable," he wrote. And then, more critically, "The appearance of a few savages would put a whole neighborhood to flight." Perhaps there was a small satisfaction in him that Frontenac's name and Frontenac's presence hadn't been quite enough. Perhaps the only one who continued to believe it would be was Frontenac himself. There must have been times when even Frontenac, with his abounding faith in himself, must have felt that confidence waver. Yet no one ever knew it. He wasn't a stupid man, except on the occasions where vanity or contentiousness made him so. Certainly he wasn't stupid in any Micawberish sense of waiting for something to turn up. He had no delusions on that score. Anything that turned up now, he realized, would be something in the bitter pattern of Lachine or La Chesnaye, unless in the interval something was done to change the thinking of the tribes. Reports from his commandants at various posts, and letters and gossip of *coureurs* and traders and, perhaps most of all, the way the fur trade had dried up and showed no hint of reviving were eloquent of a lost prestige. The Indians had about reached a decision that must have most momentous consequences—the decision that the day of France was done.

Frontenac could guess how carefully this view had been cultivated by the adroit governor of New York, Colonel Dongan, and by his no less crafty successor, Sir Edmund Andros. These shrewd gentlemen understood that conflict was imminent, that it could be no more avoided than Indians could become peace-loving citizens. They knew that of late matters had gone very much their way, and they had no thought of permitting any change in so satisfactory a situation. Frontenac realized this as well as anyone. He recognized that the plight of New France was desperate and that the Iroquois were well aware of it. In their contempt they, too, meant it to remain that way. For his part Frontenac both knew and had openly said that what was needed was a miracle, whether to make war or to help formulate a peace. But he was not overwhelmed by this recognition. Seeing no miracle about, he set himself to thinking just how to create one. The miracle he wanted was no less than a temporary peace with the Indians that would enable him to deal with the English without facing battle on two fronts.

Frontenac was not dreamer enough to go all the way with Louis in the optimistic plan to dispossess the English of their lands, take their goods, and leave them the alternatives of departure, death, or a not-so-modified form of slavery. He did recognize that in some such strategy and nowhere else was the final battleground. But here he was faced with a dilemma. He couldn't effectively attack the English without the co-operation of Indian allies and the assurance that, while so engaged, New France itself would be secure from attack. As matters stood, he couldn't be sure of either without first achieving a minor success sufficient at least to stay the declining credit of New France.

He did have one card. There was Ourehaoué, the Cayuga chief, captured and sent to France to the King's galleys by Denonville. Released at Frontenac's insistence, he had returned in the ship that brought the governor. There had been time on that voyage for a firm friendship to be born. Not every friendship turns out so well or lasts so long, for Ourehaoué never forgot or ceased to act as a friend. When a delegation of three of the other returning prisoners was sent to Onondaga they bore Ourehaoué's impassioned words to the tribes, urging them to send representatives to meet with Onontio, who was only waiting for such a group to come to ask that Ourehaoué might be returned to his own people. The tribes met this gesture with frank skepticism, stating reasonably that nothing prevented Onontio from returning their chief. For themselves, they reaffirmed their friendship with the English.

Despite the failure of this promising plan, Frontenac was not dismayed. If such a meeting could be arranged he had no doubt of his ability to sway it, as he had done so often in the past. Another message was sent by four more prisoners. Its fate was no better than the first. But in the interchange there was a word that caught the governor's attention. It was the suggestion that the Iroquois had made peace with the lake tribes. That was sobering news. If true, it meant that the colony was virtually surrounded. Certainly Durantaye's reports suggested that if it were not already true it might very quickly become so. The lake tribes were arguing that the protection of Onontio no longer had any meaning. Hadn't the French allowed the Iroquois to butcher them at Montreal without a blow struck in return? When they had attacked the Senecas, hadn't they been satisfied just to cut down corn and break canoes? Weren't Frenchmen being burned in towns all about? If they couldn't protect themselves, as it appeared, how would they protect their friends? Looked at thus practically, there was logic in their thinking that their only way of possible safety was to join hands with the Iroquois and the English. There was the threat to everything that Frontenac planned and hoped.

The aging governor was never one to concentrate long on the dark side. Here was something to get teeth into, a plan of amalgamation that, if stopped, might put an entirely different complexion on affairs. So he sent Nicholas Perrot, with his glib tongue, his courage, and his understanding, to see what could be done about it. Perrot could warn the hesitating lake tribes that the Iroquois were "like five nests of muskrats in the marsh, which the French would drain dry and whose inhabitants they would burn." But the old magic was lacking. They were bold words, and the Indians listened, as they always listened to Perrot. Probably they assessed the words, as the French themselves assessed them, as a rather doleful whistling in the dark.

For emphasis, Frontenac had followed by sending a substantial force to give bold words a tangible presence. There were a hundred and forty-three Canadians under Captain the Sieur de Louvigny, who was an important figure with the Indians in his own right. This show of force would have failed, too, except for a happening so fortunate that it might have appeared an answer to Frontenac's prayers for a miracle.

On the way to Mackinac, on the northern reaches of the Ottawa, Louvigny's command surprised a party of Iroquois hunters. The assault that followed was quick and decisive, if not very heroic. The hunters were defeated with heavy loss, and as booty there were a substantial number of scalps and one lone prisoner. This was a break indeed. It permitted an approach suggestive of a victorious army. As they neared the fort, the canoes were in procession with the one captive in the leading canoe. One captive wasn't an impressive sight, perhaps. One Iroquois captive dancing and singing at French command was something else. As for the victory he represented, that was beyond argument, with so many bloody scalps as witnesses.

It seems surprising that one poor captive should become a central figure of high strategy. Louvigny, Perrot, and the rest, however, were not slow to recognize that the fortunes of this little backwater of war had offered them a prize that, carefully used, might rather effectively forestall agreement between the lake Indians and the Iroquois. If the lake Indians could be induced to kill the captive, a possibility by no means remote, any agreement they might negotiate would be undertaken at a disadvantage, with their hands red with Iroquois blood.

The Hurons, to whom the captive had been given, seem to have sensed this strategy and were regarding the captive with quite unusual tenderness—so much so that their Jesuit missionary had to interpose and remind them sternly that unless they "put the Iroquois into the kettle" he would be taken from them. The Ottawas were angrily demanding that the captive be turned over to them. After long consultation a compromise was reached. A stake was set up, the victim tied to it, and the torturing, by both parties, began. Unlike his fellows, the captive failed to show the stoicism that gave tang to such scenes. One disgusted spectator, arguing that the victim did not deserve a warrior's death, finally dispatched him with a musket shot. Brave or no, the captive had served his purpose. He had made friendly negotiations with the Iroquois difficult, to say the least.

When Frontenac learned of this item of strategy he saw its value and acted promptly. He moved quickly because he knew that, unless the growing feeling that the day of the Frenchman was done could be changed, sooner or later—and probably sooner—the incident of the lone captive would be forgotten and negotiations between Iroquois and lake tribes would be renewed. What was needed now was a smashing blow against the English. That, it seemed, and only that, would restore French prestige. There wasn't time or opportunity for Louis' grandiose plan of taking New York and eliminating the English from the scene, even if Frontenac could have convinced himself of the plan's feasibility. But there was a chance to strike, and to strike hard enough and dramatically enough that all might realize that France was still a force to be considered and feared.

CHAPTER VI

CHALLENGE

Frontenac's plan for a three-pronged attack on New York, New Hampshire, and Maine. Ste. Hélène's desperate journey to Schenectady. Political dissensions leave that city unprepared. Scenes of massacre. Simon Schermerhorn alerts Albany. François Hertel at Salmon Falls and the Wooster River. Fort Loyal destroyed. Mounting anger of English results in a united plan. St. Castin and Port Royal.

FRONTENAC'S PLAN as finally formulated was for a three-pronged attack that would fan out to spread fear and desolation over all of England's northern colonies. One invading force, based on Montreal, would strike by way of Lake Champlain. Albany was its probable point of attack. Another force would start from Three Rivers to raid the border settlements of New Hampshire, while from Quebec the third expedition would drive toward Maine.

With the exception of Denonville's ill-starred attack on the Iroquois, the expedition against Albany was the most pretentious ever staged, judged by the character of its leadership. It was shared by Nicholas de Mantet, who with Du Lhut had provided that one small victory to lighten the darkness shrouding the land before Frontenac returned. Wherever De Mantet's name appears it is in association with swift and decisive action, as it was here. Sharing command with him was that second among the fabulous Le Moyne brothers, Jacques de Ste. Hélène. With him was his brother, Pierre d'Iberville, who stood just at the doorway of his amazing adventures.

Ste. Hélène was perhaps the most attractive of the ten Le Moyne brothers. He had less of arrogance and more of friendliness. He was a shrewd and determined fighter, but he added a gift of laughter that softened the harshness of action. He and Iberville, two years his junior, were almost inseparable until Ste. Hélène's untimely death at the age of thirty-one made separation final. They had been together in most of their adventures, first one and then the other in superior command. It had not yet appeared that of all that close-knit family Iberville was to become the greatest, as Ste. Hélène might have been the best liked. Ste. Hélène was a devoted family man, a good husband and father. Six years before, he had married Jeanne Carion. He was just short of twenty-five years, and his bride was eleven years and five months. She was eighteen when she became a widow, but she was the mother of three children.

For all his outward gentleness and humor, for all the kindliness—so noticeable that even the Indians spoke with gratitude of how he had refused to take advantage during the heat of an attack and had let thirty possible prisoners escape—he had a reputation for gallantry, enterprise, and determination.

On this occasion he needed all three. It was February when the expedition started from Montreal, and bitterly cold—so cold that few would have thought such an expedition possible. They moved on snowshoes over the frozen St. Lawrence, the hoods of their blanket coats shielding them from the full severity of the sub-zero weather. They carried their guns in mittened hands that were stiff with cold, while provisions and blankets were loaded on Indian sledges hauled by the adventurers by turns. The party was not large, 160 Frenchmen and 140 Christian Indians, so called. When sickness and cold and the drudgery of hauling the heavy sledges had taken their toll, there were no more than 250 left.

For five days they toiled along—to Chambly and up the frozen Richelieu until they reached the wind-swept reaches of Lake Champlain. There was murmuring among the Indians, who wished to know where they would attack. When they were told it was Albany, they were openly derisive. "How long is it," they asked, "since the French grew so bold?" There was the danger of lost morale, the question of whether the Indians would desert at the crucial moment. Well they might after the bitterness of the march.

A partial thaw had set in, and often they had to wade knee-deep in frozen slush, fighting sometimes to break through ice and searching with numbed feet for safe footing. Then the weather changed again. Once more the bitter cold was on them. Eight days of this brought them to the Hudson, where the roads divided; to the left for Albany, to the right for Schenectady. There was no hope in the larger venture. What chance with this cold and hungry and dispirited rabble to attack a place so well defended? Without a word of discussion De Mantet and Ste. Hélène turned to the right. They were still two leagues from their unsuspecting adversary.

It is true that Schenectady had been warned, but the citizens had chosen to meet it with derision. The warning had come from Albany, where Peter Schuyler was mayor. Peter Schuyler was known to have opposed that fanatical German immigrant, Jacob Leisler, who had set himself up in the wine business in New York, had prospered generously, and had developed a will to power. When James II had fled from his throne, Leisler, a rabid anti-Catholic, had argued that there was no legal government in the colony and had promptly set about providing one of his own. In a movement known as the Leisler Rebellion he had gained control of New York and had sent emissaries reaching out for more. They visited Albany, where the stiff rectitude of Peter Schuyler was too much for them. Moving to Schenectady, they found people ready and eager for Leisler's brand of sedition.

So it was that warnings coming from Schuyler were met with scoffing and derision. When the day of final judgment dawned on Schenectady it was on a place of fire and terror and death, a disordered place with copies of Leisler's seditious letters blowing in the wind along the bloody streets of the town. The letters had done their work. In stupidity and unbelievable folly they had done their work. There had been ample warning and no one to believe. Not many days later the Convention sitting in Albany was to pin-point the lack: "The factions and divisions which were amongst the people and their great disobedience to their officers; for they would obey no commands to keep watch . . . so that the enemy came in and broke open their very doors before any soul knew."

It was true enough. Lieutenant Enos Talmage and his twenty-four Connecticut militiamen were safe abed in their blockhouse. Abed, too, were the rest of the citizens, sleeping off the excitement of a festive gathering of early evening. No one was on guard where no one feared an attack. What did they care for Schuyler's warning? There was a ten-foot wall of logs about the place, and all but one or two of the eighty houses that sheltered four hundred persons were within its limits. But the gates—two of them—were wide open, and in a spirit of derision some town humorists had placed a snow man on each side of the entrance that looked toward Albany. There were no other guards. It was a misplaced pleasantry. It didn't delay or dissuade the men who came, their footsteps muted by the snow.

Perhaps the citizens were almost right in questioning that any sane man would order an attack from Montreal in the depth of winter. Perhaps it would have made little difference anyway had the gates been closed and guarded. The men who made that desperate march from Montreal were not men to be stopped by palisades. A few more Frenchmen dead, perhaps, but beyond that, what difference? There was no noise as they moved through the gates, past those cool sentinels of snow. There they divided, making a cordon about the homes. Only when Mantet and Ste. Hélène met at the far end of town was there any word. Then the drowsy citizens came awake with the scream of war whoops in their ears. At the guardhouse, where Mantet attacked, action was swift and bitter. Lieutenant Talmage and his men, only newly arrived, did their hopelessly gallant best to wipe out the remembrance that they had been asleep and not on guard. The doors were driven in. There was no opposition remaining when the place was set alight.

With their last defenders gone, the massacre—for there can be no other name for it—began. People rushing from their homes half clothed in the bitter night had little if any defense. "In the first fury of the attack," as the French spoke of it, few escaped. Peter Schuyler in a letter to the Convention at Albany was more explicit. "The cruelties committed—no pen can write nor tongue can express," but he does mention women, big with child, ripped up and children tossed alive into the flames or dashed to pieces against doors and window frames.

Perhaps it was no worse than what had happened at Lachine or at Le Chesnaye, but those were Indian attacks, and at Schenectady many were Frenchmen. For two hours the orgy of stabbing and looting and burning went on. The records tell us that thirty-eight men and boys were killed. Perhaps that is understandable, for this war and in those days no able-bodied man, or boy old enough to shoulder a gun, could rank as a noncombatant. It is not so easy to explain or justify the ten women and twelve children killed or the eighty or ninety captured. Few of them had arms in their hands. In those bitter hours only two Frenchmen had died and scarcely more had been wounded. Strangely enough, thirty Mohawks who were found in the town were treated with kindness.

There is the fact, too, that Iberville, going to the home of Captain John Sander Glen, well beyond the palisades, showed him the utmost courtesy. To Glen's great surprise, he and all his people were spared. He was even permitted to visit the captives to point out any relatives so that they might also be freed. He continued to discover them in such numbers that there were angry murmurs from the Indians. This was the payment of a debt. He and his wife had shown kindness to French captives taken by the Indians and on occasion had secured their release. It is this sort of contrast that makes the cruelty of an age stand out so starkly.

Yet perhaps it is wrong to speak of the cruelty of an age. War in any age is cruel. It is the manner rather than the fact that makes us recognize it. Who in this atom-bomb age can claim a sensitiveness that would justify censuring too deeply the practices of two centuries ago? Who—remembering the Warsaw ghetto of the last great war and the prison camps of Dachau and Auschwitz, Belsen and Buchenwald, can find sure ground for any age to be too critical or too complacent? There is sad truth in the words found in the *Jesuit Relations*, where Father Pierre Laurie wrote to his superior, remembering his impressions as he watched men burning at the stake. Said Father Laurie with understanding wisdom: "Our own people begin to be accustomed to this barbarous spectacle." It was true. They were no more hardhearted than most, but violence was nothing new. The sixty dead, the widows and the fatherless, these were the fortunes of such a war.

Morning came, and with it the recognition that it was time to go. What houses had not already been burned were set alight. By noon Schenectady was a smoking ruin. Fifty horses, the most prized among the captives, dragged the sleds now laden with booty as Mantet and Ste. Hélène led their forces and their captives on the long road back to Montreal. Of the ninety prisoners, twenty-seven men and boys took the road through the forest. Sixty old men and women and little children were left behind or permitted to escape with their scalps intact. The excitement of the kill was over.

In Albany the excitement had only begun. Simon Schermerhorn, up with the first wild scream at Schenectady, had managed to find a horse and to effect an escape that was almost miraculous. He roused the awakening Albany with a story of disaster that, though exaggerated in detail, essentially was sound enough. He set the attacking force at nineteen hundred, enough to startle the good people of Albany, who, however much inclined to discount this figure, would hardly have reduced it to the true two hundred and fifty. Sure that the next attack would be on Albany itself, the city fathers moved with commendable speed. The Mohawks, on whom their hopes depended, were not so easily moved. They wondered quite openly how a few Frenchmen had been able to do so much damage when they had been told again and again how invincible was the might of the English King. So early, then, was the ferment Frontenac had foreseen beginning to work. One blow and the prestige of France began to glow again, the warriors questioning once more which alliance would be more advantageous for them.

Rather reluctantly, then, the Indians were induced to set out in pursuit, spurred on by fifty young men of Albany who were eager for quick revenge. But the fifty horses for the French sleighs had permitted more speed returning, and it wasn't until many of these had been killed and eaten that the pursuers began to catch up. Almost in sight of Montreal itself they came upon a party of stragglers and killed or captured fifteen. That was the credit balance for the English: two soldiers killed and as many wounded in the first action, and a dozen more killed or trapped as they straggled home. Against that, sixty men and women and children killed and as many captured, Schenectady in ashes, and 400,000 livres in possessions gone up in blood and smoke.

The news spread throughout New England, racing like a prairie fire. Before defensive measures could be made effective, the second blow fell. This time it was François Hertel with twenty-four Frenchmen and as many Indians. They had left Three Rivers a day or two before Mantet and Ste. Hélène had set out from Montreal. Hertel's was a longer journey. It was two months before his little band neared their objective.

The country about was happy in its first real hope of peace. The years since the treaty at Casco, which seemed to end a period of almost unending fighting and savage raids that marked the Indian uprising known as King Philip's War, had been a bright promise but little more. Uncertainty and violence seemed never-ending.

At Casco Bay in the late autumn of the year, bare months before Frontenac had launched his three-pronged attack, the raw levies of

Massachusetts had met a large force of Indians and had defeated them decisively. For the first time New England breathed freely, feeling that peace had come at last.

There was a bitter awakening. It was the twenty-seventh of March, and the snow lay heavy in the forests that bordered the Salmon Falls River, which makes a convenient border between New Hampshire and Maine. The little village of Salmon Falls slept peacefully in its new security. In the borders of the forest François Hertel was waiting. Perhaps to pass the time he may have gone over some of the incidents in his life, remembering how, as a youth of eighteen, he had been captured by four Indians of the Mohawk tribe. From his home at Three Rivers young Hertel had been taken into slavery. He was always deeply religious. In a letter he managed to smuggle out of his captivity he wrote his confessor, Father le Moyne: "I would not have been taken alive if, to my sorrow, I had not feared that I was not in a state to die." Then he told how the hand that wrote had one of the fingers burned in the bowl of an Indian pipe, "to satisfy the Majesty of God which I have offended. The thumb on the other hand is cut off, but do not tell my mother of it." Probably by the same hand he sent a letter to his mother asking her forgiveness for disobedience. "It is my sins that placed me where I am," he wrote. "I owe my life to your prayers."

This was the man who was to escape from his captors to gain a reputation as a furious fighter and to be called "The Hero," and not in derision, by his fellow citizens. This, too, was the man who had mapped out his approaches to Salmon Falls with studied thoroughness; had noted that the defenses had a stockaded house at the center, a quick port of refuge, with two small forts in advance. He had noted, too, that no sentries manned the forts. At the first hint of daylight François Hertel divided his forces in three to surround the meager fortifications and, when these were taken, to round up the people from the scattered homes. It was stern work for his fifty-two men, three of them his own sons. Hertel drove relentlessly until no house was standing. Thirty persons, men and women and little children, had died by tomahawk or bullet. Fifty-four shivering women and children were captive.

Years of battling make men quick in their reactions to alarm. Hertel and his force, now cumbered by prisoners, had hardly started their retreat when scouts brought word that a force three times their number was hurrying after them. About evening the pursuers were in sight. At the Wooster River, swollen by floods and spanned by one narrow bridge, François Hertel and his sons were waiting. They stood on the bridgehead at the far shore and picked off the English as they approached. It was an exploit that Horatius might well have applauded. "We fought," says the record, "as long as we could distinguish friend from foe." Nightfall saw Hertel and his band on its way again. It is not pleasant to record that in the interests of speed some of the prisoners who could not keep up were given to the Indians. That it was common practice is none the less disturbing. It is a hard thing to remember of François Hertel, a man of deep feeling and of wide and generous kindliness, as the records of both his friends and his enemies amply prove. But it was true. It was an age of men of two soul sides, and this was the darker side.

But Hertel was still spoiling for other fighting. Hearing that a party of Frenchmen under a young officer of the Canadian noblesse named Portneuf was on its way to Casco Bay, he decided to join it. The party was the one sent from Quebec, and it too had left early in January, following the route that years later Benedict Arnold was to travel in the last attempt to take Quebec. Portneuf had seen no need for haste, and his party had stopped to hunt as opportunity arose. It was May when Hertel caught up. With his own thirty-six men and Portneuf's hundred and ten, almost half of whom were French, it was an impressive force. Soon it was joined by a large body of Indians, who thought it an opportunity too good to be missed. So as the assault force neared Casco Bay it had grown to four or five hundred. In the long months in the forest most of the Frenchmen had adopted the costume of the Indians and looked no different from their followers. There was all the outward appearance of another King Philip's War.

Fort Loyal, which was intended to dominate Casco Bay, scarcely justified the name of fort. It was a palisade surrounding a small group of buildings on a slight rise of land. It stood just where India Street comes to an end in modern Portland, Maine. Beyond the palisades the village was protected by four small blockhouses. These were not pretentious, and even the eight cannon mounted behind the palisades did not offer much security. At the moment there was no thought of such a need. The continual raiding had seemed to die down, and Captain Sylvanus Davis, who was in command, was dependable and courageous, a typical trader-soldier of the frontier. Even with his shrewd knowledge he might have been caught completely unprepared had not a nameless Scot inadvertently strolled into the forest a half mile from the village. Everything had been designed for complete surprise, but that wandering Scot with his red scalp was too tempting to resist and, once the scalp had changed ownership, it was too much to expect that there wouldn't be some gratified shouts.

This was too much for the young bloods of the garrison, yeoman soldiers new to discipline and resenting it. Young Lieutenant Thaddeus Clark, eager for glory, called for volunteers, and thirty of like spirit responded. There was courage there but little wisdom such as Captain Davis could have supplied. Shortly it would be too late to be of value. They were not long in discovering the enemy. Some cattle pointing with bovine curiosity marked their hiding place. The thirty leaped forward, hungry for the first taste of glory. Only four wounded boys returned. There was no doubt as to the glory. It belonged to the thirty, but most of their scalps belonged to the enemy.

Realizing that his small force stood little chance against that opposing him, Davis, confused by appearances, asked if there was any Frenchman with whom he might discuss terms. The terms were simple: the garrison and civilians to be given safe passage to the next town. This was agreed. How often were such agreements to be made; how little different was the result. It was idle to pretend that a few score Frenchmen could offer protection against hundreds of savage warriors. Perhaps the French meant their safe conduct, perhaps they didn't. The vanquished knew as well as the victors how slim was the chance that the guarantee would or could be observed. When the garrison filed out, the Indians took over. Some they murdered, some they carried off as captives. Only Captain Davis and one or two others remained in French hands. So ended the grim chapter of Casco Bay.

It would be idle to argue that French and English were not almost equally guilty of stirring up the Indians against their enemies. If the English seemed more dependable, it was not due to greater virtue but to the fact that they depended less on Indian allies than did the French. Governors Dongan and Andros certainly veiled thinly, if at all, their efforts to turn their Iroquois allies against the French. Frontenac quite openly offered a reward of ten écus for each scalp, whether English or Iroquois, and changed the practice only when it occurred to him that French and English scalps looked remarkably alike when detached from French and English heads. Only then did he change the offer to ten écus for a woman captive and twenty écus for a man. So humanity was served.

Bitter as the record may be, it did restore the waning prestige of France, not only among the Indians but among the French themselves. They moved with a new confidence. There was no more talk of lake Indians joining the Iroquois. The Onontio who dared attack New York and New England in one comprehensive stroke was worthy of attention when he spoke. This was indeed the old Onontio. Soon the fur cargoes would be smothering the warehouses of Montreal. Soon the Indians would be gathering in a great congress of peace and unity. Soon the stern Frontenac, seventy-one years of age, would be standing before this gathering, talking to them in his familiar terms. As if to assure them that the spirit was still the same, Frontenac was to seize a tomahawk and wave it about his head as he danced with his friends. Maybe there were those who thought such conduct unbecoming in a governor, but the Indians did not think so. They understood him. They didn't think that dignity depended on nonessentials. He was responding to a gesture of friendship with another gesture. He used their own forms. That was the essence of his strange hold over them. He didn't posture and he didn't patronize.

There was no elation throughout New York and New England. There was no fear. Perhaps there was no united feeling either. That was hard to come by in the motley collection of English colonies. In the northern group, too, the leavening of the Dutch had done little to help. But if Frontenac had, in a measure, re-established French prestige at the expense of England, he had done it at some cost. He had given these northern colonies a common cause. They weren't seeing eye to eye and wouldn't for years to come, but there was at least a burning indignation to hold in common, and sometimes that is as potent as a common enthusiasm.

They had lived through border wars and sudden and terrible forays. These they recognized as among the inescapable hazards of opening a new land. This was different. This was open war without war's uncertain amenities. This war was relentless and cruel, even for war. It attacked women and children as well as combatants. It was a threat not only to their bodies but to the new concept of freedom of body and spirit that had brought them here. The threat was from a religious form they had left their native lands to escape,

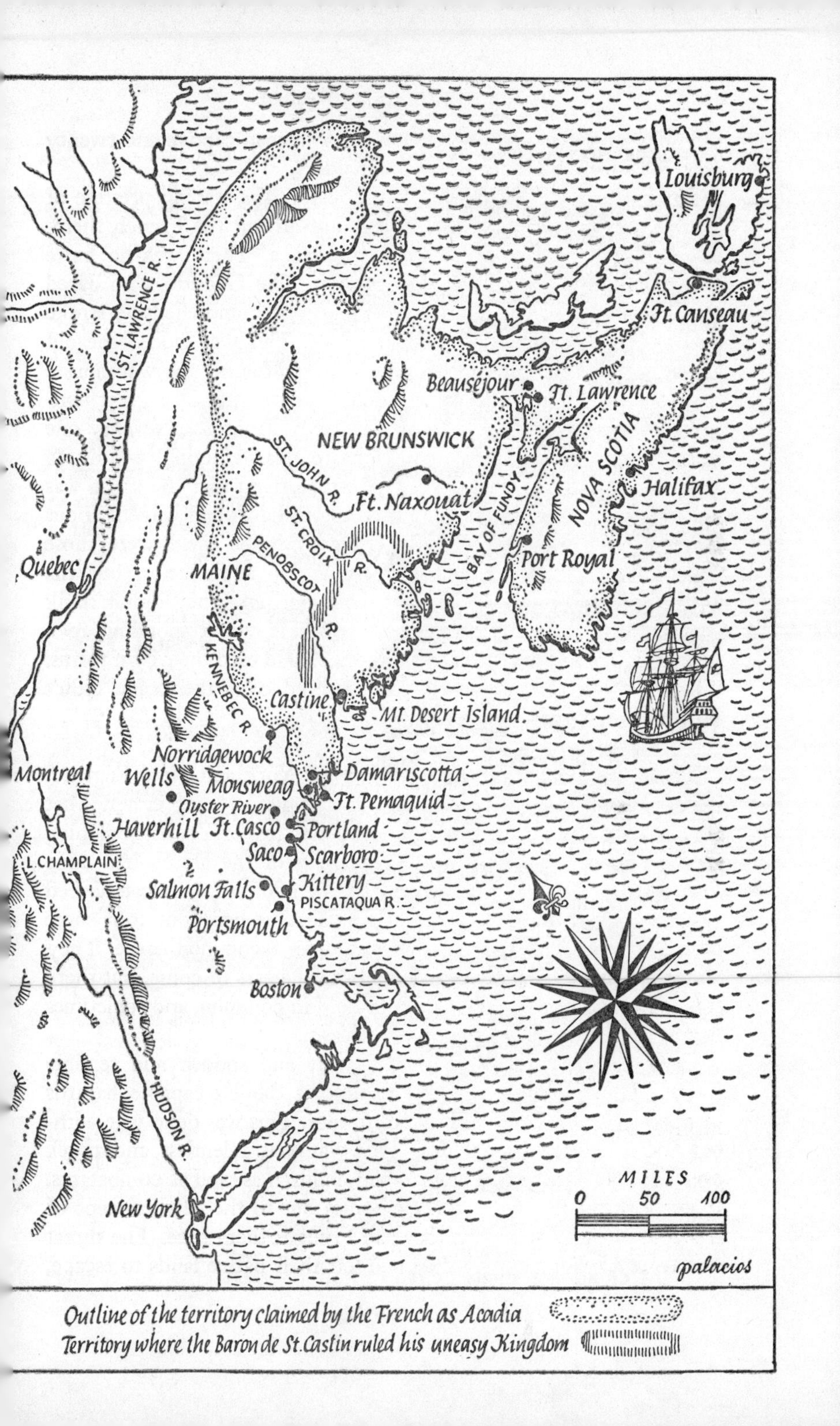

Outline of the territory claimed by the French as Acadia

Territory where the Baron de St. Castin ruled his uneasy Kingdom

a challenge to the freedom from arbitrary authority that was their solace in hours of suffering and danger. It had become a contest for survival, and stubborn English and stubborn Dutch were in no mood to submit meekly. There was growing in these northern colonies a sense of inevitability, of an absolute challenge that, unless it could be met successfully, meant that their sacrifices and their hopes had come to nothing. It was an irrepressible conflict. So if Frontenac had indeed restored the confidence of his people he had, equally surely, given them good cause to need it.

Up to this moment the English had not been thinking in terms of empire. They wanted to be left alone to establish their holdings, to till their acres, and to formulate a civil and religious government. They wanted the resources of trade, but hardly elsewhere than in Hudson's Bay, far to the north, had they thought of the acquisition of further land. They had no imperial dream. Seemingly they had only now come to the realization of how greatly the French aspired. They saw, whether they had heard of Louis' far-reaching plan or no, that the intent was there to make the continent a French preserve.

There had been no such comparable thinking with the English. There had been occasional flares of anger, when the thought of being rid of an annoying and troublesome neighbor may have been very appealing. There had been no getting down to details, and the pressure of their own affairs had promptly wiped such pleasant thoughts from their minds. Now, suddenly, they were brought face to face with the realization that it couldn't be forgotten, that sooner or later England must own New France or New France would own New England. The comforting sense that there was room for everyone ended with Casco Bay and Salmon Falls and Schenectady.

Whether Frontenac, planning his three-pronged attack on the English, had given a thought to the disturbed conditions in the colonies does not appear. It is unlikely that so shrewd a tactician would not have recognized that the colonies, which had never been warmly co-operative, were more than ever disunited. They hated Sir Edmund Andros, who ruled New England and New York with a supercilious version of an iron hand, and who with the flight of James II had lost what small support remained. Along with fifty of his more prominent followers he was seized and imprisoned. For seven weeks it was anybody's government until the general council, recognizing that this could not continue, took it upon themselves to appoint one of their number, the aged Simon Bradstreet, as governor. In New York, Jacob Leisler and his followers were able to wrest from Andros' deputy governor, Francis Nicholson, what little authority he retained. So in Boston and New England there was no officially recognized government, and New York was ruled by a usurper. The one thing that the New England provisional government could think of was economy. The hated Sir Edmund had established garrisons along the frontier. These his jailers promptly withdrew or reduced to a point of uselessness.

In New York, Leisler's authority was anything but assured. He held New York itself, but Albany kept definitely aloof. It has been seen that as a result, though there was ample warning of an attack from Canada, there was no united action, only the will to ignore or deride the threat. Presently it was impossible to do either. The ugly evidence of threescore men, women, and children killed, hundreds driven into captivity and all their goods appropriated, could not be overlooked, and it wasn't. There was animosity enough to have launched a thousand crusades, but still not unanimity enough to co-operate successfully in one. There was a conference in New York in May of 1690, in which New York and New England did co-operate to achieve a plan that was good enough. It might have succeeded had its leadership been more aggressive. It would have succeeded, even with this lack, had Frontenac been less determined.

The plan was for a twofold attack, New York and Connecticut providing a land force. Four hundred men would move by the familiar Lake George-Lake Champlain highway to attack Montreal. The New England colonies were to provide three hundred and fifty men and what Indian support they could secure and were to attack Quebec by water. New England delegates were not too enthusiastic; Boston was already engaged in a private affair from which its citizens expected much and felt that this perhaps represented their reasonable contribution. However, under some pressure, they agreed to co-operate if the support of the mother country could be secured. In the interval, however, they were pressing a private design that was nearer their hearts. It was an attack on Port Royal in Acadia, that center of privateering that represented a continuing threat to the sea-borne commerce of the colony. Port Royal, too, was the natural rallying point for adventurous spirits who were accustomed to use it as a base for harassing the New England border or instigating the depredations of the powerful Abenaki tribes. The Baron St. Castin was one of the most conscientious instigators. He had taken part in Portneuf's attack on Fort Loyal, possibly in return for Sir Edmund Andros' attack on his small principality a year or two before. If that was the reason, he had kept the account open, for there wasn't much trouble on the New England border in which the baron did not have an active hand.

There aren't many characters in this era of history more colorful than Jean Vincent de l'Abadie, Baron de St. Castin, a native of Béarn, the province of France that produced Henry of Navarre. He was a bare seventeen years of age when he came to Canada as a member of the famous Carignan-Salière regiment, which seems to have provided its full share of the great of early Canada. He was an ensign in the company commanded by Jacques de Chambly, who became the seigneur of Chambly and built Fort St. Louis, which was later to bear his name, on the Richelieu. When the regiment was disbanded a year or two later, the young baron made his way to Acadia and there set up a small kingdom of his own devising, where, barring the occasional intrusion of unfriendly English, he was the unquestioned master. The site he chose was at Pentegoet on Penobscot Bay, in what is now the state of Maine, and where his name is perpetuated in the town of Castine, which stands at what was once the center of his kingdom.

It was a kingdom by occupation rather than by authority. He considered it his on the rather dubious grounds that the French King had claimed it and had built a fort in the neighborhood to emphasize the claim. But the fort changed hands so frequently that it represented rather uncertain evidence. Added to that, the Puritan English, who liked neither the baron's presence nor his manners, claimed with rather good reason that his post was located on land granted to the Duke of York. From the Puritan standpoint there was no doubt that the baron was an unwholesome influence. He had an almost miraculous hold over the Abenaki and he missed no opportunity to co-operate with his Indian friends in carrying fire and sword to the New England firesides. The Puritans were almost equally incensed at the practical way he used New England to build up a trading fortune that is said to have run to three or four hundred thousand crowns.

Whether Baron St. Castin prospered to that extent remains a matter of question. There is no doubt whatever of his hold over the Indians. He lived with them, learned their ways, gained their confidence, and espoused their daughters in wholesale fashion. He set up his private seraglio in his forest fastness, explaining this deviation from his Catholic upbringing by saying that he was patterning his life on that of the Orientals. His innumerable children ran wild in the surrounding forests, but the baron himself maintained his courtly appearance, his capacity for business, and his unfailing hatred for the English with whom he traded.

To these unwavering qualities there might be added, strangely enough, his devoutness; for he was a sincerely devout Catholic. He had even petitioned for a resident priest who might devote himself to bringing the baron's Indian friends into the Church fold. The parish priest of Port Royal, who knew him well and knew too that he was the chief support of the Church at Port Royal, couldn't resist mentioning the request to strait-laced Bishop St. Vallier with the comment that St. Castin himself "has need of spiritual aid to sustain him in the paths of virtue." For all that, the baron made his regular twice-a-year visit to Port Royal, where he attended Mass with exemplary regularity, made his confession, which must have been quite a substantial matter, and, having received forgiveness, returned to his own people and his accustomed ways, happily conscious of a cleaned slate. There was one occasion when Governor François Perrot, who, having been removed from a similar post in Montreal on charges of peculation and having been sent to Acadia where he could continue them, had the baron arrested and imprisoned for almost two months "on pretense of a little weakness I had for some women," St. Castin explained with becoming innocence, and added, "He wanted to be the only merchant in Acadia," which was probably a shrewd enough appraisal.

The Church and Louis himself, always an exemplary moralist when dealing with the misdemeanors of others, evidently had somewhat the same estimate of St. Castin. Louis expressed the feelings of both when he sent word to Governor Meneval, who succeeded François Perrot, that he should require St. Castin to abandon his vagrant life among the Indians, cease all trading with the English, and establish a permanent settlement. If the culprit agreed to lead this better life he was assured that he might expect proofs of the King's favor. Meneval reported, after a sufficient lapse of time, that all these conditions had been met. The various squaws had been disposed in some manner, and the baron himself was reported to be living an estimable domestic life with his wife, who was the daughter of Madockawando, chief of the Penobscots.

It is difficult to establish this remarkable reformation. It was not the first of such changes of heart and conduct, so the skeptical might incline to wonder if it was the last. But history seems to have accepted it as final. Certainly the poet Longfellow did, recounting in highly romantic verse how Jean Vincent St. Castin and his Indian princess returned to the ancestral acres in the shadow of the Pyrenees, there to end their days in quietude and sanctity. So at least the story appears in the Second Student's tale in the familiar *Tales of a Wayside Inn.*

What is somewhat better authenticated is the one thing that the baron certainly did not change, his continuing lack of regard for the New Englanders whose New England he had shared for better than half a lifetime. One of the last acts of Sir Edmund Andros was an attack on St. Castin's trading post at Pentegoet. It was the third attack of the kind. Former Governor Dongan had tried it twice. But Andros was more thorough. He arrived with a considerable force, and when the baron escaped to the forest Andros proceeded to demolish the post and to remove all the possessions to his base at Pemaquid. He explained, with commendable moderation, that the baron could have his possessions back by claiming them at Pemaquid and going through the simple formula of becoming an English subject. St. Castin did go to Pemaquid to claim his possessions. He went accompanied by a considerable number of his Indian friends. He didn't take the oath. Later he proceeded to ravage the border settlements as thoroughly as he had demolished Pemaquid.

That was the general situation before Hertel had visited Salmon Falls and before he and Portneuf had reached Casco Bay. It was a situation hardly to be borne, and before the conference at New York met to formulate a general policy against Canada, New England was taking its own action against an immediate and unfriendly neighbor. The idea was to draw the teeth of Port Royal forever.

At the time a certain William Phips was patrolling the waters about Massachusetts in command of a forty-gun warship, the *Six Friends*, looking for the *Sea Rover*, a piratical craft that had been making Port Royal her headquarters and generally make life miserable for English shipping, no doubt with the tacit approval of the French authorities. The stage was set.

CHAPTER VII

THE AWFUL FROWN OF GOD

The youth and character of William Phips. His qualities and growing success. The favor of kings. Capture of Port Royal and its governor. Appointed to command the expedition against Quebec. Its hopeful promise and ignominious failure. The somber mood of Boston. The pattern of conquest set.

THE history of William Phips is one of the earliest of the continent's success stories. It has all the familiar trappings of the rags-to-riches theme. For all that, Phips himself remains a rather shadowy figure in the history in which he played a large and lively, if not too impressive, part.

He was the twenty-first child of his mother, and the youngest son, and so he remained until the death of his father when the boy was six years old. His mother marrying again, there were six more brothers and sisters. It is not difficult to understand that there could have been little luxury in his boyhood home at Monsweag Farm on the Sheepscot River. Today the country is undeniably a part of Maine. In these earlier times it lay in the disputed land between the St. Croix and Kennebec rivers, where St. Castin had his squatter kingdom and where Indian, French, and English maintained a cruel and bloody seesaw of foray and reprisal for a century and more. Young William was by turns sheep boy, farm hand, woodsman, and apprentice to a business whose chief occupation was shipbuilding.

There and not from books, of which there were none at his home, nor from schooling, for which there was little time or opportunity, came his passion for the sea and his dreams of achievement.

He was a grown man, broad-shouldered, quick-tempered, with large capable hands and a sublime confidence in himself, before it became evident that he was to be one of fortune's favorites. It is told by Cotton Mather, the great New England divine and Phips's first biographer, that when he first came to Boston in his thirtieth year he could neither read nor write. Probably the worthy minister was not wholly correct in his facts; that was his weakness. Young Phips had learned enough to be a trader and a shipbuilder and to have prospered sufficiently to give some support to the prophecy that as a twenty-first son, with the magic of that triple seven about him, he would surely stand before kings. There was no doubt in young Phips's mind, no doubt in the facts either, for the records show quite clearly that one king helped finance his earliest treasure venture, another made him a knight of the realm for his accomplishments, and a third appointed him the first "Royal Captain General and Governor in Chief of the Province of Massachusetts Bay."

When he married Mary Hull, widow of a prosperous merchant, gossip forgot about the prophecies and smiled at what they believed was a very practical arrangement. It was a happy one for Phips, and to signalize it he promised her a "faire brick house in the Green Lane of North Boston." It was Boston's social neighborhood, and there was no evidence that the promise was more than a dream. But there was no shrinking modesty in William Phips. He went on telling her that one day he would command a king's ship. "Mind you," he urged, "someday I shall have command over better men than I am myself accounted."

For all the brave words, they lived simply, almost sparingly. There was nothing to suggest that it was his wife's very modest fortune that had caught his attention. Indeed, his devotion is one of the brightest spots in the remarkable history of William Phips.

It wasn't until he came on the idea of a treasure hunt that William Phips's fortunes began to improve. This was an occupation that appealed to the hardy and adventurous. It was adventure that wasn't without promise. Spain's fabulous empire in the Indies was pouring out its gold and jewels. Not all of it reached Spain. The pirate and the privateer, who differed only nominally, took their share, and the natural hazards took even more. More than one lordly galleon had come to grief in some treacherous passage of the Bahama Banks. Somehow Captain Phips had come by a chart marking the resting place of one such submerged wreck. He went to London to petition the court for permission to head an expedition to search for the wreck and salvage its cargo.

When looked at from the standpoint of today, it seems improbable that anyone would hazard a considerable sum on such an unlikely venture. But Charles II was a gambler. Phips obtained his permission and sailed away on the *Salee Rose* for the Bahama Banks. The surprising part of the story is that after one earlier and unsuccessful attempt the gamble won. Phips found the treasure ship and relieved it of three hundred thousand pounds sterling for the royal coffers. Small wonder that Captain Phips, the adventurer, enjoyed the King's favor. The captain's own share was more modest. It totaled sixteen thousand pounds after he had fulfilled his promise to share with his men. It was a sufficient sum to go nicely with his recently acquired knighthood and the proposed "faire brick house" on Boston's Green Lane.

Lady Phips, as she had now become, was not one to let a promise lapse for lack of attention. Without waiting for Sir William's return from London, she purchased a site at Green Lane and Salem Street commanding a fine view of the harbor, and there the "faire brick house" finally took shape.

Sir Edmund Andros might speak disparagingly of Phips as the "upstart knight," but the Phips fortunes were as unmistakably going up as those of Andros were going down. Boston thought well of Phips, and the eminent divine, Cotton Mather, was keeping his friend's name constantly before the public. At the moment Sir William was cruising about in command of the *Six Friends*, keeping an eye for the *Sea Rover*. Old Governor Bradstreet and his council, however, were coming to feel that instead of attempting a feeble defense of the coast it was time to strike a blow that would chasten the French and put fear in the hearts of the Abenaki and such footloose depredators as the Baron St. Castin. Phips did not overlook such an opening. On March 22, 1690, Samuel Seawall noted the fact in his journal. "Sir William Phips offers himself to go in person," and he added, "Some feared he would not go; others that his Lady would not consent." Then the terse finale, "Court swears him Major Generall."

The new major general moved with all speed. Everyone was in

favor of action, which helped considerably, but everyone also preferred that whatever action was taken should be taken by someone else. So pronounced was this feeling that an early form of conscription was invoked, a system of impressment by which a force of eight small vessels and seven hundred men finally was secured. Phips was still in a hurry, so the force set sail from Nantasket on the twenty-eighth of April, 1690, and on the eleventh of May he reached Port Royal and promptly demanded its surrender. Governor Meneval, who ruled over Acadia, though taken by surprise, was a man of courage. But he needed more than that to defend the port with a total of seventy men against seven hundred. He made the best terms he could: private property was to be respected, the Church to be unmolested, and the soldiers returned to Quebec. Phips was happy to accede. But while the decision was pending it was discovered that some merchants had carried off goods and hidden them in the forest. Although this was private property and so free from attachment under the surrender terms, Phips decided that it was a serious offense and that all agreements were void. Perhaps he remembered that Governor Meneval had entrusted him with the governor's own money for safekeeping. In any event, all the rest of the movables, public and private, were packed in hogsheads and sent on board, some of the hogsheads, no doubt, marked for the major general commanding.

Captain Alden, at the orders of Phips, had raided and taken possession of St. Castin's post on the Penobscot and continued his raiding as far as the head of the Bay of Fundy and along the east coast as far as Chedabucto. It was a thorough if not a particularly gallant job. By May thirtieth Phips was back in Boston, having overrun all Acadia and having with him Governor Meneval, fifty-nine soldiers, two priests, and an unstated number of hogsheads of plunder.

We learn of some of the contents of these hogsheads through Governor Meneval's attempt to recover some of his possessions. There was not only the money Meneval had entrusted to Phips for safekeeping, which the doughty major general seemed reluctant to restore, but an additional and colorful collection of articles. These included "six silver spoons, six silver forks, one silver cup in the shape of a gondola, a pair of pistols, three new wigs, a gray silk vest, four pair of silk garters, two dozens of shirts, six vests of dimity, four nightcaps with lace edgings, all my table service of fine tin, all my kitchen linen." There were other items, but these will serve.

Meneval petitioned Governor Bradstreet and the council for redress, but he records: "As they have little authority and stand in fear of Phips, who is supported by the rabble, to which he himself once belonged, and of which he is now chief, they would do nothing for me." Governor Bradstreet did do something. He wrote rather stiffly to Phips demanding that he obey the council's order that Meneval's possessions be returned. Reluctantly Sir William gave up some of the money and the clothing, apparently retaining the balance, including the "table service of fine tin," which he probably felt would look well in the Green Lane home.

Such minor matters were soon forgotten in the ever-mounting resentment over the French attack on Schenectady, Salmon Falls, and Casco, and there was a grim determination to curb this recurring threat. Phips's success at Port Royal, whose importance no one had stopped to assess, marked him out for leadership. He had no notable military ability. His choice resulted not from outstanding qualities but because there was no one else whose qualities were as good. The dominant purpose of the New Englander to possess and develop the land did not tend to the development of leadership caliber as did the constant reaching out of the French, which necessitated the ability to plan and control.

As a leader, William Phips did have some qualities. He could secure the devotion of his followers or, failing that, could achieve the same end by a gusty outpouring of oaths, supplemented by the hammer blows of his hamlike fists. Even after fortune had smiled on him he had been known to strike out with hands that were now partly hidden by lace ruffles. Tall, stalwart, sharp of eye, and of a pleasant countenance, he was the proper figure for command. His success at Port Royal gave him the popular appeal that made him not only the most desirable head for the expedition against Quebec but the only possible one. If there was a single doubting mind it did not belong to Sir William. "The plan is well formed," he admitted when he first heard of it, "and I am the best man in Boston to handle it."

The one protesting voice seems to have been that of his wife, who, wifelike, felt that he had done his share and might now settle down to enjoy his "faire brick house" and his considerable honors. "There is nothing to be disturbed about," he assured her. "Did I not greatly enrich us all by my last conquest? This time I shall do better. The business is more important." Still unconvinced, the good lady probably urged that there was no need for more. For all his manifest shortcomings, there were qualities in this man. They showed in his retort: "I was born for others as well as for myself in this world. I may sit still at home if I will, and enjoy my ease for the rest of my life. But I believe I should offend God in doing so; for I am now in the prime of my age and strength, and I thank God I can endure hardship. I will now expose myself where I am able, and as far as I am able, for the service of my country." That was his final word, and had his abilities been equal to his devotion, history might have had to record a very different denouement.

To attack Quebec was a large undertaking for anyone, and the conditions that faced Sir William Phips were far from being the best. For one thing, ammunition was limited. An appeal was sent to the mother country for more adequate supplies, and the message emphasized the urgency. Storms delayed the returning vessel far beyond the scant patience of the new commander in chief. He made a careful search of the town, rounding up and requisitioning even the scantiest stocks. At best it was inadequate, as events would show soon enough. However, it was all there was, and as he expected to make as short work of Quebec as he had of Port Royal, he hopefully convinced himself that it would be more than adequate. Anyway, if he waited much longer the season would make the adventure impossible, and that wasn't to be considered.

If there was some recklessness in the chief command, there were solid qualities in his assistant commander, but they didn't happen to be qualities of military knowledge or the judgment for leadership. Major John Walley was a councilor of Barnstable and obviously a man of considerable prominence. The records of the Plymouth Colony show that by appointment of the General Convention, John Walley and Thomas Hinckley—who was governor of the County of Plymouth—were appointed commissioners to "enquire into the grounds of war against those who disturbed the peace of Their Majestys' colonies." Later, on the same authority, John Walley was empowered "to impress or otherwise provide a suitable vessel to transport the soldiers if there was occasion."

When the problematical occasion became a fact, Major Walley was associated with Major William Bradford, deputy governor of the colony, in imposing the impressment order which called for a certain number of men from each community. These duties, as far as we know, were carried out meticulously and adequately. When next we hear of Major Walley he is being spoken of by some as a lieutenant general in charge of the military forces of the expedition against Quebec, and its second-in-command. Even political importance hardly seems to justify the jump from major to lieutenant general, so we are forced to the conclusion that Walley also was chosen because there was no one better equipped.

August ninth of the year 1690 was a day of heat and sunshine. Everyone who could find a way had journeyed to Hull, a short distance out of Boston. There is some confusion, even among the participants, as to whether the starting point was Hull or Nantasket or Boston itself. It is of little moment. It had been noised about that the great expedition was ready and would sail with the first favorable wind, and this day seemed likely to provide it. Anyway, it was a sight worth seeing. There were thirty-two ships in all. Admittedly some of them in ordinary times were just fishing craft. But there were Sir William's flagship, the *Six Friends*, a ship of war mounting forty-four guns; the *John and Thomas* with twenty-six guns; the *Swan* and the *American Merchant*, whose armament is not recorded. These were the major units. There was a small group of three vessels that Jacob Leisler had gathered at New York and sent to join the expedition, one of them a frigate mounting twenty-four guns, the other two mounting four and eight. It wasn't a very heavy battery, though probably ample for the ammunition available. It was an impressive sight even if some of the vessels were pretty small. Each had its complement of men, no less than thirteen hundred riflemen in all, and an almost equal number of crew and supernumeraries, bringing the total to some twenty-two hundred men.

About six o'clock the wind veered favorably, and suddenly all was movement. Anchors were up and sails broken out and the great enterprise that was to destroy the power of France in the New World had begun.

The three small vessels New York had supplied for the attack on Quebec were recognized as a token contribution. New York's real share was to be the land expedition against Montreal, which was aimed at taking that city and diverting attention from the attack on Quebec. It was the well-tried policy, the divide-and-conquer strategy. Good as the plan was, the New York phase of it was not getting off to a very promising start. The attack on Schenectady had sent a wave of anger through the whole section, but there was so much division existing that it was difficult to achieve the unity necessary to a successful attack. In so much New York was different from New England, where the governor and council of Massachusetts could memorialize the home government that it was the "general opinion of the whole Country that there is no expectation of putting an Issue to the Indian Warr, nor will their Majestys' subjects here ever live in peace, but by the dislodging and removal of these ill neighbors." And Cotton Mather added the word that it was the general conclusion "of all who argued sensibly" that "Canada must be reduced."

In New York there was no general opinion. There were too many divided loyalties. There were the friends, or at least supporters, of the summarily removed Sir Edmund Andros. There were the followers of the usurper Jacob Leisler. There were the more devoted followers of the deposed Stuarts and those who rejoiced over the accession of the House of Orange. It didn't make for general or decisive opinion. There was even division in command, once the expedition was undertaken. It was shared by Fitz-John Winthrop of Connecticut and Robert Livingston of New York. Neither of these gentlemen had the decisiveness or the strong fists of a Phips to command the respect of seven or eight hundred English and as many Indians. The expedition was doomed almost before it started. What the Reverend Cotton Mather wrote later of the sea expedition might perhaps apply equally well here. "There was more haste than good speed in the attempt," the reverend gentleman stated, adding, "They were not enough concerned for the counsel and presence of God in the undertaking; they mainly propounded the plunder to be got among a people whose trade was that where wild beasts enriched them; so the business miscarried."

At least there could be no question about the business miscarrying. Winthrop and Livingston had indeed started on their way from Albany when word reached them from the governors of Massachusetts and Connecticut that Sir William Phips had set sail on his great adventure. This news was something of a spur. For the moment, excitement added its hint of enthusiasm. Reaching Wood Creek at the head of Lake Champlain, the commanders found that the force in charge of the canoes that were to transport the expedition up the lake had grown impatient of waiting and had returned to Albany. Smallpox had broken out among the Indian allies, as it frequently did, with an effect more deadly than bullets. This double calamity was too much for the small enthusiasm that had existed for the undertaking from the beginning. The two leaders, having had their fill of command, were anxious enough to follow the canoes back to Albany. There seems to have been only one really effective dissenting voice, that of tough John Schuyler, who had seen with his own eyes what had happened at Schenectady and still burned with a passionate desire to repay it. He got permission to take a force of twenty-nine white men and one hundred and twenty Indians to make this repayment.

As it turned out, it wasn't an attack on Montreal but on a few citizens and soldiers at La Prairie and still on the south side of the river. The reprisal party killed or captured twenty-five persons, some of them women, burned homes and haystacks, killed some cattle, and retired. As vengeance, it was understandable; as a move in the crusade to capture Canada, it was as dismal a failure as history records. So Sir William Phips must have thought when he heard the news and realized that the crusade was his, and his alone.

Frontenac was in Montreal when he received a somewhat startling letter from Quebec's town major, Prévost by name. Prévost had been charged with the strengthening of the defenses of the city during Frontenac's absence and with organizing a company of guards. His letter to Frontenac contained a bit of gossip that the town major forwarded with some reluctance. Word had come overland from Acadia that an Englishwoman taken captive by the Abenaki had said something of a great fleet sailing from Boston to attack Quebec.

Frontenac shared the dubiousness that showed in every line of the town major's letter. Still he could hardly satisfy himself that the English would be content with such a tawdry business as the attack on La Prairie. The wise course seemed to be to return to Quebec. Rain was blanketing the river, a cold misty rain, and the small vessel that was to take him turned out to be a leaky tub and all but foundered before it was well on its way. A transfer was made to the canoes that Frontenac had never liked, and the long and uncomfortable journey begun.

It was early next day that they saw another canoe approaching; the two men in it were driving it as if in desperate need for haste, as indeed they were. They bore another letter from Prévost. This time the news was disturbing enough. It was authenticated by the word of the Sieur de Cannanville, who had arrived from Tadoussac, where he had himself counted no less than twenty-four ships, eight of them of considerable size. Sending back word to Callières to come at once with every fighting man who could be spared, Frontenac pushed on, probably in some relief that the chances were that John Schuyler was by now back in Albany with his captives and Winthrop safely returned to Hartford.

It was October 10 when Frontenac had heard the first whisper of Phips's approach. It was morning on the fourteenth when he reached Quebec. The anchorage before the city was free of sail. Though it was still early the town was out to greet the governor. There were times when it had become almost a habit to criticize their turbulent master, but, come danger, that stern, assured face brought new confidence and faith.

Prévost hurried forward, eager to show the governor what precautions had been taken. He had done wonders in so short a time. The first fortification of Quebec had been begun that spring. By now it had grown into a strong defense, wrapping itself about the city. Even the vulnerable rear was secured by barricades of heavy beams and casks filled with earth. A line of palisades followed the course of the St. Charles River from the great cliff at the Saut au Matelot to the intendant's palace. Beyond that, covering the rear, were further palisades strengthened at places by towers of stone. At points along the palisades and especially at the Saut au Matelot, which guarded Lower Town, were batteries of guns. There were two small batteries in Lower Town by the river, too, but no fortifications. It would have to take its chance.

Dawn was breaking on the sixteenth of October when a sentry making his round at the Saut au Matelot suddenly sensed something new. His eyes could hardly pierce the pre-dawn mist that shrouded the river, but as the light came up and the air grew clearer his startled eyes saw shadows take shape. There were ships riding at anchor, and they were clear enough now for anxious folk to count them. Great and small, they reached the breath-taking total of thirty-two sail.

Sir William Phips had indeed arrived—but he had arrived too late. It is easy to know that now. Not so easy for a confident commander in chief who had always believed that luck was with him and who had the heart to press that luck. He knew by now of the failure of the attack on Montreal. He was shrewd enough to assess that France united was a different proposition from a France desperately struggling to maintain two bridgeheads close to two hundred miles apart. He also knew that even so fine a defensive position as Quebec needed more than two hundred trained men to maintain it. What he should have realized but didn't was the need for haste. It was the eighth of August when his expedition had set sail. It was the ninth of October before Frontenac learned of his approach. For two months Phips had had all the advantage of surprise. Such unbelievable luck he had no possible right to expect. Yet it was still six days later before the expedition cast anchor before Quebec.

It had been a long voyage. Strangely, there had been no pilot to show the way. There was the continuing necessity of waiting for slow and ill-managed vessels to catch up. There were rough days on the lower St. Lawrence, where the river fanned out to a width of thirty miles, and innumerable hazards for seamanship. But here at least William Phips was in his element. He knew ships and he knew the sea. Perhaps the greatest achievement of this strange campaign was that he *did* arrive, and with his whole fleet. None of this explains an inexcusable delay—three weeks within three days' sail of Quebec, says the second-in-command. It doesn't explain why day after day the commander in chief sat with his senior officers, now sometimes known as Lieutenant General Walley, Admiral Captain Gilbert, Vice-Admiral Captain Joseph Eldridge, and others in the cabin of the *Six Friends* in a continuing council of war that laid down rules to cover the soldier's conduct in every imaginable contingency. The result was an admirable document, as its provisions amply prove. Yet, but for it, Quebec might have been taken.

Even delay had not shaken the sure confidence of William Phips that he was a man of destiny. Winthrop's failure, which left Callières free to go to the aid of Quebec with his considerable Montreal garrison and which might have sobered a more thoughtful man, left Phips relatively untroubled. If the task had become more difficult, the glory to be achieved had grown in proportion. No thought of failure crossed his mind and, just as he believed in himself, the men who followed him believed too. Without rhyme or reason there seems to have developed among the English an overwhelming assurance of victory. It was supported by no evidence unless one saw a parallel between Port Royal and Quebec, between the seventy men captained by Meneval of the six vests of dimity and the four nightcaps with lace edging, and the tough old eagle at Quebec with the Le Moynes and the Du Lhuts and the Perrots at his back. Still, the confidence was there. There was plenty of evidence of it. The Reverend Michel de Couvert, writing to a fellow priest, tells how French captives exchanged by Phips spoke with some awe of this amazing confidence; how prior to the expedition's departure more than twenty suits at law had been settled in Boston, determining just how the rich booty won at Quebec should be distributed and, particularly, "to whom should belong the six silver Chandeliers of the Jesuit Church."

Admittedly there was no such confidence in Quebec. New France had grown used to fear, and now it was fear of famine and fear of the shortage of men. The very threat of a siege was the threat of disaster. The nuns of the Hôtel-Dieu were burying their silver and the sacred vessels in the garden and arranging for carts to take them beyond the threat of the terrible assault they feared. From the crowded lanes of Lower Town women and children, heavy with bundles, were crowding every corner of the convent. They saw in its gray walls a small security the nuns themselves had not discovered.

Strangely and promptly Frontenac's return changed all that. It wasn't the three hundred men who came with him, for they only added to the threat of famine, and already the nuns were remembering the beans and cabbages stolen from their garden and how the pile of fuel disappeared as if by magic. But something had changed. The sacred vessels were disinterred and, rather shamefacedly, the order for carts was canceled. Frontenac had said they should stay and get back to their work. Aged and crippled, the good Bishop Laval had emerged from retirement to see that the picture of the Holy Family was properly displayed on the cathedral clock tower.

There was a strange upsurge of religious fervor, as Father de Couvert reports in the *Relations*. He tells with enthusiasm of the happy thought of Father Chaumonot, one of the oldest missionaries, who urged that Masses be said for the souls in purgatory that they might be delivered from that place so they could "come to our help in our need." And Father de Couvert reports that the proposal "was extremely well received by all the people."

About ten in the morning there was a flurry of activity about the fleet, and a small boat put off from the *Six Friends*. It bore a flag of truce carried by a young subaltern with a message for Frontenac. Halfway across the river the boat was met by a French canoe and it was explained to the young officer that instructions were explicit. If he wished to go through the city to present his letter to the governor he must do so blindfolded. Rather resentfully the young officer submitted, and he was then escorted to the quay. He couldn't know that what there was to hide was the evidence of near famine, while the roundabout journey that took him over all manner of obstacles was meant to convince him that here were massive fortifications. Nor could he know that the few troops who marched to and fro across his path were meant to simulate a powerful army.

Then he stood in the great hall; the bandage was taken from his eyes. He was face to face with Frontenac, who, better than most, knew how to dress a ceremony. About that stern old governor were grouped some of the great figures of New France, the bishop and intendant and with them, garbed like their leader in their best, the men who had made it and would now defend it. There was Claude de Ramesay, who now was second-in-command and whose lineage went back not to France but to the heathered hills of Scotland. There was the Sieur de Subercase, the one man who had been ready to move that grim day at Lachine; Valrenne, who had commanded at Fort Frontenac and had destroyed it on orders. There were the Le Moyne brothers, Jacques and Charles, also named Ste. Hélène, and Longueuil. That same afternoon, slipping up the north channel in safety to Beauport, came Iberville and Maricourt with a small following back from Hudson's Bay in time to join their brothers. Vaudreuil was there, too, and Mantet and Hertel. With evening, Callières would be arriving from Montreal with eight hundred men, and the cheers that welcomed them would reach out to the waiting fleet, bearing an ominous warning. With the eight hundred were more of Canada's great, Durantaye and Du Lhut and Nicholas Perrot. Of them all, only two were missing, La Salle of the handsome face and the roving heart, whose bones were whitening somewhere on the marshy shore of Matagorda Bay, which is now Texas, and Henri Tonty, La Salle's unwavering friend, who kept his faithful watch at Fort St. Louis.

It would be small wonder if the young subaltern's voice was not quite steady as he faced this gathering of the great, alone, and read the long and colored passages that Cotton Mather had helped prepare. But it was steady enough as he demanded: "Your answer positive in an hour . . . upon the peril that will ensue."

Frontenac's face was flushed with anger. "Your general should not be surprised at the hostilities carried on by the French on the colony of Massachusetts. He should expect that my King would wish me to make war on a people who have failed in their duty to their lawful

King. . . . The Prince of Orange is but a usurper to the throne," he growled, "I do not acknowledge him."

To the request for an answer in writing he lashed out in new fury: "A man like me is not to be summoned after this fashion. Let him do his best: I will do mine."

Thomas Hutchinson, writing his history of the colony of Massachusetts some years after the event, says of the demand and its response, "If it was too pompous, the answer was too insolent."

Already the young subaltern was being blindfolded anew, to be jostled again by the few French soldiers who marched and countermarched as before. The ruse escaped him. His mind was still dazzled by what he had seen. "It is a mighty town, where I have been, sir," he reported to his commander. "The garrison there is so strong that a step cannot be taken without rubbing shoulders with some rude person. And the people speak a strange language, keeping their secrets to themselves. In the great room where I handed your letter to His Excellency, the men were dressed so splendidly that it made small difference taking the cloth from my eyes. I was dazzled by looking at them."

The time for words had passed and the men who had used them pompously or insolently had now to justify their use. The Reverend Cotton Mather saw this clearly, as clearly as he sensed the essential failure. "General Phips now saw that it must cost him dry blows and that he must roar his perswasions out of the mouths of great guns to make himself master of the city."

The day had passed and there was no hint of surrender. There remained only the dry blows and the "perswasion" of guns. The plan was good enough. Lieutenant General Walley, or plain Major Walley, whichever it might be, was to attack by way of the Beauport shoals, a plan that years later James Wolfe, a different soldier indeed, was to attempt with indifferent success. In the beginning Walley's forces did as well. Wading through slime and freezing water, sometimes to their knees, sometimes to their waists, twelve to thirteen hundred of them managed to get ashore. Strangely enough, there was little effort to stop them, though ample troops were near at hand at Beauport and Beaupré. Here, too, leadership was lacking. Ste. Hélène and Maricourt, who knew this sort of fighting well, were with the two batteries that stood alone and unprotected in Lower Town where the attack was expected.

Walley had hardly made his dispositions and sent out his "forlorns," or skirmishers, when the French levies discovered their presence and opened a galling fire on their front and flanks. The troops were raw and untrained and there had been months aboard ship to forget what little knowledge and discipline they had, but at the order to charge they responded gallantly. The French retreated slowly, finding cover in forest and swamps. By nightfall the attackers had secured a position near the St. Charles, where they could be in touch with boats that were expected to reach them with supplies. There were some houses and barns and ricks of hay and straw that provided a grateful protection against the chilling cold.

Walley was satisfied. He estimated that the attack had cost him four killed and sixty officers and men wounded. "It was a great mercy," he reflected, "that we had no more damage done us." He reported that the French had lost twenty to thirty killed and that the hospitals of the city were full of their wounded. Father de Couvert, however, who was in the city and who wrote while the attack was still fresh in his mind, set the French loss at four killed and seven wounded.

The plan of attack as agreed upon was that the ships were to await the signal that Walley was successfully across the St. Charles and had entered the city's defenses. The fleet would then begin a heavy bombardment, at the same time making quite a show of landing a force above the town, as if intent on taking it from the rear. Now, when patience was needed, Phips, who had all too patiently plodded up the St. Lawrence, had the sudden urge to attack without awaiting Walley's success. Possibly he guessed that it was uncertain. Anyway, he took the *Six Friends* within pistol shot of the shore and, with his fleet behind him, he opened with every gun that could be trained on the city.

Reverend Mother Juchereau admits, "We were more dead than alive when we heard the cannon." Nonetheless, she remained practical, superintending the collection of the cannon balls that fell in the convent yard–there were twenty-six of them–and sending them back to the gunners in the batteries for return to the English.

Phips had no such source of supply, for the cannon balls that cut through the rigging of the *Six Friends*, splintered its mizzenmast, and raked the cabin and hull ended with finality in the St. Lawrence. So telling was the plunging fire of the French batteries that Phips reluctantly had to order the *Six Friends* cut loose from her moorings so she could drift out of range.

Major Walley hadn't been more successful. If Phips was open to the criticism that he hadn't waited for his own plan of attack to take shape, Walley had possibly waited too much. His forces were just about where the initial success of their unopposed landing had left them. It wasn't wholly Walley's fault. So many faults can be attributed to this earnest and well-intentioned man that this fact should be admitted. The ships that, according to plan, were to advance up the St. Charles River to bring supplies and to aid in the crossing, had not appeared. Walley had waited hopefully and uncomfortably. "We stood our ground that night," he records, "but found it exceeding cold, it freezing that night so that the next morning the ice would bear a man." With the first light of day a small vessel did slip up the river and unloaded six field guns, twelve-pounders weighing about eight hundred pounds each. These were promptly mired beyond any hope of effectiveness, but the half barrel of musket powder and the one biscuit per man that it also unloaded before the venturesome craft stole away in the morning mist were welcome indeed.

There was no further suggestion of other ships to support Walley's attack. Perhaps their captains were too interested in what was happening elsewhere, or perhaps they suddenly remembered that they were part owners and that the river between two armies looked like an unwholesome place to take their property. Whatever the reason, the orders were overlooked.

There was some ground for this hesitancy. However much fighting might be done on the flats, eventually the river had to be crossed, and lining the high banks beyond were a thousand men or more, trained men, waiting for just such an attempt.

Walley was frankly annoyed. The twelve-pounders, which he couldn't possibly use and which had managed to become firmly mired just where they could most impede the movements of his army, emphasized the fact that no one was thinking much about his problems. He had done better thinking himself, and it was practical thinking. He had provided a considerable number of wheelbarrows that would carry two *patereros* each. True, the *patereros* were small cannon indeed, mostly used for firing salutes. Heavily loaded, they could do considerable damage in close fighting and, more to the point, they could be moved and used. While his forces waited, a council of war was called and Walley was deputed to approach the commander next day, learn the cause of delay, and get further instructions for the situation that now confronted them.

The commander had his problems too. He didn't know too much of what was happening with Walley. He did know that there was no suspicious movement in the town suggesting that Walley had become a real threat.

He must have known, too, that his own spectacular attack had been no more successful. The fire from the batteries on the cliff had not been silenced. The French guns were as strong and as destructive as they had ever been. Now he discovered that the supply of powder that, considered in Boston under the excitement of departure, had seemed quite ample to subdue a city that was sure to surrender on demand was down to about two rounds per gun. Phips had conserved it as best he could. When it became clear that Frontenac had no thought of surrendering as tamely as had Meneval at Port Royal, the load of his guns had been cut to half charges. He couldn't know, of course, that, so curtailed, his missiles rattled off the solid masonry of the town, making a terrific din but nothing much else. Father de Couvert estimated that fifteen or twenty écus would cover the damage. True, a child had been killed by a splinter of rock "between the great church and our college," but there was "no other harm."

When Walley visited the general in chief early the next morning the commander was still belligerent, still thinking of some new assault. The problem was how to get around that shortage of ammunition. There could be no further bombardment of the town, and everything depended on a flank attack. Walley's report was not encouraging. Smallpox was raging in his small army, and as no one had prepared for fighting in freezing weather, some were dying of cold. Here, too, ammunition and even food were scarce. It was the word about freezing that caught Phips's attention. It had been at the back of his mind for some time. The people who were to say that Phips might easily have succeeded if he had come a week earlier or stayed a week later, the Baron la Hontan among them, might easily have been wrong. It was true that had he arrived a week earlier he might have defeated the two hundred fighting men who were then the total of Quebec's defenders.

There was another fact, however. It was all that Quebec could do to feed this two hundred, and to feed the three thousand who finally arrived was doubly impossible. Even as a victor, Phips could have expected little else than to starve with the defeated.

Slowly this was becoming clear to him as he listened to Walley's report of shortages and sickness and particularly of the river frozen hard enough to support the weight of a man. There was no fear in him, but a native shrewdness told him that it was time to get away, to get away while he could. Reluctantly he told his anxious associate to get his men aboard ship again as promptly as he could.

It couldn't be done very promptly. With Walley away, his force by the river had got itself into a skirmish that grew until it reached the proportions of a sizable battle. It was a sorry fight that benefited no one. The English were not across the St. Charles, nor was there any suggestion that they might be. They were standing about where they were when the fighting started. All that could be said was that they had fought well, if uselessly. For the French this little outpost action was calamity.

The attack was in charge of Ste. Hélène, the second of the Le Moyne brothers, and with him was his older brother Longueuil. Le Moyne-like, they were in the thick of it. For once their fabulous luck had run out. Longueuil was hit and down. Fortunately it was a spent bullet, which had stunned but had done little permanent harm. When they came to Ste. Hélène it was different. There was a great hole in his thigh, and these men were familiar enough with wounds to recognize its seriousness. They were able to get him away and back to a bed in the Hôtel-Dieu. There was a week or two of misery ahead of him, and then rest in a quiet spot in the garden of that house of God.

It was strange that of the six or eight of Frontenac's followers who were to die in the defense of Quebec one of them should have been Ste. Hélène. For a moment when he heard the news Walley had a sudden upsurge of hope. Perhaps without such a man as Ste. Hélène his own task might be simpler. The hope flickered out. He knew that whatever Frontenac might lack it wasn't leadership. There was a momentary lag. It couldn't have lasted long, but it did last long enough for him to get away, leaving those useless twelve-pounders behind him.

There was another council of war that lamentable Sunday with all the attacking force afloat again. Other plans of attack were discussed. It was shadowboxing, as everyone knew. If victory had ever been possible, it was now too late. The council broke up with only one thing decided. There was to be a prayer gathering the next day "to seek God's guidance." Even that wasn't to be. God expressed Himself in other ways. There was a great gale of wind, and some of the ships dragged their anchors and seemed likely to end untidily as wrecks along the shore. But that wasn't to happen either, at least not here. There was some safety down-river in the lea of the Isle of Orleans. They found it at last. Frontenac sent that determined gentleman, Subercase, to watch the departure and to make abundantly sure it was a fact.

There was really no doubt of that. The fight was out of them. Even the Puritan's abiding dislike of Catholicism had somehow been forgotten in the all-pervading wish to be away.

There had been a time when thinking was different, or so it was said. Some of the returning French prisoners had brought startling reports. Whether these reports were truth or levity or just plain fiction, no one was to say. It had been planned, so this report urged, to strike a blow at the Church as well as the city. The plan was that all the nuns were to be returned to France. Some of the ecclesiastics were to be sent to Boston prisons. For the Jesuits a more colorful fate was reserved. It was proposed that these should have their ears lopped off to make chaplets for the bandoleers of the soldiers as a preliminary to knocking them on the head.

If there ever had been such a thought, which seems improbable, it got no farther than pleasant anticipation. The Jesuits retained their ears. The nuns went about their simple tasks of caring for the wounded and for the women and children who needed help. In the spring they would be in the garden again, setting out the beans and cabbages of which it had been despoiled and life would have returned to its accustomed round.

As for Phips and his command, they still faced the hazards of getting home. For once the luck that seemed to belong to him had vanished. Everywhere his assault had been a failure. He was already planning for a new assault, but in the heavy depression that was on him even this hope failed to stir him. If there was in him any sense of self-disparagement, it would not last long. While it lasted he needed support. He found it in a return to his old trade. There at least he knew himself efficient beyond any question. As a general there might be argument; as a ship's carpenter there was no one who could challenge him. Day after day the commander in chief was overside in a ship's sling, diligently patching his badly mauled flagship to make it fit for the hazardous voyage home.

Before he had gone five or six leagues from Quebec he remembered the prisoners he had picked up on the river or had brought with him from Boston, hoping that their knowledge of the coast would be of help to him. They were of doubtful advantage now. He proposed in a word to Subercase that there might be a general exchange. When the suggestion reached Frontenac, it found him amenable enough. Perhaps he realized that he would be securing fighting men and that he would be returning mainly women taken prisoner in the recent raids. This point had either escaped Phips or he had lost his will to bargain. He was as eager to be away as Frontenac was to see him go. Let the prisoners be exchanged, the governor conceded grandly. That done, he explained, he would consider the "impudent incident" closed.

It was not closed for Phips. All the way down the river misfortune dogged his path as storms harried his battered vessels. One chance was still his. Again he missed; whether through oversight or an unwillingness to attempt anything more, we do not know. He was scarcely six leagues down-river from Quebec when word was received there that three French merchantships were in the river. Swift canoes were sent to warn them, for if they were discovered and destroyed by the retreating English, starvation might well succeed in destroying New France where English might had failed. The canoes just edged out in the race, and the *Glorieux* and the *Saint François Xavier* and a frigate that composed the fleet found an uncertain shelter in the Saguenay. They had just reached it as the English fleet appeared. There were breathless moments, but if Phips or his captains noticed, they did not turn aside. Piously the French gave credit to St. Anne and St. Francis Xavier, to whom vows had been addressed for the safety of the ships.

There had been prayers for the English expedition too. They were fervent prayers, though the Reverend Cotton Mather admits a doubt "that the faithful did in their prayers arise to any assurance that the expedition should prosper in all respects." Perhaps it was that. In any event, the French ships went on their way untroubled. But that wasn't so with the great expedition. It wasn't prospering. One ship sailed into the mist and was never heard of again. One ship foundered, though its company and crew were rescued. Not so fortunate was another, which was driven ashore, where those who were not drowned fell into the hands of Indians and perchance wished they had been less fortunate. Some were driven off course, finally to make a landfall somewhere in the West Indies.

The brig *Mary*, with Captain John Rainsford in command, went ashore on Anticosti Island in a bleak night. The captain and the sixty aboard made the shore and developed a Robinson Crusoe talent for adapting the wreck to their needs. Its timbers provided rude shelter against the winter, and salvaged supplies gave a distant hope of survival. The supplies did not amount to much, but it was agreed to divide them. They ran to a weekly ration of two biscuits, a half pound of pork and as much of flour, a pint and a quarter of peas, and two small fish. Hunger and cold quickly began to take their toll, but the record points out that they were all convinced of the necessity of keeping their allowance, "unless they would at last eat each other." Early in December the surgeon died, and in a matter of a few weeks forty of the sixty followed him. At the end of March, Captain Rainsford and four of the company remaining set out in a small skiff they had lengthened to provide a cabin for two or three men. With a sail salvaged from the brig the five began their impossible voyage to Boston. It was the twenty-fifth of March. On the ninth of May the skiff with its tattered, starving crew miraculously arrived and was sighted. Soon a vessel was dispatched to Anticosti to rescue the other survivors.

The commander in chief on the *Six Friends* had reached Boston the preceding nineteenth of November, and one by one, at intervals, what remained of his fleet came limping in. This time there were no prisoners, no hogsheads filled with spoils, no aura of victory. The Reverend Cotton Mather was speaking soberly of the forty thousand pounds the expedition had cost, "and not a penny in the treasury to pay it withal." There was nothing with which to pay the soldiers or the ships' crews or the captains except some quickly devised paper money. The receivers were far from content. Shrewdly they reasoned that paper from a government that had not a penny in its treasury must have a dubious value. No one was happy. No one was satisfied. Old and wise Governor Bradstreet was urging his people to prayer that they might be relieved from this "awful frown of God."

Sir William Phips himself, speaking in a flash of self-revelation that would not last for long, was confiding, "The things which befell me on this expedition were too deep to be dived into—and in my day I have been used to diving."

Weeks later, still in the King's favor, he was petitioning for men and money for another venture. The irrepressible conflict had scarcely begun.

CHAPTER VIII

GLEAM IN THE DARKNESS

The threat of famine continues owing to marauding Indians. Massacre at Pointe aux Trembles—the counterthrust at Repentigny. Death of Bienville. Peter Schuyler attacks La Prairie, is routed by Valrenne. Quebec is fully fortified. Mantet leads attack on Mohawk towns. His success followed by the near destruction of his force through starvation. Frontenac uses a "glorious success" to impress the lake tribes. The trade of the colony restored. The first glimmer of returning confidence.

THERE was famine in the land, or something very close to it. The threat that might have reduced Quebec had Phips stayed a week longer, and that might have detroyed him in turn, was still a very present threat. Fields everywhere were lying fallow. Who was to cultivate them, with the stealthy shadows in the forests watching every movement? It was heavy work guiding a plow with musket always at the ready, and sown fields were scarce.

Out in the great gulf where the St. Lawrence meets the sea, English ships were watching as tirelessly as the Indian warriors, ready to pounce as opportunity offered. Perhaps one in three of the ships from France succeeded in running the blockade. It was the captured vessels that represented the food and arms that provided the margin beyond the bare necessities of survival.

With the coming of spring the Iroquois came again, not as cunning individuals looking for some small advantage, but in bands who were finished with their hunting and now turned to lordlier game. There were tragic decisions to be made. To leave the stockaded farm to work in the fields was to court a far from uncertain disaster. To do otherwise was to accept the almost equal threat of famine. In April the premier threat had ceased to be a promise and had become a fact. At Pointe aux Trembles, at the eastern end of the island of Montreal, and now a suburb of the city itself, there was a sudden burst of firing. Before the inhabitants were well awake thirty homes were burning fiercely. The attack was swift and ended as swiftly. The news would bring quick reprisal from the city, and the dusky warriors did not wait for it. They were satisfied with the dead and the captives that were with them.

It was a stealthy warfare of savage thrust and equally savage riposte. At Repentigny, a few miles farther down-river from Pointe aux Trembles, a party of Iroquois had found a comfortable haven in a deserted house near the fort. When scouts brought word of them Vaudreuil was quickly on the move, heading a daring band eager for revenge. There were forty or more Indians. Probably somewhere they had found brandy or had grown scornful or careless. Perhaps they felt themselves masters of the French. At least they kept no guard. Those who could crowd into the house were sleeping there. Many had preferred to sleep in the grounds about it. These last had no time to fight. One volley disposed of them. Now the sleepers in the house were broad awake. It was too late. If the end was not in doubt, the interval was grim. Young François de Bienville was of the cut of all the Le Moynes. He had learned the Indian trick of shouting his name as he attacked. But the house was spouting fire now and he fell dead with his name on his lips. The name itself was not to die. In the custom of the Le Moynes it was passed on to another brother, and it still lives in the history of the great city of Mobile. There a bronze Bienville still looks over a city that he created and where he ruled for many years.

Though six Frenchmen died that day, they had ample company. All the Indians were either killed or captured. The difference was slight. Of the five Indian survivors, only one, a boy whose family had given protection to a Jesuit missionary, survived for long. One was given to the Ottawas. His life expectancy was brief. One was given to the citizens of each of the three settlements of Repentigny, Pointe aux Trembles, and Boucherville. There the habitants, with a cold ferocity that would have done credit to their foes, stoked their fires and watched their victims burn to make the toll complete. This was the life of New France, a wicked seesaw of attack and revenge.

It was a part of the conflict that there seemed to be no avoiding. The English, momentarily chastened by the ill success of Winthrop and Phips, were satisfied to remain in the background, nudging their Indian allies to keep up the pressure. But affairs like that at Repentigny were costly and the Indian allies were shrewd. They recognized that if it was important, as the English said in response to French tactics, to keep the French in perpetual alarm, it was as important to Englishman as to Indian. The hint had a barb in it. The English would have to join in the fighting or find that they were left to provide the perpetual alarm by themselves.

The argument was convincing. Also, it fitted in with the urgings of the more restless spirits. Major Peter Schuyler was one of these. He had gathered a force of a hundred and twenty English and Dutch from about Albany, and with fifty Indians added he proposed to have his own try at Montreal. He followed the same route that John Schuyler had chosen the year before—by way of Lake George and Lake Champlain. He followed it with less of flaming anger in him and with more skill. Ten miles above Fort Chambly on the Richelieu he left his canoes and like his predecessor turned to attack La Prairie rather than hazard a larger challenge.

This time La Prairie was not unprotected. Callières had seen to that. He had eight hundred men—militia and regulars—wrapped about the place. If Callières had been with them, Major Peter Schuyler might not have reached home again. But Callières was sick with a wasting fever and could not be afoot.

Rain was falling that August night, a chilly and unpleasant rain. There was much scurrying for shelter, and even the sentries were more intent on keeping dry than on keeping alert. Who was likely to be abroad on such a night? It was said that there was a considerable drinking of French brandy for protective and other reasons. Perhaps it was used not wisely but too well. There are records that say so, but the subject was ticklish and the opponents of the brandy trade would hardly have missed so useful an argument. Certainly the sentry at the mill was awake and alert. An hour before dawn his sharp "*Qui vive?*" rang out. Before the sleepers realized that no one had answered, Peter Schuyler's men were on them. They were awake all right now, though probably not as alert as if Callières had been present. But the advantage of surprise was slipping away and St. Cirque, who commanded in Callières absence, had the regulars well in hand. Their sudden attack was met by a blast of fire. Fifty of them were down, and among the dead was the young St. Cirque. The regulars itched for revenge, and in a wild and leaderless flurry of attack they drove Schuyler's men to the shelter of a neighboring ravine. There again fate favored the English. Time to re-form, time to let disorganization work on the battered regulars, time to strike again with a new fury. Yet it is hard to understand how eight hundred trained men, even though leaderless and disorganized, could have failed to prevent the escape of Schuyler's less than two hundred. Perhaps those who raised the brandy argument had a case.

Schuyler wasn't quite away. Across his path was as stubborn a fighter as there was in all New France. It was Valrenne, he who had destroyed Fort Frontenac and had saved his forces from a hazardous situation. It had not been his idea to destroy the fort. The order had come direct from Governor Denonville, and Valrenne was a stickler for discipline. Now he had other orders and he obeyed them with a similar fidelity. Perhaps there was more of fidelity than of shrewd military judgment. He was first on the ground, and he held the fate of the canoe guard of twenty-seven men in his hand, and the canoes were Schuyler's only hope of escape. But Valrenne's instructions had been definite. He was to place his force between Schuyler and his canoes, and that was precisely what he did. It did not seem to occur to him that if he destroyed the canoes the purpose of the order would be satisfied.

Instead he placed his men in Schuyler's rear and waited for what might happen. He did it shrewdly enough. Two great trees had fallen across the path. They made an effective breastwork, and behind them Valrenne had his men in triple ranks. When Schuyler discovered this force barring his way he sent his men charging forward. They had underrated the number and the defenses of the French. A deadly volley at close quarters sent them reeling back, and for a moment the combat ceased. Schuyler and his men knew now that their one chance was to break through. They were men of courage, and desperation was also on their side. They knew now that Valrenne's purpose was to drive them back on the eight hundred troops they had escaped at La Prairie. Their only alternative was to reach their canoes and the safety they promised. So they came again, this time not to be denied. They swarmed over the breastworks. They were fighting now hand to hand; the flashes of the guns scorched the shirts of their opponents. Driven off, they still returned to the attack. For more than an hour Valrenne held his men together and barred the path. The old familiar form of Indian warfare was gone. This was bloody fighting, face to face and at arm's reach. Something had to give way, and something did. "We broke through the middle of their body," Schuyler recounted later in his Journal of the expedition, "until we got in their rear, trampling upon their dead; then faced about upon them and fought them until we made them give way—to say the truth," he added, "we were all glad to see them retreat."

If Schuyler reached his canoes in safety it was hardly Valrenne's fault. That is, if one excludes the one inexplicable question: Why were there canoes to reach? He had fought such a fight and in such a manner as had never before occurred on the continent. There were forty of Schuyler's dead to prove it and almost as many Frenchmen, and these were not women and children, as so often was the case. These were fighting men. For all that, the dead had died in vain. Nothing had been accomplished, nothing proved, unless one accepts the importance of keeping the French "in perpetual alarm." That was the sole credit item.

There was a plague of caterpillars that year. They were less vicious than the Iroquois, though scarcely less alarming. They decimated the crops that hungry Frenchmen looked to as their best promise of survival. As if to balance the account, there was also a plague of squirrels, and the French were quick to learn that, though they might prefer a different diet, hungry stomachs could adapt themselves to squirrel meat without too much complaining.

Had that been the only problem it might have been borne with fortitude. Problems were everywhere, like the Iroquois who might appear at any moment so that Frontenac had to designate three hundred of his fast-diminishing force of soldiers to guard the workmen in the fields. "We are perishing by inches," he wrote the minister in one of his few complaints against the slings and arrows of outrageous fortune. He coupled it with a request for one thousand additional fighters. There is little evidence that either the complaint or the request received sympathetic hearing. At least no soldiers appeared.

Everywhere there were threats. Sir William Phips had gone to London, and the suggestion that his purpose was to promote a new assault on Quebec sent a shiver through many hearts, even the hearts of those who did not know how narrow had been the gap between victory and defeat. To the more knowing the thought was still more disturbing. This time the tough Sir William might not be too late. This time his terrible bombardment might not have to sputter out like a damp squib because of lack of powder. This time it might be a Peter Schuyler who would march on Montreal, not a vacillating, ineffectual Fitz-John Winthrop.

Frontenac, despite the coolness toward the subject, continued to petition the King for men and money. He wanted to deliver the attack, not just await it. Louis, as always, was embroiled somewhere else and had nothing to spare. The few soldiers he did send scarcely made up the wastage of those already in Canada. No ships were available to support the tempting thought of an active attack on New York. Even money was grudgingly supplied. True, the sums were growing—in appalling fashion, to Louis' view. The attack of Phips and the threat of further attack had made the people particularly sensitive to the virtual defenselessness of their position. The hurried fortifying completed just in time by Quebec's town major, Prévost, had indeed served its purpose. But would the fortifications stand against guns fully charged? The general opinion was that they would not.

To young Gédéon de Catalogne fell the task of planning the first real defenses. Under the eye of the great French military engineer Vauban impressive works were beginning to grow, climbing up the heights of Cape Diamond itself. Quebec was to be the unassailable citadel of the New World. It cost money. Even with conscripted labor from twenty miles about, costs still mounted at a rate that brought agony to the heart of Intendant Champigny and sharp protests to his lips and pen. The year after Phips's dramatic failure the expenditure for defense reached 99,000 livres, or as many francs. In 1693 it was 193,000 livres, and a year later 750,000. Even admitting that this last figure included pay for the troops, as it probably did, the increase was indeed appalling.

Louis couldn't see the great works of Quebec growing before his eyes—the vast stone redoubt that crowned Cape Diamond and, for the first time, had become part of the defense, an impressive part mounting sixteen cannon. Frontenac himself laid the cornerstone in that year 1693. From Cape Diamond the solid earthworks now girdled the city to the St. Charles River. Prévost, with his early improvisation, had done a magnificent job, but for all that, his fortifications were a child's toy compared with the defenses that now crowned the heights. If Sir William Phips planned to come again, this was a point for him to remember.

For all the fortifications that were going up about Quebec and Montreal and Three Rivers, there was little sense of security. The immediate attack may have ended in failure, but the nibbling of little attacks wore on the patience and the nerves of the people. It was not only the recurring atrocities of the Iroquois, it was the realization that retort in kind was not enough, while New York and Boston were urging their not unwilling allies to keep the French perpetually alarmed.

There were sporadic reprisals for such attacks that added to the horror of the days without achieving other useful ends. A young regular officer, Beaucour by name, followed one party of Indians to their hunting grounds and, surprising them, killed and captured the band almost to a man. As captives brought a tidy bounty, they were taken to Quebec. There Frontenac promptly sentenced two of the captives to death. One found a knife and managed to be his own executioner. The other was less fortunate. One of the first ceremonies of the newly fortified Cape Diamond was the burning there of this luckless Iroquois. It was done by Christian Hurons but, beyond any question, at the orders of the governor, and before an interested and representative gathering of Frenchmen. So it had happened, not so long before, in the streets of Montreal when several captives were burned there by the orders of Vaudreuil, then in command of its military forces.

The recounting of such instances seems to suggest a callousness that is difficult to accept. To understand, it is necessary to adjust to the thinking of times that gave otherwise humane men the curious ability to rationalize suffering and cruelty as an instrument of grace. For all the apparent ruthlessness of the age, there was a real and vivid interest in the welfare of the soul. The records of the *Jesuit Relations* are steeped in this concern, and it would be senseless to conclude that it was not born of a deep and earnest and devoted conviction. If Jesuit fathers could watch these scenes of cruelty with untroubled hearts, it was because they could also see behind the cruelty a deep spiritual significance, even a road to salvation. It was a confident belief that was far from casuistry. "We have very rarely indeed," wrote one of these priestly fathers, "seen the burning of an

Iroquois without feeling sure that he was on the path to Paradise; and we never knew one of them to be surely on the path to Paradise without seeing him pass through this fiery punishment."

It may have been merely a comforting evasion to enable kindly men to shut their eyes to happenings too ruthless to be borne, though there is little to support that view. At least the men who could see this suffering as a means of grace were not thinking only of others. As individuals, they went through all manner of sacrifices and discomforts with a minimum of complaint, as the records prove. At need, they were as genuinely ready to give up their own lives in just such tortured fashion, upborne by the same confident hope.

But however devoted the priests, no matter how many converts they might claim, they could rarely make the conversion run as deep as the native instincts of the convert. A sudden change in the fortunes of war or peace might be sufficient to cause the convert, at least for the time, to slip away from his new allegiance. Always the missions were face to face with this insecurity, this evidence that time was needed to make conversions complete.

There had been plenty of evidence of this fact in the history of one of the oldest and most important missions, that of Sault St. Louis—or Caughnawaga, just across the river from Lachine. On more than one occasion the Mohawks had done their utmost to induce their Christian fellows to shuck off the new ways and to return to those of their fathers. Even though the converts might not leave, they were uncertain and unsettled, and there was no surety that some added word might not wipe out the efforts of years and turn friends again into enemies.

Here was one small place where Frontenac saw eye to eye with the Jesuits. Their strategy was to widen the breach between the old ways and the new. With his sure sense of the working of the Indian mind Frontenac saw that the best hope was to sow an enmity that would make this uncertain line more difficult to cross. Because the converts at Sault St. Louis were Mohawks, an expedition was prepared that would attack the Mohawk towns, take prisoners and destroy the warriors so that they should no longer trouble the mission.

The expedition was well led. Nicholas Mantet was one of the renowned leaders in New France, and his lieutenants, Courtemanche and La Noue, were men of solid reputations, With them went a hundred picked soldiers and a considerable group of Canadian militia. The bulk of the force, according to the set plan, were Christian

Indians drawn from all the missions of the colony. They made an army of 625 men.

The French were beginning to understand that there was no use in postponing all the fighting until spring. With reasonable precautions against the cold it was possible to move in winter. This gained some advantage of surprise, for it was hard to disabuse the minds of their foes that winter brought a complete assurance of peace. The force left Chambly in late January of 1693, and though it took a little more than two weeks to reach the three Mohawk towns that were the focus of attack, no word of their coming had preceded them. These towns lay in the valley of the Mohawk in what is now northern New York. Many of the warriors were away on the hunt, and though those who remained fought valiantly, the end could never have been in doubt. Twenty or thirty persons were killed and nearly three hundred captives were secured.

The hidden strategy of the campaign had been that, still hot with the enthuiasm of battle, the Indians should immediately kill all their male captives and so make a lasting breach between the mission Indians and their native fellows. While they were far away from their native sections and under the influence of their teachers, the idea had appeared reasonable to the converts, and even pleasant. Back in the familiar haunts of their people, they saw it differently. They would have none of it. They were even somewhat concerned that they had come at all. Half the purpose of the expedition, that of driving a wedge between the Christian Mohawks from the missions about Caughnawaga and their heathen fellows in the Mohawk lands of upper New York, had come to nothing.

For all its successful beginning, no part of the expedition was turning out as happily as had been hoped. In addition to the reluctance of the Christian Indians to deal summarily with their captives, scouts had brought word that Peter Schuyler, that aggressive and combative opponent of La Prairie, in the year just past, was on their heels.

The scouts, who seem to have been in close contact with the enemy, explained that they had been told Schuyler had no hostile intent and merely intended a parley. That seemed a reasonable idea to their Indian followers but left Mantet and Courtemanche frankly skeptical. They knew nothing of Peter Schuyler that suggested any leaning toward parleying. But the Indians had decided that they would wait and see what Schuyler had to say, and nothing would move them from that position.

They could remain bemused only so long. When Schuyler's force finally appeared, the correctness of Mantet's judgment could no longer be in doubt. This was no matter of words, as Schuyler's flaming muskets very promptly proved. The regulars and militia, having favored Mantet's views, were not unprepared and put up a stubborn defense. The Christian Indians, however, were frankly taken aback and showed a tendency to decamp. Their priestly leaders scourged them with bitter words. Men like Father Guy, standing before their converts, lashed out with biting words. "What are you afraid of?" he demanded stormily. "We are fighting with infidels, who have nothing human but the shape."

Father Guy's example did more than his words, for, infidel or Christian, the bullets were coming fast and the fighting was bitter. Mantet's Indians had joined in, if somewhat reluctantly. It was well for Mantet that they did, for a group of Oneidas had joined Schuyler's party, and each now had some six hundred fighters. It was bitter work that kept up with varying fortunes until night fell and put an end to it.

Morning came with a strange quietness over the frosty forests. Cautiously Schuyler sent men forward to guard against sudden surprise. These discovered the reason for the stillness. Mantet's camp was empty. The night had been a night of snow, and with it as a shield they had slipped away.

Peter Schuyler was pre-eminently a man of action. When he discovered his adversary gone he promptly ordered a pursuit. For once he met with open revolt. His force had been without food, or at least sufficient food, for a number of days. They wouldn't move until supplies came up. His Indian allies seemed to be in better case and Schuyler, seeking the reason, was welcomed at their campfires and urged to share with them. Hunger is a great cure for over-fastidiousness, and he might have shared the meal but that in ladling out the broth a human hand was disclosed. That was too much for even strong pioneer stomachs, and Schuyler declined, to the surprise of his Indian allies. They saw no reason why they should go hungry while there were dead Frenchmen to put in the pot.

Many of Schuyler's force lacked the inclination or the opportunity to satisfy their hunger thus, and they were suffering from cold as well. They would not move. It was a day later that a convoy arrived. Five sturdy biscuits doled out per man lent a more cheerful complexion to affairs. The pursuit was resumed.

The snow that first aided the French retreat now became a hazard.

It slowed progress to a walk, and the straggling of the three hundred prisoners presented a further complication. Schuyler's force, which had only the snow and little enough supplies to trouble them, all but overtook Mantet's retreating column. They could have done so, and no one knew it better than Mantet. He sent a stiff word to the pursuers. At the first hint of attack all the prisoners would be slaughtered.

Argue as he might, there was nothing that Schuyler could say that would induce his Indians to pursue further. Without them he was hopelessly outmatched. They were hungry and weary of fighting, and they pointed out that they had no collection of captives to equal Mantet's threat. As far as they were concerned, the pursuit was ended. Indeed about the only man who was burning to pursue was Peter Schuyler himself. But this was not his day.

The fact was that no enemy was needed to make the French retreat a torture. They reached the Hudson to find the ice breaking up. They managed to cross only by a miracle, the great block of ice that offered a temporary bridge disintegrating as they clambered ashore. Lake George was no better. The ice was sodden and unsafe. They had to beat their way along the shore. It was a tortured march of days. Food was almost gone, and all that drove their weary feet forward was the remembrance of the food cached at Lake Champlain for just such an emergency. When they arrived it was to find that the food had spoiled. Here was disaster.

Mantet went over his weary forces, picking out the hardiest, the most determined. Drawing heavily on what few sources of food remained, he gave it to them. On the survival of this small group, on their ability to reach Callières with a report of the plight of Mantet and Courtemanche and their men, to say nothing of the three hundred prisoners, and to secure relief their remaining hope depended. It was not a bright prospect.

This group on their way, Mantet drove his starving crew to search the forests for nuts and bark, for squirrel or rabbit or anything that could stave off famine. When such sources failed, they put their moccasins in the pot, trying to find some hint of sustenance. The forests must have teemed with game, but the men were too weak to follow it as daily they drew nearer death.

Callières, once he heard the word, moved swiftly, and men and food were promptly on their way. They were not a day too soon. Many of the men had to wait until food had restored some little measure of strength before attempting further journeying. For weeks afterward small groups of half-starved men came straggling back, tortures forgotten now that they were in sight of home.

Frontenac saw it differently. He spoke of the expedition as a "glorious success." After all, it was a success of sorts. The Mohawks had been disciplined and a wide breach driven between them and the Mohawks of the St. Louis mission and elsewhere. The three hundred captives were evidence beyond question. Of course he had not shared in the hardships, nor had he seen the pitiful scarecrows dragging themselves across the snow to food and safety. He looked beyond the facts to the hoped-for results. The prospect justified the tribute of success.

The tribes about Michilimackinac, that outpost of New France, were still uncertain where their allegiance should lie. They were practical folk and had no intention of backing a losing side. Now they were in a quandary. The great Onontio had returned, and there were evidences of his power. They had heard of the English attack on Quebec and of its failure. That was on one side. On the other was the fact that the Iroquois still swarmed along the Ottawa, bottling up the trade of the north. The French didn't seem to be able to do much about it, and if the French couldn't, the tribes had no thought of doing anything for themselves. There was still that tempting thought of combining with the Iroquois for their mutual advantage. It had come to nothing in the past and might easily again, but there was still no thought of killing it forever by unfriendly acts. So the lake tribes did nothing. Beaver skins piled up at Michilimackinac, and Canada, with its source of income all but shut off, drifted toward bankruptcy.

That was what Frontenac probably meant in describing the Mantet-Courtemanche expedition as a "glorious success." Anything that gave him a new talking point was likely to appear so. What the urging of two hundred French traders scattered through the woods about the straits had failed to do, this new evidence of an aggressive spirit might achieve. The Mohawks had been soundly disciplined. They had felt how heavy the hand of France could be when it was personalized in a man like Frontenac. This was not vain talking. There were scalps to prove it. More indisputably, there were the three hundred Mohawk prisoners.

So Frontenac played his winning card. He sent Courtemanche

with ten companions tough as himself to bear the news of the great victory. Happily there had been no opportunity for the tribes about the straits to learn of the tortured progress of that returning army of victors. They took the report at its face value. Here was the proof of Onontio's word. He had said he would teach the Iroquois a lesson. Here was the lesson taught. Give him time and he would deal with that scattering of enemies who fashioned ambuscades along the Ottawa to curtail honest trading. In their new confidence the tribes were even ready to undertake it themselves.

Frontenac couldn't know all this. He had played his card and now could do nothing else but wait. Suppose Courtemanche and his ten tough followers had not won through? Suppose the tribes had not believed? The old governor was many things, but he wasn't given to spending much time over spilled milk. He waited patiently, reasonably confident of a reward and already pondering some other plan should that reward not be forthcoming.

Then the word came. It was an exultant word. It spoke of better than two hundred canoes loaded to their last inch and escorted by other canoes bearing hundreds of Indians and *coureurs*. It was like old days. The governor, hurrying to arrive at Montreal, was caught up in the excitement. The warehouse doors were open and trade goods that had been gathering dust for a matter of years were being disgorged, their place taken by fat bundles of beaver skins. The relief was almost too much for the usual scrambling and ribaldry. Here was hope where no real hope had been for seemingly endless years. "It is impossible," wrote one observer, "to conceive the joy of the people when they beheld these riches."

Well they might rejoice. Here the wealth withheld for three long years was spilling over before their eyes. Merchants and farmers and traders, who had learned that you could die of lost hopes as well as of hunger, saw hopes revive and the threat of hunger disappear. Small wonder that they should see in the stout old governor, moving among the excited throng that bargained and bickered about the canoes, "the father of the people and the preserver of the country."

The sky was still dark with lowering clouds. In their new excitement and confidence they might forget it for the moment. It was too near and too fraught with terrifying significance to be forgotten for long. But now there was a glimmer of light lacing the clouds, and wherever the lilies of France fluttered the tired hearts were grateful.

CHAPTER IX

THE WIND BEFORE THE WHIRLWIND

Villebon launches plan to keep the Abenaki perpetually on the warpath. Father Thury heads attack on York, and Captain Convers defends Wells. A new English fort at Pemaquid. Its final capture by Iberville. Failure of the challenge to Boston. Haverhill and the hardening spirit.

If the people of New France had found a glimmer of hope of better days to be, Louis in his palace of Versailles didn't share in the discoverey. He resented bitterly the attack on Quebec with its challenge to his sublime authority. Its dismal failure did little to mollify his outraged dignity. Momentarily he was shaken from his accustomed complacency. His usual attitude was somewhat similar to that of the Pharaoh of the Israelite captivity. He expected his subjects to make bricks without straw. But the "impudent incident" of Phips's invasion had shaken him sufficiently to induce him, and almost voluntarily, to allocate twenty thousand livres toward the strengthening of Quebec to forestall another such incident. He even added twenty-four thousand more for arms and munitions.

Such openhandedness showed the temper of his thinking about as clearly as it could be shown, for Louis had no expendable surplus. He looked to New France to provide financial support rather than demand it. He didn't, of course, consider the outlay as wholly a loss. It set him thinking of offensive rather than defensive strategy, and a strategy likely to be most immediately profitable. This ruminating led him to the happy thought of ousting the persistent and pestiferous English from Newfoundland and Hudson's Bay.

Newfoundland itself could hardly be described as tempting, with its sparse population of two thousand men and a certain number of women and children that did not seem worth counting. These were scattered over the Avalon Peninsula, nowhere in any great number, and mainly dependent on the fisheries. But its position was strategic. The English knew it as well as Louis and were as determined to control it. Hudson Strait was then a great funnel through which drained much of the fur trade of the northern and western lands. Not too far south of the narrow mouth of the funnel, like a cork carelessly dropped from a bottle, was Newfoundland. Louis had assessed its importance shrewdly enough. The Hudson's Bay section, which today seems far away, perhaps did not appear quite so distant in days when a journey of any kind was a matter of personal physical effort and Newfoundland and Hudson Strait not so sharply separated. Certainly distance had no terrors for white man or Indian in the days under review. The tribes of the west and north thought nothing of trading trips that ran into many hundreds of miles.

Henry Kelsey, a factor of the Hudson's Bay Company at this time, tells in his journal of a gathering of the tribes about "Machinipi, the Great Water." The "Great Water" is identified as present Lake Winnipeg, and the road along it and down the Nelson River was a familiar highway to the French. It was the recognized overland route to the bay. Kelsey reports one trading party coming this way with six hundred canoes, one thousand men, and a few women. This was the trade on which Louis had a covetous eye. He felt that whatever cost and effort were needed to secure it would be well repaid by the probable booty.

Louis had a practical basis for this belief. D'Iberville's expedition against Port Nelson on the southwest side of the bay a year or so before had achieved no military results and provided no particular glory. The best that could be said for it was that in retreating up the shore Iberville had stumbled over Fort Churchill. There was no great glory nor much hazard involved in its capture either. It was a shabby fort, poorly armed and with a very limited garrison. It was, in fact, more a fur-storage depot than a fort. When the defenders, such as they were, saw the approach of Iberville's fleet, they realized that the thought of defense was futile. The best they could do was to fire the fort, hoping by this action to divert Iberville's attention until the barracks bulging with the season's furs were beyond rescue. But Iberville had a very practical side. He was acquisitive. He saw the bulging warehouses and set his men to salvaging the contents rather than saving the fort. Fort Churchill had a very debatable value, but the value of hundreds of bundles of furs was clearly tangible. When this cargo was landed finally at La Rochelle it brought something in the neighborhood of eighty thousand livres in beaver alone and some six thousand additional livres in other skins, a tidy fortune for the day. It was hardly surprising that Louis, who felt that the English were clearly interlopers on his property, should decide to remove them from opportunities so promising.

To all this thinking Frontenac was wholly sympathetic. He considered Hudson's Bay a part of his own province and was as sensitive as Louis himself when the English assumed the right to trade and build forts and generally to behave as owners. Even where treaties at times recognized these rights, Frontenac continued to disagree and waited with ill-concealed impatience for renewed opportunity to crystallize this disagreement in overt action.

At the moment, however, he faced a situation that seemed to him more pressing. It was Acadia. Distant as it was from the center of New France, it presented a difficult problem of defense. Actually, of course, it had hardly anything of the kind. Sir William Phips had made short work of reducing its capital city of Port Royal, imprisoning its governor, and requisitioning all of the public and much of the private property. Phips had then sent Captain John Alden roaming about the province, reducing other places of lesser importance, and finally demanding of the inhabitants an oath of loyalty to William and Mary. Anybody but Frontenac might have recognized in these facts the suggestion that Acadia was no longer within his jurisdiction.

Frontenac, for his part, recognized nothing of the sort. Perhaps he was right. Acadia had changed hands before and would do so again on more than one occasion. None of this was very permanent. Not even the loyalty oath. Phips promptly sailed away and left the Acadians to figure out the situation as best they could. Despite the oath, they figured that they were still subjects of Louis.

The fact that did give these happenings significance was that the Abenaki had taken Phips's capture of Port Royal and Captain Alden's subsequent punitive expeditions throughout the country at their face value. The Abenaki included not only the various Indian tribes of

Acadia but most of the tribes inhabiting the New England states as well. As far as they were concerned, the victory at Port Royal had been conclusive. There was no subsequent reflecting on the tangled question of whether the victory had any real substance or no. In their opinion, the Puritans of New England were masters and a force to be reckoned with and—something that was certainly not to be overlooked—they were the most immediate and most promising market for trade. It seemed so settled and final that the Abenaki began negotiations for a treaty of amity with the victors.

This was precisely the situation that Frontenac feared most. If the Abenaki were to exchange their uncertain loyalty to the French in favor of a similar attitude toward the English, the possibility of holding Acadia for the King would be slim indeed. This was not something to be accepted lightly. Once more Frontenac and the Jesuits had a common cause. Acadia had been the scene of some of the Jesuits' earliest missions, and to lose it would possibly mean the loss of these hardly won souls. The one hope of salvaging not only the souls but the colony as well was to bring about a sharp cleavage between the Abenaki and the Puritans, so that the proposed treaty of friendship might come to nothing. Even though it was the seed of so much border ruthlessness, it was the sort of strategy that did achieve a measure of the ends desired.

Acadia was a kind of no man's land. It had much more land than people, and even its boundaries were matters of constant dispute. At the time, Acadia included Nova Scotia and New Brunswick and a considerable part of the present state of Maine. The English set the southern boundary at the St. Croix River, much as it is today. The French, somewhat more generously, moved it to the line of the Kennebec River. Whatever the basic rights and wrongs of the case, there was no doubt that between these two rivers there was a no man's land that everyone claimed. That interesting and romantic figure, Baron St. Castin, had done somewhat more than claim. He had set up a trading empire based on Penobscot Bay and, backed by the nine points of the law, a more or less established possession centered at Pentegoet. It was a personal kingdom that was said to have resulted in a fortune of three to four hundred thousand crowns, while his dusky offspring helped to populate the land. Possibly his rights might have been more generally respected had they not been combined with an unwavering hatred for the English from whom he made his fortune. The feeling quickly became mutual, so that his dramatic figure was the focus of the unsparing warfare that bedeviled that land.

Acadia was not a populous place. It was a land of virgin forest, broken only by the silver thread of rivers that interlaced it. About these rivers lived the Abenaki. The white population, if the census taken by Intendant Meules in 1686 is to be believed, totaled 885. By 1693 it had grown to 1,009. It was not too difficult to count because most of it was at Port Royal with its fort and its ninety-odd homes. At the head of the Bay of Fundy were the settlements of Beaubassin and Les Minas with a settled population. What remained of the 1,009 were scattered in small groups in fishing settlements along the coast.

It was not, as anyone could see, a very defensible property, but while it could be taken it could not be held. Sir William Phips might occupy Port Royal and harry the settlements on the Bay of Fundy and the Atlantic and send St. Castin and his dusky brood skittering into the forest for safety, but his influence was as short-lived as his visit. The land remained essentially French and would so continue for a century to come.

The nub of the problem was about the same as it is today. Quebec was very distant, and Boston and New England were near. In the basic logic of trading, Boston was the market, not Quebec. The Abenaki had quickly discovered this, as had Frontenac. He saw that Acadia had never really been possessed. There the Jesuits set up their missions. There the English came to fish and to trade with the Indians. There French ships gathered to ply their desultory raiding warfare on English shipping, while buccaneers from the West Indies preyed on both in unashamed lawlessness. But nobody dominated the land. It was abundantly clear that while the Abenaki changed their loyalty with the suns or the seasons Acadia could never be firmly held, and while it remained so vulnerable to attack it was a canker rather than a blessing in the body politic of New France. Starting from there, it is not too difficult to follow Frontenac's thinking. If the loyalty of the Abenaki could be assured or, failing that, if they could be stirred to a lasting enmity against the English, the future of Acadia might be different.

A succession of Indian attacks, he saw, would certainly enrage the English, would reduce their willingness to trade with the Indians, would almost certainly divert their attention from France's growing imperialism, and would leave time for the larger schemes that Frontenac had in mind. So at least he probably reasoned. In the primary results of this scheming it might appear that he had reasoned soundly. What he overlooked was the basic fact that he who sows the wind most probably must reap the whirlwind. It was no more than a high wind in the old governor's day. Small wonder that he felt confident he could dominate it. He couldn't see it building up to whirlwind fury, a fury that inevitably would sweep away the proud lilies of France—leaving her only a small group of islands close under the shadow of Newfoundland as a base for her fishing fleet. So St. Pierre and Miquelon are the only reminders that once she had all but owned a continent.

Whenever Frontenac had a new idea its amazing virtues stood out for him like an Everest looming over the plain. Momentarily, at least, it dominated all his thinking, and he was impatient for its immediate accomplishment. He could hardly wait to impress Louis in turn. He was shrewd enough, however, to remember that other attempts to impress royalty hadn't been too successful. He decided to send a personal representative, someone who might have the necessary persuasive powers. He chose a trusted aide, the Chevalier Robineau de Villebon.

It seems that Villebon lived up to the governor's expectations. Apparently he made a more favorable impression on Louis than he has on history. The King added Acadia to his list of proposed battlegrounds and without more ado appointed Villebon as governor, charged with putting into effect Frontenac's proposals for embroiling the Abenaki with the English.

It was mid-October 1691 when Villebon, having talked the plan over with Frontenac, set sail from Quebec for his new post. The obvious first action was the retaking of Port Royal. This was no difficult task. When Phips had sailed away after taking the city two years before he had all but forgotten the matter. The French had been told they were now good English citizens owing allegiance to William and Mary instead of Louis. Phips hadn't done anything to give these instructions any body. So when Villebon appeared before the fort in the *Soleil d'Afrique*, which bore as well a substantial cargo of presents that were to influence the thinking of the Indians, Port Royal surrendered almost before the request was made. The citizens trooped in happily to be relieved of their obligation to William and Mary and to return to their rightful sovereign.

Villebon recognized that the capture of Port Royal was not a great achievement. If Sir William Phips could take the city with not too great effort and Villebon recover it with considerably less, it was evident that it wasn't a very secure stronghold for a new governor in his highly uncertain world. He decided that a place somewhat less accessible would have its advantages. With this in mind he crossed to the St. John River. Making his way upstream for some distance, he came to a point the Indians called Naxouat, across river from the present Fredericton, the attractive capital of New Brunswick. It looked a suitable place. There, whatever might be the fate of Port Royal, Villebon would be free from constant threat and ready for his important task of mustering his war parties to ravage the New England countryside. So Villebon built Fort Naxouat and stored his cargo of presents.

There is no doubt as to Villebon's instructions. They were definite and complete. He was to be the shining example. "You yourself," the minister had written, "will herein set them so good an example, that they will be animated by no other desire than that of making profit out of the enemy." He and his officers were urged to join the war parties. The Canadians of the militia who had come with him from Quebec were to be encouraged and, it is hinted, supported, so that they need have no other employment than waging incessant war against the New England countryside. Villebon, moreover, was charged to use the presents he had brought to interest the Abenaki. They were quick to discover how much easier it was to accept this support than to go hunting to provide their own. What more could be said than the minister's clear words: "There is nothing which I more strongly urge upon you than to put forth all your ability and prudence to prevent the Abenaki from occupying themselves in anything but war"? What *lettre de marque* had ever offered more encouragement or granted more license?

Villebon was deeply conscious of his new dignity. He felt himself to be a figure of destiny and was eager that others should think so too. It was late fall, however, before he reached his new parish. Winter had laid a restraining hand on the land before he had completed necessary security measures. Eager as he was to set the King's plans in motion, he knew that there would be little gain if, while he marched off leading the Abenaki on some aggressive enterprise, Phips or another appropriated Acadia. It had to be admitted, too, that the Abenaki were not exhibiting any martial ardor. They were intent on a bit of hunting, perhaps. Beyond that, they had no thought of straying far from home.

It was a certain Father Thury, rather than Governor Villebon, who finally got Louis' program into gear. Father Thury had come to Acadia as a missionary. He had been trained in the seminary in Quebec, and the training had evidently been practical. Thury had achieved a remarkable hold on his Indian converts. He was a man of action, which the Indians liked, and of strong if circumscribed views. It was an age of strong prejudices, when men's religious opinions permitted no charitable softening or qualification, whether the holder was Protestant or Catholic. The English, Father Thury firmly and sincerely believed, were the enemies of God, and so he instructed his followers. To attack them was a sure road to divine favor. It was uncomplicated thinking such as the Indian mind could quickly grasp. Probably Father Thury was of the pattern of the zealots of all ages but for the fact that he combined his zeal with a quick decisiveness. Most unquestionably he was a man well suited to keep his Indian charges from thinking of anything but war and plunder.

It was January 1692 and bitter cold, and the snow was heavy on the ground. It held the forests in a rigid grip and locked the friendly way of lake and river. The English were far away. None of these things dismayed Father Thury. He was preaching a crusade against these English, and the Abenaki listened as the peasants of Europe had listened to Peter the Hermit. Villebon had done his part, too, though his part didn't smack too much of the man of destiny. It was to hand out a generous portion of the goods that Louis had supplied, guns and powder and lead. In the end it was Thury's eloquence that mattered most. His converts listened and believed. They were ready to go where he said and when he said. Father Thury said both and said it promptly. With a hundred and fifty of his trusted converts he moved out into the winter forests looking toward the frontier and the English. At the Kennebec they met another band who, attracted by the promise of plunder, agreed to join them. It was a long march and hard, and only Thury's example kept them driving away from home toward the frontier. It was more than a month before they looked down from the heights to see the little settlement of York.

York was not a place of any strategic significance or other importance. Just why Gethsemane came to it rather than another place is hard to say. It was just a scattering of houses on a riverbank near the sea. Four or five of the houses of the settlement, as was the custom, were made stronger than the others. They were to be a rallying point and a defense when the occasion arose. It was February, and the citizens had no thought of danger. They didn't know, of course, of the plans to keep the Indians thinking of war and plunder—the plundering of just such indefensible places as the hamlet of York. There were perhaps three or four hundred persons in the settlement or in the country about. Of them all, perhaps the only one of any consequence at all was their minister, the Reverend Mr. Dummer. He was old and deeply respected. He was also a man of learning, a graduate of Harvard College, a mighty distinction for those days.

That night of February 4 Father Thury and his convert followers lay shivering in the forest. It had begun to snow again. The driving flakes obscured the view and deadened the footfalls of the approaching band. A shot and the bellow of war whoops were the first hint that this was not a day like other winter days. The first fortified house was easily taken. There were no male defenders there. Probably it made little difference. Those who resisted at all were killed. The rest were captives. With minor variations it was the same everywhere. The Reverend Mr. Dummer was awkwardly climbing on his old horse, bent on some mission of mercy, when the red fury burst about him. He didn't go on that errand then or any day thereafter. One of the warriors donned the dead minister's gown and preached a mock sermon to his shivering companions. We do not know if Father Thury was present. If he was, he made no protest. More probably he was attempting to spur his charges to attack the other fortified homes.

The enthusiasm had finally died. There were captives enough. The Indians didn't relish facing the fire of men whose evident intent was to sell their lives dearly. There was more to be gained by pillaging the houses already taken, more excitement in setting them afire and killing the horses and the cattle and ravaging the countryside about.

There had been plenty of killings that day. Even the Indians had their fill. A hundred persons dead, so the French report declared, many of them women and children, and perhaps eighty captured, better than half the population of the town. Other reports speak of forty-eight killed and seventy-three prisoners. Whatever the figure, the fact was grim enough, grim and purposeless as any tale told by an idiot—full of sound and fury, but signifying nothing.

That was February, the year 1692. The exaltation of these pitiful events persisted. In June it was still a driving force. The country about Pentegoet and Castine had become a land of wigwams as Micmacs, Malecites, and Abenaki gathered there for new adventures. With them were Father Thury's converts, who had played a stellar part at York, and others from Father Baudoin's misson at Beaubassin, at the head of Fundy. There was a small coterie of French officers, too, headed by Governor Villebon's brother Portneuf, and a group of twenty Canadians. When the expedition at last crossed Penobscot Bay and took the path for Wells, it was an army of better than four hundred.

Wells had its memories. It had been attacked the year before and had paid a price. But it had the later tragedy of York to bring experience up to date. It was warned. In so much Wells was more happily placed than York had been. In other respects it differed little. It was about the same size. It had the same number of houses prepared for defense, five in all. Only at Wells, Joseph Storer's house was larger and was surrounded by a stockade. Wells knew what was before it and was as much prepared as might be. A day before the attack was launched two sloops had come up the creek and unloaded supplies and fourteen additional men. That brought the more or less trained defenders to a total of thirty. More important still, these were led by a Captain Convers, who had been in the militia and, beyond that, was a determined man. There, then, was the setting—the sloops in the river guarded by their crews of work-toughened seamen, the townspeople gathered in the stockade, and Captain Convers and his thirty men.

For once the attacking force had little advantage of surprise. It did seem to them that the two sloops would be easy victims. But after two Canadians, one of them an officer of rank, and some Indians had died at the hands of those determined seamen the attempt assumed a somewhat different aspect. They still kept up a desultory fire at the boats, but from a distance now, while many of their number drifted away to join an attack of the Storer house, which might, after all, prove an easier victim. There were only thirty men behind the stockade and many women and children, and they were facing four hundred warriors, still a little drunk with recent success. The odds were discouraging. They might have been impossible had the four hundred been as determined as the thirty. But the Indians had no love for fighting men behind breastworks. They liked surprise and quick forays, not stockades spitting fire. They tried diplomacy. They offered terms—generous terms, could they have been believed. Convers was tough-minded. "I want nothing but men to fight with," he retorted.

They were dramatic words. Perhaps overly so. He might have been satisfied. Four hundred opponents to thirty was odds enough for anyone. But, it seemed, he meant it. Each successive attack was met by a blast of fire. It was not warfare to the Indian taste. Not even Father Thury's urging or Portneuf's promises of gifts could make them like it. They returned to the sloops. There an attempt was made to flush the defenders out by fire. It was not successful, and it cost some more Indian lives. That was enough. They remembered the one prisoner they had been able to surprise. His name was John Diamond. They had a more satisfying time torturing this poor victim to death. But that one item of misery hardly made a victory. They knew it. They knew that a few determined men had bested the most impressive attack ever made on the frontier.

It wasn't at all the lesson that Louis and Frontenac or even Villebon had hoped to teach. The retreat from Wells had none of the enthusiasm of the impressive approach. True, those who went with Thury to meet Governor Villebon had their moment of satisfaction. Seeing that the returning warriors were without captives, Villebon made his gesture of good-fellowship. He provided a prisoner for them to torture and burn at their leisure. That accomplished, there was no lift to the spirits. The Indians had ceased to think of war and were remembering instead that they had done well in their trading with the English. They had nothing against them. It was this thinking that the French feared most deeply. There was no doubt about it, the war spirit required powerful stimulation if it was to survive.

If anything was needed to add to the uncertainty momentarily bedeviling the Abenaki, it was the suggestion that the English had at last gone on the offensive. The affair at Wells had proven that with due warning and proper leadership outlying communities could be defended. That had given the Abenaki ground for thought. It had, however, done little to explain the fact that the French were unmistakably the aggressors, while the English seemed satisfied to submit to attack without thought other than to defend themselves as best they could. A suggestion of more forthright action was needed.

The man who proposed a new policy of reprisal was none other than the indomitable William Phips. Despite his sorry showing at Quebec he had not lost the royal favor. Indeed the very opposite was the case. He had been appointed governor of Massachusetts. It was an appointment that probably set a record of some sort for its complete unsuitability. It has to be admitted, however, that the new governor did have flashes of inspiration. He saw that a weak defensive policy along the frontier was playing into the hands of the French, giving validity to their claim of ownership of all the lands to the Kennebec River. If he didn't know of the settled French policy of keeping the Abenaki always on a war footing, he did realize that this was the bearing of all the facts. There was no hope of protecting a frontier piecemeal. There were too many communities. They were too isolated. They had too few defenders to be effective against concentrated attacks that could be directed anywhere. Sir William proposed taking the war into enemy territory as the best defense of home. It was the view he had presented in England on his visit there shortly before his appointment as governor. Perhaps his insistence that for the health and safety of New England Canada must be subdued may have had some part in his appointment.

As a first step in that program he proposed a network of forts on the frontier strong enough to defeat attack and to protect the surrounding territories. The London government, having no thought of financing the undertaking, were all enthusiasm. Phips was instructed to proceed with the plan as promptly as might be. With instructions combining so nicely with inclination, the governor was a happy man. He had not much more than stepped ashore from his London visit before plans for a new fort began to take shape.

It was understandable that the first fort should be at Pemaquid. It would replace the fort destroyed by the French and Indians a year or two before. It was located on no admitted frontier except that of the sea. It was well within that debatable land claimed by French, English, and Indian alike.

This was familiar ground for Phips. The Monsweag farm where he had lived as a boy was only a good stone's throw away. He was completely familiar with the Kennebec and Sheepscot river country. The new fort dominated both streams yet was far enough east of the Kennebec to be well within the area that the French had consistently claimed as their own. The stream's importance to the French lay in the fact that the Kennebec connected with a network of rivers and marshes that linked it with the Chaudière River, which enters the St. Lawrence opposite Quebec. It was, then, part of a water highway to Canada, a difficult but feasible route for an attack, as Benedict Arnold would discover three quarters of a century later.

Probably this was obscure to Phips. But the fact of the proposed fort's strategic position wasn't obscure at all, nor that here was a challenge to French aggression. Perhaps his interest, too, was partly a matter of relief. At the time there was sweeping over New England one of those strange outbreaks of hysteria that sometimes overtake both individuals and nations. New England had gone witch-hunting and its governor, Phips, could not quite detach himself from this strange and cruel persecution. A stubborn realism gave him little patience with the juvenile informers or excitement-crazy adults. Though their feverish accusations left him unmoved, he couldn't quite escape. Able men were being swept along on this wave of passion. The Reverend Cotton Mather, the governor's ardent friend, was among the credulous. He had shouted from his pulpit to his trembling congregation: "Witchcraft is the most nefarious high treason against the Majesty on high; a capital crime. A witch is not to be endured on heaven or on earth."

When the governor was inclined to question the evidence, he met a spirit of conflict even in that "faire brick house" on Green Lane. His lady retorted at one of his outbursts in words that have a strangely modern ring: "Had you attended the services in the North Church more regularly, you would know that the Bible states plainly: 'Thou shalt not suffer a witch to live.' "

The hysteria was to continue until its gossip came to point a finger at her, the governor's lady. It died because of such overstresses and because Phips moved at last to suppress it. While it lasted it sent many innocent people to the gallows, and it explained in some measure the bitter conflict between the English and French—an irrepressible conflict of clashing ideologies and interests, and a conflict equally irrepressible between the fanaticism of Puritan New England and the absolutism of a Catholic Church that had paid for its hold on Canada in the blood of its saints.

The new fort was undoubtedly a happy relief for the governor.

He was deeply interested in its construction, as well he might be, as the cost ran to twenty thousand pounds and the good citizens of New England were grumbling mightily and questioning how it was to be secured. The fort was vastly more pretentious than the two that had preceded it and that, in the passage of years, had been captured and destroyed. Phips had no thought of letting the new fort suffer a similar fate. Its walls were made of stone set in mortar. It was a stupendous undertaking for the day. Two thousand cartloads of stone were needed. The fort itself stood a few rods above high-water mark. It was quadrangular in shape, with the side walls two hundred feet long and supported by a round tower at each corner that mounted the cannon taken from the abandoned fort at Casco.

Even partially completed, the fort at Pemaquid was of importance. There was a gathering of Indian tribes from the Merrimack and the Penobscot. They came to look and see and were deeply impressed. They gladly entered into an "everlasting and solemn" treaty of peace and gravely swore allegiance to William and Mary. It seemed that New England had reason to be grateful to Sir William, even if it had been necessary to pick up the bill for twenty thousand pounds.

The hour of gratitude was short-lived. Stern old Governor Frontenac hadn't overlooked the happening, nor had its significance escaped him. Set well in advance of the boundary, the fort at Pemaquid, France was ready to admit, was certain to encourage the Abenaki in their natural leaning toward the English. The "everlasting and solemn" treaty did not disturb Frontenac too much. He knew that nothing was everlasting with the Indians, and treaties least of all. It depended on what happened next, and the next thing to Frontenac's mind was to get rid of this fort.

To achieve this end two warships were at hand, the *Poli* and the *Envieux*. They were to round out this exploit by further attacks on Wells and Portsmouth. The expedition was under the command of Iberville, the paladin of the Le Moynes. With such dynamic leadership it could hardly go wrong. It seemed a reasonable assumption. The expedition started with four hundred Canadians. They were to add two or three hundred Indians that St. Castin had ready at Pentegoet, ample, one would think, to care for the sixty defenders of Fort William Henry at Pemaquid, considering that the fort was still far from completion. But everything went wrong. First an English captive held at Quebec, John Nelson by name, managed to get word to Boston. No one had expected that, for Nelson was a bitter enemy of Phips and certainly had no love for the Puritans. But again blood was thicker than water. He may have had a low regard for the "Bostonnais," but he had no mind to have them whipped by a lot of Frenchmen. The two French deserters Nelson had bribed to carry his message got through with their warning. Discovered as gentlemen of easy virtue where money was concerned, they were induced to undertake another venture, nothing less than capturing the elusive St. Castin, the particular thorn in the side of the citizens of Boston.

This expedition did not work out as well, at least for the deserters. They were captured at Mount Desert and rather summarily shot. But before that they had provided Iberville with an assortment of information that, considering its source, might have been accepted with slightly more skepticism. They told of a thirty-six-gun ship then cruising about Port Royal that had been ordered back to Pemaquid, and of two frigates hovering in the neighborhood of the fort. Each was reported to mount twenty guns. There was talk, too, of a fleet gathering at Boston for an attack on Canada. Had it been true, such a force quite obviously could have been diverted to look after the fort at Pemaquid with a minimum of trouble. That, probably, was the gist of Iberville's thinking.

He didn't know, of course, that the two frigates were really the only fighting ships that had to be considered. Even they didn't warrant much thought, as their commanders had grown weary of their stay at Pemaquid, well before Iberville had arrived in the neighborhood, and had sailed away for the livelier interests of Boston. Iberville didn't know, either, that the fort was only partially completed and lightly manned. On every other occasion where he appears, he moves promptly and with a reckless disregard of the odds. This time it was different. That difference was part of the general ill fortune that seemed to be dogging French steps. Iberville was confused and hesitant. In all the smother of information, he couldn't see that little of it was true—that Pemaquid lay before him an easy victim, a prize to dangle before the eyes of the Abenaki, to make them quickly forget their "everlasting treaty."

It is easier to understand Frontenac's feeling than his angry implication of the cause of the great leader's inexplicable failure. Frontenac claimed that the presence of Iberville's sister on the ship—just why she was there no one can know—had somehow tempered the fighting Le Moyne blood; had made the leader timorous in accepting the natural hazards of attack. It is hard to believe that his sister's presence had changed a headlong fighter into a cautious procrastinator. Yet that is what Frontenac's criticism implies. It couldn't be true. Iberville had set out to attack and knew all the hazards in advance. Instead of fighting, however, he did nothing to suggest such intention and shortly sailed away. He left to look for privateers, an occupation that carried its own danger. He was in battle with one, captured and sank it after a brisk exchange of gunfire. Had he been unduly sensitive over his sister's presence aboard, even the normal risks of the voyage might have made him hesitate. These were not inconsiderable. They came near to being final. In a driving storm the *Poli* all but ran aground on the Nantucket Shoals. Whatever the reason of Iberville's lapse, this happening capped it all. The *Poli's* sails were set for France, and the Abenaki were left to their own devices.

Iberville's surprising retreat from Pemaquid without striking a blow had sent French prestige toppling still further. Frontenac knew it, knew something had to be done to restore it promptly. The best man he could discover for this unpromising task was a certain Charles Claude de Villieu. De Villieu had a shrewd knowledge of the Indian mind and an adroit way and a lack of scruple in using it to his own advantage. No doubt Frontenac counted on this to serve New France as well. Villieu needed all his gifts. The failure at Wells and the larger failure in not destroying the fort at Pemaquid had satisfied the Indians that England's fortunes were in the ascendant. Captain Convers, the same who had defended Wells so satisfactorily, had just finished building another fort at Saco. That seemed to settle the point. Certainly the Indians thought so. There was another great gathering at Pemaquid. Most of the tribes from the debated territory between the Kennebec and the St. Croix were present, as well as others from as far west as the Merrimack in New Hampshire. They eagerly declared for peace, blandly admitted themselves to be faithful subjects of William and Mary, and left five chiefs as hostages as evidence of the sincerity of their intentions.

The long nightmare seemed to be over. Villages and settlements had heard the word that all was now well. It bore the authority of Governor Phips himself. They could return to their quiet ways and the assurance that morning would come like a benediction rather than like a blast from hell. A great wave of relief swept over the colony.

It was a little premature. It took no account of the crafty and gifted Villieu. Villieu was quick to learn that not all the chiefs and not all the tribes had been for peace. With the help of Abbé Thury, Villieu began to foster these tribal jealousies. It was not difficult. Soon even some newly sworn English subjects were joining in a renewed clamor for English scalps. It was purest chance that turned eyes toward Oyster River, a dozen miles from Portsmouth, where the town of Durham now stands—the chance that Villieu's band was near and that supplies were running out.

The citizens of the little town slept soundly, satisfied with the governor's word. Warfare was over and peace had been assured. There were a dozen fortified homes in the town, but most of them were unprotected. No one cared about that now. There was no crowding in the palisaded defenses, and no guards were set. Sleep was deep and untroubled.

The first hint of dawn was in the air, though the moon was still up when a musket shot crashed through the silence. With it came the remembrance of other days. Already it was too late. Two of the palisaded homes that no one had thought necessary to garrison were broken open. The butchery began. Some of the other houses withstood the attack; some individuals escaped. Those who ran, half clothed, from their beds had no time to question why the governor had felt that there was no more need to fear. A hundred and four of them, and most of them women and children, had died of bullet or tomahawk, or by methods less pretty and less prompt. Twenty houses were burned and twenty-seven prisoners were taken. Then the bands broke up and went searching easier prey. "They mean," the astute Villebon wrote in his diary in commendatory vein, "to divide into bands of four or five, and knock people on the head by surprise."

More than one band converged at the settlement of Groton. It was over quickly. After all, they too were basking in the thoughts of peace. To more than forty of them it didn't matter any more.

Villebon was more than pleased. He liked thoroughness. "This stroke," he said, speaking of the grim business at Oyster River, "would break off all talk of peace between the Indians and the English." He added that the English were in despair "for," he explained with some complacency, "not even infants in the cradle are spared." He had misread the evidence, as he did so often.

What he took for despair was a slow-burning anger that grew in breadth and heat like a prairie fire. All the English had wished was to be left alone. They had not met attack with attack or cruelty with cruelty. It seemed that they either could not or would not. So Villebon thought. He was wrong, as the years were to tell. The wind was growing. Not so many years now until it would sweep over St. Castin's kingdom and over Villebon's Acadia until neither was French any longer. But before that day came the lilies of France were to have other days of greatness and of splendor.

These days began with Frontenac's decision that border raiding was not enough while Pemaquid and Boston still flouted him. The two must be taken. So it was that Iberville had his second chance. It may be doubted that this was at Frontenac's suggestion. But whether it was that his sister had not joined in this expedition or that Iberville had worked through the strange apathy that had surrounded him four years ago, he was never again to know that uncertainty.

This time Pemaquid was taken. There was not too much glory in that. The fort was commanded by one Pascho Chubb. He had neither the knowledge nor the spirit to make his strange name immortal, except in ignominy. He had ninety-five men making up his garrison. These had been permitted to bring their wives and children, so that the fort was crowded, but not with fighting men.

When St. Castin at the head of his three hundred warriors sent word demanding the fort's surrender, Chubb retorted grandiloquently that even "if the sea were covered with French ships, and the land with Indians," he would continue to fight on undismayed. The words were braver than the fact. The seas weren't covered with ships. There were only two, the *Envieux* and the *Profond*, and the land wasn't covered with Indians. There were somewhat less than four hundred all told. They were heavy odds, but no heavier than before the words were spoken. When St. Castin sent word that if the fort was not surrendered no safeguards would be given, Captain Chubb had a quick change of heart. If the French would assure the safety of garrison and dependents, he would forget those brave words. They could have the fort. Iberville agreed. As such agreements, both before and later, had too often meant less than nothing, it is worth recording that Iberville made good his promise. He sent the captives to an island in the river where a few guards could keep them safe. It was none too soon. The discovery of an Indian starving and in chains within the fort set the Indians baying for blood. Iberville's sternness safeguarded the captives for the time. He couldn't protect them forever. Months later the Indians found Captain Chubb and his wife at their Andover home, and there his inglorious story was summarily ended.

The taking of Pemaquid was an almost bloodless victory. Perhaps, therefore, few people realized how emphatic and far-reaching the victory really was. Iberville might set his men to stripping the fort of cannon and hauling them aboard ship. St. Castin might distribute the smaller arms among his followers. They might topple the walls until Fort William Henry at Pemaquid was an empty and useless shell, and the good people of Boston would not care. They hadn't wanted to build the fort. They had grudged the twenty thousand pounds it had cost them to build and maintain it. Now both money and fort were gone and nobody seemed too disturbed. Certainly there was no sorrowing in Boston. They were a stubborn breed.

They were also wrong, and shortsighted beyond belief. While Pemaquid threatened Acadia and frowned over St. Castin's uncertain kingdom, Boston was relatively safe from attack. With Pemaquid gone, it was in immediate jeopardy. In fact, it was already threatened.

The long-awaited stroke against New England was about to begin. It was to be an attack that would admit of no possibility of failure. Boston had about seven thousand people, but it was a seafaring community and much of its manpower was scattered about the seas. If it had eight hundred defenders at any time, that was a maximum.

Against this uncertain force the Marquis de Nesmond was bringing a fleet of fifteen ships, the cream of the French Navy. From Canada would come Frontenac heading his greatest expedition, starting with twice the number of Boston's defenders and reinforced as it progressed with forces gathered by Villebon, Villieu, and the redoubtable St. Castin. There were elaborate plans of attack by land and sea, and other plans, scarcely less elaborate, for the distribution of the plunder. After Boston was taken the army was to move up the coast to Salem and Portsmouth, with the fleet following along to lend assistance where it might be necessary. It reads like a fabulous dream. But it could have been true.

All through the early spring and summer Frontenac planned, collecting men and equipment for his arduous march. This was to be the attack about which he had so often dreamed. It was a campaign that would settle the ownership of a continent. In the land between the Kennebec and the St. Croix there was an unaccustomed quiet. It was a hush of part uncertainty, part expectation—and nothing happened. Spring merged into summer and summer into fall. It was not until September that Frontenac received from the marquis admiral the explanation for the delay. Headwinds had delayed the fleet, provisions were running low. It was too late in the year, the marquis argued, for such an attack to have its chance of success. For Frontenac it was complete disappointment, bitter and unavailing. He knew only too well that such a chance would hardly come again, certainly not for him. With one hope withdrawn the tired, valiant old heart began looking for another. In this man there might be petulance and unreasoning anger and a stubborn willfulness, but there was no childish repining. Though he was old he still looked forward, not back. That is one measure of the man.

For all the threatening clouds, New England had its spring and summer of content. Before the import of the threat that had hung over them was fully known, it was already a thing of the past. The people breathed again, feeling that fortune had smiled on them, presaging better days.

The days weren't so much better at Haverhill. The next spring the old pattern ran true. Settler Dunstan was out in the fields of his small farm. He had taken his seven children with him, the youngest scarcely two years old. It wasn't only the new sense of security that had come over the land that had made him take them. It was partly that his wife had just given birth to her eighth child and needed to be free of the care of her young brood while a neighbor woman cared for her and the young child. There was no thought of fear in settler Dunstan. He had no hint of it until his ear caught the first wild whoop of attack.

He moved swiftly then. Shooing his young brood before him, he made his hard choice. They must run as fast as they could to the nearest fortified house, almost a mile away. They knew the way. Now they must run for it, run for their lives. Snatching up his musket, he turned and dashed toward his own house and his wife and his newborn child. He was already too late. The Indians had passed. The house was ablaze. Desperately he turned to follow his flying children. These at least he might save. He did save the seven, keeping between them and their pursuers until they reached their haven. The Indians had no will to tangle with this bitter and desperate man.

The Indians indeed had been at the Dunstan home. They had found the baby and had smashed its small body against a nearby tree. The two women they had taken captive before the house had been fired. It was one of those hit-and-run raids, no purpose, no results—unless keeping the Indians interested in violence was a result. When the flurry of attack was over, the attackers slipped away. Haverhill and its defended homes looked too tough for capture. Also, these Indians were hunters rather than warriors. They had their women and children with them, and they had no thought of risking an all-out fight. Instead they broke up into small bands. It was easier this way for the hunters to provide for their needs. Such captives as had not been killed were divided.

So it was that Mrs. Dunstan and Mrs. Neff, her companion, and a young English boy captured in an earlier raid became the property of a band of a dozen Indians from the mission about Chaudière. The group had only two warriors, three squaws, and seven children. The presence of the squaws made little difference to the captives. The squaws were as ruthless as the warriors. The two women were not used to travel. They grew weaker as the days passed. They had made only half of the two hundred and fifty miles and already they could hardly drag themselves along. Their captors were shrewd enough to know that they were too weak to escape, even if they could survive in the wilderness. At night they slept unguarded away from the fire while their captors kept close to the warmth. So the three devised a plan. It was grim enough.

Waiting until sleep had lulled the figures by the fire, the three crept closer, two women and a boy. There was a hatchet in the hand of each. They made swift use of them. Of the party of twelve, ten would not awake again. There was only one old squaw to run wounded and screaming into the forest night. There was no one to hear her except three who were prisoners no longer and one small boy whom they had spared. Their work done, the three huddled against their victims for warmth and waited for the morning.

There was a dreadful casualness about their movements as they awoke. The food to be prepared and packed in equal bundles for the journey. Fortunately the hunters had provided food. Having eaten, they were ready to go. There was one thing more. The bodies of the ten men and women and children still lay about the smoldering fire almost as if they were still asleep. Mrs. Dunstan bent to her task with steady eyes and heart. Methodically she stripped the scalps from the ten victims. With this bloody burden swinging from her hand she turned to lead the way home.

They came home safely at last. With them still the ten bloody scalps to pay for that small crushed body by the Dunstan threshold. In the cold ferocity of that accounting there was evidenced the new hardness that was creeping into the hearts of men and women. In the fifty pounds that were paid her for those scalps was evidenced, too, the new sternness in the thinking of whole peoples.

The whirlwind was not yet, but it was brewing, leaving its cruel mark on decent people. That hardness would remain, a growing and unalterable purpose, until an old order had been swept away and a new era had been born and a continent had changed hands.

CHAPTER X

NORTHWARD THE DREAM OF EMPIRE

Louis XIV's interest caught by Newfoundland. Its strategic position. Iberville's campaign. The taking of St. John's and the despoiling of the country. Orders to retake Fort Nelson. The heroic story of the Pelican *and the* Hampshire.

EYES were turning northward. Louis was looking and thinking that way. So was his Minister of Colonies. So, indeed, was Frontenac. For the moment Acadia seemed secure. It would be finally so if the plan for taking Boston did not miscarry. This seemed improbable, with the promise of the Marquis de Nesmond's great fleet and the expedition that Frontenac was to bring from Canada.

But the irrepressible English could never be quite contained. They were still making their commercial hay about Hudson's Bay. Their reluctance to leave even after many setbacks gives some suggestion of how profitable that English venture into the bay was proving. Something obviously had to be done to assure that the bulk of these profits should find their way to Paris rather than London. Any other attitude, Louis felt, was an encroachment on his established prerogatives.

Now that the first flurry of interest over Acadia and the incidents happening thereabout had settled down to a satisfactorily stable situation, it was understandable that interest should return to a venture that obviously offered more promise of a profitable return.

It was no easier to escape the thought of the great bay than it was to escape the name of Le Moyne. As individuals and as a family they had left an indelible impression on that vast territory. Three of them had been with De Troyes as his lieutenants in the spectacular overland march to the bay in the year 1686, when Fort Albany and Fort Rupert, newly founded by the Company of Adventurers, were captured. They were Jacques, the second son of the family, known as Ste. Hélène; Pierre, the Iberville of history; and Paul, known as Maricourt. They were all in their mid-twenties. Iberville was still under thirty when he headed his own expedition to the bay in 1689. He was there again the year following. In 1694 he was once again challenging the English at Port Nelson in a more impressive and a more successful venture, a good fortune dimmed by the fact that young Louis, the first to be named Châteauguay, died there in one of the attacks. He was barely eighteen years old.

It would be hard to think of the bay of those days without bringing up such memories. It is true that Frontenac did not waste any love on the Le Moynes, nor did they return any. Yet Frontenac sensed the capacity of the brothers and used their services freely. He must have known that he was building the prestige of a family that openly opposed him, yet time after time he sent them back to share in the building of the heroic tradition that allied the family with the great bay.

Pre-eminently the tradition centered about Pierre, the third son of this fabulous family. Strangely, his name has lacked the familiar luster that clings to that of others of Canada's early great. It is perhaps because so much of his achievement attaches to the distant fringes of the New World empire that was always in his thoughts. He was born in an unpretentious house on St. Joseph Street in Montreal. As a boy of twelve he followed his father, Charles le Moyne, and several of his brothers on Frontenac's great campaign to found Fort Frontenac.

He was a persistent gadfly to the English adventurers who were trying to set up their own trading empire on the bay. He despoiled the men of Boston of their great fort at Pemaquid, which had cost twenty thousand reluctantly provided pounds, and drove them from Newfoundland. He was to found the colony of Louisiana and explore Mobile Bay and set up a city that would be called Mobile and be ruled for many long years by his brother Bienville, second of the name. He sacked the island of Nevis in the West Indies and was set to challenge the power of Spain itself when he was stricken with yellow fever in Havana, where his great fleet lay at anchor. He died aboard his flagship and was buried in the church of San Cristoval, and there he becomes part of the mystery that surrounds the last resting place of many of Canada's great—the imperishable Champlain, the far-roving La Salle, and now the fighter Iberville. Some years after his burial San Cristoval was torn down and never replaced. What happened to the bones buried there, no one knows. All that is known is that they were placed there July 9 of the year 1706 and that on that day Pierre le Moyne d'Iberville lacked only one week of being forty-five years old.

When Iberville sailed away from Pemaquid, having faithfully kept his promise to protect the fort's defeated defenders, the situation was vastly different from what it had been only a year or two before. Acadia was again firmly in French hands. The white and gold lilies of France fluttered bravely once more above Port Royal and the newer fort at Naxouat. The hesitating Abenaki had, for the moment, thought better of their decision to cast their lot with the English. The talk of capturing Boston didn't seem so wild a dream as it does in the telling. Certainly Iberville didn't think so. He had drawn up his own plan of attack and was confident that it would succeed and that he would have an important part in the great venture of separating England from New England. Well before the muddling of the Marquis de Nesmond had brought all those ambitious plans to nothing, Iberville had sailed for Newfoundland. Taking Newfoundland from the English was to be a prelude to taking Boston, and it seemed to Iberville that he might accomplish the one before he was needed to take part in the other.

It was September 12, 1696, when he finally dropped anchor in Newfoundland's Placentia Harbor. This was the one small holding of France on the island. It was to be the starting point for the conquest of the whole; a successful operation that brought little credit and no profit and that was undone almost as soon as it was accomplished.

Placentia Harbor, even though it represented the majesty of Louis XIV in this island of the New World, was not impressive. Nothing but its well-protected harbor gave it any significance at all. It was claimed that the roadstead could harbor one hundred and fifty ships had there been such a number with such a need. A ramshackle fort, named St. Louis in the King's honor, scarcely did him credit. It had a garrison of eighteen men and little else except that its all but unassailable position on the heights north of the harbor made the eighteen almost as invulnerable as the fort.

One could wonder why Louis should have been attracted to Newfoundland or why he gave it more than a passing thought. There was, of course, the fact that the English appeared to favor it. That gave it a competitive interest. There was its position too—the cork carelessly tossed aside, but still near enough to the bottle to suggest its use. Lying so close to the entrance of Hudson Strait, it lay also along one of the great treasure lanes of the fifteenth-century world. By it must sail the ships that brought the fur wealth of the north to the courts and the countries of Europe.

There were other reasons. The more utilitarian one being the need for a haven for ships coming and going between the New World and the Old where they could be safe both from nature's hazards and the predatory instincts of man. Perhaps there was still another reason. Perhaps Louis had caught something of Iberville's enthusiasm, which led him always to go and see and to claim what he saw for his royal master.

Iberville's visit didn't turn out to be a particularly auspicious one. The Sieur de Brouillon, who was governor over this minute kingdom, had little intention of sharing his small authority. His sojourn in Newfoundland had not tempered the irascibility of a naturally quarrelsome man. De Brouillon was stubborn, too, and he had a shrewd eye for any advantage—the advantage of tribute from a defeated enemy, perhaps, that would hardly increase by sharing. It must be admitted, however, that there wasn't a great deal to choose between the thinking of these two courageous and contentious men.

Fortunately, perhaps, when Iberville arrived at Placentia Harbor it was to find De Brouillon gone. A fleet of seven ships with one thousand French sailors had arrived from France a day or so before. The chance was too good to be lost; the chance to take St. John's, raze the settlements along the coast, and to have it all settled before Iberville arrived to steal part of the credit and other rewards.

There were some thirty-five English settlements on the island. They lay along the eastern coast of the Avalon Peninsula, with St. John's as the seat of what rule there was, under Governor Miners and his small court. Some of the settlements were farther afield, scattered about the shores of Conception and Trinity bays. These De Brouillan felt would fall into his hands like ripe plums once St. John's had been taken. The dispossessing of existing owners seems to have been the fixed idea of the times, and the French governor's plan was no exception. Iberville's share in it was to have been to push overland and attack the settlements from the landward side as the fleet attacked by sea.

There wasn't much wrong with the plan, as was later proven, but that the governor had done nothing to make it possible. When Iberville asked De Brouillon's deputy for supplies to supplement those exhausted in the trip from Pemaquid, the deputy merely shrugged. He had no supplies to share. Word of the dilemma was sent to Frontenac, who acted with his usual promptness, sending a provision ship that had just arrived from France. By the time it reached Newfoundland, however, many days had slipped by, and before Iberville could get away Governor Brouillon had returned. He was in an evil temper. True, he had played havoc along the coast, but St. John's had defied him. He had fallen out also with De Rocher, who headed the fleet. There were words, and De Rocher, wasting no time in adding to them, set his sails for France, leaving the governor to make his way home as best he could on the one ship remaining, the *Profond.* Naturally, the governor laid the blame for the failure on Iberville's lack of co-operation, blandly overlooking the question of how Iberville's force could have marched from Placentia Harbor to St. John's, a distance of perhaps a hundred and fifty miles as the crow flies, and much more as men must march, through virgin forest and half-frozen inlet, a vastly different matter. And they were to do it without food.

There were other dissensions—the question of who was to command whom, and the larger question of the distribution of spoils that so far were matters of the imagination. When tempers had cooled and it was possible to do some rational planning it was proposed that the original plan be used again. The governor should go by sea, taking with him such regulars as there were and some of the Canadian volunteers. Iberville would proceed by land. With him would go his young brother, Jean de Bienville, the second of the name, who was to outlive all his brothers and to become the governor of Louisiana and the founder of New Orleans. Iberville would have such of the Canadian volunteers as had not gone with the governor and a few Abenaki who had been induced to join the expedition. With them was their chief, Nescambiouit. This chief was a man of lofty soul, La Potherie assures us. The sprightly historian had ample opportunity to learn about the Newfoundland adventure. As commissary he accompanied the later expedition to recapture Fort Nelson, sailing aboard the *Pelican.* There he learned the details at first hand. In speaking of the "lofty soul" he supported his claim with a telling argument. Had not the great chief taken upward of forty scalps during his lifetime?

It wasn't a big party that set out that day of All Saints', November 1, to cross the peninsula, a hitherto unbroken land. There were some one hundred and twenty in all, counting the followers of the "lofty soul." So late a date for starting a campaign might well have seemed doubtful even in a land more noted for temperate climate. Iberville, however, had no time to spare, and winter campaigning was no novelty to him. Even so, that march across the Avalon Peninsula must have long remained in his memory. The route was almost due east, crossing the innumerable small lakes and rivers that mark the head of St. Mary's Bay. When they were not fighting their way through almost impenetrable virgin forest, they were wading waist-deep in freezing water. There were nine days of this misery before they finally reached the coast at Forillon or, as the English preferred to call it, Ferryland. It was some eight miles north of Renewes, where Governor Brouillon had proposed to make his headquarters.

Iberville's forces were all but starving when they reached the coast; only the discovery of a dozen sturdy little ponies kept it from being a fact. If somewhat tough and not too palatable, the pony meat was gratefully accepted.

A day or two of food and rest made Iberville anxious to be on the move again. He journeyed to see the governor, only to discover that official in a vile temper. It appeared to be over the division of the expected spoils of the expedition. It had been agreed before leaving Placentia Harbor that as Iberville had borne most of the cost of the expedition the greater share of its rewards should go to him. Looking at it from his new quarters, Brouillon didn't feel the same way at all. He was going to have an even division. When Iberville reminded him that the arrangement had been the governor's, the latter's temper passed all bounds. Supported by his friend, De Muy, the two drew their swords and offered to decide the question by the effective if not too logical method of running through the body anyone who objected.

Iberville was not one to be put out of countenance by such a suggestion. But he was impressed by the governor's petulant statement that if Iberville was so bent on war he could go it alone. While Iberville was as little dismayed by the thought of going it alone as by the hostility of the governor, there remained the fact that the major part of the forces available were under the governor's command. If these were withdrawn, the second attack on St. John's would be as ineffective as the first.

Iberville was, of all things, a practical man. If St. John's was not taken, both his investment in the expedition and the promise of any return on it would have gone agley. Something was always better than nothing. Realizing that it was cupidity that was presently disturbing the governor, he agreed to an even split. At once the atmosphere cleared. Before it could change, Iberville put his men on a fleet of small boats he had appropriated and made his way along the wintry shore to Bay Bulls. There Brouillon, sailing in the *Profond*, finally joined him, and on November 26 the united force of some four hundred men moved on St. John's.

Nature had been generous in protecting the capital of the island. Even without the battery of eight guns that guarded the narrow entrance to the harbor, the city could hardly have been taken from the seaward side. On the land side a series of three forts guarded the approaches. They would have been more effective if the ammunition provided had been as generous as the armament. It seems to have been easier to achieve the mighty effort necessary to provide the guns than the lesser but repeated effort to supply them, for shortage of ammunition was a prevailing lack on this and other occasions.

The attacking forces under their two commanders had not had an easy march. A heavy snow had fallen, blocking whatever roads there were along the shore, and horses and wagons had to be abandoned. Struggling through heavy drifts, they had to carry their own supplies. It was two days of such rugged marching before they came in sight of St. John's. When they did, Iberville's Canadians tossed their packs aside and went charging toward the left of the defenses. Brouillon, coming up with his heavier force, drove straight ahead. It has to be noted that the covetous and cantankerous governor was also entitled to be called courageous.

Still, the forts held out. It was evident that to take them by assault would cost an overly high price. The attackers were not aware, of course, of the shortage of ammunition, so siege tactics seemed to be the better policy. First it was decided to see what guile would do. A peremptory demand was made of Governor Miners that the place be surrendered. Miners had just one hope. He couldn't withstand a siege for long, but he knew that two powerful English ships were coming and, if they came in time, the situation might bear a very different complexion. He planned to postpone a decision until the odds were more favorable.

Rumor of a relieving force had also reached Brouillon and Iberville. They were quick to see the reason for Governor Miners' maneuvering. Speed was as important to one as delay was to the other. The method of achieving speed was cogent if not pretty. A settler named William Drew, captured in the earlier fighting, was to be the emissary charged with emphasizing the need for haste. To make the point impressive, William Drew was turned over to the Indian allies to be prepared for his mission.

According to a contemporary account, the Indians "cut all around his scalp and then by the strength of hand stripped the skin from the forehead to the crown." Thus prepared, and accompanied by Major l'Hermette to make the embassy official, the two entered the city. William Drew bore the tangible evidence and the major the word that, failing immediate surrender, all the inhabitants would be similarly served.

Governor Miners was not as familiar as the others with the refinements of border diplomacy. He was stunned by what he saw. He realized that the hope of holding out until help arrived was slight. The evidence of the result of failure he could not face. He may have had doubts if even surrendering would be enough to save his people. But Major l'Hermette was firm. The surrender must be not later than two o'clock of that day. All arms were to be left behind and only necessary clothing taken. This observed, wives and daughters would be protected from insult, and two vessels would be supplied to take the vanquished back to England.

There was no time, no basis, for argument. At two o'clock precisely on the thirtieth of November, 1696, the garrison laid down its arms and moved out. They were followed by some 160 inhabitants, again not counting women and children, the whole number something over four hundred. Late November is not sunny weather in Newfoundland, but Brouillon was a stickler for detail. The plan was to destroy the colony, so the forts were razed and all but one or two of the homes, which sheltered some sick, were put to the torch.

There had been a momentary thought of holding the city and making Newfoundland a French colony. But there were not enough men to garrison the forts and leave the forces needed to lay waste the land. So it was decided.

Grandly Brouillon offered the captives two of the ships he had taken from them. One would sail for England, taking 250 persons. The other had the dual role of bearing the news to France and of carrying the 180 prisoners that remained. From France these would find their way home as best they could. It was not the strict letter of the surrender terms, but there was gratitude that it was no worse.

There was almost a month of waiting in freezing weather and with little shelter and less food. It was the day after Christmas when the ships were ready to sail. It had not been a merry Christmas, and most of the four hundred-odd captives left Newfoundland without regret. That they left it in the hands of the French couldn't change the fact that they were glad to go before worse befell them.

Brouillon had had enough of campaigning too. He had his half share of the 220 fishing boats captured and of the 100,000 pounds of codfish that formed the major part of the loot. He was eager to get back to his comfortable quarters at Placentia Harbor. He was equally willing that Iberville should have the glory of subduing the country. He realized no doubt that there wasn't enough glory to share; little enough for anyone. As a victory over the hazards of nature, it was an achievement of note. As a challenge to the hardihood of men and to leadership under overwhelming difficulties, it had its glimmer of glory. As a conquest, it was pitiful and pitiless.

The policy was to destroy the settlements that had no defense and few defenders. Poor fisherfolk were routed from their homes and robbed of their property and possessions. The boats on which their living depended were destroyed. The homes that sheltered them from a northern winter were put to the torch. It was an inglorious victory and it was incomplete.

It was January 14 when Iberville with his army left St. John's bound for Portugal Cove. It was early spring when he again reached Placentia Bay, having covered the length and breadth of the Avalon Peninsula and everywhere leaving misery and want in his path. He had taken seven hundred prisoners, too many for him to guard, an immense amount of booty, and had destroyed most of the settlements and the fishing equipment by which the people lived.

He had taken and destroyed Portugal Cove and moved on to Harbor Main, a deep and narrow inlet at the foot of Conception Bay. It was decided there that the next point of attack should be Carbonear, well up the bay, and all the settlements that fringed that great arm of land that separates Trinity and Conception bays. It was a reaching out that demanded courage. It had almost failed in that snowy winter march from Portugal Cove. Chaplain Baudoin records in his diary that "the roads were so bad that we could find only twelve men strong enough to beat the path." That thirty-mile march had almost spelled the end of the adventure. There was no wish to repeat it. Yet to Harbour Grace was just such another challenge. They risked instead the wintry sea and made their way in three boats they had captured. The end was the same. The settlement was taken and destroyed. It was followed by Carbonear. Here Iberville ran into his first reverse, though actually it was not at Carbonear but at Carbonear Island, an all but impregnable island in Conception Bay, guarded by the sea and its precipitous cliffs. Attempts were made to reach it from the sea. Each time the attackers were thrown back, not by men but by nature, the recoil of the ground swell leaving them battered but alive, and happy at such good fortune.

They looked for an easier approach, and on the island's western side they found it. It was a narrow beach guarded by some cannon and all the defenders of the island. Too well guarded to be taken, even though Father Baudoin confided to his diary that "ten men ashore would have terrified these people." The catch was that the ten men could not get ashore in those wintry seas. In summer it might have been different. But summer was months away. Carbonear Island remained a city of refuge. Eventually there gathered there most of the prisoners Iberville had taken and had been too weak to hold.

Baffled at Carbonear Island, Iberville continued his march north to Bay de Verde at the tip of the peninsula and across the narrow stretch to Old Perlicon. They were important points where 100 and 150 men found employment in the fisheries. But there could be no fishing without boats and no living without homes, and both were destroyed.

Iberville moved on along the west coast, fringing Trinity Bay by Hant's Harbor and New Perlicon, and so to Hearts Content. It was not a happy meeting. There, after another unsuccessful approach to the fortress island, he left his army and himself made a hurried four-day march to Placentia Harbor. He had been out of touch with his world for months. Now he hoped to learn what had happened at Boston and elsewhere while he planned the last phase of his Newfoundland campaign.

That was never to be. On the nineteenth of May five ships of war dropped anchor in Placentia Harbor. They were the *Pelican*, the *Palmier*, the *Wasp*, the *Violent*, and the familiar *Profond*. With them came the sixth of the Le Moyne brothers, Joseph de Sérigny, who had been with Iberville when he had captured Fort Bourbon on the southwest coast of Hudson's Bay three years before. The English, with characteristic stubbornness, insisted on calling the place Fort Nelson. As they had recaptured it during the summer when Iberville was engaged at Pemaquid, they were entitled to call it what they would. The instructions that De Sérigny brought his brother were terse and definite. They did not refer to Newfoundland but to Fort Nelson, or Fort Bourbon, as taste prefers. They were economical in words. The instructions were to get it back.

That wrote finis to the futile Newfoundland campaign, futile, cruel, and senseless, a sop to the vanity of Louis XIV and little more. Only a few months were to pass and what had been done would be undone. An English fleet would stand by while the forts at St. John's were rebuilt, the settlements restored, and the island became again an English domain.

So the seesaw of capture and recapture went on, achieving nothing, proving nothing, settling nothing. No change, unless it was a change in the temper and thinking of a people, a hardening of purpose that made conflict inevitable and ranged England and France and the systems they represented in a last great struggle that could not end until, finally, the issues were decided.

Iberville was eager to be gone. He loved conflict, a conflict of traded blows, not the one-sided misery that the Newfoundland campaign represented. He had with him now his two brothers. The Le Moynes seemed always to be happier and more effective as a team. His young brother Bienville had acted as his aide in that rugged marching up and down the Avalon Peninsula. Now his brother Joseph had arrived. He brought orders and a fleet powerful enough to support them.

It was an impatient time. In the voyage from France the fleet had been caught in a terrible storm. It might have scattered them; instead it drove them together. Somehow the *Wasp* and the *Profond* were in collision. The heavier *Profond* escaped without too much damage. For the little *Wasp* it was a different matter. The sailors in the fleet, watching as best they could through the smother of spray, saw her slowly foundering. In such a storm there was nothing they could do to help. Sadly the rest of the fleet had to sail away, accepting her as lost. But three days after they had reached Placentia the little *Wasp* limped in, battered but still gallant. There had been other hazards to the voyage. Scurvy had broken out among the crew before they reached the Newfoundland banks. Before the men were well and the battered ships had been repaired the short northern summer was more than half gone.

Finally all was ready. Iberville took command, not only of the expedition but of the *Pelican*. He had with him again his brother Bienville. The *Pelican* was a fine stout ship. Ordinarily she carried an armament of fifty guns. Before she left France this total had been reduced to forty-six, and while at Placentia two more of her guns were given to the *Profond* to supplement her weak equipment. With the guns went twenty-seven of the *Pelican's* crew, leaving her with a bare 223 men from a normal complement of 250. These changes were to have their significance. They did not dismay Iberville. After all, he was only transferring fighting men from one fighting unit to another.

Sérigny was second-in-command of the expedition. He sailed on the *Palmier*, a ship only slightly less powerful than the *Pelican*, mounting forty cannon to the other's forty-four. The remaining units of the fleet were represented by the familiar *Profond*, commanded by Pierre du Guay, who was to follow Iberville faithfully on all his later adventures; the repaired *Wasp* and the supply ship, incongruously named the *Violent*, under the command of Ensigns Chartier and Bigot, respectively.

Fortunately perhaps for history the commissary of the fleet was none other than Claude Charles de la Potherie, who, under the pen name of Bacqueville de la Potherie, was to become one of the colorful historians of the happenings in a theater that might well have been forgotten. After all, as the great Francis Parkman has written, "These northern conflicts were but episodes—the issues of war were unimportant, compared with the momentous question whether France or England should be mistress—of the whole interior of the continent."

A mere incident it was indeed in the vast conflict for the mastery of a continent. But it was an important incident, sometimes a glowing one. Were national sympathies less restricting, some Tennyson might have found in the fight of the *Pelican* and the *Hampshire* a conflict worthy to be remembered with the story of the little

Revenge or of those six hundred riding with stubborn discipline into the valley of death.

Fortunately this backwater of conflict was to have its own graphic, if less poetic, recorders. There was young Father Gabriel Marest, who confided to his friend and guide some of his reflections and observations on the courage and resourcefulness of the men who faced this northern battlefield. Happily his recollections were recorded for present-day readers in that invaluable picture of early men and events known as the *Jesuit Relations*. "The frequent maladies and continual dangers to which people are exposed in this perilous navigation," he explained, "are such that the French did not dare to undertake without having with them a chaplain." It was so that young Gabriel Marest, newly arrived in Canada, was assigned to this dangerous and exacting office. "I will not conceal from you," he wrote his friend, "that this was contrary to my inclination."

So he became a part of Iberville's first expedition and capture of Fort Nelson in 1694. He left a graphic picture of this inhospitable land where, he wrote, "winter comes before autumn," and where, while it was still August, "we began to descry those great icebergs which float in the sea; we saw perhaps a score of them. Far away they looked like mountains of crystal and some of them like cliffs bristling with peaks."

He had to record other hazards: "Monsieur de Chateauguai—a young officer nineteen years old and brother of Monsieur d'Iberville—had gone to skirmish near the English fort in order to divert their attention and prevent their knowledge of our difficulties. Having advanced too far, he was wounded by a ball which pierced him through. He sent for me that he might confess, and I went to him immediately. At first we thought that the wound was not mortal; we were very soon undeceived, for he died the next day."

He tells then of misfortunes to the vessels from wind and ice and unknown shallows, the injury to the ship so that she took water faster than the pumps could expel it, and it seemed unlikely they would ever reach the place where they were to winter.

"So much sad news," the young priest continued, "did not dampen the courage of Monsieur d'Iberville, although he was extraordinarily touched by the death of his brother, whom he had always tenderly loved. He made this a sacrifice to God, in whom he chose to put his whole confidence. Foreseeing that the least sign of anxiety which might appear upon his countenance would throw everyone into confusion, he maintained throughout a marvelous firmness—setting everyone to work, exerting himself, and giving his orders with as much presence of mind as ever."

And Iberville's second expedition was also to have its recorder in the already mentioned Bacqueville de la Potherie, who, in addition to his duties as commander of the forces in the forecastle of the *Pelican* and administering the commissariat of the expedition, was to find time for his careful record of the incidents of the voyage.

It is small wonder that young Father Marest felt that such hazardous undertakings needed the ghostly counsel and the comfort of a spiritual guide. It was surely a small enough demand, for they asked no other concession. Today, with every modern navigational device for the safety of shipping and with elaborate charts of the shoals and the currents and the ice movement and with daily weather reports, the navigation of Hudson's Bay is not for amateurs. These adventurers with no charts, no navigational aids, with small knowledge of the weather and little more of the land to be visited, and with the uncertainty of sail pitted against the unpredictable movement of winds and ice, faced the hazards and made what even today is something of an adventure into an everyday happening. Certainly this voyage is one of the highlights of naval history. Yet, because it happened in Hudson's Bay, even so great a historian as Francis Parkman dismisses it as an episode and hurries by it in a paragraph or two. Small wonder that Pierre d'Iberville never achieved his just rating as one of the great captains of history.

Two whole weeks the fleet sailed along Newfoundland's bleak eastern shore and into the open Arctic waters, taking advantage of the favoring winds. As they neared the strait at the bay's entrance the weather changed. The bitter northern gales sheathed decks and rigging with ice and made the handling of sail a torture. Finally they were in the strait, in the lee of the snowy wastes of Baffin Land. It was unfamiliar waters for the French. La Potherie employed his time in selecting from the names of the ship's company, not forgetting his own, suitable identifications for the capes and islands passed. A day or two in the lee of the land helped to free the fleet of the encumbering burden of ice and to permit it to move again. They crossed the strait to Cape Weggs. It was August second.

A day or two of sailing brought them to Nottingham Island, and there the ice closed in. There was nothing to do but wait. Three weeks passed as if they had been three ages. One day the wind rose and cut channels of water in the field of white. Iberville moved swiftly. He slipped the cable of the *Pelican* and set her bow toward free water. He made it with bare minutes to spare. The opportunity was brief, too brief for any who hesitated. Fog settled in again and the wind blew the ice into a solid pack before others of the fleet could escape. Iberville waited. Perhaps the wind would change again. He waited there in open water, in this distant hope, for three days. They might end, he knew, in becoming weeks. The fleet would have to follow when it could. Iberville set his sails for the open bay and Fort Nelson. It was September fourth, two months since leaving Placentia Harbor, when the anchor of the *Pelican* sank into the mud of the Hayes River, only a few miles from her objective.

Iberville was anxious. He knew the hazards of those waters, but they were greater than even he knew. Scattered in the ice in the straits between Nottingham and Digges Islands, the ships could do little to help each other. Some of them, like the *Profond*, had little areas of open water about them and some hope of escape. When the fog lifted, Pierre du Guay, in command of the *Profond*, was happy. Even the three ships that were slowly sailing toward him didn't change that. It seemed that all the fleet had broken loose and was now free to follow their leader's course. Then his surprised eyes caught the flutter of red at the masthead, and he knew the ships for what they were. The Hudson's Bay Company's fleet come in time to defend Fort Nelson. Du Guay was no poltroon. His first idea was to fight—against any odds. Then he remembered that his ship carried the munitions and supplies for the expedition. Its safety was vital. Instead of attacking, Du Guay headed back into the ice, where pursuit was as impossible as was the hope of succor. The *Palmier* and the *Wasp* did their best to help, but they too were locked in the ice, and their efforts to move were fruitless. They could only watch.

Du Guay's fighting spirit was still high. If he could not get to close quarters with the enemy, neither could they reach him. As soon as it was light enough to see he opened fire on the *Deering* and the *Hudson's Bay*, the smaller and nearer ships of the fleet. All day long this interchange of gunfire continued. At the distance it could hardly be called a battle and it certainly wasn't on even terms. Locked in the ice as she was, the *Profond* could bring only two guns to bear on the enemy. These were effectively served, even if they accomplished little. The heavier and more numerous guns of the attacking fleet did no more. Evening brought the *Hampshire* to join the attack. At nightfall it died away. Captain John Fletcher of the *Hampshire* was quick to realize that it was a purposeless undertaking. While they remained locked in the ice the French ships could cause no trouble. If they escaped, they could be looked after handily. Morning found the English fleet well on its way.

At his anchorage at the mouth of the Hayes River, a bare ten miles from his destination, Iberville waited for his supporting ships to arrive. He had sent ashore an expedition of twenty-two men under his cousin, Le Moyne de Martigny. They were, if possible, to pick up some Indians and to learn from them something of the situation of the fort and whether the company's fleet had come and gone.

While he waited, part of his question was answered. At the first glint of dawn on September 5 Iberville saw three ships tacking toward his anchorage.

Now he knew the answer to the question about the fleet. He knew some other things too. He knew that there was no chance to pick up De Martigny's twenty-two if he was not to be caught like a rat in a trap, nicely bottled up in the Hayes River, where he could be disposed of at leisure. He knew that what with the scurvy-ridden men below deck he had a crew of less than a hundred and fifty to handle his sails and man his guns.

When he had turned over men and guns to the *Profond* at Placentia it hadn't occurred to him that he was doing other than distributing his forces differently. Any action, it seemed, would be a fleet action, and these men and guns would serve him. Now he knew the men could not help and that he had just forty-four guns to set against the fifty-six of the *Hampshire* and the sixty-eight shared by the *Deering* and *Hudson's Bay*. Three ships facing one, and a hundred and twenty-four guns opposed to forty-four, at least six hundred fighting men compared to a hundred and fifty. There, it seemed, were unbeatable odds.

Iberville was no counter of costs, and neither were the men who followed him. If the English fleet were permitted to relieve the fort, the prospects of capturing it would be negligible. There was a council of war. It didn't take long or use many words. The universal idea was to fight, and the quicker they got out of the bottleneck of a river and got started, the better.

The three English vessels driving forward in battle formation with the mighty *Hampshire* in the lead were a sight to see. Iberville had other problems to occupy him. His heavy set of sail heeled the *Pelican* over so that one of her broadsides seemed likely to fire over the masts of any adversary. Like many problems, that one didn't need handling. The *Pelican*, driving full-sail toward the *Hampshire*, suggested to Captain John Fletcher, who didn't know how few were the men behind the sails and guns, that Iberville was proposing to board his ship. He slipped out of range. The movement that brought the *Pelican* about and heading for the *Deering* leveled the guns so that the blast carried away much of the tackle of the *Deering's* mainsheets. For a moment she was difficult to handle. As the *Hudson's Bay* hurried up to assist she also received a broadside. For a moment it seemed as if the *Pelican* were master of the two.

But now Captain Fletcher had brought his ship about and had his guns ready. The attack was deadly. Musketry swept the forecastle, where La Potherie commanded, with dreadful results. Two shots had pierced the hull near the waterline, while others damaged the *Pelican's* fore rigging.

For three hours the roll of gunfire shattered the Arctic silence. Outnumbered and outgunned, the *Pelican* gave no sign of defeat. Captain Fletcher grew more and more impatient. The present advantage was his, but for how long? Who was to know when the French ships imprisoned in the ice at Digges Island might find a means to escape and so wipe out this advantage? The *Pelican* once sunk, that danger would be past. This firing from long range was playing the Frenchman's game. It was minimizing the advantage, an advantage of men and fire power. The obvious course was to move in and use both, rake the ship and board it while the shock was still on them.

But there were niceties even in battle. As the ships drew together Captain Fletcher called out, demanding surrender. Nothing happened. The lilies still fluttered jauntily at the masthead, and the gun ports of the *Pelican* still belched their fire. Captain Fletcher was a gallant man. More than that, he could recognize gallantry. In the courtly gesture of his age he called for wine and, standing there on his quarter-deck, he raised his glass to a worthy enemy. He went even further. A deep voice boomed out an invitation that Iberville would dine with him after the fight, should he survive.

There was no immediate answer, only the figure of Iberville standing also, glass in hand, drinking to his enemy. Such pretty gestures over, the fighting was resumed. Captain Fletcher loaded his guns with grape. As he approached, it raked the *Pelican's* decks, covering them with dead and wounded men. This was what Iberville had feared. This was why he had fought a battle at long range. If the *Hampshire* should get close enough to board, the *Pelican's* gallant story would be ended. No courage could withstand such odds.

Coming up under full sail and heeling over in the breeze, the *Hampshire* was a thing of beauty and of fear. Iberville had time for neither. He waited his one chance. As his enemy came round to close in for the kill, the wind heeled it over. It was the moment. Iberville sent his broadside crashing into the *Hampshire's* side just at the waterline. The great ship shuddered and lost way. For a moment she righted herself, then as the water rushed in at her gashed side she settled and was gone. Captain Fletcher would not keep his appointment either as victor or vanquished. Gallant, as always, he had gone down with his ship.

The *Pelican* was in little better shape. Seven shots had pierced her hull close to the waterline and others had wrecked her upper works. The lower battery and La Potherie's forecastle were a shambles. Hardly enough men remained to handle the sails, none to work the guns. Iberville didn't wait to consider these problems. He brought his ship about and headed for the *Hudson's Bay*, which had been hanging on the fringes of the fight. Momentarily unnerved by the sudden, inexplicable fate of the *Hampshire*, Captain Smithsend struck his flag without waiting for demand. The *Deering* hadn't waited for this final gesture. It was already out of gunshot range and moving rapidly as Iberville turned the *Pelican* in pursuit. But crumpled rigging and battered hull could not meet the new demand. So the *Deering* escaped.

Night came on, a dark night of gale and snow. The tangled ropes were stiff with frost and cruelly harsh to tired fingers. Below deck the wounded screamed in agony at every pitch. A doomed ship anchored on a lee shore facing an Arctic gale. By midnight one anchor had gone and they had to slip the other and try to beat to sea. But the rudder gave way, and before it could be repaired the heroic *Pelican* was hard aground on a shoal, still two leagues from land.

Iberville sent La Potherie and some half dozen sailors to try to find a possible landing place. Before they had gone far their boat, too, had gone aground on one of the innumerable shoals. There was nothing for it but to go overboard and fight their way through the surf, sometimes up to their armpits in the ice-covered water. But they did reach shore. They did show that it could be done. Soon the wounded were being taken overside and loaded on hastily assembled rafts. It was not surprising that eighteen of the wounded could not survive that ordeal.

Some days later Iberville, crossing to the Hayes River, saw his remaining ships, the *Profond*, the *Palmier*, and the *Wasp*, riding quietly at anchor, and he knew that the final moment had come.

The fort was strong, well enough manned, and plentifully supplied with artillery; better guns than Iberville could hope to produce. The storm that had destroyed the *Pelican* had also driven the *Hudson's Bay* ashore, and fifteen of its crew, Captain Smithsend among them, had reached the fort and been added to its defenders. Captain Smithsend had recovered his composure and was in no mood to surrender a second time. When Iberville sent Le Moyne de Martigny to Governor Bailey to demand that the fort be surrendered, Captain Smithsend threw his influence heavily on the other side. This attack, he assured the defenders, would be the last resort of desperate men. Many had been killed, Iberville among them. It was not a surprising deduction, and probably he believed it.

Anyway, he urged, a stout defense would quickly discourage the attackers. That was the gist of the message that De Martigny had to bring to Iberville. It fitted in nicely with the views of Governor Bailey, who was a man of courage and in no mood to surrender. It would have been better had his men been more resolute. He had offered them a year's pay if they would defend the fort. He had added a promise of forty pounds to the widow of anyone killed in action. Neither offer stimulated great enthusiasm.

The truth was that while they knew they had the preponderance in guns and could do an attacking party much damage, they also knew that the weight of numbers must tell. And the numbers, unmistakably, were with the French. Henry Kelsey, the deputy governor at the time, recorded in his journal that three times the demand for surrender was "deneyed." In the end, "finding such great force as nine hundred men and ye ill tidings of our own ships," the garrison "marcht out—and ye French took possession of ye fort, this being ye end of a tedious winter and tragical journal by me, Henry Kelsey."

Whether the "tragical journal" was quite accurate in the number of men under Iberville's command remains in doubt. Many of the original force, as Captain Smithsend had pointed out, had been killed or wounded. There was sense in his argument that a stout defense had often discouraged the attackers, but the weakness of the argument remained. Iberville wasn't dead. The forces he had were measurably more numerous, and they had the *élan* that expected victory assures. The defenders, who had firsthand knowledge of that battle of David and Goliath, had no doubt that a superior force would be used decisively. The ill tidings of their own ships, which Kelsey had mentioned, were the decisive factor. The will to continue was lacking. It wasn't lacking in Governor Bailey, who did his best. But when Sérigny was sent to him with a fourth and final demand for surrender it included a statement that time for negotiation was running out. If the governor would not surrender, the fort would be taken by assault and on the victor's terms. There would be no more delay.

The governor made one final effort to purchase the enthusiasm of his men. It was useless and he knew it. Even with the most heroic defense the garrison would still be overrun. Governor Bailey could not see the possibility of such a defense. He made the best terms he could. He was permitted the dubious benefit of the honors of war as his garrison marched out of the fort and the red ensign of England gave place to the lilies of France.

Quite possibly there was no need for either surrender or assault. The Treaty of Ryswick, signed while Iberville was still at the bay, would probably have given the fortress of the north to France without cost, just as it brought an end to eighteen years of almost constant warfare. But Iberville didn't know that. He had to settle the matter in his own way. After all, it wasn't quite an empty victory. It remained a drama of unwavering courage and endurance, an instance of inspired leadership. It was played out on the fringes of an uncertain empire and could have only a minor impact on the sweep of history.

All that is true. Yet it was a victory and a name that would be remembered in years when victories were few and leadership uncertain and when the fortunes of France had begun to decline again. Here was a captain who did not live with doubt, who was not timid of odds, who knew what he wanted and was ready to chance everything to secure it. Here was the greatest of a great family, whose courage and devotion are a living part of the history of the Canadian nation.

CHAPTER XI

IROQUOIS INCIDENT

Frontenac's new lieutenant, De la Mothe Cadillac, comes on stage. Their friendship does not help either to the good will of the Church. The Iroquois, a continuing threat demanding action. Fort Frontenac rebuilt, the great expedition undertaken. New York's Governor Fletcher acts to minimize the results.

WITH Iberville's amazing success the struggle for the north seems to have come to a momentary pause. This was given some appearance of finality by the Treaty of Ryswick, which, for the time at least, established the ownership of Fort Nelson. There was no such assurance for the rest of the continent. Frenchmen still only assumed the ownership of the north and west. They maintained their uncertain hold on the river system of the midwest mainly by the prestige of those men who commanded at the isolated forts and trading posts.

Frontenac's ability to select able lieutenants and to hold their unwavering loyalty, had he no other outstanding gifts, would still have marked him as a great commander. The intendant, Champigny, and others before him had another explanation. They were quick to insinuate that favoritism and the tangible material advantages he had to offer were certain to surround him with the most daring and aggressive spirits. There is weight in such a view, and yet the evidence is against it. Had these men been only followers of the main chance, it is surely assumable that they would have ended in an affluence greater than they achieved. No one of them, not even the governor himself, was entirely free from some selfish interest. But that was not what gave them their amazing prestige and their hold over the imagination of their savage followers. Selfishness may earn material rewards, but hardly those of the spirit. These men dominated because they themselves were dominated by something greater than desire for personal gain. Those who served the arrogant old governor must share his quality. They were not above reproach. But this at least they could claim: they were more interested in the task than in its reward.

Had such leadership been lacking, the French could not have maintained for so long their grasp on a vast and uncertain empire. They differed from the English, who, for all their adventurous strain, were not then the explorers and the colonizers. On this continent, at least, they were agriculturists and traders. They had no yearning for farther fields until they had established that those about them were unmistakably their own. They were fleeing from oppression and social inequality. They were jealous of authority. They were suspicious even of each other. It was next to impossible to unite them in any common enterprise.

It was this that helped equalize the great disparity in numbers. There was no attempt to unite the widely scattered English colonies. Each lived to itself. Gathered in small communities, the English made these the center of their lives and loyalties. It was so that New York and New England, and sometimes not even these, were the only English groups that would unite against French aggression.

The French, on the other hand, were neither traders nor agriculturists, and they were reluctant immigrants. It was the adventurous fringe of the French population, the younger sons, the near aristocrats who could recognize the privileges of a caste and never share them, who were the group ready to accept the challenge of the New World.

There were, of course, another group and another reason. It would be hard to think of New France without recognizing the amazing part that missionary zeal played in the opening of a continent. It is a debt that cannot be overstressed. Yet it is not all a credit item. Had the Huguenots, despoiled of their lands and denied religious freedom by the revocation of the Edict of Nantes, which had assured both, been permitted to find a new home in a new land, much might have been different. France would not have lost more than a million of her great artisans. They would have established themselves in communities in a new continent and might easily have grown strong enough to hold the bulk of it for France. But the bigotry that would not permit Protestantism to raise its head in France itself could hardly permit it in the New World. So the chance was lost.

Be this as it may, no one can take from the Jesuits the credit for their amazing achievements and for their unquestionable and selfless devotion. Their courage is the only light in many a dark page of Canadian history. If sometimes devotion took on a strange and cruel shape, it does not follow that by nature there was cruelty there. The total story makes that abundantly clear. Where these deviations appear it was because a single-minded devotion to a pervading idea had made all else seem inconsequential–small imperfections in a great design. The Jesuits' concern was with souls rather than bodies. They saw a danger to the soul in the mingling of races and the conflict of different cultures. They saw the results of the intercourse of untrained people with reckless and not too scrupulous men who were chancing their lives in the hope of a quick fortune.

They did their best to keep the races separated, but still the adventurous spirits continued to take to the woods, often enough to be submerged in the vastness and unfamiliarity. The King could issue rules and impose rigid penalties and the priests could inveigh against them unceasingly, yet the adventures still roamed. They had to, though officialdom was slow to see it. They had to attract the fur trade on which the life of the colony depended. They had to attract it against the pull of the easier approach, the larger population and the greater resources of the English colonies. They achieved their end by taking France to the Indians; by establishing an amazing ability to achieve the respect and dominate the thinking of a native people. In this we speak of those men who were ever extending that line of forts and trading posts, men who are remembered in the familiar place names of a continent.

There was Du Lhut, who had made the Sioux country almost a kingdom of his own. There was Courtemanche, who ruled at Fort Maimi on the Ohio River; and Henri Tonty, who had made his iron hand a symbol of justice and might in the lands about Fort St. Louis and the Illinois country. There was Nicholas Perrot, ranging the more northerly reaches of the Mississippi, observing and recording as he went, and always following his unending task of keeping the Indians at peace, among themselves, and with the French. And at Michilimackinac one of the most vibrant of these adventurers—Antoine de la Mothe Cadillac, the founder of Detroit, who later became the stormy governor of Louisiana, and whose name to most people is nothing more than the name of a car.

As he enters the story for the first time a word about him might be opportune, though the achievements that give him a place in this galaxy of men of adventure come at a somewhat later date.

Certainly Antoine de la Mothe Cadillac was not the least among these adventurers. He was born a hot-tempered Gascon who would bow to no authority, whether of Church or state. Particularly, his rebel spirit rejected the authority of the priesthood, though he was a faithful if rebellious servant of the Church. He came to Canada as an officer of the Carignan regiment, a lieutenant colonel at the age of twenty-four. He was called the "raven" by some, in deference to an impressive nose; by others the "Black Prince" because of his swarthy Spanish complexion and his imperious manner.

In truth, he was a difficult man to handle. He had been brought up as an orphan of good family, and his early memories were of penury and orphanage and a lonely childhood. It had not broken his spirit, only fixed in him the conviction that poverty must never happen to him again. It had taught him something. Now he was through with it.

Cadillac was a man of keen wit and determined character. It was reluctantly, if at all, that he could bow the knee to prelate or priest. Confident of his own qualities, with a ranging ambition and the courage to sustain it, he was not slow to attract the attention of the old governor. It was to grow into a lasting intimacy and a debt that Cadillac willingly admitted. "I am molded by your hand," he said. "What I am you have made me." It was a statement of fact, for Frontenac was as little likely to be cajoled by compliments as Cadillac was to offer them. It was a double-edged compliment, too, little likely to ingratiate either with bishop or intendant.

This friendship grew out of a shared opinion. It was when Cadillac (who had been sent to France to outline the situation in the colony to the King) told His Majesty, "The world may revolve on its axis to all eternity but Canada will no more become a France than a desert a garden," that he caught the imagination of the old governor. It was so much what the King did not want to hear. It was so close to what Frontenac himself had always believed. He had worked for a new and different world. He had always been bitterly opposed to the policy of circumscription that was implicit in almost every message received from France. Louis and his ministers wanted no reaching out. They were satisfied with a restricted community bound by all the old rules of Church and state and profiting from a trade that flowed toward it. Here was where the governor and his young associate were of one mind. Trade wouldn't come to them. If they wanted it they must reach for it.

Since Frontenac had never been popular with the bishop or his following, the addition of Cadillac to his official family at the château did little to help. Cadillac did not permit himself the dubious luxury of boredom. "The winter passed very pleasantly," he wrote in one of his letters, "especially to the officers who live together like comrades. To contribute to their honest enjoyment," he explained, "the count caused two plays to be acted." Not everyone felt that this was honest enjoyment. The bishop and his following were frankly disapproving. But when it was rumored that Molière's play, *Tartuffe*—a play that satirized certain evils existing under the mask of religion—was likely to be the next offering, the attitude went beyond disapproval. It is quite possible that Cadillac was the author of the rumor. Whether or no, the rumor brought repercussions out of all proportion to an offense that had not been committed. "Monsieur de St. Vallier," wrote the irreverent young officer, "sweated blood and water to stop a torrent that existed only in the imagination." But if it began as an imaginary challenge it grew into a fury of charge and countercharge and a smother of interdictions and excommunication that nowhere had any substantial basis. It did nothing to endear the governor and his lieutenant to the spiritual authorities, and it engendered no upsurge of affection in return. Cadillac, whose Gascon temper responded promptly to any suggestion of criticism, had a tongue as sharp as his temper, and he seemed to bask in such opposition. He spoke quite openly, charging that the Jesuit conduct "smelled of sedition a hundred yards off." When he met with opposition in return, he did not attempt to change his policies to mollify his enemies. Instead he announced that he did not intend "to pause in my way for the noise of puppies snapping and barking at my heels." They were not words likely to add harmony to associations, and they didn't. His conflict with the spiritual authorities was endless and unrelenting. Even their missionary zeal came under his sharp criticism. "One may as well knock one's head against a wall as hope to convert the Indians." He did add that the only approach was by the way of educating their children.

Cadillac, though devout enough in his own way, couldn't resist challenging methods. He felt that public policy should govern missionary zeal. Converts would come more readily if first there were respect and obedience to the civil authority. Whatever merit there may have been in the argument, there was none at all in the belligerency of its presentation. He was a staunch hater. He could think with relish of knocking off the jaw of Father Etienne Carheil, the Jesuit who had done most to oppose him at Michilimackinac, and he could chortle with joy on hearing that the good father was losing most of his converts. One would be wrong in picturing Cadillac as a wholly endearing character. All that need be said for him was that he was devoted to his far vision of a great Canada.

Perhaps in speaking of one of his nature it need hardly be said that Cadillac was in sharp opposition to the Church's attitude to the brandy trade. He admitted that it presented its problems; that there were probably three or four hundred kegs hidden in the woods about Michilimackinac by unlicensed traders. Brandy that could be bought in Montreal for three dollars a pot and turned over at Michilimackinac for twenty-five was a profit not likely to be resisted. He urged, with a viewpoint that is not unknown today, that it was next to hopeless to try to combat so natural an urge and that the best remedy was to confiscate such supplies for government uses. In his plans for founding Detroit he adopted just such a policy.

Aside from such aspects, Cadillac saw no hope of maintaining the friendship and assuring the trade of the Indians if New York and Albany offered them rum with their trading while Montreal and Michilimackinac offered them nothing. Besides, he often urged, brandy was needed "to counteract the bad, hard diet of fish" and as a protection against bitter cold and drenching rain.

That was the man whose story has hardly begun, a tough, far-reaching man who had no fear of enmities or of championing unpopular causes. He had his own ideas of the Indian situation and how it should be met, and brandy played its part. Yet he was shrewd enough to know that, despite everything bishop and priests might argue, brandy had not been lacking, and the stubborn fact remained that it had not brought enduring friendship, nor had it prevented the English from diverting much of the fur trade their way.

The crux of the situation in the New World was still the Iroquois, whose antagonism toward the French showed no sign of abating. It was true that cautious feelers, directed through various channels, suggested that the Iroquois might be happy to conclude a lasting peace. The prospect seemed promising. Various meetings were arranged, but nothing resulted. Meeting after meeting ended with an agreement on the part of the Iroquois that they would return all captives. Explanations of the reasons for failure to live up to these agreements were plausible, but the captives were not returned. There was, too, a continual insistence on the part of the Iroquois that the English should be included in the pact. As part of Frontenac's policy was to wean them from this attachment, he would have none of it. It became increasingly apparent that what had seemed like an honest yearning for peace was merely a shrewd maneuvering on the part of the Iroquois for time to regain their strength.

It was not love for the Iroquois that led the French to such peaceful approaches. It was that the Iroquois were the key group in the Indian world. The other tribes might hate them, but the hate was accompanied by fear. They had good reason to fear, as they knew very well. If this ever-present threat could be removed, it would not be too difficult for the French to maintain peaceful relations with the smaller tribes.

Some might argue, as La Mothe Cadillac did, that the friendship of these lesser tribes was always in doubt. Speaking of the Ottawas and the Hurons, who were nominally allied to the French and were most directly under their influence, he said: "They play the fox but never the lion." There was truth in that, as everyone knew. They were a shifty crew. While apparently friendly with the French, they were still dickering for an understanding with the Iroquois. While that was so, French Canada was sitting on a powder keg. There were seven thousand Indians of mixed blood centered at the vital post of Michilimackinac, and there were less than two hundred Frenchmen to maintain order.

Everywhere there were danger and uncertainty; the danger that the fur trade might dry up as it had done before; the danger that the dreadful scenes of Lachine and La Chesnaye might be repeated. So

Frontenac continued the conferences and the Iroquois sent their representatives. This was the breathing space everyone wanted. While there was a chance that something might come of the negotiations, the lake tribes were not likely to cause trouble. Frontenac spoke in his familiar tones. "My Iroquois children have been drunk," he said to one of their chiefs, Tareha by name, who had come to discuss peace, "but I will give them an opportunity to repent." But repenting seemed to be the last thing the Iroquois had in mind. They still leaned toward English trade and English rum and to the belief that by a combination of the lake tribes and those of the west and the Mississippi region the French interlopers might be driven from the land. So though there were many florid gestures, the prisoners who were to be the symbol of the repentance were not returned.

While Frontenac was holding his conferences at Quebec, Major Peter Schuyler was calling his own gatherings at Albany and was working just as assiduously to keep the Iroquois from signing any peace and to keep them in a warlike spirit. He assured his hearers that if they made peace with the French they would be slaves forever.

This talk, too, the Iroquois took with a pinch of salt. They argued that the English were happy to call them allies, but that being allies was a two-way bargain and the English had not contributed their share. They were happy to see the French attacked, but they did nothing to support their Indian allies. These argued that they could not fight the French alone, but if the English would agree to fight with them, there would be no more talk of peace with the French.

That was about how Frontenac had figured the situation. He suspected that the English had no troops to spare for such a venture as a renewed attack. Perhaps he suspected their further difficulty, that they could not come to an understanding even among themselves. Argued that way, it was quickly evident that Indian policy was to play both ends against the middle and that while this attitude persisted gestures of friendship were unlikely to get anywhere. He was not a man for half measures. There was no logical stopping point in his thinking between a negotiated peace and outright war. Now it was the latter on which he had decided.

The English wouldn't intervene in the fighting, despite their protests that the Iroquois were subjects of King William of Orange. It only remained to make sure that the wavering tribes would not make common cause with the Iroquois and attack the colony while Frontenac was engaged in his program of disciplining them. The way to assure that was to sow a spirit of bitter antagonism between them.

It was the old war of intrigue and senseless cruelty over again. How much of it resulted from the hardening sensibilities of people who had lived too long under a dire threat, how much from the prevailing assumption that duplicity was a sound and useful diplomatic practice, it is difficult to say. Undoubtedly the plan had its basis in the mistaken belief that the more prisoners the French could make their Indian allies torture and destroy, the less likelihood there was of co-operation among the various Indian groups. Such actions were encouraged even while peace negotiations were in progress. So there was little to choose between the tactics of the two parties.

It is understandable that fear and anger might press duplicity to horrifying ends. It did in the case of seven Iroquois who came to Michilimackinac. Whether they came as traders or as emissaries of the Iroquois masquerading as traders remains in doubt. There were sufficient occasions when prisoners, taken by friendly tribes, had turned out to be bearers of such messages to give color to the suspicion. But the French didn't pause for elaborate inquiries. Two of the seven were knifed as they stepped from their canoes. The Hurons immediately came to the aid of the attacked. They gave every evidence of being deeply outraged at the unprovoked assault and determined to protect the remainder of the party. A little persuasion induced them, however, to relinquish one of the number, an Iroquois chief. In order that the Ottawas might also become involved, they were invited to join in a feast to "drink the broth of an Iroquois." The truth, however, was that the unfortunate Iroquois never became broth. He was tortured with red-hot gun barrels until popular ferocity had been suitably aroused among his Indian protectors. They continued the torturing until weary, finally cutting the victim to pieces and each eating his share.

This incident happened while La Mothe Cadillac commanded at the post. No doubt the gusto belonged to the Indians. Yet it is difficult to hold the commander, who did not intervene, entirely free of guilt. Even were one so disposed, there is a letter in his own hand referring to an occasion when four prisoners were somewhat similarly treated. He wrote: "If any more prisoners are brought to me, I promise that their fate will be no sweeter."

It is not difficult to understand that such happenings could hardly create an atmosphere that encouraged peace. It is understandable, too, that the Iroquois might be too shrewd to relieve the French of all blame for such happenings. These weren't isolated cases. Frontenac himself is said to have turned over for burning a prisoner captured by his own soldiers. He wasn't burned, but that was more by chance than anything else. The soldiers had hamstrung the captive, as a precaution against escape, and he died of loss of blood before the ceremonies could begin.

Sometime later four Iroquois prisoners were burned in Montreal, with some of the citizens co-operating with their allies. There is no suggestion that Callières, governor of the city and a kindly and devoted man, would willingly countenance cruelty. Yet he did write to the minister explaining that this event was a reprisal for Indian depredations. That very well may have been true, for neither side seems to have had a monopoly of such practices.

One thing was very clear to later observers, if it wasn't at the time. This sort of thing was adding to the danger of the colony. It offered no compensating benefits. It wasn't creating an impossible barrier between the Iroquois and the lesser tribes. Such practices were more or less common among them and could be forgiven. But no such understanding covered the French. Their misdeeds would be remembered. Peace with the Iroquois was a very distant dream indeed.

Frontenac had come to see this. He recognized that the time for diplomacy had passed, even for this direct and ruthless form of diplomacy. The only way to deal with the Iroquois was to teach them a lesson they would not easily forget. It could hardly be called a new policy. La Barre had proposed it and had been negotiated out of his intention before the final stroke. Denonville had actually tried it but had fallen short of the necessary ruthlessness. This would be the third such attempted lesson in the course of a dozen years. Frontenac could be ruthless enough when the occasion demanded, and sometimes when it didn't. Yet he might be no more successful than the others. It was the chance he took.

The chance was taken with the more enthusiasm because he had convinced himself that the necessary first move in such a lesson was the rebuilding of Fort Frontenac. He was unquestionably right in this. But not always do inclination and obligation jibe so neatly.

This decision, once made, the fat was really in the fire. If the governor was convinced that Fort Frontenac should be resurrected, the intendant was unalterably opposed. It was characteristic of intendants that they should be out of sympathy with governors. In the checks and balances that autocracy needed to sustain itself this conflict of opinions was highly desirable. It kept both officials from developing delusions as to the reach of their own authority.

One reason for the two being at perpetual cross purposes was that many of the governor's activities involved expenditures, while the responsibility of the intendant was to be forever setting limits to anything of the kind. Intendant Champigny was by no means the perpetually snarling opponent that Duchesneau, intendant in Frontenac's earlier governorship, had been. Champigny had a heart and a sneaking respect and fondness for the old governor. While their conflict was incessant, it never reached the bitter hatred that had resulted in making the association of Frontenac and Duchesneau so utterly impossible that Louis, unable to untangle the question of who was most to blame, had to end by recalling both.

Champigny, though of a very different spirit, was not weak, and while the contests with the governor were less virulent they were hardly less incessant. The steady flow of charge and countercharge to the King and his Minister of Colonies might easily have set them thinking rather despairingly that all this had happened before.

The fault certainly was not all on one side. The governor was bent on keeping the record straight, and he undoubtedly felt that this required that it should be kept just as he himself wished. He wrote the minister, Pontchartrain, "If you will not be so good as to look closely into the true state of things here, I shall always be exposed to detraction, and forced to make new apologies, which is very hard for a person so full of zeal and uprightness as I am. . . . I have long tried to combat these artifices, but I confess I no longer feel strength to resist them, and must succumb at last, if you will not have the goodness to give me strong support."

Even such appeals left the minister unmoved. At least unmoved by sympathy. "This dispute you have had with M. de Champigny," he wrote with crisp decisiveness, "is without cause, and I confess I cannot comprehend how you could have acted as you have done. . . . It is deplorable," he went on almost plaintively, "that instead of using my good will to gain favors from His Majesty, you compel me to make excuses for a violence . . . in which you indulge wantonly, nobody can tell why."

The patience of the minister and the King was due to be strained still farther. Fort Frontenac was the reason. Champigny was deeply upset by the very thought of its restoration and the effort and the costs involved. He was not a soldier. He had been under the influence of Denonville who was, and who had thought the post a millstone about the neck of the colony. He did not properly assess the weakness that had resulted in this way of thought. He could not himself fully understood its strategic significance. All he could see was the cost. As for its significance, he fell back on those rather time-worn charges that the fort would be used by Frontenac and the friends he favored for purposes of private trade they might divert from Montreal, where it would be subject to the assessments of the royal treasury.

Intendant Champigny was highly vocal in the matter. He protested to the minister. He wasn't particularly scrupulous in his charges, but he was thorough; and the minister, who, like the King, was naturally opposed to the expansion of the colony, found the arguments readily believable.

Shrewdly Frontenac had expected just such a campaign. He had also anticipated what the answer would be. He proposed now to do as he willed about Fort Frontenac before authority should forbid it. He was a great believer in the forceful arguments of an accomplished fact.

Deaf to the shrill protests of the intendant, he started an expedition on its way. It was strong and it was schooled to move fast. It was composed of seven hundred men, a mixed group of artisans and soldiers. They were under the command of the Marquis de Crisasy. The marquis perhaps was not one of the most noble characters of history. He was a Neapolitan by birth, and his title stemmed from there. He had left his own country for his country's good, with an unsatisfied charge of treason hanging over his head. It was this, probably, that led him to seek service under the French King, and in a country where his presence would not be obtrusive. Little is known of his relation with Frontenac. He was not moved by the open protests of the intendant and he could act quickly and get a job done. These were qualities to win the governor's attention.

It was well that De Crisasy could act promptly. His expedition was scarcely a day on the way from Montreal when a letter was brought to Frontenac at Quebec. It bore the official signature of the Minister of Colonies. Pontchartrain had written, in words that could not well be mistaken, of the plan to restore Fort Frontenac. How much of definiteness came from the intendant's representations, how much from the King's opinion and his own, is difficult to say. It is not difficult at all to know what had been decided. The whole plan "must absolutely be abandoned."

Whether a copy went to the intendant, or whether the news just filtered along the unofficial grapevine, no one knows. But it is known that Champigny must have learned of the prohibition almost as soon as the governor. He hurried to Frontenac to demand that the expedition be recalled immediately. Most people in the governor's position would have seen the wisdom of such a course and would have followed it promptly. But Frontenac temporized. De Crisasy, he knew, would by now be a good day's travel from Montreal. It would take days even to reach Montreal with such an order, and all the time the expedition would be getting farther and farther away. Some additional days were lost in this argument until there was no longer much purpose in demanding recall.

That was quickly proven. About a month after the expedition had left, Cristasy was back in Montreal. He could report a good job done. As it turned out, the damage to the fort hadn't been as serious as had been thought. Valrenne, in his haste to obey Governor Denonville's order to destroy it and get his forces to safety, had mined the walls all right. He had heard the mines explode but he hadn't waited to see the result, and his report overstressed the destruction. With seven hundred eager workers, the task of restoration had not been too difficult. Fort Frontenac was once more a factor in the defense of New France. It now had a permanent garrison of forty-eight men and was provisioned for a year, all for the reasonable total cost of sixteen thousand francs. Frontenac was as pleased as the intendant was disapproving.

All the advantage seemed to be on the intendant's side. Pontchartrain had been definite enough about the Fort Frontenac project to satisfy anyone. The scheme "must absolutely be abandoned." Yet there Fort Frontenac was, good as new, garrisoned and provisioned for any eventuality. It was a situation that would require explaining. Even Frontenac, used to devious ways in achieving his own ends, could see that.

When the bill for sixteen thousand francs was presented for something that shouldn't have happened, the situation was likely to be difficult. There was only one strategy that gave any promise of avoiding the wrath that was due to come. It was to create a diversion; a diversion that would serve either to distract attention from this incident or give it a new justification. A final and effective lesson given the Iroquois offered just such a promise, and again it fitted in happily with the governor's inclinations.

He began at once to make plans for what he must have realized would be his last expedition. There was to be no question this time whether the wasps had been destroyed.

There was one quality that Frontenac undoubtedly had. He could always convince himself. He was quite sure now that the rebuilding of Fort Frontenac had been a necessary prelude to the great lesson that he felt the Iroquois must be taught for the final security of the colony.

There isn't much doubt that had the Iroquois waited for this lesson it would have been rather final and the Iroquois confederacy would have ceased to be an important factor in Canadian affairs. But the Iroquois were not blindly patriotic. When it appeared that fortune was against them they disappeared and prepared to fight another day.

Of course no leader could foretell this, so Frontenac set about making this expedition one that would overawe the confederacy for all time. It had to be with the forces he had available, as the Fort Frontenac affair rather suggested that it might not be a good time to make new appeals. Also, he had appealed the year before for reinforcements and had been sent some five hundred new troops. On arrival, however, these turned out to be mainly boys of fifteen or sixteen years who needed aging and conditioning before they could be useful in New World fighting. There were some four regiments of regulars, some eight hundred men, who could be used, and of course there was the Canadian militia, which would considerably more than double that number. Some five hundred Indians certainly could be secured from the surrounding missions. There was the additional probability that La Mothe Cadillac would be coming from Michilimackinac with a large contingent. Altogether it promised to be the greatest expedition ever staged on the continent, outnumbering even Denonville's great expedition of a dozen years before.

The governor was well on in his seventies, but he had no other intention than of commanding the expedition in person. With him were some stout fighters of similar determination. Callières was to lead the van. The Montreal governor was a martyr to gout, which made it an agony to put a foot to the ground. It never occurred to him, however, that this was ample reason for staying at home. All it suggested to him was that he needed a horse. Considering that the expedition must go by canoes and bateaux on an expedition that would take weeks and would eventually end in marches through all but impenetrable forest, it was not a suggestion that would have occurred to everyone. So it was that the one reluctant voyageur of the whole expedition was Callières' horse, an animal that somehow managed to ride the bateau as it leaped and swerved through racing waters, to arrive in usable condition and to become one of the unsung heroes of the expedition. There was De Ramesay, with the hint of his ancestral Scottish hills still coloring his name if not his speech. There was Vaudreuil, who had hurried up to be a last-minute addition to Denonville's great and disappointing effort. And there was Frontenac himself, with the blood running strongly in his old veins and his old skill coming back to him as he took the field again.

It was the fourth of July 1696 when the forces that had rendezvoused at Montreal set out on their great crusade. Headed by a swarm of Indian canoes, the expedition finally drew away from Lachine, just above the great rapids. Callières with his two regiments of regulars dispersed in canoes headed the more organized troops. Following them the various bateaux loaded with cannon, mortars, rockets, provisions, and Callières' horse.

Not far behind was Frontenac's canoe, surrounded by those of his staff and guard, and behind them De Ramesay and his horde of Canadians and Vaudreuil with the remaining regiments of regulars bringing up the rear. Undoubtedly it must have been an impressive sight.

Fifteen days of fighting with river and rapids brought the force to restored Fort Frontenac. They waited there a week to rest and reorganize and to receive the Indian reinforcements Cadillac had promised. When the week had passed and these had not come Frontenac lost patience and decided to go without them. On the twenty-sixth they gained the southern shore of the lake. Two days later the expedition reached the mouth of the Oswego River with their four hundred canoes and bateaux.

Here was the road that led straight to the heart of the Iroquois country. It was a rough road of white water and tangled shores. This was the road through which men must cut their way, dragging their canoes and bateaux as best they could. Two days of it, and they were faced with the great falls. At this portage everything must be carried. The old governor would have stepped ashore and taken the path with the best of them, but the Indian allies would have none of it. Sturdy braves lifted his canoe on their shoulders and bore him aloft through the forest and by the rapids, shouting and laughing as they went. Beside him stumbled and straggled his staff and bodyguard, trying vainly to maintain some semblance of order. Only the stiff old figure of the hawk-eyed governor riding high in forest paths remained unaware of any lost dignity. Torches blazed about him, lighting the path with an eerie splendor. Perhaps it seemed to him a fitting setting for the King's vice-regent riding again to the wars.

There was no dignity left for those who followed, sweating men dragging the great bateaux up the portage path on rough rollers newly cut in the forest. It was backbreaking work. It was late as the last tired workers dropped to rest above the falls. With daylight they pushed on again. Vaudreuil and his regulars were marching ahead knee-deep in water for miles on end. They reached Lake Onondaga. There, near Salina, they made their camp and built the necessary fort to protect canoes and stores. Leaving a guard there, the main force pressed forward. They were in battle order now; Callières, on his horse, commanding the first line and Vaudreuil the second.

It was not a happy experience for any of them, least of all the horse. It was nine miles to the village the Indians called "Onnontague" and the French and English "Onondaga." It might have been ten times as far. The road led through dense forest, crisscrossed with fallen trees, over outcroppings of rock by swamps and thickets matted with vines.

Progress might easily have been stopped but that the officer who pioneered the way was not given to stopping. He was Daniel d'Auger, the Sieur de Subercase. It was the same Subercase who had commanded the forces on that dreadful night at Lachine, the one man who was ready and eager to move and had been restrained only by Governor Denonville's stern order. Then the Iroquois had been attacking. Now the shoe was on the other foot and no obstacle was likely to delay him for long. Behind him, he knew, was another governor, one who didn't vacillate. He was an old man now, this governor. He rode in an armchair instead of a canoe. But still he sat erect, eyes bright, pressing forward, still in command.

When they reached the village, all that remained of it was a mass of smoldering embers among the vast surrounding maize fields. There were no defenders, unless it was the stark bodies of two dead French prisoners left behind by the retreating Indians. The Onondagas had fully planned to defend themselves, and the warriors from two adjoining villages had come to their support.

Father Jacques de Lamberville records in the *Relations* that an Iroquois who had been taken prisoner by the French three months before had managed to escape and had brought the breathless word that the French forces numbered six thousand men, a pardonable exaggeration considering the impressiveness of the expedition, and that they were fanning out in all directions to attack the various towns. This brought a change in thinking. After all, patriotism began at home, and soon the defenders were slipping away. The people of Onondaga realized that there was little possibility of a successful defense of their homes. They had fired the village and retreated.

There wasn't much left to destroy at Onondaga except the crops, and this tiresome job was thoroughly done. In the course of it the French managed to round up an old lame woman and an old man of eighty years who had been discovered hiding in a hollow tree. The old woman was claimed by some relatives and in a spirit of good will was released to them. It was perhaps too much to expect that the old man should also meet such a kindly fate. The Indians were looking for a victim, and he seemed to fill the bill. He didn't make his chances any better by deriding his captors. With considerable relish the Hurons promptly set about the task of burning him. When Frontenac heard of it he sent orders that if the victim had not been burned all over he should be spared. But the victim's tauntings had resulted in such thorough measures that there was no purpose in sparing him. The best they could do for him, to satisfy the governor's orders, was to dispatch him with a blow on the head.

He was one of the few casualties of the expedition. A Christian Iroquois and two Abenaki had strayed from the expedition and had met a somewhat similar end. There were the two French prisoners discovered in the smoldering remains of Onondaga, and some few had been drowned in the rapids. But the casualties had been almost negligible, on the whole.

Evidently the story of the six thousand fighters had gained considerable credence. The Oneidas, centered about a town called Onneiout, about forty or fifty miles distant from Onondaga, had sent a message to Frontenac suggesting a willingness to make peace before further damage was done. Frontenac replied that he would consider the suggestion on condition that the Oneidas all migrate to Canada and settle there. To give point to this suggestion he sent Vaudreuil with a detachment of seven hundred men, including three hundred Indians. But something went wrong with the negotiations. Some thirty prisoners were taken and the town and the surrounding crops were destroyed.

There was talk now of marching against the Cayugas, thus rounding out the expedition. Father Lamberville records that "Monsieur the Governor and Monsieur de Callières were of the opinion that the attack should go on, but the majority opinion was against them." He explained that the soldiers' shoes were worn out and that they wanted to get home for the harvest.

Other reports had it that Callières had offered to remain for the winter and to renew the attack in the spring but that Frontenac had vetoed the suggestion. One of the better-known historians expressed the opinion that Frontenac had no thought of letting anyone else secure too large a share of the credit. That hardly seems probable. At best, there wasn't much credit to share, though in his reports the governor did his utmost to make it appear a magnificent success. It should have been. It had cost fifty thousand écus. But certainly he had generously given Callières the major credit for the success.

Frontenac had reported glibly: "Sire, the benediction which heaven has ever showered upon Your Majesty's arms has extended even to this new world; whereof we have had proof in the expedition I have just made against the Onondagas." He spoke of the long consideration of the enterprise and of the difficulties that have made it seem imprudent, and he continued, "I should never have resolved to undertake it, if I had not last year established an entrepôt which made my communications more easy." Having thus described and justified the restoration of Fort Frontenac as the creation of an entrepôt, he went on to enlarge on the expedition and how the famine, which they had prepared for their enemies, "will destroy more than we could have killed by sword and gun."

Had there been a famine, undoubtedly that would have been true. One reason that there was no famine to act so helpfully was the prompt action of Governor Fletcher in command at New York. Possibly the recent charges of the Iroquois, that the English were happy to encourage their Indian allies to fight the French provided they demanded no assistance from the English, had flicked the governor in the raw. He had word of the expedition against the Onondagas, who had always been claimed as subjects of King William, while the lands of the Iroquois confederacy, also claimed as his, had now been invaded.

He called the council of New York to decide what was to be done. The council, after some deliberation, decided realistically, "It would be very grievous to take the people from their labor." That was the usual argument, but they had a clincher: "There is, likewise, no money to answer the charges thereof." After all, Onondaga was quite a step away from New York and even Albany. And the tendency of the day in the English colonies was mainly to disregard what they could not see.

There were, however, certain citizens with somewhat larger vision. These assured Governor Fletcher the money he needed to provide the relieving force he wished. But there was still no public enthusiasm for the undertaking. Fletcher called on Connecticut and New Jersey for support. These avoided any possible argument by simply making no reply to the appeal. So Governor Fletcher went to Albany with his scattering of forces, hoping to add to them there. Instead he received word that Frontenac was well on his way home. There was no need for him to support his Indian allies by arms, but they would need food, and this he could and did provide. So the famine that was to have supplemented the work of sword and gun never materialized. The great expedition was little more effective than those that had preceded it. Violence had not made friends. It had not even filled enemies with fear.

CHAPTER XII

MEASURE OF A MAN

Frontenac renews his bickering with the intendant. Tacitly he refuses to obey the orders to recall his lieutenants and destroy his forts and trading posts. The Treaty of Ryswick leaves many problems unsolved. Rejoicing over peace ends with a typical challenge. Frontenac's illness and death.

THE old governor returned from the wars not as a man of peace but belligerent as ever. He was quickly at odds again with the intendant, the Iroquois, and the English.

His conflict with Intendant Champigny was renewed with hardly a pause. Few would question that the governor was right in the basic issue about which the conflict centered. Being so, he emphasized how possible it was to be right in the wrong way. An iota of diplomacy might have made it possible to convince authority of the soundness of his views or, at worst, to come to a workable compromise. That was never Frontenac's way. It probably was the basic fault that withheld from him the stature of true greatness. Often as he protested his need and hope for official co-operation, the facts seemed to suggest that a hearty conflict with authority was, for him, a stimulant rather than a deterrent.

The intendant, the bishop and the Jesuits, and a considerable following of merchants and traders were for setting bounds to the colony. The intendant was probably moved by the economies this tighter organization would permit and the greater assurance that all the business of the colony would pay a substantial tribute to the

King's treasury. The bishop and clergy, concerned more with the souls than the bodies of men, resented the way less devoted persons were encroaching on their established parishes. They argued, with more than a little reason in many cases, that the debaucheries of the forest trader undid the good that men might do. The merchants and the traders had their natural stake in the local community and felt, again with some reason, that the wider the horizon the less important the local community became.

All these wanted what the King wanted, to make New France a replica of the old, compactly settled and easily controlled. He liked order. He liked authority. He liked subservience, and all these suffered as men's eyes turned more and more to the far horizons.

The far horizons were Frontenac's country. They always had been. The men who caught his fancy, quite naturally, were the daring spirits who had left the Old World because it had refused them equality and opportunity or had offered them opportunities that could not satisfy hearts as restless as theirs. These were his friends and he stood by them loyally; for his own ends, it was often claimed, but there is no hint of proof to support these charges, unless it is that these gave substance to his dreams.

He was as loyal to his Indian allies as he was to his French friends. He would deal with them as a father and defend them as a brother. The empire he had envisaged, uncertain as his claims might be, was not uncertain to him. He was ready to defend it against the encroachments of the English, who, to his thinking, were interlopers. The trading posts and forts, which marked the progress of the amazing adventurers who were the governor's friends, were slowly marking out an empire that Louis XIV didn't understand and didn't want.

Frontenac had argued for it with his blunt and pugnacious eloquence. But Champigny and the bishop argued more tellingly on the other side. It is always easier, of course, to win an argument that dovetails with preconceived opinions, and this was so with the King. He moved promptly and far more comprehensively than the intendant had planned. There were to be no more forest trading permits. All the ranging spirits were to be ordered home and compelled to stay there on pain of the less pleasant surroundings of the King's galleys. The forts and forest posts were to be abandoned and destroyed, even the newly restored Fort Frontenac. Immediate peace was to be made with the Iroquois, let happen what would to the Indian allies of France.

To have obeyed such orders would have been to return New France to the fear and despair that had been its lot before Frontenac had returned. Even the intendant knew that the orders had gone too far. There was no power in the land that could have enforced them. Somehow, whether that was made clear and they were tacitly withdrawn, or whether they were just allowed to fall into quiet oblivion, the result was the same. The adventurers were not recalled. The forts and trading posts were not destroyed. The Indian allies were not betrayed. Frontenac had lost the argument but, as so often happened, he had won his own way.

Frontenac's great lesson to the Iroquois seems to have sputtered out just as had Denonville's lesson. Yet Denonville's lesson ended with the tragedy of the Lachine massacre. Frontenac's ended with the Iroquois appearing at Quebec with overtures of peace. They had brought none of the prisoners they were holding, but they promised to return in the spring, and this time the prisoners would be brought. They left a hostage to prove it. By spring they had changed their minds and sent a message instead. They were so grief-ridden at the death of their great chief Black Kettle that they had no strength to travel. They asked for the return of their hostage and declared themselves eager to make peace with Onontio. They were very definite that this peace would not include France's Indian allies. Probably it never occurred to Frontenac that this was exactly the peace the King had ordered him to conclude. The reply didn't suggest any such intention. "Tell the chiefs," the old governor snapped, "that if they must needs stay at home to cry about a trifle, I will give them something to cry for. Let them bring me every prisoner, French and Indian, and make a treaty that shall include all my children, or they shall feel my tomahawk again."

In Europe, meanwhile, peace negotiations were finally bringing an end to eight weary years of war that had left both France and England all but bankrupt.

In the château at Ryswick, near The Hague, that summer of 1697, there was bickering and argument. At times it was so embittered that had it not been that the representatives of England sat in one wing of the château and those of France in the other, while the representatives of Sweden, acting as mediators, occupied the *salle* separating the two, conflict might have broken out again.

The compelling force toward conciliation was that Louis XIV had other irons in the fire. He was interested in getting an agreement that would assure a friend of France being accepted as the successor to the throne of Spain, presently occupied by the ailing Charles II. Such an agreement, he felt, would assure that the House of Bourbon could dominate both Europe and America. It was a lordly prospect and made him unusually tractable in what he considered matters of lesser import. It wasn't surprising that the signers of the treaty should concentrate on the matters that touched them closely rather than on distant affairs affecting another continent.

Louis, with a shrewd trade in view, was ready to recognize William as King of England now that the nuisance value of James II had worn rather thin. It was a gesture that cost little, considering that William had in fact occupied the throne for a matter of eight years. The agreement that Anne should be William's successor cost more. Anne was a Protestant, a sister of the beloved Queen Mary, and so assured of a welcome. Louis would have preferred it, of course, could the succession have gone to her younger brother, James Francis Edward, the Chevalier de St. George. He was an ardent Catholic like his father, and, like him, the chevalier had his own nuisance value really better than Louis understood. The chevalier could stir the Jacobites of the Scottish highlands. On several occasions he set them to spilling their own and England's blood. And after him his son, yet to be born, the Bonnie Prince Charlie, a figure of history and romance. Between them they would certainly cause enough problems. Of course Louis couldn't know that they would do so much better in that regard than the stubborn and intractable James II. But he was wise in his estimate that the Chevalier de St. George had a very slim chance indeed of ever reaching the throne of England, and it wasn't an issue to be raised when he was doing his best to ingratiate himself with his English neighbors.

All this was to have its bearing on a distant continent. But it was still a fact that none of the problems that had been bedeviling the new continent for those eight years was settled at Ryswick. The French continued to dominate Hudson's Bay. But there was the loophole that England had Fort Albany on the bay restored to her. It wasn't quite a French preserve. In Newfoundland the position was reversed. England dominated the country but France still had its toe hold at Placentia Harbor. Temporarily at least Acadia did come back to France, but there was no settlement or relinquishment of the French claims that she owned New York and the uncertain allegiance of the Iroquois. The claim, in the case of New York, rested on an issue of prior discovery; in the case of the Iroquois, there was the unassailable fact that the Jesuits had been more concerned over Iroquois souls than the Puritans had been. There was really no settlement of the controversial questions that were a perpetual irritant, keeping alive the spirit of conflict between New France and New England.

There could be no denying the fact that, however uncertain their welcome, the English had secured a footing on the coast of the New World. France was unwilling to concede their right to it and planned, when the opportunity arose, to push them back into the ocean and, opportunity or no, to contain them in the narrow ocean strip and to permit no straying westward.

Almost the only controversial issue that was faced at all was the question of the boundary between Acadia and New England. The English set this boundary at the St. Croix River and the French at the Kennebec, with the Baron St. Castin maintaining his dusky kingdom in the lands between. The machinery was set up to decide this vexed point, but the decision was long in coming.

Though the treaty was signed on September 20, 1697, it was July of the following year before Frontenac got the official notice. With it was the King's proclamation to his people in Canada. It began, perhaps a little overhopefully: "The moment has arrived, ordained by Heaven, to reconcile the nations." However affairs might be in Europe, there wasn't too much evidence even of a will toward reconciliation in the New World, let alone the achieved fact. Five months had passed since the signing of the treaty before Frontenac received the first hint of it in words dropped by a party of Dutch and Indian traders. They couldn't have been said to be very peaceful months. Some little time after this first whisper of peace Major Peter Schuyler arrived at Quebec bearing copies of the treaty. His arrival did indeed have some evidence of a peaceful intent. He had with him all the French prisoners who had been held by the English. There was also a courteous message from the new governor of New York, the Earl of Bellomont. He advised Frontenac that he would also order the Iroquois subjects of the English Crown to deliver all the prisoners held by them. He asked in return a repatriation of all the Iroquois prisoners held by the French. It was an olive branch of sorts, but it didn't stir any warm reciprocal feeling.

In spite of what the deliberators at Ryswick had decided, Frontenac still held to his own opinion, and he wasn't ready to accept friendly gestures on any other terms. He wrote the New York governor to give himself no trouble about prisoners held by the Iroquois. The Iroquois, he explained, were French citizens in rebellion against their King. They had seen their error and had sent word of their repentance and their wish for peace. If they did not come promptly to make good their words, he would have to use such force as was needed to compel them.

The Earl of Bellomont, his olive branch thus cavalierly treated, promptly dropped it for an approach more to his liking. This carried no hint of appeasement. He wrote, in response to Frontenac's letter, that he had warned his Indian subjects to defend themselves and had assured them that he was prepared to send soldiers to their assistance should that be necessary.

Sober second thought did less than nothing to modify the temper of his thinking. A day or two later he was writing, still more emphatically, that he had actually sent his lieutenant governor with troops to join with the Indians in opposing the proposed attack. "If need be," he added, "I will arm every man in the provinces under my government to repel you and to make reprisals for the damage which you will commit on our Indians." This while the assured blessings of peace had just begun to hover over the land!

The bearer of this missive was one not calculated to achieve for himself an overly hearty welcome. It was Captain John Schuyler, who, following the attack on Schenectady, had staged the first sanguinary and senseless raid on La Prairie. But Frontenac had the soldier's quick forgetfulness of the wounds of old wars. He received John Schuyler pleasantly enough, but not quite so well the message that he brought. "My Lord Bellomont threatens me," he said a little stiffly. "Does he think I am afraid of him?" No one seeing him could have thought anything of the kind, and obviously John Schuyler was too shrewd to think so.

The spirit of peace was about. The Sunday that followed was the day Louis had set aside for the *Te Deum* that was to mark the accomplishment of peace. It was an occasion to make a man forget small animosities. The cathedral was packed with people rejoicing that at long last peace had come to them. No one could appreciate their feeling who had not lived under the shadow of fear for so long. In the evening there was a great banquet in the château. The leaders of New France were there, and in their midst their honored guest, John Schuyler. It was a symbol of the good will that marked the gathering. In such a spirit Frontenac rose and proposed a toast to King William. Captain John Schuyler, not to be outdone, proposed the health of King Louis. There was another toast proposed by Frontenac to the esteemed governor of New York, the Earl of Bellomont. Then followed the solemn proclamation of peace as the King had ordered.

The streets were bright with lights, and bonfires blazed in every vacant space, making the fortress city stand out as a place of magic. The guns in the fort on Cape Diamond boomed out their message of peace, and the ships in the basin below the cliff sent an answering blast.

The festivities were long, and the old governor was tiring. But he still had work to do. Captain Schuyler would be leaving in the morning, and he must bear Frontenac's message to the earl. The light of the dying bonfires of peace were still casting an uncertain glow through the windows of the old governor's cabinet. He sat down to write.

Somehow the spirit of the day seemed to have grown distant and uncertain, and the hours of mutual toasting and good will seemed like something shadowy and long ago. The old governor's hand may have trembled a little as he wrote, but not his heart. "I am determined," wrote the stiff old martinet, "to pursue my course without flinching; and I request you not to try to thwart me by efforts which will prove useless. All the protection and aid you tell me that you have given and will continue to give the Iroquois against the terms of the treaty will not cause me much alarm, nor make me change my plans, but rather, on the contrary, engage me to pursue them still more."

Brave words, if perhaps they were not all wisdom, perchance brushing aside the little help and hope that peace had brought and leaving in their place an irrepressible something. It was not to be halted by glib words proclaiming peace where there was no peace, only the remorseless conflict of thinking that was worlds apart; that could find no ground for peaceful coexistence; that must subdue or be subdued. "I am determined to pursue," wrote the old governor. But the hand that traced the words shook a little. His face was gray and tired. Only his eyes looked forward, stern and unwavering.

Days passed. Outwardly the peace was not broken. Instead, the governor took up again his continuing quarrel with Intendant

Champigny. The disputes were mostly on matters of small moment, but they had deep roots. Most of them came back in the end to some phase of the old issues—whether New France should draw into itself, restricting its boundaries as the King and his ministers wished, or reach out to new and ever-widening horizons—the New World that Frontenac and his galaxy of adventurers had constantly before them.

To all appearances Frontenac fought and planned with all his old vigor and decisiveness. But when the last report for the Minister of Colonies had been written and the last ship had sailed away for France, beginning one of those periods of six months of no word coming or going between the Old World and the New, which the governor had used so often and so adroitly, there came a change in him. It seemed at first that he had just lost something of his accustomed vigor. Perhaps it was only that the immediate need for action had passed and he was tired. Perhaps it was only that the chill possessive winter was closing about the château on the heights and the snowy, perilous streets of Quebec.

Early in November he took to his bed. A little rest and his marvelous vitality would reassert itself. So he probably thought, and so others thought. As the days passed, a question grew in men's minds. It was started perhaps by the unfamiliar sight of Bishop St. Vallier entering the château. He had not been a familiar there. Nor, for that matter, had the intendant. He and the governor had been at odds since the day Frontenac had returned. It was not like the bitter broils that had marked the conflict with the earlier intendant, Duchesneau. Underneath the present bickering there was a sense of mutual respect. It did nothing, however, to qualify the definiteness or the persistency of his official opposition. Yet now the intendant was a frequent caller. Somehow it caught the attention of the people. They stood clustered in little groups, wondering perhaps why they were there at all. They had nothing much to say to one another once the first burst of comment and inquiry was over. There was none of the careless gossip of other days.

Possibly, could they have realized it, they had only come to be near one who had brought courage in days when courage seemed far away indeed. Perhaps they were remembering, not how fear had suddenly left them, but how its character had changed. The coming of one man had made the difference. It had brought resolution where before there had been only a breathless waiting for the inevitable. That, the old governor had meant to them. They had no part in the bitter controversies that had raged so constantly between authority and authority. This had nothing to do with them. The right or wrong of it seemed to depend only on who was doing the telling. But there was one thing they remembered of themselves, without needing word from anyone. This man had brought hope when hope was dead. If any looked ahead with courage, even today, wasn't it because of that old stern face and that old but steady heart? So they waited.

In his room looking down on the snowy slopes and out over the frozen river perhaps it came to Frontenac that he would not see the spring again, the spring that was always so vivid with new projects. If the thought occurred to him he set it aside for more practical things. Repining was as useless to him as counting costs. Get the thing done and let the results take care of themselves.

On the twenty-second of November he sent for his notary. Sitting straight and tall in his accustomed easy chair in his own room, he dictated his will. It was a simple enough document. It made no provision for the vast sums his enemies claimed had come to him through his close friendship with the men who had taken the names of New France to the far corners of the continent. Strangely enough, of all the people he had known, it was a one-time enemy whom he remembered in his kindness. It was to Champigny, the battling intendant, that he left the crucifix of aloewood. It had been dear to Frontenac because it had once belonged to Madame de Monmart, his sister, who had died long years ago. To Madame de Champigny he left a reliquary that he had been accustomed to wear. They were very personal gifts, but not of great value. For the rest, he left fifteen hundred livres for daily Masses on his behalf for a year, and thereafter once a year forever. And he added carefully that these Masses should be changed to include his wife upon her death.

To his wife, whom he had hardly seen in thirty years, he left all that remained of his property. It was little enough; little enough to challenge forever those who accused him of profiting at his country's cost.

There was one other request. It was that on his death his heart should be removed and encased in a small casket of lead or silver and sent to his wife, that she might have this tribute of remembrance and that she might ultimately deposit it in the family tomb of the Church of St. Nicolas des Champs.

Having set all this down, the old governor was weary and returned to his bed. Never in life would he rise from it again. His good friend, the Récollet father Olivier Goyer, came to him and with dimming eyes administered extreme unction.

Daylight was passing and candles had been lighted that late afternoon of the twenty-eighth of November. The old chieftain lay on his bed. He was like a soldier waiting for his call. It found him with his mind alert and his eyes still bright. He was nearing the end of the seventy-eighth year of a life that had been crowned with incident and successes, and many, many mistakes.

When they had encased his heart, as he had asked, they sent it by messenger to the still lovely aging lady who bore his name. Madame Frontenac still carried her head as high as any. She stood there stiffly. She did not want a heart in death, she said, that had not been hers in life. It was pride, of course, not truth. In no crisis great or small in his life had Frontenac failed to turn to her for help, and never had the help been lacking.

Yet, perhaps she was right. Perhaps the heart of every devoted man is part of the work of his life and belongs where that work belongs. It may well be that she was thinking that, more than most, that proud, courageous, stubborn, and unruly heart belonged to Canada.

So when it was returned they opened his coffin in the crypt of the church of the Récollets and returned the old heart to the body it had served so well. There are those who think this story is apocryphal. Perhaps it is, though the great Francis Parkman records it and gives his evidence. But does its truth matter so much? In spirit, if not in fact, it remains the truth.

One of the poignant records of those days is the letter Intendant Champigny wrote to the minister in December 1698.

"I venture to send this letter by way of New England," he wrote, "to tell you that Monsieur le Comte de Frontenac died on the 28th of last month, with the sentiments of a true Christian. After all the disputes we have had together, you will hardly believe, Monseigneur, how truly and deeply I am touched by his death. He treated me during his illness in a manner so obliging, that I should be utterly void of gratitude if I did not feel thankful to him."

On the Friday following his death the funeral was held. The Jesuits had hopefully believed that in his last hours he would forget the long animosities between them and ask for burial in the cathedral church. But he chose instead the church of the Récollets. The Jesuits hid their chagrin manfully, and the bishop himself officiated at the service. But it was the governor's friend, Father Olivier Goyer, who rose to make the final oration.

"I will not seek to dry your tears," he said, "for I cannot contain my own. After all, this is a time to weep, and never did a people weep for a better governor."

The words continued to fall on ears that were eager to listen or had grown suddenly charitable in the presence of death. But it couldn't last.

There is a copy of this great eulogy still extant that has a wider interest than the glowing words of Father Goyer assure. Interspersing each word of adulation are words of bitterly biting comment inscribed by some priestly hand. It is rather generally held that the priestly commentator was that Father Latour who was later to be the biographer of Bishop Laval.

"This disinterested man," said Father Goyer, "more busied with duty than with gain . . ."

And the written record of these words bears the critic's terse comment: "The less said about that the better."

"Who made the fortunes of others, but did not increase his own," went on the priestly orator.

"Not for want of trying," the cramped script interpolates, "and that very often in spite of his conscience and the King's order."

"Devoted to the service of his King," Father Goyer's glowing words go on, "whose majesty he represented, and whose person he loved . . ."

"Not at all," adds the critic, with more truth than timeliness. "How often has he opposed his orders, even with force and violence, to the great scandal of everybody."

So the oration continues and so the embittered retort. Every word of praise is followed by its detraction, a somber and conscientious if embittered challenge. Yet, if we cannot wholly believe the glowing words, no more can we believe the embittered criticism. Somewhere between the two, perhaps, lies the true measure of a man.

Frontenac had his enemies, and they were many and bitter. He had stern critics, and often enough they were right. He had his overweening vanity, his prejudices and his stubbornness, and they are difficult qualities to commend.

But he had something else. He had a far vision—a great vision. Had it been shared more widely, his reputation and his world might have been different. As it was, he was the early spearhead of a conflict of ideologies that had to come, at last, to final grips.

If his cause was not the best cause, at least he believed it best and served it with an unwavering heart. And if he had his enemies, he also had his friends. We do not speak here of the friends whose names are among the landmarks of history, but of the simple people who needed him; the people of Quebec who stood in the freezing streets, lost and bereft at his passing.

"Never be haughty to the humble, nor humble to the haughty." They are not his words. They were spoken by a very different man and centuries later. Perhaps Frontenac could not have phrased the thought so well. Quite probably he had never consciously thought in those terms at all. Yet, for all his buoyant, blustering, arrogant pride, they were part of the code by which he lived.

Too stubborn, too prideful, too wedded to his own desires and his own beliefs, too unmindful of others' thinking for true greatness, he had the next best thing—a heart that, having found a cause, could give it a life's devotion, a capacity to gather to him men who could share a vision, a strength to sustain the unnamed many in trusting without understanding, and a high purpose that until God's finger touched him set him fighting—often wrongly, but always valiantly—for what his heart believed.

CHAPTER XIII

INTERLUDE

Callières succeeds to the governorship of New France. His peace with the Iroquois highlighted by the death of the Rat. Founding of Detroit by Cadillac. His unhappy appointment to the governorship of Louisiana. His conflict with the crafty Scotsman, John Law, and the challenge to the Mississippi Company. Cadillac's disgrace. His ultimate justification and his unhappy death.

HISTORY has amply sustained the chastening judgment that no man is indispensable. Experience, however, has added the qualification that the passing of a man of force must leave an interlude of uncertainty and speculation.

In our own time the passing of Stalin, then head of the Soviet state, posed a world of questions. Who would succeed? How would the successor measure up to the man he replaced? Would new political policies emerge as a result? Would these mean a growing or a lessening threat? Until such questions and a multitude of others were answered or forgotten, there remained the suggestion of "time out" for reorganization. Time out, too, for developing new strategy to meet such changes.

The Peace of Ryswick, which had settled more disagreements in Europe and had done almost nothing to resolve any of the existing problems of the New World, provided this breathing space. It was an interlude in which it was possible to reassess existing policies; an interlude during which some more pressing problems might hope to find an answer.

On the death of Frontenac, Callières, the governor of Montreal, promptly moved to Quebec and assumed the larger post of governor of New France. There did not seem to be anyone anxious or able to dispute this assumption of office, and the King soon sustained it. That is not to say, however, that the appointment was unanimously approved. It was hardly to be expected. Certainly there had been no universal approval of Frontenac; and Callières, sound and devoted and well equipped for the office as he was, was not a Frontenac. Added to that, he was a sick man. Gout had tortured him for years without being able to keep him from active participation in affairs. Of late years dropsy had added to his misery. There was not much time ahead of him.

Intendant Champigny, who had felt an unexpected sorrow about the long embroilment with Frontenac, did not let that affect his general attitude. He promptly picked up the cudgels to trade blows with another governor. He began by announcing that he had never seen such hauteur since coming to the colony. One might discount this as coming from a temperament inordinately excitable had not both La Potherie and Vaudreuil added comments of a somewhat similar nature.

It is possible that Callières had a strain of vanity that his earlier history did not disclose. It is also possible that the enemies of Frontenac had passed on their enmity to one who admittedly had been his friend. It is very possible, too, that Philippe de Rigaud, Marquis de Vaudreuil, thought of himself as better material for the governorship. If so, he did not have long to wait. He first succeeded to Callières' position as governor of Montreal and on the latter's death in 1703 he followed also as governor of New France.

The always devoted Callières, on taking over Frontenac's honors and duties, set himself to the difficult task of completing his predecessor's plans. The most pressing of these, of course, was to bring the Iroquois to a proper state of submission. The Iroquois, shrewd negotiators that they were, quickly realized that they were not dealing with a Frontenac. Had they been sure that the English would support them with more than encouraging words, they would have renounced cheerfully any thought of agreement with the French, even should that lead to an open and active breach. However, they knew better than to expect anything of the kind.

So their policy was to maintain a nice balance of apparent friendship with the two while asserting their own complete independence.

They were startled and disturbed to learn that the Peace of Ryswick, signed by France and England, in enjoining peace between the two nations had also provided for concerted action should this be necessary to keep the Iroquois in control. Shrewd as they were, they didn't realize that a nation that could not induce its own units to combine for attack or protection against a common enemy was hardly likely to be able to combine with that potential enemy for punitive purposes.

Of all the things that the Iroquois did not want, any combination of English and French stood first. They had suffered heavily in the fighting and raiding of recent years. Their fighting strength was down to twelve hundred warriors, less than half of what it once had been. No inconsiderable part of these losses was represented by prisoners held by the French and their Indian allies. This was the nub of their thinking. They must avoid further conflict with the French until they had secured the return of these prisoners. In this mood they were more than ready to send a deputation to meet with the new Onontio. They would see how he responded to argument. They would concede only where it was unavoidable or where concessions were made to favor them.

They found, as they had hoped, that Callières was far from being as tough and astute a negotiator as Frontenac had been. When the ambassadors from the tribes arrived to discuss the exchange of prisoners, they brought with them thirteen women and children and a plausible story that the remainder of their prisoners had become so enamored of the life and of the Iroquois among whom they lived that they had no wish to return.

Callières, eager for peace, was ready to accept this highly dubious statement at its face value. Not so his Indian followers. They saw nothing in the Iroquois character to occasion such a quick change of heart. However, when the Iroquois agreed to meet again the next August, bringing all their prisoners with them, a temporary agreement was reached.

All that winter and the following spring representatives of the governor visited the tribes, urging them to attend the August meeting, bringing with them all their Iroquois prisoners. The governor's greatest support in this campaign came from none other than the great Huron chief Kondiaronk or, more familiarly, the Rat. He it was who had killed the former peace effort in Denonville's time and, in so doing, had been largely responsible for the massacre of Lachine. However, those were other days, and since then the Rat had secured and fully earned the friendship of the French. It was due in no small degree to his support that the Iroquois prisoners held by the lake tribes had been collected.

The Rat was both shrewd and able. He saw that the prisoners were brought. He was not confused in his estimate of the value of Iroquois promises. "Now let us see," he asked, "if the Iroquois have also obeyed . . . but I know they have not brought them." Of course he was right. The Iroquois had again brought plausible reasons why no prisoners were with them. There were promises that they would be released later. But while the other tribes had brought all their captives, the Iroquois had brought nothing. It was the old familiar story, demands and promises and no concessions.

It was the Rat who calmed the rising anger. He had urged his own and other tribes to relinquish their captives in the interest of lasting peace; now peace seemed as far away as ever. The aging warrior was burning with fever and too weak to stand. He was put in a chair and, seated, he addressed the angry tribes. For two long hours, with slumped shoulders but flashing eyes, he talked, urging against hasty judgment, painting the need for peace, for the establishment of some workable agreement. Then, too weak to say more, he was carried from the gathering. By midnight the Rat was dead.

How much of the accord that finally came was due to the stormy eloquence of the Rat, how much to the pageantry with which the French clothed his funeral, who is to say? It was a setting that Frontenac would have loved and one that he would have managed with consummate skill. There was the lying in state in the chief's own wigwam, a lonely figure stretched on a bed of beaver skins and wrapped in a scarlet blanket with gun and sword at his side.

Even the Iroquois, who had always been his foes, came in solemn procession. Sixty of them gathered about his bier while their great orator, Avenano, spoke of how the sun had covered its face at the passing of the great Huron.

The funeral was one continuous pageant. French troops headed the funeral procession, followed by sixteen Huron warriors garbed in beaver skins and with guns reversed. Then the clergy preceding the coffin borne high by six Huron warriors. And behind it the great chief's brothers and sons and with them Vaudreuil, escorting Madame Champigny, while every French officer soberly waited as three volleys rang out over the grave. There is nothing that can be added to Francis Parkman's graphic picturing of this strange scene.

It was a becoming honor. It was a noble pageant. It was an astute diplomatic gesture. The tribes were deeply impressed and warmly friendly to the French. They remembered, too, the words of their dead leader and were ready to be co-operative. It was as well. Callières sat in the open with thirteen hundred Indians grouped about him. They had come from as much as two thousand miles away. They had come with varied emotions and desires. Now their hearts were still stirred by the remembrance of the past hours. Nicholas Perrot and a score of Jesuits were there to interpret. They repeated the governor's message in five different languages. When it was finished, the chiefs stepped forward, their prisoners with them. Tribe after tribe was represented there. In the words of their leaders, "in the prisoners they had brought was the evidence of their good faith."

At last the Iroquois spokesmen arose, proud and short of speech and crafty as always. They approved of what had been said and done. They promised their obedience to the treaty. As for the prisoners, they could be sent for. They were at the disposal of the tribes. There was a great business of smoking the peace pipe, with Callières, Champigny, and Vaudreuil leading off. Historically minded La Potherie has the last word. "Thus," he says, "the labors of the late Count Frontenac were brought to a happy consummation."

Perhaps Callières wasn't quite sure of the happy consummation. All the tribes had brought their prisoners. The Iroquois had brought only promises. These they had already broken times beyond number. He tried his hand at diplomacy. He would keep the prisoners delivered by the tribes until the Iroquois made good their word to restore the prisoners they had taken.

It wasn't for nothing that the Iroquois had sent ambassadors to study the new governor. They had studied to good effect. There was no protest. "Keep them if you like." The Iroquois spokesman shrugged. "We will go home and think no more about them." Then in more friendly tones: "If you gave them to us without making trouble . . . we should have no reason to distrust your sincerity, and should be glad to send back the prisoners we took from your allies." They would never have dared such tactics with Frontenac, never dared this barefaced early version of the familiar confidence game. Frontenac would have recognized it. Callières, for all his fine qualities, had no such insight. He spoke to the tribes and earned their grudging assent to let the prisoners go. No prisoners were returned, of course. We do not know whether Callières really expected them. In so much it was another Iroquois victory. If it wasn't a deal that Frontenac would have liked or accepted, it did achieve the success of his policy. Never again were the Iroquois to be the deadly threat that they had been before the old governor returned.

There was another safeguard for the colony, and this also was partly Frontenac's plan. The good faith of the Iroquois was an uncertain security at best. What would make it secure was to make any other course hazardous. There were two roads marked out for Indian attack. They could strike across Lake Ontario from Oswego, as they had done in the attack on Lachine. This road was now blocked by the frowning bulk of Fort Frontenac. The other road was the longer one by way of the lakes to Michilimackinac and down the Ottawa. The enemy who had challenged the gallant Dollard des Ormeaux, whose heroic story is one of the breathless pages of *The White and the Gold*, had come that way. This open highway left a clear path to the very heart of the colony. It left the northern and lake Indians always open to attack from the Iroquois, their most dreaded foe. It made the threat of an Indian coalition more than a matter of idle imagining. Should either policy succeed, France would be left without an ally on the continent. Either would permit the Iroquois to dominate the Ottawa River from the north and, with it, the very heart of the colony. That was what had given Michilimackinac its first importance. It was a strategic outpost, on the flank of any invader from the north. It was vital to the life of the colony. It must either be sustained or replaced, and Cadillac spoke for replacement.

La Mothe Cadillac could not be considered an unprejudiced witness when it came to his opinion of Michilimackinac. He didn't like the post and he didn't like the people. He had been at the fort long enough to know. He had been in command for years. He knew that all Father Carheil said about its moral leprosy was true enough. It wasn't that the good father was above a certain tendency to exaggerate, but the facts wouldn't permit it. In the better part of six years that Cadillac spent there he had never once brought his wife. But, knowing that the Jesuits had a case, he hated the way they presented it, and Father Carheil was the bright peculiar star among the galaxy of those whom this gusty Gascon disliked.

The mission of Mackinac was very dear to the hearts of the Jesuits, and Cadillac knew it, and there is no questioning the fact that he was happy to recognize it as a failing cause. It wasn't only prejudice that moved him. He knew that the Hurons and the tribes of the North Superior country were openly trading with the English on Hudson's Bay. The Assiniboins had drifted away to sections nearer the present western border line between Canada and the United States. The Algonquins were to be found in the present Wisconsin country, and the Ottawas held an uncertain allegiance with the tribes in Michigan.

Michilimackinac had lost its pivotal place in the life of New France. No longer was it the center of the fur trade. All that was left to it was its far from savory reputation and the slowly dissipating hopes of its Jesuit missionaries.

When Cadillac had first proposed to Frontenac that a fort be built on the lower narrows linking Lake Erie with Lake Huron the old governor was profoundly unimpressed. Had the young Gascon not been a man after his own heart, the reaction would have been more violent and all discussion might have ended there. No doubt Frontenac was remembering how little official enthusiasm there had been for Fort Frontenac. He could well imagine how much less there would be for a project hundreds of miles farther afield. The gruff reaction didn't disturb Cadillac. He was not easily put out of countenance by authority, and he had an unshakable confidence in his own opinion. He went on talking. The governor would know better than anyone that the day of Michilimackinac was almost done. What had happened to the fur trade that had once centered there? The English had most of it. What they didn't draw north to the bay, they drew south to the lakes. He warmed to his subject, pointing out how a fort at the mouth of the straits linking Lake Huron and Lake Erie could attract trade that was now finding its way to Albany and New York and, for that matter, to the English on Hudson's Bay. It would be a check on the Iroquois too. . . . The old governor glanced up sharply as the confident voice went on. Hadn't these rivers and lakes been the road by which the Iroquois had approached the upper reaches of the Ottawa River, that open doorway to New

France? Put a fort across that avenue and the road would be closed for good.

The old governor's imagination was afire. He knew that enthusiasm came to him easily and that Louis knew it too. He knew of Louis' distaste for an enlarging empire. He knew that there were impressive forces in New France, the Jesuits and the *coureurs*, who for once would find a common cause in fighting such a harebrained scheme. Should it succeed it would spell the ruin of Michilimackinac and damage the fortunes of the merchants who drew their trade from it. There would be plenty of opposition. Much of the brandy trade centered at this post and, however much the Jesuits might oppose, there were powerful forces who saw in it too good an opportunity to overlook. They would not look on idly while trade was diverted elsewhere.

All this Frontenac knew well, but in his mind the merits of the scheme outranked every other circumstance. He began planning how to bring it to the favorable attention of the King. Finally it came to him. Send the irreverent Gascon to the court to argue his own case. He was not likely to be overawed even by majesty. He set about writing letters to his wife and others, urging support for the new fort. He was never to know the result, or whether his judgment had been sound. Before La Mothe could get away the old governor was dead. Cadillac's one out-and-out supporter could support him no longer.

Callières, newly appointed to his high office, inclined to move slowly. He knew that Frontenac had approved the scheme, and his inclination was to follow that lead. But the opposition was heavy and important and very disconcerting to newly vested authority. The intendant, Champigny, who was a fast friend of the Jesuits, was naturally opposed to any move that so definitely lacked their approval. Also, he had been well schooled in the policy of contracting French holdings in the New World, and by no manner of reasoning could this new proposal be made to bear the appearance of a contraction. It was expansion if ever there was such a thing. He called a meeting at the château in Quebec. Most of the leaders of the colony were present, including the governor and intendant and La Mothe Cadillac as well. It wasn't a very satisfactory gathering. There was much opposition, headed by the intendant. It was a stirring meeting, with the intendant providing most of the arguments (not always very closely related to the subject) and Cadillac most of the fireworks, while the governor occupied a neutral position. When it was over, with nothing settled, Cadillac decided to go over the heads of these officials and make his case at court, as Frontenac had suggested.

His first step was to write the minister in what for him were restrained words. "Canada is a country of cabals and intrigues and it is impossible to reconcile so many interests. You can never hope that this business will succeed if it is discussed here on the spot." He followed this as soon as might be by taking the first available ship for France.

As it turned out, he was his own best salesmen. His very brashness attracted Louis, and his discerning presentation of the plan, his softening of the obligations and dangers, and his emphasizing of the results made their appeal to the minister, Pontchartrain. He stated emphatically that the execution of this plan would ensure the safety of New France and the ruin of the British colonies.

For these large results he asked only fifty soldiers. He made his own deal or very close to it. There were to be fifty soldiers and fifty Canadians to begin the work, these to be followed the next year by other settlers. For himself, Cadillac was allowed a personal trading concession of some four thousand crowns, or roughly five thousand dollars. It seemed substantial, but out of it there were many charges to be met. When Pontchartrain agreed to the plan Cadillac wasted no time in further argument but took the first ship for Quebec, eager to be at his new venture. But the selecting of the necessary forces took time. The soldiers he knew something about, but hand-picking fifty of them was not a simple matter, and when it came to selecting fifty farmers and mechanics it was still more puzzling. In the main they were not an adventurous breed, and whispers were getting about suggesting that all was not quite well. Such hints added to the attractiveness of Montreal and Quebec, with their familiarity and relative safety. Cadillac's patience, never his long suit, had grown thin indeed by the time everything was ready for departure.

It was June 5, 1701, before the hundred Frenchmen finally had been selected and the twenty-five canoes that were to carry them had been made ready.

With Cadillac as second-in-command went Alphonse Tonty. He was a good linguist and spoke the Illinois dialects fluently. That was the reason for his selection. It was true that he was a brother of Henri Tonty, and not without the latter's courage, but there the resemblance ended. Henri Tonty was a man of almost spotless reputation, but the confusion between the two brothers robbed Henri of his full stature. Alphonse Tonty had not his brother's stern conscience. He was a man of itchy fingers and a reputation for looking after himself without too much consideration of questions of mine and thine. But he was able and courageous and he did his part. There were two young cadet lieutenants, Dugue and Chacornacle, probably chosen because their high spirits were about all they had at stake. Two priests accompanied the expedition, the Jesuit Father Vaillant and the Récollet Father Constantine.

Just why Cadillac chose to go on his great adventure by way of Michilimackinac, a matter of a thousand miles, when he could have taken the direct route of Lake Ontario and Lake Erie at about half the distance, has always been a matter of discussion and criticism—as though he had gone on one last gloating visit to what was soon to be a ghost town.

Perhaps it was a matter of the facilities of travel. Cadillac knew that twenty miles a day was good traveling for a canoe, loaded as these were and facing possible lake storms. Traveling northward by river, even allowing for current and winds, as much as forty miles a day was not impossible. Probably, however, the real reason was to pick up cannon and muskets and munitions from the deserted defenses. He did this with the King's full permission. There was a less publicized reason that might have had a bearing. Before leaving for France he had cached a hundred and ninety-eight pots of brandy in the woods near the post. These had been seized from unauthorized bushlopers and really belonged to Montreal merchants. Cadillac didn't give that a passing thought. They were too valuable trading material to be overlooked.

The expedition left Lachine by way of the Ottawa River. This was followed to its juncture with the Mattawa River and along that stream until it emptied into Lake Nipissing, so called by the Indians because of its many mists. From there they followed the course of the French River, once called the River of Sorcerers but today a place of luxury fishing camps, and so to the Georgian Bay and Lake Huron and along its northern shore to Michilimackinac.

It was a familiar route to Cadillac. More than once, while in command at the post, he had made the trip from Montreal by snowshoe in the depth of winter in order that he might be on hand when the fur brigades arrived.

It was not a completely uneventful trip. His hundred Frenchmen were a motley crew. Before they had left Lachine there were some meetings over a friendly glass and more than one sly suggestion that an adventurous fellow might do rather well for himself if he had the spirit to take things into his own hands. A few bold lads could take the canoes and their contents, and perhaps the pots of brandy, and disappear into the woods. The words fell on fertile soil. Before they had reached the Mattawa there were evidences of dissatisfaction. There was scuffling about the canoes. It hadn't got to open insubordination, but it was shaping that way. In one of these scuffles Cadillac's hat was knocked over his long nose. This was considerably more than Gascon temper could stand. His sword was out and his great voice was inviting anyone who had a mood for disagreement to come and be spitted. His reputation as a swordsman was well known and his evident relish at the thought of using his skill cooled the hottest blood. There was no more dissension.

The expedition did not spend much time at Michilimackinac. It was there just long enough to collect the goods needed and to pass some hot words with Father Carheil, the Superior of the mission. Long enough, perhaps, for Cadillac to drop a line to the minister to describe the good priest as "the most passionate and domineering man I have ever known." Had it been the good priest writing, there would have been little need to change the judgment.

The usual route from Michilimackinac to the lower lakes skirted the west shore of Lake Huron and followed the long detour about the shores of Saginaw Bay. Good weather favored Cadillac. It suggested the daring course of facing the open lake across the mouth of the bay and saving that long detour. His luck was with him, and by July 23, just short of seven weeks since they had left Lachine, the canoes drew to shore at the point chosen for the new fort.

There has been some question as to why the narrows of the Detroit River had been selected rather than those at Sarnia, where Du Lhut had once rallied the tribes. The reason was that the lower site lay across the portage trail to the more distant tribes of the Illinois and the upper Misissippi and Wisconsin rivers.

Cadillac drove his men hard. There was no rest until the stockade had taken shape. It stood about forty feet from the water at the narrowest point of the river so that a cannon shot could reach the farther side. It enclosed a square that today might be roughly bounded by the river, with Shelby and Jefferson streets as the sides, reaching back to Griswold and Wayne streets. The pickets stood twelve feet high and were fashioned of logs at least three hands' span in circumference. They had to be cut by hand and carried to their place of use. It was backbreaking work. There wasn't much promise of ease, either, in the three-quarter-acre plots of land allotted to the soldiers or in the three acres for each settler. These ran from the water, as they do today in Quebec, in long narrow strips. It is a companionable system, where a man can call to his neighbor from the center of his land.

But all was not entirely smooth sailing. Two months after they had arrived Father Vaillant, the Jesuit, was hurrying back to Quebec. It had been gossiped about that the good father had expressed, more or less openly, the opinion that the post couldn't succeed.

The suggestion that a task to which he had set his hand could possibly fail was too close to blasphemy for Cadillac's taste. He charged the priest with the words and was not satisfied when the priest hurried away without answering. Vaillant knew that his only course now was to return to Quebec.

Cadillac did not let the matter pass quite as easily. He wrote the highly devout Pontchartrain without mincing words. "I had as lief see a clown Emperor of the Moon," he wrote, "as such men in positions of responsibility at Detroit." Pontchartrain's retort was singularly gentle. It merely urged that Cadillac should keep peace with the Jesuits. Perhaps he recognized that even that was a command well beyond the ability of the man he addressed.

On September 10, 1701, not much more than a month after the fort had been begun, Madame Cadillac, accompanied by Madame Tonty, reached the post at *d'étroit*, "of the strait," and took up a more or less settled life there. Nothing about La Mothe Cadillac seems to point to the devoted husband and father, yet he was both. Where one would have expected his marriage to be as stormy as his life, it was nothing of the kind. Perhaps that was because Thérèse Guyon, whom he married in the cathedral at Quebec on June 25, 1687, was enough like her husband to understand his tempers and to share his enthusiasms. They had thirteen children in all, and five of them she brought with her to Detroit.

Thérèse Guyon was as well born as her husband. They had met first at Port Royal, where her father was superintending the erection of the stonework for the new fort. La Mothe Cadillac was posted there at the time and was a young man of position. He had been granted a holding of some thousands of acres in that land of disputed ownership between the St. Croix and the Kennebec rivers. Such grants were not too difficult to secure. Louis felt that in granting such titles he did something to establish his kingly ownership of the land. Of course Cadillac was not to hold the property too long. Eventually it returned to the English without either the gainer or the loser being too impressed or depressed by the change. After all, the property, centering about what is now Bar Harbor, Maine, and including all of Mount Desert Island and a tract of four square leagues on the opposite mainland, was generally accepted as useless land of small if any value. But whether he was landed or landless, Thérèse Guyon recognized Cadillac as a man of quality and never thereafter changed her mind.

On the long journey to Detroit, Madame Cadillac had met and spoken to Father Vaillant retreating rather ignominiously from her husband's displeasure. Perhaps that fact colored the good father's thinking, for he spoke to her in deep sympathy for the fortune that had cast her lot in such a dangerous post.

Madame's retort had been prompt. "Don't waste pity on us," she said. "When a woman loves her husband, no place where he is can be dangerous." It was a nice, if dubious, sentiment. A post that controlled all the territory as far west as Chicago could scarcely be free of hazards, husband or no.

There was the fact, too, that the Iroquois were far from pleased at this new venture. This was land they claimed as their own. It was their preferred beaver-hunting ground. In their alarm they appealed to their English allies. To get the English King fully involved in the matter, they turned over the whole territory to him, conveying the vast parcel of land from Lake Ontario northward to Lake Superior and westward as far as Chicago "unto our souveraigne Lord King William the Third." The authorities at Albany who drew up the document didn't spare anything. They outlined the properties mentioned as being about eight hundred miles long by four hundred wide, and included certain conditions that left the donors very much subject to the will of the new owners. As a matter of fact, the document didn't have a very real value. Neither Iroquois nor English had the temerity to make its terms effective over the squatter rights of the little group at the straits.

There is no blinking the fact that the purpose of the venture was highly practical. There was the political angle of putting a roadblock on one of the most important avenues of attack on Canada, but the practical phase of the matter had to do with the fur trade. King Louis had come up with an idea that to his mind had real point. If you couldn't get rid of the *coureurs*—and all the attempts to date had failed for one reason or another—it might be possible to curb their activities.

The plan was to establish recognized outlets that for the time would be restricted to Fort Frontenac and Detroit. The trading would be under the control of a trading company headed by seven directors. To salve the feelings of such former trading posts as Michilimackinac and Montreal, all Canadians there and elsewhere were to be permitted to share in the profits of the venture. The people so blessed did not respond as was hoped. They recognized that the Compagnie de la Colonie du Canada had what might be described as a bond issue ahead of the common. It was obligated to repay the eighty thousand francs that the expedition to Detroit had cost, cover some of the remaining expenses of the post, and assume a few other burdens as well as the routine trading expenses. As a whole, the Canadian people observed the opportunity with a rather jaundiced eye. There were approximately one hundred and fifty investors. In a population that had now reached 15,355, that was not an encouraging percentage.

As a matter of fact, everyone was disgruntled and openly complaining. At Michilimackinac, Father Carheil was bewailing the loss of his converts, who, now that no business was left, had followed where they expected business to be. It was a sobering thought to the clergy. Only Cadillac learned of it with satisfaction. In that mood he wrote the devout Pontchartrain words that must have startled that sober man. After reporting the news that only twenty-five Hurons were left at Michilimackinac, Cadillac didn't waste time on regrets. "I hope," he added piously, "that in the autumn I shall pluck the last feather from his wing; and I am convinced that this obstinate priest will die in his parish, without one parishioner to bury him."

Throughout Canada discontent lay heavy as threatening storm. It was everywhere. The new trading dispensation was the heart of it. It meant hardship for the honest trader and worse for the dishonest, of whom there were not a few. The trading company, being the brain child of Louis himself—at least by adoption—could not be openly attacked. It was possible to qualify its effectiveness by less direct means. The vested interests of the day had their undoubted power. They were headed by the Chevalier de Vaudreuil, at the moment governor of Montreal. He was an able, courageous, arrogant, and crafty man. He did not like the sight of other heads standing above the crowd. Somewhat of Vaudreuil's way of thinking was De Ramesay, as able and perhaps as powerful if not as crafty. With their followers they waited impatiently for any opportunity that might offer the chance to clip the wings of the blustering Gascon at the straits.

Whether this was a factor in the growing dissatisfaction of the seven directors of the company, or whether they just seized some unrelated opportunity of aggrandizement, does not appear. They were already protesting that their work was too heavy and that further privileges were needed to offset this heavy burden.

Cadillac was not in a sympathetic mood. He didn't think the burden too heavy. Indeed, he retorted testily that the directors only wanted to have a storehouse and clerks—no offices, no troops, no hospitals, no settlement, nothing in fact of the growing center of life and trade that he and Frontenac had dreamed. He suggested a counterproposal. Cadillac would himself lift this heavy burden from the shoulders of the seven and would carry it on his own. He would pay back all the money the directors and company had advanced. He put it all in writing for the minister. "I promise you," he wrote Pontchartrain, "that if they accept my proposal, and you approve it, I will make our Detroit flourish."

Not only did the seven directors rejoice at the proposed relief, but the minister also approved. Strongly as he disliked Cadillac's continuing vendetta with the Jesuits, he must have felt a sure confidence in his business acumen. At least he approved the change that made Cadillac the complete master of Detroit.

This change, which put new and extensive powers into Cadillac's hands, was far from being the change that Vaudreuil and his set had anticipated or wished. But it made one thing crystal-clear, and that was that the King and his minister thought better of Cadillac than did some of his Canadian confreres. It was fairly obvious, too, that the many efforts to discount that appreciation must have fallen on pretty stony ground. Vaudreuil was shrewd enough to understand this and to recognize that it called for a change of strategy. Deprecation had failed. Perhaps a build-up that would remove a rival to seemingly more important fields might succeed.

It was a campaign that took shrewd advantage of the King's weaknesses. He wanted the satisfaction of conferring a favor that might assure an added devotion. Such a favor, which apparently cost nothing, had an additional attraction. The argument then was that a man of Cadillac's proven ability should have a post that would call out all his powers, and not one where all that now remained was to keep a well-organized operation functioning smoothly. A larger position to keep a good man satisfied, thought the King. A more distant post, thought Vaudreuil and De Ramesay, far enough away so that an aggressive man might cease to be a thorn in their side. None of them could know that organization and operation are often closely allied. They could hardly have guessed how quickly and completely a slow progress can change into sharp recession or how comprehensive the failure could be when a Dubuisson took the place of a La Mothe Cadillac. It would be years before it would again be the Detroit of which Cadillac had dreamed; the Detroit that he had built and loved and had relinquished with such bitter regret.

The blow came in the guise of a promotion. The order was transmitted through Quebec, as was fitting. It had been engineered there. The order bore the date of September 13, 1710. It read, "Having appointed you to the governorship of Louisiana . . . it is the will of His Majesty that you should go at once." Then the official tone had softened. "It is too great a chance for you," Vaudreuil had interpolated, "not to congratulate you on the choice which His Majesty has just made." Perhaps he recognized that Cadillac would see through his spurious heartiness, for he concluded, "This is for the welfare of the service."

Cadillac had no illusions. He was not an erudite man. Most probably he had never heard the warning to beware the Greeks bearing gifts, but he understood the situation as clearly as if he had. However it might appear to be an advancement to govern a province rather than a city, he knew that appearances deceived. He knew that Louisiana had been the death of reputations as great or greater than his own; the death of men, too—La Salle and Iberville and De Soto before them. He knew that he had to face the antagonism of Bienville, the young Le Moyne who was known and loved and who, quite naturally, must feel that the post belonged to his family and to him.

Cadillac had no love of the country itself. "This territorial paradise," he was to write, "boasts twenty-five fig trees, three pears, three apples. Its wealth is a tissue of fable and lies. The whole wretched country is good for nothing. The people are no better than the country." So the disillusioned man could work off his spleen. How different the words that came to him at his first glimpse of the Detroit that was to be: "Seas of sweet water glide past our door. The banks are lovely meadows of deep green fringed with fruit trees. The vines are a roof embowering the trees in an embrace. . . . The meadows need only the plowshare to grow anything. . . . The grapevine has not strength to support the weight of its fruit, and it has not yet wept under the knife of the vine dresser. . . . The shy stag, the timid deer, the wild turkey hens, the strutting woodcock, the quail, the partridge, all in greater numbers than in a private French park."

So wrote the man of the land he loved and of the land to which he was going. He had used every effort to delay or avoid the change. It had not availed. Frontenac was dead and the men who had succeeded him had no love for Cadillac. They wanted him away. They knew, and he knew, that the change would be the end for him.

Cadillac was only forty-five when he reached his new post, the good-for-nothing country of his imagining, but already the grasshopper had become a burden and desires had failed. The glory had gone out of the job, and only the job itself remained. There would follow the years of battle with the young Bienville. In different times the young Le Moyne must have been a man after Cadillac's own liking. But such friendship was not for the bitter heart.

There was his unhappy, if distant, conflict with John Law, a Scotsman born, who achieved a strange and sinister influence both in the old France and the new. Cadillac had left Louisiana and his post as governor well before John Law made his entrance there. It would have been possible for Cadillac to argue that it was none of his business, had that been his way. It wasn't. He made things his business. John Law's contact with the New World began with Antoine Crozat's failure in Louisiana. Crozat, a rich merchant of France, had secured a fifteen-year lease of Louisiana and planned to develop its supposed vast gold and copper mines into a new Eldorado. It didn't take long for a sound merchant to realize that his dream was a will-o'-the-wisp. He was happy to surrender his charter to the Regent.

This was John Law's opportunity. The crafty and none too scrupulous Scotsman had succeeded in making himself a Paris banker of sufficient repute for him to insinuate himself into the good graces of the Duc d'Orléans, who had become Regent following the death of Louis XIV. John Law used this connection to have Crozat's concessions turned over to the Compagnie des Indes, more popularly known as the Mississippi Company. Naturally John Law was the company's controlling head and in that capacity was entitled to exploit the Louisiana colony for a matter of twenty-five years. When it came to exploiting, John Law had no thought of stopping there. By fabulous promotional schemes he developed this venture into probably the most fantastic gambling scheme in all history. In less than two years he had managed to involve in this project the royal bank, the mint, and the investing of all the royal revenues.

Among the projects was a proposal to develop a vast territory on the Arkansas River. Probably the most vivid recounting of this venture is found in the letters of young Father Paul du Poisson to his good friend, Father Louis Patouillet. Du Poisson had been sent with the expedition as a missionary to the Arkansas, and he writes with all the flavor of a new and vividly personal experience:

"The French settlement of Akenses"—so Father Poisson spells the word—"would be an important one, had Monsieur Law's reputation continued four or five years. . . . The Company of the Indies had granted him a tract sixteen leagues square. . . . His intention was to found a City, establish manufactures, to have numbers of vassals and troops, and to found a Duchy. . . . The property which he then sent into this country amounted to more than fifteen hundred thousand livres. Among other things he had means to arm and superbly equip two hundred cavalrymen. He had also brought three hundred Negroes. . . . Twelve thousand Germans were engaged for this grant. This was not a bad beginning for the first year," the young priest comments, but adds rather sadly, "Monsieur Law was disgraced."

He tells that most of the three or four thousand Germans who had landed on the continent had died and the few who remained had been recalled. That was not quite the complete story. Some two hundred of them, going down-river, intent on returning home, were persuaded to settle in a section about thirty miles above New Orleans. It became known as "the German shore." Even today a lake and an adjoining town bear the name Des Allemands. There is more than this to connect an ancient chapter of history with the more immediate present. The three hundred Negros introduced by Law were the origin of African slavery in Louisiana. Thereafter cargoes of slaves arrived through the ports of Mobile and New Orleans. They were introduced in sufficient numbers to necessitate the *Code Noir*, the collected royal edicts concerning the condition and the discipline of Negro Slaves in Louisiana.

It was none of these things that involved Cadillac in the growing web of John Law's lawless Mississippi Bubble. All France had gone mad in this wild orgy of speculation in fabulous profits that were expected to result from each uncertain venture in this new land. When money grew scarce John Law was quick to provide it. The presses of the royal bank, under Law's management, sent out a continuing stream of paper money. It was over this that the two men came in conflict. Cadillac couldn't intervene in schemes that had the blessing of the Regent of France. Had he wished, he could have gone as most officials of his age were going, buying Mississippi stock low and selling it high, reaping fabulous paper profits. He would have none of it. Blunt and tactless as ever, he announced to anyone who would listen that there would be no royal revenues, no dividends, no profits out of these ventures for long years to come. Though Crozat joined him in these protests, they were in vain. Nobody listened. They were too dazzled with the promises of vast wealth without effort. They didn't want to come awake.

Behind the dazzlement, too, there were powerful forces with much at stake, and Cadillac was a threat to safety. When in his final year as governor he demanded that the King's revenues should be paid in specie, not in paper, they realized the full extent of that threat. They couldn't meet their obligations in specie, so somehow Cadillac must be discredited. There is nothing new in the practices of crime. The methods used might have been those of today. Cadillac's demands were met all right, and in specie. But when this was passed on to the proper authorities, the specie was found to be counterfeit. It was so palpably a frame-up that it seems unbelievable the charge that Cadillac was responsible for the counterfeiting could be made to stick. But it was what the people wanted to believe. They wanted to discredit the man who had discredited their dreams of sudden wealth. So the charge was made and sustained and Cadillac was sent to the dreaded Bastille.

The crash had to come sometime. It came in May of 1720. The authorities suddenly discovered that Law's Compagnie des Indes had issued more than twice as much paper currency as there was specie in all the realm of France. The bubble had burst; the shares had no value at all. Then at last the people realized that Cadillac had been right. He was released from the Bastille. But the circumstances of his justification were not happy. They had resulted in his release, but they had almost brought his world to bankruptcy.

There was the last sad midnight when his plague-ridden body was hurried to its solitary grave at Castelsarrasin, whose governorship was his final official post. Such the beginning and the end of a man.

CHAPTER XIV

"THE WOFUL DECADE"

The War of the Spanish Succession, known on the American continent as Queen Anne's War, reopens the long feud between New France and New England. In Canada, Governor Callières is dead. Governor Vaudreuil—who is in his place—revives the old policy of keeping the Abenaki thinking only of war. The border flames again in a score of places. The raid on Deerfield becomes a vital page in Canada's story.

THE Reverend Cotton Mather, the friend and biographer of Sir William Phips and one-time devoted witch hunter, was a minister of distinction in Puritan Boston, where the ministerial rank was high. He was also quite a phrasemaker and a bit of a pedant as well. He had coined his own phrase to cover an era that in Europe has come to be known as that of the War of the Spanish Succession, and in America as Queen Anne's War.

That was some years later. Thus far the Peace of Ryswick seems to have brought a season of tranquillity. A peace that did little more than establish a status quo could hardly be expected to last, and it didn't. In something less than five years the divergent interests, which hadn't changed, set the disputants at each other's throats again. What followed was grim enough, and Cotton Mather's phrase was not without aptness. In his pedantic vein he spoke of the years between 1703 and 1713 as *decennium luctuosum*, "the woful decade." For once the great Cotton Mather had understressed. Both in the matter of the extent of time and in the tribulations covered by the years, the phrase was too mild.

And yet, for the time, it seemed the settlement that Ryswick had proposed might have become actual and lasting. Europe had been almost beggared by war. William III of England had found it necessary to pledge his personal fortune to help finance the not too fortunate campaign against Louis in the Netherlands. Louis' own situation was not much better. The gentle Abbé Fénelon, tutor of the King's grandsons, had been moved to write the King with unaccustomed frankness. "The country," he wrote, "is a vast hospital."

Factual as this statement was, that was not the consideration which moved Louis. The suffering of individuals seemed to him a necessary part of his own growing authority, to be accepted by them without complaint. Certainly the Peace of Ryswick wasn't a settlement to Louis' liking. It had compelled him, among other things, to recognize William as the rightful King of England. It had bound him to support that claim should anyone dispute it. It had also settled the English succession on Anne, who was a Protestant, rather than James II's son, who was a Catholic. Louis had agreed to these things because a new and magnificent prospect had presented itself. He knew that to achieve it he must conserve all his resources. It was no less than the dream of bringing all the once vast powers of Spain and her still far-flung possessions into the orbit of France.

It wasn't an impossible prospect. Charles II of Spain was childless and ill and mentally unstable. The vast empire over which he ruled had fallen to such low estate that little but its pride and the outer shell of power remained. To Louis, however, the prospect was bright. With the might of France supporting and being supported by the possessions of Spain, he would indeed dominate his world.

It was a heady dream, and it gave little time for the problems of his colony overseas. He knew quite well that he was toying with an idea that might once again launch the continent into war, a war that could not possibly fail to affect the colonies in Canada. He knew that William would almost certainly range both England and Holland against him. He knew that the Austrian Hapsburgs had better claim to the succession of Spain than were available to him, and that with them would go the greater part of Germany.

Matters hung in this even balance until the ailing Charles of Spain seemed to settle everything by naming as his successor a Hapsburg prince, Joseph Ferdinand of Bavaria. The settlement wasn't as final as it appeared, for the young prince died almost immediately, leaving the succession still undecided.

Louis had suffered a shock. But for the happy demise of the Hapsburg prince, his fine dream might have disappeared into thin air. Rather than risk another such hazard, he craftily proposed a Partition Treaty as a hedging of his bets. In return for an agreement not to oppose the Hapsburg claim to the Spanish throne, he negotiated concessions on the Pyrenees border and the province of Savoy bordering on Italy and Lorraine and Luxembourg in the north. It wasn't what Louis had dreamed, but it was something.

But the prideful Spaniards were bent on having a word to say about their own fortunes. Canvassing the advantages of an alliance with Hapsburg or Bourbon, the more powerful cabal chose the Bourbon side. There wasn't much time to waste. Over the bedside of the dying Charles they argued and wrangled until, worn out with the struggle, the dying man surrendered and accepted Philip, Duke of Anjou, as the legal successor to the throne of Spain. His only stipulation was that this grandson of Louis XIV should renounce any claim to the throne of France. This done, the ailing monarch died. It was November 1, 1700.

Louis faced a quandary. There was the Partition Treaty, solemnly sworn and bearing his name. It had seemed to save something from possible failure, but now the kingdom of Spain seemed ripe to fall under his sway, just as he had dreamed it. He hardly hesitated. It was two weeks later that the courtiers at Versailles saw the great doors of the King's cabinet swing open. There stood Louis in all his majesty, and beside him the young Duke of Anjou. There was no hesitancy in the King's voice as he announced, "Gentlemen, the King of Spain." Above the flutter of respectable applause Louis' voice was heard explaining that Philip of Anjou was not only King by right of birth and by the will of the Spanish people but, he added, "It is the will of heaven." He did not seem to remember that he had connived rather actively to be sure that the will of heaven should parallel his own, or perhaps it was just that he confused the two. "Be a good Spaniard," he adjured his grandson, "but remember that you are born a Frenchman."

No doubt it seems a far cry from the palace of Versailles and the kingship of France and Spain to the distant colony beyond the sea.

There does not appear to be much association between such events and "the woful decade" of which Cotton Mather was to speak. But out of this bit of kingly pomp stemmed the events that were to set a frontier ablaze again. They were to grow into a challenge that was to rob France of her colonial empire and to begin the downward course that would end a dynasty as it ended a way of thought.

Nothing happened immediately. It wasn't that England did not see the threat. It was too definite for that. It was almost sure to cost her trade with France. This was always subject to the hazards of war. But that with Spain had been more stable, and it might not so remain. England's life was in the balance. Then as now, she had to trade to live. But England was far from united. She had never quite accepted William and did not accept him now. There was impatience over a foreign policy that had brought neither glory nor gain but had driven the country close to financial ruin. England's greatest soldier, John Churchill, who was to become the Duke of Marlborough, was intriguing more or less openly against William. His plan was not to restore James II but to be rid of both James and William and to put James's daughter Anne in their place. Anne was the friend and confidante of his wife and through her, John Churchill felt, could be easily guided.

William III was a sick man, sick and troubled and embittered. No one had served England's interests more devotedly or had received such scanty thanks. No one saw the threat as he saw it. No one in England was troubled by the accession of the Duke of Anjou to the throne of Spain. He was young, they argued, he would be turned into a Spaniard by the force of events. No one seemed to resent Louis' flouting of the Partition Treaty as a scrap of paper when the Spanish King's will seemed to promise something better. "It grieves me," wrote William III in some bitterness, "that almost everyone prefers the will to the treaty."

But Louis seemed bent on pressing his luck too far. When about this time James, the deposed King of England, died in exile, Louis could not resist the large gesture. Though he had accepted William III as King of England and Anne as his successor, he promptly forgot his given word and recognized the dead James's son, the Chevalier de St. George, as James III, the rightful King of England.

This profoundly stupid gesture did what all William III's urging and efforts and devotion had been unable to do. It united England behind him, an England as bitterly determined as he to defeat the plans of France. For once it seemed that William would have the chance he deserved. But even that was not to be. Riding in the park at Kensington, he was thrown heavily from his horse. It was more than his frail remaining strength could survive. He had a few days to call Anne to him, to urge her, who had been far from true to him, to put her trust in one man who had been less true, to put John Churchill in full command of England's armies. Then he died, a tired and sick and disappointed man.

Those years, the decade between 1703 and 1713, which were to be such "woful years" on the American continent, were to be years of swelling triumph for England. At a small and almost unknown village on the Bavarian Danube the finest army France had ever raised met the united forces of John Churchill and Prince Eugene and was sent staggering home in broken and disorganized rout. Blenheim was to become one of the great names of Britain's story, and John Churchill its fabulous Duke of Marlborough. But Blenheim was not alone. The story was repeated again and again in those epic years—Ramillies and Oudenarde and Malplaquet, names to be remembered forever on the banners of Britain.

When it all ended, Louis' great dream had ended too. The young Duke of Anjou still sat on the throne of Spain, Philip V, founder of the Spanish Bourbon house. It was almost as planned. Only there was no hope of using it so that France could dominate Europe and the world. The hope had broken on the mounting strength of the enemies who now surrounded France. The dream would never live again.

In Canada, Governor Callières was dead. This man of ability and courage and a quite unusual capacity for loyalty was through with his suffering and his problems. In his place there was a man of far different character and qualities: Philippe de Rigaud, the first Marquis de Vaudreuil in the early aristocracy of Canada. He was of good family and, quite naturally, at an early age he entered the French Army and achieved there a well-established reputation as a soldier. When he was just short of fifty years of age he was sent to Canada to assume command of all the troops in the colony. He took with him eight hundred reinforcements for Denonville's campaign against the Iroquois.

Unused as Vaudreuil himself was to forest warfare, he had not reached Fort Frontenac with his command, following Denonville's advance, before he realized that it would be suicidal to take these untrained levies into such a campaign. It was characteristic of him that he made his decision promptly, leaving the contingent at the fort, though he knew the governor was expecting them. It was characteristic also that, though he was no better trained than they for this New World warfare, it did not occur to him to stay behind. He pushed on by himself and was soon operating as Denonville's chief of staff and certainly at no discredit to his position.

With Callières' death, Vaudreuil, acting with equal decisiveness, promptly had himself appointed administrator of the colony. He must have conducted his duties creditably, for a year or two later he was appointed governor. He wasn't a Frontenac; neither was he a Callières. Perhaps he resembled the former more than the latter in his love of action, his quick decisiveness, his unqualified confidence in his own decisions, and his determination to have his own way. He had not Callières' unquestioning loyalty nor his fine scrupulousness. He lacked the devoutness that characterized Frontenac, or even his much less easily recognized spiritual qualities. If the austere authority of the Jesuits had been somewhat shaken by Frontenac's continuing opposition to them, under Vaudreuil the change became startlingly noticeable. Whether this resulted from the increasing prosperity of the colony and the lighter spirit that resulted or was in part a reflection of the social leadership of the governor's court, it would be difficult to say, but the fact was there.

Admittedly Vaudreuil himself was not a pattern of all virtues, and his wife inclined to encourage the unconventional rather than resent it. This different spirit found its way into the convents. Some of the nuns were known to dine with the governor and his wife. There was no suggestion of impropriety in this, but, coupled with the increasingly frivolous nature of these gatherings, it did occasion the bishop some concern.

Madame la Marquise was Canadian by birth. She was the daughter of a Canadian officer, Pierre de Joybert. She had spent her childhood not even among the modest amenities of Port Royal but at Gensec, an obscure military post on the St. John River. Undoubtedly she must have been attractive to catch the often roving eye of the marquis. Just how Madame Vaudreuil came to attract the notice of the wife of the King is not very clear. It certainly wasn't that she was devout or circumspect enough to have earned a friendly word from the Jesuits. Her relatively humble Canadian birth was not a steppingstone of value. Obviously she had made her place in the highest social circles of the New World, and that place was secure enough to attract the favorable attention of Madame de Maintenon. The marquise was called to France to become the governess of the King's children. That was in 1709. She remained there for fifteen years and made what might appear to be a somewhat humble office into a position of undoubted power. It was said of her that she bore the air of one to whom nothing could be refused. When she returned to Canada in 1724 the old governor was close to his end.

Though Vaudreuil had achieved the top authority in the colony, he wasn't quite satisfied. The authority imposed new obligations, both political and social, but neither seemed to please him. Placidity was not a quality that he found attractive, and under Callières' careful regimen peace had been assured. It was a needed peace. In the incessant war and skirmishing along the uncertain border the land had become almost a desert, and neither French nor English seemed inclined at the moment to jeopardize that peace.

But Vaudreuil was itching for action and he was still imbued with the idea that sound policy could not overlook the wisdom of keeping the Abenaki actively hostile to the English. He had openly voiced the opinion that it was convenient to maintain a secret alliance with the Indians. Perhaps "convenient" hardly suggested the definiteness of his thinking. This was to the effect that a little quiet pressure could induce hurried forays into English territory, forays that would do considerable damage and yet leave the French free to disclaim any hint of responsibility.

It wasn't difficult to stir up this war spirit. The Indians were already nursing a grievance. It had to do with the sale of land. There was no doubt that the Indians had actually sold to the English considerable parcels of land, transactions that the purchasers considered a clear transfer of ownership. To the Indian mind it was nothing of the sort. A sale of land, in their view, meant that the purchaser was entitled to travel over it unhindered, and even to shoot or fish on it. But these English would not recognize this reasonable deal. They had a habit of fencing in the land and excluding others. This the Indians resented, feeling it a definite infringement of their overriding ownership. The French had no such possessive instinct. All their training was against it. Land hunger was for peasants.

In using these differing attitudes to create disaffection in the minds of Indian allies, Vaudreuil had a useful assistant in the Jesuit father, Sebastian Râle. Râle had come to Canada with Frontenac on the latter's return. Some years spent in various mission fields, combined with an instinct for languages, had made him proficient in several Algonquin dialects as well as the dialect of the Hurons. In 1693 he was appointed missionary to the Abenaki, living in and about their village, which then, as now, was known as Norridgewock. It lies roughly thirty miles north of Augusta, Maine.

Father Râle liked the northern migration of the English as little as did his Indian associates. The Indians saw it as an encroachment on their lands. Râle recognized it as a challenge to his missionary efforts. He knew there would be no compensating colonizing effort by the French. They were not a land-hungry breed. They wanted adventure and quick return, not the slow, plodding gain of developing communities. He was no more eager for an influx of *coureurs* than for the encroachment of the English.

A man of strong body and constructive spirit, Râle was curiously shortsighted. It stemmed from an embittered sort of patriotism and perhaps almost as bitter a creed, though between Catholic and Puritan thinking there was not so much to choose. Both were rigid and unbending.

Râle might one moment be considering the spiritual needs of his flock, and the next writing Governor Vaudreuil that, when the governor wished it, at a word from their missionary the Abenaki would be ready to lift the hatchet against the English. Or he might be voicing a bitter protest that large tracts of land were being exchanged for a bottle of rum. The fact was probably true, just as it would have been possible to provide instances where a bottle of rum had paid for many bundles of skins. If the French did not use it to buy land it was only because they preferred the rum. Certainly it did not justify his challenge to his followers that if they didn't drive the English out they would lose not only their lands but their souls.

There and in similar instances was the resowing of the seed of the bitter border strife that was so cruel in its manifestations and so purposeless in its results. There can be no question of Father Râle's devotion as there can be of his wisdom and scrupulousness. He was not a martyr as so many of his fellow Jesuits were, serving their God with an undeviating consecration that defies any criticism. Sebastian Râle chose to be not only priest but also leader. He died in one of the minute engagements of those terrible years. It was a small engagement in the total of happenings of the times. It was large enough to destroy the tribes that Râle had so sincerely wished to serve, and to leave their teacher lying among his flock with a bullet through his forehead. Perhaps there is a suggestion that good intentions, born more of bigotry and a belligerent chauvinism than of wisdom, may end in being self-destructive.

The recorded events range beyond "the woful decade" with which this chapter deals. There are plenty of incidents within its scope to more than justify the phrase, for once again the whole border and far within it blazed into woeful happenings. It was not open war, at least at first. It was a series of stealthy raids, apparently an upsurge of Indian anger, but the sad fact was that the hard core of each attack was the small group of French who accompanied each expedition and gave it direction if they could not control.

It was August 10, 1703, and the people of Wells were basking in the summer warmth. They were well used to attack. These had been frequent enough to set a kind of pattern. But there had been years of relative calm, and perhaps the alertness that once had been second nature had grown to seem less important. Even the gunshots that broke the August stillness had nothing sinister to suggest. It was probably some hunters in the bush. By the time Wells knew the truth it was too late for anything but sorrow. The wife of Thomas Wells had reached the time of her confinement. She was killed as she lay there, and two small children with her. Joseph Sayer, a neighbor, perhaps fared better. He was killed and all his family with him, a fully settled account. There were many others. When the marauders had gone and there was time to total the score it came to thirty-nine, mostly women and children killed or carried away to uncertain captivity.

The red fury swept along the border, following an unsettled course. The victims probably would not have been surprised had they known that the bulk of their assailants came from the Christian missions and usually included a small group of Frenchmen, probably along for the excitement of the chase. The settlement about the falls of Saco fell to them. Though the fort itself held out, the settlement had to report eleven killed and twenty-four captured.

One by one the settlements were reached and paid their dreadful toll; Spurwink and Scarborough, Cape Porpoise and Winter Harbor, each had its tale of horror. At Purpooduck Point, a fishing village near present-day Portland, there were nine families, but most of the men were away in their boats. When the Indians departed they had with them eight prisoners, but of the nine families there were twenty-five women and children left behind who would never know when husband or father returned.

The group that attacked Casco came from Sebastian Râle's parish. No doubt they were numbered among those whom the good father reported as ready to lift the hatchet again. If so, they weren't very successful. The fort there, with its thirty-six determined men, was not to their liking; two or three old men killed, but nothing else worth mentioning.

The Jesuit historian, Pierre Charlevoix, whose first visit to Canada had filled him with a desire to write the history of the country, passes these incidents by with a rather casual reference. "Monsieur de Vaudreuil," he wrote, "formed a party of savages to whom he joined some Frenchmen under the direction of the Sieur de Beaubassin; they effected some ravages of no great consequence; they killed, however, about three hundred men." Even this was an overstatement. A better investigator set the total of those killed and carried off at a hundred and sixty, and few of them were able-bodied men. Most of them were women and children. The dreadful thing about it is that even the casual reader comes to accept the judgment of Charlevoix, that such a total is of no great consequence.

It wasn't the end. The flames and the killing spread along two hundred miles of frontier. The stealthy attack touched Hampton and Black Point and York, which had its baptism of tragedy years before, and Berwick and Haverhill. These and others had their incidents of horror and death and unbelievable endurance.

At Haverhill the attackers burst into the house of a woman who, while near her time, was busily boiling soap. This she threw on her attackers, but while it is reported to have scalded one assailant to death, she could not protect herself against all and was taken prisoner by her rather admiring captors. It was a trick they would have liked to emulate. The bands drove their prisoners northward through the forests, stumbling under their heavy burdens. As they paused for the night the woman was safely delivered of her child. It wasn't to comfort her long. Its wailing exasperated the Indians, who quieted it by dropping hot coals in its mouth as it cried. Soon it troubled them no longer. It is strange that in so many of the stories of these days tragedy was imposed on everyday emergencies that naturally would call for human sympathy. These people could not hope for sympathy, yet they didn't succumb. They accepted what happened to them with a stoicism almost beyond our understanding. Next morning, the mother, leaving her dead child, picked up her heavy burden and without a whimper of complaint followed her captors northward.

The thought that comes to mind is, how could these happenings be permitted? It is easier asked than answered. How protect such scattered settlements where men were so few and attackers could strike without warning at a score of different points and melt away before it was possible to combine against them? The settler who lived on the frontier took his own chances and provided his own security, his only help those who shared a similar hazard.

Governor Dudley of Massachusetts did what he could. All the possible points of attack could not be defended. The only answer was attack. He sent strong parties to retaliate in kind. They were heavily armed and they had a practical incentive. The General Council of Massachusetts had authorized a bounty of forty pounds for each Indian scalp, just as today we might offer a bounty for wolf pelts. The white man hardly accepted the Indian as a human being, and perhaps the Indians shared similar opinions regarding the newcomers.

Vaudreuil had some small justification. There seemed no other way to stay the inexorable spread of English settlements creeping closer and closer to the doors of New France. Also, though the squeamish might protest at the horrors, there wasn't a great deal to choose between the two contestants. After all, it was claimed with considerable probability, the English had fostered the massacre at Lachine and Chesnaye. If they were somewhat less aggressive in this regard than the French, it was because the Englishman was digging in, establishing his own right to a holding and building a town about it, while the Frenchman preferred to remain foot-loose.

However that may be, Vaudreuil was somewhat of the opinion of Charlevoix, that these small hit-and-run expeditions didn't add up to any impressive results. He was faced with certain limitations. Though Callières had succeeded in making peace with the Iroquois, to the French mind it was a very uneasy peace that might be broken at the smallest incident. Because of that, Vaudreuil sent no war party in the direction of Albany, for that would be treading on Iroquois territories and might easily provide an incident the English could use to bring about a rupture between the French and the Iroquois.

But Boston was a different matter. The Abenaki disliked and distrusted the English for encroaching on their lands. But they were the suppliers and traders nearest at hand, and it might not be beyond hoping that this could be developed into a friendly alliance. "We must keep things astir in the direction of Boston," Vaudreuil had stated more than once, "or else the Abenaki will declare for the English." It was a well-worn bit of French foreign policy that had dominated French thinking for decades past. It hadn't achieved all the results hoped, but it had kept the English as uncertain of Abenaki actions as the French were of the possible thinking of the Iroquois. Perhaps that was how fate pointed the finger at Deerfield.

Deerfield had neither political nor strategic significance. It did not lie in any disputed territory or across any road of travel. It was close to the northwestern frontier of Massachusetts, but certainly it was too far from the Canadian border to pose any threat. The only possible excuse for attacking there must rest on the military maxim that attack should be made where least expected. Certainly Deerfield, living its quiet life in the shadow of its immemorial elms, felt itself secure. Certainly its few inhabitants had no thought that a distant conflict over the question of the occupant of the Spanish throne could possibly affect them.

They did not know Governor Vaudreuil except by name, and possibly not even so much. So they couldn't have known that there was no probability that he would be satisfied with an inconspicuous part while great events were happening in Europe. The attack on Deerfield was his first open act of aggression. It was also his greatest mistake, the mistake that spelled the doom of French power on this continent. On any other basis, what happened at Deerfield might be more a matter of New England history than a vital part of that of Canada. But, in fact, it was the fuse that brought the great explosion.

It was a quite unnecessary action, judged by any standard of conduct. Deerfield had done nothing to New France or to Frenchmen. It was not that action was demanded because of pressures elsewhere. The colony of New France was indeed enjoying probably the period of greatest prosperity in its history to this date. It was freer of alarm and more securely established than it had been in many years. Ryswick, if it hadn't suggested the solution of any problems, had brought a momentary peace in which French and English were beginning to forget their latent differences. Given time, it could have been that a boundary as unguarded as it is today could have been as inviolate and as friendly.

To Canada's great misfortune she had as her governor an able man but also a vain and aggressive one. He couldn't leave well enough alone or remain inactive while action was fomenting in Europe. It has been argued that there were justifications, that there had been English depredations against the colony, both provoked and unprovoked. The attacks on La Prairie and the massacres at Lachine and La Chesnaye were there to prove it. But these had all stemmed from New York, not Boston. The Phips expeditions against Port Royal and Quebec were the only outright aggressions against admittedly French territory that had their origin in Boston. For these there had been provocation enough. Also, they had been met effectively enough to satisfy any grudge.

There was another consideration that might well have stayed Vaudreuil's hand. France was powerful on all her borders save one, and that one the southeast. She was firmly entrenched on the Ohio and the Mississippi, at Fort Frontenac and Niagara and Detroit, the possible roads of aggression. Du Lhut dominated the far west, and Iberville had emphatically established France's control of Hudson's Bay. Only Acadia, representing as it then did present-day New Brunswick and much of southern Maine, was distant and indifferently protected. It was there that peace was needed most. It was there that it was least certain. That policy of keeping the Abenaki embroiled with the English dominated Vaudreuil's thinking as it had that of Frontenac. Its revival was the culminating blunder of French policy. For that reason the history of Deerfield is a vital page in Canada's story.

There might be some question as to the responsibility for the hit-and-run raids of "the woful decade." How many of these were conceived by the Indians themselves, how many were instigated by some bold and irresponsible young Frenchmen interested in excitement and plunder are questions that are not easily decided. Deerfield was another matter. The attack was ordered by Vaudreuil and was commanded by a young Frenchman of some note, none other than Hertel de Rouville, son of François Hertel, who years before had led the attack on Salmon Falls and had fought with heroism at the Wooster River. With De Rouville, who in later years was to be a respected judge in Canada after the conquest, went four of his brothers and a total of fifty Frenchmen and two hundred Indians, Abenaki and converts from the mission at Caughnawaga.

There is so little credit for Canada in the story of this expedition that it is only fair to record that the march itself was a fine example of undaunted courage. It began from Montreal in the bitterest month of a bitter winter. It led the force across the entire length of New Hampshire, three hundred miles of unbroken snow where every step had to be taken on snowshoes and dragging the heavy sleds of supplies. It was the twenty-eighth of February when De Rouville finally halted his command at Petty's Plain, two miles beyond the outskirts of Deerfield. Night was at hand and he felt that it was too late to attack that day. It was a decision that was met with grumbling; provisions were gone and the prospects of another foodless night in the freezing cold were not cheering. They dared not light fires for fear of alerting their victims. Chilled and ferocious, they waited for the twenty-ninth to dawn, for this was leap year, and the last day of February, 1704, was to be a day of grim remembrance.

Deerfield had few defenses. Most of its forty-one homes were grouped about the Badley-Hatfield road, which formed the main street of the village, a pleasant, elm-shaded place. There was a center of defense, a palisade enclosing fifteen homes that was to be a city of refuge for all the people. But the winter had been harsh and had limited its usefulness. Snow had blanketed the fields about the village to a depth of three feet and had drifted heavily so that the north wall of the palisade was almost covered and offered no protection from an agile foe who could easily leap the remaining barrier. In numbers De Rouville's force about equaled the population of the village, with the difference that De Rouville's two hundred and fifty were seasoned warriors while much more than half of the Deerfield population were women and children.

There was a small garrison posted there, yeoman soldiers to the number of twenty. While the citizens slept these were supposed to keep watch. But the cold and the boredom of keeping an apparently aimless watch where no enemy threatened lulled them to sleep with the rest.

Two hours before dawn, while the yeoman soldiers still slumbered peacefully, De Rouville and his men were broad awake. They were weary and cold and savage with hunger. But they were also used to this sort of work. The snow was crusted enough to bear their weight, so packs and snowshoes were discarded and the men moved forward, stopping now and then so that if anyone was awake in the village the sound of the coming enemy might seem like the rising and falling of the wind. The caution was needless. No one awoke until the attackers had climbed the drift and were within the stockade and men with axes were battering the doors.

No need to recount again the familiar, desperate story of such attacks. It varies only in names and in minor details from the story of a score of other such attacks. When it was ended there was the usual assessing of losses–forty-eight dead, some of them smothered in the cellars of their burning homes, and a hundred and eleven prisoners. The total was substantially more than the number of those who escaped.

What makes the Deerfield story more interesting and vivid is that the record is fuller and the incidents more detailed. This is not so true of the lurid events of that grim twenty-ninth of February as of the days that followed. This odyssey had its minor Homer.

Sixteen years before, there had come to Deerfield a young Harvard graduate, the Reverend John Williams, to minister to this little Puritan community. He was a man of courage and clear vision and of extreme, if narrow, devotion. He had also a gift of insight and expression. The record he left behind of the captives' journey into captivity, their treatment there, and their return is elaborately titled *The Redeemed Captive Returning to Zion*, and so on for an additional fifty-odd words. But if the title is long the record itself is clear and memorable and singularly free from the animus one might expect. Only where Puritan and Catholic views collide does this simple record become biased and disputatious.

The report begins with a preachment of importance. The singular fact is that, though these outpost villagers lived in daily threat of their lives, the attack, when it came, in most cases fell on an unguarded and unwarned community. "Not long before break of day," Parson Williams records, "the enemy came in flood upon us; our watch being unfaithful, an evil whose awful effect in the surprisal of our fort should bespeak all watchmen to avoid, as they would not bring the charge of blood upon themselves."

He records his awakening, his bold effort at defense, and of being seized and bound while two of his eight children were killed. Of the eight children, one was away from the village, but the remaining five with himself and his wife were hurried across the river to join the remainder of the captives "to the number of one hundred, nineteen of whom were afterwards murdered by the way and two starved to death near Cowass in a time of great scarcity or famine that the savages underwent there."

The story of that march is an unbelievable medley of harshness and cruelty and consideration. As the weaker members among the captives began to lag they were killed. This was done reluctantly, for prisoners had a sound commercial value living; dead, at best they were worth only a scalp. It was not possible to permit them to slow the retreat. Already from the towns adjoining Deerfield men were gathering in pursuit.

John Williams tells with simple pathos of his efforts to help his wife, who had borne a child the week before and was in no condition for this rugged march. Finally being ordered forward, he writes he "had to take a last farewell of my dear wife, the desire of my eyes and companion of many mercies and afflictions."

Her end was not distant. Coming to the Green River, which was shallow and too swift to freeze, the whole company had to wade through. Stumbling in the stream, Mrs. Williams had barely strength to reach the shore, none to mount the stream's bank. Realizing that she could never survive the march, her Indian captor killed her with one stroke of his hatchet. It was not quite as ruthless as it appears. There was no time to waste or provisions to spare. Progress had to be swift or captives and captors alike would have perished. There was no soft alternative for those who could not keep up. To be left behind meant slow starvation or death by frost. More merciful, perhaps, the hatchet stroke that ended all quickly.

At best these were ruthless days. Human life had not the value we set upon it today. A man might be hanged and quartered in England for the theft of a sheep. In France one who was annoying to the favored class might rot in prison for a lifetime. Women were being hanged for the delectation of the crowds on Boston Common for no better reasons than that they had used herbs to cure the sick or, as the Reverend John Norton, a contemporary observer, argued, "for having more wit than her neighbors" or on the trumped-up complaints of excited and irresponsible children.

While many died, as Mrs. Williams died on this hazardous march, and while De Rouville most certainly dispelled further hope of escape, after Joseph Alexander had successfully achieved it, by warning that further attempts would result in the remaining prisoners being burned alive, these facts do not support the evidence of a cruelty beyond believing. Certainly the record of the personal observer, the Redeemed Captive who did return to Zion, bears no such implication.

"My youngest daughter," he writes, "aged seven years, was carried all the journey and looked after with a great deal of tenderness. My youngest son, aged four years, was wonderfully preserved from death, for though they that carried him or drawed him on sleighs were tired with their journey, yet their savage cruel tempers were so over-ruled by God, that they did not kill him; but in their pity he was spared and others would take care of him; so that four times on the journey he was thus preserved, till at last he arrived in Montreal, where a French gentlewoman, pitying the child, redeemed it out of the hands of the heathen."

But it was the seven-year-old Eunice Williams who is the shining example of this unique example of cruelty and kindness. There was a young brave among those who followed De Rouville and probably he was no less active in the tragedy of Deerfield than were the others. But his heart warmed to a child. For all those tortured three hundred miles he carried her tenderly. She went with him to the mission at Caughnawaga, where she was protected and educated, and finally married her young captor. Several times in the years that followed Eunice Williams revisited Deerfield and her father, but no argument or pleading could induce her to remain. She had chosen her life and was completely satisfied.

The Reverend John Williams, pastor of Deerfield, was a man of understanding and, above all, just. But humor had no part in Puritan theology, and John Williams was poorly supplied. He could record that when he came to Montreal eight weeks after his capture, "Governor Vaudreuil redeemed me out of the hands of the Indians, gave me good clothes, took me to his table, gave me the use of a very good chamber and was in all respects relating to the outward man, courteous and charitable to admiration." This was not an isolated reference. It must have impressed him deeply, for it recurs in the record again and again.

After his lengthy stay at Château Richer he speaks of the Jesuit priests, whose persons he liked and whose doctrines he detested. "I am persuaded," he writes, "that the priests of that parish abhorred their sending down the heathen to commit outrages against the English, saying it is more like committing murders than managing a war."

Despite the balanced judgment, which made him give generous credit where credit was due, John Williams was not an easy visitor. The Jesuits, supported perhaps by the feeling that retrieving the soul of a Puritan minister would be an outstanding accomplishment, were happy to entertain him. They made him their honored guest, invited him to their table, and showed him innumerable kindnesses. It was true of his stays at Fort St. Francis, at Quebec, and at Château Richer. But when the pleasantries were over and the disputations began, John Williams proved himself an able and truculent defender of his beliefs and belligerently defiant of those of others. If the good Jesuit fathers had received him with courtesy and kindness, it was with ill-contained relief that they saw him depart, a still belligerent, still unwavering Puritan.

It was February of 1704 that saw that miserable company of one hundred and nineteen captives start on their long march to Canada. It was the end of November of 1706 when arrangements were finally completed for the exchange of such prisoners as had survived, less the few, like Eunice Williams, who had decided to remain. The Reverend John Williams writes: "We came away from Quebec in October 25 (1706) and by contrary winds and a great storm we were retarded and then driven back near the city and had a great deliverance from shipwreck, the vessel striking twice on a rock in that storm. But through God's goodness, we all arrived safely at Boston, November 21; the number of captives 57, two of whom were my children."

The instances recounted may seem to have only a sentimental association with the history of Canada. But they are more, much more than that. It isn't the record of one calamity but of a score, all stemming from the same source and adding up to a bitter total of cruelty and wrong. An attitude of mind completely foreign to the orderly and peaceful growth of political territories and institutions that is the English way. It resulted in the hardening of the purposes of a people traditionally sensitive to any form of injustice and never overly apt at turning the other cheek. Distant as these events may seem to be from the main current of history, they represented, as nothing else could, the irrepressible character of the conflict that was slowly building up to an all-out challenge, where one or other contestant inevitably must relinquish the field.

CHAPTER XV

CHALLENGE

Recurring border raids give a semblance of success that Beaucour's venture against Connecticut does nothing to sustain. These renewed raids stir the English to a determination that Canada must be taken. Benjamin's inglorious campaign in Acadia is followed by the less glorious one of Colonel March. Samuel Vetch brings a new spirit to the challenge. Associated with Colonel Nicholson, the first proposed assault of Canada fails dismally. The determination born to take Acadia as the steppingstone to Canada. Subercase's small force bested. Port Royal becomes Annapolis and Acadia passes to the English, and so remains.

DEERFIELD was a memory of the past. In a grass-grown plot on the eastern edge of the little town the forty-eight who had died there that morning of February 29, 1704, were sleeping quietly. A year or two and the fifty-seven redeemed captives would return to these accustomed scenes and it would seem that Deerfield would become just another poignant memory that it was better to forget.

Yet occasions do arise when for no apparent reason incidents no more important than scores that have preceded seem to produce an impact on heart and conscience that no facts will explain. Deerfield was like that. Its story seemed to have an arresting quality that incidents of larger import could not achieve. The Reverend John Williams sensed a phase of it and set down his feeling in his record of the Redeemed Captive's return. He saw his captors as "wonderfully lifted up with pride." There was not much room for pride in the capture of a sleeping and undefended village peopled mostly with women and children. Perhaps it was that there was no reaction in kind that gave this happening a prophetic quality, as if the dominance France had claimed for so long finally had been acknowledged. John Williams heard the boasting. The next raid would be so impressive, would bring so many captives, that the problem would be what to do with them. He saw the expedition that was to bring this about start on its way. De Beaucour, an officer of outstanding courage and ability, was at its head. From bits of casual gossip overheard Williams learned of its purpose. It was to take the challenge farther afield and harry the settlements in Connecticut. It was sobering news, for Beaucour had under his command a force of a hundred and twenty Frenchmen and enough mission Indians to make a total of eight hundred experienced fighters. It was more than three times the force Hertel de Rouville had led against Deerfield.

Yet John Williams saw them depart with a heart that was strong in his unshakable Puritan faith. Their boasting and high spirits couldn't touch that. He listened, as he records, "with great hopes God would discover and disappoint their designs." Happily for the settlements in Connecticut, his faith was amply justified. There is no discoverable reason why this great force should not have achieved its objective. It was not a matter of opposition. Connecticut was wholly unaware of Beaucour's expedition or that it was only a day's march away. But Beaucour's Indians took fright. The only apparent reason was that one soldier had deserted. He might have gone to warn the settlements; he might also, of course, merely have taken to the bush or be trekking his independent way homeward. Warned or unwarned, the Connecticut settlements would have been easy prey for a force that could strike anywhere or at two or three points at once. That was not Indian thinking, however. They liked sleeping enemies, not enemies aroused. So the great expedition broke up and went streaming home, satisfying itself for lack of prisoners with a few scalps taken from outlying farms. Pastor Williams had been right. God had disappointed their designs.

That was not the explanation of the French. They laid the full blame on their Indian allies and still felt themselves completely masters of the situation. In a sense they were, at least on their chosen battlefield. It wasn't that the English colonies lacked the will to resist or conceded for a moment French Canada's assumption of dominance. Their weakness wasn't fear. It was disunion. Petty jealousies and divided counsels made combination against a common enemy next to impossible. This conflict of counsels was not the whole problem. It was rather that this hit-and-run policy the French had favored put all the advantage on the French side. There was little if any defense against this sort of raiding. In the winter before Deerfield a force of six hundred English militia had traveled the woods all winter without ever seeing an Indian. In the following summer nineteen hundred men were posted along the border. It was a useless precaution and ruinously costly. Shrouded as the country was by all but impenetrable forests, it was easy to confuse the defenders. The French had only to attack, as they had done at Deerfield, far afield from the scene of former attacks, and the elaborate precautions came to nothing.

There was also a vulnerability in the situation of the English colonies that did not exist with the French. The difference stemmed from a different way of thinking that resulted in a different way of life. The English were colonizers. They were forever reaching out, stopping as they went to build new settlements, each of which became a potential point of attack. The French did nothing of the kind. By and large they were not settlers but adventurers. The center of their lives was the well-defended towns where authority resided—Quebec, Three Rivers, Montreal. Such settlements as existed were merely satellites of these larger centers.

That was the difference that gave the French so sharp an advantage in this border warfare. One might think of this border war as starting with a basic triangle formation. The French assaults began from the apex of the triangle. As the march continued it could fan out to any point on that extensive territory that formed the base of the triangle. It represented a possible field of operation stretching from perhaps Oswego on Lake Ontario to Boston and Portland on the Atlantic coast.

To visualize similar attacks by the English on Canada, the triangle remains the same. Only the concentration for attack is at the triangle's base. On that long line had to be assembled a striking force gathered in the face of divided interests and prejudices and from such scattered centers as Albany and New York and Hartford and

Boston and Portland. Should this be accomplished, there still remained the disturbing fact that such a force must move against a constantly narrowing front until it came to a focus at one or other end of that hundred-and-sixty-mile stretch between Montreal and Quebec. Always the French enjoyed the advantage of their interior lines; always the English had to defend a field of possible attack three times as long that had not three possible points of assault but scores of such points. It was small wonder that the French should feel themselves favorably placed for such strategy and were determined to exploit it to the limit.

What they didn't see was that the English colonies' quiescence did not spring from fear or from any sense that New France could actually dominate. It was rather that there was no central guiding force, no common purposes to bring the separate colonies together. There was little love lost between the new aristocrats of Virginia and the Puritans of New England or between the settlers of Maine and the traders of New York; little realization as yet that they must all hang together or hang separately. For long it would remain a struggle between the stubborn New England spirit—sometimes supported by New York, which shared the hazards—and the land-free, adventure-hungry Frenchman, whose interest and pleasure were not in colonizing but in trading and fighting.

New France couldn't see that English patience had come to an end. How Deerfield could be the spark to set that slow-burning fire alight, who can say? There had been other attacks more vicious and more destructive. If it is to be explained, perhaps it is no more than this, that a mounting load of fury must have a final straw. That back-breaking straw was Deerfield.

Governor Vaudreuil simply couldn't realize this. He couldn't understand that these nibbling attacks on one frontier settlement after another were as stupid as they were cruel. They built up an antagonism out of all proportion to their negligible accomplishment. When Frontenac had started such raids they were just as ruthless, but they had a purpose. The Iroquois threat to the life of the colony was real and imminent. The Five Nations had come to believe France's day was done. She could be attacked without the hazard of reprisal. It was the English who dominated the continent. New France had lost the will to fight back. She had no confidence that she could survive and conquer. For the morale of her people, for a check on the Iroquois, some challenge to a powerful enemy was imperative. There was that much justification to Frontenac's raiding. It wasn't just killing. It had a purpose, and the purpose was achieved.

No such excuse remained. New France was prosperous and successful and freer from threat than it had been for years past. The morale of the people had never been higher, the need to impress the Indians never less. So the raids had no large purpose and achieved no end unless it was to forge a determination that henceforth was never to waver for long. But for the present, the task facing the English colonies, of protecting themselves against the ever-recurring horror, was beyond their powers. One alternative remained, and only one. There was no more thought of peaceful co-existence. The people responsible must be destroyed.

The ministers of a great vengeance do not always seem to be appropriate. The first man to give the burning anger of the English colonies a physical presence was scarcely so. Major Benjamin Church had some qualities that the times sorely needed. He had a will to challenge these unjust border attacks and he could think and act quickly. Major Church had earned a stout reputation as an Indian fighter in King Philip's War, but that was some time past and, while his courage hadn't suffered in those years, his figure had. He had grown so fat that when he now took the trail there had to be a soldier to accompany him; to lever him over fallen trees or hoist him to his horse. He was sixty-five years of age. But if the years had qualified his physical charm they had done nothing to his spirit. He could still blaze into quick anger that happily left him still a man of action and of sharp decisiveness.

When the news of Deerfield reached his home in Tiverton, Rhode Island, Church didn't accept the judgment of so many of his fellows, that Deerfield was quite a piece away and was someone else's problem. Immediately he adopted the problem as his own and, sputtering with rage, had himself hoisted on his horse. Undismayed by distance or disability, he was going to see Governor Dudley at Boston, and with a definite plan of retaliation to present.

Governor Dudley received the proposals in the favorable spirit in which they were offered. He promptly advanced Major Church to a colonelcy and gave him command of his proposed expedition with an authorization to collect such forces as he could for the venture.

It is rather sad to relate that this prompt and vigorous action had almost negligible results. The will was there, but it was complicated by an overly tender attitude toward the most likely and most strategic target—Acadia, and particularly its fortress center, Port Royal.

The many vicissitudes of Acadia had invariably ended with it once again in French hands. Yet, though part of Canada, it was a distant and difficult province to govern and defend from Quebec. Its interests, too, if not its sympathies, might almost be said to be more nearly allied with New England than with Quebec. To a considerable extent its trade outlet was through Boston, and thence also it drew an appreciable part of its supplies. Its contact with Canada was the long sea road by way of the gulf and river St. Lawrence, or the difficult and hazardous overland route of the Kennebec and Chaudière rivers.

While Acadia remained in French hands it was an example of the "fleet in being" challenging both these avenues of possible attack on Canada. This left only the border as a point of attack. There Vaudreuil's commandos were still carrying on their harrying tactics and there, for the reasons explaned, any attack by the English was sharply handicapped. But Acadia was wide open, and the humbling of Port Royal was the first and necessary step in the attack on the heart of New France itself.

Colonel Church had been shrewd enough to know that Port Royal was the logical objective. When this was suggested, however, he received a quick rejection. There were rather lame excuses that plans for a major attack on the fortress were even then before Queen Anne, and nothing could be done before her permission was received. There was gossip, somewhat less generous, that said Governor Dudley and other nabobs of Boston had a substantial interest in the trade with Port Royal and were satisfied to see it remain in French hands. So Colonel Church set out on his roving commission with no very definite objective. Having got his force of seven hundred, mainly sailors and Indians from about his native Duxbury and from Plymouth, he moved up the coast to Mount Desert Island. There a little conferring suggested Fort St. Castin, lying in that debated land between the Kennebec and the St. Croix, might well be destroyed. As usual, most of the inhabitants promptly disappeared into the forests, where the redoubtable Indian fighter found it difficult to follow. A few men were killed and a few surrendered Frenchmen were added to that number by inadvertence when Church's disorderly mob took one of his choleric outbursts too literally. It couldn't be described as an impressive victory.

The avenging band sailed up the Bay of Fundy, and Church himself led a part of his force against Grand Pré and sent another column against Beaubassin. Both places were set afire and the dikes were breached to let the sea water flood the cultivated land. It was harsh enough treatment, and Church blustered mightily about what he would return and do if "Deerfield" were repeated elsewhere; then, taking a few prisoners to exchange, he sailed away for Port Royal. So far there was little glory in this and no accomplishment whatever. About the best that could be said was that Church had kept both his Indian allies and his rough levies well in hand.

The thought of Port Royal was still in Church's mind. He was smart enough to know that burning houses and cutting dikes were rather empty gestures. Port Royal would be different. There was just the possibility, too, that it could be reduced by a threat of force, or even force itself, should a favorable opportunity occur. Of course there were the orders that the place should not be attacked, but orders were held rather lightly by the Indian-fighting community. So on reaching the vicinity of the port he held a council of war as to whether or not the orders should be obeyed. It was the practical considerations that decided the point. There were only four hundred men available for assault, and it was felt that this was not enough to assure success. Therefore, the governor's orders should be obeyed.

Colonel Church did make his final gesture. It was a demand for the surrender of the fort. This being haughtily refused, there was no alternative remaining but to embark with as good grace as he could and sail away for home, his whole effort an example of sound intentions more destitute of results than such intentions should be.

The failure of this mission somehow increased rather than diminished the gossiping over Governor Dudley's interest in Port Royal. This grew to such volume in the next year or two that it seemed essential that he should quiet these voices. Also, he was a little bit caught by the force of his own arguments. He had rather publicly urged that in the past two years "the Assembly of Massachusetts had spent about £50,000 in defending the provinces, whereas three or four of the Queen's ships and fifteen hundred New England men would rid us of the French and make further outlay needless."

This view may have been overly sanguine, but it wasn't one that permitted the utterer to sit about doing nothing. In 1707 Dudley himself proposed an all-out attack on Port Royal. The General Court promptly ordered it and authorized the raising of a force of one thousand men. It was to be under the command of Colonel John March of Newbury. The force was raw and undisciplined and as inexperienced in concerted action as was its leader.

All through the years of conflict, leadership had been the one great lack of the English colonists. Individually they were the equal of any men anywhere, but they were just individuals of courage and determination, without a rudiment of training in warfare or the leadership of men. They were colonizers rather than soldiers; businessmen, traders, farmers, but not military leaders. With the French it was quite the opposite. Command was something they understood and wanted. Most of the young aristocrats who came to Canada were army-trained. Where they weren't, the very nature of their roving life and perpetual struggle with the Indians soon developed qualities of leadership.

It might have been possible for the English colonies to make good their lack by calling on the mother country for trained military leadership. It has to be admitted that in later years, when they did depend on others, leadership frequently failed them, as will be seen as this history unfolds. But there was also an innate prejudice against imported command. The Puritans wanted no direction that wasn't in tune with their own thinking, and they believed the English regular soldier to be of "a crew that began to teach New England to Drab, Drink, Blaspheme, Curse and Damn." So they developed the hard way: by the teaching of innumerable mistakes.

When Colonel John March was appointed to lead the great expedition against Port Royal that Dudley had suggested, this policy reached its zenith. At first all went well. If Connecticut would not co-operate in the expedition, Rhode Island did better, supplying eighty men, while New Hampshire added sixty. There was beginning to be some semblance of united effort. When the total force was finally aboard the frigate *Deptford*, impressed for the purpose, it was a considerable body of one thousand and seventy-six soldiers and four hundred and fifty sailors, the biggest expeditionary force since Phips had sailed for Quebec.

If ever there was a less expert army commanded by a less knowing leader, it is difficult to remember where or when. It consisted of an odd assortment of plowboys, fishermen, mechanics, village officials, church dignitaries, and farmers, as is the way with armies. In this case, however, there was no attempt to weld the whole into a fighting unit. As they were in the beginning, so they remained, individualists accustomed to attend to their own affairs and abnormally reluctant to accept direction. Courage they had aplenty, but it was the courage of the mob.

As the men were, so was their leader. Though he was personally brave and possessed many popular qualities, these, sadly enough, did not include the quality of leadership. John March had seen some frontier service and could probably have managed a handful of men with reasonable credit, but to handle a thousand was completely beyond him. To the question of why he was chosen there is just one answer, and that another question, "Where were the colonies to look for anyone better qualified?"

It was early June of 1707 when the *Deptford* with its supporting warships sailed into Port Royal basin. An impressive and alarming sight it must have been for the few defenders and townsfolk. Impressive, too, the speed with which this motley little army prepared for attack. Probably the plan had been well enough conceived. Some three hundred and fifty men were landed on the north shore a few miles below the fort. Their landing was unopposed and they immediately began their march. At the mouth of the Annapolis River they blundered into an ambush, but they had swarmed over in such numbers that the few defenders had no alternative but to retreat, leaving the attackers breathless and as elated as if a major victory had been assured.

While this heroic passage was in progress Colonel March had landed seven hundred and fifty men on the south shore. This attack he would command in person. They had advanced only a short way when they met an outpost of two hundred Frenchmen. These were under the command of Governor Subercase himself. He will be remembered as the soldier who didn't panic in that dreadful night and early morning when the Iroquois burned and ravaged Lachine. He it was who had commanded the advance in Frontenac's last campaign against the Iroquois. Certainly he was not a man to be easily pushed about. So when we learn that March's seven hundred and fifty men drove Subercase's forces from their entrenchments, even with the sharp disparity in numbers, there is still evidence that the attack was made with courage.

But after these small successes the whole program bogged down. No one knew just what to do or how to do it. Councils of war did nothing but add angry disputation. French deserters from the fort added to the uncertainty by reporting Subercase's forces as already numbering five hundred with an equal number expected any day. He had forty-two heavy guns, the deserters reported, better than anything the besieging expedition could produce.

What the deserters didn't report was that all was not peace and harmony within the city itself, and certainly the defenders were less numerous than reported. Governor Subercase seldom had more than three hundred soldiers at his command, while the expected reinforcements existed mainly in the minds of the deserters. In truth, morale was low. The soldiers stationed there were not infrequently left without pay for years on end, never an encouraging policy. There was a prosperous minority among Port Royal citizens, largely involving those who had certain piratical interests, but poverty was the more general state. There are records to show that Governor Subercase gave away some of his own shirts and even the sheets from his bed and, on one occasion, some of his own furniture to meet the more pressing need of those he governed, which is farther than most administrators would be disposed to go.

Tempers were no more secure than circumstances. There was incessant bickering over inconsequential issues, in which the governor himself was inclined to join. Nothing was too small; cows straying in a neighbor's garden, a quarrel at the church door where a fourteen-year-old got his ears soundly boxed, the price of a canoe charged against the governor's salary, the virtue or the lack of it in a certain lady—all became matters of high policy. High enough, at least, to be referred to the ministry in France. There was the usual bickering with the Church. The chaplain was heard to remark that he cared no more for the governor than for the mud on his shoes, while the acting intendant of Acadia, De Goutin by name, writing of his efforts to keep on good terms with the governor, records: "I walk as if in the chamber of a sick prince whose sleep is of the lightest."

Governor Subercase was sending his own letters, in which he urged that what he really needed was a madhouse for some of his people, adding a final personal opinion: "There is no country on the earth where I would not rather live than in this, by reason of the ill-disposed persons who inhabit it." Nothing in this record to suggest a community easily moved to a common enthusiasm in defending their homes!

But not knowing what else to do, Colonel March did nothing. In a day or so he gave orders to destroy storehouses and other buildings outside the fort, and the men went to the task with such vim that one observer was to remark, "They would have taken the fort if the officers had shown any spirit." This might have been true, considering the situation within. But Colonel March had no such thought. He was thinking of getting away. Very shortly thereafter he sailed with his whole force for Casco Bay, from which safe haven he notified Governor Dudley that the great expedition was not going very well.

Governor Dudley, having no better leader at hand, did not recall March but adopted the more doubtful course of sending three commissioners to advise him. Two belonged to the militia and the third, John Leverett, was a bachelor of divinity who was soon to become president of Harvard College. What the expedition certainly didn't need was more sources of opinion when already it had almost as many as there were members. About the sanest word to come from the expedition was that of Captain Stuckley, commander of the British frigate, who wrote Governor Dudley: "I don't see what good I can do by lying here, where I am almost murdered by mosquitoes."

Finally the three commissioners arrived at Casco Bay with another frigate and an additional hundred recruits. There was a lot of talk and recriminations and finally in high ill humor the expedition headed back for Port Royal. This was to be the acid test. But it turned out to be more of the same, a few minor skirmishes, a few more buildings burned, and reams of talk and nothing of the slightest importance. Probably John March made the wisest decision of his whole command when he ordered his forces to re-embark and return to Boston.

It may be difficult to see how the union of England and Scotland in 1707 could have any possible bearing on these affairs or the long conflict between England and France in the New World. Admittedly the connection is tenuous, but it did exist. In opening expanding horizons to a hardy and acquisitive race it influenced many situations. Up to that time England, realizing that the aggressive Scot might prove tough competition, had definitely shut him out of all her colonial plans.

With union, it was soon discovered that this most patriotic of nations balanced its aggressiveness with an urge to migrate. Being shut out of the English colonial zone, these adventurous Scots determined to create a new Scotland on the Isthmus of Darien, now better known as Panama. This elaborate scheme cannily envisioned a New Scotland bathed by two oceans and enjoying the trade that stemmed from both. The results were not quite as happy as the thought. Even the hardy Scot soon found that the twofold challenge of imperial Spain, who had first claim on the land and had no thought of relinquishing it, and the tropical climate was a bit more than had been anticipated. The grand dream came to a rather sad and summary end.

Among the captains of this ambitious undertaking was one Samuel Vetch. He survived the fate that befell so many of these adventurers by finding his way to New York. There he thoughtfully married into one of its prominent families, that of Robert Livingston.

A little later he went to Boston, where his background of forbears, which included several covenanting ministers, assured him a ready acceptance. Soon he was one of Boston's prominent traders. True, this trading was lacking in stern covenanting rectitude. It was a little tinged with the suspicion of illicit dealings with New France, and openly he was charged and fined for trading with Acadia. Unlike many of his fellow merchants, however, who felt their trading interests more important than patriotism and who had no wish to see a profitable business destroyed, Samuel Vetch was ready to risk all for a larger dream. That dream nothing less than a proposal to drive both France and Spain from North America. When Newfoundland and all Canada had been secured, he proposed to wrest Pensacola from the Spaniards and so leave Queen Anne "sole Empress of the vast North American continent."

Samuel Vetch was an aggressive salesman as well as a dreamer. He went to London and to the Queen's ministers and, whether owing to the heady dream itself or Vetch's persuasive tongue, when he left London it was with the promise of a British fleet and a force of five seasoned regiments to support an all-out attack on Canada that would wipe out the memory of the rather sorry episodes of Church and March.

With Britain's contribution on such a large scale, she expected substantial support from the colonies. Again it was to be the familiar two-pronged attack, by land and by sea. New York was to provide eight hundred men, Pennsylvania a hundred and fifty, New Jersey two hundred, and Connecticut three hundred and fifty. This force was to follow the accustomed route by Lake Champlain and the Richelieu River and assault Montreal. New England was to raise a force of twelve hundred men to add to the five seasoned regiments and the fleet to attack Quebec by sea. It was Phips's plan all over again, but this time with more careful preparation and possibly better leadership.

Certainly the land attack had a much better promise. More men, more determined men, while Colonel Francis Nicholson, who was to lead, was a very great improvement over Fitz-John Winthrop, who had commanded the land forces in Phips's attack on Canada. Though his experience was political rather than military, Colonel Nicholson had played an important part in colonial affairs, having been governor at various times of Virginia, Maryland, and lieutenant governor of New York. He was practical-minded, with a capacity for thinking in broader terms than was customary among his contemporaries. If his private life was not without flaw, there was no hint of lack of character in his administration of public affairs. Perhaps more important for the work in hand, as a leader he was both bold and vigorous, something Winthrop had not been; and if he was somewhat overly headstrong and ambitious, it was qualified by a real devotion to the colonies and the mother land. Perhaps even more important as a strictly practical matter was the fact that he was the one man who would be satisfactory to the various interests of his diverse command.

Nicholson acted with swiftness and determination. He moved up the Hudson to a spot known as Great Carrying Place. There he disembarked his forces and set them to cutting a rough roadway through the forest to Wood Creek. It was not a name of very good omen, nor was it to improve in that regard. But for John Schuyler's attack on La Prairie, it had been the farthest point reached by Fitz-John Winthrop's expedition. Its strategic importance was that it led directly to Lake Champlain and thence to Chambly on the Richelieu and so to Montreal.

It was hard to keep such an expedition secret. Vaudreuil soon learned of it and promptly sent De Ramesay with fifteen hundred troops to surprise and destroy the invader. For that purpose he landed a little south of Crown Point. Immediately confusion seemed to surround the expedition. Trained soldier that he was, De Ramesay got himself hopelessly lost in the forest. When he rediscovered his command it was to find that Nicholson was well aware of their approach. The possibility of surprise was gone, and there was much disagreement among his officers as to the wisdom of attacking so large a force so far from home. The French forces finally returned to Chambly, having accomplished nothing and having lost nothing but the initiative.

Beyond any doubt the initiative lay with Nicholson, but this advantage was qualified by the fact that his attack was to coincide with the fleet attack on Quebec, and as yet the fleet had not appeared. All through the heat of summer and early fall Nicholson's force camped at Wood Creek, waiting word of the fleet's arrival at Boston, which was to be the signal for advance.

Waiting was much more dangerous than marching, even with De Ramesay barring the way. The troops began to sicken and the Iroquois allies to grow restive. They might give up the association altogether. There were even darker suspicions. The Iroquois found the conflict of French and English a condition distinctly to their advantage, and they were not happy when it turned sharply to the disadvantage of either side, as now it appeared to be doing against the French. There were rumors that to adjust the balance they had poisoned the streams about Wood Creek. Little evidence supports the theory except that it might easily have been done. It was suggested that the Indians had achieved this result, perhaps inadvertently merely by tossing the skins and offal from animals captured in the hunt into the streams and so polluting them. It seems, however, that, possible as this might be, it was not needed to explain the sudden upsurge of malignant dysentery that attacked the expedition. The heat, the flies and mosquitoes that blanketed the neighborhood, the disorderly and unsanitary conditions of the camp itself provide explanation enough.

The consternation that had swept over New France at the first hint of this attack had quickly grown into something bordering on hysteria. Governor Vaudreuil had written Pontchartrain of "the most bloody war" that was about to overtake the colony. There was talk of giving up Chambly and even Fort Frontenac and of concentrating forces for a last-ditch defense of the colony. But days passed and nothing seemed to happen. Slowly panic gave way to wonder.

For the weeks and months that Nicholson's levies had been lying in their pestilence-ridden camp the New England contingent had been waiting too, though in somewhat better circumstances. The fleet with its five seasoned regiments was to have reached Boston by the middle of May. But though Samuel Vetch was writing to London with growing urgency by every post and though Governor

Dudley was adding his petition for haste, these appeals apparently fell on deaf ears.

It was the eleventh of October 1709 when Governor Dudley received a reply from the Earl of Sunderland. There were no apologies, merely a statement that, owing to the exigencies of the European war, the fleet had been sent to Portugal instead of Canada. The letter had been written on the twenty-seventh of July. But no one thought to explain why a fleet that was due in Boston in early May should have remained unreported for so long. It was part of the very casual treatment that was considered good enough for the colonies.

Before the letter had arrived Nicholson had disbanded his force, knowing that it was now too late to attack with any hope of success, and had warehoused his stores in Albany. Wood Creek returned to its customary anonymity.

The New England forces were no happier. They had waited and drilled for months on end, neglecting their businesses and their lands for no purpose whatsoever. The governments of the eastern colonies were acutely aware that they had spent forty-six thousand pounds in preparing for the attack and maintaining their forces. For the day it was a figure of real consequence. They wanted something to show for it. If the destruction of all Canada must be postponed, they saw no reason why Port Royal, at least, might not be taken, so ending that ever-present threat.

Nicholson went to London to present the case, and Peter Schuyler soon followed. He took with him five Mohawk chiefs. Regrettably, one of the chiefs died on the voyage, reducing the number to four. Even so, this promotional effort did more than all the oratory to bring the American war to public attention. The four chiefs were clad, at the Queen's expense, in magnificent robes designed by a theater costumer who had given his fancy free rein. Their own tribes would scarcely have recognized them, but they did achieve the objective of gaining attention. That in turn resulted in Nicholson's plan being accepted. He was to command the attack against Port Royal, with Vetch as his adjutant general.

The naval force that was to spearhead the expedition was to have been in Boston early in March. But New England, having learned something from past experience, did not plan to begin raising her proposed forces until the fleet arrived. It was as well, for it was July before the ships actually appeared. Recruiting was not easy, and it was September 18, 1710, before the expedition finally sailed from Boston. It consisted of five small warships and thirty still smaller transport and service ships. Though the vessels were not large it was quite an impressive armada.

It was the twenty-fourth of September when they reached Port Royal. One of the ships, caught in the swift-running tide of the harbor entrance, went on the rocks and twenty-six men were drowned. The rest made it safely. The following day the troops were ashore.

It was a sizable attacking force, for Nicholson had heard that Subercase had been reinforced. This was not true to any large extent. Perhaps happily for him, for in a letter to Pontchartrain he had explained that personally he had been compelled to borrow enough to maintain the garrison for the past two years and now had not a sou remaining.

The landing force consisted of four hundred British marines and about fifteen hundred provincials divided into four battalions, half commanded by Nicholson and half by Vetch. With two hundred and fifty defenders within the fort and nearly two thousand attackers without, the result could not long be in doubt. But Subercase, always a stout fighter, put on such an impressive show that there was no attempt to take the fort by assault. It was several days before there was even a demand for surrender, and October 2 before the lilies of France were finally run down from the flagstaff and the red ensign run up. With no little ceremony Subercase and his forces were permitted to march out with all the honors of war, to be returned to France in British ships.

After innumerable changes of fortune Port Royal was now British and would so remain. Samuel Vetch, the good Scotsman, was at last to be governor of a province that could be named for his native land—Nova Scotia. And its capital was no longer Port Royal, but Annapolis Royal. But the royalty involved was a British queen rather than a French king. There was the beginning of the challenge. It would face New France with varying fortunes until the challenge was complete.

Queen Anne, a rather dull and supremely stubborn woman, had said that she must have Acadia. Now it was hers. But she had advanced her sights. Now she was saying with equal stubbornness, so the French heard, that she must have all of Canada.

CHAPTER XVI

THE MAGNIFICENT FIASCO

The greatest challenge yet to face New France. An important yet almost forgotten chapter in the history of Canada. The mixed motives that fostered the expedition and assured its unexpected strength. The palace intrigue that put incompetency in command. Two notable misfits—their fortune and their fate. An empty victory that favors the vanquished. The Peace of Utrecht where France signs away her hope of empire and decides the character of the now inevitable conflict.

IT still seems strange that one of the greatest threats ever to cast its shadow over early Canada should remain an almost forgotten chapter of her history. Probably not even the names of the leading actors in these events will be wholly familiar to the average reader. Sir Hovenden Walker, commander of the threatening force, was an admiral of the Royal Navy, though there is nothing in his record, public or private, to suggest why or how he came to that rank. Jack Hill, who, as second-in-command of the expedition, had almost twelve thousand troops under his command, was a brigadier who wasn't really a soldier—a man about town, a pleasant fellow with all the social graces and no military graces at all.

There is no real reason why anyone should remember either of them. No doubt this explains today's lack of knowledge. It springs from the quite natural tendency to understress those incidents that lend no credit to either friend or foe, for it is easier to be magnanimous, at least after the event, than to be left without respect for anyone.

If glory or even credit was wholly lacking in this abortive effort to seize Canada, it was not because in concept, in the strategy proposed, or in the forces employed the project was foredoomed to failure. Never in the history of Canada, to this date, had the threat been more actual or the possibility of success more real. The fleet was the strongest and best equipped ever to sail these northern waters. The troops that reinforced the fleet provided a fighting force almost equal to the total population of Canada. For the Canada of the day, in all its widely scattered sections—from New Brunswick, Maine, and Cape Breton, which France still claimed, to Detroit and Duluth, and from Hudson's Bay to the Gulf of Mexico—still could not boast a combined population of twenty thousand of all ages.

Walker's great fleet of nine warships and more than sixty transports, in addition to the complement of sailors to set the sails and man the guns, had fifty-five hundred regulars from the choicest troops in Europe, trained under the great Marlborough himself, and five hundred marines, almost as choice. Also there were some fifteen hundred provincial militia and enough other allies to bring the total to twelve thousand men. The supporting force that Francis Nicholson was leading against Montreal, in the old and tried policy of divide and conquer, represented no less than twenty-three hundred skilled fighters.

All in all, it was a mighty undertaking that no one could discount. Certainly the French did nothing of the kind. They realized it as a threat not only to their political life but to their spiritual life as well. Father Joseph Germain, Superior General of the Canadian Missions, writing from Quebec to a friend under date of November 5, 1711, records: "All the inhabitants of Canada . . . without a single exception were convinced that not only the preservation of their temporal goods, of their wives, of their children and of their lives was at stake, but also of the Catholic apostolic Roman religion, which would be utterly destroyed throughout the colony if the English became masters of it. They were sure that in all the churches they would witness naught but sacrilege and profanation: altars overturned; images broken; priests and laymen ill-treated, murdered or sent as slaves to other foreign heretical countries; and everywhere the utmost desolation." The defense of the country quickly became something in the nature of a crusade. They were ready to shed "the last drop of their blood rather than yield, or enter into any agreement with these perfidious enemies of God and of the Church; and if God permitted that they should die in battle, they looked upon such a death as a glorious martyrdom."

This wasn't the perfervid thinking of a zealous priest alone. There was no doubt that a new determination, born of a very desperate need, touched every part of the community. Masses and processions and an almost unending succession of fasts were the order of the days, though it must be admitted that, if the outward manifestations were different, the prayers that ascended to heaven from Boston beseeching aid for English arms were probably no less sincere or devout than those that arose from Quebec for quite different ends.

Mother Juchereau noted with satisfaction that many of the ladies of Montreal gave up their ornaments and became more modest and pious. There is a touch of local pride, too, in her recognition that the Montreal ladies outdid even those of Quebec, "for they bound themselves by oath to wear neither ribbon nor lace, to keep their throats covered and to observe various holy practices for the space of a year."

On the more strictly practical side Father Germain records that "Monsieur the Marquis de Vaudreuil, Governor of Canada, had taken such effective measures to increase our forces that he had gathered together more than twelve hundred savages of various nations . . . for whom he had caused cabins to be prepared in the vicinity of Quebec. He had, too, so well prepared all the settlers who live with their families in the country, outside the towns, that they erected stockades in the depths of the forests, at places which the enemy could not or would not venture to approach, in which to put the women, children, cattle, furniture and effects, with strong guards—leaving in their homes nothing that could be of use to their foes. All the settlers capable of bearing arms were to proceed to Quebec, where there was a very abundant supply of provisions and of munitions of war; for all were convinced that by saving Quebec the colony would be saved, and that by losing it all would be lost."

At Montreal similar precautions had been taken. There more than twelve hundred men, "both French and savages, had been left under the command of a very valiant captain, Monsieur de Longueuil, a member of one of the leading families of Canada."

To provide against the possibility that the enemy might approach from above after the manner of former Indian attacks, "ambushes were set to harass them wherever they might pass."

There is no doubting the fact that, whatever future generations might think, the Canada of that day knew itself to be facing its greatest challenge. Even looking back after the event, Father Germain was to record the simple fact: "Had they come as they intended and as we feared, the victory was very uncertain though we had prepared ourselves in every possible way."

In essence, the plan of attack was admirably sound but for one major lack. Unfortunately for the planners, the lack was crucial. It was a matter of faulty leadership. There were other qualifying factors, of course. The objectives were not only those that appeared on the surface. Certainly Britain was not playing the game suggested by the New England colonies. She was not thinking only of the New World and its problems but had involved with these the politics of home. Undoubtedly the Walker expedition was a move in the crafty political maneuvering of the day. It was not this, however, that determined the results. If the motives were not as single-minded as they were made to appear, the actual planning was sound enough. Sir Hovenden Walker could have achieved the conquest of Canada a half century ahead of the actual fact. Had he been a different man he could have changed the history of a continent.

There were a number of forces influencing the decision to send an expedition to drive the French from the New World. Only one of them, the capture of Acadia, had any very definite bearing on Canada itself.

There was the continuing threat of Louis XIV's ambition, which had to be curbed in some way. Louis' grandson was sitting on the throne of Spain as Philip V. The English people, who had accepted this fact without protest when William III had urged against it, had changed their thinking. Marlborough's victories had put them in a far stronger negotiating position. They were not now ready to accept Louis' assurance that he would forgo any Bourbon claim to the throne of Spain. They saw in this changed attitude not the evidence of a more peaceful intent but only the necessary, and perhaps momentary, readjustments of a nation despoiled by war and other kingly extravagances. They were convinced, too, that even this momentary change of heart was not shared by Philip. He had tasted kingship and found it to his liking. Certainly he had no thought of relinquishing his throne, no matter what pressures were brought to bear. The English Whigs, recognizing that, whatever Louis might say, a Bourbon France and Spain represented an extending threat in Europe, demanded that as Louis had been responsible at least in part for Philip's being on the Spanish throne he should use his powers now to eject his protégé. With a shrewdness that sometimes marked his diplomacy Louis argued that if it was a matter of fighting anyway he might better make war against his customary enemies than against his kith and kin. So deciding, he discovered the one cause to appeal to a war-weary French nation.

In Britain politics had entered on a very bitter phase. The Whigs, with the prestige of the great Marlborough behind them, had developed an autocratic attitude the Tories were quick to recognize as both a threat and an opportunity. It had never been difficult to stir the English into action at any hint of a developing autocracy. This time it might be possible to convince them that they were face to face not only with the autocrat but with a conqueror who might be a Cromwell all over again.

Changes of large significance were in the making. The Whigs had grown arrogant. They were confident that their day had no end. Marlborough himself was no one to advocate caution, and his duchess was no more tractable than he. Thus came the change. For years as lady of the Queen's bedchamber, the duchess had fostered an intimacy that wiped out the suggestion of rank. The queen was Mrs. Morley and the duchess Mrs. Freeman in all their intercourse. The difference was no more than that, or so it appeared. But the duchess was a masterful woman. She would have dominated a far stronger character than the dull and indolent Queen Anne. As it was, she ruled her sovereign with a rod of iron. It was small wonder that the Whigs should feel themselves too strong to be assailed.

It was this growing arrogance of a lady of the bedchamber toward her Queen that finally brought the change. It reached through the outward show of intimacy and touched Queen Anne's one great strength, her obstinate sense of royal dignity. It was the year 1710 that saw the friendship of Mrs. Morley and Mrs. Freeman come to an end, never to be revived. But it wasn't the end of play-acting. Poor Queen Anne, who had borne fifteen children and had no child living, needed a friend. She found one in Abigail Hill, like the duchess, one of the ladies of the Queen's bedchamber. There was no need to think of a new name for Abigail Hill. She had provided it by her marriage. She was Mrs. Masham, the Queen's new and dear favorite.

The pendulum was swinging in other than court circles. England was tired of war, even victorious war, where each new success seemed only to bring the country nearer to financial ruin. She was tired even of her great conqueror. War-weariness was turning men from the Whig camp to that of the Tories, where Lord Treasurer Harley, who would become Earl of Oxford, and Secretary of State St. John, who would become Lord Bolingbroke, had just achieved the long-desired office in a landslide victory that left no doubt of Britain's opinion.

But though governments might change and even a popular idol become almost a figure of fear and a challenge to a people always restless under a threat of power it might not be able to control, the prestige still remained. It might not be too difficult to retrieve what little had been lost. This was the shadow behind the Tory successes. How was this imminent challenge to be met? Certainly not by any embroilment with colonies overseas.

The sound strategy that had sent Francis Nicholson and Samuel Vetch to London at just this crucial time paid off. Here were men of ability and determination who knew what they wanted. They had come to urge that the capture of Acadia should be more than an isolated action that some new treaty might bring to nothing in the give-and-take of negotiations, as had happened more than once. It should be a starting point in a war of conquest that should finally drive the last Frenchman from the continent.

Suddenly Harley and Bolingbroke had their answer, the one achievement that could assure their continuance in office. If it were possible to set against the victories of Marlborough the conquest of a new continent, that would be victory indeed. It would be an achievement profiting the home land rather than the various countries of Europe that, another year, might be allied to someone else. The invasion plan disclosed new merits as it took shape. It minimized the shadow of Marlborough in that every regiment diverted to America reduced the forces available to that impressive figure. Small wonder that Harley and Bolingbroke listened with growing enthusiasm to the representations of Vetch and Nicholson outlining the plan for an English continent, or that they moved with quite unaccustomed promptness to make the dream come true.

In the New World rumors were everywhere; rumors of an attack on Boston, rumors of an attack on Canada, rumors of a possible effort to retake Acadia. The last wasn't surprising, because Samuel Vetch, the newly appointed governor, was having anything but a happy time. The English colonies, once Acadia had been captured, quickly withdrew the bulk of their troops, thus relieving themselves of the financial burden and leaving to competent Governor Vetch the tangled problems of what to do next. What Governor Vetch had to do was to spend considerable sums of his own money, as Subercase had been compelled to do before him. It was the only way of financing the government and of keeping his handful of troops sufficiently paid and satisfied to prevent them from siding with Acadia's alien and hostile population.

Wherever anyone went there was talk of conflict. Monsieur de Costebelle, the French commandant at Placentia Harbor, Newfoundland, heard through a couple of Irish deserters from the fort at St. John's of elaborate plans for an English attack on Canada. Others had heard this rumor also, among them a Frenchman, La Ronde Denys, who had lived and studied in Boston. Whether these studies had developed a native craftiness does not appear, nor does it appear how he was in touch with the French commandant in Newfoundland. But in some way he had suggested to Costebelle that this rumor might be given a useful twist by suggesting to the Bostonians that the English forces, sent ostensibly to assist in the conquest of Canada, might in reality be more concerned in seeing that New York and New England didn't develop any republican ideas of their own.

In reporting to Pontchartrain the rumor of the proposed English attack on Canada, Costebelle had passed on the suggestion of La Ronde Denys that success for Queen Anne in Canada would result in the colonies being surrounded, and under these changed circumstances they might find themselves relieved of many of the liberties they now enjoyed. To add another string to this useful bow, he suggested that gossip might also be set a-simmer in London to the effect that the American colonies were beginning to think of shaking off the yoke of England and of establishing their own republican democracy.

Half a century later this would have been an effective approach. At the moment Boston was more interested in the rumor of attack and the suggestion that the city was to be given over to pillage. New England was troubled, too, by the open hints that its chief settlements and citizens must pay heavy tribute or share a similar fate.

As in every great undertaking, the question of leadership was to become a matter of first importance. For the moment, however, parliamentarians were too busy with the details of organization to give it more than passing attention. When they did come to it, it was to find that the matter was already closed. Mrs. Masham, the Queen's new intimate, had found the time to consider the subject. She also had a candidate whom she considered suitable. It was her brother, John Hill. He was a versatile fellow, a man about town, with the pleasant easy virtues of his class and the happy faculty of making friends more readily than enemies. Whether this came from strength or weakness, it was certainly a fact that Jack Hill, as he was known, was a likable character if nothing else. One of the very few definite references to him appears in the journal of Colonel Richard King, the quartermaster general of the expedition. While Viscount Bolingbroke, who had been largely responsible for planning the undertaking and had learned of its arrival at Boston, was writing a friend, "I believe you may depend on our being masters at this time of all North America," Colonel King was writing less enthusiastically. He had managed to embroil himself with almost everyone with whom he came in contact in the colony and naturally spoke with more frankness than friendliness of the "in nature and Sowerness of these People, whose government, Doctrines and Manners, whose Hypocracy and canting are insupportable." Then follows the word of commendation: "No man living but one of Gen'l Hill's good Sense and good Nature could have managed them." Let this rest as the final judgment on Jack Hill, for no other as friendly or as gentle will be found.

General Hill, if he had no active enemies, had an appreciative friend in his sister. Through her good offices with the Queen, Hill was first appointed colonel and, shortly after, brigadier. The great Marlborough had once described him as "good for nothing," but possibly that opinion may have been colored by the fact that Hill was a protégé of Mrs. Masham rather than Mrs. Freeman, and that the former had succeeded to the friendship that Mrs. Freeman, who was also the Duchess of Marlborough, had lost.

Possibly, in urging the appointment of General Hill to command the land forces of the expedition, Mrs. Masham may have remembered that her erstwhile rival had benefited largely from the military reputation of her husband and felt that here was an advantage that was not to be taken lightly.

Just who was the sponsor for the more surprising choice of Sir Hovenden Walker as over-all commander of the expedition does not appear, nor does the reason for so surprising a choice. Quite obviously no one had given leadership much thought. Officialdom was still bemused with its great idea and with planning an undertaking whose overwhelming strength would be decisive under any conditions. The stakes were too large for any other explanation to have weight.

However poor the leadership, the fleet that dropped anchor in Nantasket Roads just two days better than seven weeks after leaving Plymouth was the mightiest fleet England had ever sent on one enterprise. There were fifteen armed vessels, nine of them ships of the line, and forty transports carrying seven British regiments with their artillery trains. To this would be added a considerable group of ships to carry the colonial forces.

The fleet had left Plymouth under sealed orders. There were speculations that it was destined for the West Indies or the South Seas, or perhaps both. Even the commanding admiral, Sir Hovenden Walker, was not to know its destination until the orders were opened when he was well at sea. How suitable that was for an admiral who, as it will appear, was never anything else.

It was June 24, 1711, when the fleet arrived, and no effort was spared to get it on its way with the utmost promptness. There was no love lost between the seamen and soldiers of the mother country and the colonists, and the sooner the expedition moved on, the happier everyone would be. The colonies' support, however, was both prompt and generous. Some forty thousand pounds in credits were voted by the Massachusetts Assembly. The same body vested rather extensive powers in the Queen's officers, powers that would not have been tolerated a few years hence. Willy-nilly, raw levies were quartered on the citizens at a rate of eighteen pence per man per day. This didn't make for happy relations. Prices of provisions and necessities were set, and authorities were empowered to search the homes for food and liquor and to seize such supplies as were not willingly relinquished by their owners at the established prices.

At Albany, Francis Nicholson, who was to head the supporting expedition against Montreal, was distributing among his new levies the arms and equipment he had stored there after the failure of the former expedition. There were some twenty-three hundred men, almost evenly divided between English and Indians. He had marched his forces as far as the ill-omened Wood Creek near the head of Lake George and there eagerly awaited the word that would tell him that the naval forces were well on their way upriver. That was to be the signal for his dash up Lake Champlain to the attack on Montreal. This time there was every reason to expect success. If in the policy of border raiding the French enjoyed all the advantage, in these dual all-out attacks the advantage lay the other way. The two logical striking points, Quebec and Montreal, were too distant from one another for troops to be quickly moved from one point to the other. The French colony, therefore, had to fight on two fronts with limited forces. It was a strategy that must win in the end and this, if ever, seemed to be the time.

True, a similar strategy had signally failed even with the highly aggressive Sir William Phips in command. But there were sharp differences. Then the fleet, but for the four leading vessels, had been mainly unarmed fishing boats hurriedly adapted for conflict. They were also very sparsely supplied with ammunition. The army Phips's ships convoyed consisted of slightly more than two thousand untrained levies in place of the twelve thousand under Walker's command, half of them veteran regiments.

In the land attack against Montreal under the divided command of Fitz-John Winthrop and Robert Livingston, there had been only half the forces available to Francis Nicholson. But the sharpest difference was one of leadership, the vacillation and general incompetence of Winthrop and Livingston against the knowledge and decisiveness of Nicholson. There was good reason to believe that the final hour of New France had come.

For long months New France lay under the shadow of this latest threat without quite knowing what the threat was or where it would first be felt. All they surely knew was that the New Englanders had taken Acadia with so little effort that the suggestion that Canada should be taken too, as Queen Anne had demanded, did not seem to be out of the way.

On July 30, 1711, the fleet sailed away from Nantasket Roads on its great adventure. All it lacked were pilots who knew the river. Samuel Vetch had been called from his governorship at Annapolis

Royal to command the provincial forces and, though not a seaman, he had made the journey up the river on several occasions. It was felt his experience would be of value.

Fortunately or unfortunately—it is hard to decide which—one of Walker's ships, the *Chester*, which had been sent ahead to gain such knowledge as it could, had captured a French vessel commanded by a Frenchman named Paradis, who knew the river well. Whether his intentions were to save his skin and line his pockets or merely to deceive is not wholly clear. What is clear is that he accepted a bribe of five hundred pistoles, roughly two thousand dollars, a sum that might possibly give patriotism a hard jolt. Whatever Paradis' intent, there was no question that he was highly vocal. He talked all the time, providing a wealth of information that Paul Bunyan might have envied. He told of the rugged Canadian winter, of the river freezing solid to the bottom, of vessels crushed flat by the pressure of ice, and of such crewmen as were fortunate enough to escape this hazard dying in the slow misery of starvation.

It was mid-August when the tales were told, and it might have been remembered that less than three weeks ago, when the fleet had sailed away, Boston had been sweltering in the heat. But Sir Hovenden, if he lacked many qualities, did not lack a colorful imagination. When shortly after he wrote his journal of the affair, Paradis' words were very fresh in his mind. So he spoke of his melancholy contemplation of "seas and earth locked up by adamantine frosts and swoln with high mountains of snow, in a barren and uncultivated region," and more poignantly still of "great numbers of brave men famishing with hunger, and drawing lots who should die first to feed the rest."

It was August 18 when the fleet reached Gaspé Bay. So far the voyage had been uneventful. But fate was drawing in. It did not come by reason of the "adamantine frosts" that Walker so much feared, but by sheer human carelessness. It seems apparent that what Phips had done twenty years before, Admiral Walker might have repeated. He had Phips's journal with him as some sort of guide. But complete confusion had settled on the whole expedition. On August 22 it was somewhere in the neighborhood of Anticosti Island, where the river is some seventy miles wide, giving ample room. For some reason the admiral had decided they were near the south bank. Shortly after, the captain of Walker's flagship, the *Edgar*, reported that land had been sighted. Still confident that it was the south shore, the admiral ordered that all the fleet should be brought to with their bows headed northward. Having so arranged matters with reasonable care for a situation that didn't exist, the admiral retired to his cabin.

He was not yet asleep when the captain of one of the regiments burst in to announce that there were breakers on all sides. Admiral Walker may have had his limitations, but he was not going to be told his business by another, and a landsman at that. Stiffly he ordered the officer from the room and returned to his rest. Moments later the captain was back, demanding that the admiral come on deck and see for himself.

Garbed in dressing gown and slippers and smoldering with anger, Admiral Walker went on deck. What he saw set him calling for the French pilot, Paradis. When finally aroused, Paradis took one look and announced that they were faced against the treacherous north shore. It was that hazardous bit of water surrounding the Seven Islands group and particularly the Isle aux Oeufs.

Once aroused, Admiral Walker seems to have acted promptly enough. He managed to save his warships. The transports were not so fortunate. Eight of them, with two of the service ships, were dashed to pieces on the rocks. Two days later, when what could be done had been done and when the survivors from these wrecked vessels, said by Walker to be four hundred and ninety-nine, had been rescued from the rocks a council of war was called aboard the general's ship, the *Windsor*. It was not much of a council. All were of one opinion, and the leaders seemed bent on only one thing, to get away.

There could be no denying the seriousness of the calamity. The admiral set his losses at just short of a thousand men. Later reports set the figure at seven hundred and fifty men and ten ships. It was a serious setback, but many a general has suffered a worse reverse and has gone on to conquer. There were still more than sixty vessels, including all the warships, and the forces that remained were still almost equal to the entire population of New France and certainly more than equal to any troops that could be brought to withstand them. But the will to fight had vanished as completely in general and admiral as in the humblest private. The makeshift pilots, too, had seen enough. Except for the Frenchman, Paradis, who knew better, there was complete agreement that navigation of the river was impossible. Neither Walker nor Hill urged or commanded any further action. Only one voice was raised against a prompt withdrawal. When Samuel Vetch heard next day of the decision to withdraw without striking a blow, he approached the admiral and spoke his mind bluntly. "The late disaster," he argued, "cannot, in my humble opinion, be anyways imputed to the difficulties of navigation, but to the wrong course we steered, which most unavoidably carried us upon the north shore. Who directed that course, you best know; and as our return without any further attempt would be a vast reflection upon the conduct of this affair, so it would be of very fatal consequences to the interests of the Crown and all the British colonies upon this continent."

It was bravely spoken, but it accomplished nothing. The commanders wanted no more of the hazards of distant waters. They edged their way cautiously to the gulf and steered for Spanish River, which is now the harbor of Sydney.

At Sydney the forces divided, and Samuel Vetch with his provincials made his disappointed way to Boston. Admiral Walker set his course for home, consoling himself with the reflection that the disaster was really a blessing in disguise, a merciful interposition of Providence by which the whole expedition was spared the freezing and starvation, the fate that had taken such control of all his thinking.

At Wood Creek, Francis Nicholson still waited word of the progress of the naval forces that was to be the signal for his advance. When it finally came he could hardly credit it. Success was so certain, and now nothing remained but retreat, unless he should attempt the patently impossible, of conquering Canada alone, with only his small and ill-trained force to back him. When the full significance of what had happened became clear to him his reaction was understandable. It is recorded that he tore off his wig, hurled it on the ground, and danced on it in a passion of rage, crying out, "Roguery! Treachery!" Here was a man of ability and courage and decisiveness who lacks a larger place in history because it was his fate to be dependent on the actions of men of smaller caliber. The only thing that was left for him to do, he did. He burned the wooden fortifications he had erected with patient care. Leaving a strong detachment to guard the border against raiding parties, he marched his army back to Albany and disbanded it.

In New France the people still waited, uncertain of the fate in store for them or when it might be known. Long after the events just recorded, "on the vigil of St. Michael's day, the 28th of September," as Father Germain explains, "a strong wind arose from the northeast." Quebec took this as an omen. It was the favored wind for vessels moving upriver to Quebec. In two or three days now, they said, the English fleet would be in the basin of Quebec.

There was a sudden upsurge of anxiety when on October 2 two horsemen were seen approaching the city. They turned out to be officers from France, Claude du Tisné and Pierre Plasson by name. To the anxious crowd that surrounded their horses they explained that they had come from France on the King's ship *Héros*, which had anchored twelve leagues below the city, waiting a favorable wind. In their impatience they had found horses and come ahead. But they had nothing startling to report; had seen no enemy ships either in the gulf or in the river.

Some day later, however, scouts arrived with more startling news. The huge fleet actually had been in the river, sixty or seventy leagues below the city. There it had been caught in a sudden and dreadful storm. Seven or eight of the larger vessels had pounded to pieces on the rocks. "The admiral's flagship, in particular, had split open at the keel and all aboard had been drowned with the leader of the expedition and his principal troops."

This was exaggeration, as was the news that followed of dead bodies, three thousand of them, lining the shore. There were bodies enough, the red-coated men of England who had stood dauntlessly at Oudenarde and Malplaquet, now soiled with the river slime and swaying slowly in its moving tides.

Good Father Joseph Germain had time to lament that "inasmuch as they had all died in heresy, there are so many souls that are damned." He was glad to report that the firing of guns was a matter not of aggression but of rejoicing, while he reflected that had they come as expected "a great deal of blood would have been shed on both sides." And he added with a quick change of heart, "We would never have done them as much injury as did the storm which prevented them from reaching us. . . . God has preferred to show us that He alone is the author of this victory." There is room here, perhaps, for the thought that Heaven is given the credit for a defeat that belonged somewhat more to the blundering of vast incompetence and lack of heart.

Sometime before the fleet's expected approach Governor Vaudreuil had sent the Sieur de la Valtrie to keep watch at the mouth of the St. Lawrence and to report its movements. Apparently he missed it there, but on his way homeward he landed from his canoe at the Isle aux Oeufs and there discovered the hulls of lost ships and fifteen to sixteen hundred dead bodies. A total twice that of Walker's official estimate. Whichever it was, a mute evidence of a vast disaster. He hurried onward with his tidings. By the time he and his two companions had reached Quebec the story had grown with many tellings. There was talk of three thousand of "these wretches" who died after reaching land, not counting the multitudes drowned in the attempt or the livid corpses of many women.

Perhaps Father Germain was less credulous than some. He speaks of the collection of "chests large and small, puncheons of wine and brandy, oxen and horses, pigs, dogs and sheep and many fowl, some dead, some alive, which swam to shore."

While this was being recorded the fleet, its warships not strewed along the shore as Father Germain records, nor with its flagship split at the keel and all its men, including the admiral, drowned, had arrived safely in the Thames. But even this was not quite safe, for as it lay at anchor its flagship did blow up suddenly. Dean Swift, recounting this strange happening, suggests that it was due to the "carelessness of some rogue, who was going, as they think, to steal some gunpowder." He adds a terse conclusion: "Five hundred men are lost."

But even this lacks the final touch of poetic justice. The men might die, but not the admiral. He was safely ashore. For the record it must be said that Walker's glib stories of good fortune in having lost only a thousand men where he might so easily have lost them all, in a land where rivers froze solid to the bottom, fell on unsympathetic ears. He was relieved both of his command and of his half pay. He went to the New World and then to the Barbados, where he died inconspicuously a few years later. Brigadier Hill, better placed as the brother of the Queen's reigning favorite, took up his ordered life again: the business of being a man about town, which suited him so much better than more heroic roles.

It might appear that the incidents recorded are just another tragic example of how the Colonel Blimps can destroy great undertakings and bring to nothing the most elaborate sacrifices. It might be argued that this magnificent tragedy of bumbling inefficiency, wrong thinking, and timorous judgments might mark it as something best forgotten, a discreditable incident that has no real bearing on the story of Canada.

But that would be scarcely the whole truth, for these events did have their influence on the history of this continent. There was the influence of men like Nicholson and Vetch, too great to be disregarded, that helped to foster a bitter resentment and indignation. They had not lost men, but there were lost time and lost money to be considered, and neither was acceptable to the English colonists. Still less could they accept without concern their lost confidence in the mother country. Either she was not sincere in her agreement to help against an aggressive New France or the assistance was not competent enough to be of value. None of this thinking tended to soften the antagonism toward a northern neighbor or to change the almost accepted opinion that a continent was not large enough to sustain such antagonistic interests.

If the English colonies were embittered, the French were hardly less so. They might thank Providence for their present safety, but they still remembered that for months they had been under a shadow more vast than they had ever known before. It had been made abundantly clear to them that they were in a trap. They couldn't anticipate that they would always be so fortunate.

On the continent, too, there was a changing situation. Louis XIV was aging fast. Much as he still might desire a union of France and Spain, he realized it was not for him. The opposition was too widespread, the resources of France too sharply depleted. Momentarily there was freedom from war. In Britain the Whigs, who wanted war, and the great Marlborough, whose natural element it was, were both in disfavor. Sir Hovenden Walker's unhappy expedition was not likely to turn a nation's thoughts to further conflict.

So peace came. At the placid little Holland town of Utrecht on April 11, 1713, the representatives of the powers put their signatures to a treaty that was to have a profound bearing on the fortunes of the New World. Unknowingly, perhaps, or perhaps unavoidably, France was making concessions that must eventually be the end of her vast empire in America.

Louis was negotiating from weakness. His son, the Dauphin, had died rather mysteriously two years before the peace. The Dauphin's eldest son had also died only a year after his father. Louis knew that the succession now depended on a child of three. He was shrewd enough to know that it was not a time to embroil France in further wars.

One thing he had set his heart on. It was to retain Acadia, one of the earliest possessions in the New World. To achieve this end he was ready to sacrifice much. The great Hudson's Bay region, the scene of many French triumphs, was to become English territory, with all that meant of domination of the western reaches of a continent whose rivers emptied into the great bay. He was ready to forgo all but some fishing privileges in Newfoundland. But still England was adamant about Acadia. She held it now. At Annapolis Royal, Francis Nicholson had succeeded Samuel Vetch as governor, and probably both had made it clear that the colonies would have no truck with such a deal.

The best Louis could achieve was a compromise, with France conceding to Britain "Acadia according to its ancient boundaries." It was an uncertain phrase that would be bickered over for half a century. All that France was able to retain of these Atlantic holdings was what the French knew as Isle Royale and Isle St. Jean, uncertain and unprofitable lands.

This was the end of an era. The magnificent fiasco of Walker and Hill was not wholly meaningless. It was a milestone in the history of a continent. Failure and mistakes there still might be, but there would be no further turning back. Battle lines had been drawn. There would be no lasting peace until the lilies of France had ceased to wave over an acre of Canadian soil.

CHAPTER XVII

THE GREAT FORTRESS

The Treaty of Utrecht—which cost France Acadia and Newfoundland and Hudson's Bay—leaves her hopelessly surrounded; her ancient highway of the St. Lawrence almost closed to her. The vital need for an outlet on the sea points to Isle Royale, now Cape Breton, her one remaining foothold on the Atlantic. Here, at English Harbor, rechristened Louisburg for the King, an invulnerable fortress is planned. The reluctance of people to face starvation on this "wild and Barren Island." The fortress grows slowly, and not very nobly. Here at last, in an atmosphere of craft and chicanery, appears the friend of Pompadour.

TIME was when France claimed the Atlantic seaboard of this continent almost as far south as Boston. The small foothold in Newfoundland at Plaisance, better known as Placentia Harbor, coupled with the successful ventures of Iberville, had given a sure sense of ownership over all the coast north from the St. Lawrence to Hudson Strait and indeed over the Great Bay itself. From the St. Lawrence to the St. Croix River—on the present boundary between Maine and New Brunswick—French ownership was well established. From there to the Kennebec River, however, was a no man's land that everyone claimed, and no one with enough authority to make the claim effective.

The Treaty of Utrecht brought many changes. While the ignominious fate of Sir Hovenden Walker's expedition could hardly have been designated a French victory (one contestant having turned tail before the battle began), it was a victory in effect. France still remained in undisputed control of the field. Even this, however, didn't make it much of a triumph, because, as not infrequently happens, the negotiators managed to appropriate whatever fruits of victory there might have been.

With Acadia held by the English and its ownership made official by the terms of the treaty, with England also controlling Hudson's Bay and Newfoundland by the same authority, New France was bottled up decisively. It might, and did, continue to claim control of the center of the continent with a show of reasonableness. Offsetting that, however, was the fact that its contact with the mother land involved increasing hazards. There were other disadvantages almost equally grave. It was more difficult now for Canada to keep herself informed of the happenings and the thinking of the New England colonies. Canada could be attacked from that direction without warning. Canada could only attack in return by the arduous overland route, where its intentions would be recognized long before an attacking force could reach a vulnerable point.

Unfavorable as were the terms of the treaty to France in the New World, Louis had to accept them. He was in no position to fight on, hoping for something better. What he wanted from the negotiations, as far as these affected New France, seemed reasonable enough, considering what he was ready to concede in return. He wanted Acadia restored to France. Acadia had been given back before for less valuable considerations. This time, however, the English were not in a conciliatory mood. Had they been so, they would still have realized that, the feeling of New England being what it was, concessions would be highly ill advised. The best that Louis was able to secure in return for the loss of Acadia and Hudson's Bay and Newfoundland —plus the long-opposed recognition of the Iroquois as the unquestioned subjects of England—was hardly encouraging. It was territory that France had always claimed without ever thinking of it as of any tangible value at all. This was the rocky and inhospitable island bordering on the Atlantic that the French had solemnly christened Isle Royale, more as a gesture than anything else, and Isle St. Jean farther up the gulf, which today is Canada's small garden province of Prince Edward Island.

To Louis' thinking, Isle Royale, which we know as Cape Breton Island, certainly was not a plum. It was distant from the center of Canada. It had no population. Strangely enough, neither it nor Isle St. Jean had been able to attract either the land-hungry or the adventurous. Indeed, the thinking of the day inclined to question whether there was enough arable land to support a population had it appeared.

It was the threat inherent in this virtually complete encirclement that had dominated Canada's thinking for close on half a century. Now, with Newfoundland to the north and Acadia to the south in British hands, it gained a new urgency. For half a century the threat had suggested a policy. It was the proposal to capture New York or Boston or, better still, both. With such a blow New France could cripple her one great enemy, could settle the Iroquois menace, and could secure year-round ports on open water. It had been a plan that was highly doubtful at any time and never more so than at this moment. But, failing this, there remained only the obvious and imperative alternative: New France must create a foothold on the narrow seacoast frontier that remained to her.

It was out of this vital need that Louisburg was born. It was to be the fortress harbor on the sea, to protect French commerce, to challenge her enemies, to guard the ancient life line of the St. Lawrence. It was to live its gallant, crowded, colorful forty years and pass into history—a place now visited mainly by wandering tourists. They view the little town that still remains, that still bears the name of a French king, gaze curiously at the carefully preserved remnants of one of the great fortresses of the world, scarcely remembering that its passing was something more than a landmark gone. But here the hopes of New France died and the history of a continent was changed and, perhaps it is not too much to say, the history of a world.

Isle Royale—the Cape Breton of today, a prosperous part of the province of Nova Scotia, with its own vast resources of coal and steel and wood products, not to mention an expanding tourist business—in the year 1720 was still a wilderness. It could boast only one French family and perhaps a hundred Indians. Nothing much to set the pulses beating—a land of barren hills cloaked with spruce and pine, of lakes and broad marshes afloat with moss. But beggars can't be choosers, and French Canada had nowhere else to look for a threshold on the sea. There was no question that Isle Royale was the logical and the only place for such a fortress as was planned. The question was at just what point? There were good harbors at Spanish Bay, where now stands the city of Sydney, and at Port à l'Anglois. This latter was more strategically placed on the open ocean, a year-round port free from the winter ice that troubled Spanish Bay.

The landlocked English Harbor, where a fleet could ride at anchor, decided the point. Graciously, perhaps also because Louis was paying all the costs, the name was changed to Louisburg. Louis was not a particularly stupid man. He was quick to realize that, dream as he might of recovering Acadia, he needed a starting point. Louisburg was the best available. For the moment, however, he was picking up the pieces of his defeated armies and planning new projects. The fortress would have to bide its time.

In Tory England there were other adjustments to be made. England was less belligerent than it had been under the Whigs. It was intent on converting the gains of war into a growing world of commerce. Queen Anne, too, if she hadn't quite secured Canada, momentarily was satisfied. There had been a long step in that direction. An uneasy quiet reigned in Europe and was reflected in the New World. It wasn't that men had become more peacefully inclined but only that other interests had intervened and needed settled ways for their development. Then, too, the disputants needed to recuperate from past efforts and perhaps even to find a compelling motive to set them at each other's throat again.

In the semi-quiet of this hollow peace seven years were to pass and with them Louis himself, and still Louisburg was only a dream. Governor Vaudreuil was fostering a periodic snapping at English heels as a means of keeping the Abenaki interested and employed and attached to French interests. He was quite frank about it. A secret alliance with the Indians, he explained, permitted a subtle incitement to acts of violence that provided embarrassment for the enemy but, properly managed, could be disclaimed before they become damaging to French interests, and certainly before they fostered an open breach. There was a small reason for these depredations; partly habit, of course, but partly because English tactics were becoming more aggressive. This was not easily borne by the French in territories that they considered their own. True, when they had held Acadia they had boldly asserted that it included not only the section now known as the Nova Scotia mainland but most of New Brunswick and much of Maine, as far at least as the Kennebec River. But when Acadia was finally ceded to England this thinking changed. Now the French asserted just as bluntly that Acadia ended with the peninsula of present-day Nova Scotia, and they said the sections of New Brunswick and Maine as far as the Kennebec still remained their property. If they had been content just to lay claim to and establish a mild occupation, probably no one, at least for the time, would have raised any active objections. In the twenty years of border raiding this disputed land had become a virtual desert. Now with peace on the land it was beginning to blossom again. That was enough of a hint for the land-loving English. They began pressing northward in this restored country, building their settlements as they went, exactly what Vaudreuil feared most. Already their encroachment on this debated land was challenging French ownership. More than that, they were drawing nearer and nearer to the line where acknowledged French territory began. Some way must be found to discourage such policies. Possibly the best way was to make them hazardous. So the border flamed again with its purposeless half war.

These happenings, and especially the steady northward trek of the English, were disturbing developments. They emphasized the weakness of the French position, with no port to challenge a possible aggressor. Canada began pressing for such a fortress. Its building was beyond the resources of the colony. Moreover, no one had given such a policy a thought. It was the custom to lean on the King's beneficences, and no one thought of questioning that the King would not pay the shot. It can be admitted that Louis had no love for such thinking, but he had no love either for bowing out and letting his hereditary enemy win the day. So it was agreed. The fortress could be built, and about it a town would grow. When the great Louis had died his successor accepted the obligation, but its fruition was still in the future. Eventually the one French family at Louisburg would become better than four thousand persons dedicated to the service of France, to Mother Church, and to the cause of a fully restored Acadia—of which Isle Royale would be an effective part.

Years before, when Quebec was under threat, Louis had sent the greatest military engineer of his day to design its defenses. He was none other than Sébastien Le Prestre, Seigneur de Vauban. He was a marquis and a marshal of France. It was not a French boast alone, but a generally accepted belief—one that the years have not challenged—that he had carried the art of fortification to a degree of perfection unknown before his time. As he worked on the defenses of Quebec and the less important post at Three Rivers he seems to have toyed with the idea of building another mighty fortress at some such point as Isle Royale. If so, the great Vauban died before the plan had got beyond the drawing board. Fortunately, however, there was still in New France another expert engineer, who had been Vauban's assistant at Quebec and had done much of the practical work. It was Gédéon de Catalogne. He it was who would now take up the work on the master's plan for Louisburg and who would die there when his work was finished and before he could know that the impregnable fortress he had fashioned was not impregnable at all.

De Catalogne had every reason to think it so, and it was an opinion that was shared by friend and foe alike. Indeed it was said that, with just the possible exceptions of Quebec and the new fortress of Gibraltar, Louisburg was the strongest position in the world. When completed, the great fortress would lie across a narrow peninsula jutting out into the Atlantic; on one side, the harbor that could shelter the mightiest of fleets, with an entrance protected by island batteries and Batterie Royale directly facing that entrance. Here the defending French ships could lie in complete safety. On the other side was the rock-ribbed shore of the open Atlantic, and on the landward side, across the broad angle formed by the fortress itself, there was mountain country, a difficult and treacherous battleground.

Vauban's plan called for a fortress of stone. Walls ten feet thick and thirty feet high would rise above a deep moat eighty feet wide. There were embrasures for a hundred and forty-eight guns, though ninety guns were the most ever mounted, with other guns on the island batteries. All this the King was to provide, along with eight companies of trained soldiers for its defense.

But the King's obligations were not to stop there. He was to set up a government and a town. There was to be a hospital generously endowed from the King's purse, and schools and churches for both Jesuit and Récollets. Louis had also agreed to send out companies of young women to become the wives of the soldiers, as had been done in the earlier days of the colony. In addition he would also send some families and would provide their support for two years.

It was an ambitious program as it was envisioned, and one not easily accomplished. The English, who were natural colonizers, never did quite understand the difficulties faced by France in setting up her colonial empire. For that reason they were prone to overestimate the strength and unity of their foe. They did not understand that French officials, with almost negligible exceptions, looked upon service outside France as virtually an order of banishment, to be resisted as long as possible and to be escaped at the first opportunity. The only real exceptions to this attitude were the adventurous spirits for whom far places had an inescapable allure, or the somewhat larger group of practical-minded folk who expected to use their exile in providing the feathering for nests that ultimately were to be built in France.

It was hard for outsiders also to realize that there was very little positive authority existing in New France, or to appreciate the complications involved in the tangle of overlapping obligations and responsibilities in such authority as did exist. Occasionally a Frontenac would arise, stubborn and opinionated and daring enough to formulate his own plans and policies. But even men of this caliber understood that there were definite limits to evasion. They knew that any and every encroachment on the King's orders or prerogatives would be promptly reported by a watchful intendant who generally recognized, as indeed he was expected to do, that his first duty was to be alert to just such happenings.

The government of Louisburg was made still more complex by the fact that it had its own governor and intendant, who were subordinate to the governor and intendant at Quebec. Disagreement by this higher authority on any problems presented to them meant that the issues must be referred to the Minister of Colonies or the King. Such delaying actions might extend into months before a decision could be secured on even the most minor matters. It is small wonder that the harassed Gédéon de Catalogne was twenty years in seeing the fortress plans finally come to life. Small wonder, either, if he realized that with so little authority the result could hardly be all that had been hoped.

Obviously the first problem was to secure the necessary population to support the fortress. Nobody, apparently, had any inclination toward Isle Royale. Even its garrison had to be paid a special bounty. A quarter century after the foundations had been laid the regulars in the post numbered a bare six hundred, and almost half of them Swiss mercenaries.

As France had relinquished any claim in Newfoundland beyond the small holding at Placentia Harbor, it was natural that in seeking citizens for the fortress island authority should think of those remaining in Newfoundland. These represented no more than twenty or thirty families, and they were no more eager for a pioneer life about the one-time English Harbor, now rechristened Louisburg, than was anyone else. They had been through their pioneering days and had settled themselves in a place of their own choosing where they were doing modestly well and were happy and contented.

But Louis needed settlers, so he wrote to Costebelle, then governor at Placentia Harbor, to move his authority and his citizens to Isle Royale. Louis was definite. "I have caused my order to be given you," he wrote, "to evacuate the town and forts of Plaisance and other places of your government of Newfoundland. . . . I have given my orders for the equipment of vessels necessary to make the evacuation and transport you, with the officers, garrison and inhabitants of Plaisance and other places of Newfoundland, to my Isle Royale, vulgarly called Cape Breton."

It being late September of the year 1713 before this missive was sent, His Majesty had made a small concession. To prevent the deportees "perishing from cold and misery," he had decided to postpone the implementing of the order until the next spring.

Even this consideration, however, did not make the inhabitants of Plaisance—or Placentia—more content with the proposed change. They were ready to do everything possible to remain, ready indeed to change their allegiance and become British subjects rather than accept the removal order. Costebelle, though after all he was only changing the governorship of Placentia for a somewhat more promising post at Isle Royale, was frankly puzzled at this attitude. He wrote to the ministry, explaining his problem rather plaintively: "Nothing can cure them of the error, to which they obstinately cling, that they are free to stay or go as best suits their interests."

Obviously he found means of making it clear that there was no alternative. As he was in command of the troops, who were also to be transferred, that should not have been too difficult. In any event, the transfer to Isle Royale was made and for a time at least the settlers suffered extremely in the change, just as they had expected. But they provided a nucleus of the population that Louisburg needed, and nothing else mattered.

This, then, was the first actual instance in the New World of a ruthless uprooting of French citizens against their will. It was not at the order of the English but at that of the French King and his accredited ministers and officials. In all the romantic hubbub that grew up about the later expulsion of the Acadians, no one stopped to remember that the policy was not new. It had been set in France with the Huguenots and again at Placentia.

Undoubtedly the King also would have ordered immediately a forced migration to Louisburg from Acadia had there been any promise of success, but no such evidence existed. According to the treaty agreement, the Acadians were free to go or stay as they wished. Queen Anne had even made a generous gesture in that direction by stating that any who might wish to leave were to be permitted to sell their lands. It was probably a bona fide evidence of good will. She was scarcely shrewd enough to realize that a permission to sell had value only where purchasers were available and that there were none in Acadia. The local government had no inducement to help out, much as they might have liked to see the end of these troublesome citizens who, as Governor Phillips was to report later, were "growne so insolente as to say that they will neither sweare allegiance nor leave the Country."

It was still true, as Governor Vetch had pointed out some years earlier, that, troublesome as they might be, it was better to keep them than to let them go. "One hundred French natives of America," he argued, "familiar with the woods, able to march on snowshoes and accustomed to the use of birch canoes, are of more value and service than five times their number of raw men newly come from Europe."

There were other considerations too, as Governor Vetch explained. "They will no doubt gladly remain upon their plantations (some of which are considerable) provided they may be protected and encouraged by the Crown, and as no country is of value without Inhabitants, so the removal of them and their cattle to Cape Brittoun would be a great addition to the new colony, so it would wholly ruine Nova Scotia unless supplied with a British Colony, which could not be done in several years."

The Acadians were patriotic beyond a doubt, but this was mixed with a solid practicality. One priest who read to his flock Pontchartrain's letter on the need for transferring the Acadian population to Louisburg reported a united unwillingness. They were being more than reluctant to "leave their rich farms and risk starvation on a wild and barren island."

To the French as well as to the English the attitude presented its problems. There was the urgent need at Louisburg for just such population as the industrious and frugal Acadians assured. But there remained the qualifying thought that Acadia was to be recovered at the first opportunity, and there would be undoubted advantages in having accomplices on the ground. This thinking perhaps was something of an afterthought, to explain away the failure to entice the Acadians from English control, for neither enticement nor enforcement was more than nominally successful.

The Church was the spearhead of these efforts. It believed, or pretended to believe, that the souls of its followers were in jeopardy as a result of their continued close association with the English. There is no indication, however, that the English did not live up to the last letter in that clause of the treaty that assured the Acadians the full enjoyment of their religion.

Perhaps the mild treatment of a conquered enemy cannot be credited to an overwhelming good will. There was little to justify such an attitude. But this much is beyond question. Had the Acadians wished to escape from English rule they could have gone when and where they wished. There was no force in Acadia capable of coercing them in any way.

Finally the French authorities themselves took stronger measures, and French officers warned the reluctant Acadians that they would be treated as rebels if they did not agree to move as they were ordered. Under such compulsion a considerable number accepted the inevitable, signed an agreement that they would live and die as faithful servants of the French King. As an evidence of their good faith some hundred and forty-six heads of families from Annapolis, a hundred and thirty-nine from Minas, and seventeen from Cobequid agreed to go to Isle Royale. That represented almost half of the Acadian population. As a matter of fact, all but a bare dozen of the families somehow managed to overlook this promise before the boats for their transfer arrived. Possibly dissuaded by the English authorities, who certainly had no other means of preventing their departure, most of them had again changed their minds, and Colonel Vetch records, "By what I can learn there is not many of them removed."

The truth was that nobody was at Louisburg because of any inclination of his own, so there was little open enthusiasm to tempt any newcomers. Those who were there were so either because of the compulsion of military duty—the necessities of the case, as in the instance of the Newfoundland deportees—or with a shrewd eye for some immediate personal advantage.

A project that was to run to a total cost of thirty million livres represented a vast sum, probably more than as many dollars of our present currency. This offered enormous opportunities for speculation both in the operation itself and in the exploiting of those concerned. The harpies gathered from far and near, tempted by the promise of quick profit. Scamped effort and scamped materials were the order of the day. It wasn't that sound enough materials were not provided. Good stone went into the construction of the quarters of governor and intendant, on whose instruction we do not know. But when it came to the fortress itself, soft stone, easily quarried nearby, took its place, and sea sand, which was worthless and cheap, was used in the mortar that bound the stones. It too was at hand and to be secured at nominal cost. It left a neat margin for profit. The fishing fleets from France came over with cut stone and bricks as ballast, had been doing so for many years, so good stone was available. But it was discovered that there was a market for this stone in New England, so, understandably enough, the builders interested in turning a quick penny, dishonest or no, did not overlook this small opportunity. French stone was a procurable commodity in Boston but not in Louisburg.

Trading between New England and New France was strictly forbidden by the laws of both countries, and by both the rule was openly violated. When it was profitable, official eyes were considerately turned the other way. New England did a highly remunerative trade with Isle Royale in wines and brandy and foodstuffs and tobacco and in building materials for the new fortress.

It not infrequently happened that the wines and brandy had been consigned to Louisburg from France, but the astute merchandisers of Louisburg found it more profitable to ship these products to Boston, making their gain on the transactions. From Boston they would be shipped back to Louisburg under a license that allowed another gain. Traders grew fat on this traffic.

The Acadians participated in the business to a degree. They might not have wanted to share the life of Isle Royale, but they had no objection to providing supplies for those who did, at a generous profit. It was a sure business, for few persons in Isle Royale had any thought of developing its arable land or of discovering its resources. Their thought was of getting away, and the sooner the better. So they leaned to occupations like smuggling, where the profits were generous, rather than to fishing, where the hazards were high and the returns small. No one was interested in the resources about them or in the slow and onerous work of building a country.

They preferred Louisburg. With all its lacks, it didn't lack for taverns and drinking. Gambling and brawling were familiar occupations. One thing Louisburg did lack was a police force and a jail. Indeed, one of the residents was known to complain rather bitterly that there was no hangman. Not even "a tormenter to rack the criminals or inflict other appropriate tortures."

Pirates infested the seas about. To offset them there grew up a breed of privateers who used Louisburg as a base and preyed upon these lawbreakers and quickly became almost as lawless as they.

It seems that the blight laid its fingers on almost everyone. Even the servants of the Church were not quite immune. They bickered among themselves, and charges flew about describing the Récollet friars as drunken, ignorant, and lazy. It was undoubtedly prejudiced talk and probably Louisburg was just about as any barrack town where authority was far away and the bars were down. Any married soldier was entitled to open a tavern, and there were few bachelors in Louisburg. The officers, too, were said to do a brisk trade in spirits and wines from France, growing prosperous enough to have Negro servants of their own.

There were devout men whom the laxities could not affect, except perhaps in making them more critical and more lacking in the smaller generosities that should have made them see shortcomings against the bitter loneliness that helped to breed them. The Abbé Maillard was unquestionably a man beyond personal reproach. Yet he was unsparing in his reproach of others. He spoke of Louisburg as a den of infamy where the Christian standards he represented were largely flouted, where nothing much more than the appearance of faith remained, and where impiety stood as an evidence of broad-mindedness.

It wasn't only the common soldier or the common people. The canteens of the officers, said the good abbé, were schools of Satan where every sort of ribaldry and blasphemy was common and where the Church was the butt of every obscene jest.

Perhaps judgments should be qualified. Perhaps, to men of high standards living in a world barren of any refinement of thinking or of life, evil might look more evil than it actually was. It is not hard to understand what years of living in such an atmosphere might do to the spirit of men whose one pervading wish had always been to be almost anywhere else. If the officers and the builders, with their shabby devices, were making of what was supposed to be an impregnable fortress something vastly less than that, was the deterioration to end there? What were ennui and bitterness and disillusionment doing to the men who were supposed to defend the fort? That, the years were to tell.

On looking at that rather sordid picture, it perhaps might be possible to lay a finger on one man who epitomized the distemper of mind and body and heart that was Louisburg. It was not of his creating. He had come from France when the fortress was nearing completion, to be part of its life. Clearly he did not intend Louisburg to be his final goal. It was for him, too, a starting point. He was its intendant. He would be closely involved with the destiny of which Louisburg was only a part. He was undoubtedly the cleverest, the most devious, the most important man in the city. He was more important than the governor, because he was more able. He did not devise the chicanery, the fraud, the cheating, and the depravity. It was all there when he arrived, a well-beaten path. It can only be said of him that he discovered the path quickly and followed it assiduously.

He was a coming man, as anyone could see. He chose his friends with a careful eye for their value to him. One of them one day was to become the Marquis de Pompadour, the invaluable companion of that fifteenth Louis who was to follow, if with less dignity and less devotion, in his great-grandfather's footsteps. With all his shortcomings, Louis XIV had never delegated his own responsibilities, while Madame de Pompadour was to exercise many that remained to Louis XV.

She was to coin an apt and well-remembered phrase. It might have been used as reasonably by her protégé, who in the closing days of Louisburg was getting his introduction to the opportunity that appealed to him.

"After us the deluge!" laughed the disillusioned Pompadour. These could well have been his words. For this was François Bigot, and if any one individual can be held largely responsible for the downfall of France in the New World, most certainly he is that man.

CHAPTER XVIII

THE WESTERN SEA

The eyes of New France still look to the far horizons. From the Gulf of Mexico men follow the great river systems—the Red, the Arkansas, the Missouri. Opening a new domain, they almost touch hands with other men who, facing unbelievable obstacles, still dream of a Western Sea. Pierre de la Vérendrye and his four sons open the lands beyond the lake head. They build forts on unknown lakes and rivers and see the vast prairies. They find lakes Winnipeg and Manitoba and follow the great Saskatchewan River. They move into Minnesota and the Dakotas to the fringes of the Rocky Mountains. Then bitter disillusionment as once again there emerges the sinister figure of François Bigot.

LOUISBURG was not typical of the spirit of New France. There it seemed that some strange malady had deadened a spirit that once had been bright and aspiring, leaving in its place only the crafty and predaceous. But elsewhere the challenge of a new land still called to men with a continuing urgency and met the old, undaunted response. The names of the actors in these scenes are not as familiar as are the names of Iberville or Cadillac or Tonty or Du Lhut or that Le Moyne de Bienville who is forever associated with the Gulf Coast; with Biloxi, and Mobile, which he governed so long, and the great city of New Orleans, which he founded.

Probably few have heard of Juchereau de St. Denis. Yet he was the first to venture far beyond the mouth of the Red River. This is not our Red River of the North, but the lowest western branch of the Mississippi and a mighty stream in itself, thirteen hundred miles long. Many long miles beyond where any white man had been before, he founded the present city of Natchitoches, Louisiana. It was to be the starting point of all the later adventuring in the Southwest. One of these adventurers, Bénard de la Harpe, starting from this point, followed the river to its juncture with the Arkansas and journeyed far up that lonely stream. And there was Du Tisné, who, almost alone, traveled the Missouri to its juncture with the Grand River; and Bourgmont, who followed Du Tisné's footsteps and built a trading post there and a fort that he called Fort Orleans. And there was St. Ange, and many others of lesser note, who pushed the frontiers farther and farther back, adding vastness to the realm of France.

It may seem strange that these names should appear in a Canadian history when their exploits occurred so far afield. Yet they have their place. They are part of the history of those lands about the Gulf of Mexico. And it was the defense of the ancient river highways linking Canada to the Gulf that brought the conflict between France and England to its inevitable climax.

Nearer home, the story was little different. There, too, the great unknown lands were still calling to men to come and see. Other rewards were scant, as their stories tell. Weariness and danger and sacrifice were the common wage. Yet the land did not call in vain.

The famed Carignan-Salière regiment, which had come to Canada years before, brought with it a young lieutenant, René Gaultier de Varennes. When finally the regiment was recalled, young René Gaultier remained to accept the grant of land given those officers who wished to make their home in Canada. He chose lands that were near to Montreal but near also to Boucherville, the property of Pierre Bouchard, a man of substance who had once been governor of Three Rivers, then Canada's third city.

Perhaps it was inevitable that young René Gaultier should be attracted to Marie Bouchard. Perhaps, indeed, it had shaped his decision to stay. Whether or no, he was shortly to marry her, when she was not quite thirteen years old, and they had a family of sturdy sons. In 1685, when another son was born, it was decided to call him Pierre after his grandfather, no one suspecting that the younger Pierre would be the greater.

This young Pierre was barely nineteen when, with others of the young Canadian noblesse, he followed Hertel de Rouville in the grim adventure against Deerfield. A year later he was campaigning in Newfoundland.

When that was over he went to France to join the armies of Louis XIV and to become a soldier indeed. By this time he was called La Vérendrye, like his older brother Louis. He was in time to take part in the battle of Malplaquet, which the great Duke of Marlborough himself spoke of as a "very murdering battle." It came near to being the final battle for young Pierre de la Vérendrye. He was left for dead on the field that had cost even the victor twenty thousand men. He had been shot three times through the body and had six saber wounds, evidence that he had not missed being where good blows were being traded. In addition to his wounds, he had a citation in the orders of the day. This did him little good, as his riddled body had already been collected by the allied armies as among the dubious spoils of war. Pierre de la Vérendrye, for all his wounds, did not die.

When finally, after more than a year in an English military prison, he was released and returned to France, it was to find that for his gallantry Louis had appointed him to the rank of lieutenant. But in those dark days of France—with her decimated armies licking their wounds and wondering when and where another blow would fall, with a country almost bankrupt, and even the Sun King shaken for the moment from his belief in his divine destiny—there wasn't a much emptier occupation in the world, or one less profitable, than a lieutenantship in the French Army.

But Pierre had his friend at court, none other than the Marquise de Vaudreuil, wife of the Marquis de Vaudreuil, then governor of Canada. The marquise, it will be remembered, had gone to France to become the governess of the King's children and to make quite a place for herself. No doubt she knew of the young Vérendrye, for both his grandfather and his father were men of consequence. She found the young lieutenant nearly penniless and still pale from his wounds and his long imprisonment. Using her considerable influence, she secured him the reduced rank of ensign in the service of New France. Here he was almost free of competition. None of the young bloods were attracted to a service that took them away from France.

But Pierre de la Vérendyre was glad to be back in Canada and to take up his modest job of soldiering. It wasn't very demanding, and he had time to meet and to marry Marie Anne Dandonneau. That was in 1712. In the next dozen years she had borne him six children, and his four sons were to play an active part in his fortunes.

Before he went to Europe, young Vérendrye had caught the eye of Governor Vaudreuil, who had granted him a small trading post called La Gabelle, on the upper reaches of the St. Maurice River, on which Three Rivers is located.

It gave him a modest affluence and a growing reputation. He spent the next dozen years after his return mostly at La Gabelle, always a little better off at the end of each season. He was learning, too—a working knowledge of the Indian tongues and an understanding of their ways.

His post at La Gabelle buzzed with rumors, tales of mighty rivers and vast lakes and strange peoples. Over the years he listened, trying to sift the little truth from the colorful additions resulting from many tellings. There was a certain pattern in the stories that, however the surroundings might vary, seemed to remain the same. It was this recurring note that caught the attention of Pierre de la Vérendrye. There wasn't too much time for thinking. He had caught the attention of the newly appointed governor, the Marquis de Beauharnois, who commissioned him to one of the vacant posts on Lake Nipigon. He was given the rather impressive title of "Commandant of the Northwest," of which his isolated post represented the largest known part.

In the two years he spent at the Nipigon post the tales he had first heard at La Gabelle began to repeat themselves with a growing emphasis. He heard again of the vast lakes beyond the great Superior and of a river that flowed from it to the Western Sea. But this time there was an Indian chief from the Kaministiquia who gave a new and personal twist to the story. He had followed the river until he came to waters that ebbed and flowed. He had been seized with terror at the sight and had hurried to return. There were other stories that seemed to grow with the telling—the talk of cities and fortresses in the lands to the west, and people whose skins were white and who rode on horses and were clothed in metal.

Slowly the mind of Pierre de la Vérendrye took fire at that suggestion of a Western Sea. It was not that he was credulous or accepted these stories at their face value. "These people," he said to his friend, the Father Dogonnor, "are great liars, but now and then they tell the truth." And Father Dogonnor, who had just returned from a mission to the Sioux, nodded in agreement.

No dream was ever more elusive than that dream of a Western Sea; and none ever more persistent. It had begun with the early explorers, who had thought of the St. Lawrence as a great waterway leading straight to a more westerly sea than any known to their world. No one had seen it, yet the thought of it had disturbed the peace of men for many years. It had been the dream of the early explorers. Jacques Cartier had thought of the St. Lawrence as a great waterway to a more westerly sea than any known to him. The lashing threat of the Lachine rapids had somehow called to the mind of the early voyageurs the thought that it might be an outer guardian to the gates of the East that could be reached by going west. China was the goal. So they called this fretted stairway of white water after that country, La Chine. Marquette and Joliet had this Western Sea in mind as they pressed into the unknown. So, no doubt, had Radisson. It was never very far from the thoughts of La Salle, even when he was finding his way down the mighty Mississippi to his lonely death on the shores of another great water. More than likely it was part of the urge that had suddenly moved Du Lhut to sell his fine home in the better part of primitive Montreal to follow his fortunes into the Sioux country.

But La Vérendrye started a new pattern. Piecing together the stray rumors that had come to him at La Gabelle and that had grown to substantial proportions in his diary as he gathered them at the trading posts on Lake Nipigon, he had come to his own confident belief. However much of confusion and wild thinking the stories and gossip might reveal, one thing was certain. There was a Western Sea, and it lay due west, not south. If he was to find it, he must seek it through the country of the Christineau and Assiniboin tribes rather than the lands of the Sioux. That was the introduction to our West of today.

Of course Vérendrye knew that, ten years before his appointment to the post on Lake Nipigon, Governor Vaudreuil and his intendant, Bégon, had proposed a common plan for an expedition. The fact that it was a common plan was itself unusual enough to call for comment; it was still more surprising that this wholly unusual collaboration should have had to do with the Western Sea.

However, the suggestion had been impressive enough to secure the permission to send out a trial expedition. It was under the command of a young lieutenant of colonial troops, Monsieur de la Noué. He was hardly experienced enough for the work in hand. Even had he been, his orders were such as to permit him little opportunity.

He did make the first gesture toward that chain of forts that the governor's and intendant's plan had suggested, by building at the mouth of the Kaministiquia River a rude stockade that hardly seemed to justify the rather pretentious name of Fort Kaministiquia or the honor of being the ancestor of present-day Fort William.

These were the years when Vérendrye was growing up. They were not bountiful years in the New World any more than in the Old. He had to struggle for even a modest place in the sun. For all that, it never crossed his mind to do other than look ahead and to dream of a great future. We know from the words of the newly arrived Governor Beauharnois, who quickly became his friend, that Vérendrye was a man who was mild but firm and who dealt with the Indians with consummate tact.

He was not driven by the lure of gold that dominated the thinking of many of the lesser greats. "Money has never inspired my aims," he said of himself. "It is for the service of the King and for the good of the colony that I have sacrificed myself and my sons." This was when he had learned how lacking in gratitude could be the King and the country he had sought to serve.

While he was still at his Nipigon post he was writing Governor Beauharnois that he would undertake the search for the Western Sea if the King would provide a hundred men and supply canoes and arms and provisions. But the governor's power to obligate the King was limited indeed. The best he could do was to pass on the suggestion with his full endorsement.

Neither the young King nor his young Minister of Marine, whose duties included the government of the colonies, was deeply moved by appeals that did not minister to the King's inclinations or appetites, and Governor Beauharnois' appeal did neither. It represented immediate outgo for an intangible return, and it was also an appeal from far afield.

As a lad of fourteen, the young Comte de Maurepas had succeeded his father, the Comte de Pontchartrain, as was the custom of a day when nepotism had been elevated to a fine art. At the time of this appeal he had reached the mature age of twenty-six and a sure place in the favor of the King. He was by no means lacking in ability, as his record shows. He supplemented this by an adroit use of every advantage. As his duties included the control of the city of Paris, the story of the life of the city—its gossip, its scandal, its record of crime—passed through his office, and De Maurepas used his skill in collecting the spicier bits of information that came his way for the pleasure of the King, who combined in one person all the more unpleasant attributes. De Maurepas cultivated the King's taste for the unsavory with a loving care worthy of a better cause. But it did this much. It earned the favor of the King. When Vérendrye's proposals came before him, De Maurepas did not hesitate. If it had been a matter of petty scandal in the colony, a matter of precedence, or a question of whether a farmer should be permitted to engage in business, he would have given the matter thought and a comprehensive answer. But this was a matter of spending, and De Maurepas knew that in refusing this he was on safe ground. Vérendrye's petition was to be granted in part. It was the part that permitted him to discover as he saw fit, but at his own risk and expense. The King, so De Maurepas assured the governor, would have nothing to do with the financing of the proposed expedition, providing the men, building the necessary forts, or underwriting the trading effort. The best that he would do was grant Vérendrye a monopoly of the fur trade in the country occupied.

Knowing nothing of the hazards and hardships and the outlay implicit in such great adventures, the young Minister of Marine and Colonies no doubt felt that he was being generous. He did not consider whether the country would be productive of furs, or what the sales price would be when they were finally delivered, or how the trade goods necessary to success were to be secured and the personnel of the expedition paid and supported. All this was to be covered by the monopoly of the trade in a land that, for the most part, no one had yet seen. On this, Vérendrye was to venture all he had in material goods and his reputation present and to come.

De Maurepas was cynical-minded toward the talk of great adventure. "The officials of Canada," he had said, "are looking not for the Western Sea, but for the sea of beaver." The Jesuit Father Francis Nou, writing to a friend, told of a conversation with Vérendrye at the Lake Nipigon post in which the latter had said somewhat the same thing—that the Western Sea would have been discovered long ago if the people had wished it.

It was typical of Vérendrye that when the decision was finally presented to him he didn't hesitate. No one was in a better position than he to assess the bargain offered or to know that it was bad. If he succeeded, the major part of what gains accrued must go to someone else. If he failed, his reputation would suffer too, and with it the opportunity to recoup his losses.

In the years of trading since his return from Malplaquet he had probably built up a modest competence beyond the needs of his growing family. There was also his share in the two seigneuries of Varennes and Tremblay left by his father. This, but for a small share for the subsistence of his family, he was prepared to risk in a venture on which his heart was set. But it wasn't enough. He had to interest others, and men of substance were relatively few, and those who were had grown so by crafty dealing.

Vérendrye's demands were not small. Men were needed, a substantial number. They had to be fed and paid. There were forts to be built to protect the ever-lengthening line of communications. They were costly both in time and money; and time, in this instance, was money. There were great canoes to be provided, ninety feet long and broad enough so that at the portages two husky voyageurs could walk abreast at front and rear, their heads disappearing in the inverted canoe.

No less a force than fifty men would be needed. And the promise that the great canoes would return laden with furs was uncertain. Only one thing was certain—that, whether successful or no, it would be two or three years before anyone could return to show the profit or loss of the venture. The hazards of underwriting such an undertaking were not imaginary. If voyageurs had been known to venture into the wilderness with trade goods to the value of a couple of thousand dollars and return a year or two later with profits of a cool quarter million, the hazards were in proportion. The trade goods could fall into the hands of an enemy. It had happened to those English traders, McGregory and Rooseboom, in Governor Denonville's day. This was not an isolated instance. Somebody had to pick up the tab for such losses. This the Montreal merchants knew quite well. The forces of nature were a hazard too. When La Salle had watched the little *Griffin* sail away from Green Bay, in what is now Wisconsin, with its fabulous cargo of furs he had reason to feel elated. But the *Griffin* never arrived at any destination. More than once, also, mutiny had broken out on such expeditions as proposed and the trade goods had been stolen or scattered and the leader had been deserted or even killed. La Salle had died so at the hands of Duhaut, his trusted follower.

Despite all this, the unwavering enthusiasm of Vérendrye decided the issue. The merchants might still be hesitant, but at least they subscribed. Vérendrye had no thought of giving their enthusiasm time to cool. He appointed Christophe Dufros de la Jemeraye as his second-in-command. Young De Jemeraye was the son of Vérendrye's sister but, beyond that, he had considerable experience and training as an ensign of marines. He was twenty-three years of age at the time. Indeed, despite the grizzled looks of the fifty voyageurs who had been gathered, all of them were young. Vérendrye himself was only forty-five when he began his search for the Western Sea. He had with him three of his sons: Jean Baptiste, who was a ripe eighteen; Pierre, who was seventeen; and François, known as the Chevalier, who was sixteen. Only Louis Joseph, who was only fourteen, was still considered too young to share the hazards of the great search.

It was a sweltering day that June 8, 1731. Sweat streamed from the faces of even the grizzled yet youthful adventurers. They were not all hardened as were the fighting men. Among them was a scattering of blacksmiths and carpenters who would be useful when it came to building forts. They would be tough enough by then.

The gates of Montreal swung open and disgorged most of its citizens. Some must have remained, for the church bells set up a cheerful clatter. The people cheered and priests in their black and brown robes looked on with hands upraised in blessing as the fifty adventurers swung the great canoes over their shoulders and set out on the road to Ste. Anne on the Ottawa, where the first stage of their journey would really begin.

There were some among those watching the departure who did so with mixed feelings. The merchants of Montreal were not quite convinced that they had acted wisely. The Western Sea meant little to them compared with present profits. They were sending out stores of trade goods in the hope of handsome profit that might run as high as a thousand per cent. Such profits were not unknown. But, also, the merchants of this earlier day were closer to their sources of trade. The hazards involved were not unknown to them. They might be saying farewell to their fellows, these adventurous few. They might be seeing the last of both trade goods and profits. It was a troublesome thought that would recur.

As the canoe-bearers reached Ste. Anne and thankfully set their burden down, others arrived, great shoulders slumping under heavy loads of trade goods and tools and the munitions and provisions for the long months to come. Soon the great canoes were loaded. The paddlers took their places two abreast on the four benches, with the steersman in the rear and a bowman up front to watch for possible hazards. They were on their way. It was heavy work and dangerous, loaded as they were, gunwale almost at the water edge. Probably the paddlers, as they drove the heavy craft northwestward, would be singing a version of the oldest of Canadian chansons, the sad tale of Cadieux, the white hunter who, in the days of the Iroquois threat, had been set ashore to divert the Indians' attention while his companions made their escape. Instead of Indians, so the chanson tells, he was to meet a danger far more dreaded–the *folie des bois*, which was a product of solitude and long years of lonely living, dissipation, perhaps, and unending danger–the folly of the woods, which set a man traveling in circles until weariness and solitude and hunger brought their inevitable end. Somewhere along this riverbank, so the legend goes, Cadieux was resting at last. And not too many miles away was the end of the Long Sault portage, where the men must shoulder their heavy loads again, perhaps remembering that here it was that young Dollard des Ormeaux and his sixteen companions had given their lives for New France only seventy years before.

For a month the travelers lived through unending days of fighting the current and the hazards of white water until they came to a small stream that led to Lake Nipissing. It was familiar ground to many, more than familiar to Vérendrye, for years of his youth had been spent here. So by the French River and the bay and Lake Huron they came to the shadowy ghost of that once flourishing Sodom that was Michilimackinac, the center of all evil, as Father Carheil had explained at such exhausting length. Now it was showing signs that Cadillac's fervent hope that the good father might have no more parishioners than were needed to bury him was beginning to take shape. Vérendrye had known the place well when, newly returned from Europe, he had been stationed at Lake Nipigon for two weary, disillusioned years, listening to the tales of great rivers flowing westward, of a vast, flat country peopled with great herds of animals like nothing ever seen–*folie des bois*, indeed, and yet Vérendrye could not help believe.

But Michilimackinac was no place to linger. It took another month to reach the desolate fort at Kaministiquia that La Noue had built years before, seventy-eight weary days since the sound of the bells of Montreal had died in the voyagers' ears. This fort had always seemed the logical starting point for any westward adventuring. Vérendrye thought differently. He pushed on another forty miles to the southwest until he came to the mouth of the Pigeon River. Here was his doorway to the West.

The crews were sulky. Seventy-eight days might be a long time, but it had allowed no room for loitering. They were tired of the constant forward drive and resentful over the brief stop at Michilimackinac. It would appear that the Pigeon River route had not been an altogether happy choice. A few miles from its mouth the river broke into wild rapids, miles in length. Faced with the heavy task of loading all their possessions over this great portage, the voyageurs broke into open revolt. They were more than weary, autumn was at hand, and soon the ice and snow would follow, and the men knew what was before them. It was the first time Vérendrye had faced revolt, and it would be the last, but for the moment it was definite. They had not his faith. To them, this Western Sea was a mirage, a will-o'-the-wisp that might well lead so large a party to its destruction. Vérendrye argued with them to no end, and Father Messager, who had joined the party as chaplain, added his word with equally slim results. A few of the bolder spirits were ready to continue, but most held sullenly aloof. It was hopeless, as Vérendrye well knew, to drive such men too hard. Finally it was agreed that some of the boatmen, those who wished, might go ahead, provided the leader would stay behind and wait for spring.

La Vérendrye had a peculiar capacity for dealing with men. To drive was folly. A better way was to teach them to share his vision. What other course could succeed? Regretfully he gave the word to turn back for Kaministiquia. Before he did so, however, he had set the small expedition in motion. It would be under the command of one who was only twenty-three years of age, his nephew Christophe de la Jemeraye. With him went Jean Baptiste de la Vérendrye, the commander's oldest son. He was second-in-command and he was eighteen years of age. There were thirty men in all, including the boyish leaders, and they went in four heavily laden canoes. It was well that the reluctant had remained behind and that the eager had pressed on too far to turn back, for there were forty more back-breaking portages before they crossed the height of land and came to Rainy Lake, whose farther rivers flowed west, not east.

It was here that they were to build the first of the forts that had been planned to assure their communications. The work was pressed with vigor, for winter was approaching and shelter was needed for survival. Half stockade, half fort, it enclosed cabins of logs that were warm enough. And soon the Indians were coming with their furs to this fort in the clearing that had been named Fort St. Pierre after the older Vérendrye.

The arrival of the older Vérendrye at the fort on July 14, 1732, was quite an event. It impressed the Crees mightily. It wasn't only the friendly giving of gifts, important as this was. The Crees were neighbors, but far from friends, of the more warlike Sioux. Vérendrye's presence started speculation as to whether the Crees, allied with the French, might not be able to deal with these neighbors on more equal terms. To show their good will they collected fifty canoes manned with braves and offered to lead Vérendrye westward to other great waters. It was a chance hardly to be missed, even though Vérendrye's forces had just arrived and his men were weary with long paddling. Before arguments could arise, they were started on their way again.

It was August before they reached the Lake of the Woods. They were a large party now with the fifty Indian canoes added, and Vérendrye considered his diminishing supplies with a troubled mind. Everything now depended on whether Jean, not yet twenty years old, who was hurrying from Michilimackinac with supplies, would arrive before winter set in. It was a profitless business, guessing on such matters when there were practical things to be done, a fort to be built as a shelter against the winter. Skirting what is now the Minnesota shore of the lake, they came to its western end and camped there. They were probably about four miles up the Northwest Angle Inlet, west of American Point and Buckete Island. There Vérendrye built the second of his chain of forts and named it Fort St. Charles after Governor Beauharnois, whose Christian name it was. It was a defensible place with rows of palisades fifteen feet high. Vérendrye watched its building with modest pride, knowing better than anyone that it was not proof against their greatest enemy —not Indians, not cold, but hunger. Day after day passed. The light night frosts put a thin surface on the water and disappeared with the dawn; this now turned into something sterner, a film of ice that grew deeper day by day until it would bear a man's weight. Vérendrye was forced to face the fact that the canoes could not get through. It was not an unfamiliar hazard and it has hardly changed with the centuries. Today, with all our knowledge and all our modern devices, man must still wait on nature with what patience he may, recognizing, now as then, that freezing cold and sudden breakup present problems and hazards that he cannot master.

The wintry afternoon was drawing in. Vérendrye leaped to his feet at the sound of a shout. He reached the doorway of the fort to see young Jean de la Vérendrye burst from the woods. Behind him staggered his snowshoe army bent under heavy loads. Here were the provisions, brought from canoes that indeed were locked in the ice fifty miles away.

Vérendrye did not spend much time in rejoicing. They had been near catastrophe and they could be again. The certainty grew in him that the merchants in Montreal were growing lukewarm in their interest. Another year and there might be no interest at all. That danger had to be faced, and promptly. He sent his nephew Jemeraye to Montreal to tell of their progress and explain their difficulties, and to kindle enthusiasm again. With Jemeraye went the Jesuit Messager to support his arguments. These two were not long in discovering that the merchants in truth had lost both heart and faith. True, they had received two cargoes of furs–a modest return where they had expected a fortune. Almost three years had passed and this was all. There were murmurs that Vérendrye might be doing better for himself. They were the practical men of an earlier age, these merchants of Montreal. They proposed now to advance supplies in proportion to returns. That this might mean starvation to the fifty or more adventurers, that it might forever close that dream of a Western Sea troubled them very little. As has been said, they were practical men.

Others were practical in another way. While Jemeraye was facing this problem, young Jean and Pierre de la Vérendrye, approaching their twentieth and nineteenth birthdays, were pushing up the long reaches of the Winnipeg River to where it opens on Lake Winnipeg. There, while Jemeraye did his unsuccessful best with the practical men of Montreal, the two with their companions built the third of their chain of forts and named it after the Comte de Maurepas, who had done less than nothing to deserve the honor.

With the return of Jemeraye, it became clear that the situation of Vérendrye's expedition was little less than desperate. The merchants had called the tune. As far as they were concerned, gold or furs in the hand spoke louder than any intangible Western Sea.

There was just one chance. Leaving Jean and Pierre at Fort Maurepas and with Jemeraye in general command at Fort St. Charles, Vérendrye secured a light canoe and with a few companions set off for Quebec to see the governor and to argue the case himself. By the time he had reached his destination and had done his best, it was too late to return.

It had been summer in 1734 when he started for Quebec. It wouldn't be too much of a trip today. Something better than two thousand miles. You could drive it, without pressing too hard, in a week's time. But not by the roundabout route a canoe must travel and with human muscle the only motive power. For all the haste, the trip took months. There were other weeks of planning and discussion. Vérendrye, impatient, eager to be gone, tortured with the thought of what might be happening in his absence, had to put a curb on himself. Already rivers and lakes were feeling the iron bonds of frost. There was no hope of getting away until spring released them.

The governor had done his generous best to help. He wrote with feeling to De Maurepas, "He is facing so many difficulties alone." And he went on to explain, "He has failed to secure any associate who, like himself, prefers the glory of success to gain in money." De Maurepas was unimpressed. Unfamiliar with the hardships, and certainly not sharing them, he could be impatient with one who was undergoing both. Vérendrye received peremptory orders to forgo his interest in trading. What was expected of him was to find a route to the Western Sea.

The merchants, of course, were of another mind, and they inadequately, it is true, but solely were paying thc costs. Thcy wanted their pound of flesh. Probably between the two Vérendrye lost patience. Speaking coolly, he made it clear to the reluctant merchants that alternatives were few. They could lose their investment completely or they could continue their support in the hope of something better. The practical men had little choice but to continue. They exacted hard terms, however. Vérendrye was to be responsible for any loss, and again there was no alternative.

Returning, Vérendrye made still another investment. He took with him his youngest son, Louis Joseph, who had now reached eighteen years and was to be restrained no longer. With them also, as chaplain, went a young Jesuit father, Pierre Aulneau. They made the return trip at a terrific pace. The June day when they set out was one of oppressive heat, and everywhere as they progressed the forests seemed to be afire and a pall of smoke blanketed everything. It was September when they finally reached Lake of the Woods, but the supply canoes could hold no such pace, and if they would arrive, or when they would arrive, was still a matter of pressing importance.

Vérendrye did what he could. He split up the party; half would remain at Fort St. Charles and half, under the command of Jemeraye and the two older Vérendryes, Jean and Pierre, would winter at Fort Maurepas. Thus the hunting and fishing grounds would be broadened and the possibility of survival improved. There also was to be considered the extra advantage in trading.

Fate did not seem to favor Vérendrye. The frost closed in before the canoes had passed well into Lake Superior. There they could still make some progress, but the rivers were closed. The winter prisoners at the two forts ate roots and moccasin leather, and even their hunting dogs, when fishing was poor and game had disappeared, but they survived. With the coming of spring, hope began to blossom again. Young Father Aulneau, who had made that hurried return trip with Vérendrye and since had known nothing but half starvation, took up his pen to write to his good friend, Julien Bonin, to whom he confided all his observations and opinions. He headed his letter with a small flourish, "Fort St. Charle among the Kiristineaux." He had not been deeply impressed with his surroundings and he said so with some frankness. The fort was "merely an enclosure made with four rows of posts of 12 to 15 feet in height in the form of an oblong square. Within are a few rough cabins, constructed of logs and clay and covered with bark. Several streams," he wrote, "put it in communication with other lakes, all of which empty into another which the savages say is larger. . . . They call it *Ouinipignon*." Nothing here to offset the memories of struggle and starvation. Later he added his heartfelt comment: "This is all the information I am able to give you at present concerning this wretched country." It was not to trouble him much longer. He wrote on April 30, 1736. Less than two months later he was dead.

In the spring, when the whole company gathered again at Fort St. Charles, one face was missing. Jean and Pierre were there, but their cousin, young Christophe de la Jemeraye, who had commanded the group at Fort Maurepas, was not with them. Earlier, hearing of the plight of the forces at Fort St. Charles, he had gathered the winter's furs and what provisions remained and hurried with all his forces to their relief. He did not improve, and on the way he died of some unknown illness that may have been just the outcome of weariness and privation. There is something pathetic in a youth of such capacity and such unflinching devotion, so little remembered that his name is not even mentioned in many an important history. He lies buried somewhere by a northern river, wrapped in his hunting robe. He had seen much and suffered much. He had known the glory of being numbered among that "lone grey company before the pioneers." He was only twenty-seven years old.

It was a heavy blow to Vérendrye. Christophe de la Jemeraye was his sister's son. He was also a man who recognized the magnitude of the undertaking and had gladly chosen to share the heavy burden. Now the burden must be borne by fewer shoulders, unless one remembers Louis Joseph, the youngest of the Vérendryes.

There was no time for weakness. Checking over their resources, the Vérendryes, father and sons, discovered with dismay that powder was running short. There was scarcely sufficient for a month, and already the Crees were beginning to arrive for the trading. Should they learn how weak were the forces that they hoped to have on their side against the Sioux, they might think it better to seize what they could and go it alone.

This was very clear to Vérendrye, and out of it came the decision to send three swift canoes with twenty men to Michilimackinac to trade the winter store of furs for food and munitions. With La Jemeraye gone, there was one choice for leader. It was Jean, oldest of the Vérendrye sons. With him would go the young priest, Father Aulneau. It had been a hard year for him, not yet quite hardened to the rugged life of the colony. He needed rest and the spiritual uplift of a retreat. This trip would assure both. It would have, that is, but for a little byplay that had unhappy results.

Pleased with some new firearms, a small group of Crees could not resist the impulse to try a shot at some Sioux who were in the neighborhood. They were not expert marksmen, and the pleasantry did no harm except to offend the dignity of those who had been the target. They demanded to know who had fired the shots. Recognizing that matters had gone beyond a joke, the Crees retorted craftily that some Frenchmen had done the shooting. There the small incident seemed to end.

It was June 8 when Jean de la Vérendrye got his little force of four canoes and twenty men in motion. Once started, they moved fast. They made twenty miles in what remained of that day. At one of the myriad islands in Lake of the Woods they stopped for the night and lit their campfires.

It was probably the fire that led the Sioux, still incensed at the pleasantry of the Crees, to this one island. A fortnight later a party of French and Indians discovered by chance why the voyageurs had gone no farther.

The twenty-one still lay in a group about the dead fire as if they had been engaged in council or perhaps joining in evening prayer. Certainly young Father Aulneau had been so engaged. He was still on his knees, his left hand on the earth and his right still upraised in a gesture of invocation. An Indian arrow protruding from the back of his head supplied the only discordant note in that figure of peace and worship. Elsewhere there was no evidence of peace. The leader, Jean de la Vérendrye, now aged twenty-three, lay face down on the earth. His back was hacked and torn unbelievably, and the headless body was mockingly decorated with gaily colored porcupine quills. All were there, victims of their own trust and courage, and all were scalpless.

Late that fall the bodies were brought to Fort St. Charles to be buried at last in the shadow of the little Catholic chapel. Eight hundred Crees had gathered for the occasion. They were hopeful that, with such a challenge, the French could now be counted on to destroy the Sioux. They had come prepared for such an eventuality and now urgently demanded that the murders be avenged. It was a hard argument to resist. There was bitter grief in Vérendrye for the death of his first-born. There was anger at the senseless treachery. But when he spoke it was for peace. It was not timidity. That could hardly be charged to one who had collected nine wounds at Malplaquet. He knew that such a war would set the whole country ablaze. It would put an end to the hope of searching for any unknown sea. Young Jean de la Vérendrye had died in that cause, and his father could not turn his back on it. So it was decided.

The shortage of provisions and arms that had been almost forgotten was relieved when on July 17 Louis Joseph, youngest of the

Vérendrye brothers, arrived with the long-delayed supplies. For all his desire for haste, it was February 8, 1737, before Vérendrye was ready to start his followers from Fort St. Charles toward Fort Maurepas. After all, those practical men, the merchants of Montreal, had to be considered. Also, unless there were furs, there would be no supplies and no likelihood of accomplishment, so he could only wait. When the day came, there was no promise of an easy journey. The wind, blowing gustily from the north, had sent the temperature to a cruel forty below zero. There was word, too, that all along what is now the Minnesota borderland that they must travel the snow lay in twelve-foot drifts in the forest. It was not a time to dawdle. Ordinarily the trip by canoe was expected to take twenty-one days. But fighting their way through heavy drifts on the seventeenth day, Pierre de la Vérendrye, who was in the lead, saw the fort in the distance facing on a great body of water that was to be known as Lake Winnipeg.

When he had made it clear to the Indians that he had not come with any warlike intent and had warned them to beware of the English, who were the bringers of the plague of smallpox they so dreaded, he listened to the report of his sons, who told of the Indian gossip of a meeting of rivers where game was boundless. The hint of a river that might possibly flow westward caught his imagination, and he sent his sons to investigate the gossip. Then wearily he turned his face toward the east again and the dreary continuing conflict with niggardliness that had no outlook beyond the figures in the account books. This was the third trip over those thousands of miles since the expedition had begun. Truly had he written that the Western Sea might have been discovered any time had the people really wished it. But what argument would convince stubborn men who would haggle over every penny spent, no matter what the returns?

It was well that Vérendrye had with him on his return fourteen heavily laden canoes. This was tangible evidence and it was needed. Even Governor Beauharnois seemed to be growing a little uncertain, demanding new pledges of immediate progress, while he reported to the minister: "I told him that if he didn't keep his word, I would recall him."

The merchants were even more dubious. They took little thought that Vérendrye had not only invested all his own substance in this venture but had lost his first-born son while his other sons were leading lives of constant hazard. These were intangible things, but fur cargoes were tangible. The fourteen canoeloads of furs were something, but they only made greedy eyes glitter the more. The merchants decided to send one of their number to represent them in the enterprise. It was the Sieur de la Marque, and he was himself a considerable investor.

Obviously, if anything was to be done that year, it had to be done quickly. The reception he had received could hardly be called inspiring, but Vérendrye put it behind him. He must get back. He was at Michilimackinac early in July of 1738, and by the twentieth he had secured twenty-two men and six canoes made for speed and was on his way again. They passed the established posts with hardly a pause, and on September 24 he was with his sons, camped at the confluence of the Red and Assiniboine rivers, where now stands the great city of Winnipeg.

Even there the stay was brief. The Assiniboine seemed to give some promise of leading westward. But as it is, so it was, an unpredictable stream. There was little hope in its westerly bearing. Soon it was too shallow for the canoes, heavily laden as they were. So the company was divided, the "useless people"—those who could not rank as fighting men—went with the canoes and the stores; the rest marched on foot, the first Caucasian feet to tread those illimitable miles of prairie.

But before they left they built a rude stockade at their camping, another in that growing list of fortress trading posts that marked their passage. They called it Fort Rouge, after the color of the river.

Driving the heavy canoes with paddle and pole was tough work for the "useless people," and the others made better time across the prairie grass. A week after leaving the newly created Fort Rouge, the party came to what was to be known as the Portage of the Prairie. When the "useless people" caught up they were set to work building still another fort on the site of what is now Portage La Prairie. They named it Fort La Reine. It is to be hoped that the sad little Polish Queen of Louis XV heard of this honor, for little else that was heartening came her way.

The fort was hardly built when the Sieur de la Marque, who had been sent to keep Vérendrye on the move, finally caught up. With him came his brother Nolant and eight followers. Caution suggested that it was late to be setting out across a wind-swept prairie toward an unknown destination. But caution had never stood very high with Vérendrye, and now with La Marque as a reminder of the court's demand for results, he thought of it not at all.

October 16 came, and the unfamiliar beat of drums startled the prairie wildfowl. When all had gathered to learn the reason, Vérendrye told them of his decision to move at once to the country of the Mandans—which covered much of present-day Minnesota and the Dakotas—of whom he had heard many things and, not least, that they might lead him to the Western Sea.

It was obvious that the whole party could not go, yet the selection was made with difficulty. With Vérendrye would go two of his sons, Pierre and the Chevalier. Also, La Marque and his brother and their small following could hardly be overlooked. In all, a score of Frenchmen were chosen to share in the adventure, and with them, as many Assiniboins to act as guides and interpreters.

They went by way of the Souris River, finally striking across the prairie to the Mandan lands. Food was not now the problem. Buffalo ranged the prairie lands in almost limitless herds, and the hunters killed and cured ample supplies. It was as well that this was so, for the party had grown to six hundred as group after group of Cree and Assiniboin joined them, unable to resist having a share in so impressive a party.

It was the end of November before they reached the outskirts of the Mandan country and saw the delegation of Mandan tribesmen who had been sent to welcome them. Vérendrye had expected much of the Mandans. In all the reports he had received the Mandans were said to be just like Frenchmen in appearance and manners and to have knowledge of the Western Sea. But these men, coming with their sparse gifts of corn and tobacco, hardly met these specifications. They were, in Vérendrye's disappointed words, "just like the Assiniboins; they are naked; a buffalo robe may be thrown carelessly about them but they have not even a breechcloth." His surprise and disappointment taught him a useful lesson. "From that moment," he wrote in his journal, "I resolved that we must discount all that we had heard."

It was as well, for difficulties dogged his footsteps. At the outskirts of the Mandan country an Assiniboin youth managed to abscond with his bag of personal effects. In the celebrations of welcome another youth decamped with the bags containing the gifts, without which no welcome was ever assured. Momentarily the lack was

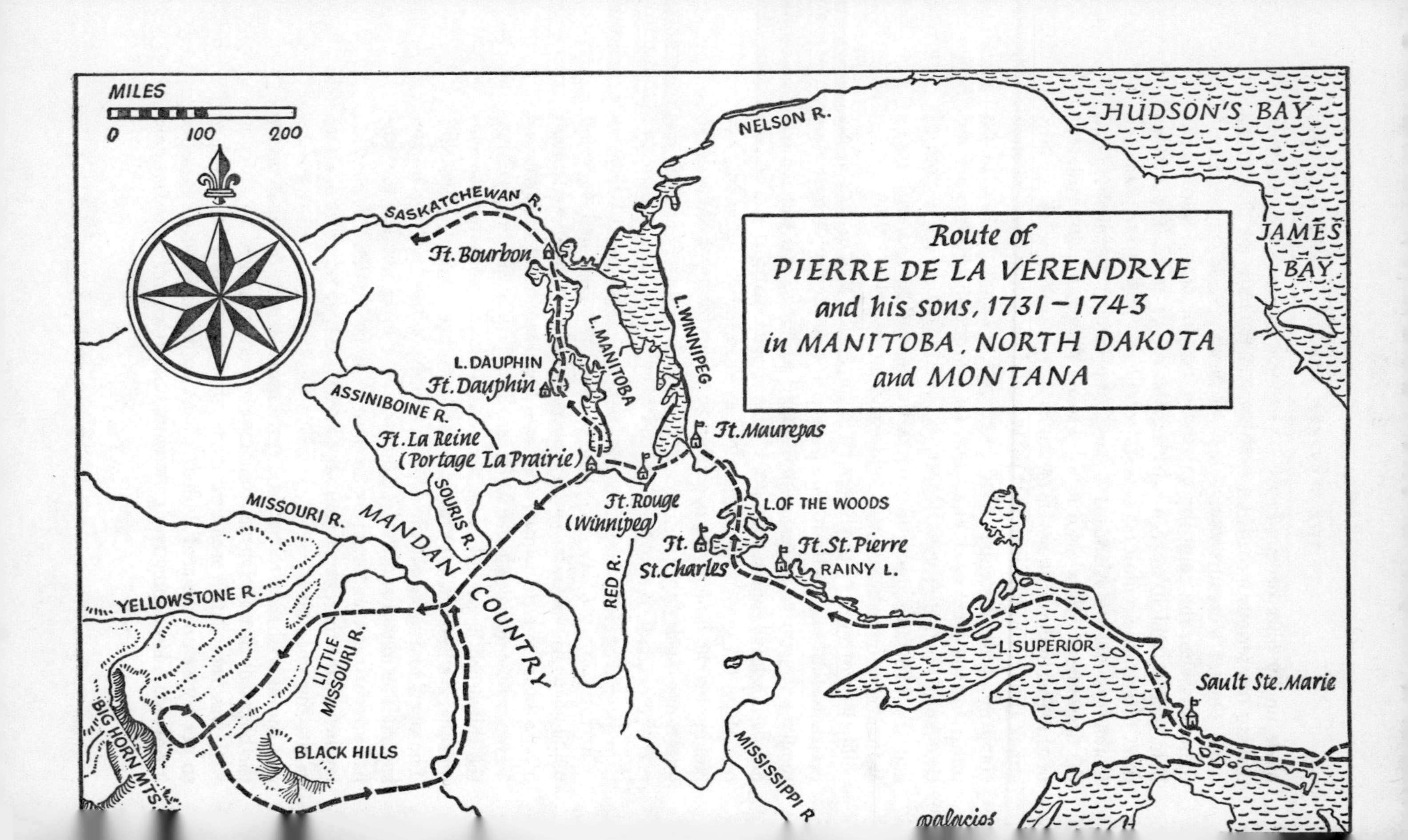
Route of
PIERRE DE LA VÉRENDRYE
and his sons, 1731–1743
in MANITOBA, NORTH DAKOTA
and MONTANA
MILES
0
100
200
HUDSON'S BAY
JAMES BAY
NELSON R.
SASKATCHEWAN R.
Ft. Bourbon
L. WINNIPEG
L. MANITOBA
L. DAUPHIN
Ft. Dauphin
ASSINIBOINE R.
Ft. La Reine
(Portage La Prairie)
Ft. Maurepas
Ft. Rouge
(Winnipeg)
L. OF THE WOODS
Ft.
St. Charles
Ft. St. Pierre
RAINY L.
SOURIS R.
MISSOURI R.
MANDAN COUNTRY
RED R.
YELLOWSTONE R.
LITTLE MISSOURI R.
BLACK HILLS
BIG HORN MTS.
MISSISSIPPI R.
L. SUPERIOR
Sault Ste. Marie
palacios

made up by gifts of munitions. This could not continue without making too serious inroads on vital necessities. Then the final blow came. One of Vérendrye's sons could speak the Cree language, and there was with the company a young Cree who spoke the Assiniboin tongue, which, in turn, was understood by some of the Mandans. By this circuitous route contact was maintained between Vérendrye and the Mandans. It was a peculiar ill fortune that led this important young Cree to fall deeply in love with a daughter of the Assiniboins. These latter, having heard a rumor of a Sioux attack thoughtfully spread by the Mandans, who had tired of their company, were hastening back to their homelands. This was too much for the lovelorn youth, who set out in ardent pursuit. This seemingly small defection left two groups of people, the French and the Mandans, the latter friendly enough and ready to be of assistance, without any means of communication.

Obviously, under these conditions little was to be gained by remaining. It was rather too much to expect that the Mandans would be ready to support the party through the winter. It was decided to leave two of the party, Vérendrye's personal servant and one of La Marque's followers, who had shown themselves quick at picking up the Indian tongues, to learn what they could of the language and such other information as might be useful when the party returned in the spring.

It was January 8 when they decided to start for Fort La Reine, which they had come to look upon as home. It was the very heart of the bitter prairie winter. The strain and hardship had told on Vérendrye, and when the day dawned, he was too ill to travel. By the thirteenth he seemed somewhat better, sufficiently so to decide him that his best chance was to proceed. It was a sobering decision. The open prairie in midwinter was something to daunt the boldest spirits. The moose and the buffalo were no longer to be seen. They had sought the comparative shelter of distant river bottoms. What lay before the marchers was a world of unbroken white that glared in the sun with blinding force. There were no trees for firewood, and the only shelter to be found was the great drifts piled up by the blizzards that also made it difficult to hold a course.

"I was very ill," Vérendrye recorded in his journal, "but hoped to get better on the way." That was a rather improbable hope, as it proved. A later entry reads, "It would be impossible to suffer more than I did. It seemed that nothing but death could release me from such misery." A sick man, improperly protected and fed, plodding through the snow in bitter weather for almost a month—certainly death would have seemed probable enough, and Vérendrye knew it. "I do not know how God preserves us," he wrote. But God did preserve them. A fortnight after he had reached Fort La Reine, Vérendrye was reporting himself "a little restored."

As he grew better, the tantalizing suggestion of a river that would flow westward was ever in his mind. One of his first acts was to send a small expedition to a lake that was familiar to the Indians because it was on their road to Hudson's Bay and the English traders. It would be useful to have a fort farther north than La Reine. So, though this expedition discovered little else, they did build such a fort on one of the northern lakes and called it Fort Dauphin. It was named as an indication of their loyalty to the French Crown and they didn't know that a growing town of the English one day would take its place.

But the thought of a river flowing westward was not to be forgotten. Perhaps it might flow from that great northern lake of Winnipeg. He sent his son, the Chevalier, to find it. It was April 16, 1739, when the young Chevalier and one dusky companion headed their canoe toward Lake Winnipeg. Once, as they neared the northerly fringe of the lake, it seemed as if the dream might have come true, for half concealed in the swamps that marked its mouth was a great river, greater than they had dreamed. Only it didn't flow from Lake Winnipeg toward the west; it flowed to the east and ended there.

Nothing daunted, the two set out to find its source. Day after day for many long miles they paddled against the current until at last they came to a point where the river broke in two. These were the two rivers that came together to form the mighty Saskatchewan. Near the present-day Le Pas, they made their final camp before turning back.

Probably none of the undertakings of Vérendrye was more important than this. Here the two voyageurs heard again from the Crees of the vast mountains many long leagues away, and beyond the mountains the water that came and went and was too brackish for man to drink. So many will-o'-the-wisps they had followed. This time it was true. But who was to know that?

Not long after, at the scene of their most westerly camp, just where the Pasquia River merges with the Saskatchewan, another fort was built and named Fort Bourbon. Under its shadow there was a trading post that was to spell dark days for the English traders on Hudson's Bay. For, the Crees argued sensibly enough, why travel a thousand miles with furs while Fort Bourbon was close at hand?

Vérendrye heard of the Chevalier's discoveries with only moderate interest. His mind was still set on the stories from the Mandan country to the exclusion of all other evidence.

In September the two Frenchmen who had been left to learn the Mandan language arrived at Fort La Reine with more stories of men who rode horses, whose skin was white and who lived in forts made of brick and stone. The word set the senses tingling. But before Vérendrye was the more pedestrian task of making both ends meet. He had to go once more to Montreal to stir again the lagging enthusiasm and ensure the essential supplies.

By the end of the year 1741 they were all once more united at Fort La Reine and eager to move. There was no hope of financing such an expedition as had gone before, but an expedition of some sort there must be. In the end it simmered down to just four men. There would be the Chevalier, apparently the most aggressive of the brothers, and with him Louis Joseph, a lad of less than fourteen years when Vérendrye first set out, and too young to join that expedition. Now he was a man grown. With the two Vérendryes went two other Frenchmen, probably the two who had been left with the Mandans to learn their language. That was the total of the expedition that left Fort La Reine on April 29, 1742.

The trail followed by the four was fairly familiar. It led by way of the Souris River to the watershed of the Missouri. It was the more or less familiar highway to Hudson's Bay.

Three weeks of paddling brought them to the Mandan villages, and they waited there awhile. By July 23 their patience was exhausted. With two Mandans as guides they struck out across the prairie in a southwesterly direction. Loaded as they were with provisions and trade goods and gifts, they moved slowly. Weeks passed, and still no hint of human beings. They came at last to what their Mandan guides called the "Mountain of the Horse People." Weariness and the hope engendered by the name decided them to stop here and build a signal fire. Such temerity was too much for their guides, who saw nothing but risk in so announcing their presence. They slipped away during the night.

At last, on September 14, there was the welcome sight of an answering smoke column. Advancing toward it, the Frenchmen found curiosity but not hostility. The tribe was known as the Handsome Men, the reason not being too apparent. From then on it was a matter of being passed from one tribe to another. The Horse Indians were finally reached after a month's traveling. They did not belie their name. There were horses, and the travelers, if they did not secure the information they had hoped, did secure mounts that made traveling easier. Somewhat later they passed on to a tribe known as Men of the Bow, who were preparing to attack their great enemy, the Serpents. The Frenchmen were given no option but to join the party, and for many days they plodded on toward the blue mountains that now marked the distance.

They had reached the foothills when returning scouts announced that the Serpents had decamped. This apparently happy news appeared differently to the devious Indian mind. To those of the expedition it meant but one thing. If the Serpents had departed, they undoubtedly were making a wide sweep and were heading back to the camp where the women and children had been left. Despite the argument of the chiefs, they would accept no other view. They turned tail with a magnificent unanimity. It was a grim retreat that became more grim as panic was added to the bitter winter that piled snow in two-foot drifts. At last the quiet camp was reached and apprehension disappeared among much brave talk of a discomfited enemy.

The Frenchmen did not wait for the proposed second attack but set out on their own. By March they came to a tribe known as the Little Cherry Indians, who lived far south of the Mandan country. But for this happy meeting there might be no real evidence at all as to just where the Chevalier and his companions had actually been. No one knows exactly just what were the high mountains they had reached—which were, as the young Chevalier recorded, "for the most part well wooded and seem very high." Perhaps they were just the Black Hills of South Dakota, though that seems unlikely. The most probable assumption is that they had actually reached the Big Horn range of the Rocky Mountains.

Probable as this is, it is still only an assumption. But while they were with the Little Cherry Indians the Chevalier and his associates had followed a custom usual with French explorers of leaving a leaden plate in a sort of "Kilroy was here" gesture, to notify the world at large, or such part of it as was interested, that this was now French territory.

A hundred and seventy years later, on a February Sunday of 1913, some young folk taking an afternoon stroll in the fields near Pierre on the Missouri River, the capital city of South Dakota, turned up a bit of history. Kicking the turf, as exuberant young folk will, a boot toe connected with something that was not Dakota clay. Closer examination showed it to be a plate of some unknown material. It was heavy like lead and there were marks on it that looked like a flower, and some words in a foreign language.

It turned out to be one of the lead plates entrusted by the Marquis de Beauharnois to Vérendrye for just this purpose. The script was in Latin and was clear enough, and the flowers were the French fleur-de-lis. There was more than that. Scratched on the back of the plate was this inscription in French: "Placed by the Chevalier de la Vérendrye—the 30th of March 1743." This much, then, is established history.

It was the end of March when the plate was buried. It was July 2 when the little party reached Fort La Reine, just a year and three months since their canoe had slipped down the Souris River into a vast silence. Vérendrye had lost one son in this great venture, and it is not hard to understand how he must have felt as month after month passed and there was no word to tell whether two of his three remaining sons were still alive.

The price of achievement is always high, and so with the dream of the Western Sea. In hardship and suffering and anxiety and loss it took its heavy toll. One would think that the vast territory opened by Vérendrye and his sons would have brought the highest honors. That was not the case. When after the return of his sons he made his final journey to Montreal, it was not to receive the award of the victor but the disgrace and ignominy of the defeated. He found himself supplanted, his only continuing association with the great undertaking the obligation to pay his successor three thousand livres a year out of the fortune in profits, profits that existed nowhere but in the Maurepas mind.

But Governor Beauharnois, not overly brave in challenging authority, did stress Vérendrye's manifold accomplishments, his blameless life, and the great difficulties he had faced. The tales of wealth, he explained, were untrue. After twelve years of arduous labor, Vérendrye's sole remaining capital was four thousand livres. But Maurepas remained unmoved either by this appeal or Vérendrye's own quiet remonstrance.

But that star was not to rise again, though it flickered for a moment in the uncertain happenings of those days. The friendly Governor Beauharnois was recalled and the Marquis de la Jonquière appointed in his place. The marquis, however, had the misfortune to be captured by the English and so the post fell, in the interim, to the Comte de la Galissonière. The *comte* was small and deformed in body, but the cramped body held a fighting heart. He wrote the minister without qualification: "My opinion is that the stories are wholly false that you have been told about the Sieur de la Vérendrye preferring his own gain to the task of exploration. Any officer must give some attention to trade so long as the King does not supply the means of subsistence." It was a challenge to no purpose.

Maurepas retorted: "I form this opinion from his own journals." It was almost his last official word. There is, perhaps, a melancholy sort of justice in the fact that Maurepas, who had served his King well, was to receive the same treatment he was ready to impose on others. With hardly a word he was sent into a banishment that was to last for twenty-five years, and his place was promptly filled by a less able and less accomplished man. Minister Rouillé, who took Maurepas' place, promptly reversed his decisions. The King, he said, would allow Vérendrye to go again to the west, but added with a hint of Maurepas' disbelief that he must be watched closely to see that he did not neglect the explorations. Happy at the apparent change of fortune, Vérendrye almost failed to notice the qualification. He wrote gratefully to the minister, and possibly in return Rouillé saw that he received the coveted Cross of St. Louis, little enough payment for almost half a continent.

The earliest date he could set for the new venture would be May of 1750, and he set about his preparations with renewed vigor. "He spared nothing," wrote the Chevalier, "which might bring success; he bought and prepared the needed goods; he inspired me and my brothers with his own enthusiasm."

But it was not to be. As night fell on Montreal that December 6, 1749, the tired body of Pierre de Varennes, Sieur de la Vérendrye, reached the end of its long road and its unfinished dream. It found rest at last in the chapel of Ste. Anne in the Church of Notre Dame.

At Quebec the Marquis de la Jonquière had at last arrived. It was to him, the new governor, to whom the great explorer's sons must look for justice. And justice they might have received, for La Jonquière was a just and able man. But at his elbow was one who, though able enough, was also one to whom justice and right and honesty and honor were words empty of any meaning. François Bigot, the friend of La Pompadour, the protégé of Maurepas who, as intendant of Louisburg, had seen the fortress destroyed and had thought only of what he had been able to gain, was now intendant of all New France. Never in all its history had any appointment been as disastrous. There had been weak men where he was not weak. There had been men, perhaps, as selfish as he, but never had there been one in whom evil was so personified.

It was hopeless to expect, with the official belief in the fortunes to be made in such an expedition as Vérendrye had proposed, that Bigot would let that chance fall into the hands of Vérendrye's sons.

The Chevalier, who had been ill in Montreal when his father had died, did his best. He wrote the governor that he was responsible for contracts made by his father and that he hoped to succeed to his father's place. The governor replied that Legardeur de St. Pierre had already been appointed to continue the long search. The Chevalier hurried to Quebec to urge his case in person, even agreeing that he and his brothers would be happy to serve under St. Pierre. It was a forlorn hope. The governor was firm. There was no place in the west for the Vérendrye name.

There is little remaining to the story, but that little surely should tell of Marie Anne Dandonneau, who as little more than a child had become Madame Vérendrye. She bore two daughters, and four sons whose valiant story is almost her only monument. Perhaps the girl-wife, who had known so much of separation, was satisfied that it should be so. Perhaps she was one of the Marthas of the world, content to serve, happy to give her all without self-pity and without reward. So much one may hope, for there is little more that is known of her.

For the sons, too, the record grows sparse. Pierre, the oldest brother, survived his father only a bare half dozen years. For Louis Joseph, youngest of the four, there was no change in Fate's averted face. When the war with Britain was over and there was no longer any New France, many Frenchmen wished to return to their heart's home. With such went Louis Joseph de la Vérendrye on the good ship *Auguste*. She never got beyond sight of that Isle Royale that now was definitely Cape Breton. Shipwrecked on the rocky coast, more than three hundred Frenchmen perished, among them the young Vérendrye.

Only François, better known as the Chevalier, survived for long. He fought with all the gallantry of his father through the Seven Years' War. And when the issue was decided, he accepted it. Canada was his life and he would not leave it. For thirty-four years he lived under British rule, a quiet and uneventful life, a bachelor to his death. With him a great name came to an end. But before he died he was to know of a dream's accomplishment. Alexander Mackenzie had found the Western Sea.

CHAPTER XIX

"A PROJECT OF WILD AUDACITY"

Conflicting claims to the Austrian succession involve Europe in further war. Duquesnel, governor of Louisburg, entangles Canada by destroying the English settlement at Canseau. Attack on Annapolis repulsed by Mascarene. New England aroused. William Vaughan urges attack on Louisburg, and Governor Shirley of Massachusetts takes up the cause. William Pepperrell appointed commander of expedition. Commodore Warren commands the navy. Death of Duquesnel and Duchambon's succession. Investment of the fortress. The problems of amateur soldiering. Royal Battery taken and the attack on Island Battery a disastrous failure. Its last capture sets stage for final assault. Duchambon capitulates. New mutiny follows capture. France's retort the calamitous D'Anville expedition. Peace and its historic mistake.

IF Louisburg might stand for the nadir of the French spirit in the New World, there were few knowing or willing enough to admit the fact. To the French, Louisburg was a great gesture, a new guardian of the gates of Canada. To the English it was a challenge in part to their vanity but, more importantly, to their trade with the American continent. To the American colonies it was a never-ending threat, to their lives, to their seagoing commerce, and to the fisheries that were the backbone of that trade.

For the peoples of the New World threat was nothing new. Antagonism began with the advent of the English on this continent. Their presence was looked upon as an encroachment on lands that the French considered their own. The English, never a people to submit tamely to authorities that appeared ill founded, were far from ready to accept the broad generalization that the French owned a continent because they had been the first to discover a relatively small segment of its northern fringe.

The happenings of the century that had passed had done nothing to encourage a better relationship. Throughout the English colonies roots had been firmly established and a conviction was hardening that a continent was not large enough for two such bitterly antagonistic groups. If this was true of the English, it was doubly true of the French, to whom the growth of the English colonies and their expanding claims were a challenge that could not be accepted. French pride was hurt. The numerous threats to Boston and the incessant French depredations against the New England colonies might seem amply to justify the English seizure of Acadia, but not to French thinking. They might bide their time, but they proposed to return. The creation of Louisburg was the first move in that campaign. The next would be the recovery of Acadia itself.

As a matter of fact, both contestants were itching to precipitate a conflict. Governor Beauharnois, like his predecessor, was more than a little inclined to turn the momentary cold war that followed the Peace of Utrecht into something really explosive. He found little encouragement in the homeland. All Europe seemed to be leaning toward peace. It was not a peace of restored good feeling but purely one of exhaustion, and the difference in the New World did not appear important enough to become a *casus belli.* Until someone rattled the saber again in Europe, the uncertain peace would remain and would be reflected in affairs in the New World.

It was not Louisburg or the smoldering antagonisms of French and English colonists that finally brought matters to a head. It was the vanity of Frederick II, newly succeeded to the throne of Prussia. This was the Frederick who was to be known as "The Great," and it was his shadow that was to dominate Europe for years to come.

The Emperor of Germany and Austria, Charles VI, had recently died, leaving no male heir. His later years had been devoted to gaining the agreement of the great powers of Europe for the pragmatic sanction that assured the succession to his daughter, Maria Theresa.

He had not been long dead, however, before it seemed that the sanction might be almost as dead as he. They were rugged days and perhaps there was reason in the view that it was no time to vest the rulership in a woman's hands, even though those hands were to prove themselves competent enough.

Probably the real issues were somewhat more complicated. Frederick of Prussia had large dreams, in which Prussia's star was to rise as Austria's declined. As the first step toward this goal he laid claim as the male heir to the Austrian province of Silesia. Before Austria could either agree or disagree, and before his declaration of intent had reached Vienna, Frederick had marched his army into Silesia and in two quick battles had effectively decided his point.

So began the Silesian Wars, which were to continue for years to come and were to embroil most of Europe for another generation. France, of course, was quick to espouse the cause of an already successful ally. And of course she had never been friendly with Austria. In addition she allied herself with the Bourbon King of Spain, who was quite ready to declare Maria Theresa a usurper and himself the heir to all the Hapsburg lands.

By one of those strange turns of fate Britain was at this time at war with Spain, in a dispute that has sometimes been called the War of Jenkins' Ear. The Jenkins in question was a rather inconspicuous English merchant sea captain who got himself into an altercation with a Spanish coast guard. One hot word led to another until the Spaniard finally boarded the English ship and, as the argument grew more heated, made a cut at Captain Jenkins that neatly sliced off his ear. This the angry coast guard retrieved and tossed into the captain's face and, with some uncomplimentary words for the English King, departed.

It was an incident nicely in tune with the vigorous politics of the day. The opponents of the Prime Minister, Sir Robert Walpole, urged that he had shown himself too eager to amass money and too timid to entertain the thought of war. Then Captain Jenkins appeared in Parliament, his severed ear neatly packed in wool and packaged in a box. The resulting hysterical demand for war was not to be resisted. Years afterward Edmund Burke was to assert that when the good Captain Jenkins died it was discovered that both his ears were intact and in their appointed place. But in the interval Britain was again at war with Spain and so felt that it could not very well be at peace with a France that was Spain's ally. So it is that Captain Jenkins may be said to have his small and distant place in Canadian history.

Always it was difficult for the mother countries to feel that the colonies had any life or interests that were peculiarly their own. Usually news of pending great events reached the colonies slowly. For once, however, the French minister had been prompt and on May 5, 1744, Governor Duquesnel at Louisburg received the word that France and Britain were again at war. Receiving it, he moved with decision.

Let us allow him this small credit, for the one observer who reports of this at first hand, Habitant of Louisburg, will allow him little else. This eyewitness, who left his careful account of the first capture of Louisburg, excuses himself for remaining anonymous. "It is often unsafe to tell the truth," he explains, "and especially with the artless candor which will guide my pen." Of the "candor" there can be little doubt, but whether it was "artless" is still a moot point. Certainly it hardly could be called free of bias. He writes: "As soon as our governor learned of the declaration of war he formed vast projects which have resulted in our present misfortune. God keep his soul in peace! Poor man, we owe him little; he was whimsical, changeable, given to drink, and when in his cups knowing no restraint or decency. He had affronted nearly all the officers of Louisburg and destroyed their authority with the soldiers. It was because his affairs were in disorder and he was ruined that he had been given the government of Cape Breton."

"Poor man" indeed. He is not even allowed the small credit of having moved promptly when the moment came. All the observer will admit is that "the foolish enterprise against Canseau . . . is the first cause of the loss of a colony so useful to the King," a judgment that is open to debate. He will not even grant Duquesnel the uncertain dignity of death. Here the record is abrupt. The governor "died suddenly in the month of October, regretted as little as he deserved to be."

To give Governor Duquesnel the barest justice, it might be conceded that to appoint a superior official because his affairs were in disorder and himself ruined can hardly reflect only on the recipient of the appointment. It is also true that when the word of the outbreak of war reached him he did move with admirable celerity, and on the offensive and at least with some sort of plan.

It is difficult to agree with the Louisburg observer that the attack on Canseau was a strategic blunder. Canseau was hardly a shining mark, but it was not without some importance. It was a small settlement located on an island at the mouth of the Strait of Canseau—now Canso—which separated Acadia and Cape Breton. It was the closest English settlement to Louisburg, about fifty miles distant. In a small way it had its considerable importance as an outpost of observation and a fishing post of value. In no other way was it impressive. It was a scattering of houses about a wooden redoubt, built by the fishermen. It had some eighty defenders.

These defenders were blissfully unaware that events of importance were pending. The English authorities had not shared France's promptness in notifying their colonies that war now existed between England and France. No hint of it had reached Canseau. The first notice there was the arrival of Duquesnel's expedition. It was a small fleet, a motley collection of vessels, only two of them armed. But they did carry six hundred men under the command of Captain Duvivier. His orders were to destroy the post and bring its inhabitants to Louisburg as captives. The issue was not long in doubt. The English forces surrendered on the undertaking that they would be returned to Port Royal or to Boston. There was one small qualification to this. They must first spend the year as prisoners at Louisburg. This qualification more than undid whatever advantage had lain in the destruction of Canseau, since it soon became evident that Louisburg could not support so many additional persons. The prisoners had to be returned. But now they went armed with the valuable knowledge that the impregnable fortress was far from impregnable. Behind an impressive façade a heart was lacking. This, not Duquesnel's adventuring, lost the French King his useful colony. The returned prisoners bore with them specific details that leadership at Louisburg was incompetent and venal, that the pay of the Swiss mercenaries, a considerable part of its garrison, was long overdue, that mutual distrust existed and continual shortages of provisions and munitions. Here was the seed of that "project of wild audacity" that was beginning to grow in the minds of the English colonists.

Unhappily for himself, Duquesnel had not the capacity to assess this situation. To him Canseau was a victory from which he had secured prestige, prisoners, and an important supply of provisions. He thirsted for more. He was going to make his name immortal by recovering Acadia for Louis XV. The first step was to recover Annapolis, the Port Royal of old.

As a sober fact, Annapolis was not so much more impressive than Canseau had been. Since its capture from the French no one had paid it more than passing attention. Its ramparts and moats had fallen into disuse, save as the favorite grazing ground for the garrison cows.

But Annapolis had something. It had Major Paul Mascarene. Under his careful eye it was beginning to assume a more martial aspect. He was one of the reasons why the French wanted Annapolis, and he was certainly the major reason that they did not get it. The French hated him because Paul Mascarene was a Frenchman born, Protestant born too. His parents were Huguenots and had been among the 400,000 French men and women who had been terrorized and ruthlessly driven from France when Louis XIV revoked the Edict of Nantes, which had permitted Protestants religious freedom. Paul Mascarene had not been taught to love France.

When Governor Duquesnel, pleased with the success at Canseau, sent Captain Duvivier to repeat the success at Annapolis, Duvivier had with him a modest army of four French officers and ninety regular troops. To this force were added some three or four hundred Micmac Indians, under the command, so it was said, of their missionary father, Le Loutre. It is well to remember that name because it stands out in the history of those days with a rather dark significance. Probably he fought as hard, as devotedly, and as ruthlessly as anyone for what he believed to be the best interests of the Acadian people. Equally it is true that he as much as anyone was responsible for the ultimate expulsion of the people he loved so sincerely, drove with such a sternly mistaken patriotism, and, in the end, served so simply and so well.

If there was still evidence of crumbling in the defenses of Annapolis it was not in the hundred defenders who stood behind Mascarene. True, Governor Shirley of Massachusetts did send him a small reinforcement from the state militia, but these men were of little value, as no arms had come with them and Mascarene had none to spare. Yet though outnumbered the defenders were not discouraged. Three weeks of desultory attacks had achieved nothing. Duvivier had failed even to interest the Acadians in active participation. The most they could be induced to do was to construct one hundred and fifty scaling ladders for the proposed final assault as an evidence of their good will. As they insisted on being paid for the work, it was evidence, too, of the canny nature of the Acadian mind.

The attack on Annapolis just petered out. Duvivier did his best.

He sent word to Mascarene that two ships were coming from Louisburg and that their arrival with additional troops would make the English position untenable. He asked for surrender. Mascarene retorted placidly that he would make up his mind what to do when the ships actually arrived. He did not have to make this decision. Governor Duquesnel had come to loggerheads with the two captains, and they had sailed away in high dudgeon, but not in the direction of Annapolis. When instead two vessels arrived from Boston, bringing fifty Indian rangers to reinforce the fort, what little heart remained to the attackers melted away. With it went the besieging army. The expedition was a failure, the Habitant of Louisburg confided to his journal, "though it was to be expected that it would succeed, because the enemy were very ill equipped to resist us." And he added at another point, "The English would perhaps not have troubled us if we had not first affronted them. It is our love of aggression that has cost us dearly."

That was a sound enough judgment. The English colonies had their own financial problems and they had no money and no time or enthusiasm for war. Left alone, in all probability they would have left others alone. But the destruction of Canseau and the attack on Annapolis put a different complexion on the matter. It raised "in some heated brains," as Francis Parkman has said, "a project of wild audacity."

Perhaps this germ of audacity had been there all the while, at least since the French had moved into Isle Royale in earnest and had begun building an impressive fortress there. Such a fortress could have no other reason than to challenge the English. So probably from the beginning there had been a feeling that sooner or later Louisburg must be destroyed. Canseau and Annapolis only added new fire to those already "heated brains."

Many claims have been made as to who was the first to demand that the impregnable fortress should be attacked. The major opinion favors William Vaughan of Damariscotta as the first to urge Governor Shirley of Massachusetts to make the attempt. Certainly William Vaughan was just the man to provide the wild audacity that such a project demanded. In youth he had established a fishing post at Matinicus Island, off the coast of Maine, and from that had gone on to control the lands about the Damariscotta River, where he built a wooden fort and established a considerable settlement. He was headstrong and foolhardy and a man of vast self-confidence. Then, too, the background of all his success had been his fishing enterprises and he was acutely alive to the threat Louisburg presented to the fishing interests of the English colonies.

In William Shirley, the newly appointed governor of Massachusetts, he found a man very much to his liking, a ready listener, a man of sense and wisdom, yet one also who could take fire with quick enthusiasms. Vaughan knew something of Louisburg and he caught the governor's interest with his report of the winters there, where the snowdrifts banked against the ramparts like scaling ladders, so that much of their defensive value was lost. All that was needed for a successful winter attack was an expedition that could brave the winter storms and fog. It was an appealing project, but Shirley rightly decided it unfeasible. Also, he knew nothing could be done without consent of the members of the General Court.

The proposals made them, the sober merchants and farmers and fishermen and artisans who composed the convention, listen with strained attention. They remembered that the mother country had been more than cool when the plan was broached many months before. That proposal, as Governor Shirley had presented it to his patron, the Duke of Newcastle, was that fifteen hundred or two thousand men would suffice to capture Louisburg once a fleet of half a dozen warships had forced the harbor.

The demand didn't seem too extravagant, but Britain hadn't a man or a ship to spare. At outs with Prussia and now with Spain over that matter of Captain Jenkins' ear, she had also to contend with France. France's great soldier, Marshal Saxe, was ready to use his country's obligation to Spain as an excuse to plan an invasion of England. It was to have as its nominal head Charles Stuart, the Bonnie Prince Charlie of romance. This proposed invasion, like many another, came to nothing. The French fleet, conveying the Prince's army to Kent, found the British fleet waiting and had to retire discomfited. But if Marshal Saxe didn't sail up the Thames, he did meet the allied British, Dutch, and Austrian army at Fontenoy in Belgium and compelled its rather precipitous retreat. And if Bonnie Prince Charlie didn't keep his appointment in Kent months later, he *did* land in the Hebrides with his seven followers and raised the Stuart standard at Glenfinnan. It wasn't England that was invaded, but emphatically it was Scotland, with the clans joyfully rallying to support their own King. It was a great though swiftly passing moment. Gray old Edinburgh was a carpet of white roses, and the white cockades on the highland bonnets waved with a jaunty gallantry. It mattered little that Edinburgh Castle was held against them and even less that, under its guns, good Mr. McVicar of the West Kirk might mount his pulpit and raise his voice in earnest prayer, beseeching that "for the young man who comes seeking an earthly crown, may Heaven speedily send him a Heavenly one."

The cheering and the singing and even the prayers died away. The White Rose Court was a memory and in its place was "Butcher" Cumberland waiting at Culloden Moor, hard by Inverness. That was the end—and the sad remembrance of "the brave and noble that have died, in vain, for me."

This was still long months in the future. Only the portent cast its shadow on English hearts, leaving no room for thoughts of more distant adventuring. The good councilors of Massachusetts knew it quite well. There were days of careful reflection and discussion on Shirley's eloquent appeal backed by the reports of the Canseau prisoners who had spent weary weeks in Louisburg. They could tell that the impregnable fortress was not quite that—that food and munitions were scarce, that the defenses were not yet completed, that the defenders were unpaid and mutinous. None of it changed the councilors' thinking. They decided against the venture.

Governor Shirley was not a man easily turned from a chosen course, and still less so was William Vaughan. They and others went about arguing that Louisburg could be captured if taken by surprise. It was not hard in Puritan New England to be stirred against Catholic Louisburg. Self-interest and the spirit of a religious crusade had a quick and powerful appeal to devout and narrow men. This thinking gained many followers, though wise old Ben Franklin was to remind his brother: "Fortified towns are hard nuts to crack, and your teeth are not accustomed to it." It was a voice crying in the wilderness. The crusading spirit had taken hold, and Shirley and his followers used it to urge the Court to reconsider its decision. After much argument and disputing the plan to attack Louisburg was carried by a single vote. The more devout saw that as an unmistakable answer to prayer and supported their belief by a happening that seemed to them too timely to be a mere matter of chance. A tie vote of the Court, which could well have changed the history of the times, might easily have been had not a member hurrying to cast his contrary vote fallen and broken his leg instead. Whether viewed from the standpoint of the prayerful or the skeptic, the fact remained. The Court had decided for war.

Once this decision was reached, opinions changed unbelievably. It was hard to discover an opponent of the plan. It was too much to expect, however, that such a common opinion should result in a common purpose. While states as far south as Pennsylvania favored the proposal, when asked to participate with funds and fighting men they were curiously deaf. They might approve, but the doing was a matter for the New England colonies. In the main that was how it remained.

Massachusetts, at the time including the present state of Maine, being the instigator and promoter of the scheme, with perhaps the most to gain or lose, shouldered the heaviest burden. She would raise three thousand men. New Hampshire promised about five hundred. Connecticut also was interested and ready to supply an equal number, though she coupled this with the proviso that their commander, Roger Wolcott, should rank second in the expedition. Without giving the matter unnecessary thought Wolcott was made a major general and everyone was satisfied. Caught in the enthusiasm, Rhode Island decided to go along to the extent of one hundred and fifty men, thought better of it, and decided to contribute instead the services of the armed vessel *Tartar*. New York lent some guns to the expedition as her share.

Now with this decided, and with the enthusiasm for war become tangible, the burning question was who was to lead. Everyone who had been involved in publicizing the idea felt that his early enthusiasm represented a claim. There was no doubt of the importance of William Vaughan's services. There was no doubt either that he would have liked the post and felt himself equal to it, but he did not press his claim. There were others who were not as moderate. But Governor Shirley held impressive cards: the bulk of the financing and the fighting men came from his colony. Without hesitation he chose William Pepperrell, second of the name and a prominent merchant of Kittery in Maine. He was named lieutenant general and commander of the land forces of the expedition. Undoubtedly, had the King's regulations permitted, he would have been supreme commander. But that would have placed a colonel in command over a high British officer. Such a course was intolerable. The best alternative was to make each of equal rank in his own department.

It was an almost impossible situation that Pepperrell faced. Not only had he little or nothing to say in the direction of the small fleet that was vital to the success of his operation, but his appointment as lieutenant general did not stem from one authority. His commission came in turn from Massachusetts, New Hampshire, and Connecticut, each of which appointed him to his office and maintained some authority over his actions. That some measure of unanimity was achieved was almost as miraculous as was the eventual success of the venture.

Quite rightly did Francis Parkman speak of the expedition against Louisburg as "a mad scheme." No other phrase would fit it as well. It was a project that would have given pause to the finest armies in Europe. Here was one of the greatest fortresses in the world, planned by the greatest military engineer of his day, manned by professional soldiers of the dominant military nation of the day. It was defended not only by the works of man but by a harsh and unfriendly sea that gave a safe haven to a defending fleet in an admirably protected harbor while an attacking force must ride out ocean storm on a rugged lee shore.

It was a scheme planned by an astute and able man, for no one could deny so much to Governor Shirley of Massachusetts. Nor could they deny that he was trained as a lawyer and had as little knowledge of military affairs as had the wholly untrained volunteers. They were all happily ignorant of the nature and extent of this great undertaking. Excitement and enthusiasm completely took the place of any considered judgment. The unnamed writer of the first report of the expedition, as recorded in the *Louisbourg Journals*, compiled for the Society of Colonial Wars, mentions the generally current belief that Louisburg must be reduced because it was "like to prove detrimental if not destroying to our country." The result was an almost hysterical enthusiasm for enlisting that took no account of circumstances or of age. It is recorded that John Storer, major in the Maine militia, raised a company of sixty-one in a single day, their ages running from sixteen to sixty. This latter age came closer to being the rule than the exception. The author of the record already mentioned, during his recounting of the siege, records the death of a volunteer from Bolton, Maine, "who died with a feavour. He was about eighty years old."

It is true that the actual leader of the expedition, William Pepperrell, had not yet reached the age of fifty when he took command. He had also enjoyed some military honors from his colony, finally reaching a colonelship in the state militia. But this occurred in the interlude of peace and represented almost nothing in the way of active knowledge of military affairs. All that could be said in favor of his choice, from a military angle, was that those who had more or better experience were already dead.

One thing was certain. There was no one brash enough to challenge the appointment of William Pepperrell. Men of that name had gained too firm a place in the confidence of their fellows. They had achieved a settled position, too, a financial and social and political position, and that in a relatively short stretch of years.

The father of the new commander had been born on England's Devon coast, though Wales also has laid some claim to him. The actual place of his nativity is of relatively small moment, for he came to the Isle of Shoals about 1667 as a lad of twenty, and thereafter it remained the center of his life. He had almost no capital, but ambition and ability took its place and served him well. He quickly became a responsible trader whose small schooners nosed into every inlet up and down the coast. When his time came to marry, his position was sufficiently secure that he married into one of the ranking families of Boston.

William, Jr., was the son of his parents' later years, but the death of his older brother Andrew made him a figure of importance at an age when most young men have still to find themselves. At seventeen years he was his father's partner, and as the father began to withdraw from the business, young William's authority grew in proportion. Shipping became his major interest. Many of his ships were fitted and loaded at Piscataqua and from there sailed the coast of America as far north as Newfoundland and made their place in the trade with Europe. His finger was in every profitable pie that appeared. Before he had outgrown his early manhood he was a figure of first importance, and his marriage to Mary Hirst, from another of Boston's leading families, established his position that much more firmly. He was now a man of wealth, with his great house overlooking the water at Kittery Point, a center of the social life of his colony.

His influence had quickly gone beyond the strictly material. He had barely reached his majority when he was appointed a justice of the peace, and by the age of thirty he was heading the military levies of the state. Shortly thereafter he became a member of the governing council, and three years later he was named chief justice of the

Court of Common Pleas, an honor that came to him in his thirty-fourth year and that he retained until his death, thirty years later.

It is hardly surprising that when men looked for a leader for this great undertaking the name of William Pepperrell should occur to them. It was a name that had stood for success for two generations, for success and unsought public service. He had energy, good sense, and tact, but he was not a genius. There was nothing to separate him from his fellows. He was a man who belonged both to the city and the town and could speak the language and share the feelings of each. It was possible to be proud of his success without being awed by it. He had not clamored for the post of first captain. He had not wanted it. He was not too sure that success was possible. Even had he been, there was in him no longing for military glory. He had no wish to leave his wife and children or his business. It was Governor Shirley who selected him, realizing the difficulties of the undertaking, its conflicting interests and jealousies. If anyone could make a fighting unit out of such unpromising material, it was this man, whose friendliness and understanding and moderation had already made him a leader among his fellows. So it was decided and so it proved.

It is difficult to understand the sudden wave of enthusiasm for the expedition. It was more than a matter of leadership, more than a realization that while Louisburg remained French, New England could never be free of threat. Perhaps it was partially idleness and the boredom natural to winter months in a primitive community that fostered the fervor of a naturally devout people into something approaching a crusading spirit. The eagerness to participate was almost universal. There were other factors, of course. Recruiting agents were paid a half crown for every man enlisted. These agents enlivened the winter scene by marching through towns and villages to the beat of drums. The twenty-five shillings' pay a month was an item not to be overlooked. There was always, too, the pleasant thought of sharing the spoils of Louisburg. Rumor had it—without supporting evidence—that the fortress was vastly rich. It was an alluring prospect for communities long accustomed to look with favor on privateering ventures as a familiar and highly profitable source of income.

So, for one reason or another, volunteers shouldered old muskets and followed every road leading to the enlistment posts. They were eager to secure the blanket, the only issue that the government supplied, that would mark them as an accepted recruit.

It was always possible in New England to find a fleet of sorts for any undertaking. By March 24, 1745, a hundred ships were gathered in Nantasket Roads. Every sort of vessel was there, from the fishing sloop turned transport to the more impressive armed vessels of the individual government navies. The rendezvous for the actual assault was to be the unfortunate port of Canseau, only some fifty miles from Louisburg, and there was a great itching to be on the way. Actually there wasn't much to be gained by haste. When the New Hampshire men, the first contingent to be away, reached Canseau on April 4 it was to learn that Louisburg was still isolated by the ice of winter and as secure behind its icy barriers as if it hadn't an enemy in the world. The situation was unchanged when the contingent from Massachusetts arrived a day or two later, and though it was two weeks before the Connecticut forces arrived, there was still no hurry.

Perhaps it was as well; the contingents had suffered considerably on the voyage and needed time to recuperate. The vessels limped in one by one, each with its record of storm and illness and intolerable crowding. Those experiences are reported soberly by a young and anonymous writer whose account appears in the *Louisbourg Journals*. The young narrator had not found the experience inspiring. Even when his ship stopped for a time on Nova Scotia's eastern shore he was not tempted to investigate. "I went not ashore," he writes, "but it appear'd a hidious country, as I found the Eastern Shore generally was." However, the weather improving, spirits improved with it. By the weekend he was recording: "Most or all of us recovered of our sickness and had a good stomach for our victuals."

Only a day or so later he was reporting his arrival. "This day I went ashore and saw the ruins of Canso. It is much larger i.e. had consisted of more buildings than I expected but it was reduced to ashes (the sight of which fill'd me with some indignation against the people of Cape Breton). It was a very pleasant place, and the land was good."

It was well that it was pleasant, for the whole expedition had to spend some weeks there and the resources of the place were few. The young journalist records that, the fleet having mainly arrived, it was a large band that was ordered to go ashore and train. Among others, there were thirty-six drummers who were ordered to beat at once, though he explains that he knew of no reason for it. He was a serious-minded crusader, as many were. He reflects on this occasion about the drums and adds of the "fidlers" and "trumpeters" that they were pleasant but that "considering the occasion of our being together prevented, in a great measure, the delight we otherwise could have took."

The whole expedition was again ashore two days later—a Sunday —"to be viewed concerning our arms and ammunition." But the young narrator adds that there were two sermons "preatch'd" that day. In the morning by Samuel Langdon and in the evening by the Reverend Samuel Moody. "I judged," he records, "that there was'ent less than four thousand men that heard him."

This indeed was an unusual army, where the necessary military preparations could be set aside to provide for divine service that could be assured a hundred per cent attendance, where chaplains were as numerous as drums, and where earnest young soldiers would set down in their journals meticulous details of each sermon, its text and the substance of its thought, sometimes adding other details, as of the Reverend Samuel Moody that "he also was led to speak of swearing and cautioned against it, for he speaks of almost everything in every sermon."

This Reverend Mr. Moody was the minister of York. Francis Parkman speaks of him as a "rough little village pope," an appellation that certainly would not have pleased one who, when one of his parishioners attempted to slip away from his interminable address, was wont to roar: "Come back, you graceless sinner, come back."

This same puritanical fanatic, unswerving after his seventy years' experience with a jealous God made in his own fanatical image, took with him on the expedition an ax, for the purpose, as he explained, of cutting down the "idols" in the Louisburg churches. Actually he did manage something of the kind.

In the intervals of preaching, some effort was made to inculcate the rudiments of drill. It was not very elaborate nor taken very seriously. These were volunteers. They were also individuals who, when the time came, might move somewhat clumsily, but would move without hesitation and at some hazard to their lives.

It was obvious by now that if so much could be learned of Louisburg, four thousand men gathered at Canseau could hardly have escaped the notice of the fortress. Surprise was no longer possible. But if this much was lost, much also was gained, and the gain was vital to success.

When the expedition was first planned, Governor Shirley had written Commodore Warren, who commanded the small British West Indian squadron based on Antigua, asking for his co-operation. Though a British officer, Commodore Peter Warren was more than friendly with the English colonists, an attitude that was rather rare. Warren had grown interested in the country and had secured for himself large holdings on the Mohawk River. He had other close ties and interests. He had married a Miss De Lancey, the sister of the then Chief Justice of New York's Supreme Court. It has been suggested that this had led him to the pleasant thought that, with any sort of luck, he might be the governor's successor. To join with Shirley would not only have been his personal inclination but might have furthered these personal plans. When he discussed the matter with his officers, however, they were unanimous in their opinion that existing orders would not permit such action. Reluctantly Warren had to report this to Shirley. It must have been a bad moment for the Massachusetts governor. Even a layman could see that the capture of Louisburg without the co-operation of a fleet was next to impossible. Even Shirley's confidence in Pepperrell could hardly convince him that the scattering of small ships that represented the provincial navies could hope to make good that lack. Why, one French line-of-battle ship could more than look after the whole.

Luck had been with the governor in the selection of a leader. It was to stay with him. Something in Shirley's direct action had impressed the home officials. There was a midnight meeting at the Admiralty, at which new instructions were prepared for Warren. He was to concert measures with Governor Shirley "for the annoyance of the enemy, and His Majesty's service in North America." It might have occurred to Commodore Warren that this cryptic message could be interpreted many ways and that it would certainly leave him holding the bag if anything went wrong. Without giving that too much thought, Warren interpreted it in line with his own inclinations. He ordered his fleet to crowd on sail for the voyage to Boston. Meeting an English schooner on the way, he learned that Pepperrell had already sailed for Canseau. Without a moment's hesitation he changed his own course to follow.

On April 22 there was a great fluttering in the anchorage at Canseau—an unfamiliar sail was descried in the distance. It was obviously a ship of war, very possibly one of the French ships that were expected. There was no doubt of the relief when the red ensign fluttered out. It was His Majesty's ship *Eltham*, of forty guns, the regular escort that followed the spring merchant fleet to England. Counting the costs and possible benefits, Commodore Warren had canceled its instructions and sent it to Canseau. It bore the first news that Warren and his fleet were on the way. They arrived shortly after, Warren on his flagship, the sixty-gun *Superbe*, and with him the *Mermaid* and the *Launceston*, of forty guns each. Now the stage was fully set.

It was the twenty-ninth of April when the expedition left Canseau. Word had been received that at last the ice was out of Gabarus Bay, the open roadstead a few miles to the west and south of the fortress. Shirley's plan had been to attack Louisburg while everyone was asleep. That meant that the fleet should reach its destination by late evening. But a turn of the wind caused much delay, and it was between nine and ten in the morning when the main body of the fleet came to anchor at Flat Point Cove in Gabarus Bay.

The last vestige of hope that anyone would be surprised vanished when a few guns opened from the fortress and the bells of the city began calling to those who lived beyond the walls. But if the defenders were not surprised, neither were they prepared. There was no body of skirmishers awaiting a possible landing.

The natural obstacles were greater than the human. The surf was running high and there were still great hummocks of ice on the shore to make the footing difficult. It was tough work indeed wading through the icy surf, dragging the few cannon behind.

The first landing at Louisburg tempts the reflection as to how different the situation might have been had there been a Frontenac in command. But Duchambon, who had succeeded to the governorship on Duquesnel's death, was certainly of no such stature. He was not even a Duquesnel. It is idle to argue that the impressive Louisburg was not defensible. It was not impregnable, but a few determined men could have made it measurably close to it. It was vastly more so than Quebec had been when Sir William Phips had made his grand attack. Had Frontenac been here, he would not have stood idly by, or almost idly, while Pepperrell landed four thousand men on what the young journalist of Louisburg described as the "most stony of any place on earth." Frontenac would not have sent a handful of men to meet the spearhead of this great invasion. Had such as he been present, Sir William Pepperrell's name might have been added to that of Sir William Phips as among the spectacular failures.

A very simple ruse seems to have confused the leaders of the repelling force. Governor Mesillac Duchambon was there with twenty-four regulars and Port Captain Morpain with fifty civilians. To feint at one point and to attack at another was not a very complicated operation, but it seems to have left the two defenders hopelessly bewildered. Before they realized that the actual landing would be at Freshwater Cove, a number of the attackers had reached shore—seventeen, according to the young reporter. It was enough to meet Morpain's band as they came blundering along. The fire of the colonials rushing to the attack killed six and resulted in the capture of as many more. It was all over before it had more than commenced. Boats were swarming all along the rocky shore and men were leaping overside and dashing through the icy water. The bridgehead had been held long enough to let two thousand men ashore. The rest could land at their ease the following morning.

The young reporter of the *Louisbourg Journals* tells how they climbed a high hill a mile and a quarter west of the city, which they could now overlook. They were met by some uncertain artillery fire that the attackers took in very good part—"One of the balls we took up while it was a roalling—wee judge'd it to be a 24 pounder."

They cut boughs to make beds and listened to the "froggs peep," and "there was singing and great rejoicing" and a vastly comfortable night's lodging. They had no specific orders, "but everyone did what was right in his own eyes."

There were some orders, however. Governor Shirley, working out his careful plan of conquest well ahead of the event, had recognized that next to the fortress itself the Royal Battery, sometimes called the Grand Battery, which lay outside the fortress on the north shore of the harbor, was the heart of the defense. It looked straight down it to the entrance, so that its guns covered every ship that sought the harbor. The importance of taking this battery was only secondary to getting ashore.

Chance put this undertaking into the hands of William Vaughan. Vaughan, it will be remembered, had suggested attacking Louisburg in the winter and using the snowdrifts as scaling ladders. It was a task cut to measure for a man who had no liking for waiting for the propitious moment and whose rash self-confidence had perhaps kept him from a more important role in the expedition.

Colonel Vaughan had taken some four hundred men through the woods about the town and behind the Royal Battery. There were several houses filled with naval stores, pitch and tar and sails and cables. This was not pillage to the liking of his men, and in a spirit of impatient lightheartedness they set the whole ablaze. It was a costly bonfire. Some claimed that it represented a hundred thousand livres. "They were much blamed for destroying so much," records the young reporter of the *Louisbourg Journals*, and he adds his own word of disapprobation: "I can't suppose they had any prospect of doing any good thereby." Very possibly he was correct in his judgment, but good did result. The smoke and fire and the movement of so many men convinced the defenders that an all-out attack was about to begin and it was time to get out. "From that moment," records Habitant within the city, "the talk was of abandoning this splendid battery, which would have been our chief defence had we known how to make use of it. . . . Not a single musket had been fired against this battery. . . . Unless it was from a panic fear which never left us again during the siege, it would be difficult to give any reason for such an extraordinary action . . . and so on the 13th by order of the council, a battery of thirty pieces of cannon, which had cost the King immense sums, was abandoned without undergoing the slightest fire."

William Vaughan, returning from the not unpleasant task of making a bonfire from the French stores, happened to note that no flag flew from the flagstaff of the Royal Battery, nor was there any smoke from the barracks chimney. It was possibly a ruse of sorts, but Vaughan wasn't one to pass up a chance because it happened to be unlikely. There was an Indian in the party, and a flask of brandy that Vaughan just happened to have with him was sufficient to tempt this dusky ally to chance a closer investigation. Climbing in through an embrasure that was completely unguarded, he was dumfounded to discover no one about. Soon William Vaughan and his thirteen followers were all gathered there. The Royal Battery was theirs without a blow. The flag was down, the guns were spiked, the place was empty. It was here that eighteen-year-old William Tufts had his modest immortality. He climbed the flagpole, his coat in his hand, and fastened it at the peak. If there was no red banner of England, at least the red coat of a British infantryman flew there with unconscious dignity.

That was at nine in the morning. Soon four boats set out from the town. There had been time for some reconsideration. This was the garrison returning at least to complete its work of destruction. But

Vaughan and his thirteen had no thought of leaving. They stood on the beach, under fire from both the town and island batteries, coolly trading musket shots with the men in the boats. The defense was so spirited that even the sharp disparity in numbers left the Frenchmen uncertain of their course. Before their minds were made up reinforcements had arrived and it was too late.

Among the newcomers was another man with an important part to play. It was Major Seth Pomeroy. He was an adventurer by instinct and a gunsmith by vocation. He soon collected some twenty men of similar bent from among the reinforcing troops. It was an age of handy men. Soon they were at work on the spiked cannon. It had been an inexpert job of despoiling, and shortly the guns were free—twenty-eight forty-two-pounders and two eighteen-pounders. The fact that Pepperrell had brought along cannon shot too large for any guns he had now ceased to be a matter of levity. By the next morning the guns of the Royal Battery were busily lobbing Pepperrell's shot into the fortress.

The ring about this Gibraltar of the West was closing, slowly indeed, but with a sobering relentlessness. Batteries were appearing at every point of vantage. It was incredible work. West of the town there were steep hills guarded on all sides by swamp and forest and pathless rocks. Horses and oxen that were used in the early attempts to move the guns bogged down and were hopeless. But over the marshes and through the forest and up the heavy grades went the New England volunteers. They depended on human muscle power alone, just as the early Egyptians who built the pyramids, except that these were free men. They worked at night that they might remain unseen and safe as might be of fire from the town. Harnessed together in gangs, sometimes two hundred strong, they did the impossible. In the morning a new battery would open on the luckless citadel. A projecting spit of sand, well in the inner harbor and nudging the fortress, was known as the Barachois. To reach it the guns had to be dragged halfway round the fortress, four interminable, roadless miles through forest and muskeg from Gabarus Bay. The French had no fear of the obviously impossible, yet here, too, another battery appeared before the unbelieving eyes of the disheartened defenders.

The fortress was still relatively unharmed. It was too big a job for weary men and limited equipment. They needed the heavy guns of the fleet to breach the walls. But while the Island Battery guarding the entrance held out, success was hardly possible. So far the fleet had mainly stood off at sea, guarding the entrance against a possible relieving force. It was a dangerous and unrewarding work. There were occasions when merchant ships bringing supplies attempted to slip by. They could boast of little success. Warren was watchful. He took four of them that way, and they were needed prizes for an expedition whose guns were often silent because ammunition was lacking. In the beginning that lack was partially the fault of the green recruits. They blazed away at anything. In their exuberance, too, they sometimes argued that if a load of gunpowder would do so much damage, a double load would do more. This was proven sadly true on numerous occasions when the overloaded guns would burst, scattering death among the enthusiasts. It was a hard lesson to learn. Three of the heavy cannon of the Royal Battery exploded from this cause.

The shortage of supplies made the commanding general impatient to get it over. This impatience brought Pepperrell to his one disastrous decision. If the Island Battery was the key, his men would take it.

It was midnight of May 26 when his three hundred men started from the Royal Battery. They were joined by a force half as large from Lighthouse Point. Progress was slow because they used paddles instead of oars for the heavy boats, lest the sound of the oarlocks should warn the garrison. The surf had risen and the landing stage permitted no more than three boats to approach at one time. Even ashore the force still faced the battery, walled on all sides, manned by a hundred and eighty men, thirty cannon, and nine smaller pieces.

A hundred and fifty men were already ashore and Captain d'Aillebout, in command, was unaware of the threat. He might have remained so had the leaders remembered their instructions to make no sound. But the early success was too much. The excitement found a voice in three hearty cheers. The cheers came too soon. A moment of astonished silence, then the Island Battery flamed into life as its guns were turned on the group ashore and the boats clustered near the landing stage and outlined now by the gun flashes.

For all their desperate situation, the landing party did more than cheer. They went storming in, planted their twelve ladders against the walls. But they couldn't succeed and had to retreat. There was no protection for them in the waiting boats. The boats farthest away managed to draw off, but many of those nearer in were shattered and sunk.

What remained of the first landing party, not cheering now, were firing doggedly. It had little effect. With the coming of dawn the alternative was clear. It was death or surrender. They chose the latter course. A hundred and nineteen surrendered, many of them wounded. The total cost in those killed, drowned, and captured was a hundred and eighty-nine—nearly half the attacking party, as Pepperrell himself pointed out.

There was rejoicing in Louisburg, and the reports of the victory grew with each telling. Governor Duchambon was one of the most enthusiastic. He wrote the minister that the battery was attacked by a thousand men supported by eight hundred reserves. There were thirty-five boats in the attack, he recorded, and only two of them got away, bearing thirty men, the only survivors of the thousand attackers. It was a good story. It aroused enthusiasm and gained some credence. The enthusiasm didn't last long, for a day or so after came the news that the great French man of war, the *Vigilant*, with her sixty-four great guns and her five hundred and sixty men, had been lured into the midst of Warren's fleet, sixty of her crew killed and the ship herself disabled and captured. It was a splendid victory. The ship was heavily laden with munitions for the garrison, supplies that now would be joyfully used by the attackers.

Despite such notable achievements, Warren was growing weary of the constant watchfulness and danger—of standing off a stormy, dangerous shore and bombarding from a distance a fortress almost invisible in the prevailing fog. Some of his shots took effect. Some fell short and, as our young journalist tells, struck in the water near the shore and sent great geysers over the walls. Warren's patience at last gave out altogether. "For God's sake," he wrote to Pepperrell in the most direct words he had permitted himself, "let us do something and not waste our time in indolence."

It wasn't exactly indolence. There was sickness too. At one time fifteen hundred men were down with fever, and wounds were deadlier still. There are records in the *Louisbourg Journals* that there were other hazards. Small groups that lagged or strayed into the woods might be found later with their scalps missing. Also, there were rumors about a certain partisan, Marin by name, who had come from Quebec with a band of Frenchmen and Indians to await the arrival of some hopefully expected forces. He had made a preliminary attack on Annapolis. There word had reached him from Duchambon to come quickly to the aid of Louisburg. Marin was crafty enough to know that it would be a hopeless gesture, and hopeless gestures were not in his line. But Pepperrell could not know this. These factors, however, did hurry developments.

The general could not agree with Warren's impatient proposal for a joint attack on the Island Battery. He did see that it had to be silenced before Louisburg could be secured. For that purpose he built up the artillery at Lighthouse Point, which commanded the Island Battery across the harbor entrance. Soon, with plodding insistence, it was being pounded to pieces. At the same time the batteries surrounding the town were keeping up a perpetual bombardment. The citizens were finding their only security in artificial caves or bomb shelters. These were simple enough, but effective. They were made of long pieces of lumber, the Habitant of Louisburg explains, slanting from the casement, "deadening the force of the bombs and turning them aside that their momentum had no effect. It was underneath this that we had, as it were, buried them"–the "them," of course, referring to the women and children. Though with this protection the citizens were relatively safe, only one house in the entire town escaped major damage. "We feared at every moment," the Habitant continues, "that the enemy, waking from their blindness, would press forward and carry the place by assault. I am able to affirm," he adds, "that we had not enough [powder] left for three charges." Later it was discovered that this was correct. The reserves of powder were thirty-seven kegs of a hundred pounds each.

The one French hope seemed to be a sortie from the fortress that might silence some of the nagging batteries and give time for some relief. We know, however, that relief was not in sight. Even had it been, the move required more determination than Duchambon could muster. He was not a last-ditch soldier. Probably the end would have been no different had he been. He was completely convinced, probably with some reason, that if the Swiss regulars were used they would desert to the English.

No matter what anyone did, the end was near. The Island Battery had been all but silenced, and that surprise fleet of eleven new ships from England had been added to Warren's fleet, already numbering six powerful warships plus the smaller vessels of the provincial navies. A combined sea and land attack was in the making. Its probable date was June 16.

The defenders had done their best. Everything considered, it was a very commendable best, but the end could not be long delayed. Governor Duchambon was not one to await the inevitable. He asked for terms of surrender, and after some negotiations the terms were accepted. They had reason to be. They were generous. The French were to be permitted to march out of the fortress with flags flying and drums beating, carrying their arms, which would be surrendered later. The full honors of war. It was a colorful gesture that the French loved. The troops were to be returned to France and bound not to fight against the English for a year.

Indeed the terms were more than generous. All private property was to be respected. Strangely, included in the terms was a very unusual clause that no one seems to have thought of explaining. It is Clause 6 of the surrender terms. "If there be any persons in the town or garrison, which you shall desire may not be seen by us, they shall be permitted to go off mask'd."

Could it be that there was some English deserter among the garrison to whom the French felt committed, or perhaps some depredators who had earned the hatred of the English? One may speculate endlessly, but still the reason remains obscure.

There was no doubt of the acceptance of the terms. Because of their leniency the excitement was shared almost equally. It was as if there had been two victors and no losers. That would pass, but for the moment all was excitement and relief. The sight of the great fleet sailing into the harbor, sails glistening in the sun, was too much for anyone to resist. At night the habitable homes were brightly lighted as if for a homecoming, and bonfires blazed in the streets. There were friendly dinners, too, for the officers.

By morning there had been a marked decline in the sense of relief and the spirit of good will. The French were remembering that they were seeing an evidence of the growing strength of the English. The victors, too, had lost some of their first exuberance and had begun counting costs. In one sense the manpower losses seem entirely out of proportion to the vastness of the effort. Though Pepperrell reports that over "9,000 cannon balls and 600 bombs" had been used against the fortress, not to speak of the musketry and hand-to-hand conflicts, those killed in the siege totaled about one hundred on each side, though many others had died of wounds. The Habitant set the loss of the French at one hundred and thirty and of the English at two thousand killed, but that is certainly an exaggeration.

Discontent was growing. The Reverend Samuel Moody was probably the most contented member of the British force. He was doing his duty as he saw it, and that included the use of the hatchet he had brought with him. He had visited the parish church and had hacked away happily at some of the figures that he insisted on considering idols.

On the whole, discontent was widespread and was growing with every day. Pepperrell had got the best from his men. In the fighting they had proved themselves the equal of the professional soldier. But they weren't that. They had done what they had come to do, and now it was finished. They were going home. They were discontented with what they had gained from their effort and far from satisfied with the peace terms that protected the private property of the defeated. It was, they thought, the rightful property of the victor. The feeling was emphasized by the fact that the prize money of the navy had been substantial, while the foot soldiers felt that the real burden, the hunger and the cold and the wounds and death, had been theirs. There was a growing ugliness in their mood when it became evident they weren't to be allowed to go home, that long months of guard duty were before them. Even Pepperrell's generous personal gift of ten thousand pounds to be distributed in place of the expected prize money could not for long change the situation.

The diarist in the *Louisbourg Journals* records that seven hundred had agreed to lay down their arms. In fact, it was more serious than that. A general mutiny was in the making. The troops had been kept over their enlistment period. Clothing, rum, and other necessities were lacking. The men were unpaid, and in addition to that the method and amounts of payment as between Massachusetts and New Hampshire, and Rhode Island and Connecticut, were sharply different. That, and the fact that the navy had done rather well for itself, led to very hard feeling indeed.

Fortunately, before there was any serious outbreak, Governor Shirley arrived and made the malcontents a stirring speech. He had sent to New York and Philadelphia for adequate supplies of clothing. The garrison force would be paid five pounds a month and would be steadily reduced so that by October it would be down to two thousand. This, with appeals to their patriotism and strong words about the ignominy that would follow any other course, almost turned the trick. It was completely turned when the governor added two hogsheads of rum to drink His Majesty's health. It might not have been quite so satisfying could they have foreseen that before the spring, when British regiments from Gibraltar would arrive to take over the guardianship, more than nine hundred of the occupation force would have died from illness.

With the capture of Louisburg an accomplished fact, Governor Shirley yearned for another great cause. This may have been due to the fact that the distribution of honors, which had made Warren a rear admiral and Pepperrell a baronet, had passed the governor by. It is to his credit that, far from making him disgruntled, rewards to his colleagues only stirred him to new ventures. He found his great cause in a plan to capture Canada. English mother country and English colonies were in happy agreement over this project, a unanimity that may have resulted in part from the circumstance that the mother country had stepped in and footed the bill for the efforts of the various colonies in the Louisburg matter. Also, it seemed that if the one conquest could be accomplished, why not another? All the figures were on that side of the argument. The English colonies combined could now number a total fighting force of three hundred thousand men. Canada, calling on her last fighting man, could have counted perhaps fifteen thousand. The numbers spoke eloquently, but not with entire conclusiveness. The French were a united force, deeply imbued with the conviction that Canada was theirs by right and by God's will, and they were under a central and supreme head. The English colonies, on the other hand, were groups of ardent individualists, scattered and contentious.

All the colonies, however, except perhaps Quaker Pennsylvania, thought well of any plan that would forever end the threat that had cast its shadow over the northern settlements for more than a century. With Louisburg for a base, with the mother country seemingly properly interested in the enterprise and the colonies burning with a new confidence, success seemed assured.

The plan was the accustomed one—a two-pronged attack, one over the frontier by the familiar, if somewhat ill-omened, Lake Champlain route against Montreal. This to be supported by volunteers from the southern and western colonies with the usual high percentage of Indians. The other attack would follow the equally familiar route by the St. Lawrence to Quebec. This would be manned by the New England colonies, supported by the English fleet and the eight battalions of seasoned troops that the Duke of Newcastle, now head of the British government, had promised.

Weeks went by and grew into months, and still no fleet and no battalions. The colonial levies, ready and eager to move, were becoming impatient. The Lake Champlain expedition, never too heartily supported, seemed to melt away. By mid-August Governor Shirley was writing to Newcastle that the proposed expedition could hardly reach Quebec before October, and that would be too late. Newcastle explained, but the explanations were unconvincing. They suggested that he had never been enthusiastic. His instructions support this conclusion. Shirley was told to get rid of the colonial soldiers "as cheap as possible" and to attempt no further conquests.

If this bold gesture, which might so easily have succeeded, was to end in an ignominious anticlimax, what remains to be said of France's spectacular riposte? This was to be the great counterstroke that would wipe out the shame of Louisburg and see that stronghold safely back in French hands again, and with it all Acadia. Meanwhile the English colonies would be taught a sobering lesson, their seacoast so thoroughly ravaged that there would be no further inclination to tamper again with what France believed to be her own.

It seemed almost beyond believing that there could be two "magnificent fiascos" in a matter of thirty-odd years. Yet Sir Hovenden Walker certainly proposed to destroy New France, while the Duc d'Anville was to make it dominant and secure. Both were to fail with lamentable thoroughness.

France's navy had long been her pride; now, leagued with Spain, she felt herself invincible. This was the time to decide the fortunes of Canada once and for all. D'Anville's fleet was impressive, eleven ships of the line, twenty frigates, and some thirty-five transports and fire ships. It carried close to six thousand sailors and half as many trained soldiers. D'Anville sailed from France on June 20, 1746, on what must hold the record as the most calamity-ridden of any human voyage. Slow ships and calm followed by tropic heat retarded the voyage. Lightning damaged some ships, killing members of their crews. Fogs resulted in delay and collisions. Unending storms added their varying hazards. Pestilence broke out on many ships, and soon—for days on end—fifty bodies a day were going over the side with the scantest of ceremony. The fleet had been almost three months in the crossing. Food was growing scarce. In some ships famine was already present. As they drew near land the mightiest of all the storms struck them. Some few ships were sunk with all on board, others were dismasted, all were scattered. Some were too lost and beaten to think of rejoining the fleet and instead set sail for France. When D'Anville finally reached his destination at Chebucto, soon to be known as Halifax, his great fleet had been reduced to two ships, and most of his crews were ill or dying. It was to learn, too, that Admiral Constant and his West Indian fleet, which was to rendezvous there to join in the recapture of Louisburg, had come and waited and finally sailed away.

Near the entrance of what is now Halifax Harbor, the sick were put ashore to die or get well as best they could. Most of them were to die, and among them their leader, the Duc d'Anville. But whether he died of the plague that September 26, or by his own hand, worn out by hardship and disappointment, is still an open question.

The first news that greeted D'Estournel, the vice-admiral, when his flagship finally found the harbor, was that death had made him commander. His first official act was to follow his former leader's body to a small island in the harbor where it was buried, again with the barest ceremony. It was to rest there until, long years later, it was returned to France.

Sickness increased and famine as well. Dissensions arose. The King's orders called for an attack on Louisburg, and D'Estournel, urging that with shattered fleet, depleted forces, and famine staring them in the face such an attack was madness, found himself, whether from jealousy or nobler motives, at variance with most of his remaining officers. It was too much for the worried admiral. Those who heard groans from his cabin and burst open the door found him dying. In desperation he had fallen on his own sword.

In his place there was still another vice-admiral, the Marquis de la Jonquière. He was of sterner stuff, able, courageous, determined, and if his later record shows him to have been somewhat too eager for his own well-being, it does not change these facts. Though it was said that La Jonquière had less than a thousand men in fighting condition, he determined on action. Louisburg was impossible, but not Annapolis. At least so he thought until, reaching there, he found in the harbor the English fifty-gun ship *Chester* and the frigate *Shirley* from Massachusetts. With his sick and starving crews, the odds were impossible. For all his courage, La Jonquière decided he had no choice but to return to France.

That was not quite the end. French vanity was stronger than

France's proverbial common sense. They could not, or would not, read the writing on the wall. In May of the following year La Jonquière was given command of a new fleet. It was to convoy the merchant ships that annually, at this time of year, reprovisioned New France. This service rendered, the fleet could turn its attention to Louisburg and the other plans of destroying England's hold on the New World. But this time the English were ready. Admiral Anson caught up with Jonquière's new fleet off Cape Finisterre. With his bevy of merchantmen to defend and his six ships to Admiral Anson's seventeen, La Jonquière decided to accept the unequal contest. Only by fighting a delaying action could he give the merchantmen a chance of escape. When he finally struck his flag on his flagship, *Le Sérieux,* he had fought for five hours. There was ten feet of water in his ship's hold and it refused to answer its helm. The remainder of his small fleet was in little better shape, but the merchantmen had made good their escape. With La Jonquière's surrender the French fleet had virtually ceased to be.

It is difficult to be a colonial power without a navy, as France quickly realized. She knew that she would have to counter force with craftiness. The opportunity came quickly. With another peace treaty to be signed, France remembered that with an English fleet based at Louisburg there was little hope that her colonies in the New World could be kept alive.

At Aix-la-Chapelle she made a broad and friendly gesture, a policy of give-and-take. What better peace measure than the return of the conquests of war? Hadn't France taken Madras and the English Louisburg? What better than a fair exchange? Now the English colonists learned a bitter lesson they were to remember—that English thinking and English interests were very different from their own.

This Louisburg, which had been given away for an unknown port in distant India that meant nothing to them; this Louisburg was indeed "the people's darling conquest." But they knew well, these people, that it was more than a conquest. Louisburg was the colonists' guarantee of security. With it gone there could be no peace—no safety. The irrepressible conflict must be fought out to the bitter end. For Governor Shirley was right. England and France could not live peacefully together on the same continent.

CHAPTER XX

LIFE LINES

France's hold on the New World depends on her ability to control her life lines, east and west. The restoration of Louisburg protects the one, subject to the challenge of the newly built Halifax. The English, spreading out everywhere, offer a new challenge to the life line linking Quebec and Louisiana. Acting Governor Galissonière plans a series of forts to protect the Ohio-Louisiana line and sends Céleron to locate the forts. Appointment of Duquesne as governor lends a new hardness to French thinking. He moves promptly to build the forts and drive the English back. Governor Dinwiddie of Virginia counters with an expedition under Washington against Fort Duquesne. The death of Jumonville breaks the uncertain peace. Retreat of Washington and surrender of Fort Necessity.

NEW FRANCE had two life lines. One was the ancient highway of the St. Lawrence River, which, with the Atlantic, linked New France with the old. By it came subsistence for the colony, a benefit balanced in part by returning cargoes of furs. By it came also some measure of protection as France found herself able to supply added manpower. And always it was a highway carrying the evidence of an absolute authority.

The other life line was one integrating New France itself. It was a network of rivers flowing mainly southward, particularly the Mississippi, the Ohio, and the Illinois. Those linked Canada with that far outpost of French Empire centering about the Gulf of Mexico and named Louisiana after the Sun King. Either life line could be threatened. Both had been and would be again, for both were vital to the survival of New France.

For the moment, danger to the one seemed to have passed. The adroit maneuvering at Aix-la-Chapelle had seen Louisburg returned to her former owners, while England stood astounded. Britain's then First Sea Lord, the Duke of Bedford, had spoken the thought of the British people when he had announced bluntly that he would hang the first man who so much as proposed the return of Louisburg. Unfortunately he lacked the power to carry the threat beyond his own command, and those above him were less forthright. Despite public opinion, Louisburg was safely in French hands.

There was no such safeguard for the life line running south; that was far away and less easily defended. For all the peace now existing, the most adventurous of the English colonists were pressing steadily westward beyond the containment of the Alleghenies that was to have been the utmost limit of English and Dutch encroachment. There was a tacit threat in this westward surge even though peace did still govern the land. The French were not slow to see it. They had always known it must come. They must have known, even if they would not admit that their ownership of the land was not much better established than the English claim to the same acres. The Indian, whose right to the land was based on centuries of occupation, was recognized by neither contender. He was to be a real factor in the conflict, and his position was clear. "We have not ceded our lands to anybody," the Indian spokesman urged, "and we have no mind to obey any king." So rested the threefold claim to the West. Conflict was brewing there between those who would acquire and those who must defend. But for the moment attention was elsewhere.

Even with Louisburg restored, the French, remembering their almost nonexistent fleet, were apprehensive over the flurry of activity about Chebucto Bay in what had once been Acadia. It was here that the unhappy Duc d'Anville had found refuge for his shattered fleet and his plague-ridden forces, and here he had died and found a resting place. The French sensed that a king's move was in the making.

England was conscious that with the return of Louisburg she had lost caste with her colonies. She was beginning to realize, too late, that the trade of the fortress for Madras was an exchange of a present asset for one that was distant and dubious. This thinking was followed by a rather spectacular change in Britain's colonial policy.

In all probability it was induced by the growing resentment of the American colonies rather than by any notable change of heart. Britain was aware that the trade she had accepted at Aix-la-Chapelle had been far from sagacious. It benefited no one but the traditional enemy. Governor Shirley of Massachusetts was perhaps the one who made this unpleasant realization abundantly clear. Shirley was well aware that with the French once more strongly entrenched at Louisburg, with nothing to oppose them, the New England coast would continue to be a ready and promising target. Particularly was this so while the French, numerically speaking, still dominated Acadia. It was almost forty years since the Acadians had assured their Récollet missionary, Felix Pain: "We will never take the oath of fidelity to the Queen of Great Britain to the prejudice of what we owe to our King, to our country and to our religion."

In the years that followed, there was little change. Paul Mascarene, shortly before the fall of Louisburg, was reporting to the British Secretary of State: "These inhabitants cannot be depended on for assistance in case of a rupture with France; it is as much as we can expect if we can keep them from joining the enemy or being stirred up by them to rebel." Mascarene was by no means a hard master. His policy was one of conciliation, but he didn't vary in his opinion that "this province is in a worse condition of defense than the other American plantations which have inhabitants to defend them." Still later he was writing Governor Shirley suggesting that English settlers might be introduced to replace some of the Acadians. It was not a new thought. Nicholson had given voice to it after he had captured Port Royal. "Upon the whole it is most humbly submitted whether the said French inhabitants may not be transported out of the province of Nova Scotia, to be replaced by good Protestant subjects." That was in 1710. Yet these reluctant citizens, who had been granted ample time to prove that such drastic remedies were unnecessary, had done nothing at all in that direction.

Governor Shirley was no less eager to see Acadia strongly settled and preferably by colonists from the New England colonies. He wrote the Duke of Bedford, who had now become Secretary of State, that Nova Scotia should be made a British colony in fact as well as in name. He argued for New England settlers as being familiar with the cultivation of new lands, staunchly Protestant, with an unwavering allegiance to the British Crown. These, with New England troops in garrison, convinced Shirley that within ten years there would be an English-speaking population strong enough for self-government.

Paul Mascarene loyally supported these views, and it was he who continued to urge the Lords of Trade that it would be a wise step to establish a number of English families on the Atlantic coast and to erect the necessary fortifications for their security. So Paul Mascarene, a Frenchman, was the actual father of the great fortress city of Halifax.

The members of the British government, in their attitude of newly discovered humility, listened to all the advice and then took the course they thought best. They by-passed Governor Shirley's suggestion of using New Englanders to colonize the country, and instead decided to send some twenty-three hundred settlers from England. To secure the number, rather generous terms were offered. This was not all loss, because England at the time was undergoing a minor unemployment crisis. There were large numbers of soldiers and sailors who had no employment owing to the unaccustomed circumstance that Europe momentarily was at peace. To distribute these citizens, who might easily become a burden, it was decided to encourage them to be colonists. Colonists were assured a grant of fifty acres of land, to which they would be transported free, and to overcome their lack of knowledge of frontier life, subsistence for a year was included. It was close to being a free grant, for no taxes on the land were to be imposed for a matter of ten years. Thereafter for another ten years the tax would be a modest shilling a year. This was for the private soldier and the like, while their officers were granted holdings that would make them great landowners at the scratch of a pen.

Thirteen transports carried the colonists to their new home. They reached Chebucto on July 2 of the year 1749. By winter all were comfortably settled in their log homes. There were other sources of population: there was the dispossessed garrison of Louisburg and those who had served them, and there were citizens of New England who had listened to their Governor Shirley and had become convinced enough by his eloquence to give up a pioneering that had grown familiar and almost comfortable for one that was still rugged and adventurous. Altogether, when Chebucto was renamed Halifax after the Earl of Halifax, who as First Lord of Trade and Plantations was responsible for the settlement, it was already a thriving town.

Edward Cornwallis was the newly appointed governor, succeeding Paul Mascarene, who after many frustrating years was ready enough to go and find a quiet haven in Boston. Cornwallis had arrived at Chebucto well ahead of his convoy of colonists. Perhaps his first impression was one of the strangeness and loneliness. Almost on his arrival he was writing the Duke of Bedford, Secretary of State, "The country is one continual wood, and no clear spot is to be seen or heard of." But his enthusiasm grew as he discovered the harbor. "The finest, perhaps, in the world," he wrote. Edward Cornwallis was an able, sensitive, and generous-spirited man, though less known to history than his more publicized nephew, the general who thirty years later was to surrender Yorktown to General George Washington and to gain a reputation for ineffectiveness that he in no wise deserved.

Edward Cornwallis didn't surrender anything. He was barely thirty-five when he took up his work at Halifax, saw to the welfare of the colonists, and began the fortification of the city, fortifications so well planned and strong that in all their history they were never seriously challenged. The town itself was carefully laid out by the same engineers who had planned the fortifications. The colonists drew lots for the holdings they favored and were soon actively building their homes. Before winter came, Halifax had taken on the appearance of a new but well-settled town, while the fortifications were manned by British regulars sent to relieve the New Englanders who had taken Louisburg.

One of the first activities of the new governor was an attempt to conciliate the Acadians and to urge them to take the oath of allegiance. He approached this task with perhaps something more than an open mind. It was almost a bemused mind. He reported that neighboring French settlers, who had been living for years on well-established British territory, "showed an unfeigned joy in hearing of the new settlement." It is impossible not to conclude either that these French citizens were willfully deluding the friendly governor or that he was doing the same for himself.

Undoubtedly Cornwallis met the problem of Acadian expatriates with understanding and sympathy. "We know," he wrote reasonably, "that a forced service is worth nothing, and that a subject compelled to be so against his will is not very far from being an enemy." Events were soon to prove the soundness of this thinking. But Cornwallis did his sober best to establish good feeling. "This province is your country," he said, speaking to the stubborn-faced Acadians. "You and your fathers cultivated it; naturally you ought yourselves to enjoy the fruits of your labour. Such was the desire of the King our master. You know that we have to follow his orders. You know that we have done everything to secure to you not only the occupation of your lands, but the ownership of them for all time. We have given you every possible assurance of the enjoyment of your religion, and the full and public exercise of the Roman Catholic faith."

Nothing, surely, could have been fairer, but he went on: "We are sorry to find in our government persons whom it is impossible to please, and upon whom our declaration has produced nothing but discontent, jealousies and murmurings. We must not complain of all the inhabitants; we know very well that there are ill-disposed interests and mischievous persons among you who corrupt the others."

It was no use. Soft words fell as purposelessly on stubborn hearts as had the harsher words of Vetch and Nicholson. This was a breed who would neither concede not conciliate, and the day when action must take the place of threat or promise was almost at hand. But people who have listened to the cry of "Wolf!" for forty years are poorly equipped to assess properly the portents of change.

The French were deeply disturbed at the growing interest in what had once been Acadia. They recognized the building of Halifax for what it was, a move to limit the effectiveness of Louisburg and to renew the challenge to their eastern life line. The harbor of Halifax, they knew, might easily shelter a fleet that would be a standing challenge to the protection of Louisburg. It was the promise of eventual conflict.

But France had other problems. The English were everywhere breaking out from the encirclement that France had proposed for them. Rather than being driven into the sea, they were like its waves, encroaching ever farther and farther inland. It was not deliberate in the sense that it was aimed at annoying the French. It was rather an expression of national characteristics and the outcome of differing political backgrounds.

As has been said already, the gain the French sought was not a home in the New World but a fortune that would stand them in good stead in the Old. They were brave men, none braver in all history. But they were adventurers, not builders. They didn't colonize the land; at best they garrisoned it. They followed the vast network of waterways Nature had provided and left no reminder of themselves, save the lead plates that they buried to mark their passing, to claim a land that they made scarcely a gesture of holding. They left their names as a slim reminder of their part in the brave story. They cut few roads and built few towns, for they were travelers who did not propose to stay. Only a few forts dotting the wilderness marked their passage. The center of their living changed little from their first settlement–Quebec, Montreal, Three Rivers, and now Louisburg taking the place of the lost Plaisance. These were their homes. The rest were only indistinguishable dots on an ever-enlarging road map.

The English might not travel so far nor so imaginatively, but where they went they left their mark. They had no easily available network of lake and river planned by a bountiful Nature. So they must make roads, and roads lead to places, and places become settlements, and the possession of the land becomes a driving incentive. The French were quick to visit, but they had no inclination to stay. To exploit the fur resources to the limit and to move on and repeat the performance elsewhere meant that always they had to look farther and farther afield. But the paths they traveled were marked by few settlements. For their purposes forts were best. Only on the far-off Gulf of Mexico did their coming create a lasting habitation.

The English produced no La Salle, no Le Moynes, no Vérendryes, no Cadillac, no Du Lhut, no Nicholas Perrot, no Henri Tonty. Look at the place names about their long trails. Others passed that way, but the names remain predominantly French. They mark the passage of men who came to see, to discover, to trade, until trading grew thin and they looked for new pastures.

When they moved, the English moved by roads their own callused hands had built. They were served by lumbering carts that could not for a moment compete with the swift canoe. But they were solid and dependable and could carry vast loads. So they went to the ends of the roads and settled down and built a settlement and tilled the soil and raised their crops and families, until other unsatisfied folk came along, pushed the trail farther into the wilderness, and followed it until they, in turn, found what they sought and became part of the network of habitations that were spreading over the land.

In the north, New England and New York, freed for the moment from the threat of force, were pressing slowly but inexorably toward the great waterway of the St. Lawrence and Lake Ontario. They were fiercely individualistic and cared as little for the French claims as they did for those of the great Five Nations—the Oneidas, the Mohawks, the Onondagas, the Cayugas, and the Senecas—and later the Tuscaroras, making thus the Six Nations, who claimed the lands from Albany to Lake Ontario. The Dutch and English were pushing west from the land of William Penn into the lands that France had claimed and had done nothing to occupy. From Philadelphia and Baltimore others were following the rough roads to the shores of Lake Erie and from there to the Ohio River, where now stands Pittsburgh. Years before, Governor Spotswood of Virginia had been pressing the same way. His Knights of the Golden Horseshoe, those who had drunk His Majesty's health on Mount George in the Blue Mountains, had set alight a new spirit of adventuring that was beckoning bold spirits to see what lay beyond the Blue Ridge, beyond the Alleghenies and into the lands of the Ohio River that led straight to the great Mississippi Valley. Here was the threat the French had feared. There was the challenge to the life line that linked Louisiana with Quebec. To defend this line, France claimed all the lands drained by the waters of the St. Lawrence and the Mississippi. It was not a claim that could be made good, for it covered areas that had been in English hands for generations. But defensible or no, the claim had to be supported. It was that, or relinquish the French lands of the south.

Fortunately for her, France had as administrator of Canada a man of courage and determination and more than the average astuteness. The Marquis de la Galissonière had assumed office shortly before the peace of Aix-la-Chapelle, when it became clear that La Jonquière, who had been appointed governor, being lodged in an English prison following his defeat at Cape Finisterre, had his present usefulness limited.

Galissonière was a naval officer and, momentarily, somewhat more successful than La Jonquière. He was also a man of equal determination, if not of equal physical appearance. The new appointee could not depend on any charm. He was ill shaped, almost to the extent of deformity. But the deformity ended at the outer shell of the man. Inside he had not only a courageous heart but a shrewd, agile, and constructive mind. The strategist in the naval officer was quick to see how vulnerable was a life line of better than a thousand miles in length dotted by a few isolated posts, largely indefensible against more than a sudden surprise attack. No wonder the English were breaking their bounds when the challenge was so tempting.

As Galissonière thought of it a plan took shape in his mind. If Louisburg could check the English on the Atlantic, a dozen smaller Louisburgs, strategically placed, might make the other life line secure. The plan, as it took shape in his mind, was to safeguard the most vulnerable part of that line running through a certain no man's land, which everyone claimed and no one possessed, from the head-waters of the great river system at Lake Erie to the Ohio River and its confluence with the Mississippi.

With this vast plan in mind, Galissonière, in the early summer of 1749, sent out a preliminary expedition. It was too small to attract attention or antagonism, but strong enough to protect itself against the Indians. It consisted of fourteen officers and cadets, the adventurous nucleus of any expedition; twenty French regulars, a little better than a hundred Canadians, and a few Indians. It was really a prospecting party to report on the best location for the line of forts Galissonière had proposed. The expedition was under the command of a seasoned veteran, a member of the Canadian noblesse and a captain in the Canadian militia, Céleron de Bienville. He was a figure of dispute. Father Jean de Bonnécamps, a professor in the Jesuit college of Quebec, who accompanied the expedition in the interests of his studies of hydrography, left a careful record of events and persons. In his report he speaks of Céleron as a man "attentive, clear-sighted and active, firm, but pliant when necessary; fertile in resources and full of resolution—a man, in fine, made to command." He adds, "I am no flatterer and I do not fear that what I have said should make me pass for one."

But Governor Jonquière, who had finally been released from imprisonment and had assumed his post in Canada, relieving Galissonière, was not so impressed. He described Céleron as haughty and insubordinate. Perhaps both were right. It is understandable that a man trained in the ways of Canada might consider his own judgment preferable to that of one so newly arrived.

If Céleron was haughty, Jonquière was certainly no less so. In an early statement he had asserted vehemently that the English had no right to a single foot of territory in North America. It was an echo of his master, Louis XV, who with as little knowledge had announced, "I will not endure the English on my land." It was understandable, therefore, that these same English might find it difficult to see in Céleron's expedition a gesture free from any hostile suggestion. Equally, it did not suggest any open hostility.

The expedition that had set out from Lachine on the fifteenth of June reached Niagara three weeks later, and from there left familiar territory. Lake Erie was generally unknown and not less so the deep forests about Lake Chautauqua, where Father Bonnécamps records that "Monsieur Chaubert on that day caught seven rattlesnakes." It was an experience that impressed the good father and he spends many pages of his journal telling how dangerous they are and suggesting precautions. He recommends saliva mixed with a little sea salt as a sovereign remedy. Fortunately there was no need to try it.

At last they reached the river they were seeking, "La Belle Rivière," now somewhat less graciously named the Allegheny. As the lead disks that Céleron buried ceremoniously and in numbers claimed the land, named the Ohio River and all the streams that fall into it, and all the lands on both sides of it as the possession of Louis XV, the Ohio was also a focal point in the defense of the life line. Such defense involved a friendly relationship with the Indians. This was not too easy. The chief of the most powerful of the tribes, the Miami, was well known to be more than friendly with the English, so much so indeed that they were wont to speak of him as "Old Britain" and the town in which he lived, less understandably, as Pickawillany. The French had a different name for him, though the reason for it is more obscure. They called him "La Demoiselle." It could hardly have been in derision, as he was a person of consequence and one whose favor they were eager to secure. Céleron traveled the Ohio to its meeting with the Great Miami River, not too far from present-day Cincinnati. Following that stream, they finally came to the town of La Demoiselle on Laramie Creek.

Old Britain, or the Demoiselle, had moved his village toward the Ohio to be within easier reach of the English traders. Céleron's plan was to break up this friendly association that was unfavorable to French plans. He used all his skill and innumerable gifts to induce La Demoiselle to return to his old location farther away from English influence.

The Demoiselle accepted both gifts and advice with profuse promises that Céleron was too experienced to take at their face value. When he reached Montreal again after three thousand miles of traveling, it was with the uneasy conviction that more than leaden plates were needed for an effectual repossession of the land. English traders were in almost every town. They were underselling French goods and undermining French prestige. They could be ordered out, but once French backs were turned they would be back.

La Demoiselle, instead of retreating to his old encampment, gathered his friends about him at Pickawillany. It became a really impressive menace to French plans. Not perhaps because of the unassailable loyalty of Old Britain, but because of his shrewd recognition that it represented the side on which his bread was buttered.

Two years after Céleron's return, a French trader of mixed birth from Green Bay, Charles de Langlade, followed somewhat the same route. His reasons were probably personal. The Demoiselle had disturbed the trading habits of the region in a way that Langlade could not approve. He gathered a force of Ojibways and Ottawas, who didn't need any specific reason, and led them against Pickawillany. Most of its male inhabitants were away on the hunt, and the attackers were unannounced, so the end was quick and complete. The victors prepared a great feast. Perhaps it is indelicate to record that the chief dainty at that hilarious feast was nothing less than La Demoiselle himself. Broiled to the savage taste, he was eaten by the victors, who gave every evidence of a hearty appetite.

This incident, quite apart from any regrets for the Demoiselle's unceremonious passing, brought the question of the ownership of the territory into considerable prominence. The French, of course, claimed it all. They had been the first to reach the Ohio. But then the Virginians, who had occupied their lands for some hundred and fifty years, had set no boundaries to their claims and had accepted none. Recently they had established a certain equity in these lands, based on a charter given by George II to an Ohio Company, of Virginia origin, entitling them to trade and settle the Ohio territory regardless of the claims of Louis XV. Both cases would have been stronger if anyone had thought to plant some tangible evidence of claim, some fort or village impressive enough to leave no doubt of ownership. But the buried disks, which weren't discovered until a couple of centuries later, and many of them not then, were almost the only tangible evidence that this was part of the life line that linked Louisiana with New France.

The sudden death of Governor Jonquière just at this time must have been reckoned a serious loss, as no doubt it was. It might have been more serious but for the character of the man who succeeded. He was of very different temper. He was stern and uncompromising where Jonquière had tended toward the frivolous, and a rigid disciplinarian where the former had been easily pleased and, it was rumored, had himself been somewhat light-fingered.

The Marquis de Duquesne de Menneville emphatically was a man of action and looked the part. He was a soldier, not a colonizer. In an early argument he made the difference very clear. Addressing a group of Iroquois shortly after his arrival, he asked them, "Do you know what is the difference between the King of France and the Englishman? Go look at the forts which the King has set up and you will see that the land beneath his walls is still a hunting ground, he having chosen the spots frequented by you simply to serve your need. The Englishman, on the other hand, is no sooner in possession of land than the game is forced to quit, the woods are felled, the soil is uncovered, and you can scarcely find the wherewithal to shelter yourselves at night." Seldom had the difference in two ways of thought been so clearly stated.

The new governor had no doubt as to his mission, and his authority exceeded that of most of the governors who had preceded him. It is said by Madame d'Hausset, one of the innumerable gossips of the day, that his instructions were in the handwriting of Madame de Pompadour, though they bore the signature of the King. From the same source comes the story that, prior to his leaving Versailles, Duquesne was sent for by the King's favorite, who presented him with a magnificent ring with his seal cut into a great ruby. "Monsieur le Marquis," she said, "I want you to put that seal on articles of capitulation from Boston, New York, and Philadelphia. France must be supreme in the New World, and you must make her so."

The marquis did his best. He was haughty and zealous in a way that the happy-go-lucky Canadian militia found it difficult to understand. But he had his way. He quickly whipped them into a real fighting unit. He meant to use them to fight, tough and relentless fighting. He had nothing but praise for Langlade's destruction of Pickawillany and its ruler. He rewarded the trader as seemed right to Duquesne's haughty spirit. "As he is not in the King's service," he wrote, "and has married a squaw, I will ask for him only a pension of two hundred francs, which will flatter him infinitely."

The exploit that was to be so modestly repaid was to be the pattern of others to come. Duquesne had no sooner taken office than he was planning to put teeth in the project that had led Galissonière to send Céleron to spy out the lands of the Ohio. Governor Duquesne was less sensitive about angering his opponents than his predecessor had been. The English were encroaching on French land, he reasoned. More than that, they showed evidence of doing just what Duquesne had told his Indian friends they would do, settle down and make the land their own. Duquesne was in no mind to sit quietly by and watch it happen. He decided on an expedition that would do something more than plan the location of forts to protect the southern life line. This expedition was to build the forts.

It is true that there was a beginning already to the chain that was to link Louisiana with Quebec. The fort at Niagara was an important post, and across Lake Erie, close to the location of present-day Erie, there was another. It wasn't much more than a stockade, but it served notice that the French were intent on making good their claim to the Ohio country. A road led from this for leagues through the bush to a stream now known as French Creek. Here another fort was built close to the present site of the thriving, present-day city of Meadville. They called it Fort Le Boeuf. It was a good step on the way to the Allegheny River, which led to the vital roadway of the Ohio River.

Originally Duquesne's expedition had been under the command of the noted partisan fighter, Marin, the same who had been too wily to go to the aid of Duchambon in Louisburg and so had lived to fight another day. But Marin fell ill and was replaced by another who had an earlier part in this record. It was Legardeur de St. Pierre, who, it will be remembered, had been sent to complete the work of Vérendrye and had used his authority to see that none of that name would have a further part in the opening of the great West. St. Pierre was aging, too, but he was still the picture of a soldier and still a man of decisiveness and courage.

The movement of fighting men into these lands claimed by English as well as French was a disturbing thought. New York and New England, which had suffered most in the bloody border forays, might have been expected to be the first to act. They were as disinclined as other sections to unite in common action. They had some measure of excuse. Bordering them on the left was the powerful Indian confederation, the Six Nations. They were a powerful threat in themselves. The colonists knew, too, that the French would be likely to stop at nothing that gave promise of alienating this important group from their uncertain friendship with the English. Should that happen, Oswego, the only English post on the Great Lakes, would easily fall into French hands. Not unnaturally, when Governor Clinton of New York suggested to his Assembly that they should assist Pennsylvania in this crisis, the suggestion was coolly received. The gist of the Assembly's thinking was that New York was looking after her own Indian problems and it wasn't unreasonable to expect Pennsylvania to do the same.

It was all part of the very loose integration of the various colonies. In their thinking they were almost as much at odds with one another as they were with the French, or at least they were extremely reluctant to become involved in each other's affairs, particularly where such involvement might cost money. The feeling was fairly general that if Pennsylvania laid claim to these more western lands she should decide what to do about defending them.

As a matter of fact, the Pennsylvania of the day was a very mixed brew. Dutchmen were at odds with their English confreres. Puritans were at odds with more liberal religious views. The Puritans had come to America seeking peace and they were generously, if mistakenly, ready to offer it to anyone. They were the earliest and least successful of pacifists. There was the Royalist group, too, who thought it next to high treason to take any action, especially an action as drastic as setting up a British frontier without first securing authority from home. And there was, as always, that restless residue eager for new lands and ready to accept any hazard to acquire them. In such a medley of opinion there was little chance of effective action, and there was none.

St. Pierre was troubled by no such handicaps. Under the King, Governor Duquesne had absolute authority, and he was not one to permit an enemy to recover peacefully from his mistakes. When Duquesne said "March," St. Pierre could move without fear of qualifying direction. He moved, and moved fast.

If Pennsylvania watched these happenings with a concern that ended short of action, that was not so with another colonial official. The Scotsman, Robert Dinwiddie, who had fought his way up through many inconspicuous posts to become lieutenant governor of Virginia, was not on much better terms with his House of Burgesses than deputy governor Hamilton of Pennsylvania was with his Assembly. The difference was that Dinwiddie was better schooled in the give-and-take of practical politics than was his Pennsylvania counterpart. Also, Virginia had in its Ohio Company a more personal and material stake in the Ohio lands and had a charter from the King to prove it. Naturally Dinwiddie found all this coming and going disturbing. He wanted to know more about it. He acted promptly to achieve this desired end. The company he proposed to send to investigate would be small, to rob it of any warlike intention. There was Christopher Gist, chosen because he knew the country well and was on reasonably good terms with the French. He would guide the small expedition. A dutchman named Vanbraam would act as interpreter with the French, and a trader—Davison—would do as much for the Indians they might meet; and there were four woodsmen who would do most of the heavy work. The youngest member of the expedition—twenty-one years of age, but already one whose bearing and shrewd appreciation of affairs marked him as a figure of importance, and who held the friendship of Dinwiddie and the respect of his fellows—was the obvious leader. His name was George Washington.

The little party, with Washington at its head, reached Fort Le Boeuf on December 11 after a rough journey. The two hundred canoes that marked the shore about the fort were evidence that St. Pierre proposed to start early in the spring and to move far, and in some force. For all that, the little party was courteously received. Even when he received Dinwiddie's message and came to the paragraph that read, "It becomes my duty to require your peaceable departure, and that you would forbear prosecuting a purpose so interruptive of the harmony and good understanding which His Majesty is desirous to continue," St. Pierre made no retort in kind. He explained gravely that he would have to submit the letter to the Marquis Duquesne and await his orders.

The orders did not come, or if they did, the fact was not made known, and after some delay Washington's party began their return journey. The results did not seem very important, but Governor Dinwiddie appeared satisfied. After all, it was established that his letter of warning had been delivered. That brought the situation within the scope of the King's further instructions, or so Dinwiddie permitted himself to believe. These instructions read: "If you should find that any number of persons shall presume to erect any fort or forts within the limits of the province of Virginia, you are first to require of them peaceably to depart; and if, notwithstanding your admonitions, they do still endeavor to carry out any such unlawful designs, we do hereby strictly charge and command you to drive them off by force of arms."

Obviously the orders applied specifically to the "limits of the province of Virginia," and Fort Le Boeuf was certainly a far cry from Virginian soil. Dinwiddie, however, decided to interpret the Ohio Company charter as widening the boundaries of Virginia to include anything that might possibly be covered by the charter's terms. He felt, now that St. Pierre hadn't promptly turned tail at his order, that the British had full authorization to attack.

Most of the colonies would probably have agreed with this judgment, although agreeing and acting were very different things. But for Dinwiddie, probably the whole matter would have died out like a damp squib. The governor was not one to let anything die of inanition. So it came about that Horace Walpole was to say with complete truth, "A volley fired by a young Virginian in the backwoods of America set the world on fire."

In the beginning the fire wasn't apparent. Governor Dinwiddie was almost alone in his desire for action. In his journey of the previous year Washington's quick eye had recognized the strategic importance of that point where two great streams, the Allegheny and the Monongahela, met to form the mighty Ohio. He had mentioned it to the governor, who kept the thought in mind. In the early spring of 1754 Dinwiddie gathered a little group of forty woodsmen under the command of a young ensign named Ward and sent them to build a small stockade at this point, as evidence of ownership. Here was the threat the French feared most. The post surely commanded the Ohio River, a vital part of their life line. Duquesne didn't hesitate as to his course of action. It might be a warlike gesture, but it had to be made. He sent the Sieur de Contrecoeur to dispossess the young ensign, Ward. There couldn't be much argument—Ward with his weary forty men and Contrecoeur with his well-trained command of five hundred men. The little band was soon in full retreat.

Contrecoeur didn't waste time in pursuit. It was obvious that the

English would resent his action. It was best to face them with a fully accomplished fact. He set about building at the same location a French fort of vastly more impressive strength. When the fort was completed he took command with his five hundred men, having named the post Fort Duquesne in honor of the governor. Later it would be renamed Fort Pitt. Well it might, for it was the Great Commoner, William Pitt, who was responsible for retrieving it, and as the great city of Pittsburgh it still bears his name.

The immediate history was another matter. Dinwiddie had been wise in his decision to build a fort there, and young Ensign Ward, it might be remembered, had done his best, but as often happens the sound plan was too little supported and too late in its accomplishment. Dinwiddie spoke of it bitterly in words whose like have rung down the ages to challenge man's procrastination. "If our Assembly," he said, "had voted the money in November that they did in February, the fort would have been built and garrisoned before the French had approached; but these things cannot be done without money."

The governor did his best to retrieve the loss. He gathered a force of some three hundred men. They were called the Virginia Regiment. It was under the command of an English gentleman, an M.A. of Oxford who had more scholarly attributes than military. However, Joshua Fry was a man of position, and the lack of military training might be overcome by appointing him a colonel of Virginia troops. As the colonel didn't long survive the hardships of frontier campaigning, we do not know how this solution might have worked out. Perhaps it would have been saved in any event by the appointment of Major George Washington as the second-in-command.

They had proceeded as far as Will's Creek, still almost a hundred and fifty miles from Fort Duquesne, before Colonel Fry became so seriously ill that the command devolved on Washington. It wasn't an easy command and it couldn't be swift. There were less than three hundred men to guard against surprise, to build roads, and to drag wagons and cannon. Often the best they could do was a march of a mile a day. It was a great relief to emerge finally from the encompassing forests into a vast treeless plain known as Great Meadows, even though the force had been reduced to little more than half of the original three hundred.

They were soon joined, however, by a band of Indians whose chief was known as the Half-King. The reason for the name is not clear, unless it might suggest a rather shifty gentleman with a sharp eye for the main chance who was ready to change sides on the slightest provocation. For the moment he was favoring the English, and he brought word that a force of Frenchmen were in the neighborhood, presumably waiting for the English. It seemed that the advantage would lie with the party who first attacked. With the help of the Half-King and his followers the Frenchmen were soon discovered lurking in a ravine in the neighborhood. Both forces fired at once, but it wasn't the Frenchmen's lucky day. At the first volley ten of them were killed or wounded; among the killed their leader, Coulon de Jumonville. This was the exact volley that Horace Walpole felt had set fire to a world. Perhaps it had, for this small French force came to assume an importance that its size scarcely justified. Not only were there ten killed, but the remaining twenty-one were taken prisoner. Some of the Half-King's followers had complicated matters by tampering with the wounded, while the Half-King himself openly boasted that it was his tomahawk that had dispatched Jumonville.

The French promptly charged that Washington's men had fired on a group whose peaceful intent was only to warn the English that they were encroaching on French territory. They also pointed to the fact that Washington had been courteously treated when he had approached St. Pierre just a year before.

It is true that Jumonville did have a letter on his person at the time of his death, but it wasn't, as the French claimed, authorizing no more than an order to vacate. It ordered him to expel forcibly such English as he should meet. His actual actions were by no means as innocent as many Frenchmen undoubtedly believed. His party had remained in hiding for two days near Washington's force and without making any effort to present the warning. He just waited and watched, sending word back to Contrecoeur, who was moving up with five hundred men, to press on quickly.

Learning of the fate of this advance force, Contrecoeur sent out another advance party with Coulon de Villiers, Jumonville's brother, in command. There was no doubt of the orders this time. They were to destroy the English party.

Undoubtedly Washington expected something of the kind. He had immediately moved his forces back to Great Meadows, free of the forests where an enemy could approach without warning. They began throwing up entrenchments, and word was sent to the ailing

Fry to send on such men as he could. Fifty additional men soon arrived, but they still left Washington's force not much more than the three hundred with which he had started. It was all he could expect.

When De Villiers' force finally debouched from the forest it was seen to number, with its Indian allies, better than nine hundred fighters. The presence of an enemy quickly disclosed that the rough fort that Washington had named Fort Necessity did not have a very hopeful position. It was overlooked by a ridge that permitted the French to riddle the place with musket shot and prevent the use of its three cannon. To add to that, rain began to fall in cloudburst force. Soon the defenders were up to their knees in watery mud. Food was growing scarce, for there had been no provision for the additional fifty men. The crowning difficulty came when it was discovered that some of the priceless ammunition was water-soaked and useless.

For nine long hours the musketry battle kept up in that smoking deluge of rain. It was deadly business. When Fort Necessity could hold out no longer and parleys brought the fighting to an end, a hundred English had died. The French losses, though less severe, were serious enough. It is a little hard to remember that the two nations involved in this bitter affray were still nominally at peace.

There was an ugly incident in the surrender arrangements, which otherwise were generous enough. The surrender documents used the phrase "*l'assassinat du Sieur de Jumonville.*" Washington, who knew no French, was assured that the phrase merely stated that Jumonville had been killed. He signed the document without hesitation, not knowing he had thereby accepted a charge of assassination that the French would remember. There was nothing too creditable to anyone in the whole affair. Perhaps the best summing up was that voiced by the crafty Half-King. "The French," he said with open scorn, "had behaved like cowards, and the English like fools."

CHAPTER XXI

"WE ARE NO LONGER A NATION"

A game of political cross-purposes begins. Britain and France appear to be at peace while each prepares for war. Admiral Boscawen provides the overt act that ends the pretense. General Braddock arrives at Williamsburg, calls an assembly at Albany to formulate plans and provide a united front. A not overly successful gathering. An expedition starts on its ill-omened way. The many delays. The Battle of the Monongahela and the death of Braddock culminate a crushing defeat. The Indians write off the English as of no more consequence. Two years of border outrage follow. English courage and confidence are dissipated in the New World and the Old. The emergence of William Pitt.

From a strictly practical standpoint, there is little doubt that both the victory and the defeat at Fort Necessity were vastly overstressed. Yet this small engagement in an isolated backwater did profoundly affect the happenings of two continents.

English prestige had ebbed very low. If the Half-King's judgment reflected on both French and English, the Indian tribes, in the main, had assessed the situation differently. The English had been the aggressors, or so it seemed to the Indian mind. They had been defeated and compelled to retreat. There were now no English forces beyond the Alleghenies, and the Father of Waters did indeed "roll untroubled to the sea." France's life line was assured, and apparently the English colonies were content to do nothing but bicker among themselves. With so much evidence of division and failure, it was small wonder that the tribes should feel that the turn of Fortune's wheel undeniably had favored the French. So when this strange truce, in which men fought and killed and took land and lost it, finally burst into open war, it was to find most of the Indian tribes aligned with the French.

Well before that time came, the Indians, with few exceptions, considered the English cause lost. In all the border sections, terror and rapine were constant companions. In the remote settlements men and women and children laid down their lives, not because their cause was lost, but because the Indians thought it was.

This was the almost unbelievable. If numbers counted for anything, the English colonies were in an unassailable position. The colonies from Maine to Georgia at the time had a population in excess of 1,600,000, including some 200,000 slaves. Of the available white males, there were better than 200,000 of military age.

Against that, the total white population of French Canada, including Louisiana, was estimated by Voltaire at 80,000, while other authorities put the figure considerably lower. Governor Duquesne, who had a reason for accuracy, estimated that in addition to the regular military garrisons of 3,000 to 3,500, there were some 19,000 men of military age, thus setting a comparative basis of ten to one. To this, of course, must be added the number of available Indian allies, in which the French were superior. Mainly, the colonies could look to a highly uncertain support from the Iroquois, whose numbers were set by Sir William Johnson at nineteen thousand.

More than that. There were sharp economic disparities. New France was not self-supporting, as were the English colonies. There never was a time in its history when New France produced the amount of foodstuffs needed for her own support. Speaking of these years of the mid-1750s, Voltaire again was rather loudly proclaiming that the policy of expending so much blood and treasure in maintaining and defending so unprofitable a dependency was unstatesmanlike and wrong. He argued that if one tenth of the money squandered there had been used to improve the wasteland of France there would have been a considerable profit.

There was no profit in Canada. But he argued with customary

cynicism, "The King must amuse himself, and this ruinous colony is one of his playthings. It is," he urged in a burst of passion, "a sink-hole for money and a sponge for the blood of France."

There was some reason for this passion in the comparison of a country that, despite its prosperous fur trade, had to import three times what it exported, while the neighboring English colonies could export almost twice what they had need to import.

Striking as these comparisons are, impressive in their evidence of an unarguable disparity, the facts did not greatly depress the French nor, seemingly, encourage the English. The French were wholly confident that the English colonies would never forget their differences long enough to permit them to combine against a common enemy. It was a reasonable assumption, with much evidence to support it. The one thing the argument lacked was the recognition of that peculiar attribute of the English race that has saved it on more than one desperate occasion, an overwhelming reluctance to accept defeat. The French entirely failed to recognize that such thinking could offset innumerable errors and disadvantages.

The British government, usually too immersed in its own affairs to be deeply concerned over those in the New World, was interested enough to recommend some form of union that would permit the colonies to bring the weight of their greater resources against the French. So much could be done without jeopardizing the uneasy peace then existing. Though the suggestion had the support of strong men–Benjamin Franklin, who had come to be a power in Pennsylvania, and the energetic Governor Shirley of Massachusetts–not all the colonies were so minded. Seven of them did send commissioners to the convention at Albany, but Virginia, despite the aggressive part played by its Governor Dinwiddie in recent unhappy events, would have none of it, while New Jersey, too, remained coolly aloof.

The conference could scarcely be called a success. Franklin might point dramatically to the picture of a snake cut into many slices and liken this to the divided provinces, ending with a burst of impassioned eloquence, "Join, or die," but the commissioners remained cool and aloof. They preferred to discuss their relations with the Iroquois. Hendrick, the Indian who spoke for the Mohawks, left little room for complacency even here. The colonists, he complained, were encroaching on Indian lands, building their towns without warrant on lands secured by barefaced trickery. The English were too driven by personal greed to take effective action against the French. "You English," he said with mounting scorn, "are all like women, and the French may come and turn you out." There was not much encouragement in conferring. The participants knew it as well as anyone else. They were united in their recognition of the menace of France but on nothing else. There were halfhearted resolutions that came to nothing. So ended the first congress in the New World.

The failure of this attempt at united action left the management of affairs almost completely in the hands of the home government. It was an unhappy result. In the centuries of history the motherland had known many first ministers, some good, some negligible, some bad. Never, perhaps, had she been so dismally served as at this particular juncture. Her Prime Minister, the Duke of Newcastle, was admittedly a man without capacity, without knowledge, and without understanding. Horace Walpole, who knew him well, spoke of his qualities—perhaps with more wit than charity—as "a borrowed importance and real insignificance." But beyond any question, Newcastle's basic theory of government was that everything must give way to the importance of retaining the power that he loved by the crafty use of patronage and preferment that would not bear the light of day. He was petty, often ridiculous, while his appointments, honest in the sense that he used them to sustain his position rather than to line his purse, were miracles of misjudgment. He selected as his Minister of Colonies at this critical time Sir Thomas Robinson. It was said of this appointment that it was Newcastle's crowning achievement, for who could have believed it possible that he could find as an assistant a greater fool than himself?

These were the men on whom the responsibility of retrieving British prestige was to rest. How much this resulted in the acceptance of a plan that France had certainly encouraged is difficult to say. That plan involved the dissipation of English power in minor actions on the fringes of France's American empire. It left the heart still strong and untouched. The same effort directed at Quebec and Montreal might easily have changed the course of history.

In mid-January of 1755 a group of transports carrying the 44th and 48th regiments of the line boarded ship at Cork and sailed away for an unnamed destination. The Colonial Minister, Sir Thomas Robinson, was meeting the disturbed protests of France by a bland statement that the troops and ships were not intended to disturb the peace of any nation even while he must have known that the commander of these troops bore with him definite instructions to attack a French garrison.

It was a game of cross-purposes, for while the French were accepting Robinson's explanation with apparent relief, and explaining that they also were innocent of any martial intent, they were gathering a force of eighteen warships and supplementing their crews with six battalions of troops, three thousand men in all. It was not possible to be quite so unobtrusive about the destination of these forces as were the English, for in addition to Baron Dieskau, who commanded the troops, there went also a new governor for Canada to replace the ailing Duquesne. It was the Marquis de Vaudreuil, son of the former governor. So the preparations for conflict went on in this smog of subterfuge and deceit.

Learning of this new move in the campaign of misrepresentation, Newcastle hurried Admirals Boscawen and Holborne in pursuit with an equal number of ships of the line. For all the protested innocence of this sailing, Boscawen carried secret instructions to capture and destroy any French vessels that might come his way. More lightly laden, the English fleet made better sailing than the French and was waiting off Newfoundland for the French fleet's arrival. But the fog that often blankets those seas favored the French. Dieskau and his three thousand troops reached Quebec safely, while the remainder of the fleet found shelter in Louisburg harbor. Only three small vessels of the fleet had lost contact in the fog. When it lifted, the three saw the sails of Boscawan's fleet only a mile or so away.

All the to-and-fro talk of peaceful intent had left its aura of uncertainty. "Are we at peace or war?" signaled puzzled Captain Hocquart of the *Alcide*, one of the lost ships. But Boscawen was not confused. He had his orders to capture or destroy. A broadside from one of his ships soon settled that point. One of the smaller ships escaped, but two were taken.

This was something different from a skirmish in the Pennsylvania woods. These weren't colonists dead or captured. They were French ships and French soldiers and sailors. Pretense no longer availed. This was war.

With such happenings close at hand it was not difficult to overlook the less dramatic. When a small British fleet dropped anchor in Hampton Roads, Virginia, disembarked a few individuals, and proceeded on its way upriver to Alexandria on the Potomac, it didn't create much of a stir. Yet even without his military following General Braddock was an impressively military figure. His short erect figure portrayed his calling, and his sharp eye and stern bearing marked a man confident in himself and one not lightly turned from his way. He had come to visit Virginia's energetic Governor Dinwiddie, and for some time he lodged with the governor in the palace at Williamsburg.

General Braddock, whose major general's stars were still only a few months old, was a typical product of his day and age. It has become rather a habit to think of him as a rough, stupid, stubborn, and generally incompetent officer who covered his failings with a rude and blustering exterior. It is a picture that is far from the truth. He was a man of competence in a time when the forms of war were sometimes deemed more important than the substance. There were traditions of behavior that ranked almost equal with achieved results. Advancement went by favor, and wealth and position often decided command. Braddock had neither, so it must be assumed that he was selected for commander for more impressive reasons. He had been an officer in the crack Coldstream Guards, and he had a private income of three hundred pounds a year, enough to suggest some small claim to social position without being enough to support that claim. He has been charged with being a spendthrift, but at his death this patrimony was a little larger than when it had come to him. Like many of his class, he had once fought a duel and, being worsted, he refused stubbornly to beg for his life. He had been governor of Gibraltar, where he had made himself popular with the common soldier. Whatever he may have been with his equals—uncompromising, stubborn, truculent—he was never overbearing with his soldiers, asking of them only obedience and the acceptance of a rigid discipline.

Horace Walpole, who was the gadfly commentator of his age, wrote of Braddock: "Desperate in his fortunes, brutal in his behaviour, obstinate in his sentiments, he was still intrepid and capable." Obstinate undoubtedly he was; desperate he may have been; capable is even today a matter of argument, but brutal he was not.

Most of the thinking of this continent has pictured Braddock as a stupid, arbitrary character and a bumbling and ineffective soldier. Little of this can be substantiated. He was a product of his age, and if it was one of spit and polish, he belonged to it. But it was more than that. It was an outward form that stood for a devotion that permitted no qualification. He was put in command by no other than the Duke of Cumberland, who, as well as being the favorite son of George II, was the best soldier the House of Hanover had produced. It was not a political appointment, for Cumberland appointed Braddock commander in chief of all the British forces in North America without waiting to consult with the Prime Minister, the "thick-witted" Duke of Newcastle. Braddock had many critics, but he also had the respect of Britain's best soldier, who recognized his fidelity and his wholly unchallenged courage.

It was the end of March when the streets of Williamsburg were stirred to a sudden excitement. The governor's carriage came rattling down Duke of Gloucester Street on its way to a momentous conference. The watchers were not very sure of what the conference might portend, but the sight of the stern-faced little major general sitting beside the governor, with Commodore Keppel facing them, indicated that it was an occasion of more than usual importance. The bevy of soldiers and civilians who rode their horses about the carriage, clop-clopping down the cobbled street, added to the impression that great events were in the making, as indeed they were. The general had called a conference of the provincial governors at the Carlisle House in Alexandria to discuss the forthcoming campaign. The citizens guessed as much, if they did not actually know. When the cavalcade reached its destination, it was to find most of the governors already arrived. There were Dobbs of North Carolina, Morris of Pennsylvania, Sharpe of Maryland, De Lancey of New York, and perhaps most important, the ever-active Governor Shirley of Massachusetts. They were still very far from a united group. Governor Shirley was convinced that Nova Scotia was the crux of the military situation.

After some heated argument it was decided to send Colonel Monckton to dislodge the French from their fort at Beauséjour, from which they had been threatening the countryside. That would still leave Louisburg unchallenged and so would achieve little, but it seemed of importance, and perhaps it was as the first suggestion of sterner measures in the coming Acadian tragedy. Governor Morris was still supporting the pacifist views of his state and, while favoring some action, preferred not to be involved. New York thought the attack should be launched by the favored war road—Lake Champlain to the heart of Canada, Quebec and Montreal. Governor Shirley had his mind set on cutting the French road westward by taking Niagara.

And of course Fort Duquesne stood out, not only as a point of threat to the westward movement of the English, but as a challenge to their pride.

In the end it was decided to challenge everywhere. The main thrust would be against Fort Duquesne, with General Braddock leading his regulars in what everyone believed would be a decisive action. But to make it doubly sure, in addition to Colonel Monckton's attack on Beauséjour, it was decided also to create a diversion by way of Lake Champlain. This time there was a man to lead who gave great promise of success. It was a young Irishman, William Johnson, who had come to America to manage the lands along the Mohawk River belonging to his uncle, Admiral Warren, the same who had traded good blows at Louisburg. Young Johnson had made himself a power with the Iroquois tribes. Perhaps if the attack had been concentrated on this vulnerable point success might have been achieved, but there was no such wise judgment available. So it was decided that the capture of the wilderness stronghold of Fort Duquesne should be the center of effort. The curtain was about to rise.

If the convening governors, watching the 44th and 48th regiments of the line go through their paces, felt that nothing could stand against them, it was not surprising. Few, if any, who saw them thought differently. Their numbers had been increased by enlistment to seven hundred men each, and the recruits had quickly and proudly picked up the skill of veterans.

In their spotless red coats and immaculate white helmets, which would have looked like a bishop's miter but for the accompanying gleam of steel, and their white bandoleers, they did indeed seem invulnerable. Even the shrewd Benjamin Franklin was too impressed to question when Braddock explained to him: "After taking Fort Duquesne, I am to proceed to Niagara; and having taken that, to Frontenac . . . for Duquesne can hardly detain me above three or four days, and then I see nothing that can obstruct my march on Niagara."

He might have been more nearly correct had his expedition been directed to a more northerly port than Williamsburg. A straight road across populous Pennsylvania with its opulent land and generous resources would have shortened the journey and eliminated many of the problems of the barren and mountainous southern route. Probably Governor Dinwiddie may have thought differently, and as the

Ohio Company had a Virginian origin and as most of the preliminary action in the Fort Duquesne theater of operations had been conducted by Virginians, the governor's opinion obviously carried weight.

The decision, however, had some sharp drawbacks, as Benjamin Franklin was to point out. In the petty bickering of the times it threw the chief onus for the success of the expedition on the shoulders of Virginia, with Pennsylvania, which presented the closest road and the most immediate interest, standing coolly aloof.

The expedition presented the first need for sustenance and support, on a grand scale, that the colonies had known, but Pennsylvania showed no inclination to accept their white man's burden. Though advised of the need months in advance, they did nothing. There wasn't sufficient food for men or horses, and if there had been, there were neither the horses nor the wagons to transport it. The *Colonial Records* of Pennsylvania report that the quartermaster general of the expedition, Sir John Sinclair, "stormed like a lion rampant." If the fact is correctly reported, he had ample cause, but his anger achieved no useful result. There were only twenty-five teams and wagons for the whole army.

Horace Walpole, the gossip who missed few opportunities of disparagement, commented that Braddock "seemed in no hurry to be scalped." As it actually was, Braddock, never an overly patient man, seemed more likely to die from fury and frustration than from enemy action. But he did approach the one man who could and would be of service. Benjamin Franklin, deputy postmaster general of the colonies and one of their important citizens, having first made the point that Braddock should have landed at Philadelphia and marched westward through Pennsylvania, did stir his home state to the needs of the situation. Such was his prestige that soon there were a hundred and fifty wagons to add to the existing twenty-five, and all the horses needed. There were now better than six hundred of them, far more than enough for the slim pasturage available. They were not flourishing on the diet of leaves, the best fodder available.

The situation might have been somewhat better had the one man who could have helped him most, the one man who was unhappily familiar with the route to be taken, been asked to help. But army red tape was as real as at any time in history. Colonel George Washington knew more than anyone else what problems were to be faced and what hazards must be accepted. But he was a provincial officer.

By the rules, he was ranked alongside the most beardless sub-lieutenant of the two regiments of the line. Braddock did not challenge this doctrine. He had been brought up in it and it did not occur to him to question its wisdom. But somewhere native shrewdness came to his aid. Recognizing his need for help, he appointed young Washington to his staff, where red tape could be most conveniently handled.

It was a wise move, perhaps Braddock's wisest. It is probable that Washington was the one to suggest that some of the independent companies should be sent ahead to prepare a camp that would be the starting point for the great thrust that was to drive the French forever from the path of the advancing English. This force reached an old trading post of the Ohio Company on Will's Creek, near where it enters the Potomac, and there on a plateau of rising ground they made a vast clearing. In the midst of it they set up their palisades, an enclosure of logs surrounding barracks and magazines, for the force that was to come. The walls were pierced with loopholes for the ten small cannon they had brought with them. All was now ready.

Braddock started his expedition toward their new base at what was known as Fort Cumberland. It was some hundred miles westward. For himself, he followed across the Blue Ridge into the valley of the Shenandoah in his coach and six. Moving northward, he rejoined his army at Fort Cumberland on May 10, 1755. It was the most pretentious force that had yet been seen on the continent. There were fifteen hundred regulars, the flower of the British army. To these were added four hundred and fifty militiamen from New York, Virginia, Maryland, and the Carolinas, staunch fighters, though their lack of order and discipline was little to Braddock's liking. There was a motley gathering of other arms; three troops of the independent companies in the King's pay. These were the men who had built Fort Cumberland. There were some thirty men of the Virginia Light Horse and thirty sailors of the *Centurion*, the ship that had brought Braddock to the New World. Not wishing to miss the excitement, they had joined the expedition. These, with ten men as guides and a scattering of Indians, made up a total force of something in excess of 2,150, as the figure appears in the journal of Captain Orme of Braddock's staff.

The whole was commanded by Braddock in person. Of the two regiments of regulars, the 44th was commanded by Colonel Sir Peter Halket, a brave and able officer, and the 48th by Colonel Thomas

Dunbar, of whom the less said the better. Lieutenant Colonel Burton commanded the provincial troops and was to follow their fortunes gallantly to the end.

It was June 10 before preparations were all completed and the army was ready to start on its great adventure. The route taken would be roughly that followed by Washington the year before. Now there would be a difference; then a few men trained to the woods could follow almost invisible paths, but this was an army moving with artillery and clumsy tumbrels of ammunition, and long wagon trains with provisions, with droves of scrubby cattle lumbering behind. There was not only an army to be fed but a fort to be provisioned once it had been taken.

The progress was bitterly slow. It was a good day when the force made ten miles. Often enough it was only four, with the trains stretching back for other miles behind. Every step of the way was forest or rocky mountainous terrain, river or marshland. The heat blistered faces, and insects made life a torment to men who were new to the frontier.

Following the axmen went Sir Peter Halket leading the 44th. Their tight scarlet tunics and bandoleers, pipe-clayed to a shining white, were bright spots of color against the forest gloom; their black-gaitered legs moving in unison flashed in the sunlight until they merged with the forest. Slogging along behind, without pretense at style, came the provincials headed by Burton, and then Colonel Dunbar with the 48th, moving with the precision that showed their training. Braddock, riding with them ahead of the long line of wagons that stretched back for miles, was happy at the sight. These indeed were soldiers.

It is customary to speak of the leader as if he were careless and inefficient, and he was neither. Flankers followed the army on either side, keeping pace as best they could in the untouched forest. At first they grumbled at such precautions where the forests seemed silent and tenantless, but the occasional discovery of a soldier dead in the forest underbrush, with his scalp lock missing, soon stilled any argument.

Eight days' marching brought the army to Little Meadows, less than twenty miles from its starting point. It was evident that at such a pace winter would overtake the venture before they had mastered the hundred rugged miles that still stood between them and Fort Duquesne. It was a grimly challenging thought.

The present-day traveler who follows U.S. Route 40 out of Cumberland, where the far corner of Maryland abuts Pennsylvania, may follow almost in the footsteps of Braddock's army and may wonder how a journey of a few hours should have taken weeks. But this hundred-odd miles is studded with history. Some fifty hilly miles out of Cumberland, going westward, is present-day Farmington, the site of that Fort Necessity that Washington built and had to surrender. A few miles farther west was Rock Fort, where Dunbar had his reserve camp and close by the spot where the wounded Braddock came to die. And not far from Chalk Hill, almost midway between Farmington and Uniontown, lies the rocky glen where young Coulon de Jumonville was killed, to put a new and sterner note into the crafty maneuvering of English and French to possess this land.

But all that was many yesterdays ago. The land was new and rugged and unmapped, and Braddock's great army could not make the pace of the traveler on Route 40. It was so evident that it was finally decided the army must be cut down and stripped of all unnecessary impedimenta. The decision was given added weight by the report that heavy reinforcements were on the way to Contrecoeur at Fort Duquesne. Six hundred men, including the sick, the weaker horses and much of the supplies would be left with Colonel Dunbar, who would follow at the best pace possible. The place where he then camped was known as Rock Fort.

With his army now reduced to twelve hundred regulars under Colonel Halket and two hundred provincials under Colonel Burton, Braddock did not change his cautious advance. To move forward following the banks of the Monongahela River was certainly the shortest route, it was also the most hazardous. The land was rough and broken with plenty of positions for a defending force. He decided to follow the cautious course. He would move his army across to the river's other shore, where he would not be expected, move some miles up the bank and nearer the fortress, and recross the river when the rough terrain had been passed. The plan seemed to succeed beyond all hopes. The army forded the river in safety and soon learned from Colonel Gage, who had been sent ahead, that the return ford was in his hands. Still not a hint of action, and Gage's force of three hundred men and two guns seemed adequate to protect the recrossing.

No one interfered. It was not unnatural to conclude that so obvious

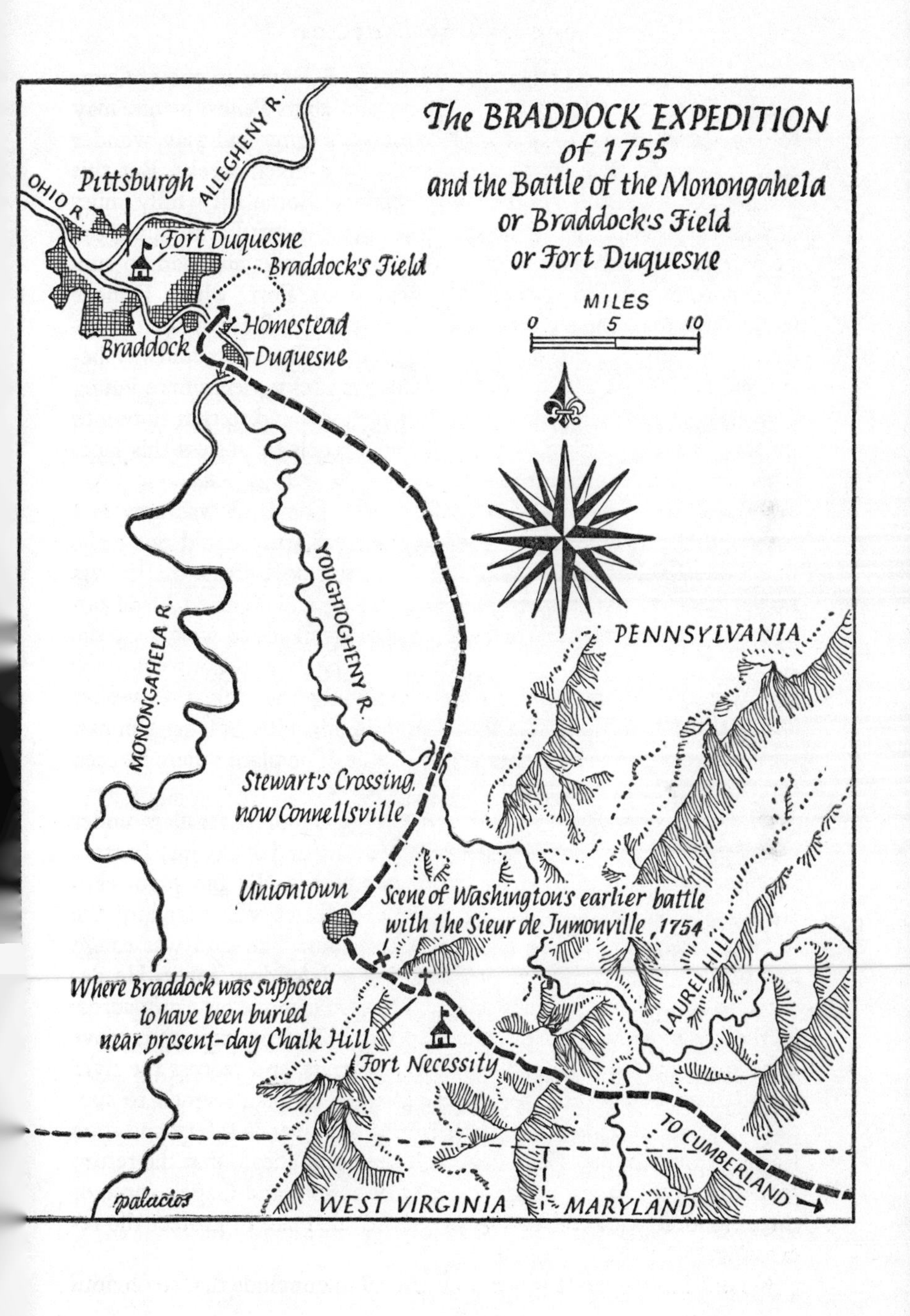
The BRADDOCK EXPEDITION
of 1755
and the Battle of the Monongahela
or Braddock's Field
or Fort Duquesne
MILES
0 5 10
Pittsburgh
OHIO R.
ALLEGHENY R.
Fort Duquesne
Braddock's Field
Homestead
Braddock
Duquesne
YOUGHIOGHENY R.
MONONGAHELA R.
PENNSYLVANIA
Stewart's Crossing,
now Connellsville
Uniontown
Scene of Washington's earlier battle
with the Sieur de Jumonville, 1754
LAUREL HILL
Where Braddock was supposed
to have been buried
near present-day Chalk Hill
Fort Necessity
TO CUMBERLAND
palacios
WEST VIRGINIA
MARYLAND

a failure to protect the approaches to the fort was a confession of weakness. Early afternoon found Braddock's command ready to recross the river. He made quite a ceremony of it. The army forded the river by companies in precise formation with flags flying and bugles blowing. Still there was no one to stop them. When they moved forward it seemed as though the lands and woods about were free of hostile intent. The intent was there, however. It had been with Captain Beaujeu from the beginning. He had urged Contrecoeur to challenge the passage of the river. But the Indians on whom he must depend had been impressed with Braddock's strategy, and still more so by the numbers and equipment of his command. They had no love for artillery and no wish to join in Beaujeu's mistaken heroics. It was long hours before Beaujeu had them convinced enough to help, and by then the river was passed. But there was still the forest.

Braddock's force moved forward. Some Indians and light-horsemen skirmished ahead. They had moved forward perhaps a mile from the ford, with Gage's three hundred men and his two guns following, and still little sign of the enemy. There was yet time before the three o'clock hour, when their orders were to camp and rest for the morrow's attack.

Suddenly, in a gap in the forest, a figure appeared. It was in Indian garb, but strangely enough it wore also the insignia of a French officer. The figure waved its hat and, as if this were a signal, the forest came alive with warriors firing from every vantage point. It was a happy moment for the Indians. Never had they known such shining red marks for their musket fire, and never had they been safer than in the inexperienced fire of the regulars. But Captain Gage quickly evened the count with his two guns loaded with grape and canister.

For a moment, had they known it, Fort Duquesne was almost in their grasp. The young Beaujeu, with his way with the Indians, lay dead in the underbrush, and the guns these Indians most feared were speaking with authority. They began to slip way into the shadows. But there were seventy-five French regulars there under Captain Dumas, and with him was that half-breed leader, Langlade, the same who had challenged the Demoiselle and had been of the party who had dined off her (or him!). These were not men to be frightened, and they knew the Indian and his ways.

This head-on sort of fighting was not to their liking. Covered by the smoke of Gage's guns and further protected by the underbrush, Dumas and Langlade, leaving the French regulars to protect the front, positioned their Indian allies in mile-long skirmish lines on both flanks of the attack. Here they were out of the field of fire of the guns they dreaded and conveniently hidden from their foes.

Hearing the swelling fire that swept over his van guard, Braddock, like the courageous if not too brilliant soldier he was, moved to the sound of the guns. Leaving Colonel Halket with four hundred men, including most of the provincials, to cover the rear and guard the baggage, Braddock and his regulars marched to the front. Give these men the accolade of courage if not of wisdom. They moved forward in serried lines, their red banners flying and their marching step as if on parade. This was not Dettingen or Fontenoy or the mannered fighting of Europe. From the quiet forests surrounding, a pandemonium of shrieks and gunfire greeted them. Still they went forward. Still Braddock, stout and high-hearted, rode at their head. He had forgotten the many suggestions that Washington had poured out to him: how the Indians fought; how they should be fought in return; a warfare of hiding and confusing, the very antithesis of all experience had taught him. In this hour of crisis it was all forgotten. Perhaps that is the ultimate judgment of Braddock; he was slow to learn.

In this crisis it came back to him that discipline won battles. Time and again, in his own experience, it had been proved. What he seemingly could not realize was that those battles were fought under rules accepted by both sides. Here there were no rules but every man for himself. Discipline, the sort of discipline he understood, did not count any more.

They reached Gage's company. These had suffered enough; they had faced hidden fire with unbelievable bravery. Now the fire was turned on other targets. They had time to think. Their thinking told them to get away. Back through Braddock's ranks they raced, breaking the formation and shaking the steadiness of even these veterans. The newer recruits began to falter. Braddock was riding along his lines, his sword in hand, shepherding and encouraging them and, where needed, emphasizing his orders with the flat of his sword. The mounting panic paused. Officers were planting regimental colors as a gathering point for confused men who needed to find their familiar place again. Rarely has any continent seen more gallantry than that day as officers gathered their men, dressed them in lines, and led them against a hidden foe with bayonets flashing.

Never had there been such a shining target for those who could find their mark even in the forest dusk. A blaze of red coats set off with pipe-clayed belts and leggings bright as on parade. Shoulder to shoulder they fired calmly at a target they could not see, doing perhaps as much damage to friend as to foe. Time after time Braddock seemed down as his horse was shot under him, but he was up again on another horse, a stout figure waving his sword aloft and shouting to his men, his voice growing hoarse in the surrounding din. Officer after officer was hit. Companies were commanded by sergeants or less. Still they stood firm; in little groups now instead of the "thin red line," but they still faced ahead, firing at an unseen foe.

It was not a battle but a massacre—a massacre of men who knew the meaning of devotion better than they knew the meaning of fear. Long years would follow when the embittered French would pour their abuse on these luckless regiments. But Captain Dumas, who took command of the French and Indian forces when his fellow captain, Beaujeu, fell dead, remained to speak for the defense. He had been there and he knew. He told how a red line had stood without flinching for two long, obstinate, courageous hours while about them their fellows dropped in rows like ripe corn.

It couldn't last. Even discipline is not infinite. There was no hope but to save the few who remained. His voice hoarse with weariness and bitter with regret, Braddock gave the order to retire. As he turned, his horse—the fifth he had ridden that day—stumbled. This time Braddock could not leap from the saddle. He fell with it, a bullet tearing his lung. Two wounded members of his staff struggled up. A tumbrel was brought, the injured general was moved as gently as could be, and the little group was caught up in the turmoil of retreat.

They fell back on Colonel Halket's rear guard, but it too had suffered. Colonel Halket had fallen. They found his body there and in his arms that of his young son, who had hurried up to aid. Each had his own Indian bullet.

Hysteria began to take command. Rifles were dropped as men raced away. As they recrossed the ford they had passed that morning Braddock called out that it must be held, but discipline was as weak now as the voice that issued the order. Again, as the retreat reached the earlier crossing of the Monongahela, Braddock tried again, beseeching his men to stay and make a stand. They hesitated a moment, but there was no fight remaining. Braddock called for Washington, his only unwounded aide. He was to hurry to Colonel Dunbar's camp some sixty miles away and urge him to hurry up men and supplies. But already some of the wagon drivers had burst into the reserve camp with wild stories of rout and ruin.

Colonel Dunbar was no last-ditch soldier. He did nothing to help. When Braddock arrived, carried in a litter by two men who had to be bribed for the task, he was too weak to assume control. Colonel Dunbar knew the end when he saw it. His orders were to strike camp, destroy everything that could not be moved, and make Fort Cumberland as best they could.

Braddock couldn't command; Dunbar wouldn't. So once again Washington had the unhappy part of leading a beaten army home. Before they reached Rock Fort, a few miles west of Great Meadows and Fort Necessity, Braddock lapsed into unconsciousness. Once he roused himself enough to say, as his young aide, Captain Orme, records, "Who would have thought it?" and a little later, in a dazed voice, "We shall better know how to deal with them another time." The spirit was not defeated if the general was. The spirit was still looking to other and better campaigns. Poor, brave, and not too brilliant Braddock, for him there would be no "other time."

They reached Little Meadows, and close to it he died. He was buried there with Washington reading a brief service. Then the foreign earth closed over him. The wagons and the guns and the footsore men of the retreating army tramped over that lonely grave, blotting out every mark of it, lest someone find it and despoil it. It was the least and the best they could do for a brave man.

Ahead of them Dunbar drove his reserve army, pressing away from any threat of pursuit. But there was no pursuit. Why would there be, when on the deserted battleground there was wealth beyond Indian imagining? Everything had been abandoned; wagons and guns and horses and cattle, and even the specie for the payment of the King's regiments. In the glades and the forest shadows where the regiments of the line had fought, the dead lay thick as leaves would lie that coming autumn. Of 1,460 officers and men who had made up Braddock's army, there remained only 483 who were fit for duty, and many of these were walking wounded.

The figures tell the grim story. Out of eighty-nine officers, sixty-three were killed or seriously wounded. Out of thirteen hundred rank and file, not five hundred remained unscathed. Perhaps most of those wounded were left on the field, died there, or were carried off for future torture and death. Why pursue a retreating five hundred when such rich plunder was at hand?

While Washington was leading the fragments of the provincial army back to Virginia and safety, Governor Dinwiddie was writing to exhort Colonel Dunbar to make a second attempt. But Dunbar, who, though he missed the actual fighting, had seen enough to know it would not be to his liking, wrote in return a stiff official note that said he was marching his army to Philadelphia, as Washington had assured the governor he would.

In bitter words the governor wrote to his young friend, Captain Orme of Braddock's staff, "I was not brought up to arms, but I think common sense would have prevailed not to leave the frontier exposed after having opened a road over the mountains to the Ohio, by which the enemy can the more easily invade us.

"Your great colonel," he added, "is gone to a peaceful colony and left our frontier open. . . . The whole conduct of Colonel Dunbar appears to me monstrous. . . . To march off all the regulars, and leave the fort and frontiers to be defended by four hundred sick and wounded and the poor remains of our provincial forces appears to me absurd." So it might have appeared to anyone. And one is led to wonder whether the ignominy of one man might not have cast its shadow over another who, if he was not great, was at least devoted and did have a great man's heart.

History's bitter record was to prove how sound the Virginia governor's judgment had been. Dunbar reached Philadelphia, quickly embarked his men, and sailed away. A breathlessness fell on the western frontier, where Pennsylvania and Virginia waited fearful and disturbed for what might come. The great expedition that was to drive the French from the land had trickled down to a bare thousand half-trained militiamen. Many of them had been with Braddock and still trembled at the thought of that catastrophe. There was little spirit in them and no aggressiveness at all.

The only officer with rank and experience was just twenty-three years old. Twice he had brought a beaten army from the frontier. That men still believed in him, that he still believed in himself, is a tribute to the quality of the man. But what man, no matter what his qualities, could hold so long a line with supporters so pitifully few and with every forest glade swarming with excited Indians eager for the blow that would be final? And in the reckless young partisans who had chosen the forest and adventure rather than the humdrum securities and the settled life, the Indians had men to lead them.

Even the hardy pioneers who had forced their way into the wilderness—English and Scotch and German and Irish—taking their chances, had come to know that the chance was too slim for anyone. They were streaming back from the frontier. In three days, so Washington's own journal records, he had counted three hundred wagons fleeing from what everyone knew would come now that France's claim to all the land from Canada to Louisiana lay untroubled by any threat. Already, Washington records, the road Braddock had built was beaten hard with the prints of moccasined feet.

The few might escape, but not the many. Like a visitation of locusts, blood-maddened Indians swarmed across the frontier, killing and burning and destroying. From the Ohio lands to Virginia's west and southern borders, and from the Carolinas to western New York, the dreadful work went on as frontier settlement after settlement flamed up and died. The children who escaped the first frenzy were driven into captivity, to death, or lifelong banishment. For a year, for almost two years, the work of butchery and destruction went on. There was little retaliation. It was as if the spirit of men of the English tongue had died in them. The funds that Philadelphia had gathered in advance for the fireworks that would suitably celebrate Braddock's great victory lay unused. There was no spirit to suggest that such funds could be put to sterner use. There was still no thought of combining with whole hearts against a common foe. Minds were still set on individual security, individual gain, nothing more. This spirit could not end there. It reached across the seas and found men glancing apprehensively at other narrow seas that seemed now their only safeguard. It was left for Chesterfield to speak for them all; Chesterfield the impassive, the cynical, who could write to his son such bland and worldly-wise advice, spoke now for all who dreaded and despaired. "We are no longer a nation," he said, and it seemed that he might be speaking truth.

But the great Frederick of Prussia, who had no great love for a land that had been both his friend and his foe, had a surer insight. He had seen a new figure emerge and had sensed a changing attitude. "England has been a long time in labor," he said, "but she has at last brought forth a man."

As he came to power in that troubled and fearful age, that man spoke with a new purpose and unassailable confidence. "I want to call England out of that enervated state in which twenty thousand men from France can shake her." And over and over again that tingling challenge: "Be one people. Be one people." So men remember—the undismayed. His name was William Pitt.

CHAPTER XXII

THE LOST DISPATCH

A seemingly useless paper, found on the tragic field of Braddock's discomfiture at the forks of the Ohio, lays bare the larger strategy and alerts Vaudreuil to meet it. The timely coming of Baron Dieskau with four famous regiments equips him for the task. Shirley is lamentably lacking at Oswego—saved by the threat to Crown Point. Here a strangely romantic figure commands: William Johnson and his story. Dieskau's early attack and success—the death of Ephraim Williams and King Hendrick of the Mohawks. Fort William Henry begun. Its first defense. Defeat and capture of Dieskau. The strange wild enthusiasm at an empty victory.

ON the site of what is sometimes called the Battle of Braddock's Field, a dark and bloody ground indeed, now stand the thriving towns of North Braddock and Braddock Hills and Rankin. Here so many years ago Fate played one of its strangest tricks. Yet perhaps it is not so strange. Those versed in the history of the great War between the States will remember the almost unbelievable story of three cigars wrapped in a bit of crumpled paper that may well have changed a fragment of history. For the paper was General Lee's army order No. 191, the order that outlined the proposed movements of his army as it moved to invade Pennsylvania. Coming into the hands of General George B. McClellan, it changed a chronic delayer into a man of quick and decisive action and made an almost unknown creek, the Antietam, in the shadow of the little Pennsylvania town of Sharpsburg, a name of greatness and of bitter and unavailing tragedy.

Almost a century earlier and still in Pennsylvania and less than two hundred miles away, there was another happening equally strange, equally decisive. The exulting Indians swarming over the Monongahela battlefield in the wake of Braddock's army, or the small remaining part of it that had not died where it stood, were not thinking in terms of strategy. It is doubtful if anyone was. Contrecoeur had not expected victory. The jaunty and reckless Beaujeu who had led the first attack was dead, and the Canadians who had been with him had fled from the field, crying as they ran, "*Sauve qui peut* [Save yourselves]!" Dumas, who had taken full command in the heart of the battle, had only that heart to sustain him. "I advanced," he says in his own report, "with the assurance that comes from despair." There had been victory beyond any possible question, but still the victors were glad to be alive.

There were no thoughts of future plans. The thoughts were of here and now. It was an Indian battle headed by seven French regular officers. It was over. There were bloody scalps to be reaped, fabulous booty to be shared, or acquired by force from either friend or foe. They knew nothing of Niagara or Crown Point and cared considerably less. And when the wave of rapine and death had flowed over these fields of dead and wounded, of crippled wagons and deserted guns and all the tragic fragments of war, it swept over Braddock's headquarters too, burning and destroying. Surely nothing there could escape—no dispatch, no papers, no scrap of warning? What possible hope was there, even had anything of the like existed, that it would have caught the eye of some wandering warrior among so much booty? What possible hope of its reaching anyone with the authority to receive or the knowledge to understand?

Obviously there was no such chance. Yet the paper did appear and in due time reached the hands of the new governor, Vaudreuil. History is cloudy on the matter of how. All it records is that from that tortured battlefield came the information that was to pile defeat on defeat. For the colonial plans to attack Niagara and Crown Point thus became known and, inconspicuous soldier that he was, Vaudreuil made careful and exact plans to meet the threat.

It was in July of 1755 that Governor Shirley, able and confident and eager for some military acclaim, was ready to move. He had as his second-in-command Sir William Pepperrell. The capture of Louisburg, which had been planned by the one and carried out by the other, had resulted in a good deal of prestige to which neither was wholly entitled. Able men they were, but men of military skill they were not. Even the success at Louisburg, which had undoubtedly taught the able Pepperrell at least some rudiments of the military art, was not the conclusive argument that it appeared. The success of that expedition might be credited as much to French incompetency as to colonial military skill. Pepperrell would undoubtedly have been a most valuable assistant to a skilled commander. Shirley had enthusiasm but no skill and nothing even distantly related to military genius. As it was, the plan that they were to follow would have required military qualities of the first order. In its place was an undoubted will to serve their country. Governor Shirley, now major general, had another motive. As the expedition was setting out he learned that the son of his hopes, young William, who had been Braddock's secretary and a lad of great promise, was lying somewhere on those grisly fields the defeated Braddock had relinquished, a bullet through his head.

Shirley had reason enough to wish to strike a shrewd blow to French prestige. He had not the skill or the equipment, and now he had lost his one advantage of surprise. The lost dispatch had come to Governor Vaudreuil's hands and made everything fully known.

It would have seemed that some measure of co-operation between the expedition that aimed to sever a French life line by the capture of Fort Niagara and Johnson's proposed attack on Crown Point on the main artery between Canada and the New England states might have benefited both. If anyone thought so, nothing was done about it. If the plan for a double assault had any influence at all it was to induce Shirley to get his own task done before that farmer from the Mohawk Valley, as he liked to think of Johnson, could play his part in making history.

Johnson was not a good hater, but he did have a sound knowledge of men. Some years later he was to write to Lord Amherst: "Shirley hates me. I am sorry for him; I almost pity him. He has many good traits that are good and useful, but he has also a few small traits that are bad and harmful–more to himself than to anyone else. His trouble lies in his tendency to subordinate the great traits to the little ones. I do not know of another instance where the making of a great character has been so spoiled by foibles." Then, as later, it was a sound and not unfriendly judgment.

Even had Shirley been gifted with more skill and fewer foibles, the task before him would have been all but impossible at the time. The French knew quite well how vitally significant Niagara was to them, and they knew of the plan to take it. They knew also that it was a long, long road for any enemy, and their own hearts were high with victory.

There were trails between Canada and the frontiers of New England and New York that had been made clear in many a bloody foray. Adequate enough they might be for a score or two of raiders trained to the woods. But this was different. This was an army, an army that might have a final strength of twenty-five hundred men—and not woodsmen, but merchants and artisans and farmers with little knowledge of soldiering. They were formed now into three regiments, and their gay uniforms did something to lift the hearts of their owners. There was a regiment of New Jersey provincials in splendid regimentals known as the "Jersey Blues" and rated as regulars, more because of the uniform than because of the training. Yet it was a sturdy body of men, about five hundred in number. They were doubly appreciated, not only because of their sturdy worth, but because Shirley had managed to divert them from William Johnson's expedition against Crown Point. There were, too, the 50th and 51st regiments of the line, so called. Despite their new uniforms, many months were to pass before these yeoman farmers and artisans became seasoned soldiers to match their title. They were paid by the King and as an added incentive were named, respectively, as Shirley's and Pepperrell's regiments. These and a scattering of other forces and the necessary camp followers brought the total to somewhere about twenty-five hundred men. It was a pretentious force for the day.

Albany was the natural starting point for all such expeditions. It was the meeting place of the trails. One led northward to Canada by way of Lake Champlain, the ancient highway that had seen so much bloodshed and was destined to see so much more. The other followed the Mohawk River westward until it finally reached Lake Ontario at the remote trading post of Oswego, which the English had appropriated and fortified thirty years before, to the bitter vexation of the French.

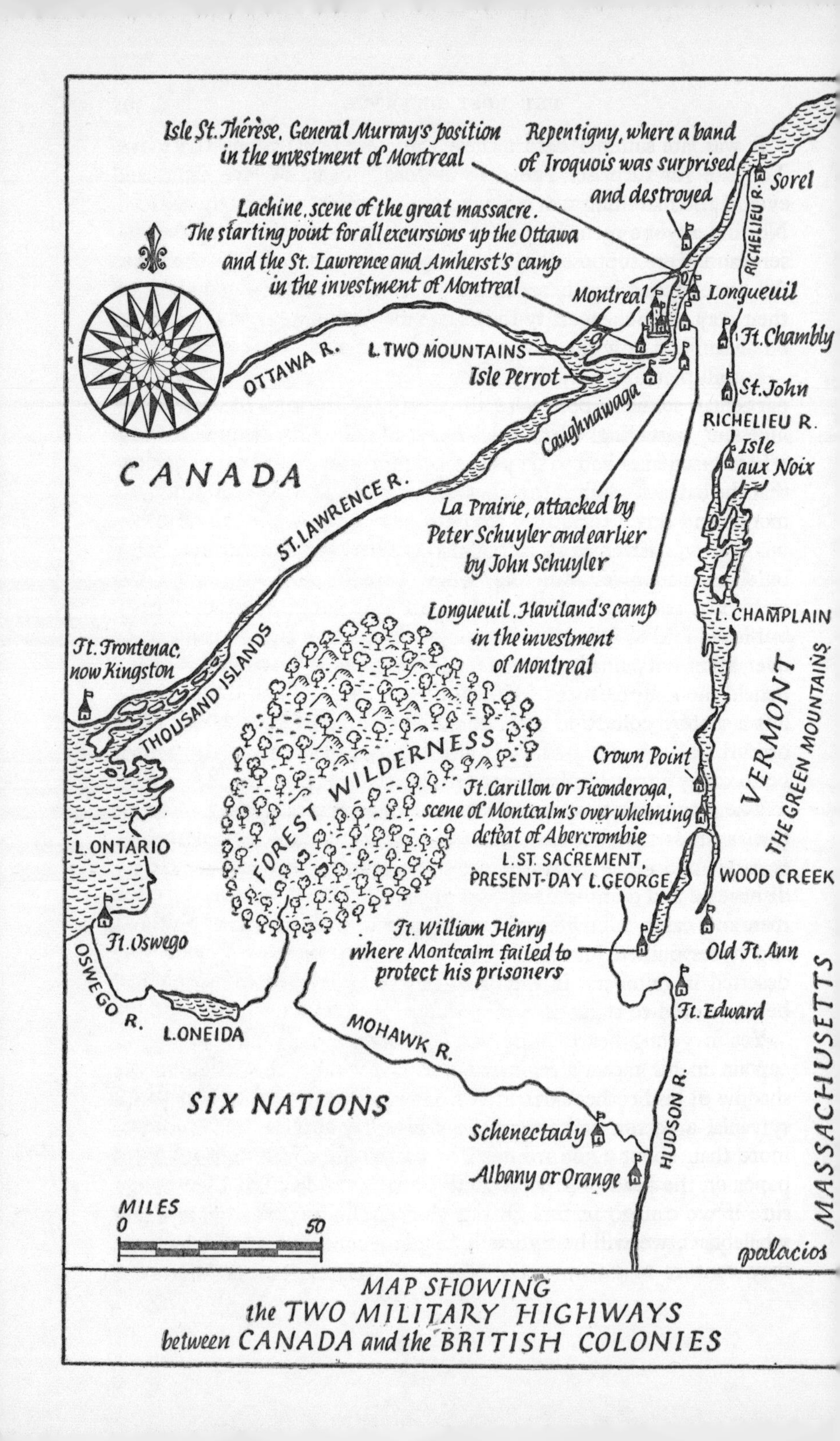

MAP SHOWING
the TWO MILITARY HIGHWAYS
between CANADA and the BRITISH COLONIES

It was late summer before these forces were at last on the move. Too late for surprise. The new uniforms made a brave sight, and even if the marching was a bit ragged for regulars, nobody noticed. Nor did anyone record whether it was the day of the week that the sergeants were supposed to have their hair powdered like subalterns. All were loaded into bateaux and boats of every kind and were on their way. At Schenectady they were met by Shirley, who had gone on ahead, and now the adventure really began.

For all that theirs was a familiar track, it was not familiar to these particular soldiers, nor were the rough going and the seemingly incessant portaging. Sixty long miles it was through a wilderness where often axes had to be used to clear the overhanging boughs so that the bateaux might proceed. Over this height of land and the vast morass and scrub forest the rivers, such as they were, flowed westward. It was bitter work to put the bateaux on sleds and drag them by sheer manpower over long miles of such going. Even when the creek was reached, it too was clogged and matted with fallen trees, but it did lead to Lake Oneida. Such was an experience met over and over again until finally they reached the broader Oswego River and beheld the long reaches of Lake Ontario. On the bare hillside to the left a shabby collection of buildings rudely fortified bore the name of Fort Oswego. They had been three weeks on a journey that would be to today's traveler little more than three hours.

The men were sick, exhausted, and disheartened. Word of Braddock's disaster had reached them and brought a sudden panic fear. It passed and became a slow discouragement that fine uniforms, now disheveled and damp-stained, had no further power to change. Boatmen and camp followers, whose task it was to see that provisions and stores pushed forward, were bewildered and fearful. They had deserted in numbers. It was late August before enough order had been restored to think of pressing on.

Yet in young hearts hope was still high. Young Jack Shirley, a captain in his father's regiment, was not disheartened, despite the shadow of his brother's death. Writing to Governor Morris of Pennsylvania, a patron and friend, he was still confident. "We are not more than about 1,500 men fit for duty," he wrote, balancing his paper on the head of a pork barrel, as he records. "But I am pretty sure if we can go in time in our sloop, schooner, row-galleys and whaleboats, we will be sufficient to take Frontenac, after which we may venture to go upon the attack of Niagara, but not before. I have not the least doubt with myself of knocking down both these places yet this fall, if we can get away in a week."

But before the week was up Governor Vaudreuil, who had brought with him from France three thousand special troops, was pouring many of them into Fort Frontenac. These were not ordinary regiments. The very names of them sing their way through French history, a challenge to glory—the regiments of Béarn and La Reine and Guienne and Languedoc. They were to have their part in the requiem of France in the New World.

There could be no more thought of attacking Fort Frontenac; no more thought of attacking Niagara and leaving the road clear for such forces to swarm over all the English lands. Shirley knew it in all his pride and vanity. Pepperrell knew it in his soberer way.

Shirley was not content to forget the whole affair. Lack of courage or overcaution had never been charged to him. He gathered a council of his officers and pointed out to them that he still had 1,376 men fit for duty. He proposed to start for Niagara with six hundred men, leaving the balance to hold the frontier and defend Oswego. To his Indian allies he made a great speech telling them of General Johnson's achievements and, after enthusiasm had been whipped up by high words, he gave them a bullock for a feast. The Indians received it with enthusiasm and when it was roasted ate it with relish that was the more for telling each other that the subject of their repast was actually the governor of Canada.

Even such encouraging thoughts could not change the situation. Young Jack Shirley understood it; knew that the men had been on half rations of bread for three weeks now and, worse still, no rum ration had been available at all to make the deprivation bearable. The weather was as bad as could be expected so late in the year. The larger vessels would not hold half of the force of six hundred and the bateaux were made for river travel and could not weather stormy lake waters. All the field officers thought the proposal too rash. Young Jack Shirley records reluctantly: "I think it is my duty to let my father know what I hear." That information led to another conference and the decision to postpone the attempt. Seven hundred men were to be left at the fort to protect it against possible attack and to build other vessels for next year's expeditions. Shirley and the remainder of his forces returned to Albany.

Young Jack Shirley was never to know the result of his advice. Nor was he to receive an answer to his letter from Governor Morris.

We learn it from Governor Morris himself. He tells how the post from New York reported the death there of young Shirley "of a Flux and Fever that he had contracted at Oswego." He adds his final word, perhaps the best appraisal of a hapless undertaking, "the loss of two sons in one campaign scarcely admits of consolation."

Even had Governor and Major General Shirley's courage taken precedence of his judgment, it seems unlikely that anything could have been gained. Troops from Fort Duquesne were streaming back eastward in numbers. Any time since Braddock's defeat Fort Niagara would have been bulging with more troops than Shirley could bring against it. Also, no sooner had he succeeded the ailing Governor Duquesne than Vaudreuil had begun making plans of his own. Like his father before him, he saw as the logical mark the point where the English were most strongly entrenched, where the blow might do the most lasting damage. Because Oswego covered the territories of the Iroquois long house, it was apparent that a serious blow there might easily weaken the Iroquois' uncertain loyalty to the English —not unreasonable thinking. Carrying the thought into action, Vaudreuil proposed to send some of the troops that had come with him from France. They would be well fed, for German-born Baron Dieskau would be in command, a French officer who had learned his trade under the great Marshal Saxe himself. Dubious about the value of provincial troops, Dieskau knew how to use them and would most certainly have struck a decisive blow at Oswego.

Just at this time, however, there came to Vaudreuil's hand the fateful lost dispatch that told of the proposed attack on Crown Point. No one would claim that Vaudreuil was a man of more than average acumen, but he did realize, as Braddock and all his gubernatorial advisers apparently did not, that an attack on a perimeter could never equal an attack on the heart. It was at the heart that the assault along the ancient highway of Champlain and the Richelieu was directed. Promptly Vaudreuil changed both his plan and his order. Dieskau was to scrap what plans he had made and to lead his troops to Crown Point instead. Being very human, Vaudreuil gave up a cherished plan reluctantly. "Make all haste," he wrote his new general in chief, "for when you return we shall send you to Oswego to execute our first design." That Dieskau might not return was a contingency that quite obviously did not cross his mind.

The men whose rather surprising task it was to face the French general, that soldier of outstanding ability and protégé of the great Marshal Saxe, had no military training at all. True, there were relatively few men in the colonies who had, outside of those who had been at Louisburg or had some knowledge of the disorganized butchery that represented the Indian raids. There the basic military maxim was to kill before you were killed, a forthright idea requiring little elaboration.

There were some men, however, who had shown unusual astuteness in dealing with others, or a capacity for accepting responsibility and making the most of it, or working harmoniously with their fellows, and particularly with their more difficult fellows, the Indians.

With such capacities to take the place of military training, William Johnson was a marked man. William Johnson indeed would have been a marked man in almost any circle. He had been born in Warrenpoint, County Down, Ireland, the son of an obscure Irish schoolmaster. The schoolmaster, it is true, had once been an officer in Cadogan's Horse, a regiment of note, and had remained with it until a wound received at Oudenarde made him a cripple. Young Johnson was a nephew of Sir Peter Warren, who, it will be remembered, had played a considerable part in the taking of Louisburg and had made himself wealthy by the purchase of vast holdings of land in the Mohawk River Valley. Warren had married the daughter of the governor of New York and in secret nursed the hope that he might succeed to that position. The hope never came to fruition, but Sir Peter Warren's shrewd venture into real estate did when Palatine German and Holland Dutch began to move into the Mohawk River lowlands and the valueless land began to become valuable. It was then that Admiral Warren remembered that, if he was to profit by the influx of new citizens, his lands had to be looked after. And then it was that there had come to his mind the picture of his young nephew, a red-haired Irish lad six feet tall and suitably broad of beam, a man of quick action and ready laughter and friendly as a puppy, but a man with a great head, as his portraits show, and with the evidence of great physical strength about him.

To the well-born and inpecunious of that day it was the accepted practice to belong to the "King's Own," which of course bespoke employment in either the army or the navy. Young Johnson, who always had in him a strain of the rebel against the accustomed, decided on the law, which, good as it might be, could not equal the standing of the King's services. He had been listed to appear for examination at the spring assizes for admission as a junior barrister when Sir Peter Warren's letter reached him. Young Johnson wasted no time in regretting the law. Quickly as might be he set sail for the New World. He spent the winter in New York as the guest of his uncle, enjoying the best society of the day, and in the early spring he was off for Sir Peter's lands along the Mohawk. He was twenty-three years of age and out to make his fortune.

Contrary to the spirit of the time, young Johnson urged his uncle to sell part of his immense acreage in parcels of one hundred and fifty and three hundred acres. He interested numbers of Scotch-Irish farmers to come to that section and to build homes on large tracts of land. As the vast Mohawk Valley area filled up it made huge profits for the astute commodore, who had been farsighted enough not only to secure the valuable lands but to find one to manage them with skill, understanding, and imagination.

Young William Johnson had his own dream of the future. Partly it grew from a bitter indignation at the way white traders exploited the Indians—perhaps defrauded would be a better word. Certainly the concept that the Indian had any rights that a white man need respect was quite new. Until William Johnson suggested it, there is little doubt that it would have been considered a counsel of weakness. When Johnson decided that he would open a trading post of his own, it was not only with the idea of money-making but of dealing fairly with all—Indian and white alike. It is not improbable that he realized what was very soon made plain—that this changed attitude would pay off handsomely.

In applying to the governor for a license to trade, he wrote: "I wish to create this trading-post not any more for the profits it may bring to me than to show by actual example that trade with the Indians can be conducted honestly as well as any other commercial business."

This trading post did not conflict with the interests of his uncle, who had indeed helped substantially in financing the venture. The site was at Oquawgo in the Oneida territory in the valley of the Susquehanna, near what is now the town of Windsor, Broome County. It was selected by Ezra Buell, Jr., who had been in Johnson's employ as a surveyor and who became the first manager of the venture. But though Johnson found his uncle's interests too onerous and the distance of a hundred miles too exacting to permit him to visit his trading post with any frequency, he did direct its operations, and this the Indians were made to understand. His policy was simple and direct enough. Never deal with an Indian except when he was completely sober. Once a deal was made or a promise given, it must be honored without any quibbling. If an answer was "No," no effort of argument or solicitation or Indian guile should be of any avail. The answer had been "No" and would so remain. So, equally, if the answer had been "Yes" there was no room for withdrawing.

The treatment was new enough to be startling. Suspicious at first, the Indians quickly came to recognize that here was a man whose word was good, even to his own hurt. But it was the speculative trader, the exploiters of the Indians, who were hurt most. Rapidly their ventures became unprofitable as Johnson's fortunes improved.

Young Johnson had been five years on his uncle's lands, living in a modest log shack near Warrensbush, when he was attracted to a young girl named Catharine Weisenberg. She was the daughter of a Lutheran clergyman, who had managed to give her a passable education. However, the family fortunes were at a very low ebb and Catharine, when about fourteen years of age, had been "bound out" as a servant to one of the affluent citizens. Young Johnson, no lover of any form of legal dominance, bought her indenture. That made him her legal owner. Making no point of this, the young man promptly married her, the service being performed by an Anglican clergyman. She bore him three children.

With his new status and growing wealth, it wasn't long before Johnson was building himself a fine home of stone that, when completed, was to be called Mount Johnson. In addition to his other activities he was breeding horses and raising sheep, and his establishment was growing apace. By one deal he fell heir to nineteen slaves, and though the system was not to his liking, by the time of his death the nineteen had grown to sixty or seventy, making Johnson the largest slaveholder in New York.

A year after Johnson had moved to Mount Johnson his wife died and he was left with three young children, the oldest barely five. Then began the rather strange marital relationships that were to mark the greater part of his life. In these years Johnson espoused, in a manner, two Indian women.

It is understandable that a man left with three very young children to be cared for should look for assistance. It is not quite so understandable that a man with every social grace, with an entree into any group of society, and with wealth and good connections should have sought for his mate an Indian girl, but so it was. When his first wife died, or a year or two thereafter, he brought into his house Caroline Hendrick, the niece of the chief of the Mohawks and sister of the wife of Nicklaus Brant, the father of Joseph and Molly Brant. Nicklaus Brant was known far and wide as a "man of prodigious silence," so presumably he had nothing to say in regard to this situation. For some years Caroline reigned as undoubted mistress of his home and bore Johnson three more children. When Caroline Hendrick was in her fatal illness, her sister came to nurse her and brought her daughter, Molly Brant. When Caroline died, Molly Brant seemed to slip into her place quite naturally. She remained in that place for well over twenty happy years.

In those years both the wealth and the prestige of William Johnson steadily increased. When his first home, Mount Johnson, became too small for his growing family, he built a great stone house that was called Fort Johnson. It still stands on Highway 5, a few miles west of Amsterdam, New York. Even this grew inadequate as the years passed, and he built Johnson Hall at what is now Johnstown, New York. Here Molly Brant, the "Brown Lady Johnson," as she was known, reigned for the better part of her life. If she felt any sensitiveness over her anomalous position, she showed no sign of it, and it would hardly have been guessed from any action or gesture of Johnson himself. They lived a life of baronial splendor, with the great dining-hall table always groaning under food for whoever might come, and rarely was it lacking guests. The highest in the land came there and sat with men of dusky hue. Hendrick, the retired chief of the Mohawks, venerable and noble-looking as one should look who was known to all as King Hendrick; or Nicklaus Brant, or his son Joseph—and all presided over with dignity and grace by the Brown Lady Johnson, who was not quite a wife.

Because of these strange family arrangements, it is inevitable that it should be made to appear that, combined with the luxury of living, there were less laudable circumstances. Neither gossip nor history sustains such suppositions. Why Johnson, a man of wealth and social standing, should have left his marital relationships subject to such conclusions; why he should have remained a generous supporter of the Church of England and deeply interested in its missionaries and its missionary effort and yet have been so careless of his personal relationships that it was necessary for him to write in his will of "my natural children by my housekeeper Mary Brant" will always remain a puzzling question.

Singular as his relations were, he was always devotedly attached to his home and deeply fond of his Indian companion and his half-breed children. He lived with the Brown Lady Johnson for better than twenty years without any suspicion of unfaithfulness. He was an ardent church member, and if he left the outward observances to his family and the practical administrations of affairs to himself, he did see that his family strictly observed the rituals and formalities of the church, while devoting himself to promoting missions along the Mohawk, printing an Indian prayer book, and helping finance the erection of several churches.

Why, then, the seeming carelessness in observing the customary practices of a Christian society? Perhaps from negligence or from a feeling that marrying Indian women under somewhat the same practices as obtained in the tribes might draw him closer to the Indians themselves, for that was the obvious driving motive of his life. He was free from pretentiousness, friendly and easy in his manner, decorous in his speech and actions, and temperate in all things.

When under some pressure he had resigned as agent of the New York Council to deal with the tribes, there was a breathless hush in all the lands of the Six Nations. Then they gathered themselves to beg that he be restored to his place. With Chief Abraham of the Mohawks and King Hendrick, the most influential leaders of the confederacy, speaking for them, they urged that Johnson should be reinstated and have the management of Indian affairs, "for we love him," they urged, "and he us, and he has always been our good and trusty friend."

This was the man, then, who was suddenly chosen to face the protégé of one of Europe's greatest soldiers, Marshal Saxe. The man chosen had shown unusual astuteness in dealing with his fellows, of whatever color, along with a capacity to accept authority and make the most of it. He was known and respected, but of specific military training he had not a scrap. Yet in that regard there was no one who had more, and this man was the best known and most generally well regarded. So the colonial authorities made him a major general without more ado and suggested that he might have an army of six thousand men less trained than himself, a figure that ultimately simmered down to about half the number. What Johnson was supposed to do with his army was about as unlikely as his own appointment. He was to take from the French their fortress of Crown Point, a fortress perched on a high promontory on the southwest shores of Lake Champlain and, having accomplished that all but impossible feat, he was to cap it by driving every Frenchman from the lake that they considered their own, though Crown Point was their most southerly post.

To accomplish this, he was to have an army considerably less martial than its leader. Like Shirley's army, it was made up of mechanics and fishermen and farmers who had left their homes reluctantly and were thinking mainly of getting back. They would fight well enough when the occasion arose, but in their own way. They were men of sturdy independence, accustomed to making their own decisions, and naturally reluctant to accept them from any other source. It was a characteristic that did not make for discipline, however much it might suggest a capacity for adapting themselves to the sort of forest warfare that the Frenchmen were wont to call *la petite guerre*.

It is open to doubt if Johnson ever questioned his complete ability to accomplish what he had been sent to do. He started out bravely, not knowing that Baron Dieskau, who had proposed to attack Oswego, had been suddenly redirected to bar that open road to Canada. He didn't know that the powerful fortress of Crown Point that he was supposed to subdue had a garrison of twelve hundred troops, and in addition the forces that Baron Dieskau was bringing to its support. These were two hundred and eighty crack troops from the famous Régiment de la Reine, some eight hundred Canadian militia, and seven hundred Indians. Altogether the forces available to defend Crown Point were equal to any the attackers could bring against it.

The original plan called for Massachusetts, New Hampshire, and Connecticut to supply some twenty-five hundred provincial troops, with New York adding another thousand, added to which there would be a thousand or more Indians. By the end of July all the colonial troops had arrived at Albany, the jumping-off point, and if they were considerably less than the original estimates, they still represented a very substantial army for the day.

Of Johnson's group, New Hampshire had sent seven companies, a total of five hundred men under their own Colonel Blanchard.

Colonel Phineas Lyman commanded the contingent from Connecticut, while Ephraim Williams, a colonel who had been a captain in the attack on Louisburg and hence could boast some military experience, commanded the Massachusetts regiments.

The men brought their own rifles and in the main wore their own clothes, which made no pretense at being uniforms. Thoughtfully, most of them carried a hatchet in their belts in lieu of bayonets.

It was a devout army, if inexperienced. There were sermons twice weekly, and psalm singing interspersed the perhaps more necessary work of drilling. True, there must have been some exceptions to so laudable a characteristic. Colonel Williams wrote to his brother: "We are a wicked, profane army, especially the New York and Rhode Island troops. Nothing to be heard among a great part of them but the language of Hell. If Crown Point is taken, it will not be for our sakes, but for those good people left behind." But experienced or no, spiritually minded or no, the colonial levies were on hand, reluctant, but prepared to go.

Johnson's greatest disappointment was in his Indian contingent. He had expected over a thousand. King Hendrick, chief sachem of the Mohawks and senior chief of all the Iroquois, had promised him at least that many when the preparatory conference had met sometime earlier at Mount Johnson. More than a thousand Indians had gathered there, and they had discussed the plans endlessly. It was the largest conference of Indian tribes ever gathered, and they remained for days. Indeed Mount Johnson, noted for its limitless hospitality, had to send out appeals to neighbors for twenty miles about to help with the food supply.

Despite this enthusiasm, those who turned up for the fighting were less than six hundred in number, owing mainly to the fact that the Senecas had failed to provide their quota. The Senecas had been the weakest link in the Iroquois friendship with the English. The tribe had been an especial target of French propaganda, and some of its warriors had even been part of Beaujeu's striking force at Fort Duquesne. Now these had returned, bringing the fateful news of the discomfiture of the English. These reports left the tribe almost as thoroughly convinced as was Lord Chesterfield that England was no longer a nation, and neither Johnson's amazing influence nor the pleadings of their own leaders could change that feeling. They had no wish to be a part of a defeated cause.

Hi-o-ka-to, the valiant chief of the Senecas, who at Mount Johnson had pledged himself to provide four hundred warriors, was considerably out of countenance. He proposed to remain with his people and make good his promise even if he had to "drag every mother's son of them by the scalp lock." Even such protestations got nowhere, and finally Johnson grew impatient and would wait no longer for such temperamental allies.

On August 6, 1755, he sent an advance party of New York and Massachusetts troops under Colonel Lyman to start the movement north. They were to follow the Hudson River from Albany for some forty miles to where it turned sharply to the left. This was the beginning of the long portage that was a bitterly remembered part of many an expedition. This landing point had become a place of increasingly strategic importance, and part of Colonel Lyman's instructions were to build a fort there. The building hadn't progressed very far when Johnson himself arrived with the balance of his forces. Even though the fort was still a very nondescript affair, Johnson found a name for it. He called it Fort Edward, after a member of the royal family. He set two thousand of his own men to cutting a passable road across the fifteen-mile portage so that the necessary supplies for such an army could be transported. Even so, it took his army two days to make the trip, and it was the twenty-eighth of August before they saw the first glimmer of water and knew that the heaviest work was over. It was Lake St. Sacrement, so called by the devoted Father Isaac Jogues, whose name was to be associated with it forever, for about it he had had his mission to the Iroquois and he had been martyred by them not far away.

Johnson seems to have come under a sudden urge of patriotic feeling that led him to rename many points after his royal masters. So St. Sacrement became Lake George after George III. "I have given it the name of Lake George," he wrote the Lords of Trade, "not only in honor of His Majesty the King, but to assure his undoubted dominion here." The undoubted dominion turned out to be rather sharply limited, as some twenty years later the King's authority ceased to run there, though his name still remains.

When all Johnson's troops had finally reached the lake, he built there a rude defense that ultimately was to develop into an impressive fortification bearing a name that would be a bitter memory in Canada's early history. It was called Fort William Henry.

Dieskau, ordered to forget Oswego and to concentrate on Johnson's expedition against Crown Point, which had been a taunting challenge to the English colonists for almost a quarter century, quickly moved his headquarters and his considerable army there. His was not a nature to sit quietly waiting an attack under any circumstances, particularly when he had a force at least equal to the attackers in numbers and unmistakably better both in experience and leadership. He had learned from his scouts that Johnson was busily fortifying both ends of the fifteen-mile portage from the Hudson River to Lake George, and while he was not familiar with the terrain, military experience suggested that this posed a formidable threat. Obviously his course was to attack before the enemy could make this challenge good.

From his relieving force of almost three thousand he detached a substantial striking force. It included two hundred regulars from the Régiment de la Reine, about seven hundred Canadian militia, and six hundred Indians. With this force he proposed to start hunting the hunter. His orders were exemplary in their thoroughness. Officers were to take with them only one spare shirt, a second pair of shoes, a blanket, a bearskin—presumably for comfort—and provisions for twelve days. With his Indian followers he was even more explicit. They were not to amuse themselves by taking scalps until the enemy was entirely defeated. His careful instructions made it clear that the purpose of this order was realistic rather than humane. Indeed, he explained reasonably, it was possible to kill ten men in the time it took to scalp one, an evidence of how thoroughly he had mastered some of the details of his new command.

Crown Point was about fifty miles from Johnson's position on Lake George, but Dieskau had discovered it was possible to approach the enemy without disclosing his plans. Wood Creek, a long arm of Lake Champlain, almost paralleled the southerly course of Lake George. By following the creek to its southerly end he would be able to throw his small army across the road built by Johnson's forces. This would place him almost midway between Fort Edward and the new camp that was soon to become Fort William Henry and to acquire an unhappy memory for all the years to come. At the moment it was only a rudely fashioned camp protected by the few cannon that Colonel Lyman had brought with him from Fort Edward.

Dieskau, now strategically placed between the two forts, chose to attack the latest. The decision was made for him by the fact that the Indians were reluctant to attack any place protected by artillery.

He believed that the guns had been left at Fort Edward, a misjudgment that cost him dearly.

Johnson was not a timid character and he learned belatedly of Dieskau's approach without being unduly disturbed. He had ample resources of men, he thought, to control the situation. He did, however, send out a force under Colonel Ephraim Williams to feel out the enemy. Colonel Williams, who is better known as the founder of Williams College than as a soldier, was the same man who had criticized the ungodliness of the army, which he seemed to feel was more serious than its lack of military training. With him went King Hendrick, in his eightieth year and too fat to walk, who was mounted on a pony that Johnson had provided. He wore for the occasion a ceremonial dress that his English friends had given him. It was a coat of scarlet and gold surmounted by a cocked hat, such as the dandies of the town favored, but it was less suited to forest warfare. However, these were the days when redcoats like those of Braddock marched in steady rows to meet the enemy, and why not a chieftain?

It wasn't that Hendrick underestimated the enemy. He was too wise for that. When informed that Colonel Williams' command would number a thousand men, he protested gruffly, "Too few to be successful; too many to be killed." However, when he could not change the plan he rode out in resplendent gallantry, leading his two hundred warriors.

It seems unbelievable that Colonel Williams, who might not have been a military expert but who did have some background of Indian fighting, would start out through this unfamiliar country marching with as little precaution as one might march through the streets of a home town. But all the records say that he did just that.

Dieskau, who had no experience of this kind of fighting at all, felt his way along as a trained Indian fighter might do. It was not because he was cautious by nature. He was indeed daring beyond the bounds of reason. Particularly was this so on this occasion. He was bent on repeating at these New England lakes the story that had been written at the forks of the Ohio. When some of his officers remonstrated, pointing out that they were advancing against an enemy that was much more numerous, he silenced them with a sharp word. "The more there are, the more we shall kill."

He made his plans with care: an ambush in which the unwary could march to find themselves completely surrounded on the flanks while closely engaged at the front. It couldn't be quite that complete a surprise even with Colonel Williams' jaunty and unconcerned approach. Though Dieskau's men had been warned to hold their fire until the approaching force was completely surrounded, one of them, whether through excitement or as a warning to some friend in the approaching marchers, let off his musket before the trap was quite closed.

It was closed enough. King Hendrick, riding ahead of his Indian detachment, too shining a mark for anyone to miss, caught the full force of the first blast of gunfire. A great and good man, and one of the best friends the English had, pitched from his saddle. He tried to rise, but his great weight impeded him. Then a sudden bayonet and he was still.

On the left, where Colonel Williams led his New England infantry, the firing was severe. Williams had ridden into it—stupidly, perhaps, but with a high and untroubled heart. Now he would use the one to pay for the other. His horse shot under him, he climbed a great rock where he could see, a conspicuous figure calling to his men to go forward. There he died. Of the men who followed, Dieskau himself speaks of them in his report as "crumpling like a pack of cards." Those who had not joined their leader in death were hurrying back to the slim protection of the fort.

This protection was indeed slim enough—a barrier of felled trees quickly pushed in front of the camp to delay an advance; it was the best they could do on short notice. It was barely completed when up the road came the white-coated regulars of the crack Régiment de la Reine, bayonets flashing in the sun. They paid no attention to the hail of fire that met them, but they were falling in groups, and they were pitifully few. They were, however, all the troops that Dieskau could control. The rest, militia and Indians alike, were a wild rabble combing the morning battlefield for plunder or screaming through the forest, unconscious of any orders.

As surely as the morning hours had gone against the English, the afternoon sun saw the fortunes of battle change. The men of the Régiment de la Reine could not face it alone, though they tried valiantly. They didn't retreat. They just died where they were, holding their place and falling one by one. Soon all the officers were down, killed or wounded. The men fought on until less than a quarter of them could stand, as unavailing a gallantry as history records. Dieskau himself was wounded and wounded again and finally captured.

Johnson also was hit, but his wound was more painful than serious, and Colonel Lyman was in command.

It was not a battle any longer. It was the sort of fighting that the defenders understood better than any famous regiment. It was a matter of sudden forays against isolated groups as the colonial militia burst through their own barriers to harry the retreating foe. Some of Dieskau's men were still engaged in robbing and scalping on the morning battlefield when a scanty force pushing up from Fort Edward came upon them and all but destroyed the plunderers. The bodies of the killed were tossed into an adjoining pond that to this day bears the ill-omened name of the "Bloody Pond."

For Dieskau, the defeated, there was generous treatment. When Johnson learned of his wounding and capture he had the discomfited Frenchman brought to his own tent and had the defeated general's wounds cared for ahead of his own. But wounds were the least of Dieskau's dangers. Scarcely were they dressed when Johnson's tent was invaded by a horde of screaming warriors. There were too many of their fellows lying dead for them to be patient, and even Johnson's prestige was all but unequal to the challenge. Dieskau was puzzled but undisturbed. "What is it they want?" he asked in a momentary lull. Johnson turned on him with hot words. "To burn you, by God," he explained, "eat you and smoke you in their pipes, in revenge for three or four of their chiefs that were killed." These are Dieskau's words as they ultimately appeared in his report, where he also reports Johnson's conclusion. "Never fear, you shall be safe with me, or else they shall kill us both."

It seemed that Crown Point or Ticonderoga, or both, could now be taken. Colonel Lyman thought so and urged that he be allowed to try. Governor Shirley, though wanting in success himself, could see an easily achievable success for another and wrote Johnson to that effect. To all, Johnson made the same retort. It wasn't the time to hazard more. Perhaps this attitude was characteristic with him; perhaps it is why it was said of him that though he never achieved a great or decisive victory he was never whipped. There was a possibility of further attacks. The troops available to Governor Vaudreuil had suffered little in any of their campaigns. Their morale was high and that of the English correspondingly low. Johnson was astute enough to know that while leaders might be eager for action the people as a whole only wanted to be left alone. Winter was almost come and his troops were slipping away. The opportunity for decisive action, if such there had been, had passed. More sacrifice, more suffering, and nothing accomplished.

For the moment, however, people thought differently. They were hungry for some suggestion of victory, and this at least was not defeat. Men who dearly need something to cheer for are not likely to be too discriminating. In all the long campaign of 1755 this was the only hint of colonial success. Empty of all results as it might be, it was still a victory. Baron Dieskau a prisoner in Albany certainly proved it. When Johnson visited New York in December the exultation still remained. He was given a hero's welcome. Ticker tape was still far in the future, but what the city could do to acclaim a victor it did. There were illuminations and the firing of guns and "Acclamations of Joy and Congratulation thro every street he passed." as the narrative of Daniel Claus, an interested observer, attests.

Not to be outdone, the court provided further honors. Johnson was created a baronet in recognition of his achievements, and this was supplemented, perhaps more practically, by a grant of five thousand pounds. But there was even more. He was appointed by the Crown, Superintendent of Indian Affairs in the Northern Department and colonel of the Six Nations. Rarely has so much honor crowned such limited achievement. Johnson was a man of unusual qualities, but there was nothing in his Crown Point campaign to prove it. It was just another item in a bitter and unhappy year when British arms and British diplomacy achieved nothing.

CHAPTER XXIII

THIS STUBBORN BREED

Losing Acadia, the French still claim much of the ancient lands once so called, especially the isthmus of Chignecto, the winter route between Louisburg and Quebec. The Abbé le Loutre, a darkly sinister figure, emerges. He whips into flame Acadian antagonism to the English and helps make agreement impossible. Capture of Fort Beauséjour and defeat of its unscrupulous commander, De Vergor, reflect a hardening in the English policy. Governor Lawrence demands an unqualified oath of loyalty. The Acadian refusal gives point to the continuing threat in Acadia and makes necessary the policy of expulsion.

THE conference Braddock had called at Alexandria to formulate a general plan of campaign seems to have been conceived under an unlucky star. It might have brought about a union of provinces able to show a solid front to any enemy. It might even have resulted in a United States without the necessity of revolution. But it didn't, for each colony brought to the gathering its prevailing prejudices and piques; its conviction that its own interests were paramount, and its reluctance to combine or contribute to any less self-centered purpose. So the results were something less than negligible.

Braddock had died miserably and unavailingly at the forks of the Ohio. Governor Shirley of Massachusetts, possibly the shrewdest politician of the conference, had introduced a plan for an attack on Niagara. It was sound in conception and might have brought him the military glory longed for. Instead it was easily checkmated by Canada's new governor, Vaudreuil, who was hardly even Shirley's equal as a strategist but who recognized the importance of this threat. William Johnson, sachem of the Mohawk tribe and named by them Warrachijagey, "he who does much business," did indeed gain a victory over Baron Dieskau. This bit of business, however, had been achieved more by inadvertence than by military skill, of which Johnson had little, or by shrewd planning, which for once seemed to be lacking. So even Johnson's victory was without tangible results. It left him fifty miles short of Crown Point, his objective, and it left the fortress itself still firmly in French hands.

There had been other plans proposed and approved at Alexandria. The most important of these again stemmed from Governor Shirley. It covered one phase of a belief that dominated all his actions. He was married to a French wife whom he had met some years before while on a mission to Paris, but this association had not changed his view that the French influence in the New World must be completely destroyed so that Canada could never again be a threat to the English colonies.

The first move in that campaign should be the destruction of Fort Beauséjour, which dominated the isthmus joining Acadia to the mainland. Shirley was convinced that the intrusion of this fort on what was rather obviously Acadian territory was an initial move in a plan to regain the whole. He believed, as had several governors of English Acadia, that the French would never rest until this land had been restored to them. His own thinking and all experience had convinced him that New England would never be safe should France once more control Acadia. Shirley may quite possibly have gone even a step farther and have feared that the British, who had been content to trade Louisburg for Madras for reasons of their own, might on some other occasion be ready to exchange Acadia for some remote advantage, thus again sacrificing the interests of the colonists.

That is pure assumption. But it is a possible one. It gives support to Shirley's open determination to make Acadia as completely and effectively British as might be, as it was now almost completely French. This as an assurance against just such a possibility. The forty-odd years since the Treaty of Utrecht had awarded Nova Scotia to the British had not achieved that end. This partially because the terms of the treaty, thus loosely defined, had set the limits of Acadia "according to its ancient boundries." These boundaries themselves were highly uncertain. The French had included in Acadia almost everything in sight. While they possessed it, they argued that not only did it comprise the whole Acadian peninsula but also Isle Royale, later Cape Breton, as well as present-day New Brunswick and a substantial part of the state of Maine. Thus it appears in early French maps and documents, while four separate censuses had included the mainland in the enumeration.

But when the Treaty of Utrecht awarded Acadia to the British, it shrank amazingly, and overnight. According to the revised views of French authorities, Acadia really included only the outer part of the peninsula. Obviously, they argued, it could not include the isthmus of Chignecto, which was the only possible route between Cape Breton and the mainland. This, of course, left Cape Breton, as well as the lands of New Brunswick and Maine, outside the new confines of Acadia.

All this resulted in a highly complicated argument. British and French commissioners meeting in lengthy session in Paris explored all the views and took evidence that filled four large volumes. They then dispersed, having decided nothing, so that eventually the boundaries had to be sought in less dignified ways.

If ever a conquered people were treated with consideration by their captors, it was the Acadians. That is not to argue any exceptional virtue on the part of the conquerors but rather a shrewd understanding of the situation that existed and a reasonable appraisal of the best way to meet it. If the reasons were practical rather than sentimental, the net result was generous and understanding treatment for people who represented a very stubborn breed indeed. This conquered people retained their land and freedom and the assurance of the exercise of their religion. The loyalty oath required of them was generous to a fault. If they preferred to leave, there was nothing to hinder them and they were permitted to take their goods and chattels with them.

The often-repeated French claim that they were refused permission to leave the country simply will not hold water. There were roughly nine thousand Acadians congregated in five or six centers. They outnumbered their captors more than three to one, and the latter were scattered everywhere about the country.

Unquestionably the English would have regretted to see the

Acadians leave, for the double reason that their going would leave the country all but devoid of sustenance, while if they moved with their possessions to Cape Breton they would increase the strength of Louisburg and so make an attack on Acadia appear almost a probability. If the Acadians didn't go, it was because they did not want to go.

As early as 1720 Governor Phillips, then in command in Acadia, wrote the British Secretary of State explaining the utter impossibility of preventing the Acadians from leaving. "Once joined in a body," he wrote, "with the help of the Indians to favor their retreat, they can march off at their leisure, by way of Bay Verte, with their effects, and destroy what they leave behind without danger of being molested."

The problem was not one of keeping them, for French efforts to induce them to move to Cape Breton or New Brunswick were effective only where force was used or where they were threatened with the anger of the Church. The problem was to assure their loyalty while they remained.

A few years before the conference at Alexandria, Shirley had written the British Prime Minister, the Duke of Newcastle, that if a thousand French troops should land in Nova Scotia all the Acadians and all the Indians would rise and join them. Since he felt so strongly, it was reasonable to assume that the New England governor was somewhat prejudiced. In that same year—1745—however, the French governor and intendant were expressing similar views. Writing the Colonial Minister, they urged: "The inhabitants wish to remain under the French dominion and will not hesitate to take up arms as soon as they see themselves free to do so . . . that is as soon as they have powder and other munitions of war and are backed by troops for their protection against the resentment of the English."

The beating heart of this continuing antagonism to the English was not any governor or official, whether English or French, but a priest, as strange and malignant a figure as appears in Canadian history. It was the Abbé Joseph Louis le Loutre. He had come from the Seminary of the Holy Spirit in Paris to be a missionary to the Micmacs at Shubenacadie. He became the vicar-general of the Bishop of Quebec, with the whole of Acadia as his parish. While he was serving at Shubenacadie he blandly pledged himself to the governor of Nova Scotia that he would maintain good order and keep the

French inhabitants faithful to their allegiance to Britain. The promise troubled him not at all. The Abbé le Loutre, whatever else he might have been, was a strong man, dowered with all the less admirable human qualities. He was a man of boundless egotism, with a lust for domination. There is no softer word to describe it. He was a man of unwavering opinion. His hatred of the English, even if we do not know what passion of mistaken patriotism caused it, was deep and abiding. It was bitterness and fanaticism in its very essence, and it was the moving spirit of his life.

He was a priest who had come to think in terms of violence. He could order a man scalped and with satisfaction could mark with his own hand and his own knife the course the scalping knife should take. He could set a price on such cruelty—a hundred livres for each English scalp—and could record with obvious care his two-year total, eleven thousand livres for "expenses and scalps."

He was not sensitive to treachery. It was to him a skilled profession. He could and did send emissaries under the flag of truce to the rough breastworks the English had raised at Beaubassin, and when Captain Howe came forward to meet them he could have his minions shoot him down in cold blood and then disown the act and lay the blame on savage exuberance. He could use his religion as a weapon to achieve his ends. When the unhappy Acadians had been induced by craft to cross from Beaubassin into French lands and, finding no subsistence there, pined for their deserted farms and petitioned Governor Duquesne for permission to return, he dealt with them sternly. They could remove their signatures from the appeal or have "neither sacrament in this life nor heaven in the next." He sent the Micmacs, to whom he had come as missionary, to watch the settlements at Chignecto and Windsor and Shubenacadie, and to destroy anyone who strayed beyond the slim protection these afforded. There were few, if any, like him in the great company of priests who move through the pages of Canadian history, more often than not adorning them with unparalleled accomplishment and sometimes touching them with a selfless devotion that has its own lonely splendor.

The Abbé le Loutre was not of this number. He did not do God's will but his own. He did not serve the Acadian people in wisdom or kindness or understanding. He worked to make his dream of dominion come true at whatever cost. A strange, strange figure of seemingly unvarnished evil. Yet in the day of Acadia's deepest sorrow, when some exiled themselves to a France they did not know and could not understand—a France that had no place for them—there Le Loutre found them at last and served them with a simple and unselfish devotion.

But one cannot think of him so. There are too many dark shadows in his past, and Governor Cornwallis, a man of gentle and generous impulse, was to describe him best: "a good for nothing scoundrel" —this he said as he placed an offer of a hundred pounds on his head.

It is understandable that where Le Loutre was, there also was trouble. His activities centered about Beaubassin near the head of the Cumberland Basin, an offshoot of Chignecto Bay. Here was the easiest point to lure the Acadians back to French lands, where they could be held pending the time that the word went out to retake Acadia for France.

Governor Cornwallis recognized this danger and moved to meet it. He sent Major Lawrence with four hundred men to take Beaubassin and to set up a post there to control this strategic territory. It was a bigger force than Le Loutre controlled, but the wily priest was far from beaten. If he couldn't hold the land, he could make it a desert. With his own hands he fired his village church, where he had said Mass so often. He urged his white and Indian followers to do as much for the village, and soon a hundred and forty homes were in flames. Too late the Acadians realized that they had been tricked again. There was no other course left but to follow where Le Loutre might lead.

He led to misery and to long months of cold, hunger, and loneliness. Even their fellow Frenchmen of the region were wearying of them and were happy when the authorities began to erect a post to face Fort Lawrence across the Missuguash River. Here Le Loutre put his dispossessed Acadians to work. It was a deal not unlike some we have known in our world today, in that the workers were fed—sparsely, it is true, but fed—but they were not paid. They were thinly clad, and winter was upon them. Soon it became obvious that they must receive wages enough to provide their most pressing needs. There were certainly those who still looked longingly homeward. For these Le Loutre had another approach. "If you go," he said, "you will have neither priests nor sacraments, but will die like miserable wretches." That was not true, of course, for under English rule they always had been guaranteed, and actually had, their priests and sacraments. But in their current misery, who was to remember that?

By spring those who survived saw the fort taking martial shape, and in the months following it became a place of first importance, commanding as it did the isthmus from Bay Verte to that of Fundy. On the strength of this new authority, Governor Jonquière issued an order. All Acadians were forthwith commanded to "take an oath of fidelity to the King of France, and to enroll themselves in the French militia on pain of being treated as rebels."

Small wonder that Governor Shirley, learning of such words, should have felt that the attempt to reoccupy Acadia, which he had feared for so long, was closer than he had thought. There was ample evidence. Only the year before the then Governor Duquesne had written to the Abbé le Loutre at Beauséjour: "I write both yourself and M. Vergor to devise a plausible pretext for attacking them." Meaning, of course, the unsuspecting English.

The M. Vergor mentioned was the commander of the fortress of Beauséjour, a dingy creature if there ever was one. He was the friend and confidant, the henchman of François Bigot, the intendant who did not pick men for their courage or their character, and so could use Louis duPont Chambon, Sieur de Vergor, who certainly had neither; but Vergor's day in the sun was drawing to a close, as will appear.

In Halifax, Major Lawrence, now Colonel, had also become the acting governor of Nova Scotia. He was the same who had taken Beaubassin and had built Fort Lawrence. He was a man shaped in a less gentle mold than his predecessor, Cornwallis. Perhaps he had seen that turning the other cheek had not served with people trained under the cracking whip of the Abbé le Loutre. Just as Shirley had wanted to move against the French and needed Cornwallis' aid, Lawrence now wanted to move and needed the aid of Shirley. He sent Lieutenant Colonel Monckton to Boston with a letter. It was direct and forceful: "Being informed that the French have designs of encroaching still further upon His Majesty's rights in the province," the letter said, ". . . I think it high time to make some effort to drive them from the north side of the Bay of Fundy." As a practical detail he suggested that Shirley should supply two thousand men for the purpose.

Never was there a happier exchange of opinion, for Shirley's letter, which crossed that borne by Monckton, suggested that the French of Canada might be driven out of Nova Scotia, and Shirley added: "I will endeavor to send you such assistance from this province as you shall want."

With two men of direct action sharing the same opinion there was little suggestion of delay. Shirley, as commander in chief of Massachusetts as well as governor, commissioned John Winslow to raise two thousand volunteers. Rather characteristically, perhaps, when the first regiment was formed Shirley appointed himself its colonel. He still had the thirst for glory. However, he admitted rather sadly that it was a nominal rank. The real commander of the first battalion was Winslow, with George Scott heading the second and Lieutenant Colonel Monckton in over-all command.

It was five o'clock on the morning of June 2, 1755, when a settler who lived near the Bay of Fundy, about two leagues from the fort, appeared before the startled sentry at the gateway. What he had to say was scarcely believable. He had been up before dawn at the hopeless task of tilling his infertile acres when, looking up where the morning mists were lifting from the water, his startled eyes saw an impossible vision—a great fleet of forty ships riding at anchor, waiting for the tide to permit them to enter Beaubassin.

Startled as they were, unbelieving as they were, the guards hurried him in to the presence of the equally startled Sieur de Vergor, who commanded the fort with its thirty-two guns and mortars and its one hundred and fifty regulars of the Canadian marines.

Vergor was all but paralyzed with fear, and his first and almost only thought was to hurry off couriers to Quebec, to the St. John River, to Louisburg, and to Isle St. Jean, the only points from which he might hope to secure assistance. So intent on enterprises more profitable to himself, he had done nothing toward strengthening the defenses of Beauséjour, which should have been equal to challenging the attacking force—something in the neighborhood of two thousand, including the garrison of Fort Lawrence.

It was a strong position and might readily have been made virtually impregnable but for the acquisitiveness of De Vergor and the fact that the Abbé le Loutre was more interested in pressing some buildings at Rivière du Lac. This left few of the Acadians except the old and the incompetent to work at the fort itself.

Jacau de Fiedmont, there being no military engineer present, had been deputed to act in that capacity. He did his best, but it was in the face of a vast spirit of inertia. He writes in his journal of the siege that "the confidence that peace would continue was so deeply impressed on the minds of those who lived in the district that it was impossible to awaken the slightest alarm. We continued," he observes, "to enjoy a sense of security as perfect as though we were residing in the center of Paris."

That happy sense of security was ill founded. Perhaps, had the fort been strengthened in accordance with the original plans, or if leadership had been different, there might have been a more heroic story. But the Sieur de Vergor had wasted no money or effort in strengthening defenses; nothing, at least, beyond some wails for help.

There was no reason to expect that he would. Louis duPont Chambon, Sieur de Vergor, was the son of that Governor Duchambon who had been in command at Louisburg when that great fortress was attacked by William Pepperrell and Commodore Warren. The father's far from inspired defense of that great fortress can only be considered minutely impressive in comparison with the even feebler showing of the son at Fort Beauséjour.

It must be admitted that De Vergor was not given command by reason of outstanding military qualities. It was an appointment straight from what we of today would speak of as "the pork barrel." While acting as a young officer at Louisburg, De Vergor had met and become an intimate of one who, among other notable qualities, was a capable debaucher of his associates. François Bigot, then intendant at Louisburg, had discovered young De Vergor and found in him a kindred spirit. As intendant of all Canada, Bigot had succeeded in having his favorite appointed to the command at Beauséjour. It was one of the plums that were within his gift. He did even better than that. He saw to it that De Vergor was also given charge of its supply and financing. This provided opportunities neither very complex nor very novel. Loyalty to the French King, it appeared, did not always mean that one might not at the same time defraud him. The practice was often simple. Sometimes it involved charging the King for supplies that existed only in the mind of the commander; sometimes selling actual supplies that had been sent to meet the requirements of the garrison.

De Vergor had not devised these niceties of administration for himself. Prior to his departure to his new post Bigot had written him with a candor that bespeaks their community of thinking. "Profit, my dear Vergor, by your opportunities," wrote the intendant. "Trim, cut—you have the power—in order that you may very soon join me in France and purchase an estate near me."

De Vergor had cut and trimmed as ordered. So nothing was finished, nothing was adequate. We know of these lacks through the journal of Lieutenant Jacau de Fiedmont, which has remained to tell of these events. De Fiedmont was working feverishly to repair the lack in the face of an overwhelming apathy. "It was after seven in the morning," he writes, "before the men came to work, and very few of them did a hand's turn." There were some more determined spirits. It is recorded that Abbé le Loutre was to be seen about "in his shirt sleeves, with a pipe in his mouth, directing the Acadians in their work of strengthening the fortifications." De Fiedmont and Le Loutre had this much in common—a single-minded will to defeat the English. It was not so with the Acadian defenders. When word came from the governor of Louisburg that no help was to be expected from that source, these defenders were profoundly unwilling to sacrifice in vain.

When their lesser protests were disregarded, De Fiedmont's journal records, "The settlers went in a body to the commandant, to demand that he should capitulate, saying that if there were any opposition to the decision they had reached in the matter, they would no longer respect the garrison, whose threats they did not fear in the least, and would turn their arms against the officers and the soldiers, and deliver the fort to the English."

It was not a laudable gesture, but it had become rather typical of a people who through terror and misunderstanding had grown accustomed to siding with the winner. At least it was a challenge that demanded some courage. The commandant had no equal courage to reply; no decisiveness to meet an open threat. There had been no direct assault, and the cannon fire that had touched the fort had done relatively little damage and occasioned few casualties, yet De Vergor had seen enough. When in reply to his request for terms Monckton agreed that the commander and his garrison could march out with "arms, baggage, drums beating, fuses burning," he was satisfied.

So also were the Acadians. They had been treated with customary gentleness. They were assured that they "would not be molested for having taken up arms," on the assumption that they were compelled to do so.

Commander de Vergor did not fare so well. He lost a profitable position that he had not yet fully capitalized. On his return to Quebec he was tried by court-martial but was acquitted, possibly through the support of his good friend Intendant Bigot. One more inglorious moment was reserved for Louis Chambon de Vergor before his name was happily forgotten. It was he who raised the curtain on almost the last dramatic scene of New France in the New World.

The fall of Beauséjour and the adjoining fort of Gaspereau, which was even more hurriedly abandoned, hadn't settled anything. The three hundred Acadians, supposed subjects of Britain, who had been part of the garrison, had been forgiven and permitted to return to their old lands and presumably to their old allegiance. Probably it seemed to them that everything had settled down into the accustomed ways as had happened so often.

There were factors, however, that the simple-minded Acadians simply could not evaluate. There was Governor Shirley's fixed conviction that France was still planning to repossess Acadia. Shirley would argue for the removal of the priests and the most troublesome of the Acadians and the substitution of colonists from New England. There was the fact that, for the time at least, Charles Lawrence was the acting governor, and Lawrence had been brought up a soldier and had imbibed the strict traditions of that caste and the belief that sentiment was not a sound substitute for basic realities.

He had learned by long association that the Acadians were an obdurate people, impossible as allies and dangerous as the neutrals they claimed to be. There was threat of stormy action in Europe and there was the more present threat of a great French fleet harboring at Louisburg. There was the knowledge, too, that Halifax, born with such high hopes, had not been able to keep its people enthused. Men had grown older and many of the colonists had been too old in the beginning. The hard reality of clearing the forest and sowing the land, and waiting endlessly for the harvest, had been too much for many.

The innumerable Micmac raids, stimulated by Le Loutre, that had bloodied pioneer doorsteps had been too hard a challenge for the uncertain and timid. They had drifted away. Halifax, after six years, was scarcely as large as it had been when the new colonists had first landed. Now word had come that the great expedition of Braddock, which was to have challenged the power of the French in the west, had ended in Braddock's death and his overwhelming defeat. And while all this was so, Lawrence had word that the French at Louisburg were receiving both information and supplies from the so-called neutral French in Acadia.

Lawrence was a stern but not a hard man. He merely held to a seemingly undebatable point stated long ago on unchallengeable authority: "He that is not with me is against me." He decided to put an end forever to a neutrality that wasn't neutral. He sent word to Monckton to hold his forces at Beauséjour, and he ordered the elected delegates of the Acadians to appear at Halifax for an accounting.

Lawrence met the delegates with a stern face. He told them he had but one word for them: Their people must take the oath of allegiance without qualification. The representatives were not unduly disturbed. Faced with such demands before, they had refused and the roof had not fallen on them. A night to think over their answer didn't change their opinion, though it sobered them a little. They protested that they would do nothing against the British. It was a familiar response. It had been given before, but at a word from Le Loutre or the suggestion of pressure they had done what they were told. Reluctantly perhaps, at times, but still as they were told. Now once again the representatives of the people faced authority and refused to take the oath.

Lawrence was in an unenviable position. Given a blank refusal, he had relatively little authority to challenge it. There had indeed been such refusals in the past, and Britain had done nothing on those occasions. Perhaps they had considered some definite action, but there had always been the fact that it would probably be costly. If Lawrence gave any of this a thought it does not appear. He notified the Board of Trade in England that he had ordered the Acadians to elect a new group of representatives to appear before him to accept the oath for their people. Should these also refuse—he did not ask permission but stated—he would "rid the province of such perfidious subjects."

There is nothing new in this proposal to expel a difficult and intractable population as a necessary measure of successful conflict. It has been part of warfare through all generations, and it certainly was not unknown in the days under review. Louis XIV, sending Frontenac back to Canada, had accepted with enthusiasm Callières' proposal to dispossess the English in New York and either deport them entirely or scatter them among the various colonies so that never again could they be united. Louis had actually charged

Frontenac to put this plan into effect and, had it been possible, it would have been done.

Sir William Phips, had he been successful at Quebec, might have done something of the kind. There are documents relating the various plans, if not of moving the whole Canadian population, at least of removing their spiritual leaders. With a people so devout this was almost the same thing. Louisburg when first built had needed population sorely, and when the Acadians about Canseau, and more or less under the protection of the English, had refused to go, the King's thoughts had turned to the small French settlement at Placentia Bay, Newfoundland. These people had had no will to leave, but Governor Costebelle had received orders from Louis XIV's own hand that willy-nilly they should be moved to Louisburg.

Perhaps it might even be remembered that the United Empire Loyalists, who could not see eye to eye with the American colonists in revolutionary attitudes, may not have been expelled by law, but being profoundly out of accord with the thinking of the majority, they found life intolerable and they had no option but to leave their lands and possessions and to seek the shelter of a political system with which they could agree.

This is not to argue that a strict right existed to justify such happenings, only that it was accepted practice. Indeed the evacuation of whole populations certainly has been known in our day and, had these actions been carried out with a patience and humanity equal to that evident in this sad incident, it is not doubtful that a world conscience might have accepted it, regretfully perhaps, as a necessary military precaution.

The sober truth is that most of our thinking on this unhappy incident is not derived from accepted records but from the imaginings of a New England poet more deeply moved by a romantic situation than by the truth of history. He made Evangeline a living figure of protest of whom people might think with nostalgic fervor. He built that imaginary figure into a reality that could be crystallized in poignant monuments. He spoke to his own New England world that, with him, could still see the embattled farmers standing nearby and could still hear the shot that echoed round a world. This was something he knew, something that flowed in his blood, coloring his thinking and perhaps distorting it a little, however he tried to make his record just.

Henry Wadsworth Longfellow knew Concord well and perhaps

couldn't be quite free of the prejudice that made the Englishman the traditional enemy. He didn't know Grand Pré or Beaubassin and could not recognize the patience that, however great, must sometimes have an end. And Acadia had known it for thirty-odd years. But Longfellow, whose great romantic story has moved generations of people, never thought to make it clear that there had been a long probation and that its sad end was the result of a failure to understand that no one can serve two masters.

The poet's story failed, too, in making what to history is an obvious point—that the English had no will or wish to dispossess the Acadians. They did not even realize that when they had returned Louisburg to the French they had made expulsion inevitable, since it left the threat of French imperial dreams on this continent naked for anyone to see; and William Shirley and his like saw it clearly. Should France recover not only Louisburg but Acadia as well, the "woful years" would begin again. New England could not be safe, nor could any of the coastal colonies, with an unassimilated enemy on their defenseless flanks. That was the judgment, and not any act of Monckton or Lawrence or Winslow.

Argue it however one may, tragedy isn't less tragic because in a considerable measure it is deserved. So there remains the bitter final chapter of a devoted people, who were gentle and industrious and kind and devout, but who added to those qualities an amazing stubbornness and a wholly blind loyalty. All that they really asked was to be left alone. That could so easily have been had they not entrusted these loyalties to the man who could destroy them, the Abbé le Loutre. Of him that fine historian, Dr. George M. Wrong, was to write a fitting evaluation: "He was the priest in politics, who brings to secular affairs the burning conviction that his enemies are the enemies of God."

The new representatives of the Acadians had been elected. They understood why, and were not unduly perturbed by the knowledge that they would again be asked to take the oath of allegiance. It was a game with which they were more than passing familiar. Always in the past refusal to agree had resulted in compromise of one sort or another, and there was no realization that the situation had changed. They were not people of learning or experience, these Acadians. They were simple folk whose horizons were their own farms' acres. How could they sense that a life-and-death struggle of two warring ideologies was shaping before their eyes? Perhaps it is not surprising that after almost forty years of efforts to conciliate them they should not recognize easily that the days of conciliation were over.

Governor Lawrence had met with his council, and the word had gone out throughout the province that an unqualified oath of allegiance should be demanded of everyone who had not already taken it. The Acadians responded according to their old accepted practice. Deputations from various districts went to Halifax to protest the stern directness of the oath. They wanted a stipulation freeing them from the obligation of bearing arms. They argued that their priests should be free of any form of supervision. They completely overlooked that it was the Abbé le Loutre and those who were under his direction who had brought them to this pass. They had no explanation as to why many among them had joined with French troops to defend strongholds or to attack English garrisons. They did not recognize, apparently, that among them were those who actively or passively had been a part of many a bloody raid on an English community.

Governor Lawrence was a stern man, but he had no wish to push the Acadians to desperate action. He was ready to make some concession for the moment in regard to demanding military service from the Acadians. He reminded them of the long years of considerate treatment with no compensating results. He urged them to understand how impossible it was to continue such treatment without the assurance that they would be loyal to the English Crown. It was to no end. Le Loutre and his associates had done their work too well. In the hearts of a simple and deeply devout people, the English had been made to appear a people beyond the pale of God. Subservience to such had but one end, eternal damnation. So the Acadians had been taught, and so they believed. The sum of it was that the representatives of a people stolidly refused to take the oath. One cannot escape a grudging admiration for a stupidity so consistent.

Governor Lawrence, standing before them white-faced and stern and unrelenting, spoke his quiet words of doom. "Then," he said, "you are no longer subjects of the King of England but of the King of France. You will be treated as such and removed from the country."

They could not believe the words they heard. They were so different, so direct, so final. But little by little the sense of reality came to them. It was the time to appear to submit. Such an attitude had not failed in the past. So the delegates returned and again faced the governor, but now it was a sterner figure. He didn't plead or argue any more. He faced them gravely, realizing only too well that these were old tactics. Concede only where concessions become imperative.

It was mid-July, and Acadia basked in the sun, a promised land indeed. But there was no promise for frozen hearts. They waited for what might come. It came with the march of feet. The King's soldiers in five companies covering the favored lands the Acadians had made their own. For a while they seemed to do nothing. At Fort Cumberland, which had once been known as Beauséjour, young Colonel Monckton waited for the hour while John Winslow and his blue-uniformed New England soldiery sailed away for the Basin of Minas.

The men of the section were bringing in the harvest when Winslow's summons came to them. They were to gather at the church in Grand Pré to hear the King's orders. Winslow was a kindly man and had no love for his task, but he was a soldier under orders, and he was supported by the bayonets of his New England militia. He read the sober words to a hushed and unbelieving people.

"Your lands and tenements and cattle and livestock of all kinds are forfeit to the Crown with all your other effects, except money and household goods, and that you yourselves are to be removed from this province."

Over the murmur of words his voice went on:

"Through His Majesty's goodness I am directed to allow you the liberty of carrying with you your money and as many of your household goods as you can take without overloading the vessels you go in."

There were other details. "I shall do everything in my power that all these goods be secured to you–and also that whole families shall go in the same vessel; so that this removal . . . may be made as easy as His Majesty's service will permit. . . ." And the words went on. "It is His Majesty's pleasure that you remain in security under the inspection and direction of the troops that I have the honor to command."

Day followed day and the "prisoners of the King" still waited, still unbelieving. There was danger in the growing desperation of this group. So they were separated; the younger and more dangerous were sent aboard five Boston ships then lying in the river nearby. Thinking they were being separated from their families, they had to be prodded aboard by the bayonets of Winslow's soldiery. It was weeks later that the ships, laden with united families, sailed away. Winslow sighed in relief. "This affair," he wrote to a friend, "is more grievous to me than any service I was ever employed in."

From his post not so far distant Captain Murray wrote to Winslow, congratulating him on the success of this first movement. "I am extremely pleased," he wrote, "that the poor devils are so resigned. Here they were more patient than I would have expected." He added, "But I long to see the poor wretches embarked and our affairs a little settled."

Ships were few and slow. In November, Winslow reported that nine vessels had sailed, carrying fifteen hundred and ten persons. It was December before all the six hundred remaining had been at last embarked. Winslow, too, was happy to see the end of an unpleasant task. "It hurts me to hear them weeping and wailing," he said. "Thank God, the transports are gone at last."

When the last of the vessels had sailed away to distribute their unhappy burden among the English colonies, their cargoes of human souls were totaled. It was a little over six thousand. Many had escaped and had joined with the guerrilla bands or had gone to Canada or Isle St. Jean. Many lurked in the forests and eventually drifted back to their old haunts.

Maybe it was the end of an ordeal for these, as it was for Winslow, but the ordeal did not end so swiftly for the many. It was idle to expect that the English colonies would rejoice at their coming. They were a troublesome people; all the reports made this very clear. They were Catholics in what were mainly Protestant communities, and in days when tolerance wasn't ranked among the virtues. Virginia would have nothing to do with them but promptly shipped the six hundred who were assigned to her to England, where they languished until the end of the Seven Years' War permitted their return to France. South Carolina felt the same way, as did Georgia. The best the Carolina governor would do was provide a couple of ships and send them on their way. These finally found a harborage about the St. John River.

The colonies that were more familiar with the Acadians treated them no better. Maryland, it is true, with its large Catholic population, did treat them with some humanity, but it could not care for many. New England did its sober unappreciative best. It accepted the expatriates because somebody had to, but it scattered them in unhappy little groups in scores of localities so that they might not form their own communities again. Many took the long road to Quebec.

Perhaps a quarter of them reached there or scattered near the border. They had no better treatment here, and many were close to starvation. The intendant Bigot did see in their unhappy plight an opportunity to approach the French court for aid. But when the aid arrived he saw to it that little was wasted on these unhappy exiles, while the bulk of it found its way into his own coffers.

In the story of Evangeline, many of the Acadians reached Louisiana, as indeed they did, drawn by the need to be with other Frenchmen. In the bayou country about St. Martinsville they created, as closely as they could, a replica of their old home. There they are living today much as they lived in Acadia two centuries ago, for the real desire of their hearts was for a status quo—a world that didn't change.

When one remembers their lovely country along the shores of Fundy, it is not hard to understand. But it was a hopeless ideal. Worlds do change and people cannot continue to live in the past, however gracious. When the wars were over, many found their way back and were not disturbed. After them came many others of this lonely, stubborn breed, to find their homes again, home to the old life, and the old lovely land, and the old certain religion—but not to the old priest.

The Abbé le Loutre, whom Captain John Knox had known well and was to speak of as "a most remarkable character of inhumanity," had suffered the chastening of eight years in a Jersey Island castle, a prisoner of the English he hated, and had then returned to the service of his people in France.

But in the Acadian pulpit where the bitter man once stood was another abbé speaking to these returned folk. The Abbé Jean Sigoigne had a different message. "To France may go your hearts," he said, "but to England must go your fealty and faith." How easily such words two centuries earlier might have taken from the book of history one of its unhappiest chapters.

CHAPTER XXIV

CAPTAINS COURAGEOUS

The "magnificent conspiracy" in Europe brings war to America also. Montcalm is given command and meets the embittered antagonism of Governor Vaudreuil. Oswego's capture leads to the challenge to Fort William Henry; its tragic story a blot on Montcalm's great name. Pitt, coming to power in Britain, brings new vigor. Death of Lord Howe and Abercrombie's amazing stubbornness result in a great victory for Montcalm. It is France's last flash of glory, followed by the loss of Fort Frontenac and of Fort Duquesne. The only hope is peace.

THE winter of 1755–56 was not a happy one, either in the New World or the Old. In New France harvests had been scant and the threat of famine hung over the land. This threat was always present in varying degrees. How could it be otherwise with a people so few in number and so indifferent to the cultivation of the soil? This year they had to hope for more generous treatment than usual from the homeland, though there was little evidence to justify the expectation.

The events of recent months, happening as they did in the piping days of peace, were certainly warlike enough to jeopardize the always uncertain friendships of Europe. If war didn't come immediately, it wasn't due to friendliness. Peace would last for a moment, until someone again rattled a saber in Europe, and neither England nor France was ready for such a gesture. But Europe had just the man for it in Frederick of Prussia. He would be known later, and with very good reason, as "The Great," though his greatness was a matter of earned power rather than of diplomacy.

Saber rattling from such a source was music to the ears of one sovereign of Europe. Maria Theresa of Austria had her own score to settle with Frederick, and this would offer the opportunity. At the moment she was busily and secretly using her own not inconsiderable diplomatic gifts aligning Europe against him. It was not a difficult task. Maria Theresa, of course, was bent on recovering Silesia, which Frederick had taken from Austria, and though other attempts had failed she was still determined to succeed.

No one did more to help her than Frederick himself. He had a corrosive sense of humor and a capacity for using it in the wrong places. At that time it might be said that three women dominated the politics of Europe. There was nothing that Frederick could do to establish himself in the favor of Maria Theresa short of returning Silesia, which he had not the slightest intention of doing. He could, however, have spared himself the open enmity of the other two. It did not occur to him. Madame la Pompadour was all too frequently the subject of his jests. It must be admitted these were somewhat lacking in refinement. They made no pretense of overlooking her anomalous position. Unlike Maria Theresa, who wrote La Pompadour frequently with every evidence of good will, addressing her as "My Dear Cousin," Frederick, on receiving a letter of congratulation from her, returned it with the terse comment that he did not know this person. But Madame la Pompadour, whatever her virtues or lack of them, did govern the indolent and—to her—docile Louis XV. Through him she as surely governed his ministers and the realm of France.

As if that unwise sally weren't enough, Frederick's pleasantries played with another royal lady's predilection for personable grenadiers. This was undeniably injudicious, for whatever her tastes, Elizabeth Petrovna was Empress of Russia, with the arbitrary powers that suggests.

These three women, then, for varying reasons, shared a common desire to humble Frederick and to remove the ever-present threat he represented. It was a chance too promising to be missed, and soon the three were joined by others—by Sweden and Saxony and most of the German states, producing what William Pitt was to call "the most powerful and malignant confederacy that ever yet has threatened the independence of mankind."

Against this "malignant confederacy" there was only Prussia with Frederick at its head, Frederick with his impoverished kingdom, his five million subjects, and his amazing military skill. It could not have seemed that to side with the one against the many was a very attractive prospect, and it is doubtful if anyone but Pitt was to see in these events the one false move that would destroy France's dream of an empire of the West or to recognize in Frederick the genius who might make a mockery of impossible odds.

Britain's position was almost determined by her traditional policy of opposition to France. But there was one other and more practical reason. George II had his cherished principality of Hanover to consider, and without Frederick's aid it would not be very happily situated.

If France also had little to gain and much to lose by siding against Frederick, there were still arguments that ranked high with Louis XV. It would please La Pompadour, who on her part would go to any lengths to please an empress who had treated her so graciously. Also, Prussia, like England, was Protestant. That made Louis ready to include it among his foes. He had a conscience that had never prevented him from doing anything he wished, but he couldn't escape so readily the fear that the result might be ultimate damnation. He therefore held the hope that joining Catholic Austria against Protestant Britain and Prussia might weigh the scales a little to his advantage. It became to him, therefore, a holy war, and he entered it with an exaltation that was hardly justified and with a shocking lack of foresight.

Apparently it hadn't occurred to Louis that the fortunes of France lay in the West rather than in a bickering Europe. It didn't even occur to him to make his contribution moderate; that, having promised to contribute twenty-four thousand men to the cause, it might have been left at that. Instead he immediately increased the force to a hundred thousand and added cash that France could not afford. He didn't recognize that, in doing so, he had crossed his Rubicon.

In May, France signed her treaty of alliance with Austria, and a little more than two weeks later Britain countered by declaring war on France. Both acts were futile gestures in themselves. France was joining Austria to recover Silesia from Frederick of Prussia, who probably wouldn't have had it but that France had helped him secure it. For herself, France had little to gain, and if she had a continent to lose, she hadn't yet discovered it.

Britain's position was little better. She had even less to gain and smaller chance of achieving it. It was the same Britain of which Lord Chesterfield had tearfully complained that it was "no longer a nation." It still had as its head the pompous and weak and arrogant Duke of Newcastle. He was so little prepared for the step his government had taken that it was said that in all England there were only three regiments fit and ready for service. There was nothing in Britain's recent history to encourage an attitude of optimism. Dieskau may have been defeated, various forts taken, and the Acadians expelled from their lands. These were happenings that touched only the fringes. It was still quite clear that France in the New World was unassailed and apparently unassailable—from Louisiana on its southern gulf to Louisburg guarding another—a frontier of almost four thousand miles that nowhere was really challenged.

No one in France seemed to have a very deep interest in what was happening in the New World. Even if Louis had entered a costly war on the side of Austria, with whom France had mainly been at odds, and if the only possible tangible gain was a troublesome bit of Belgium that Austria might concede as France's share of the possible loot, still France was undoubtedly with him.

To the young noblesse and the private soldier with whom dying was too familiar to occasion much thought, there were still preferences. If it had to be, better in the fields of Flanders, which were at least reasonably near Paris, than in a more highly unpleasant fashion in the distant forests of New France.

So while Louis was gathering a hundred thousand men and much money for this new and unprofitable venture in the Old World, a much more modest force was being sent to the New. It consisted of only two regiments, though they were tough and well-trained troops with a fine reputation. The regiments were the La Sarre and the Royal Roussillon. These, added to the five seasoned regiments that had accompanied Dieskau (and had suffered relatively little loss since his defeat and capture), made up a force that the harried military authorities in Paris believed would be ample to meet any situation that might arise.

There was, of course, a matter of leadership to be considered. With Dieskau's capture, the military forces in Canada were under the command of Governor Vaudreuil. It is true that he considered himself more than equal to this added task, but it was not a confidence shared by the authorities in France.

That was the situation in the late fall of 1755 when the Marquis de Montcalm, a brigadier in the French Army, happening to be in Paris, dropped in for a word with an old friend, D'Argenson, the Minister of War. The visit was merely a social gesture, a word of farewell as Montcalm returned to his estate at Candiac, but it served to recall him to the minister's attention. Whether through this or because Montcalm had already been considered, the minister hinted that there was just a possibility of an appointment to command the forces in Canada. The marquis accepted it as a friendly gesture, nothing more. He had no wish for such a charge. His only thought was to return to his family and the warmth of his own lands, and the oak and the olive groves that surrounded his Château of Candiac not far from the city of Nîmes.

It was the end of January when the letter came that was to separate Montcalm forever from all that he loved best: his devoted mother, his wife, his six living children, and from Candiac, which had been a part of the lives of the Montcalms for more years than men could remember.

The letter was dated from Versailles at midnight of the twenty-fifth of January. "Perhaps, monsieur," it began, "you did not expect to hear from me again on the subject of the conversation I had with you the day you came to bid me farewell at Paris. Nevertheless, I have not forgotten for a moment the suggestion I then made you; and it is with the greatest pleasure that I announce to you that my views have prevailed. The King has chosen you to command his troops in North America, and will honor you on your departure with the rank of major general."

Louis Joseph, Marquis de Montcalm-Gozon de St. Véran, came from a line almost as old as France itself. Always they had served their King as soldiers. They were good soldiers, as the records tell. But they were not always fortunate. There is a maxim that attaches to the name that suggests it. "War," it says, "is the grave of the Montcalms."

The child who was born at Candiac on the twenty-ninth of February, 1712, was to hold his home in his abiding love through all his life. He was a studious child with an early delight in books. Perhaps this taste was encouraged by his tutor, one Dumas, a relative. In reporting a certain shortcoming in Greek and Latin, the tutor notes philosophically that it is better to be ignorant of these than to be without knowledge of "how to read, write, and speak French well." At other times he records that his charge has "great need of docility, industry, and willingness to take advice." Obviously the tutor is not in a happy mood, for he concludes in sorrow, "What will become of him?" a thought that must have crossed the mind of many a dominie before and since with as little reason for despair.

It must be, too, that the encouragement to read and write had its reward in the easy grace of his letters. In one of the earliest of these young Montcalm writes to his father his own estimate of what his aims should be. "First, to be an honorable man, of good morals, brave, and a Christian. Secondly, to read in moderation: to know as much Greek and Latin as most men of the world; also the four rules of arithmetic, and something of history, geography, and French *belles-lettres*, as well as to have good taste for the arts and sciences. Thirdly, and above all, to be obedient, docile, and very submissive to your orders and those of my dear mother; and also to defer to the advice of M. Dumas. Fourthly, to fence and ride as well as my small abilities will permit."

If these aims seem a little too pat, a little too perfect to be the thoughts of an average growing boy, it is to be remembered that in an age rather notable for its licentiousness and self-seeking and pandering to authority, none of these things appears in his record either as boy or man.

At the age of fifteen he joined the army as a lieutenant and was a captain two years later, a commission purchased by his father, as was the custom of the day. Within six years his father was dead and young Montcalm had acceded to the title and the estate of Candiac, which was substantial in size and as substantially embarrassed by debt.

Not long after his father's death the young marquis married Angélique Louise Talon du Boulay. Strangely enough, she was a near relative of Talon, Canada's great intendant. It was an advantageous marriage, as the custom of the time would have argued. The bride's connections were influential, and she brought some property to add to that of Candiac. But if it was an arranged marriage, history records few that have been happier or marked by a greater mutual devotion. There were ten children born of the marriage, but only six were living in 1752 when Montcalm was confessing in his journal that even that number "is large for so moderate a fortune, especially as four of them are girls." But he added his own sober thanks. "May God preserve them all and make them prosper for this world and the next."

The years that followed were mostly years of war and wounds and slow promotion. Montcalm was beginning to be noticed. When the campaign in Bohemia ended he was invested with a knighthood in the Order of St. Louis and was given the command of a regiment. He fought with it, almost continuously, for three years. In the terrific battle with the Austrians under the walls of Piacenza he was seriously wounded, captured, and finally paroled. While still on parole he was made a brigadier, so that on his rejoining the army he could command more than one regiment. When his parole arrived he went to the army in Italy, where he was again badly wounded. Before he was recovered peace had been signed at Aix-la-Chapelle. There followed seven years of peace with his family at Candiac. They were perhaps the happiest years of his life. It is easy to believe that he was reluctant to accept a promotion that took him so far afield. But duty was too firmly ingrained for any argument.

That was not so with his wife. Through her relationship with Talon she knew something of the life in the New World and its continuing hazards, and it is not impossible that from the same source she may have learned something of the slow deterioration under Vaudreuil and Bigot. She feared the fate that might meet Montcalm in this distant land. Angélique Montcalm did her best to persuade her husband to find some way of evading the appointment. But, deep as was his love for her, his obedience was to his mother, who lived with them at Candiac. The aged Marquise de St. Véran would have nothing to do with such weakness. In her spartan code the word of the King was an inescapable obligation. There was only one course: to obey without question.

Montcalm was quickly away and, like any deeply devoted son and husband, was reporting promptly on all his actions. "Last night I came from Versailles, and am going back tomorrow. The King gives me twenty-five thousand francs a year, as he did M. Dieskau, besides twelve thousand for my equipment, which will cost me about a thousand crowns more; but I cannot stop for that. I embrace my dearest and all the family."

On the eighteenth of March he writes from Rennes to his wife, like any tourist: "I arrived, dearest, this morning, and stay here all day. I shall be at Brest on the twenty-first and everything will be on board on the twenty-sixth." He tells of meeting with his son, whose increased rank requires a new uniform, and of his own plans to take his leave wearing his own embroidered coat—of his fears that he might leave debts behind—and his impatience to see the bills. There is a last word, too, about his will. His health, he reports, is good, and adds that there will be time to rest on the voyage. It is all human and actual and familiar. "I embrace you," he adds to his mother, "and my dearest," so he speaks always of and to his wife, "and my daughters. Love to all the family. I shall write up to the last moment." Truly a picture of a simple, affectionate, dedicated man.

Montcalm was fortunate in his staff, or he had chosen well. His second-in-command is Gaston François, Chevalier de Lévis, who later was to be created a duke and a marshal of France. "I like the Chevalier de Lévis," Montcalm recorded simply, "and I think he likes me." How very human that is. Bourlamaque was the third in line. He was a quiet, reserved man and mainly silent. Montcalm with his volatile temper found him hard to understand at first. But he was to recognize quickly the keen mind and the discriminating observer behind the silent exterior; recognize, too, that here was another fine soldier to be trusted implicitly.

Young Louis Antoine, Comte de Bougainville, was a man after Montcalm's own heart. He was new to the army, but newness did not depress him. Everything he saw pleased and excited him. It was not the pleasure of an inactive mind, for young Bougainville, who was not yet twenty-six, had been for some years the author of a treatise on the integral calculus and was already well known in the world of science. So much so, indeed, that even as a youth, and a French youth at that, he had been elected a fellow of the Royal Society of England.

Montcalm, himself of a studious mind, could readily find himself in accord with a man of intelligence who had also a cheerful and contented mind. It was Bougainville who wrote a graphic record of the voyage to Canada and the happenings then and after. He tells of the troops marching into Brest and going aboard ship "with an incredible gaiety," a record that may have been a reflection of his own happy heart. "What a nation is ours," he writes. "Happy he who commands it, and commands it worthily." Bougainville must also have had an innocent heart to be able to reflect on Louis XV commanding anything worthily.

But if there were good friends there were also enemies. Montcalm did not know of it as he wrote his wife of the long voyage with the word that he had not been ill though the weather had been rough, filling in the details of fog and iceberg, and the taste of the cod that had been caught and eaten with a fine relish. He told that his plan had been to eat little and drink much lemonade, and other homely details. But there were two men who, while he was writing his simple story, were planning how best to meet this new challenge. Through no fault of his they were to be his implacable enemies, and they both outranked him. They were the governor and the intendant, the two highest officers of the Crown.

Governor Vaudreuil's antagonism stemmed from the fact that he was a vain, jealous, and opinionated man. He had been chosen for the post, not because of abilities that anyone could see, but because he was a man of station who had been born in Canada. The son of the first Governor Vaudreuil, he was never his father's equal. The father had been too big to find any jealousy in his heart. Not so the son. He did his assiduous best to undermine a better man.

The other enemy was not far to seek. François Bigot, the shrewdest, craftiest knave of all Canadian history, knew that Montcalm posed the first real threat to his far-reaching power. Bigot had no fear of the people. They were too poor and helpless, too lacking in any voice that authority would respect to be anything but victims of such as he. He didn't fear the noblesse. He had tampered with them, given them dreams of wealth and position and pleasure. Some he had silenced by fear of his displeasure and his ranging power to harm. More he had debauched. They were in his power, one way or another, compounding his evil acts, sharing in the avails of wickedness.

He had nothing to fear from a governor whom he could outmatch in cleverness, whose vanity made him an easy dupe of a wily man.

Bigot had been feeling his way carefully before Vaudreuil came. Duquesne was not a man with whom anyone would tangle. But there had been others who were more amenable, and there would be again. Bigot could wait, making small, crafty turns, toying with minor depravity, always keeping within the distant shadow of the law. But when he had appraised the new governor he knew that precautions were no longer necessary. He had somebody who could be handled as only Bigot knew how. The governor was jealous and small-minded. He loved pomp and the semblance of power and, more than all, he loved adulation. Thinking of himself as a great man, he was easily won to anyone who would build up his impression of power, by whatever means.

With such subtle approaches the governor was happy to sign any orders that the astutely deferential intendant might ask. Bigot did not fear France. It was too far away and too easily confused by the apparent accord between governor and intendant to be a danger. The only thing that gave Bigot pause was an incorruptible man and, shrewd appraiser that he was, Bigot sensed that Montcalm was that man.

Governor Vaudreuil was in Montreal when Montcalm arrived, but Bigot was on hand and, with his consummate guile, was prepared to lend a tone of rejoicing to the occasion. A great banquet was held in the intendant's palace. Most of the elite of New France were there, if one excludes the governor. Despite his absence, it was a lavish affair. Forty guests sat down to a banquet that obviously was meant to impress the new commander. Perhaps there was the thought, too, that he might be sufficiently impressed to fall under the spell that Bigot undoubtedly held for those who were ready to accept without too much questioning. Montcalm was not one of these. As yet his stay had been too short for a full understanding either of the needs of the colony or the character of its leaders, but he must have known that the colony was never very far from the fringes of starvation, and the years at Candiac had taught him that hospitality of this kind was costly. There is a suggestion of such thinking in the letter he wrote home describing the affair. It couldn't hide his solid, country common sense. "Even a Parisian," he wrote, "would have been astonished at the profusion of good things on the table. Such splendor and good cheer show how much the intendant's place is worth." There was another comment that gives these words further point. "Everything is horribly dear in this country," he wrote, "and I shall find it hard to make the two ends of the year meet, with the twenty-five thousand francs the King gives me." Obviously Bigot's large gesture had missed achieving its purpose.

Montcalm had sent a courier to the governor announcing his arrival, and shortly after he followed his message in person. It was the first time the two had met. What Vaudreuil saw before him did not change his opinion—a man of rather small stature whose quick eye seemed to take in everything at a glance and whose interest and excitement showed in gesture and word. Nothing of it pleased the governor. Nothing suggested a man of ready subservience or a willingness to see himself divested of power.

Before the governor had even heard of Montcalm's appointment he had been urging considerations that he believed made such an appointment unnecessary. Dieskau's unhappy experience had given Vaudreuil a splendid background for his arguments. The gist of them was the broad assumption that he was capable and willing to command the French forces himself and that no general officer was needed. He had explained with considerable care that such officers were handicapped from the beginning because of their lack of familiarity with conditions in Canada, which were so sharply different from anything they had known. It was beyond any possibility that they should understand the temper of Canadian troops, and hence the frequent belief that such troops were of no value. Lack of understanding was the reason for the failure to call out the best from heroic men. It was only when such men were under their own leaders and were not resentful of harsh and unfamiliar discipline that they showed at their best.

The Indians, too, must be handled with peculiar tact. They were allies rather than soldiers under discipline. Their methods were their own. They had to be consulted, not commanded. They could not be driven, as European officers so frequently tried to do. They could not be stayed in courses they had determined for themselves. Over and over again, in letter after letter, Vaudreuil returned to this attack. Severity with Indian allies was the very antithesis of the treatment required. They needed to be encouraged, not denied. They needed officers who were accustomed to them and knew their ways. Over and over again the same arguments, supporting the vanity of the weak by discrediting the capacity of the strong.

The man who faced Montcalm was one who had failed to convince with all his arguments, or had only succeeded in sowing a nagging spirit of criticism with his half-truths. He had seen a man appointed contrary to his will. Envy and rivalry were stirring in him, creating the will to make his destructive thinking come true. These were the qualities that everywhere were eating into French morale—pride and vainglory and a selfish and sensitive egotism. These had made Vaudreuil an implacable, relentless enemy of the new general; they made his task all but impossible. This did not immediately appear, for the governor had learned from Bigot the useful trick of concealing his purposes with the appearance of co-operativeness. But never from the moment of Montcalm's arrival was he left free to carry out his plans unhindered.

The governor, beyond the matter of his dominant position, had many ways to make opposition both inconspicuous and effective. Montcalm was nominally in control of all the troops in Canada, yet it was only the small nucleus of regular troops, perhaps three thousand in number, that gave him unqualified attention and obedience. The far more numerous Canadian militia, good fighters though they might be, were completely lacking in organization and discipline and were deeply resentful when anyone tried to supply it. Particularly was this true when criticism stemmed from regular officers. There was another and smaller group attached to the Department of Marines. They, like the militia, had been untrained and unruly until Duquesne's iron hand had taught them some measure of discipline. They were Canadians by birth and were officered by Canadians, and both were even more resentful of outside interference than were the militia. These two branches of the fighting forces lived and moved in a circle where Vaudreuil was King and where a sly reference to acts of regular officers could spread and fester.

Vaudreuil, urged on by his wife to show his authority, did his best to undermine the general. With the opportunities presented, the amazement grows that anyone could make head against such a cabal. Yet Montcalm did, because he was a good soldier, as even his opponents guessed, and because he had with him in command devoted and able men whom neither the wiliness of a Vaudreuil nor the craft of a Bigot could make disloyal.

Montcalm did not waste much time in considering these difficulties. As yet both the governor and intendant presented a surface friendliness, and he took them at face value.

Reports that the English were preparing a new attack on Ticonderoga and Crown Point took him there in a hurry. He made the capable soldier's careful study of the ground, a survey that was to stand him in good stead in days to come; then, deciding that there was more talk than substance in the rumors, he posted Lévis with three thousand men at Ticonderoga and secretly hurried back to Montreal.

In the years that were ahead it was not often that governor and general were in accord. Before the general had arrived Vaudreuil had been planning to attack Oswego. When Montcalm found the plan good he moved promptly to make it effective. Within a week he was at Fort Frontenac. The regiments of La Sarre and Guienne had preceded him there from Montreal, and that of Béarn had been returned from Niagara for the task. Added to this sound core of trained fighters there was a larger group of militia and marines and a substantial detachment of Indians. These Montcalm was beginning to understand, though the knowledge came slowly and without enthusiasm. "They make war with astounding cruelty," he wrote to his wife, "sparing neither men, women, nor children, and take off your scalp very neatly–an operation that generally kills you." Despite his lack of enthusiasm, however, they did represent a good percentage of his force of three thousand.

Whatever the self-confidence of the Canadian militia, it didn't have too sound a justification. The captains of militia, so called, were really civil officials who called up and dispatched men as demanded. To use them as soldiers was like sending an alderman to direct a strategic military movement. Not unnaturally the men selected were equally lacking in military qualities. They were unofficered, untrained, and almost unclothed. All the work of turning them into soldiers had to be crowded into a matter of weeks or days. Montcalm and his officers would have been more than human if a certain sharpness hadn't intruded at times on that necessary work. As happens not infrequently in other spheres, what the members of the Canadian militia lacked in training and discipline they made up in pride that turned into resentment at any hint of criticism. Vaudreuil kept these things in his heart and used them to support his continuing argument that the spirit of the Canadian forces was being broken by the arrogance and futility of Montcalm's command.

Vaudreuil was eloquent, too, on the subject of the tactful handling of their dangerous allies, the Indians. Trained in Canada, he shared with the bulk of the Canadian-trained officers a lack of sensitiveness to the atrocities committed by their Indian allies. Long before another great general had declared that "war is hell," Vaudreuil had done his best to see that it was so. The more terrible the war, he reasoned, the quicker the victory. In reporting to the minister, his favorite bit of statistics was the number of scalps taken. With such attitudes dominating the thinking, it wasn't surprising that the governor should consider any effort to control these savage allies as disastrous, a policy likely to cost the friendship of these useful if unpredictable allies.

As a fort, Oswego wasn't too promising. As one French officer put it, "the English were exposed to their shoe buckles." The fort had defenses only on the landward side and was open on the river front except for a rather pitiful array of pork barrels to give a semblance of security. There were two small and insignificant supporting forts on either side of the Oswego River. Altogether the most impressive thing about the fort was Colonel Mercer, its commander. He was brave and resourceful and had no thought of giving in, no matter how meager his resources. He did have a thousand soldiers and some six hundred civilians, but only a part of the soldiers had been left there when Shirley's attack on Niagara fizzled out. They had been too weak to move, and almost a quarter of the civilians were women and children.

The garrison was blissfully unaware of the fate in store for them until Montcalm's guns opened on the fort. But Mercer made so gallant and effective a defense that the only remaining chance seemed to be to take the place by storm. Just then, however, a French round shot found the gallant colonel. With Mercer dead, the whole defense fell apart. The heart was out of it, and the decision was to surrender. In all, 1,650 prisoners were taken and most of them were safely forwarded to Canada. They were fortunate. The Indian allies, defrauded as they felt of the reasonable plunder of a defeated garrison, threatened to move in and collect vengeance if nothing else. All Montcalm's efforts and those of his officers were needed to keep control. The Canadians, of whatever rank, watched the happenings with a detached interest and took no part. Their attitude was, better some dead enemies than many disgruntled allies. Despite that, however, it seems that only the few prisoners who sought escape through the forest actually suffered at the hands of the Indians.

Montcalm had been so thoroughly warned against jeopardizing the good will of his Indian allies by too rigid discipline that he did his best to sit on the two stools of protecting his prisoners and yet satisfying the Indians. Finding large stores of wine and brandy in the fort, he took the wise course of emptying the liquor into Lake Ontario. The Indians, disgruntled at so patent a waste, were the more reluctant to give up such prisoners as they had captured, but they were somewhat softened when Montcalm offered generous presents for their return.

"I am afraid," Montcalm wrote the Minister of War, "my promises will cost ten thousand francs." Much of it was his own money. "The keeping of them," he explained, "will keep the Indians more on our side. In any case, there is nothing I would not have done to prevent any breach of faith with the enemy."

Anyway you looked at it, Oswego had been a great success. It had been swift and complete. Twelve days after the siege had begun Montcalm was marching his victorious army back to Montreal, his name on everyone's lips. That was true of both French and English. For the English, who had begun the year with confidence and a determination to push back the French in a swift surge of action, had retired to their forts and were settling down to protect them as best they could.

Montcalm, too, had tried out his army and knew now what it could do and on whom he could depend. He had assessed his subordinates with care and had made his detailed and none too enthusiastic record of their qualities. Among his leading officers were some he obviously didn't think worth a comment; among them, Rigaud de Vaudreuil, the governor's brother. The governor himself made up that deficiency by writing to the minister his own version. Montcalm's conduct of affairs, he explained, had been disappointingly halting and ineffective. The happy result was due to the governor's wise insistence on his own plan and the military skill of the governor's brother in carrying out the plan. It would be understandable if the Minister of War found himself somewhat confused by such conflicting evidence.

The governor so convinced himself with his own eloquent commendation that he decided to send his brother to command another venture: nothing less indeed than the capture of Fort William Henry, which lay at the northern end of the long portage from the Hudson River to Lake George. Rigaud made two attacks on the fort and both of them failed. He did manage a vast bonfire, however, in which a large number of English boats, a few ships, and a vast store of provisions went up in smoke. But Bigot had seen to it that the expedition itself should cost a pretty penny, and what with the members of the expedition getting almost lost in the snow returning to Montreal, the advantages and the debits were about even.

If the venture did not bring much credit to the Vaudreuils, the Indian tribes forgot this in their deep consciousness of Montcalm. They saw in him the one who would sweep the English from their particular bit of earth. They were deeply interested in meeting the man who would accomplish this. At first they were disappointed as tribe after tribe came to visit. They had expected a man whose very presence would be as gigantic as their expectations, and Montcalm was short rather than tall. Speaking his disappointment, one of the chiefs addressed him. "We thought your head would be lost in the clouds," he said. Then, looking up, he caught the soldier's eye. Forgetting his image of a great man whose head would be lost in the clouds, he went on, "Yet when we look into your eyes we see the height of the pine and the wings of the eagle." A man's greatness, it seems, must show in his face, even if the days to come were to cast a fleeting shadow.

Word was about of a great English expedition again directed against Louisburg. It left Montcalm more pleased than troubled. He had no fear for the great fortress. It could take good care of itself, and while the English were attacking there, they would be drawing men from more vulnerable points. This was the time, he thought, to do what Rigaud Vaudreuil had failed to do: to put a final barrier across the war road to Canada. They had Carillon, as they spoke of Ticonderoga, and they had Crown Point. The English had a counter in Fort Edward and Fort William Henry. Take these and the road would be effectively closed.

The main difficulty was that Rigaud's folly and Bigot's rapacity had used up much of the country's resources, and Montcalm knew that there was no time to waste. Already there were twenty-two hundred men at Fort William Henry under that staunch Scotsman, Colonel Munro. Fourteen miles away the timorous Colonel Webb had more than half as many again, and still farther back in another small fort there were nine hundred more, and other forces were building up in the colonies. Give them time and there would be vastly more than any force Montcalm could bring against them. The best he could hope for was what he now had. This included his regulars—at best three thousand men—and as many more of the rather uncertain militia; this and some two thousand Indians gathered from fifty different tribes. Mainly these were wholly unaccustomed to fighting with white men, but they were the best he had available. The total was perhaps eight thousand fighting men.

Montcalm's best hope was to strike fast and hard. He had to have victory before his Indians grew tired and began to scatter and before his militia had to return to the more mundane but vital task of making a harvest. Ticonderoga must be strong to be a city of refuge when that time came. That was Bourlamaque's task, and he did it well.

By the end of July Montcalm's eight thousand were spread out for miles along the lower reaches of Lake George. By August 3 they were moving purposefully. The column of Lévis, his Indians leading the way, was making a rough path through the forests to the rear of the fort while Montcalm with the main body was approaching by water after toilsome days of portaging the boats and cannon and stores over innumerable obstacles.

Fort William Henry was not an imposing edifice, but it had its strength. It was an embankment of gravel surmounted by a rampart of heavy logs laid in tiers, and its natural defenses were many. To the north it was protected by the lake, while on the east was an almost impenetrable swamp. On the south and west it was protected by ditches and an intricate barrier of sharpened stakes. It had seventeen cannon, but best of its defenses was Colonel Munro, a Scottish veteran of the 35th Regiment who had with him part of his own regiment, a Massachusetts regiment, and an assortment of less dependable troops. And at Fort Edward, only fourteen miles south along the carrying place, was General Webb. Webb had come as second-in-command with General Abercrombie, who recently had been sent to command the troops in America. There had not yet been time to assess the complete incapacity of the two, so not unnaturally Munro felt happy at having a senior officer so close at hand. Webb had even visited Fort William Henry, given some orders, and in time had sent some additional troops, so that the garrison now numbered close to twenty-five hundred. That was more than there were with Webb at Fort Edward, but he had the resources of many smaller forts to call upon at need and the prospect of considerable reinforcements from the nearby colonies. After Montcalm had invested the fort, Munro, a punctilious officer who knew the respect due a general, wrote to Webb, "I believe you will think it proper to send reinforcements as soon as possible." When this invoked no reply he wrote again, telling of the odds of four to one and of heavy fire from the enemy's artillery, adding, "I make no doubt you will soon send us reinforcements." A doubt must have been creeping into his mind, but still the old confidence remained with him that a soldier would certainly move if convinced of the necessity. "We are very certain," he wrote to Webb with this in mind, "that a part of the enemy has got between you and us upon the high road, and would therefore be glad (if it meets with your approbation) that the whole army was marched."

Webb wasn't idle. He was sending persistent couriers asking reinforcements for himself, explaining to Governor Loudon, the dull and lethargic officer who had replaced Governor Shirley, "I did not think it prudent to pursue my first intention of marching to their assistance." Prudent that course might not be; essential it certainly was, and at almost any risk. But Webb was not a risk-taker.

Montcalm had asked for the surrender of the fort. Staunch old Munro retorted tersely that his soldiers would defend the place to the last. But the last was swiftly approaching. Most of his cannon had been disabled or had burst from overuse. Three hundred of the defenders had been killed or wounded. Still worse, smallpox was raging in the fort, growing more virulent with each passing day in the confined and unsanitary quarters; while Montcalm's trenches were creeping closer and closer to the dismantled walls.

Finally Webb replied to Munro's urgently deferential word. Or rather, his aide replied for him. "The general has ordered me to acquaint you he does not think it prudent to attempt a junction or to assist you till reinforced by the militia of the colonies. . . ."

Prudent was a word that bulked large in General Webb's thinking. Yet that letter itself hadn't been prudent. When it was located on the scalpless body of the emissary who had carried it and brought to Montcalm, it was one more bit of evidence that the days of defense were numbered. It was carefully forwarded to Colonel Munro so that he might know it too. There was another day of bombardment that grew in intensity, with the fort's gallant defenders replying as briskly as their few small guns now permitted. But it was heroic folly, and everyone knew it. In the morning a council of war determined that the garrison had had its fill of valor and were prepared to surrender. A white flag was raised.

Montcalm, like the decent gentleman he was, conceded all that he could. On their agreement not to serve again for eighteen months the English troops should march out with the honors of war and would be safely escorted to Fort Edward. They would be allowed to take one fieldpiece in recognition of their unavailing gallantry.

Montcalm, not yet used to the grim ways of Indian fighting, did sense the danger. Young Bougainville recorded in his journal: "We shall be but too happy if we can prevent a massacre." And he speaks with bitterness of happenings "which make victory itself a sorrow to the victors."

Munro had been advised to see that every ounce of rum was poured out lest the Indians should find it and become more inflamed. It was useful advice, if not wholly effective. Once the fort was surrendered, it was evacuated by the garrison, who went to the entrenched camp nearby. The Indians swarmed in, looking for rum. Finding none, they located the hospital where those too sick to be moved were still in their beds. The guard of Canadian militia watched with unconcern as their allies butchered and scalped these undefended victims.

Though man might not intervene, Fate stepped in to strike a balance, for some of those scalps were taken from men already dying of smallpox. So vengeance raced through the Indian villages, taking a terrible price for every white man and woman lost in those few bitter days.

Crazed men were swarming over the entrenched camp when Montcalm arrived. He brought some sense of authority to the militia, who, placed on guard, had again made no effort to keep the rabble out or to restrain them. Montcalm's presence, his great prestige, did prevent confusion and disorder taking a more crucial turn. By evening the worst was over. Now that the threat of immediate violence was passed, Montcalm set about the difficult task of guarding against a recurrence. The Indian leaders were all readiness to co-operate. They readily agreed that two chiefs from each tribe should go with the escort which was to see that the garrison reached Fort Edward safely, as Montcalm had promised.

There was a long night ahead, a time to think and prepare, but fear rather than wisdom was in command. There were faults on the English side. Some of them started off long before the hour appointed, so that the line of march stretched an unbelievable length. Some of them, balancing urgent warnings against the long tramp ahead of them, filled their canteens, thinking it a wicked waste to throw good spirits away. When the Indians demanded rum, they shared it, hoping so to encourage a certain camaraderie. It wasn't wise thinking and it didn't convince the Indians. The owner was happy if he lost no more than the rum.

It was early morning when the long procession began to move from the fort. The escort of two hundred regulars marched at the head, well out of sight of anything that was happening at the rear. It was too much to hope that nothing would happen. It began early when seventeen wounded men, too weak to join the march, were discovered by some roving Indians. There was a French guard within forty feet, so the records prove, and numerous French officers standing about, one of them St. Luc de la Corne, an able partisan leader. The French doctor in charge stated later under oath that when the slaughter of these unfortunates began not an officer or soldier made the slightest gesture of interfering. It was almost, as one commentator says, as though they felt pleasantly satisfied at being relieved of a troublesome responsibility.

The English on this long march were allowed to keep their rifles and such possessions as they could manage, but the rifles were not loaded and there were few bayonets. Perhaps it was as well, for an inadequate show of force might have resulted more bitterly than anything that happened. As it was, it was bitter enough. Sometimes an Indian caught a glance at a rifle or some other possession that he coveted. Perhaps it was the canteen that was seized. The owner, if he resisted, was quickly doomed. The handy tomahawk played its great part that day, settling many an argument of possession. Men and women and children were attacked and larger groups driven off as captives. No one knows just how many died. All that is known is that twenty-two hundred started on the march and fourteen hundred reached Fort Edward. The rest were not all casualties; hundreds of them were taken away as prisoners, to be later rescued or released. The closest estimate sets the actually killed at a little more than a hundred, though many authorities put it much higher. It would have been much higher had not Montcalm and Lévis and Bourlamaque and many other French officers stepped in to curb the growing slaughter. Perhaps it was Montcalm's "Kill me, but spare the English who are under my protection" that finally brought some end.

The happening was not soon forgotten. Almost a hundred years after the events mentioned here the American novelist James Fenimore Cooper, in *The Last of the Mohicans*, voiced his chilling judgment. He spoke of "The Massacre of Fort William Henry" as if it had earned a lonely eminence as colonial history's most terrible chapter. That is scarcely the case, yet the judgment remains. This one scene, he urges, "so far deepened the stain which a previous and very similar event had left upon the reputation of the French commander, that it was not entirely erased by his early and glorious death. It is now becoming obscured by time; and thousands who know that

Montcalm died like a hero on the Plains of Abraham have yet to learn how much he was deficient in that moral courage without which no man can be truly great. Pages might be written to prove, from this illustrious example, the defects of human excellence; to show how easy it is for generous sentiments, high courtesy, and chivalrous courage to lose their influence beneath the chilling blight of selfishness, and to exhibit to the world a man who was great in all the minor attributes of character, but who was found wanting when it became necessary to prove how much principle is superior to policy."

A chilling judgment indeed, and one that would leave few great figures great enough for such a pinnacle of virtue. For Montcalm's shortcomings must rest not on ill things done but on the few things that he might have done yet failed to do. And even for these there might be some defense.

He was a soldier moved quickly into a character of warfare of which he had no experience whatever. He had, at best, only a very superficial knowledge of Indian behavior. With that lack there was the constant insidious challenge carried by every note Vaudreuil sent to authority and every changing expression on Bigot's crafty face—that you couldn't treat Indians as you could white men, you couldn't discipline them as you could your own, for they were allies and not subjects and were sensitive to any suggestion of authority.

He had an army, too, which he couldn't completely control. Most of the militia was ready to accept with complete unconcern horrors that had become commonplace events. There is no forgetting, either, that this attitude was not one that was peculiarly French. The colonial English also were inured to horrors and accepted them as a part of their lives. They were as given to putting a price on human heads as were the French. Within a year of the happenings here recorded the pacifist legislature of Pennsylvania had authorized payments representing in our currency one hundred and fifty dollars for the scalp of a hostile male Indian, and fifty dollars for that of a female.

There is the evidence that, on the two occasions on which James Fenimore Cooper's stern judgment is based, Montcalm had been quite openly risking and offering his life to protect the obligations he had assumed; while in both cases General Webb, whose very office implied as sharp a moral obligation, was sitting safely behind his breastworks writing shrill letters of appeal and sacrificing forces that might not have been defeated had he acted at all.

Argue it as one may, question the total validity of such a scathing challenge as one must, there still remains the unassailable fact that the French regulars at least might have been sacrificed, if necessary, to defend a given word, and it was not done. So that bar sinister remains on the escutcheon of one of the noblest, most unselfish and courageous men to move through the pages of the history of this continent. That Fort William Henry was never to rise again changes that sad fact not at all.

Why Montcalm did not immediately press on and take Fort Edward, or even Albany, as had been planned, will always remain a question. Vaudreuil had ordered it. He was already speaking of the success at Fort William Henry as "my victory" and was hinting very broadly in official circles that had his brother Rigaud been in command the victory would have been even more conclusive.

It is true that Fort Edward now was well defended. In addition to the arrival of the two thousand reinforcements that General Webb had been expecting, there were the prisoners from Fort William Henry, almost as many in number, who certainly, in view of past facts, would not be likely to surrender again. Understandably, the British Government had relieved them of any obligation they had assumed on surrendering. Montcalm's troops, on the other hand, had been seriously reduced. His Indian allies had decamped with such booty as they had been able to collect. Many of the militia had returned to their farms, taking their horses with them, where both were badly needed. If Montcalm had wished to bring up his guns for an attack on Fort Edward, a good part of his available force would have been needed for that task alone.

Governor Loudon had just arrived when he heard of the fate of Fort William Henry. He sent a hurried word to General Webb to hold on until further help arrived. Fortunately there was no need for heroics. Montcalm did not attack. A sense of shock had overtaken him. Also, he was beginning to realize the viciousness of the attacks that were being made on him; recognizing, too, that now they were being believed. The new Minister of War, the Marquis de Paulney, wrote him in mild rebuke. It wasn't a complaint over the bloody happenings of the days just passed, quite the opposite. It might have been dictated by Vaudreuil. The minister warned that Montcalm and his officers of the regular army should show more tact in their handling of the Canadian and Indian forces.

Montcalm was deeply hurt, but his policy wasn't changed. He set his men to erasing the last trace of Fort William Henry. Soon nothing was left but a roughly cleared space where the fort had once stood. Other armies would camp there again, and not in the very distant future, but it would be a camp on cleared ground free from fortification. This work accomplished and Montcalm and his forces safe behind the fortification of Fort Carillon, called by the English Ticonderoga, the general sat down quietly and sent in his resignation.

Had the resignation come to Vaudreuil it would no doubt have been accepted promptly and the story would have been shortened. But De Paulney, new as he was to his Ministry of War, was quick to see and to understand. Everywhere he looked in the New World the fleur-de-lis was floating triumphantly. There was no breach anywhere in the long frontier line of France. He ignored the resignation.

Governor Loudon, except for his title, was not an impressive man. He was a delayer by temperament, and nothing could change that important fact. He had the happy idea of attacking and capturing Louisburg. Nothing could have been sounder. He had gathered for the task an army of twelve thousand men, which should have been ample. All through the summer days, when Montcalm was disposing first of Oswego and then Fort William Henry, Loudon was busy drilling his expeditionary force. It could have been used to save both the attacked points and yet have been in time for its major task, but Loudon had a one-track mind, and all he could think of was Louisburg. When the drilling was over the soldiers were set to digging vegetable gardens. It was an idea that was admirable enough in itself —for the sick needed fresh vegetables—but perhaps lacking in a sense of timing. Attacks won't wait for growth, and perhaps Loudon was overzealous in putting Sir Charles Hay under arrest for suggesting that all the money was being spent in fighting sham battles and planting out cabbages. It may not have been a diplomatic remark, but it was the truth.

When Admiral Holborne with his supporting fleet sailed into Halifax Harbor there was more delay in an effort to get news of how things stood at Louisburg. Finally a Newfoundland vessel arrived with some captured dispatches. These showed that the French admiral, La Motte, had succeeded in uniting his squadrons of twenty-two ships of the line and some frigates, carrying in all some 1,360 guns, while it was reported that the ground forces numbered seven thousand. This was too much for Loudon. As far as he was concerned, the proposed attack was off and, forgetting his cabbage gardens, he hurried his army back to New York.

It is rather pleasant to remember that Admiral Holborne, who had no such fleet as had Admiral la Motte, decided to have a look at Louisburg and maybe tempt some of the French ships out of the harbor to give battle. It wasn't to be. La Motte was somewhat of Loudon's temper. Both wanted to be sure the odds were all on his side before venturing. A September hurricane almost arranged that for him. One of Holborne's ships was lost and nine dismasted and others had to jettison their guns, but happily La Motte let the advantage slip by.

From Louisiana to Louisburg, France held its unbroken line and it looked very much as if that line would remain unchallenged, at least for the foreseeable future. Probably that would have been so but for the emergence of the one man who could say without arrogance, "I can save this country, and I know no other man who can." One might look back on this statement as an example of flamboyant bombast but that, almost as the words were spoken, history began to record how truthful they were.

William Pitt followed a long line of parliamentary leaders who at best were incompetent. His immediate predecessor was more interested in the distribution of patronage and the benefits to be achieved thereby than in the conduct of affairs. He used Parliament rather than served it. Pitt was an anomaly, an honest, devoted, and able man who had the capacity to find like men and to inspire them to like minds. He had his faults. He was theatrical, self-assured, sometimes pompous. He was often extravagant, to his own cost, and he had an overweening pride. But it was not the arrogance or the pride that his own people, at home or in the colonies, had learned to know. The English hated and feared the Scots. They had a long memory for the Jacobite story. It was hardly more than a dozen years since the clans had threatened England's security. They wanted the restrictions against them maintained. Pitt answered by employing Scotsmen in the services of their country. He didn't destroy the clans. He raised regiments from among them to serve a common country. It would not be long before these highlanders would be playing their dramatic part in the story of Canada. And when Pitt dealt with the colonies his first act was to wipe out that stupid social snobbery which gave a regular officer rank over anything the colonies had to offer.

Pitt not only believed implicitly that Britain was great, but he believed also that he could bring that greatness into action. His people began to feel with him. They had almost given up hope of finding a man who would lead them; a man with clean hands and an undivided heart and whose only purpose was to serve. Perhaps they were slow to recognize that here was the one challenge that France's unconquered border could not meet. Now for the first time there was a glimmer of such a hope.

Almost the first act of Pitt affecting Canada was his prompt recall of the Earl of Loudon, who had managed in so short a time to demonstrate his complete incompetence. General Abercrombie, readily and happily and for about the same reason, might have met the same fate, but he had better or more aggressive friends. Rather than stir up too much dissension in so short a space of time, Pitt decided on another course. He would send out as a second-in-command one who was certain to dominate the older man and so assume command in fact, if not in name. His choice was Lord Howe. Wolfe, writing his father, had called Howe "the noblest Englishman that has appeared in my time and the best soldier in the army." Pitt must have been satisfied at such a word. He had no small confidence in his young brigadier's judgment.

There can't be much doubt that both were right. Howe seemed to have been born for army life. He was as popular with the rank and file as he was with his fellow officers. He was quick to learn, as most English regular officers had not been. He also had nothing of the spit-and-polish tradition about him. He quickly got the idea of forest fighting, and if he didn't do away with red uniform coats, he did cut off their tails to make traveling in the forest more easy, and he did extemporize leather leggings for the same reason. Also, he cut down the amount of baggage and inaugurated a system of having the men carry meal in their knapsacks, a sort of iron ration that they could cook for themselves at need. He had hair cut short in an earlier day crew cut instead of the neatly powdered wigs heretofore thought essential. He painted rifle barrels to protect against their revealing sparkle in the forest. The fine pageantry of war was gone, the pageantry that had marched Braddock's men to destruction. Officers might write home that their friends would laugh to see "the droll figures we made." But a day or so on the march and they were happy to let it go at that.

Pitt had called on the colonies for twenty thousand men to take Ticonderoga, offering to equip and arm them. The colonies had caught the fire of the new spirit that was stirring in the land and responded handsomely. Massachusetts alone sent seven thousand men, and New York, New Jersey, and the rest of New England added ten thousand more. If the total was down to fifteen thousand men by the time they reached Fort Edward about the end of June, it was still an impressive army.

It was the more impressive when one thinks of the army that opposed it. Vaudreuil had sent Lévis off on a wild-goose chase that reduced Montcalm's army to less than three thousand. Fortunately word got about of Abercrombie's impressive force, and Lévis was hurried back in time. Even so, the general could count only thirty-six hundred men.

Montcalm fully recognized the importance of this post and exerted every effort to see that it was properly defended. This was the best he could do. Vaudreuil would not provide the men and Bigot would not assure the necessary supplies except at exorbitant cost. But beyond that was the fact, patent to a soldier of Montcalm's experience, that, placed as he was, any general, good or bad, was bound to attempt to cut him off from his base. Ticonderoga, stretching out into the lake, made it next to impossible for an enterprising man to fail. Montcalm saw it all too clearly. Instead of attempting the impossible, he moved his force backward to a ridge about half a mile west of the fort. On it he built a rough embankment made of trunks of trees piled on one another to a height of nine feet. In front the trees had been leveled for perhaps five hundred feet. They lay where they had fallen, their tangle of branches leaning forward, sharpened and dreadful. On either side the land fell away in bottomless marshy ground that was almost as effective. As a fortification it didn't look impressive. It remained to be proven whether behind even so formidable a barrier three and a half thousand men could possibly make head against fifteen thousand.

Abercrombie's army, making its way up Lake George in a great armada, was a stirring sight. It moved to enthusiasm, even those who had joined it with darkness in their hearts and their lips moving with the bitter words, "Remember William Henry." There were nine hundred bateaux loaded deep with men, the scarlet of the regulars framed with the blue of the provincials on the flanks. They lay across the lake in even rows, so that as it narrowed they reached from shore to shore and stretched back into the distance beyond man's sight. Behind them followed the great whaleboats, linked two by two and floored with planks so that the heavy guns could be carried.

It was July 6, a steaming day under a blazing sun, as the great column moved forward. There was little need for secrecy with such a force, and there came laughter and the music of bands and the unfamiliar skirling of the bagpipes from the thousand men of the Black Watch who moved with the van. There was no hesitancy in them or in the Major Campbell of Inverawe who led them, knowing that he was leading them to his own death. For hadn't he been told years before that he would die at a place with the impossible name of Ticonderoga?

Waiting for the attackers, Montcalm had placed himself and most of his regulars near the little river joining the two lakes. There was a bridge at this point, about two miles below the fort. It was the natural approach and led across the portage to reach the river below the rapids. Here Bourlamaque had been stationed to await their coming and to assess the number of the attackers. He had also sent the partisan leader, Langy by name, through the deep forests to Lake George on the same errand. The news Langy brought back made it quite evident that any attempt at a delaying action would be utter folly. So Bourlamaque was withdrawn, and when he had joined Montcalm the bridge was burned and both retired to their makeshift defenses. Langy was left still ranging the forests and, strangely enough, it was this simple decision that was to be decisive.

There were two routes linking Lake George and Lake Champlain. One was across the narrow portage that led to the bridge and sawmill where Montcalm had been. This had been partially closed when the bridge was destroyed. Another route led around the curve of the river. It was double the length and led through all but impenetrable forests, yet it had the advantage that Lord Howe must have been quick to see. By it one might by-pass Ticonderoga entirely and reach Crown Point instead. Such an action would have meant ruin for Montcalm and his forces, for it was his line of retreat as it was his line of supply.

Knowing this and accomplishing that result were different matters. They were different because of the all-encompassing forest. Heading his light infantry and preceded by a corps of rangers trained to the woods, Lord Howe pushed on with all possible speed. Trained as they were, it was not long before it became abundantly clear that the

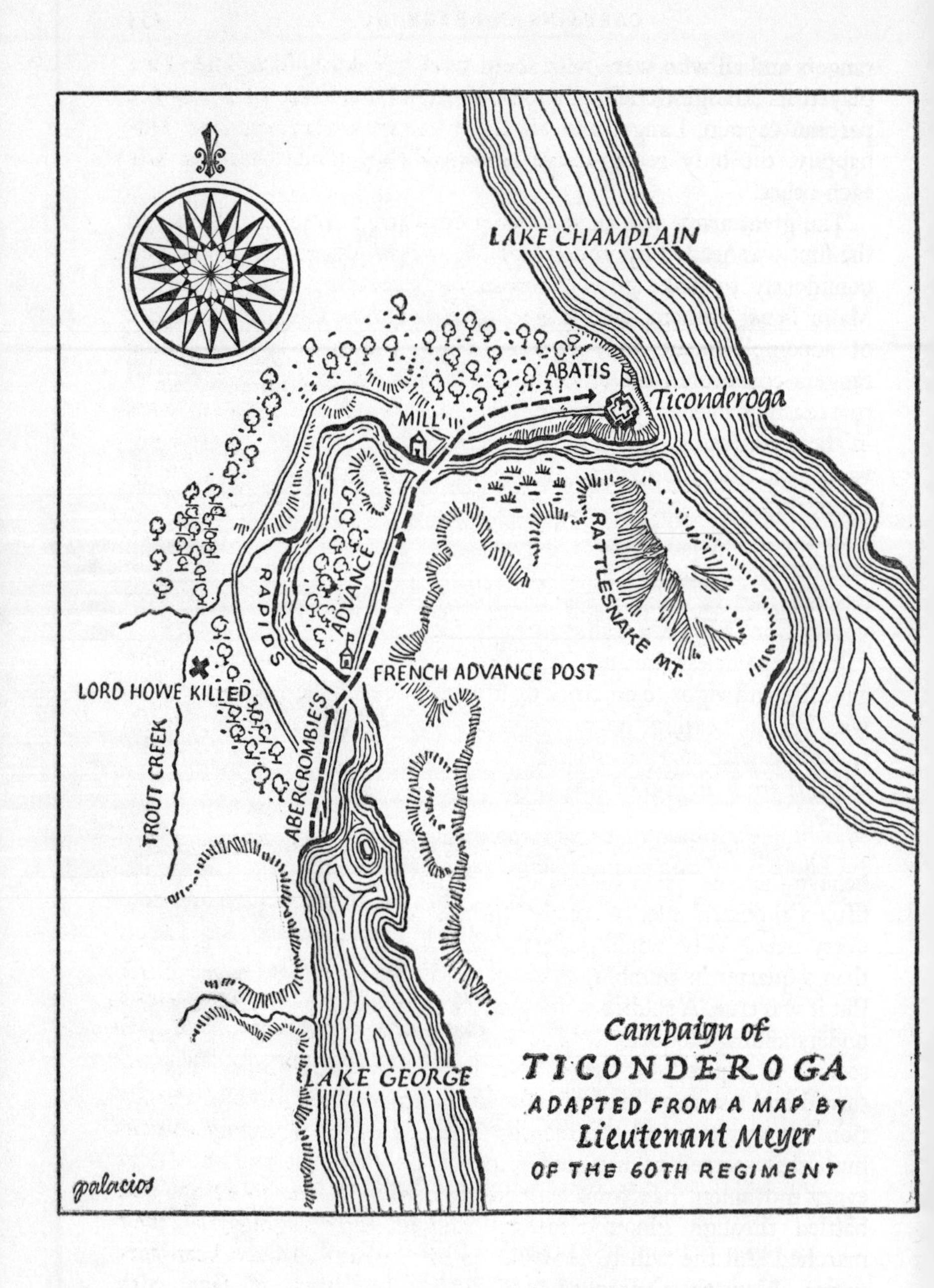

Campaign of
TICONDEROGA
ADAPTED FROM A MAP BY
Lieutenant Meyer
OF THE 60TH REGIMENT

rangers and all who were with them were hopelessly lost. Then Fate played its strangest trick, for somewhere in that maze of forest the partisan captain, Langy, and his three hundred were also lost. Unhappily, the only recognizable landmark they could discover was each other.

The great army was now moving forward in four divisions, and the first was headed by young Lord Howe, whom Pitt had relied on confidently to make good Abercrombie's mistakes. With him was Major Israel Putnam, who was to become almost a legendary figure of accomplishment and courage. These and some two hundred rangers constituted the advance guard. Suddenly the forest echoed to a crash of musketry. It came from Langy's puzzled partisans who, in their confusion, had discovered themselves between Howe's advance and the following columns of Abercrombie's whole force. Firing in such a maze of forest and underbrush did not serve them well. Some fifty of Langy's force melted away in the bush and were seen no more. The rest were killed or captured. But one of their bullets did find its shining mark. Among the few English dead was young Lord Howe, a bullet through his heart.

In this nameless skirmish near Trout Brook died the one man who gave life and vigor to an army of fifteen thousand men whose idol he was. Wolfe, hearing the rumor in the lines about far-off Louisburg, was filled with sorrow and consternation. "If the report is true," he said, "there is an end of that expedition, for he was the spirit of that army."

Few words have been so quickly and so fully justified. Who could believe that the death of one man could mean ruin to a vast army; fifteen thousand men virtually untouched and amply supplied for every need? Who could understand its hesitation before a force less than a quarter its number, so dangerously placed and so ill supplied? But it was true. A soldier writing at the time spoke with a strange and understanding eloquence. "The soul of General Abercrombie's army seemed to expire," he wrote. "Neither order nor discipline was observed and a strange kind of infatuation usurped the place of resolution." It was true; all the records speak of it, the strangely solemn hush that seemed to hang over men. The *élan* that had shown in every movement had forsaken those who only a few hours ago had battled through gloomy forests, singing and laughing as they marched. All the will to repay an injury seemed to have been forgotten. Now they marched, not singing, but stony of face, with the name of Fort William Henry in their remembering hearts.

All waited for some decisive word that would renew their confidence in victory and send them storming against Montcalm's beleaguered forces, still unready, still in desperate plight. Montcalm was writing to one of the few friends in Quebec he knew he could trust, Doreil, the commissary of war. "We have only eight days' provisions," he wrote. "I have no Canadians and no Indians. The British have a very strong army. From the movements of the British I can see that they are in doubt." And then the perceptive word: "If they are slow enough to let me entrench the heights of Ticonderoga, I shall beat them."

Abercrombie had had but one idea, to bring back the advance column that Howe's death had left leaderless and uncertain, uniting his army again against possible attack, from what source no one thought to consider. By nightfall they were again united about the first landing place, and the general held them there all night long under arms. A whole day and night wasted while Montcalm's forces worked feverishly to make their entrenchments equal to the challenge. With them their young officers were to be seen, for once forgetful of their dignity, shirt-sleeved and grimy, working side by side with their men.

By next evening Abercrombie had his army across the portage and based by the bridge that a short while back had marked Montcalm's advance post. Unexplainably he had left behind his artillery, which had been brought along with such elaborate effort. He was within two miles of the entrenched camp where Frenchmen were working their hearts out to prepare for him. Not knowing what to do himself, he did nothing.

It was next morning when he decided to find out just what the French defenses were like and whether they could be carried by assault. He did not go himself to see. Instead he sent his chief engineer, a young man named Clerk, to discover and report. This is one of the incidents that give to the action at Ticonderoga its bewildering sense of madness. Clerk was not much more than a boy. He had been commissioned lieutenant and sub-engineer only six months before. Of actual experience of warfare he had almost none. Now he was sent to decide an army's course of action, while the general rested in his tent, out of sight of the proposed happenings.

From a height across the stream from the army headquarters, which was named Mount Defiance or more colloquially Rattlesnake Mountain, Lieutenant Clerk surveyed the rough fortification of logs and sod and sandbags crowning a rise that fell away on all sides and was commanded on its front by the guns of Ticonderoga itself. He was not impressed. What he could not see was that before, between, and around that deadly smother of felled trees were deadlier counterparts of today's entanglements of barbed wire. These were known as *cheveaux-de-frise*, sharpened spikes set in wood on four sides, so that movement would present only another challenge. An advancing force, striking them unaware, would impale itself on these prongs.

On his return the young lieutenant reported, as best he could from his untrained obesrvation, that in his opinion the position could be taken by assault without artillery support. Who can know if next day, his young body pinned on one of those cruel spikes, he had time to realize that his first important military judgment had been wrong?

His general hadn't thought so. The report had dovetailed neatly with Abercrombie's own desires and fears. He had word that reinforcements which would double Montcalm's forces—which he had already overestimated—were on their way. The report did not suggest whence the reinforcements would come. Perhaps it had in mind Lévis' six hundred, but these had already arrived and were included in the total of thirty-six hundred defenders. However that may be, Abercrombie, who had already delayed so long, was impatient to have it over and to be away. No one could question his courage, and the course he chose was the dangerous course, if possibly the quickest. He was essentially a one-idea man, so, having decided his course, he did not think of any other. Yet there were many. Mount Defiance or Rattlesnake Mountain was in his hands. Sir William Johnson, arriving late with his Indian following, was on guard there. Owing to the Indian reluctance to attack fortifications, they took no other part but remained disapproving observers. The position was within easy cannon range of Montcalm's new entrenchments. Placed there, his artillery would have made that last defense untenable. Provisions were limited among the French, and there was no hope of augmenting them. Abercrombie could easily have thrown his army across any road of possible escape. He had only to wait a week to starve the French forces into abject surrender.

Montcalm was too shrewd and experienced a soldier not to have known this when he made the decision to give battle there. His one hope was for a blunder. He could hardly have dreamed of so complete a blunderer. For with so many courses open to him, Abercrombie chose the one that offered almost the only chance of failure.

Having chosen it, he followed it with that credulous determination that so often in warfare has led commanders to commit themselves beyond reason to a once-decided course, as General Burnside did at Fredericksburg or Lord Raglan at Balaclava.

No one complained. No one urged that the simpler course should be taken, or protested when it was not. "I think we were all infatuated by the notion of carrying every obstacle by a mere *coup de mousqueterie*," wrote a young officer to a friend. Perhaps it was true; perhaps more than the general should bear a part of the responsibility.

A single gun boomed from the Ticonderoga fort. At the signal every Frenchman laid down his tools and reached for his musket. The hour had come. It was almost noon. Along the bristling barrier that faced the enemy like a zigzag fence for a matter of five hundred yards until it turned on each flank, not a defender could be seen from below. But they were there, with Montcalm himself in command. There was a glint of blue where the Royal Roussillon stood in the center, waiting.

Out from the forest came the light infantry and the rangers. They were eager to attack. There was a score to settle. They had been with Howe when the bullet from one of Langy's frightened men had found that brave and generous heart. Their task was to drive in the pickets that guarded the front of the tangled maze of trees that was Montcalm's last fortress. This done, they would stand aside and watch the grand assault sweep over the barrier. The Black Watch would lead it, and the thousand men of them were itching to be at it. So were the grenadiers, who would go with them in a drive that nothing could withstand. Their bayonets were fixed, for this was to be an assault of cold steel. There would be no stopping to fire until the work was done.

But nothing went quite as expected. The line that broke from the woods was straight enough, but as it reached that maze of timber no one could keep a line. Men dashed ahead in a cold fury, but now through gaps in the logs flames were spurting and men were falling. Here and there a gun loaded with grape sprayed its contents into the straggling advance. Time after time they came on, a black fury driving them, a fury that fear could not touch. But courage had no effect on the cruel *chevaux-de-frise*. They broke the ranks as men fell screaming on their points, driven forward by the mad fury of those behind. Human nature can stand just so much. Gallantry had done its utmost. Now without thinking, men were falling back in disorder. They knew now that it couldn't be done.

But Abercrombie, down at his headquarters by the sawmill and the bridge, didn't know or would not believe. His orders were clear enough. The assault should be made again, and so it was. There never was any questioning. Screaming, fighting, and dying, the men drove forward there in that hot July sunlight on a height overlooking one of the loveliest views in the world.

There was no time to think of that or to remember the matter of the bayonet alone; time only to discover there were limits to endurance and that theirs had been reached.

There was a small diversion when Abercrombie did attempt a sensible turning move. He sent twenty bateaux filled with troops to strike at the left, where Bourlamaque himself was holding his trained marksmen in hand. In this more open field of fire they did not miss. Bourlamaque was down, seriously wounded, but he still commanded there. His men didn't waver. Soon plunging shots from the fortress itself were finding the bateaux and discouraging the men who must depend on them. The attack just ceased to be.

The reverse quickly decided Abercrombie he had been right in his first main decision. The ground could be taken and he would take it —by assault. Five o'clock came. Once again the attack was ordered; the highlanders again and the grenadiers. They were to smash at the right of the line, where Lévis and the regiments of Béarn and Guienne were waiting. It was an attack to end all attacks, made by men who would not be stayed. Time and again they almost reached the barricades behind the maze of felled trees behind the *chevaux-de-frise*. Major Campbell of Inverawe charged with the black prophecy in his mind. Years ago he had heard that he would die at Ticonderoga, a name he had never heard. Now he knew that name well, and knew his fate as it came to meet him that day. In a black fury some of his highlanders reached the abatis, climbed it, and leaped among their foes. They died there on French bayonets.

As twilight came, the last attack dwindled away. Brave men withdrew, leaving their dead behind. Killed, wounded, and missing—and most of them killed—they totaled 1,944 officers and men. But they had taken their toll. Out of less than 3,600 men, the French had lost 377 dead and wounded.

The threat was still there. Deducting his losses, Abercrombie had still 13,000 men. Reckoning his own, Montcalm could count only a little better than three thousand, and this time even a bemused general would not attack without his guns.

Montcalm sent a detachment to discover the enemy's intent. They found the sawmill ablaze and the bridge once more destroyed. Much had been left behind, hundreds of barrels of provisions and other property. But stranger than these to the reconnoiterers were the marshy flats before them. They had blossomed strangely—with the shoes of men, panic-stricken—unpursued but desperate to get away.

It was a victory, overwhelming and complete, and Vaudreuil was garnering the praise. He was also hurrying forward reinforcements when now they were useless and only a drain on depleted supplies. With them came letters ordering Montcalm to follow up the success by invading English lands. For once the quiet soldier was stung to sharp retort. "I think it very strange," he wrote the governor, "that you find yourself, at a distance of a hundred and fifty miles, so well able to make war in a country you have never seen."

Vaudreuil might make his bold claims to victory, but Canada knew to whom it owed acclaim. Ticonderoga has been called the least remembered, the most desperate, and the most dramatic battle of our history, and it was truly Montcalm's victory. For one brief remaining moment this unavailing valor might suggest that France had found herself again and that to British humbling there could be no end. Such might have been a plausible judgment, as plausible as it was without any substance. Even as victory hung in the air the net was closing with inexorable thoroughness.

Colonel John Bradstreet had headed the armed boatmen at Ticonderoga. Their record had not been spectacular, but neither had it been the reverse. Now he talked to Abercrombie of a plan he had for capturing Fort Frontenac. The poor harried general, reaching for anything that might mitigate defeat, agreed to let him have three thousand men. It did not turn out to be a dramatic victory, however impressive its aftereffects. De Noyan, who commanded at Frontenac, was there because it was the practice in the case of persons of long service and good family to find them a position of seeming prominence and some pecuniary advantage. It was the least that authority could do.

But De Noyan, if old, was not without courage, and when he heard of Bradstreet's coming he did his best. He sent to the governor for troops necessary for defense. But habit was too strong in Vaudreuil. He had systematically denuded the fort of troops for other purposes until now the garrison was down to less than a hundred. At De Noyan's appeal, the governor, perhaps in a spirit of untimely levity, sent him an adviser to aid in planning the defense. It was a reinforcement of but one man, and the man had but one arm.

The end was to be foreseen. There was no option but surrender. The gains were large in a practical sense, if not in glittering victory. There were vast supplies, for Frontenac was the main dispersal point. Too late Vaudreuil sent off a relieving force. It had gone but a short distance when news of the surrender made continuance a purposeless gesture. Characteristically, Vaudreuil let the blame fall on the aging and courageous De Noyan. But, forgetting praise or blame, the Indians received the news with awed respect for a nation that could challenge so great a fortress.

Farther west, a tired and sick man, General John Forbes, whose heart was sturdier than his body, was charged with doing what Braddock had failed to do, capture Fort Duquesne. Forbes was a sick man when he took command, but he was well served in his assistants, among them Colonel George Washington and Colonel Henry Bouquet, a brave and able Swiss who commanded one of the battalions of the Royal American Regiment.

The campaign did not begin auspiciously. As usual, the colonies were reluctant to contribute money or men and, in this case, many who did come were unwilling and untrained. A goodly number of them had never fired a musket in their lives. Writing to Pitt, General Forbes reported that even the officers of these provincial levies were "an extremely bad collection of broken innkeepers, horse-jockeys and Indian traders," and he was no more favorably impressed by the men they led. It was a bickering crowd in which Henry Bouquet plodded ahead, pushing roads through what Forbes called "an immense uninhabited wilderness." No one could call it so today. At Raystown, Bouquet built a base and named it Fort Bedford. From there he crossed the Alleghenies and Laurel Hill and there, on a little stream called Loyalhannon Creek, he built his final advance post about fifty miles short of Fort Duquesne.

They were close now to their quarry, though Vaudreuil was still reporting that he had provided for the safety of the fort by sending ample troops and provisions sufficient, he wrote, "to keep the English out of that country."

The statement, like many of the statements of the governor, lacked essential truth. The English had not been kept out. They had made close contact with the adjoining Indian tribes that had decided at last that England's star was in the ascendant and cheerfully joined the most promising side.

In the end the capture of Fort Duquesne was an anticlimax. De Ligneris was a brave man but not too astute a commander. Vaudreuil had not supplied ample resorces of men, as he stated. The fort was understaffed and ill supplied with provender. Facing this situation and deciding that no attack would be made that winter, the commander released a good percentage of his forces to conserve supplies for the three hundred who would hold the fort through the winter.

But General Forbes, though he wrote to Pitt rather pathetically that his time was "disagreeably spent between business and medicine," had used his business time well. He was pushing forward, winter or no. De Ligneris, outguessed, found nothing left to do but topple the guns into the river and destroy the fortress.

Forbes had a new stockade built there. He named it Fort Pitt, and as Pittsburgh it still remains. That done, he started back for Philadelphia. It was a torturing trip for a man who had to be carried in a litter all the way. Only a dauntless spirit had kept him at his post so long. Even dauntlessness must give way in time. In March of that year of victory they laid him in the graveyard of Christ Church in Philadelphia, where his unmarked bones still rest.

If the achievement was not brilliant, it was decisive. For France it was a year of vast and far-reaching defeat relieved only by that lonely and perhaps unwarranted victory at Ticonderoga. It was hard to believe that anyone could fail to see the writing on the wall. Doreil, friend of Montcalm and commissioner of war in Canada, saw it clearly. Addressing the Minister of War, he wrote: "Peace, monseigneur, give us peace! Pardon me, but I cannot repeat that word too often." It was well to repeat. Peace was the last lingering hope.

CHAPTER XXV

EVIL GENIUS

François Bigot, once intendant at Louisburg, returns as intendant of all New France. Young Marguerite de la Jemeraye has a vision of service that results in conflict with Bigot and her successful promotion of the Grey Nuns.

Bigot's career of knavery. His friendship with Governor Vaudreuil and his long conflict with Montcalm. His knavish following becomes a canker eating at the heart of New France. His deeds. His luxuries. His dissipations. His friendship with Madame Péan. His final arrest and conviction.

THERE could be but one name in all Canadian history to which the phrase "evil genius" might apply. There were others perhaps evil enough to set themselves apart. But in the main they lacked even the most distant semblance of genius; and the record of others, dark as it might be, was lighted too often with some sudden flash of nobler attitudes to mark them wholly evil. Perhaps the phrase is too ambitious even for François Bigot, the last intendant of France's lost continent. Astute he was; able, intelligent, constructive within his own limited view. When he wished, he had an easy graciousness that defied criticism, and he could earn from associates and friends an almost idolatrous admiration. So much must be granted.

Yet there had been at least one abler intendant than he in New France. Whatever might be argued for him, François Bigot could never have equaled the solid qualities of heart and imagination and devotion and integrity that marked Jean Baptiste Talon, the Great Intendant. In the matter of astuteness and ability there is little doubt that Bigot would rank next to Talon. In honor and integrity he would be far behind even the weakest and most venal of the fourteen intendants who preceded him in office. For Bigot's genius, such as it was, emerged as a genius for evil, in that there was no one at all to challenge his complete ascendancy.

He had two driving motives, his own pleasure and his own profit. It might be argued that these, at worst, are venial shortcomings. They were not so with Bigot. His pleasure was to debauch. His profiting was achieved at the expense of the all too limited virtues of his friends.

It isn't to be said that François Bigot was responsible for all the evil that burgeoned in New France during his ten-year intendancy. He found a country in which a canker of loose living was beginning to challenge the old sure and simple faith, and he accelerated the pace of that growing decadence unbelievably. This country of his adoption was one where men came seeking quick wealth that would enable them to spread wings more widely on their return. He showed them how to let down the barriers of scruples that might delay that end. He found men grown cynical of the tenets of honor and faithfulness and integrity, and he did his best to destroy what little faith remained. He taught by example as well as words that the humble were there to be exploited and the land to be betrayed. He wasn't the creator of evil, so even that genius is denied him; he was merely the propagator, the disseminator, and the eager and faithful advocate.

Lest this should seem to argue that a growing evil was the only active force in the new land, it should be recorded that in the very year that François Bigot was forsaking his less lucrative official position in France to sail for Louisburg and an intendantship that he hoped would favor him, a child was born who was to do as much for the good of Canada as Bigot was to do evil, and who at times was to challenge the intendant himself.

Marie Marguerite de le Jemeraye belongs among the truly great of Canada. She was the niece of Pierre de Varennes, the Vérendrye whose name is forever associated with the lands of the west and the great search for its Western Sea. She was the older sister of Christophe de la Jemeraye, who, until his untimely death, was Vérendrye's second-in-command. She was no less a patriot than they and certainly lacked none of their courage.

Her life was the life of any young and spirited girl of her day who belonged to a wide connection. Her mother had been the friend and schoolmate of the wife of Governor Vaudreuil, and they were familiar guests at the home of Claude de Ramesay, who was governor of Montreal, then a city of three thousand people.

It is believed that Vaudreuil himself had something to do with deciding her future husband—none other than his protégé, young, handsome, and highly eligible François d'Youville. But François' graces were all on the outside, as Madame d'Youville was to discover. He had no interest in his home and none for his five children. Their upbringing, and later their very sustenance, was to depend on the mother. It was not necessary for D'Youville to follow the baser practices of the traders. He had resources enough. When his father died, these improved. He came into money as he came into all the shoddy practices that his father had made profitable in administering Vaudreuil's estate on the island of Tourles, northwest of Montreal. When young D'Youville's mother died also and her fortune was added, he was freed from the necessity of work. Relinquishing his family as well, he turned to a life of dissipation, using his wealth to secure an entry into the most profligate society.

Perhaps there are some relieving factors in an otherwise useless life. At least one failure led to another success. Madame d'Youville, left with the responsibility of her young family, had to develop her own resources and in doing so she developed her own sympathies. Perhaps, had things been different, the poor of New France would not have been as well remembered and the Congregation of the Grey Nuns would not today be carrying on its devoted work about this continent and other continents as well.

Less than a year before Bigot returned as intendant of all Canada, aspersions resulting from the fall of Louisburg having been offset by his friendly patron, Governor Beauharnois named Madame d'Youville directress of the General Hospital in Montreal. This was her opening opportunity, and she said then, as she had said often before, "The people must know that we never refuse to serve."

Most probably the people did know, but Bigot didn't favor the people being treated with too much consideration. It might lead them to attitudes of mind unfriendly to such as he. Also, it involved a considerable outlay of money that the intendant felt might better be directed in other channels. He decided to combine the hospitals of Montreal and Quebec at the latter city, where it would be more under his eye. It took time and a good deal of scheming, but ultimately the hospital was moved. The resultant controversy didn't end with so-called consolidation. Eventually Bigot had to return to Madame d'Youville certain contents taken from the Montreal hospital. Rather shamefacedly he complied.

Bigot did not like complying and soon he had another cause of complaint. Before his attempt to remove the hospital, he had wished to interfere with one of its functions, that of looking after certain unfortunate women who for economic reasons were living sinful lives. Madame d'Youville had urged the former intendant, Hocquart, to permit her to make a place for them in the hospital. He did better than that. He agreed to find the money to support the plan, and Madame d'Youville set aside twelve private rooms. This new department, for rather uncertain reasons, was named Jericho. Bigot was far from being a patron of virtue, nor were the bulk of his intimates, but they were highly vocal and they wanted no reform that might infringe on vices they considered their prerogative.

Quickly responsive to those who thought as he did, Bigot wrote sternly to Madame d'Youville:

"I have been informed that Jericho is beginning to cause abuses which might be of considerable consequence in the future if I do not establish order there. . . . To prevent similar abuses I expressly forbid you to take any girl or woman at this Jericho except by my order, which I shall send you in writing when I consider it expedient to confine any of them; and maintenance will be furnished at the King's expense. I trust that you will not fall again into the fault that you have committed; otherwise I shall effectively remedy the situation."

The worst abuse charged against Madame d'Youville was that of cutting the hair of some of her charges, possibly so making them less attractive to Bigot's favorite henchmen. But we have no knowledge either that Bigot sent any unhappy women into her charge or that Madame d'Youville changed either her will to help or her methods of helping. Yet one fact is assured. Her monuments still remain, whether in Montreal or in the La Vérendrye hospital of today at Fort Frances, where centuries ago her young brother built one of the steppingstones to the discovery of the west and called it Fort St. Pierre, or in the hospitals of China and Africa and Alaska and the

United States where the Congregation of the Grey Nuns carry on her record of untiring good. Assured, too, is the sobering fact that after two hundred years of absence her adversary is still a living memory that all men scorn.

If there were any extenuating circumstances in Bigot's rise to fortune and infamy, they do not appear. He did not belong to the aristocracy, nor was he born to exceptional wealth. But he did have the advantage of high connections and a sound tradition of service. At the time of his birth in 1703 his father, Louis Amable Bigot, was serving as a respected member of the Parliament of Bordeaux, as the father's father had also served. With at least two generations of integrity and honest service behind him, there is no evidence that these were reflected in his own life. Perhaps life was too easy for him. Through influence he secured lucrative offices at court. They provided an entry to persons who might be of service to him, among them the powerful Minister of Colonies, the Comte de Maurepas. It was his unhappy part to introduce François Bigot to New France. There was another patron who shared that dubious honor. This time it was a woman.

Rather strangely, throughout his life Bigot had a very definite attraction for women. It was not because he was personally attractive, at least in appearance. He was short and stout, with reddish hair and a pimply complexion. These are not generally considered attractive attributes. It might be argued that what the ladies saw in him was what the ladies could get out of him. That certainly was not the whole truth. He had a ready wit and graceful manners. He was of a friendly nature and generous, if one accepts that virtually all his generosity was at a cost to someone else. He had a continuing delight in luxury. He was good-natured and untiring in his pursuit of pleasure and lavish in his hospitality. Perhaps there is some association between these extroverted qualities and the fact that feminine levity, which had never been pronounced in all the days of New France, was to blossom suddenly and startlingly under Bigot's skillful tuition.

In fairness it must also be admitted that Bigot had other qualities than these. His health was indifferent, but he drove himself as exhaustingly and as persistently in his work as in his pleasures. He had a boundless energy and a wealth of experience. He was shrewd and skillful and good-natured always. With his capabilities it was in him to have left as fine a reputation as had Talon. But the one thought of France and the other, despite his outward graces, only of himself. So Talon's name occupies an undisputed place of honor in the story of Canada, while Bigot, a man of even superior talent, is remembered as a destroyer.

Bigot, while at court in France, had not failed to pay his homage to the reigning favorite, and Madame la Pompadour was caught by his easy and deferential manners. It was she, perhaps, who suggested to Maurepas that a place might be found for Bigot in New France. So it was that he was sent to that Devil's Island of Louisburg to absorb the miasma of the place and, no doubt, to add to it.

It was certainly not Bigot's intention to remain in a spot so little to his natural liking. Not too much is known as to why he stayed six years or how he occupied them. The young Louisburg Habitant, whose report of the first siege is almost the only firsthand record from the French side, does report one or two incidents that are curiously like the activities of a later-day Bigot. There is the suggestion of juggling with the books covering the soldiers' pay; that soldiers were being worked on the fortifications, work for which the King would be charged but for which the soldier workers would receive no benefit. There was the mutiny of Swiss and even French troops over the fact, among others, that provisions sent by the King for the soldiers' use were being sold to the officers. All these items would naturally come under Bigot's attention, and it is perhaps not too cynical to feel that such happenings might suggest a man preparing himself for larger opportunities of the same unsavory kind. Even the fact that there is still evidence in his letters of a very real interest in the fortunes of New France does not preclude the possibility that there were other interests. There is indeed evidence of fire amid the smoke. On his return to France, eager to pick up his fortunes, instead of opportunities he was faced with charges of misappropriated public funds. But his powerful friends, still powerful and still friendly, managed to have him returned to Canada. Indeed, it is true, if difficult to understand, that, having come suspiciously close to proven guilt of malfeasance in one office, he was given another, similar but of larger opportunity for spoils. He was now to be intendant of all New France, second only to the governor in official powers. In skill and ability to dominate other men he was unmistakably superior.

It was undoubtedly the conjunction of two such men—a governor who was indolent, weak, vacillating, enormously vain, and wholly tractable, and Bigot, conscienceless, able, industrious, and adept at using the weaknesses of others to his own advantage—that brought iniquity to full bloom and New France to such a sorry place.

Finding so credulous a superior was manna in the wilderness to one of Bigot's temperament. There was now, as he saw it, no barrier to restrict his activities. There was just a proud and arrogant man, not a vicious man in the sense that Bigot was vicious. The governor's vices were those of the weak and the pompous, not those of the predator. Vaudreuil was not dishonest, in the very loose sense that honesty was estimated at the time. He was sincerely devoted to Canada. Had he turned to Montcalm, as he did to Bigot, his name might have stood as high in the annals of Canada as did that of his father, the former governor. But Montcalm, completely unassuming as he was, could not but take some measure of honor and glory from a superior who believed all glory and honor belonged to him, and to him alone. So an antagonism that verged on hatred began, and ended in the governor's falling into the wily hands of one always ready to forgo glory in the interest of profit.

Bigot replaced Gillis Hocquart, who, first as commissary general of New France and finally as intendant, had devoted his energies with complete unselfishness to the service of his country. Hocquart's twenty years of devoted service had brought a wide respect for the intendant's office. If Bigot gave that any thought, it was not to emulate the pattern but to consider how a resourceful man could use such feeling to his advantage.

In the tight little society of Quebec a man of Bigot's social nature and high position could hardly fail to make a place for himself. The open friendship of the governor made it doubly assured. Perhaps it was not an overcritical society. It was receptive to the idea that every office had its perquisites. Young Bougainville, that careful and slightly cynical observer, was to point out that to be offered the command of a fort carried with it so many financial advantages that a three-year assignment was considered an ample prospect for matrimonial intentions. He records, perhaps in support of this, that Marin and Rigaud, two partisan officers, the latter the governor's brother stationed at Green Bay, in a relatively short time had managed a profit for themselves of 312,000 francs, and no questions asked.

Young Bougainville does mention the names of certain officers who were exceptions to the general demoralization. He adds sadly that there were not enough of them "to save Sodom."

It is clear, then, that Bigot followed a path already well beaten by erring feet. It could not be said that he created depravity; he merely remodeled and expanded it. For one thing, he was a gregarious character; when he profited he liked his friends to profit with him. His letter to his friend De Vergor, then commanding at Beauséjour, will be remembered. "Profit by your place, my dear Vergor . . . so that you can come soon to join me in France and buy an estate near me." Indeed he was, as has been said, "a very prince of corruptionists."

De Vergor, amenable as he was to such suggestions, was of too small caliber to hold Bigot's interest for long, but shortly he did find a man after his own heart. It was Joseph Cadet, son of a Quebec butcher, who until old enough to take up his father's trade kept the cows for the good people of Charlesbourg. Cadet's aspirations were not as humble as his early surroundings. He dreamed of becoming a noble of France and, strangely enough, he did. In the end he was known as the Baron de la Touche d'Arrigny, happily too late to enjoy the honor for long. How Bigot discovered Cadet's peculiar genius for peculation does not appear. But the facts are that he did and was duly impressed and charmed thereby. He appointed Cadet to the post of commissary general of the colony, a post where those gifts would have their amplest scope.

In Bigot's select company of rogues there were other figures of note. There was Deschenaux, son of the local shoemaker, who obviously had profited by his schooling as Bigot's secretary, and Imbert, the treasurer general. And no one could omit Hugues Péan, the town major, who was delighted when his wife, who had been the glamorous Angélique des Méloizes, caught the roving eye of the intendant and quickly became a permanent part of the intendant's establishment. Hugues Péan, no moralist himself, was satisfied to be husband in name when the emoluments resulting were so satisfactory. There was Varin, commissary of marines, who was Bigot's representative and cat's-paw in Montreal and who had secretly decided to supplant him until he found it, or rather thought to find it, more to his advantage to turn informer on his fellow knaves. There was Martel, who was the King's storekeeper in Montreal, and Maurin, who was physically as well as spiritually humpbacked. There was Corpron, a clerk who, despite the fact that he had been dismissed by various employers for dishonesty, managed to become a wholly satisfactory assistant to Cadet, who was not so sensitive on such matters. It was not a fastidious group, nor were the lesser figures who moved in its orbit—the multitude of dissolute young bucks of the Canadian noblesse, so called, who were the juvenile delinquents of their day and gloried in the fact.

The record would be unbelievable if it was not so thoroughly documented. It would be difficult to conceive that people would submit so tamely to being robbed and despoiled unless it is remembered how deeply they were imbued with the absoluteness of an authority against which there was no appeal. And here, at the heart of the knavery, were the King's representative and his duly appointed officials. The people could not help knowing what was happening to them. They realized that they were suffering and starving and without hope while lights burned brightly in the intendant's palace and men and women dined and gamed there in an opulence that staggers the imagination. A great lassitude had settled on them. They were Frenchmen who knew that other Frenchmen were slowly draining them of the last drop of lifeblood. But they had no will or power or understanding of how to resist. This was the canker gnawing at the heart of New France. It was too deep to be resisted, too all-pervasive to be survived.

Fraud and chicanery had become a way of life, so customary that almost no one thought to question it. It was two years after Cadet had become commissary general that he, Péan, Maurin, Corpron, and Penisseault, as crafty a set of knaves as ever graced the pages of history, conceived the idea of doing a bit of business with the King. They would buy the crops produced by the habitants at what today would be called depression prices. The habitants had no other option. Perhaps they were happy at being paid at all. Cadet and his assorted rogues were happier still. What they had purchased they sold to the King for his needy armies in Europe at a profit on this one transaction of twelve million francs. Bigot's name does not appear in this profitable venture, but wherever there was a profit there was never any doubt that somehow he managed to share.

For himself he operated, at least in the beginning, with a shade more finesse, trusting to his high position to assure success. Under the shadow of the intendant's palace, which crowned the top of

Palace Hill and crowned it worthily with its great mass covering more than two city blocks, there was a large but somewhat less pretentious building near where St. Vallier and St. Nicholas streets now meet. In front it appeared to be a modest retail store presided over by one Claverie, clerk of Martel, the royal storekeeper. Actually, Bigot was the spirit of the place. In fact, the little store was only a blind for the vast warehouse behind. The blind was scarcely successful, for the familiar name of the warehouse was La Friponne, "the place of cheatery." It was well named. Into its empty vastness went all the goods received from the King to supply his colony. They would be disposed of later at a handsome profit. From it, too, went the goods that were sold to the King. By plausible arguments Bigot had convinced the minister, and the King as well, that there were ample resources within the colony to meet its needs for three years at least. It was his helpful idea that from this pool of resources the King might buy what was needed for his colony, saving himself the cost and the hazard of shipping goods from France. It was an idea so reasonable that no one could help agreeing. This arranged, Bigot approached his agent in Bordeaux, bought there what was needed, having the goods shipped to him under the King's name so that there was no difficulty with the customs. These goods were sold eventually to the King at a more than substantial profit. It was later disclosed that in one such operation—supplying the necessary stores for the post at Miramichi—the profit had been just short of nine hundred thousand francs.

Bigot liked to use his accomplices according to their greatest capabilities, and Cadet's gifts ran to the falsification of books. Between them a profitable arrangement was devised. When supplies were requested by military posts, the commandant had to specify the nature and quality of goods before payment could be secured from France. These transactions were hedged about with elaborate formalities. The requisition and the final receipt must bear the signature of the commandant at the post, but they must also be authenticated by the signatures of the King's storekeeper, the local commissary and a general supervisor, and finally that of Bigot himself. The commandant was Cadet's business. He was made amenable by a nice mixture of threats and gifts of brandy or money. For the rest, being all members of Bigot's clique, they presented no problem. It was just a matter of adjudicating the share of each in the resulting profit. The principle was simplicity itself. It was merely to deliver a half or less of what was called for in the requisition and to receive a receipt for the whole. The opportunities of profit are obvious.

There were rumors that the people were hoarding grain, and Cadet was provided with the money to demand its surrender for the King's need. The King was then sold the grain at a handsome profit. It was to be stored in the colony for the benefit of his people. Later, when the pinch of starvation had made these people tractable, their grain was sold back to them again at a princely profit.

There was indeed no avenue of fraud that was not carefully explored. The practice of the King of giving presents to the native tribes was an action to be encouraged. His Majesty could be charged for the gifts purchased at high costs. He could even be informed of their supposedly happy effect. It was the perfect arrangement, profit without attendant cost, for the presents need never leave La Friponne, indeed need never exist at all. The King could be asked to pay for twice the number of soldiers available in the colonies. Even his generosities could provide a profit, and did. The million francs he contributed to help his Indian subjects during a smallpox epidemic, a nice attention suggested by Bigot, got no farther than the grasping hands of the servants of the King.

The record is endless and ugly and did not culminate in fraud alone. It reached out to the sorrier business of demeaning a people. Those who had hardly known what it was to be beyond the fringes of want were taught its full impact. There was no flour for them, though Cadet's chickens waxed fat on the supplies of grain so lavishly provided. There was no beef for starving people. The best they were allowed was half a pound of horse meat a day, and this applied also to Montcalm and the soldiers who were fighting for the life of New France. Because these demands reduced the supply of horses almost to the vanishing point, women and children were made to draw heavy loads while their menfolk fought or did their best to scratch a sparse living from the soil. Yet after the fall of Quebec General Murray was to report large herds of fat cattle. This, while some of the people were eating grass to keep a semblance of life.

And all the while, in the vast palace at the head of Palace Hill, Bigot lived his life of luxury and ease and spreading iniquity. There the little coterie of the elect danced and dined and intrigued without a thought of how brief was the time before them. It was the coming of Montcalm that introduced the first wry note in that harmony of indulgence. At first he was impressed.

Writing in his journal some months after his arrival, the general was to record, "M. l'Intendant lives there—in Quebec—in grandeur and has given two fine balls where I have seen over eighty very charming ladies, beautifully dressed. I think Quebec a town of very good style and I don't believe we have in France more than a dozen cities that could rank higher as regards society. As for numbers, the population is not more than 12,000." Then a graver note interjects itself on his early enthusiasm. "The strange taste of M. l'Intendant for gambling, the extreme complaisance of M. de Vaudreuil, and the regard that I must show for two men vested with the King's authority, have caused gambling of the most dangerous kind to take place. Many officers will feel it bitterly before long." Indeed, more than the young officers would know that bitterness, for Bigot was devoted to gambling. It was part of his shrewd money sense. Many of the young officers of whom Montcalm had spoken were the scions of wealthy families. They were a source of plunder Bigot could not resist. Then, too, many of his own associates had grown wealthy beyond imagining. Here was a way to restore some of their ill-gotten gains to the hand and brain that had put opportunity in their way.

Montcalm, fearful for his young officers, could have the play forbidden in Lower Town, but all regulations stopped short of the intendant's palace. Night after night the intendant's vast salon was bright with candlelight and the rich coloring of silks and satins and the gay splendor of the uniforms of those who danced or played there. From the gallery above, a few favored citizens, who had not reached the social pinnacle of Bigot's guests, looked down on those who had, as they might have looked at royalty. There was a dance hall in the palace, too, for such as they. Bigot was shrewd even in his rascality. He knew that one might keep a place in the hearts of people, even as one defrauded them. There was a never-ending gaiety here. Night after night Bigot's table was lined with twenty to forty favored guests, for what were costs to one who had no thought of paying? And over all these gatherings, wherever they might be, there ruled Angélique des Méloizes, the young, the gay, the beautiful. She was the product of the Canadian noblesse, a figure of charm and wit and the ambition that made her the perfect flower of a perverted system.

For a time the ambition of Angélique looked no higher than the town major, the mayor of his day. Major Hugues Péan, who, if he had earned few laurels as a soldier, had still a sound position to offer—a coming man. So for a while Angélique ruled his small court as wife and hostess, until, indeed, her attentive eyes fell on the new intendant, small and stout and nearing sixty. But what was that to a woman of expansive dreams? There was no protest from her crafty husband when she left his arms for those of the intendant. Both husband and wife recognized that the change might have its practical side. So Madame Péan left the small court of the town major to queen it over the impressive social world of the intendant. Soon she became its indispensable hostess and knew that in fact as well as in desire she had become the Pompadour of the New World.

There was no friendliness between the intendant and the general, but Montcalm could hardly have been omitted from the list of guests at the palace. He was a somewhat critical guest, as the record of his journal shows. "The gambling has been so great and so much beyond the means of the players that I thought I was looking at fools, or rather people sick with a burning fever. I don't think I have ever seen a bigger game except the King's game. There were three tables which would accommodate eighty guests. The rooms were well lighted, and everything would have been perfect if the lord of the house, munificent in all details, had shown more tact and been more attentive to have his splendid supper served earlier. But the game held him so that in spite of his taste for feasting and his desire to please his guests, the supper prepared for nine was served only at twelve."

With the passing hours the airs of gentility began to grow thin. "I left at one o'clock," Montcalm adds, "annoyed at seeing so much play and gambling." The gathering had become riotous, he goes on to explain, and all the talk was of winning or losing. Manners were steadily deteriorating and the gaiety at the end of the banquet "smacked of the tavern."

Such happenings may have interested Montcalm, but they also profoundly disturbed him. He did not fail to see how conditions where "knaves grow rich and honest men are ruined," as he wrote, were undermining the strength and integrity of the country. Montcalm was present when Bigot himself lost fifteen hundred livres in three quarters of an hour. Bigot would not suffer. He knew too well where more was to be secured. But the general knew that many of his own officers were being cashiered for failure to meet their gambling debts.

"My heart and my stomach are both ill at ease, the latter being the worst," he wrote to his faithful assistant, Bourlemaque. But to his wife he wrote more soberly. "The price of everything is rising. I am ruining myself; I owe the treasurer twelve thousand francs. I long for peace and for you." With the growing sense of futility there was a growing nostalgia. "When shall I be at the Château of Candiac, with my plantation, my groves of oak, my oil mill, my mulberry trees?" And then, in the last word he was ever to send his wife, he wrote, "The moment when I shall see you again will be the most beautiful in my life. Adieu, my heart, I believe I love you more than ever before."

Montcalm had done his best. He had written the Minister of War outlining the situation in Canada without reserve. It was an ugly story of fraud and thievery and misgovernment. "It seems," he wrote, "as if they were all hastening to make their fortunes before the loss of the colony; which many of them perhaps desire as a veil to their conduct."

Perhaps this and other letters he had sent did have some effect. Berryer, the new Minister of Marine, did write to Bigot outlining many instances of fraud in Canada. "I no longer wonder," he wrote, "at the immense fortunes made in the colony. You pay bills without examination, and then find an error in your accounts of three million six hundred francs. . . . For the last time, I exhort you to give these things your serious attention, for they will not escape from mine."

Governor Vaudreuil hurried to his friend's defense. "I cannot conceal from you, monseigneur," he wrote, almost with tears in the words, "how deeply M. Bigot feels the suspicions expressed in your letters to him. He does not deserve them, I am sure. He is full of zeal for the service of the King; but as he is rich, or passes for such, and as he has merit, the ill-disposed are jealous and insinuate that he has prospered at the expense of His Majesty. I am certain that it is not true and that nobody is a better citizen than he, or has the King's interest more at heart."

The defense came too late. For one thing, Bougainville had been sent to France to urge upon the minister the need for a proper naval force in New France. The harried minister retorted that one does not try to save the stable when the house is on fire, and undoubtedly France had her own urgent needs. Undoubtedly, however, he would have had his questions regarding happenings and conditions in New France. Possibly as a result of this visit, supplementing as it did the substance of Montcalm's reports, he sent Monsieur Querdisien-Tremais to investigate the rumors. It was too late for anything but judgment.

For Bigot there was no turning back, even had there been any leaning that way. There wasn't. Even to the last minute he was doing his utmost to turn a dishonest penny. As a rogue he was completely consistent. So the candles still burned in the intendant's palace and the gaming went on. If it was not in his palace, it was in the discreet hideaway the intendant maintained for less publicized social gatherings. It bore various names and there is confusion in their use. It was called at times the Château Bigot or Beaumanoir, or sometimes the Hermitage. This latter in derision, perhaps, for certainly Bigot was not a hermit.

At Beaumanoir or the Hermitage, Angélique des Méloizes ruled in all her doubtful splendor among the less demure of the ladies of Quebec. There are many tales of Beaumanoir and its curious history. They have grown with the years and have added adornments with time, so that if there ever was truth in them it has been overlaid long since with colorful fiction—the story of Bigot lost in the forest and rescued by an Algonquin maiden who returned him to Beaumanoir and as a reward was kept a prisoner in Bigot's seraglio. The name that has been given her is Caroline, but that, too, was borne by the beautiful daughter of the Baron St. Castin, who also was said to have had a share of Bigot's vagrant affections. All that we know is that Angélique was there, wherever this hide-out was, and that Bigot and she and others made much and evil use of it.

So the story of Bigot draws to a close. Little remains of him but the report of Monsieur Tremais and the judgment that resulted. Bigot would have defended Quebec in the end, but possibly only out of fear of the future, for he remains an unusually consistent figure in whom duplicity was not to be denied. For it must be remembered that when in a last desperate effort to destroy the English fleet Montcalm had fire ships sent among them it was Bigot who supplied the ships for the abortive effort and charged his King three prices for them.

When the Peace of Paris was signed and Frenchmen were free to return to France there were some of the defeated who found a less than hearty welcome. Those who went from the ships to the somber shadows of the Bastille composed the whole evil company that had sold out New France. Among those who waited for trial were Vaudreuil and Bigot and Cadet and Péan and with them Breard, Varin, Le Mercier, Penisseault, Maurin, Corpron, and some lesser predators.

Long months later twenty-six judges sat in the court of the Châtelet and for fifteen months considered the evidence of evildoing. Vaudreuil was quickly released. His bearing, his argument that he had no part in theft and defalcation made him believed. It was not difficult to recognize that he had not the craft to be adept in iniquity. Of the others, Cadet, with his matchless effrontery, fared best. Unblushingly he declared himself innocent. When that plea failed he undertook to help the prosecution. He was banished from France for nine years and ordered to return six million francs. That must have been the smaller percentage of his winnings, for the butcher of Quebec did end as a baron of France, his sins apparently forgotten or forgiven.

Bigot did not show up so well. In his extremity he turned on all his former friends, now friends no longer. The public prosecutor, could he have had his way, would have been thorough. He asked that, labeled as a thief with a rope around his neck, Bigot should be taken by the public executioner to the principal gate of the Tuileries and there, kneeling, barefooted, bareheaded, and clad only in a shirt, he should declare himself a thief in a voice that all men could hear. That was not the end. He should restore eleven million francs to the treasury and have all his property forfeited to the crown. Finally he was to be taken to the Place de Grève and there beheaded.

But French justice was tougher in the talking than in the doing. The final judgment on the last intendant of New France was that he should pay back not eleven million francs but 1,600,000, and with it all his property, and thereafter he should be banished from France forever.

So he passes from history. If he returned to France after long years and lived in some comfort, as some records say, it was not the same France but only the same Bigot. His place was set. He was the man who had utterly betrayed his countrymen and his country.

CHAPTER XXVI

THE PATHS OF GLORY

Louisburg falls, isolating New France. Her danger, extreme as it is, intensified by declining morale of the people and dissension among her leaders. Wolfe's success at Louisburg brings him command of Britain's supreme threat to New France. His background, his health, his character. Disaster at Beauport followed by decision to attack the heights. An unheralded change of plan, and attack by way of the Anse au Foulon. Vergor's continued failure or worse and Vaudreuil's ineptitude permit the British to reach the Plains of Abraham. The battle. Death of Wolfe and Montcalm. De Ramesay surrenders city.

THE situation of New France could never be wholly desperate while Louisburg guarded its eastern portal. That was the knowledge that was at the heart of all her later thinking. Louisburg guarded the precious life line. Without it New France was hopelessly alone. Recognizing this, no effort had been spared to make it as nearly invulnerable as possible. The fortress itself had been strengthened, and this time there was no Bigot on hand to scamp the work. The garrison had been increased. Now there were nearly three thousand regulars, and with them a thousand militia and half as many Indians. The armament had been strengthened too. There were two hundred cannon actually mounted in the defenses, not to mention the seventeen heavy mortars. A sizable French fleet was there. It doubled the number of guns and of men.

More important than this, there was a new governor, not timid and uncertain and blundering as Duchambon had been when Pepperrell and Warren had headed the attack. The Chevalier de Drucour was of a different breed, stern, courageous, determined. He had a courageous wife, too, which is not to be discounted when the wife is among the defenders. Every day Madame Drucour took her place on the ramparts, and when the fighting began she actually assisted in handling the guns and in firing them herself. There was no lack of courage, as sometimes there had been in the past, no will to fail. And yet failure was foredoomed. It was not Drucour's fault. Probably no one could have done more than he. It was just that a Canada under Vaudreuil and Bigot was no match at all for an empire under Pitt. But even that wasn't the whole story. It was more than a difference in leadership. New France rarely, if ever, had been better led. It was a difference in people. In Canada greed was dominant in high places. In the lesser people hope and faith had died into a dull acceptance of authority that had betrayed them. No matter how long the contest lasted, no matter what successes might still be achieved, failure waited in the wings, ready to appear at any moment.

The English hardly ever before had been so united and so well served. England had indeed brought forth a man, a man of competent judgment and untarnished integrity. He was human enough to make mistakes and great enough to assure that they would be relatively few. For this particular undertaking he had chosen Jeffrey Amherst to head the land forces and had joined with the great Admiral Anson, now the Navy's First Sea Lord, to place the fleet under Admiral Edward Boscawen. Both were able men in their own fields. More happily still, they were long-time friends. As brigadiers under Amherst in this undertaking were Whitmore, of whom we know little except that he was to take over Drucour's post as the governor of Louisburg; Lawrence, who was instrumental in the necessary expulsion of the Acadian dissidents; and that strange, pitiful, dramatic genius, Brigadier James Wolfe. It is he who has the leading role in the events that follow.

Impressive as the number of French defenders might appear compared with other days, they were not facing other days but a present where Britain was using every effort against a consistent enemy. General Amherst's army numbered almost twelve thousand troops, most of them regulars, while the manpower of Boscawen's fleet of

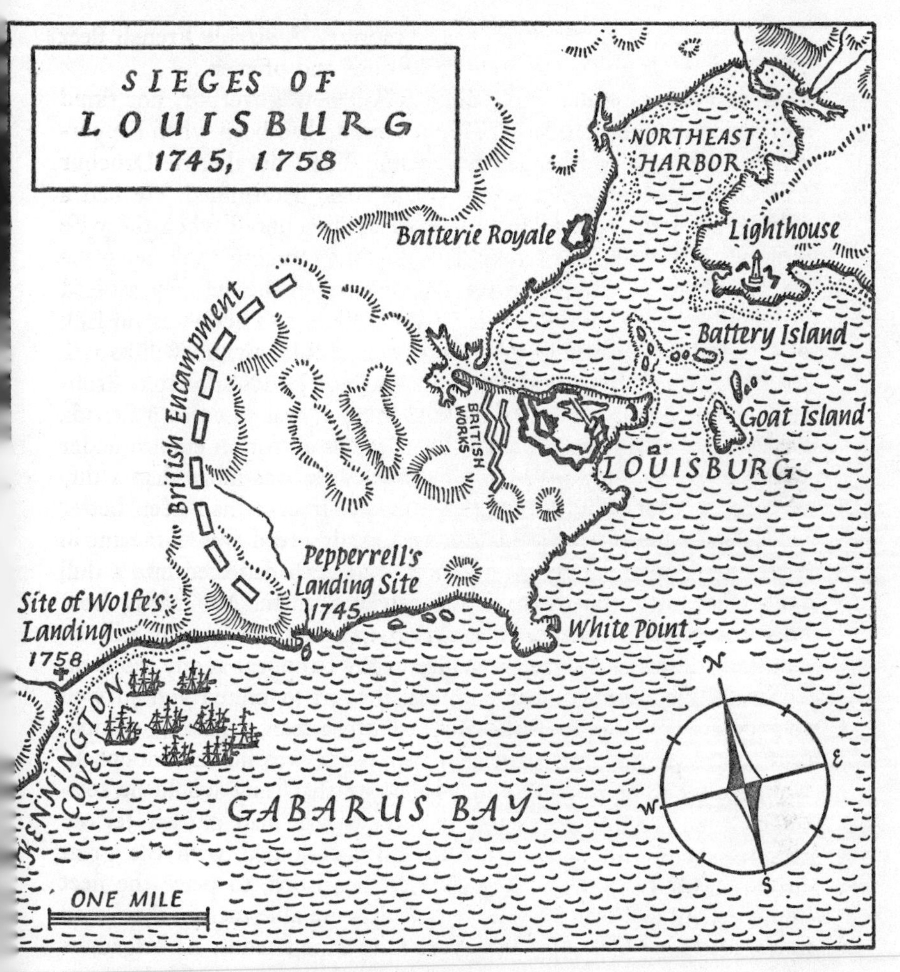

thirty-nine ships, great and small, would have raised the total to twelve thousand more. The defending force, then, numbered hardly a third of the attackers. The fortress itself, of course, was to be considered. Even though no one now believed it quite impregnable, it was a factor offsetting to a considerable degree the disparity in numbers. Yet the best protection Drucour had was the rugged coast line that guarded the only available landing points. Unlike the former attacks, where landings were almost unopposed, stout old Drucour proposed to contest ownership of every foot of solid ground, and he was fully prepared.

It was June 1, 1758, when his anxious sentinels, straining their eyes to pierce the fog, felt a sudden breeze on their cheeks and saw the fog begin to lift. They had waited long for just such a sight, but its coming left them breathless. There, in a mighty crescent in Gabarus Bay, Boscawen's fleet rode at anchor. The challenge had come.

At the first warning Drucour set his plan in motion. He had two thousand men spread along the four miles of possible attack. They were supported by hidden guns. A thousand men faced the quarter mile of beach that offered the most promising approach, between the two promontories that outlined Freshwater or Kennington Cove.

There followed a whole week of waiting, a week of storm and fog and smashing surf where no boat could live. On the eighth day the sea looked more calm and the impatient Wolfe got his men aboard boats. It was two in the morning and bitterly cold and the sea was far from smooth, though it might appear so from shipboard. But if wind and sea were cold, there was nothing cold in the welcome of Drucour's men. They let the boats come close in shore where the breakers would catch them, then the whole cove flamed with gun- and rifle fire. Small chance of replying from that smother of water. Even the restless and intrepid Wolfe could only wave to his men to get away. But one small group to the east of the beach, taking what advantage they could of the turmoil of attack, had managed to make shore, more dead than alive, among the cruel rocks. Wolfe might appear to be retreating, but even in retreat his eye was searching for some possible advantage. He saw the scattering of men seeking some shelter among the boulders and he waited for nothing else but drove his boats for that one bit of shore. When the breakers caught them he was overboard, cane in hand, fighting his way through the surf, with those who could following.

That was the real end. The siege might continue for days and weeks. The defenders might stubbornly contest every move with fire and musketry and the steady day-by-day blast of cannon. Ships might be sunk in the harbor mouth to deny Boscawen entrance, four at first, then two more. Ships might be sent for aid that couldn't come. Ship by ship the French fleet might dwindle to nothing, but the end was still the same.

Stout old Drucour would have fought on, hoping to prolong the siege, hoping at worst to hold the attackers on that rugged landing shore until it was too late to attack elsewhere. But there were not many of his mind. Most were fearful of what might come to a fortress taken by assault. So the door closed. The last hope of New France. It was July 27, 1758.

In Canada the internecine struggle continued. Montcalm did his best to end it, realizing that internal dissension was more dangerous than any open force that could be brought against him. Shortly after Ticonderoga he wrote the governor what he certainly intended as a conciliatory letter: "I think the real trouble lies with the people who compose your letters, and with the mischief-makers who are trying to set you against me. You may be sure that none of the things which are being done against me will ever lessen my zeal for the good of the country or my respect toward you. Why not change your secretary's style? Why not give me more of your confidence? I take the liberty of saying that the King's service would gain by it, and we should no longer appear so disunited that even the British know all about it."

It was a well-intended letter, if perhaps its phrasing was not calculated to achieve the best results with a hopelessly vain man. At least it didn't. Vaudreuil's letters to the minister in Paris left no suggestion of a change of heart. "I beseech you," he wrote the minister, "to ask the King to recall the Marquis de Montcalm. He desires it himself." It became a constant refrain. "I cannot help warning you," he wrote again, "of the unhappy consequences that would follow if the Marquis de Montcalm should remain here."

Obviously the home authorities were neither impressed nor pleased. Instead of the recall of Montcalm, the governor who had pleaded so earnestly received peremptory instructions from the King to defer to Montcalm "in all questions of war, or of civil administration bearing upon war."

The governor was sufficiently impressed by this and the steady deterioration of the situation to agree with Montcalm on a plan to send two officers to France to explain the situation to the King. The officers chosen were Bougainville and Doreil. They carried a letter in the governor's own hand. It read: "Colonel Bougainville is in all respects better fitted than anyone else to inform you of the state of the colony. I have given him my orders, and you can trust entirely in everything he tells you." Of Doreil he wrote almost as effusively. 'M. Doreil, the Commissary of War, may be entirely trusted. Everybody likes him here."

Lest his words should be taken seriously, Vaudreuil wrote again to the minister. The letter went by the same ship that carried the two emissaries with their word of introduction, but it was of somewhat different import. It explained, "In order to condescend to the Marquis de Montcalm and do all I can to keep on good terms with him I have given letters to Colonel Bougainville and M. Doreil. But I must tell you that they do not really know Canada well, and I warn you that they are nothing but creatures of the Marquis de Montcalm."

With such diplomatic duplicity added to the more practical opposition of Bigot, it is small wonder that Montcalm should confide to Bourlamaque, "I should like as well as anybody to be Marshal of France; but to buy the honor with the life I am leading here would be too much."

It is not always recognized that the conflict that was soon to be at Quebec was not one of equal warfare. It was also a conflict in which attitudes played their decisive part. Beyond the broader differences between authoritarianism and freedom there was the difference of a conflicting leadership opposed to one united in a common end. There was New France with its people starving. There were Bigot and his carrion crew robbing King and countrymen alike and using their winnings on their delights and their debaucheries. There was a devoted man striving to save and restore. And there was a governor nibbling at the only hope that remained, too vain and incompetent to know what he was doing. How could that stand against an England under Pitt leading the people toward the greatest unanimity they had known in centuries?

Here were no whimpering voices of challenge. Walpole, the wit of his day, might still gibe and phrase the truth jauntily, but it was still the truth. "Our unanimity," he said, "is prodigious. You would as soon hear a 'no' from an old maid as from the House of Commons."

And it was more than unanimity. It was a resurgence of devotion. Men's hearts were in what they did. No more the feeling that incompetence was good enough, no more decisions and choices made, as Newcastle had made them, because the chosen were rich in their control of votes or because they were related to a duke, as someone phrased it. Basically it was simple enough. Instead of a James Abercrombie there was a James Wolfe.

James Wolfe, to become one of the most notable figures in Canadian history, was a frail, inhibited, uncomely child. Born of a soldier father and a mother who was beautiful and devoted and something of a martinet, with a flair for intruding on her son's innocent enough affairs of the heart, Wolfe grew into a not very pleasant little boy. Yet he was a devoted son who received in return the continuing affection of his parents. His was, one must assume, a happy childhood. His admiration for his father early turned his mind toward military affairs. His devotion to his mother made him easily subservient to her will, a guidance sometimes more interested than it was wise. He added an easy capacity for making and holding friends.

He turned into a man no more prepossessing than the boy, lean, tall, red-haired, with a beaklike nose and a receding chin. As he was a frail child, so he became a frail and sickly man. This weakness accounted, in part at least, for an excitable temper. He could be arrogant. He could be fierce and needlessly stern at times, and at others considerate and understanding. He could be imperiously irritable and again be deeply hurt, and set the hurt aside because he believed it interfered with his duty. He could command affection among his associates and hold it. He could earn respect and confidence of his men. He could set them an example of a courage that never wavered. Quite early in his soldiering he said, "My utmost desire and ambition is to look steadily upon danger." He had this heart's desire. Wherever danger was, Wolfe was not far away. He received his ensign's commission when he was scarcely fifteen. A year later he shared in the great victory over the French at Dettingen as the adjutant of his regiment. He was thirty-two when he was called to Hayes, Pitt's country seat near London, and was told he was to command the expedition against Quebec with the temporary rank of major general. He was not yet thirty-three when he learned, as he had expected, that the paths of glory have their somber end. But, young as he was, already he was recognized as one of the great soldiers of his own or any age.

Wolfe was a man who had no time to waste, and certainly he knew it. During the Louisburg campaign his impatience with delay was the only source of friction between him and General Amherst, who was a great soldier but not a hurrying one. Amherst knew that Wolfe had been the life of the siege of Louisburg. From the beginning Wolfe had urged, "When the army is landed the business is half done." There was no waiting to get ashore. There was no lagging in his desperate drive to get the business finished. Every day that passed was a day that could have been used for other conquests. When finally it was over he was still in a hurry to be gone. "This damned French garrison," he complained, "takes up our time and attention that could be better bestowed."

He sent Amherst a note asking what the general proposed to do next. Amherst replied, "What I most wish is to go to Quebec." But he went on to explain that the admiral did not think the plan practicable. The word may have satisfied Amherst, but it was not to Wolfe's liking. He said so bluntly, and with every evidence of irritation. He was critical of both his senior officers and did not hesitate to let it appear. "If the admiral will not carry us to Quebec, reinforcements should certainly be sent to the continent without losing a moment."

As he continued, his annoyance grew. "I beg pardon for the freedom," he wrote, "but I cannot look coolly upon the bloody inroads of those hell-hounds the Canadians; and if nothing further is to be done, I must desire leave to quit the army."

Amherst seems to have been more than ordinarily patient for a general, and possibly he had grown used to some idiosyncrasies. His reply was firm but placating. "Whatever schemes you have, or information that you can give to quicken our motions, your communicating them will be very acceptable, and will be of much more service than your thought of quitting the army, which I can by no means agree to, as all my thought and wishes are confined at present to pursuing our operations for the good of His Majesty's service, and I know nothing that can tend more to it than your assisting in it."

If a reproof, even a mild reproof, was intended, it wasn't so received. Learning that Amherst planned to join Abercrombie on Lake George and to settle matters in that section, Wolfe could not forgo another word of advice. It was sound enough, if uncalled for. "An offensive daring kind of war will awe the Indians and ruin the French. Blockhouses and a trembling defensive encourage the meanest scoundrels to attack us. If you will attempt to cut up New France by the roots, I will come with pleasure to assist."

Apparently Amherst had grown weary of the correspondence, for he did not reply. Instead Wolfe received orders to destroy the settlements on the Gulf of St. Lawrence. It was a task little to his liking, but he went at it with his customary vigor. By the end of September he was back in Louisburg writing his report.

The report was succinct. "I have done a great deal of mischief," it said, "and spread the terror of His Majesty's arms through the Gulf, but have added nothing to the reputation of them." It was true enough. About all that had been accomplished was the destruction of the homes of many innocent people facing the approach of a rigid winter and large stores of food that would be urgently needed. It seems beyond question that no reputation had been enhanced.

Before entering on the Louisburg campaign Wolfe had received assurance that he would be permitted to return as soon as the campaign was ended. So without further ado he sailed for England, somewhat to the annoyance of Pitt, who did not know of the arrangement and wanted Wolfe in Canada, not in England. However, this misunderstanding was easily explained and, in the general rejoicing and adulation, was quickly forgotten. In a letter to Pitt, Wolfe asked that sufficient time be given him to repair the injury done to his health before he was assigned to another task. When one of his friends in a report commented on his pallor, Wolfe replied, "I have this day signified to Mr. Pitt that he may dispose of my slight carcass as he pleases and that I am ready for any undertaking within my skill and cunning. I am in a very bad condition both with the gravel and with rheumatism; but I had much rather die than decline any kind of service that offers."

However, with the idea of benefiting his health as best he could, he went to Bath to take advantage of its mineral springs and found a place on Queen's Square. Whether Bath was just a shot in the dark or whether he remembered that the year before he had met there a Miss Katharine Lowther is nowhere stated, but it can be inferred even from a letter he wrote his father. "I have got in the square to be more at leisure, more in the air and nearer the country. The women are not remarkable, nor the men neither; however," he adds philosophically, or because he had inside knowledge, "a man must be very hard to please, if he does not find some that will suit him."

Wolfe was not hard to please. He found, as probably he expected he would, that Katharine Lowther was also in Bath. He must have felt, too, that he had little time to lose, for, unlike his usual hesitancy in the presence of women, he pressed his suit with a vigor reminiscent of his military tactics. There was no public announcement of an engagement, but equally there has never been any doubt that it existed. He carried Katharine's picture with him always, and she a locket containing a lock of that often disparaged red hair. Also, she gained the quick enmity of Wolfe's mother, as was his mother's way with every woman acquaintance her son favored. There was no outward reason for such antagonism. Katharine Lowther was a woman of beauty, as her portrait shows; she was of a wealthy and socially prominent family. But Wolfe's mother had no thought of sharing his affections with any woman, or so it appeared. This time she could not decide.

Neither romance nor the climate of England seemed to do the young soldier much good. Perhaps neither lasted long enough. His stay was interrupted by that imperative message from Hayes. Hastening there, young Wolfe heard from Pitt that he had been chosen to command the expedition against Quebec, the key operation of the coming campaign in America. Undoubtedly Pitt knew of the almost insurmountable obstacles to be overcome. He knew of no one else with the persistence and the temper to goad his followers to accomplishment. If Louisburg had done nothing else, it had proven the man.

Wolfe's own regiment was fighting on the continent and he had hoped for orders to rejoin it, but when the situation made other demands he accepted them without question. For all his argumentative manner that sometimes ran to arrogance, he was, in fact, simple and unassuming. Perhaps it was the flaming hair that left the suggestion of swagger attached to his name. There was nothing of that in a letter written to a favorite uncle, but rather the suggestion of one somewhat overwhelmed by the responsibility placed on him. "I shall do my best," he wrote, "and leave the rest to fortune, as perforce we must when there is not the most commanding abilities." And he concluded his letter: "If I have health and constitution enough for the campaign, I shall think myself a lucky man; what happens afterwards is of no great consequence."

In December he was back in Bath, probably for some final words with Katharine Lowther, his intended wife. The remainder of the time he spent in London in the urgent duties of preparation. He did not go to his home again but sent his mother a stiffly affectionate letter of farewell in which he included his "best duty to the General," his father.

On February 17, 1759, Wolfe stood with Admiral Charles Saunders on the bridge of the *Neptune*, flagship of the great fleet, and watched England recede into the mist, more than half knowing that he would never see those shores again.

Saunders, with Wolfe and the twenty-two ships of the line and many frigates and sloops of war, reached Louisburg after a voyage of more than two months to find the harbor completely ice-blocked. He had no alternative but to go on to Halifax, where the great fleet arrived on April 30. The army was still to be gathered. Brigadiers Monckton and Murray had been in the colonies all winter, and the forces that were to be used against Quebec were also to be drawn from there. Mainly these were the forces employed against Louisburg; they consisted of ten battalions of infantry of the line, six companies of American rangers, and some forces drawn from the Louisburg garrison itself. When the troopships had all rendezvoused there in the latter part of May it was discovered that instead of the 12,000 troops proposed, the available force was no more than 9,280. When this was learned in England there was an immense wave of depression, and it was generally held that failure was inevitable. Wolfe himself was more optimistic. He didn't care much for the rangers, never having liked American troops, but in the main he felt that if the men were few they were mostly first-rate. He wrote to Pitt, "If valor can make amends for lack of numbers, we shall probably succeed."

It was a more optimistic judgment than might have been expected, for Montcalm had with him some fifteen thousand regulars and a thousand militia and he was defending a position heretofore considered impregnable. From the citadel westward the heights presented an almost unapproachable barrier, easily guarded with a limited number of men. Down the river it was a different matter. There was lowland there that, if difficult of approach, was possible of assault. Once secured, it might offer a more practicable route for attack. Montcalm, then, even after detaching two thousand men to hold the city, had fourteen thousand remaining to defend the seven miles of defenses running all the way from the city to the Montmorency, a deep and difficult stream, itself a sound anchorage for the left of Montcalm's line. This line was well entrenched and had behind it a ridge of ground presenting another natural defense, and in front were the muddy tidal flats along the Beauport shore, which on an earlier day had been too much for Major Walley commanding the land forces under Sir William Phips.

One advantage there was on which Wolfe counted. It is frequently overlooked and yet it was impressive. That was that General Amherst was steadily driving up Lake Champlain to attack Montreal. This threat was undermining the already badly shaken morale of the French and if it continued would compel the detachment of considerable troops to assure the protection of Montreal, for the survival of either position determined that of the other.

Montcalm, having made everything as secure as he could, decided to remain on the defensive as he had done at Ticonderoga and let the enemy break themselves to pieces on his lines. The only thing he didn't quite realize was that Wolfe was a very different opponent from Abercrombie. Yet perhaps he did. "We keep on fighting," he wrote the Minister of War, "and we will bury ourselves, if necessary, under the ruins of the colony."

Wolfe had his own comment and it bespoke a vastly different feeling. "If General Montcalm succeeds again this year in frustrating our hopes," he said, "he may be considered an able man; either the colony has resources that nobody knows of, or our generals are worse than usual."

New France had no hidden resources; that much was sure. She did have a superlative general and, at the first, it did not seem that the English could match him at all. Wolfe was sick, and much of the driving spirit that had characterized his every movement seemed to have deserted him. He did move to capture the heights across the river from the city. They were of vital importance, for only from them could Quebec be effectively bombarded. Why they were not fortified before the English arrived is hard to understand. Probably Vaudreuil didn't want it and Montcalm knew that the strength of his north-shore defenses was vital to his ultimate success. Let failure happen there and it mattered little what success there might be at other points. So the great heights of Pointe-aux-Pères were taken and fortified. Wolfe's guns commanded the city; more than that, they commanded the roadstead where Admiral Saunders' fleet rode at anchor. They gave him freedom to move up as well as down the river. In so much they were vital to victory.

Wolfe had done his best to find a vital point at which he might strike with some hope of success. Upriver for eight miles, until the fortifications at Cap Rouge were reached, the cliff rose almost straight from the river, two hundred feet in height. At only two or three points was the precipitous height broken by gullies into something slightly less formidable. A bare scattering of resolute men could hold such natural defenses against an army. And there was the city itself, with fortifications mounting over a hundred guns. Below the city, down to the Montmorency, was that steep and rocky ridge with the entrenchments before them, and before these again those dreadful tidal flats protecting the possible landing ground. To take the entrenchments, even should an army get ashore, would be a useless hazard. Formidable as they were toward the river, they were useless if taken, for the ridge beyond overlooked every inch of them. Small wonder that the commander should have written rather plaintively to Pitt, "I have only a choice of difficulties left."

He did what he could. He offered Montcalm many chances to attack in detail. He had his main force on the Isle of Orleans, but he attacked and finally secured a landing beyond the Montmorency. He had his batteries at Pointe-aux-Pères across from the city, challenging Vaudreuil to attack them. Now he had Saunders detach a part of his fleet under Admiral Holmes to see what could be done about the defenses at Cap Rouge, where Bougainville was in command. They proved too strong to be attacked, but Holmes quickly discovered that by sailing his fleet up and down the river he could keep Bougainville forever on the move, never knowing at which of those possible paths of ascent the enemy might be proposing to attack.

Many of the French commanders were pleading with him to strike the enemy somewhere, anywhere on that extended line that had been spread so thin. Montcalm only shook his head. His plan was working; days and weeks were passing. If the enemy could be stalled a few more weeks, Quebec might be safe, as more than once the coming of winter had given it last-minute security. "Let him amuse himself where he is," said Montcalm, thinking of his opponent with his choice of difficulties. "If we drive him away from there"—he was thinking of the Montmorency landing—"he may go someplace where he can do us more harm."

Lower Town was a mass of rubble from bombardment, but that had been anticipated; food was still plentiful, and there was no indication that the enemy had made any tangible gains except for those batteries at Point-aux-Pères and a certain mobility in the fleet. Time was wearing on and these small gains could be forgotten.

Sickness had quieted Wolfe's imperious temper, but it couldn't last. The frustration was too much for his eager spirit. After weeks of waiting for some opening or for the enemy to move against him, the troops as well as their general had strained their patience to the

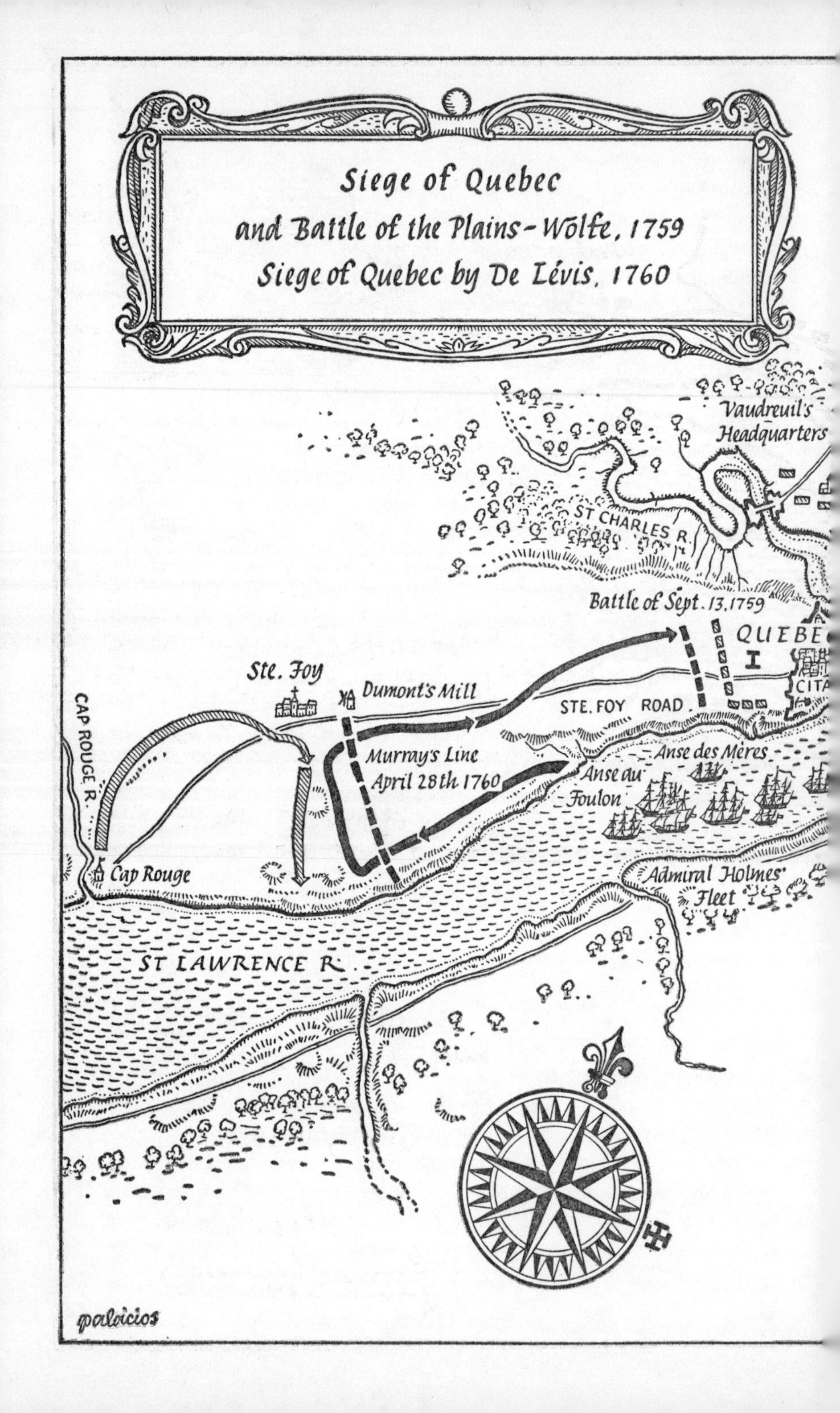
Siege of Quebec
and Battle of the Plains - Wolfe, 1759
Siege of Quebec by De Lévis, 1760
Vaudreuil's
Headquarters
ST CHARLES R.
Battle of Sept. 13. 1759
QUEBE
CITA
Ste. Foy
Dumont's Mill
STE. FOY ROAD
CAP ROUGE R.
Murray's Line
April 28th 1760
Anse des Mères
Anse au
Foulon
Cap Rouge
Admiral Holmes'
Fleet
ST LAWRENCE R.
palacios

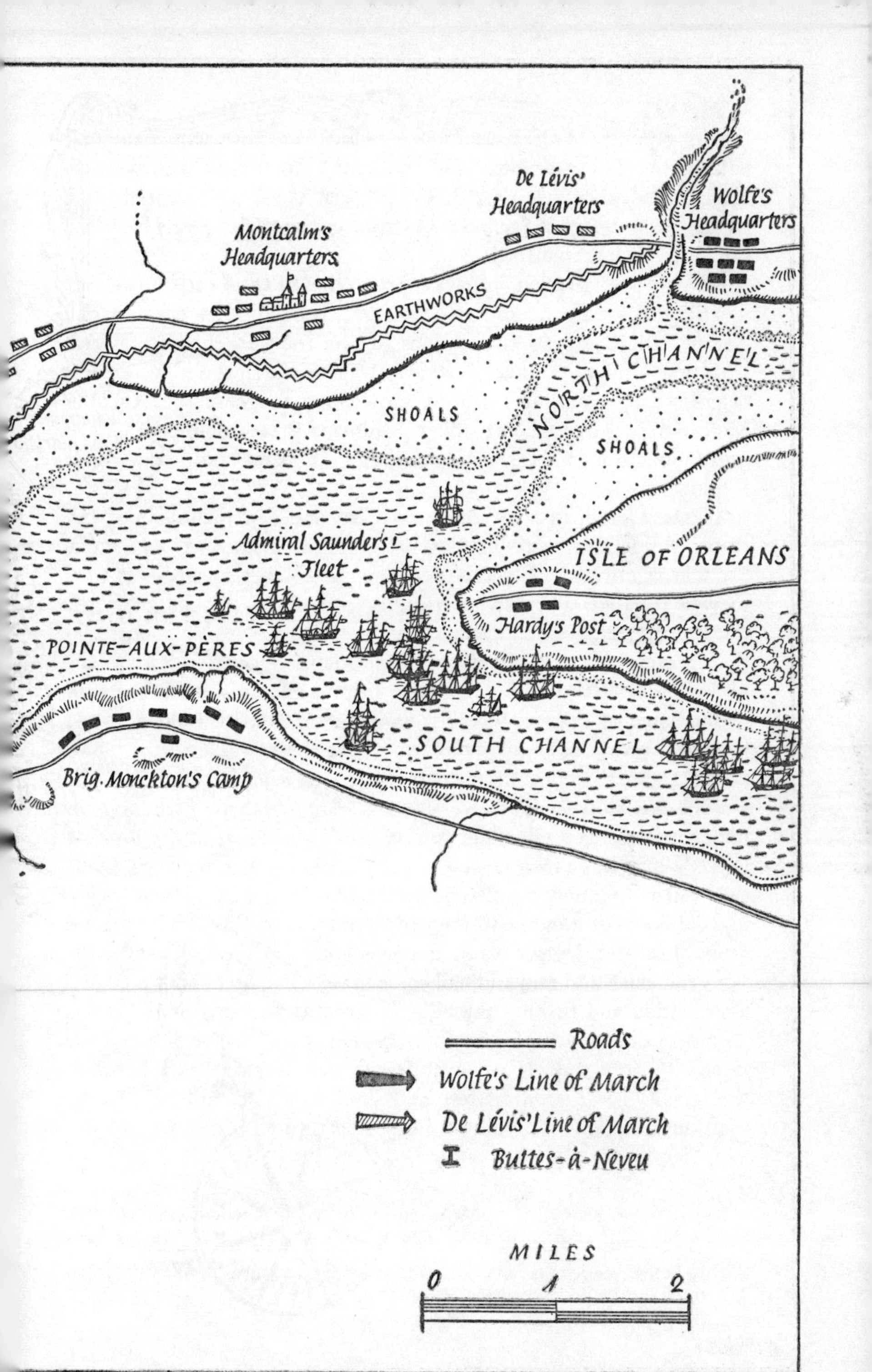
De Lévis' Headquarters
Wolfe's Headquarters
Montcalm's Headquarters
EARTHWORKS
NORTH CHANNEL
SHOALS
SHOALS
Admiral Saunders's Fleet
ISLE OF ORLEANS
Hardy's Post
POINTE-AUX-PERES
SOUTH CHANNEL
Brig. Monckton's Camp
Roads
Wolfe's Line of March
De Lévis' Line of March
Buttes-à-Neveu
MILES
0
1
2

breaking point. Wolfe's decision to attack was met with delighted enthusiasm. The grenadiers and the Royal Americans who were to head the advance felt that they had been especially favored. The attack was to be made from the Montmorency bridgehead, where low tide left a vulnerable ford.

At half-past five on July 31, from the batteries at the Montmorency, from the heights at Lévis, and from ships anchored in the channel, there came a tremendous fire on the French defenses and batteries. Under its cover boats drew into the shallow water and began setting their men ashore. Downstream, where the receding Montmorency had made fording possible, a great column of almost two thousand men was slogging through the water and mud to surer footing.

Thirteen companies of the grenadiers and a detachment of the Royal Americans were first ashore. Following them would come Monckton's brigade. But the grenadiers and Americans had no time to wait for that. They struck the first redoubt with such fury that the French relinquished it almost without a struggle. No sooner had the cheering advance swept over it and come face to face with the towering heights ahead than those heights blazed with a sheet of flame. Some of France's greatest regiments manned that height, and they had no thought of giving way. Yet there was no thought of possible retreat among those charging troops who dug heels into the treacherous slopes and drove upward. Among them, swinging his useless stick, was a tall slight figure, red hair shining in the evening light. Wolfe was a man possessed as he urged his men forward, while the dead and wounded rolled down the bloody slope together, breaking the lines for a moment, only to have them re-form and come on again. Just as it seemed valor might accomplish the impossible, the sky grew dark and rain and hail came in torrents, drenching men and ammunition and turning the hill into an ascent as impossible as ice. The men dropped back into the forsaken redoubt. Even there they were only in a trap. It was madness to persist and Wolfe knew it. Regretfully he ordered the retreat. Killed, wounded, and missing, the total ran to 443. It would have been a costly victory. It was a catastrophic defeat.

There is no record that Montcalm exulted in the victory, though it was his policy that had assured it. But Vaudreuil, as usual, was highly vocal, eager to have a major share in any credit. He wrote to

Bourlamaque, who had his own problems with Amherst on his trail, "I have no more anxiety about Quebec. M. Wolfe, I can assure you, will make no progress." Like other amateur prophets, his opinions lacked validity, true as they might appear at the moment.

The excitement, the strain, the endless delays, and the resultant dejection of spirit had not helped General Wolfe. Moreover, he was confined to his bare pallet in a habitant hut. His brigadiers could not veil their impatience. They felt, and probably quite rightly, that they should know more of the general's plans than he had confided to them.

In late August he made his general policy clear and urged them to consider what he wrote, to discuss it and offer their suggestions. His basic points were these: "If the French army is attacked and defeated the general concludes the town would immediately surrender, because he does not find that they have any provisions in the place. The general is of the opinion that the army should be attacked in preference to the place, because of the difficulties of penetrating from the lower to the upper town."

From this policy, undoubtedly, had sprung the attack at Beauport and the Montmorency. It had not succeeded, but the basic thinking was still unchanged. Wolfe had tried below the town, where his attack was more or less expected. Now he would try above, where it would be less so. His health, he knew, was the crux of his situation. There is small doubt that he knew death was very near him. What he needed was time, and it was running out. "I know perfectly well," he explained to his surgeon, "you cannot cure my complaint; but patch me up so that I may be able to do my duty for the next few days, and I shall be content."

It was undoubtedly the general's intention to take whatever desperate chance was needed to gain a foothold on the heights about Quebec. There is every evidence that the point of proposed attack was to be at Pointe-aux-Trembles. Perhaps a dozen miles upstream from Cap Rouge. It was so supposed by all the brigadiers and had their full support. That point was probably chosen because it was the junction point where all the roads leading westward to the interior of the colony merged into one that led on to Quebec. It was a point where a victory, if achieved, would have been decisive, for from there the defending army could have been encompassed. These factors explain the decision and leave still unexplained the sudden decision, made by Wolfe alone, to attack elsewhere. It seems from the evidence that Wolfe must have received a message important enough not only to change the proposed attack completely but to delay it some days, though to get the matter finished was the need that must have bulked most largely in all the general's thinking.

The point of attack selected was open to every question. It was the Anse au Foulon, less than three miles from the citadel itself and so closer to observation and to quick reprisal. Then the ascent was known to be almost perpendicular and to be cumbered with felled trees and abatis. Obviously the assistant commanders were startled at the change. An item in Townshend's diary dated September 10 states: "By some intelligence the general has had, he has changed his mind as to the place he intended to land; heard we had some deserters from the enemy's camp at Beauport." This seemingly unrelated conjunction of ideas has a more than possible implication—that some informant, some disgruntled person—and there must have been multitudes of them—or some member of the galaxy of brigands who had claimed the country must have suggested a new route, and suggested also that it would not be contested.

Major General Mahon, in his exhaustive biography of General James Murray, hazards a guess that it was Cadet who was the interested party in betraying his country. Just what he had to gain is a little obscure. Others have suggested Bigot himself, on the theory that he hoped, through the fall of New France, to cover his own vast depredations. This, too, seems a little farfetched, for New France did fall and Bigot did not escape.

Bougainville, too, was a factor to be considered. He had a large mobile defense force of better than a thousand men based on Cap Rouge and covering the whole area. He had even a small detachment of thirty horsemen. No one has ever suggested, or could suggest, that he was not wholly devoted both to his country and to his commander. Yet the sober fact remains that on the occasion when he was most needed he was not present. It is possible that he was busy about Pointe-aux-Trembles, a dozen miles away, where an attack was expected. It may have been that he had grown irritated at the constant task of following the movement of the fleet up and down the river and had become careless. There is even gossip that a quite innocent bit of gallantry involving a Madame de Vienne, who needed to be set on the road from Quebec to Montreal, may have drawn him farther from his post than he should have been. Whatever the reason, it was not treasonable and it was not sound.

Montcalm, with no suspicion of anyone but conscious that something was happening upriver, was somewhat troubled. Still he was convinced the point of danger was the Beauport shore and the St. Charles River, by which route the fortress could have been taken in the rear. This was the threatened point, and that was where he stayed. Admiral Saunders was giving good ground for that suspicion by a heavy bombardment along that shore. It might or might not be the forerunner of another assault. But Montcalm took the precaution of ordering the battalion of Guienne to a position on the Plains of Abraham close to the Anse au Foulon. When Governor Vaudreuil heard of it he was incensed. His friend De Vergor was in command there, and at the governor's own instructions. Testily he countermanded Montcalm's order. "The English haven't wings," he said. "Let the regiment of Guienne stay where it is." Those were the fatal words. He would look into it in the morning. In the meantime De Vergor was there in command.

If the friendly governor remembered for a moment that De Vergor had also been in command at Fort Beauséjour when that place had been surrendered virtually without a hint of struggle and that he had been tried and censured for his action, it seems to have entirely slipped his memory. Whether De Vergor had a part in any plot or not, there is certainly no question that it would be hard to find a less competent guardian. He hadn't advised the governor that he had allowed some of his command belonging to the militia of Lorette to return to their farms for some days and had himself retired to sleep. De Vergor was awakened by a couple of shots from his frightened sentries as the redcoats began pulling themselves over the brink. Without more ado he fled, his nightshirt trailing grotesquely behind him. He was promptly captured and goes down in history as the Major André of the history of New France, though without Major André's character or courage or possible justification. Nowhere in history will one find a good word for Duchambon de Vergor.

Among the first to reach the crest of that almost perpendicular climb was the slight, pain-ridden body that was the commander. Following him, the troops came swarming up the heights, forming ranks as they could and marching off in the early daylight, going inland until their march crossed the Ste. Foy road. There they turned east and deployed, facing the city hidden from them by a long ridge.

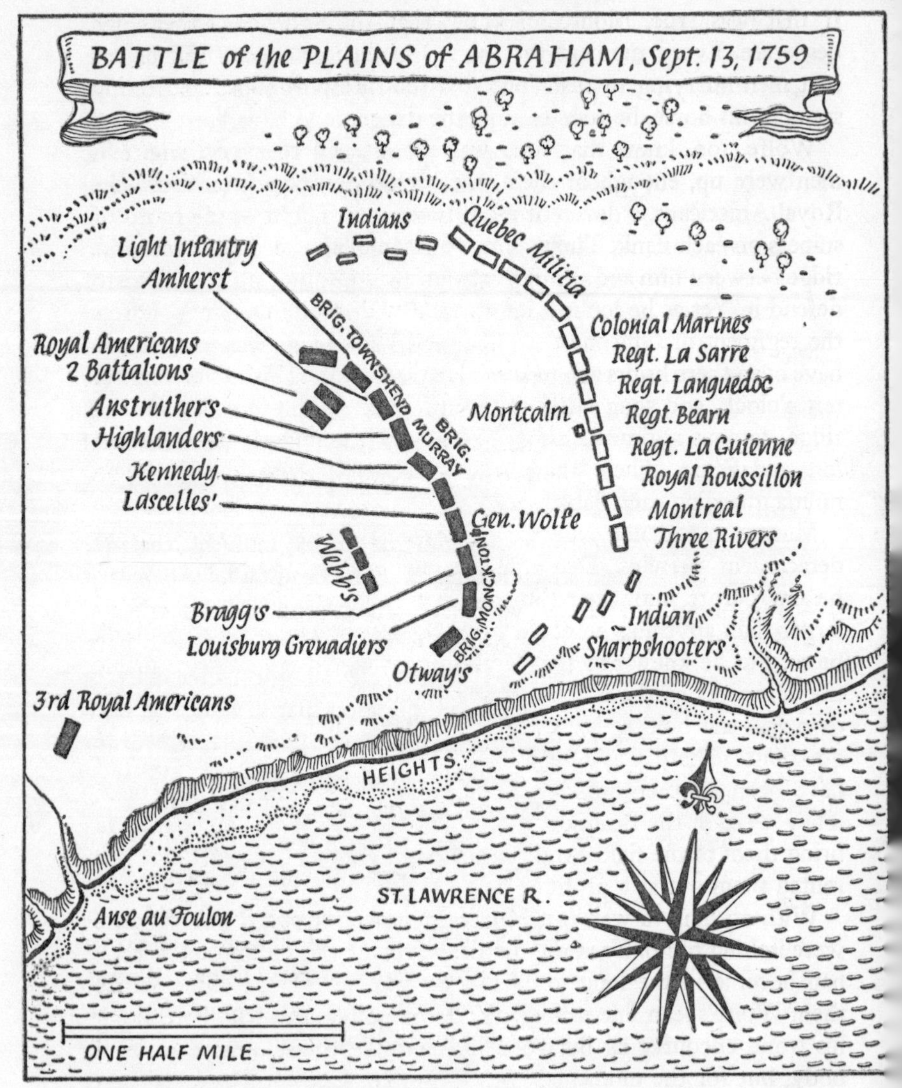

A sound of distant firing had come to Montcalm at his post near Beauport. He had been awake all night. Now he mounted his horse and rode toward the city. As he neared the St. Charles River with its bridge of boats he met an officer, Boishevert, who had been invalided in Quebec for some weeks. He had disturbing news. "I have seen the British drawn up in line of battle in front of Borgia's house," he said.

If that was true, Montcalm knew that the situation had grown desperate. Every moment that passed made it more so. His orders sent men hurrying to rush forces to the threatened section. Setting spurs to his horse, he rode toward the danger.

Wolfe, too, knew that time was the essence of everything. His men were up, enough of them, the highlanders, the grenadiers, the Royal Americans, a dozen or more battalions. There were groups of snipers on each flank. They were worrisome but not dangerous. The ridge between him and the city was bare, almost as if no one cared to defend it. Yet as he looked, it swarmed with white uniforms. It was the regiment of Guienne that, but for Vaudreuil's petulance, would have been there hours ago to make a British success impossible. It was ten o'clock, and soon other regiments were falling into line on the ridge—famous regiments, those of La Sarre, and Languedoc, Roussillon, and Béarn. They stood in ranks six deep, with the Canadian militia guarding each flank.

Montcalm had not expected an army. A strong and adventurous detachment, perhaps. That could be handled. But the regiments that he saw before him, their thin red line only two men deep, looked larger than anything he could bring against it. He knew it couldn't be so. But he knew also that De Ramesay would not make available the defenders of the city. And Vaudreuil, as usual, had plans of his own and was holding back regiments. Again there was the puzzling question: Where was Bougainville? Where were the guns? might have been another question, though Montcalm knew the answer. They were in the Beauport works, because there were no horses to bring them to the field. And there were no horses because Bigot had rented them out at a profit.

With nothing to wait for, Montcalm moved forward. His regulars were itching to go. Even the militia, reluctant and indifferent as they had become in the long years of privation, caught the fire. Before them Wolfe's lean line waited. Wolfe himself was everywhere along his front, encouraging by word and example. Fever burned his frail body, but for the moment it was forgotten. They had patched him up as he had asked, and he had his day. He had a couple of guns with him, dragged up the heights with incredible effort. These were shotted with grape.

The French line was moving now, their precision broken by the militiamen who would fall on their knees to reload. But they came on steadily enough, firing as they advanced. There was no answering fire from the thin line facing them. It stood there quiet and unmoving. The French drew closer. Now they were within forty yards of each other, a narrow strip of sod between. A sharp command and from the long line, as from one invisible hand, a crash of musketry. Many who spoke of it later said that it sounded more like a cannon shot, but perhaps that was imagination. Moments later another volley crashed into those heavy lines of advancing men. When the smoke cleared, it could be seen that both flanks were in full retreat. In the center, where the ghastly heaps of dead and wounded lay, regiments were still coming forward, struggling to regain their formation. They were not defeated, not yet.

Wolfe was at the head of the Louisburg grenadiers. With the highlanders on their left and the Royal Americans on their right, these went forward at a run. A shot shattered Wolfe's wrist. He paid no attention. Another bullet hit him, but the wild fury of the charge bore him along. The next time the shot found his breast. His fall was hardly noticed in the fury of the conflict. It was as he had asked. No one should be told except the officer who must take command. That was Monckton, but he too was struck, and now Townshend was in command.

There was not much anyone could do for Wolfe. No one knew it better than he. They carried him to the rear and sent for a surgeon. But the general raised himself and shook his head. "It's all over with me," he said. His eyes still followed the battle. He heard the cry. "See, they run," and his clouding mind responded to it. In moments his gallant, pain-ridden, dying body could see no more. Wolfe was dead. His job was done and he had said himself that what happened afterward was of no great consequence.

Another great figure on a dark horse was coming close to destiny. Montcalm was desperately trying to stay the rout when the bullet found him. He heard the cry, "*Le marquis est tué*." "It's nothing," he said. Trying to straighten himself in his saddle, he called: "All is not lost," and again, "All is not lost." But it was too late. The panic of the militia, which had little wish to fight at all, was too much. Even the steady tones of a well-loved voice could not change that fact. Through the St. Louis Gate and down St. Louis Street they supported him on his dark horse to the home of Dr. Arnoux, which once stood close to where the St. Louis Hotel now stands. Gently they lifted him down and took him inside.

One look at the grisly wound and Dr. Arnoux knew there was little time remaining. De Ramesay came. The city was his charge and he was eager for advice. Montcalm excused himself, smiling faintly—his time was so short. But, short as it was, it was enough for him to send a word to Townshend, now commanding the British forces, on behalf of the prisoners and the Canadian people. "Be their protector," he ends his appeal, "as I have been their father." There are those who quarrel with these words, urging that they were not his. Perhaps the objection is true, but it is also true that they were like enough to all his thinking to have been his words. For us, let them so remain.

It was a time of mourning. Bishop Pontbriand, himself a dying man, came to Dr. Arnoux's home for the last sacraments. It was only a few hours later that they carried Montcalm to his last resting place, in the Convent of the Ursulines, where a bursting shell had made a fitting grave for him beneath the chapel floor. There was no sound of guns, no peal of bells, only the sound of sobbing, for all there knew that in mourning for Montcalm they mourned for the passing of New France.

There was gunfire as the *Royal William* sailed into Portsmouth Harbor bearing a nation's hero. The minute guns of the fleet kept time to the muffled bells that followed the cortege to London and on to Greenwick, where they laid James Wolfe to rest in the quiet churchyard beside his father. He would have been the first to say a word for a task well done.

At Quebec there were four days of waiting, then gallant old De Ramesay, who had never turned his back on an enemy but who knew that with most of the regiments returned to France and most that remained escaped to join Lévis and his desperate fortunes, defense was an aimless gesture. So the lilies of France that had fluttered so long and so gallantly above the city came down, and in their place the red ensign of a British people.

CHAPTER XXVII

"NOW THE KING CAN SLEEP"

With the capture of Quebec, General Murray assumes command of the city. A bitter winter of hunger and cold and sickness and overhanging threat culminates in the spring with Lévis' approach. Murray's daring assault brings on the sanguinary battle of Ste. Foy, which leaves the English defeated and Lévis uncertain of the wisdom of attack. The siege and relief. The retirement of Lévis. Amherst's three-pronged attack on Montreal. Its surrender. The Peace of Paris, the end of the French empire of the West.

QUEBEC, the gray city on the hill, had been challenged many times. It was captured at last. The cost of that accomplishment had been heavy. Two great men had laid down their lives there, one in victory, one in defeat. To most people it might seem that this was the logical end, the time for the actors to leave the stage.

It was not quite the end, however. On that date, September 19, 1759, General James Murray was writing in his diary, "This day I marched into town, or more properly the ruins of it, with the battalions of Amherst, Bragg and Otway." The city that had been won at so great cost had now to be held in the face of immeasurably stronger forces determined to get it back. It was not an easy task Murray had assumed, though happily it was to his liking. Admirals Saunders and Holmes were sailing away, and with them the other brigadiers who had followed Wolfe to Quebec. For help Murray could only turn to the distant Champlain corridor where the constitutionally tardy General Amherst, commanding all the forces in North America, was maturing his plans.

Opposing him, Murray knew, were all Montcalm's able brigadiers, Lévis, Bourlamaque, Bougainville, men whose affections combined with their duty to enlist them in the cause for which their friend and leader had died. But, most of all, he had to face the greatest and least familiar of enemies, winter.

It would be winter in Quebec, and the city was in a sorry plight. More than a third of the houses had been completely destroyed, and those remaining were mainly in a semi-battered state. The thought of winter could hardly have been a stirring one. Of the top command, General Wolfe was dead and Brigadier Monckton had received a bullet through the lung and needed a warmer climate if he was not to share Wolfe's fate. Admiral Saunders had delayed his departure as long as was possible. But when mid-October came it was evident that he had left himself no more than enough leeway to escape the frost. With him went Townshend. Townshend was a fine soldier but not a diplomatic one. Invariably he criticized his commanders and so he had commented to his wife: "General Wolfe's health is very bad, and in my opinion his generalship is not a bit better." Not long after he was to say: "If the world were sensible at how dear a price we purchased Quebec in his death, it would damp the general joy." An aristocrat with a sharp tongue, Townshend saw no pleasure ahead and little prestige. Enemies have attempted to discredit him because he sailed away with Admiral Saunders. There was no discredit involved. That was as it had been arranged before the campaign began. He merely followed a prearranged plan that, happily, was to his liking. He had explained to General Amherst, now in chief command, "I cannot, whenever the army becomes a garrison, be of any use here." He needed more action and he did not foresee it in Canada. In that, of course, he was completely wrong.

General Murray notes in his diary under date of September 21, two days after the city had been occupied: "This night it was resolved in a council of war, consisting of the admiral and generals, that we should keep possession of Canada, and that I should remain in command."

It was hardly a post that he or anyone else would have chosen. The departure of the fleet would leave him almost completely isolated. General Amherst, it was true, was moving up the old Lake Champlain route, with his customary tantalizing deliberateness, to attack Bourlamaque at Ticonderoga. Too good a soldier to confuse Amherst with Abercrombie, Bourlamaque had not attempted to repeat Montcalm's tactics but had decided instead to defend the fortress itself. He might have been successful in this plan. He would certainly have delayed Amherst's advance had there been need to do more where Amherst himself could provide so many delays. But at Ticonderoga there were orders from Vaudreuil. They left no alternative, and after exchanging a few shots in the early dusk Bourlamaque blew up enough of the fortress to make it untenable and departed in the night.

Amherst, characteristically, stayed to investigate and repair. When he again took up his leisurely pursuit and finally reached Crown Point, he found to his surprise that it too had been abandoned. He discovered something else, unforeseen in his careful plans. The French had four small armed vessels on Lake Champlain.

Possibly he might have marched around the lake and have invested Bourlamaque's new position at Isle-aux-Noix on the Richelieu just beyond its juncture with the lake. But Amherst had planned to proceed by water, and he was not a man lightly to change a plan carefully made. Perhaps the seeming alternative was not possible. In any event, he delayed his advance for months while he built an armed sloop to challenge the small French ships. The delay afforded him time also to improve the fortifications at Crown Point and to give Lévis the leeway he so much needed, and it did little to encourage General Murray, locked up with his pressing problems in a dilapidated Quebec.

The records of October 4 of that year 1759 show that General Murray had a garrison force of 340 officers and 6,973 of other ranks. The figures, moreover, were deceptive, for sickness was prevalent and curtailed sharply the number available for duty. By midwinter this had reduced the total to barely half.

The momentary problem, however, was not one of numbers but of how whatever numbers there were might be fed and housed. This problem was made the more acute by the fact that it must also include close to four thousand citizens who had chosen to remain and who had taken the necessary oath of allegiance. The virtual destruction of the city had taken from the larger part their means of livelihood. Quebec had become a city of almost universal unemployment and poverty. The food resources of the city had grown sparse in the intendancy of Bigot, and the months of siege had used up what resources there had been. Even for the army supplies were limited, and, stretched to cover the needs of a civilian population as well, they were short indeed.

Winter came to add its own misery. No one had foreseen this contingency, it seemed. The troops had not been clothed to face a Canadian winter, and their suffering was beyond imagining. Day after day great drifts piled against the ramparts, making them useless for defense. They had to be shoveled clear while men's hands froze to the shovel handles. Fuel, too, was short and, in the dilapidated state of all the buildings, more than ever fuel was acutely necessary. It was a backbreaking task.

Companies of men were constantly in the forests about Ste. Foy. There had to be heavy guards to protect the workers, for raiding parties were constantly attacking. Without this or the cold, the work would have been arduous enough. Eight men, harnessed in pairs, dragged the heavy-laden sleighs the five miles to the city, and with the drifting snow they must always be breaking new trails. The highlanders suffered most. The kilts that Scottish vanity would not permit them to forgo were not made for such winter campaigning.

Had General Murray been able in the pleasant days of autumn to foresee all this, he might not have been so confident. He had a background of Scottish stubbornness, however, that held no hint of introspection. Situations would arise as they must. He would meet them to the best of his ability and accept the results with an untroubled mind. He was not a complex character. At least he was free from disputes and dissensions, and the problems he must face would be his own.

"Everybody is cheerful and happy in having Quebec," he wrote General Amherst. "All those that did not like it are, thank God, gone to places they like better." Rather obviously James Murray "liked it," though it is somewhat difficult to understand why. He could hardly have described Quebec as Montcalm had done, only a few years earlier, as being "as good as the best cities of France, except for ten or so." Just now it would have been hard to find its equal for desolation in any of the cities of Europe, let alone France. Lower Town was a wilderness of rubble inhabited only by rats, and the desolation climbed up Mountain Street where the bishop's one-time palace stood a naked skeleton against the sky. Even in Upper Town few buildings had escaped entirely and many were wrecked almost beyond recognition. The cathedral was a blackened shell. The college and church of the Jesuits seemed only a little better, while that of the Récollets was almost beyond repair. Even the Hôtel-Dieu, well on the outskirts of the city, had been pierced by a score of shells, and everywhere the humbler buildings had suffered their heavy share of destruction.

"Quebec is nothing but a shapeless mass of ruin," reported the French commissary general who had remained in the city, "confusion, disorder, pillage reign even among the inhabitants . . . each searches for his possessions and, not finding his own, seizes those of other people. English and French, all in chaos alike."

It was all true enough, but it was no fault of the new governor. In fact, no one claimed that it was. All the French complaints were aimed at Vaudreuil, what he had done or had not done and how he had first sacrificed and then deserted them. Between the French and English there was no such animus, rather civility and, often enough, a friendly cordiality. Even the soldiers, with few exceptions, behaved as occupying garrisons were hardly expected to behave in those brave days. When the time came to reap what harvests there were in the fields about the city, English soldiers were to be seen working in the fields with the French habitants. Perhaps they were farm boys, hungry for the smell of the producing earth. Certainly it was not a matter of pay. None was asked. Everyone knew there was no money for payment of any services.

General Murray, a kindly-spirited man, did everything possible to see the French were well treated. He was high-principled and genuinely humane. Indeed the only criticism that has been brought against him is that he was recklessly unthinking in his courage. Whatever there may be in that charge, he did do his best to soften the harshness of occupation for those who had entrusted themselves to his care. They were to be treated with consideration and justice. But Murray was stern enough in this. An English soldier found guilty of robbing a French citizen was promptly hanged, and lesser offenses met with only slightly less rigorous punishments.

Murray was as eager to see that the sensibilities of the people were not hurt as to protect their persons and their possessions. One of his orders covered the behavior of those meeting one of the numerous religious processions. It read: "Officers are to pay them the compliment of the hat, because it is a civility due to the people who have chosen to live under the protection of our laws. Should this piece of ceremony be repugnant to the conscience of anyone they must retire when the procession approaches."

As spring drew near, the question of available manpower became highly important. Potentially at least Lévis was immensely superior. Except for those who had elected to remain in the city, he could draw from all the remaining population. True, this advantage was more apparent than real. Once involved in battle, the French militia would fight because they were of a race of fighters by tradition. No real will to fight, however, remained. The flame of patriotism that once burned high had all but died out, smothered by the long years of starvation and suffering and hopes that died at last at the hands of Bigot and his crew, who had drained them of everything but misery. To expect them to die for a cause, if dying was to be avoided, was asking the impossible.

Lévis knew this as well as anyone. Hearing that General Amherst had given up the thought of capping the season's successes by the capture of Isle-aux-Noix, and even Montreal itself, he was immensely relieved. While Bourlamaque held that important post on the Richelieu near the outlet of Lake Champlain, some freedom of action remained. Once lost, that freedom ended. "I don't know how General Amherst will excuse himself to his court," he wrote to Bourlamaque, "but I am very glad he let us alone, because the Canadians are so backward that you could count on nobody but the regulars."

Lévis had enjoyed more happy breaks than he knew. Had General John Prideaux not been killed in a freak accident of an exploding cannon, he might long since have been attacking Montreal. Sir William Johnson did indeed carry the Niagara undertaking to a successful conclusion, but Amherst was far from sure of his capacity for handling singlehanded an expedition such as that against Montreal, and probably he was right in this, if not in the selection of the one to replace Johnson. General Gage was undoubtedly a good soldier, but Gage was a constitutional delayer like his commander. Being fearful that should he succeed in taking Montreal he might only perish there miserably in the hard winter, he felt there was no need to hurry. He got as far as Oswego and paused there. He paused so long that winter was actually upon him before his mind was made up. Once again Lévis escaped this hazard.

He spent an untroubled winter in Montreal planning his next

move. It was ambitious enough. None other than to recover the city that his great friend and leader had lost. To this end he sent young Bougainville to replace Bourlamaque at Isle-aux-Noix and brought that steady, careful soldier to assist him in his great project.

General Murray had been thinking, too, and he was soldier enough to recognize that he would have to fight for Quebec. He did his best to strengthen his outposts at Cap Rouge, Lorette, and Ste. Foy, but soon it became evident that Lévis was moving with increasing confidence. The French commander had reasoned that the threat from Champlain or Oswego could not become dangerous until midsummer. As soon as the river opened, therefore, Lévis proposed to bring all his forces against Quebec, still believing he would have time to defeat the worn-out garrison and be back on the Richelieu in time to join Bougainville in defeating Amherst. It was a good plan, made better by Lévis' sound knowledge of the terrain and by reason of a manpower that far exceeded anything Murray could bring to oppose him. More than that, the quiet efficiency of Bourlamaque and the cheerful conciliatory attitude of Lévis worked some minor wonders in gathering and revitalizing his forces. So when finally spring arrived there was a passable army ready to move. It numbered something over seven thousand men. More than ample, it seemed, to meet the sickly and depleted forces that Murray might be able to collect even should these not be taken completely by surprise. Lévis' hope was to launch an attack that would be as completely secret as Wolfe's had been. Happily, Murray was a watchful Scot and was as prepared as might be. He could have been less so but for one of those strange happenings that sometimes disturb the plans of both mice and men.

It was a wild night of wind and rain when Lévis arrived and, almost despairing of surprise, he decided to land his forces near Cap Rouge and march inland around the end of the promontory, hoping to reach the heights from the north. Landing from boats in the swift and ice-filled river was cruel and hazardous work, and an artilleryman was jostled into the water and swept away. Reaching despairingly for any possible aid, the man's arm caught on a passing ice floe. His desperate appeals, however, were lost in the movement of heavy columns slogging along the sodden roads.

It was a lookout on one of General Murray's two sloops of war anchored far downstream before the city who heard the despairing cry from the river. He heard and acted. Shortly the rescued soldier was being dragged aboard. Teeth chattering so he could barely speak, the rescued man babbled excitedly of his adventure, and out of it came the story of the marching men. Whether he spoke by inadventure or excitement or from lack of interest in the expedition's fate, his well-authenticated story does not say. It does tell that at three o'clock in the morning he was haled before Murray to repeat the tale. That he did, cheerfully enough. After all, he was still alive.

Murray was quick to appraise the significance of what he heard. He realized it was too late now to defend the heights, too late to support his outpost in force, too late to protect the munitions stored in the village church of Ste. Foy. Scouting forces should watch the progress of the advancing columns; the rest of the forces would fall back on Quebec. As to the munitions—well, there had been no thought in Murray's mind of actually endangering the church, but now the course was obvious: blow it up, destroy everything.

Murray was gathering his forces on the Buttes-à-Neveu, a line of defenses eight hundred yards beyond the wall built that winter with incredible effort for just such an emergency. The force grew and grew as sick, half-starved, half-frozen men hurried to join. There was no defensive spirit in Quebec. Everyone hoped that at last there would be action. They had no wish to be bottled up in the city like rats in a trap. They would attack. The Buttes-à-Neveu was good enough to come back to if they lost.

It was half-past six on the morning of April 28 when Murray's small army of almost three thousand men left what little security the walls of Quebec suggested. They had with them much artillery, twenty-five fieldpieces in all and two howitzers. This represented not only an advantage but a hazard. There were no horses to draw them. Bigot had seen to that. Spring though it was, there was little sign of spring. The earth before them was sodden inches deep, a quagmire of snowy slush with frozen ground beneath, and in the hollows were still deep drifts of snow. Over this ground they must move to attack, dragging the heavy guns by sheer manpower. They did not realize that, hard as it was with the ground falling before them, it would be harder coming back.

Far off on the right as they advanced they could see the little village of Ste. Foy with its blackened church beyond and the house of one Dumont, with the mill and fortified windmill adjoining. French troops were forming there and other columns marched along the rising ground where Wolfe had fought his last battle. They were moving toward the twin blockhouses built that winter to defend the Anse au Foulon, the hard road by which Wolfe had reached the plains. This was the vanguard of Lévis' army, and behind them others followed until an army of well over ten thousand men would be engaged there.

To Murray the advancing columns had the look of opportunity, the "lucky minute"—an opponent caught off guard and maneuvering for position. So he took his rather desperate chance. The long line that heard his relayed command was happy to go, eight regiments of "half-starved scorbutic skeletons," as one of their own number described them, with two regiments of similar character in reserve. Skeletons or no, they moved forward at the word, an assault force of less than two thousand men, five hundred of whom were needed to haul the guns. They were almost on the line where Wolfe's army had stood only a few months before when their guns began to fire. It was a destructive challenge at short distance. Lévis on horseback at the center of the field saw the newly restored discipline of his troops begin to waver. He ordered them back to the cover of the woods. More than ever it seemed to Murray the "lucky minute," and he pushed forward boldly. It was somewhat too boldly, for the move took his half-starved battalions from the ridge where their guns had commanded the field to the low ground beyond where the sodden snow lay in knee-deep drifts, bogging them down beyond recovery, and where a flanking fire caught them from all directions.

Immovable the guns might be, but they were not yet out of action. They could turn their fire on Dumont's mill, where five companies of French grenadiers were making the ground about too dangerous to approach. Time and again Murray's tattered forces attempted it, only to be repulsed and to come again. The snow was trampled and scarlet about the mill. At last the French gave way. Waiting for no orders, Murray's troops streamed forward to complete the victory. But instead of disorganized foes they came face to face with staunch old Colonel Dalquier and his regiment of Béarn, part of the corps that Lévis had withdrawn early in the battle. Behind them were other regiments. "We held them back," said a sergeant of the light infantry, "as long as there was ammunition for the cannon." Now there was none. The tumbrels bringing it were themselves "bogged in deep pits of snow."

The "lucky minute" had turned into two long hours. While the right was facing the seasoned regiment of Béarn, on the left toward the Anse au Foulon the fortunes were no better. Lévis' swelling columns were all about. The right and the left of the British lines were overlapped. The men were falling in growing numbers. Murray recognized his luck had run out, that this was not the short decisive action of the Plains of Abraham; this was an ordeal too stern to be faced by his skeleton crew. Yet when the order came for them to fall back there was no hurry of retreat. "Damn it," a voice was heard, "what is falling back but retreating?" Methodically, in the face of the enemy, they spiked the guns they couldn't move and, carrying some of the less desperately wounded, they moved back, a retreating but still not a beaten army. De Lévis recognized the difference, recognized, too, that, made desperate, they might turn on him again, and wisely stayed the pursuit.

The army was back again on the Buttes-à-Neveu, those that came at all. Out there in the reddened snow there were almost a thousand men, killed, wounded, or missing. They would not be wounded or missing long, as was evident enough when Lévis' Indians had done their part, for the bushes about Ste. Foy were heavy, not with leaves, but with the red scalps of the wounded and the missing, and an almost unremembered battle was one of the cruelest and bloodiest of our history. If Murray lost a thousand men, almost a third of his total, Lévis lost almost as many, though his percentage of loss was much different.

Perhaps the whole attempt had been nothing but a story of "mad, enthusiastic zeal," as one of the participants had called it. There were many who spoke that way, many who still contend that to attack at all was a stupid if gallant gesture, to leave the protection of the Buttes-à-Neveu a suicidal mistake. Yet there are others who contend that but for Murray's "lucky minute" De Lévis might have been in Quebec and Wolfe have died in vain.

Perhaps many fail to recognize that Ste. Foy was a Pyrrhic victory for Lévis. He had won decisively, but neither he nor his troops were equal to the final test of challenging Quebec by assault. And that, as we must realize, was Lévis' one hope. Time was running out for France.

Had Lévis come fresh on the field, facing only a ruined city with its sick and starving defenders grown sicker by weeks of exposure on the Buttes-à-Neveu, the chance to carry Quebec by assault would surely have been too much for him to resist, and almost certainly that would have been the advice of Bourlamaque. Such must have been Murray's thinking, too, as he wrote to Pitt: "The enemy was greatly superior in numbers, it is true; but when I consider that our little army was in the habit of beating the enemy, and had a very fine train of field artillery; that shutting ourselves at once within the walls was putting all upon the single chance of holding for a considerable time a wretched fortification, I resolved to give them battle."

To some it may seem the wildest recklessness, yet the fact remains, Lévis now did not attack. Perhaps, brave as he was, he lacked the decisiveness that Bourlamaque might have supplied. But Bourlamaque had been gravely wounded in the battle, and it was for Lévis to decide alone. He determined to invest the city and starve it into submission. But that required time, and time he did not have. Rather he had a hope that the ships promised from France would come promptly and help decide the issue.

It was almost noon of May 9, and the siege had lasted just ten days, when the eager watchers in both camps saw the tall sails of a frigate rounding the Island of Orleans. This was the hoped and the feared, but for whom? As if to settle that point, a flag fluttered from the masthead and there was a clamor of guns. It was His Britannic Majesty's ship *Lowestoffe* saluting a Quebec still in British hands.

There was a nagging fear with the rejoicing. Still some days must pass before the remainder of the fleet could arrive. There was still time to take the fortress by assault. It was Lévis' last desperate chance, and Murray feared that it might be taken. On the eleventh Lévis launched a terrific bombardment. It crumbled the old walls, and Murray's small garrison waited for the attack they were sure would follow, but Lévis waited too. Surprisingly, he couldn't make up his mind to risk the hazard. Then on the fifteenth it was too late. As the night began to fall, three great ships rounded the head of the Island of Orleans. These, like the *Lowestoffe*, were the forerunners of Commodore Swanton's squadrons, which were pressing all sail to reach Quebec in time.

All the next day Lévis waited. For what, does not appear. Perhaps it was to give confidence to the small French fleet that had wintered in Canada. If so, the action achieved nothing. The French ships anchored near the Foulon in his support fell an easy victim to the British ships. Lévis' retreat by water thus cut off made it evident it was time he should be gone. He read the signs aright. A day or two later when the dawn broke, sentries looking from the citadel saw no movement in the trenches on the Buttes-à-Neveu, no smoke of cooking fires. Scouts picked up the trail. It led over the old battlefield of Ste. Foy. There were no Frenchmen there, only those English scalps crowning the bushes, swaying a little in the wind that ruffled the growing grass on this field where brave men had died.

Every tide seemed to bring new ships. They swung at anchor along the river at Quebec, and nothing seemed to happen. Certainly nothing to restore French confidence. In the long trek back to Montreal, Lévis' army seemed to melt away. It was as if the Canadians had seen in the possible retaking of Quebec their one last hope. It had failed. Always a practical people, the habitants had accepted the inevitable and had scattered to their homes.

All through the summer, while Lévis worked feverishly to prepare some last defense, the Canadians on whom he must depend kept slipping away. Governor Vaudreuil was busy too. He was writing letters to the minister. The letters, couched in his grandiloquent style, were supposedly keeping the minister informed of the changing situation. "I am taking the most just measures to unite our forces," the governor wrote, "and, if our situation permits, to fight a battle or several battles. But if we succumb in the battles we shall fight, I shall apply myself to obtaining a capitulation which may avert the ruin of the people. . . . It is with this view that I shall remain within the town, the Chevalier de Lévis having represented to me that it would be an evil past remedying if anything should happen to me." Having so relieved himself of this precious encumbrance, Lévis was free to make the best disposition he could.

It was May when his retreating army reached Montreal, and all through the summer the slow attrition went on. There was really very little that could be done to assure the defense of a city as indefensible as Montreal. It was a long narrow strip between the river and Mount Royal. There was a redoubt at the lower end that mounted a few cannon, and the whole was surrounded by a rough bastion with a shallow moat before it. These had been planned as a defense against the Indians that had been Montreal's only expected assailants. They were a hopeless defense against cannon or any serious assault. All the reports indicated that Amherst was taking no chances and that, when finally he did arrive, it would be in such force as to make such defenses of little consequence.

Lévis did his capable best. He stationed small delaying forces along the river with more impressive defenses at Jacques-Cartier and Three Rivers to slow up General Murray's approach. But there were three spearheads of attack, and each had to be met. Bougainville was at Isle-aux-Noix, ready to challenge any approach by way of Lake Champlain, and Captain Pouchot was defending the rapids well above Montreal. It was the best Lévis could do with his depleted forces, but both he and Bourlamaque knew how inadequate it was. Far from showing the least timidity, Governor Vaudreuil was still writing in the grand manner. "I have taken positions," he wrote, "such as may hide our weakness from the enemy."

The vital questions remained. How long before the English attack would begin? Would it be a combined attack, or isolated assaults that would offer a better hope of a successful defense? It seemed a combined attack was almost beyond the possibilities. Yet it wasn't. Amherst might be slow, but he was highly competent. He recognized the danger of a divided attack and did his best to provide against it. Whether through shrewd planning or a happy inadvertence, he was amazingly successful. Never since Denonville's unbelievable mobilization at Irondequoit Bay had any concentration turned out so successfully.

Amherst had given himself the most difficult assignment. He had spent the winter at Oswego gathering his main army of almost ten thousand men, to which was added Sir William Johnson's Indian contingent of 1,350. It was the largest force of Indians ever gathered on the continent and, as it turned out, the most orderly.

Brigadier Haviland was at Crown Point, waiting the word to move up lake and river to Isle-aux-Noix, where Bougainville was waiting for him. To Murray's weathered veterans was allotted the easier task of coming upriver from Quebec.

Amherst began his march on the ninth of August. It was a long trail and not without opposition. A small fort had been built the previous winter at the head of the rapids well beyond Fort Frontenac. It was called Fort Lévis and it was in the experienced hands of Captain Pouchot. He had been at Fort Niagara the year before, and now it was his ill fortune to meet Sir William Johnson again. It wasn't a pretentious place, and Amherst could probably have slipped by without difficulty but for a constitutional reluctance to leave an enemy in his rear. There was the still more important reason that he needed rivermen to take his loaded boats down the river, and where a likelier spot to find them than here? Lévis himself had counted on

Amherst's thoroughness. As he wrote Bourlamaque, "We shall be fortunate if the enemy amuse themselves with capturing it. My chief anxiety is lest Amherst should reach Montreal so soon that we may not have time to unite our forces to attack Haviland and Murray." As a fact, Fort Lévis did delay Amherst until the twenty-fifth, when Pouchot gave up the unequal struggle. It seems also that Amherst must have found his boatmen, for the first of the rapids were negotiated with relatively little difficulty, but either they grew careless or the rapids grew more hazardous. Passing the rapids now known as the Cedar and Cascades, he lost fifty of his boats and some eighty-five men. Eventually, on September 6, he made a landing at Lachine and could see the church spires of the city in the distance. By mid-afternoon he was before its western defenses.

Murray had been coming too. He by-passed Jacques-Cartier, where Lévis had prepared a warm reception, and proceeded upriver. Where the expedition stopped for food or rest, though the French forces might be following along the shore, the habitants welcomed the English gladly and with apparent friendliness. Whether this was the result of good feeling or a shrewd trading instinct, who can say? Three Rivers was by-passed, too, and at nightfall the forces came to land close to the village of Sorel. Bourlamaque was in command in this area, and most of the male inhabitants were with him. He had not the necessary force to meet Murray in open combat. He could only fight and run. As a lesson the town was burned. Murray was a kindly man and the necessity disturbed him. "I pray God," he wrote to Pitt, "this example may suffice, for my nature revolts when this becomes a necessary part of my duty."

The example seems to have had its effect. The Canadians were deserting Bourlamaque by scores and by hundreds. By the end of August the force at his command was more than cut in half. It permitted Murray to make greater speed. So on September 6, when Amherst was landing at Lachine on the west of the city, Murray was making camp on Ile Ste. Thérèse near the eastern end of Montreal Island.

Brigadier Haviland, forcing his way along the familiar highway from the south, by late August had driven Bougainville from Isle-aux-Noix and, giving him no chance to entrench at St. John or Chambly, had finally reached camp at Longueuil across river from the city, and just one day late. Now the city was ringed by a force of twenty thousand men.

That night the governor called a council of war. He had indeed been busy. He had been writing the articles of capitulation. There were fifty-five clauses. Most of them were innocent enough, and nothing could becloud the fact that this was surrender. All the officers present agreed with the terms. When they were presented to Amherst, that generous man was almost equally complaisant, until he came to the article stipulating that the French troops should march out with arms, cannon, and the honors of war. Generous-minded as he was, Amherst would have no part of that. "The whole garrison of Montreal," he wrote in return, "and all other French troops in Canada must lay down their arms, and shall not serve during the present war."

Lévis was outraged, and young Bougainville tried his best to have this condition modified. When he failed, Lévis sent his own personal emissary. Amherst had grown tired of argument. His answer was definite and final. "I am fully resolved," he replied, "for the infamous part the troops of France have acted in exciting the savages to perpetrate the most horrid and unheard of barbarities in the whole progress of the war, and for other open treacheries and flagrant breaches of faith, to manifest to all the world by this capitulation my detestation of such practices."

Hot with anger, Lévis told the governor that rather than accept such terms he would move to St. Helen's Island and there fight to the finish. It was a futile gesture and well he must have known it. That island in the river by Montreal, named for the sad young wife of Champlain who could not stand the harshness and loneliness of the great land of her husband's love, was indefensible before such forces as Amherst had at hand. Petulant at that knowledge, Lévis did the one thing that left a slight tarnish on a great name. He burned the captured banners of the regiments of France that were part of the capitulation. They were still in his keeping until surrendered. They were no longer his to honor or defame.

In closing his great study of Danton, Hilaire Belloc used these poignant words: "And I will close this book by the last duty of mourning, as we who hold to immortality yet break our hearts for the dead."

So, surely, must anyone feel on reaching the end of this record of New France. So small an end to come of so much courage, so much daring, so much devotion and self-sacrifice. Once it had been an empire that reached from the stormy gray rocks of Isle Royale to the very shadow of the Rockies, and from the fog-bound Hudson Strait to the smiling shores of the Gulf of Mexico. An empire to remember, every foot of it grown rich with the blood of saints and soldiers and patriots. To come to this—a little strip of ground about a river mouth and a town that men will call New Orleans. That and two little islands in the Gulf of St. Lawrence, like milestones on that ancient highway. They are called St. Pierre and Miquelon, and the flag of France still flies there. Little islands well out in the gulf. Yet no man may build there even the smallest fortress or raise an army greater than the thirty stout policemen that the law permits. This was the empire that remained, and one must be hard of heart to lack a hint of heartbreak for the dead.

But those who were dying didn't think to mourn. There was no vision left and, without it, peoples perish. They were blind to the promise of a new country, being embittered by the declining fortunes of the old. They went their way, scornfully confident that what was lost by battle, as often before, might be restored by treaty. But that of Paris would teach them differently.

The great Voltaire, wise man and cynic, could be as blind as any. He gave a magnificent fete to acclaim the deliverance of France "from a vast stretch of frozen country." Even Madame la Pompadour came closer the truth than that. She spoke and thought for those who lived only for the present and the personal. She could sense the compensations. No more importunities, no more arguments and quarreling, no more obligations. It was a closed book, not to be reopened. Yet she could find it in her heart to be satisfied. She put it all in a phrase. "Now the King can sleep," she said.

In so few words Madame la Pompadour epitomized much of the story told here, of a society and an ideology that lacked the final capacity to rule; that had so lost its way that a King's sleep could become more vitally important than the well-being of a people or a land.

Yet in that "great frozen country" that Voltaire was so glad to see relinquished there was a stirring of new life that he would have approved, where freedom would take the place of absolutism, where two peoples could each bring their own contribution to such an end. All the glory, all the achievement of the storied past would not be lost and forgotten but would become a part of a common heritage. The love of freedom would grow into a tradition of liberty and democracy to make a common inheritance. There is the common pride in the nation to be. This is the great and dramatic story that still remains to be told.

INDEX